SABAN'S

MIGHTY MORPHIN POWER RANGERS

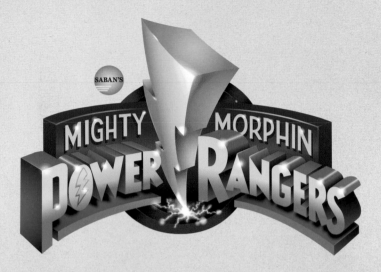

SHATTERED GRID

HIGGINS • PARROTT • DI NICUOLO • GALINDO
BAIAMONTE • COSTA

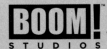

BOOM! STUDIOS

SERIES DESIGNER
SCOTT NEWMAN

COLLECTION DESIGNER
JILLIAN CRAB

SERIES ASSISTANT EDITOR
MICHAEL MOCCIO

COLLECTION ASSISTANT EDITOR
GWEN WALLER

SERIES ASSOCIATE EDITOR
MATTHEW LEVINE

EDITOR
DAFNA PLEBAN

HASBRO SPECIAL THANKS
MELISSA FLORES, PAUL STRICKLAND, ED LANE, BETH ARTALE, AND MICHAEL KELLY

Ross Richie CEO & Founder
Joy Huffman CFO
Matt Gagnon Editor-in-Chief
Filip Sablik President, Publishing & Marketing
Stephen Christy President, Development
Lance Kreiter Vice President, Licensing & Merchandising
Arune Singh Vice President, Marketing
Bryce Carlson Vice President, Editorial & Creative Strategy
Scott Newman Manager, Production Design
Kate Henning Manager, Operations
Spencer Simpson Manager, Sales
Elyse Strandberg Manager, Finance
Sierra Hahn Executive Editor
Jeanine Schaefer Executive Editor
Dafna Pleban Senior Editor

Shannon Watters Senior Editor
Eric Harburn Senior Editor
Chris Rosa Editor
Matthew Levine Editor
Sophie Phillips-Roberts Associate Editor
Amanda LaFranco Associate Editor
Jonathan Manning Associate Editor
Gavin Gronenthal Assistant Editor
Gwen Waller Assistant Editor
Allyson Gronowitz Assistant Editor
Jillian Crab Design Coordinator
Michelle Ankley Design Coordinator
Kara Leopard Production Designer
Marie Krupina Production Designer
Grace Park Production Designer

Chelsea Roberts Production Design Assistant
Samantha Knapp Production Design Assistant
José Meza Live Events Lead
Stephanie Hocutt Digital Marketing Lead
Esther Kim Marketing Coordinator
Cat O'Grady Digital Marketing Coordinator
Amanda Lawson Marketing Assistant
Holly Aitchison Digital Sales Coordinator
Morgan Perry Retail Sales Coordinator
Megan Christopher Operations Coordinator
Rodrigo Hernandez Mailroom Assistant
Zipporah Smith Operations Assistant
Sabrina Lesin Accounting Assistant
Breanna Sarpy Executive Assistant

Licensed by:

MIGHTY MORPHIN POWER RANGERS: Shattered Grid, January 2020. Published by BOOM! Studios, a division of Boom Entertainment, Inc. ™ & © 2020 SCG Power Rangers LLC and Hasbro. HASBRO and its logo, Power Rangers and all related logos, characters, names, and distinctive likenesses thereof are the exclusive property of SCG Power Rangers LLC. All Rights Reserved. Used Under Authorization. Originally published in single magazine form as MIGHTY MORPHIN POWER RANGERS No. 25-30, MIGHTY MORPHIN POWER RANGERS FREE COMIC BOOK DAY SPECIAL 2018, and MIGHTY MORPHIN POWER RANGERS: SHATTERED GRID No. 1 ™ & © 2018 SCG Power Rangers LLC and Hasbro. All rights reserved. BOOM! Studios™ and the BOOM! Studios logo are trademarks of Boom Entertainment, Inc., registered in various countries and categories. All characters, events, and institutions depicted herein are fictional. Any similarity between any of the names, characters, persons, events, and/or institutions in this publication to actual names, characters, and persons, whether living or dead, events, and/or institutions is unintended and purely coincidental. BOOM! Studios does not read or accept unsolicited submissions of ideas, stories, or artwork.

BOOM! Studios, 5670 Wilshire Boulevard, Suite 400, Los Angeles, CA 90036-5679. Printed in China. Second Printing.

ISBN: 978-1-68415-390-9, eISBN: 978-1-64144-373-9

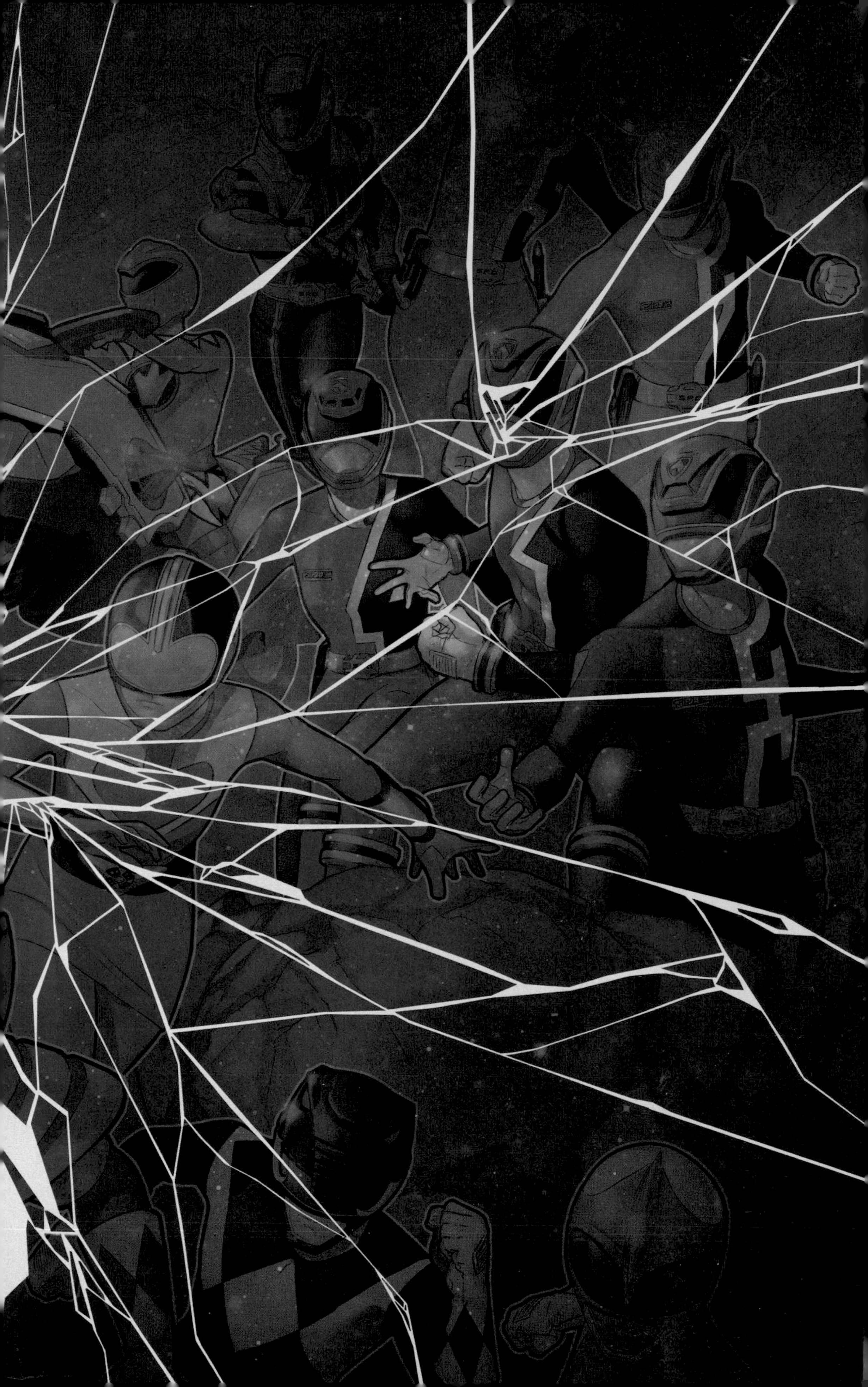

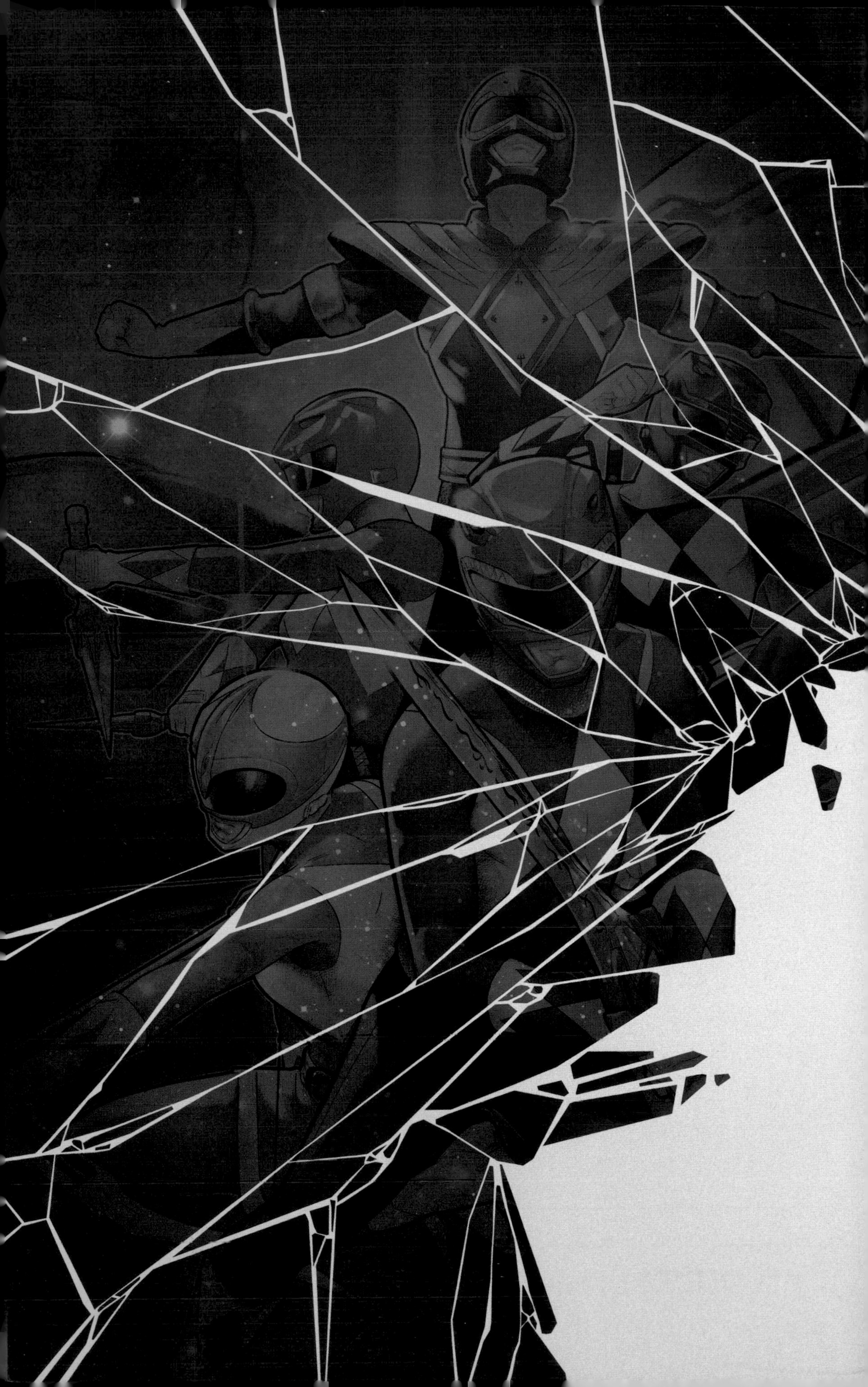

S H A T T E R E D   G R I D

WRITTEN BY
KYLE HIGGINS

ILLUSTRATED BY
DANIELE DI NICUOLO
WITH INK ASSISTANCE BY **SIMONA DI GIANFELICE**
& DIEGO GALINDO

COLORS BY
WALTER BAIAMONTE
WITH ASSISTANCE BY **FRANCESCO SEGALA**
& MARCELO COSTA

LETTERS BY
ED DUKESHIRE

*MIGHTY MORPHIN POWER RANGERS
FREE COMIC BOOK DAY 2018 SPECIAL*

WRITTEN BY
KYLE HIGGINS
& RYAN PARROTT

ILLUSTRATED BY
DIEGO GALINDO

COLORS BY
MARCELO COSTA

LETTERS BY
ED DUKESHIRE

COVER BY
GOÑI MONTES

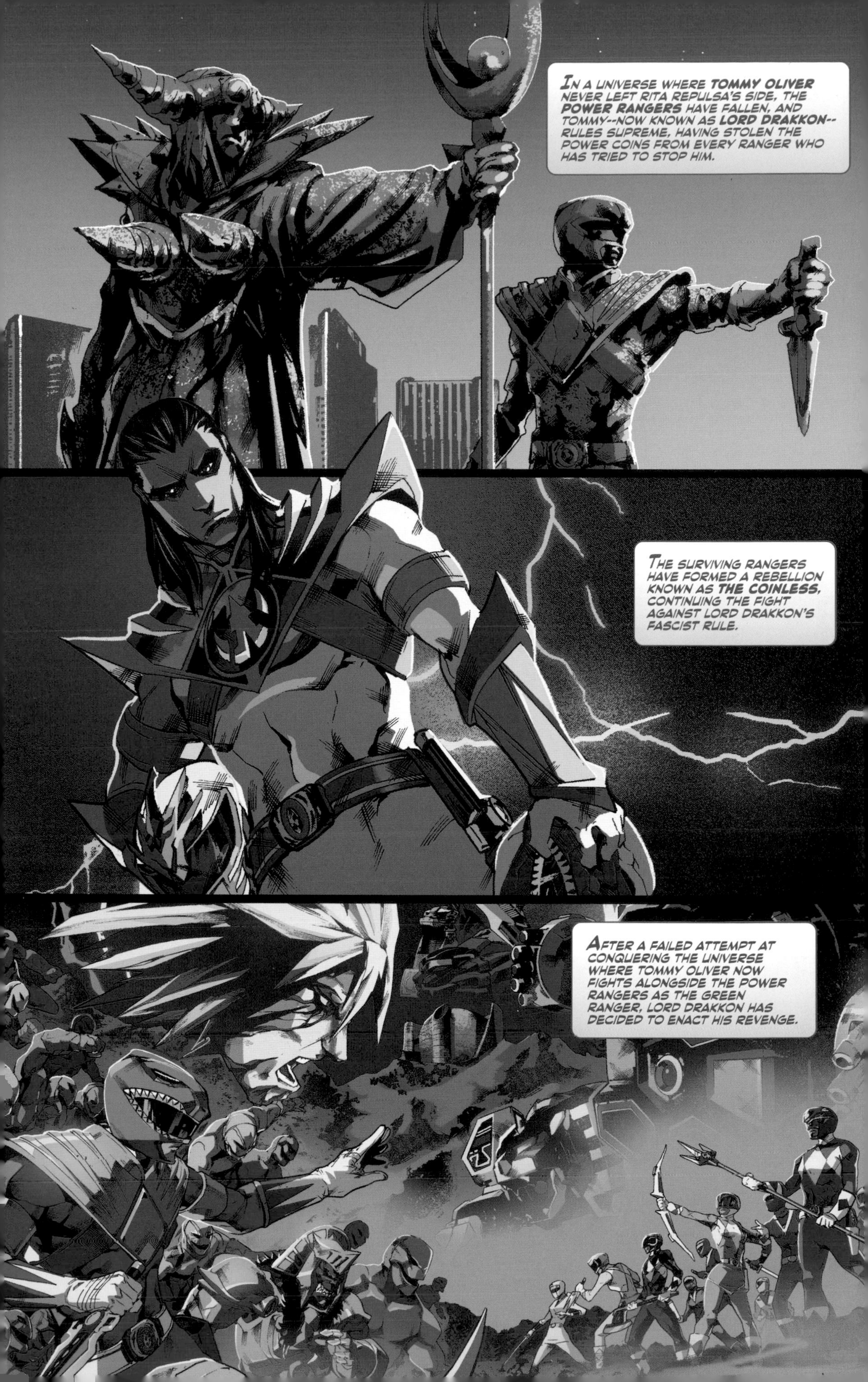
IN A UNIVERSE WHERE TOMMY OLIVER NEVER LEFT RITA REPULSA'S SIDE, THE POWER RANGERS HAVE FALLEN, AND TOMMY--NOW KNOWN AS LORD DRAKKON--RULES SUPREME, HAVING STOLEN THE POWER COINS FROM EVERY RANGER WHO HAS TRIED TO STOP HIM.
THE SURVIVING RANGERS HAVE FORMED A REBELLION KNOWN AS THE COINLESS, CONTINUING THE FIGHT AGAINST LORD DRAKKON'S FASCIST RULE.
AFTER A FAILED ATTEMPT AT CONQUERING THE UNIVERSE WHERE TOMMY OLIVER NOW FIGHTS ALONGSIDE THE POWER RANGERS AS THE GREEN RANGER, LORD DRAKKON HAS DECIDED TO ENACT HIS REVENGE.

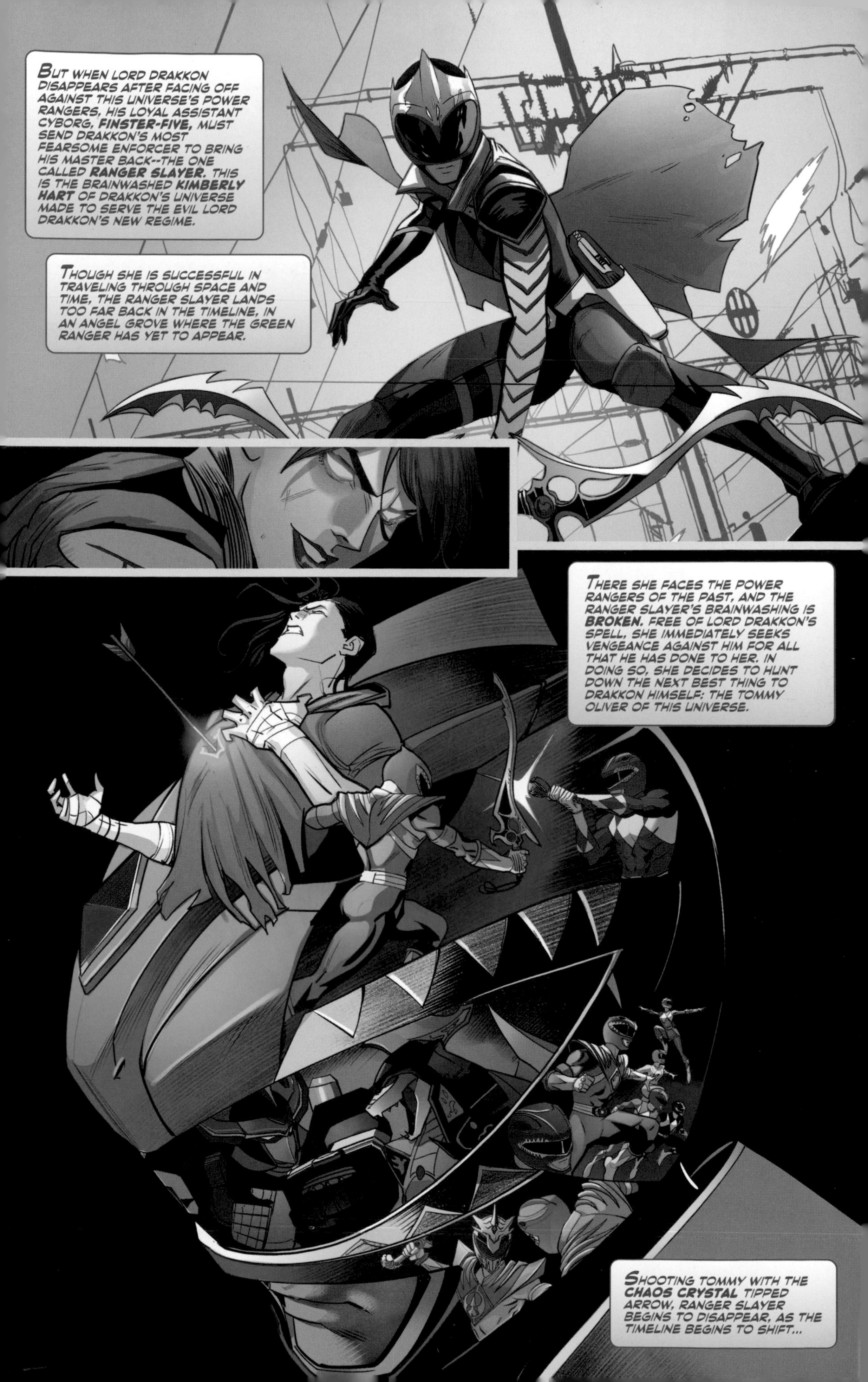
But when Lord Drakkon disappears after facing off against this universe's Power Rangers, his loyal assistant cyborg, **Finster-Five,** must send Drakkon's most fearsome enforcer to bring his master back--the one called **Ranger Slayer.** This is the brainwashed **Kimberly Hart** of Drakkon's universe made to serve the evil Lord Drakkon's new regime.
Though she is successful in traveling through space and time, the Ranger Slayer lands too far back in the timeline, in an Angel Grove where the Green Ranger has yet to appear.
There she faces the Power Rangers of the past, and the Ranger Slayer's brainwashing is **broken.** Free of Lord Drakkon's spell, she immediately seeks vengeance against him for all that he has done to her. In doing so, she decides to hunt down the next best thing to Drakkon himself: the Tommy Oliver of this universe.
Shooting Tommy with the **Chaos Crystal** tipped arrow, Ranger Slayer begins to disappear, as the timeline begins to shift...

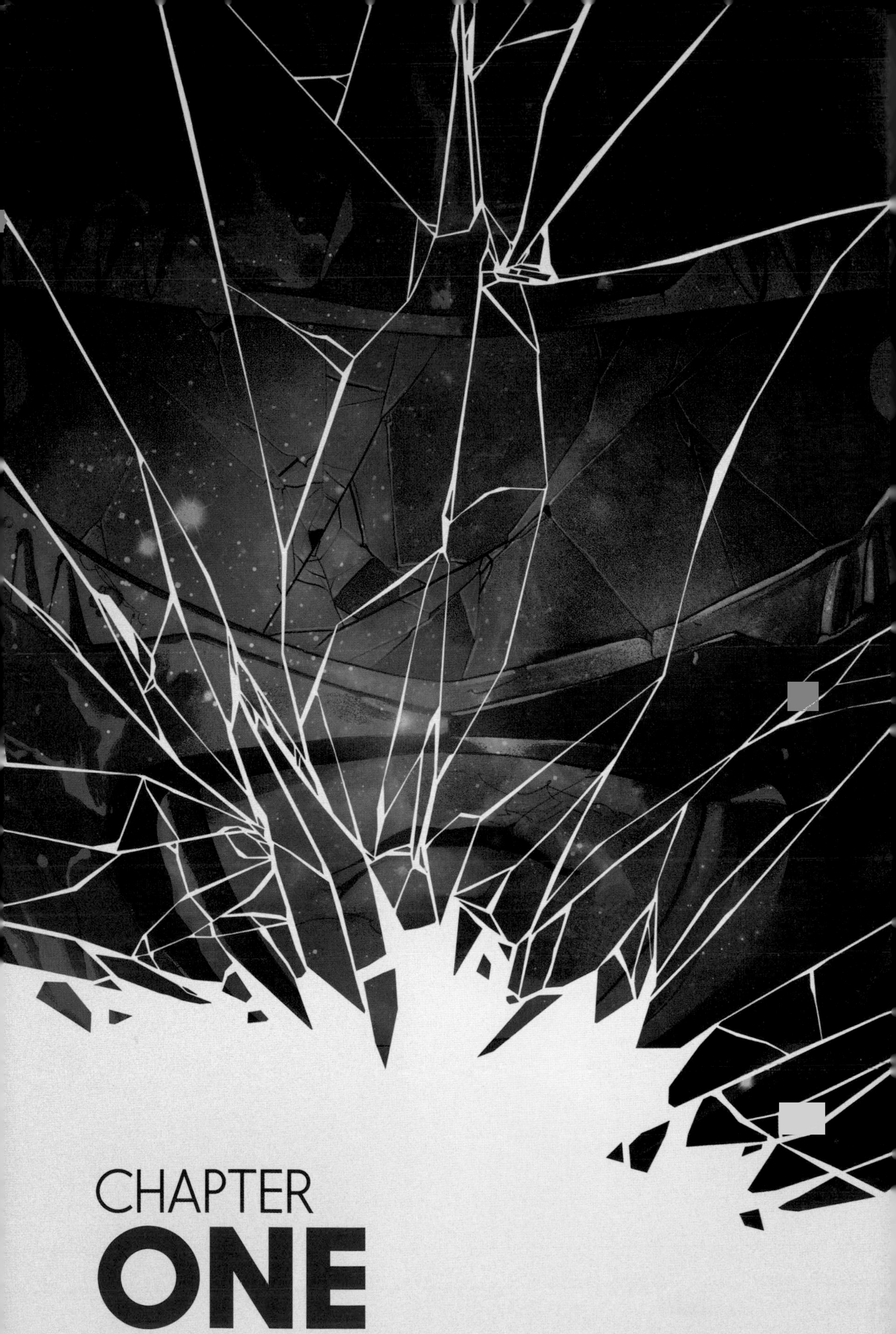

CHAPTER ONE

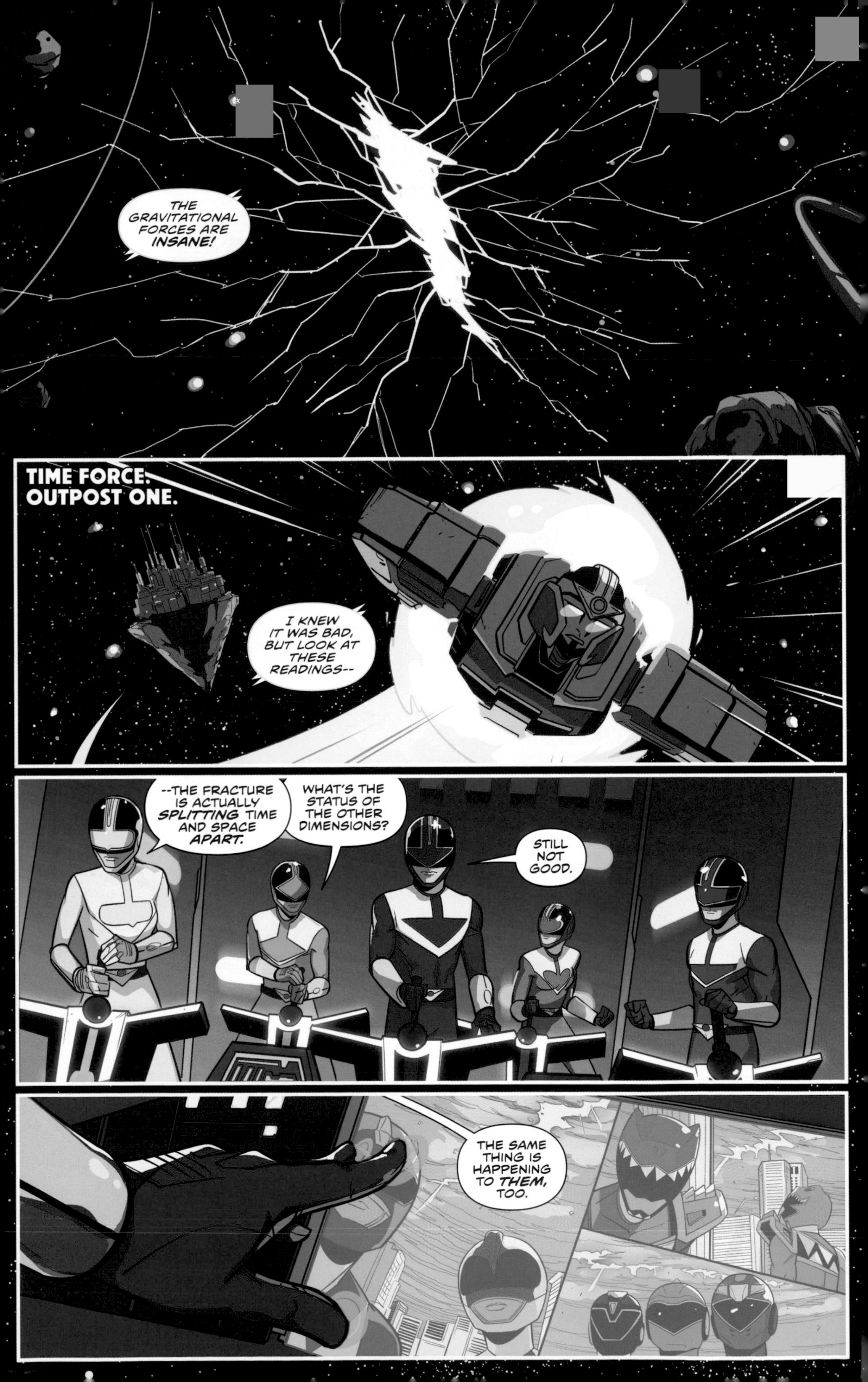
THE GRAVITATIONAL FORCES ARE INSANE!
TIME FORCE. OUTPOST ONE.
I KNEW IT WAS BAD, BUT LOOK AT THESE READINGS--
--THE FRACTURE IS ACTUALLY SPLITTING TIME AND SPACE APART.
WHAT'S THE STATUS OF THE OTHER DIMENSIONS?
STILL NOT GOOD.
THE SAME THING IS HAPPENING TO THEM, TOO.

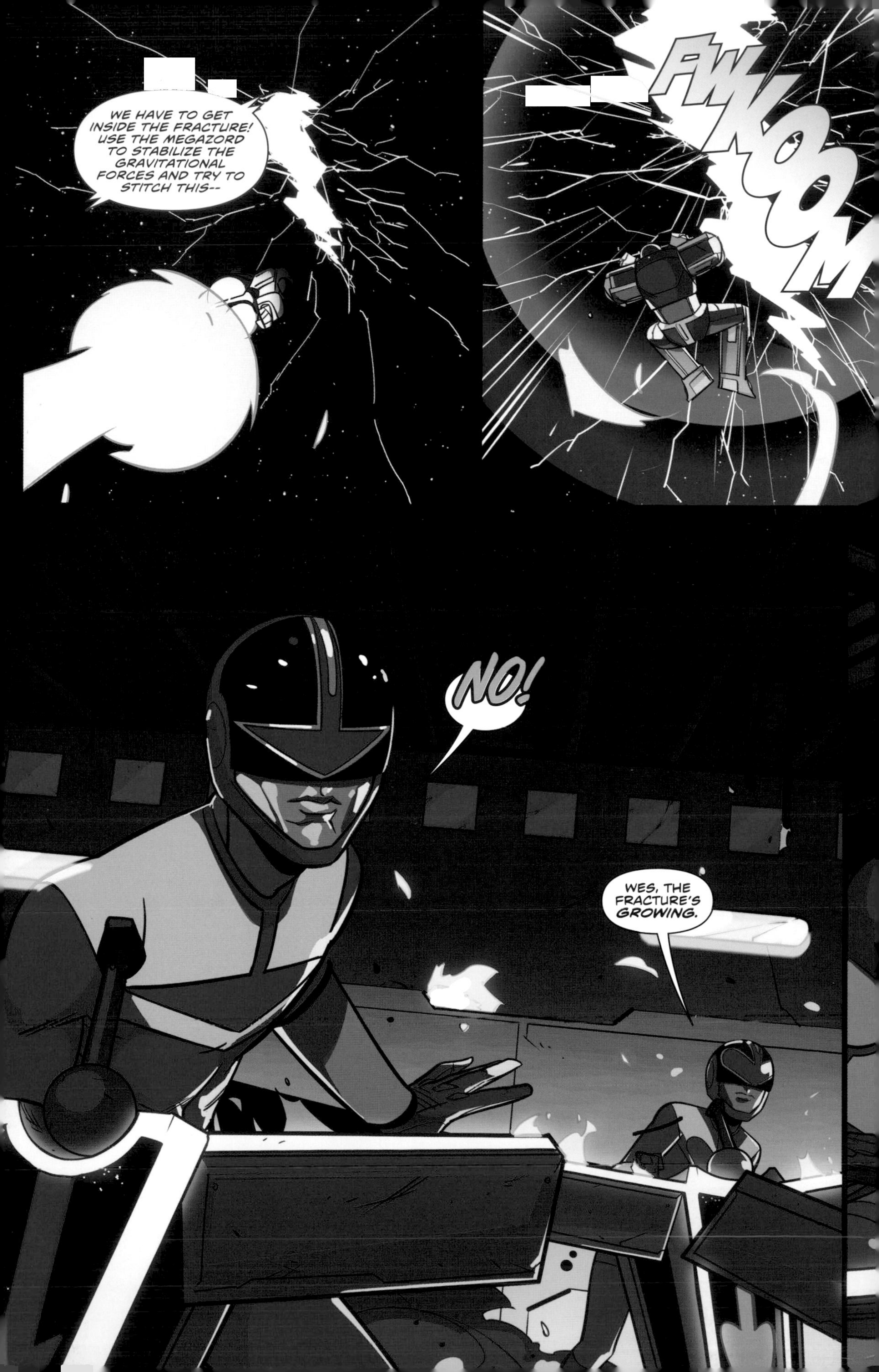
WE HAVE TO GET INSIDE THE FRACTURE! USE THE MEGAZORD TO STABILIZE THE GRAVITATIONAL FORCES AND TRY TO STITCH THIS--
FWKOOM
NO!
WES, THE FRACTURE'S GROWING.

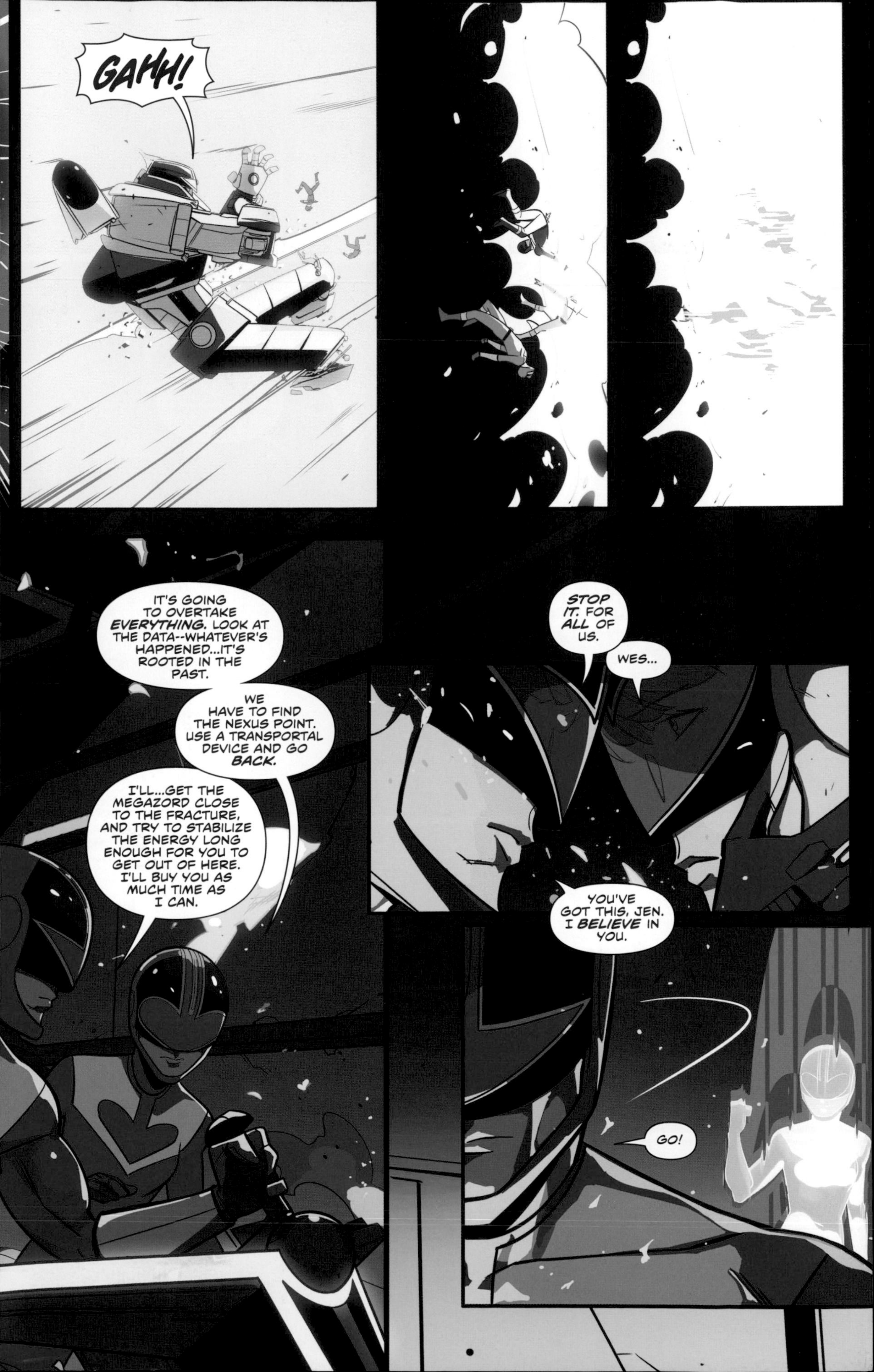

GAHH!
IT'S GOING TO OVERTAKE EVERYTHING. LOOK AT THE DATA--WHATEVER'S HAPPENED...IT'S ROOTED IN THE PAST.
WE HAVE TO FIND THE NEXUS POINT. USE A TRANSPORTAL DEVICE AND GO BACK.
I'LL...GET THE MEGAZORD CLOSE TO THE FRACTURE, AND TRY TO STABILIZE THE ENERGY LONG ENOUGH FOR YOU TO GET OUT OF HERE. I'LL BUY YOU AS MUCH TIME AS I CAN.
STOP IT. FOR ALL OF US.
WES...
YOU'VE GOT THIS, JEN. I BELIEVE IN YOU.
GO!

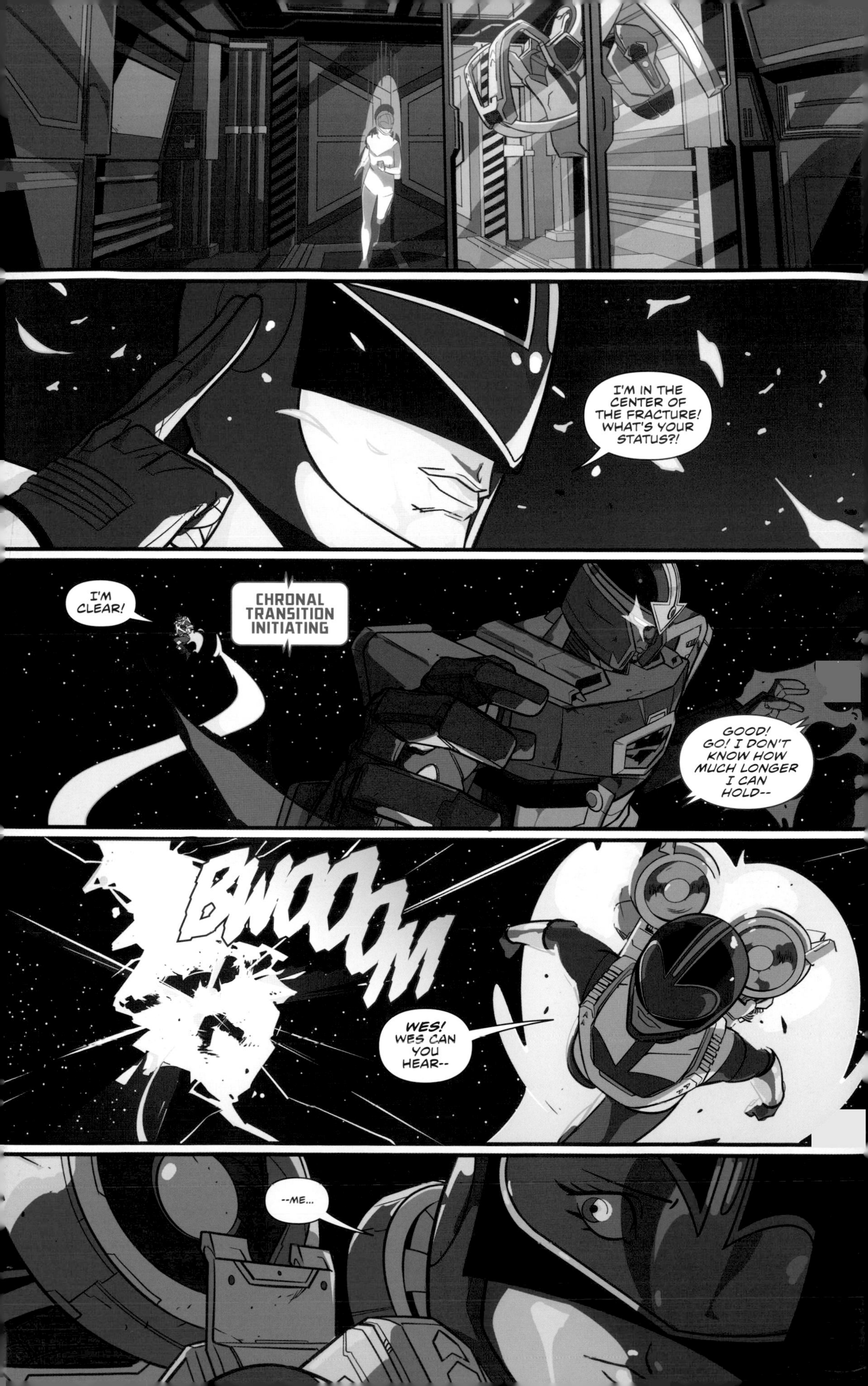
I'M IN THE CENTER OF THE FRACTURE! WHAT'S YOUR STATUS?!
I'M CLEAR!
CHRONAL TRANSITION INITIATING
GOOD! GO! I DON'T KNOW HOW MUCH LONGER I CAN HOLD--
BWOOOM
WES! WES CAN YOU HEAR--
--ME...

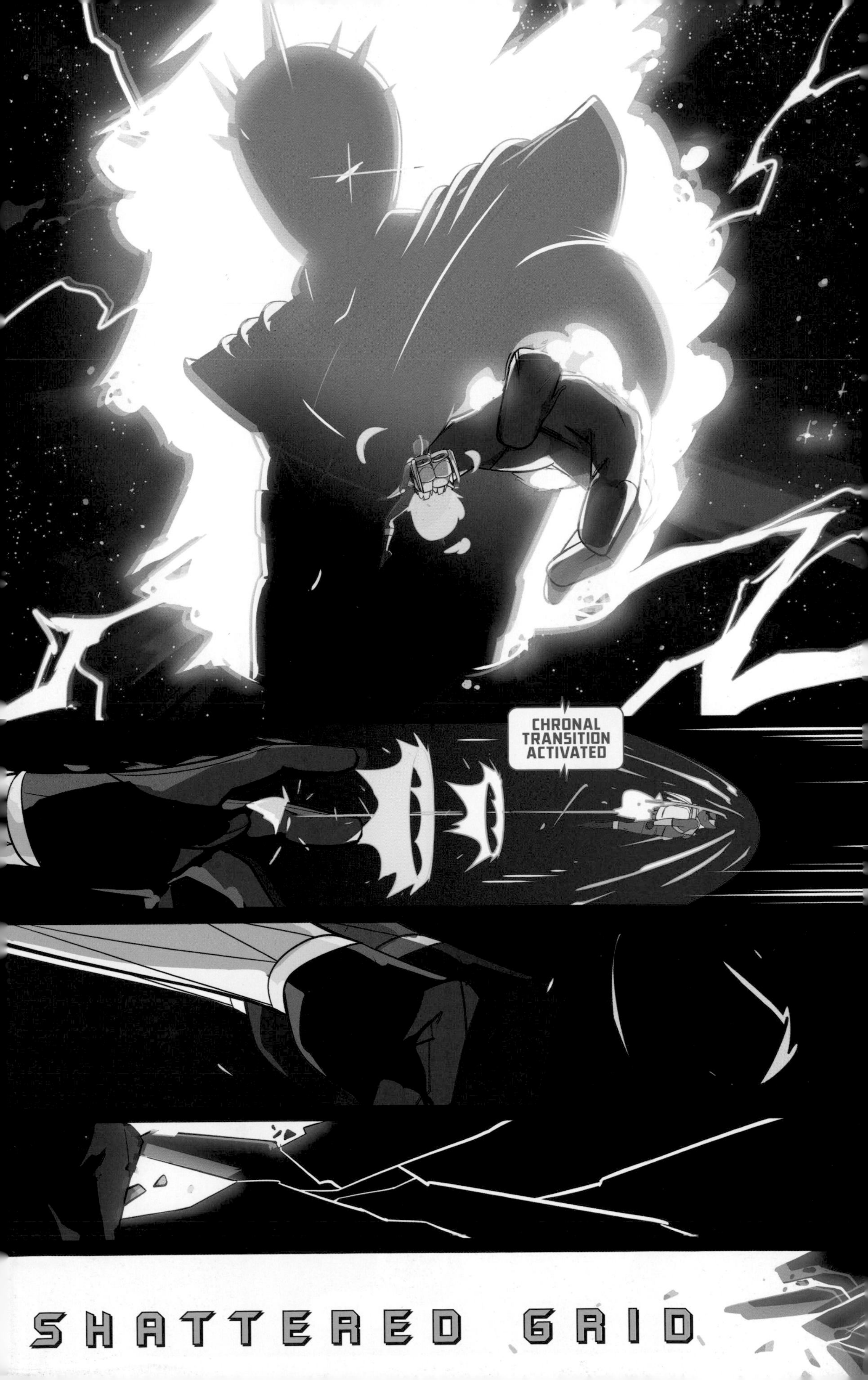
CHRONAL TRANSITION ACTIVATED
SHATTERED GRID

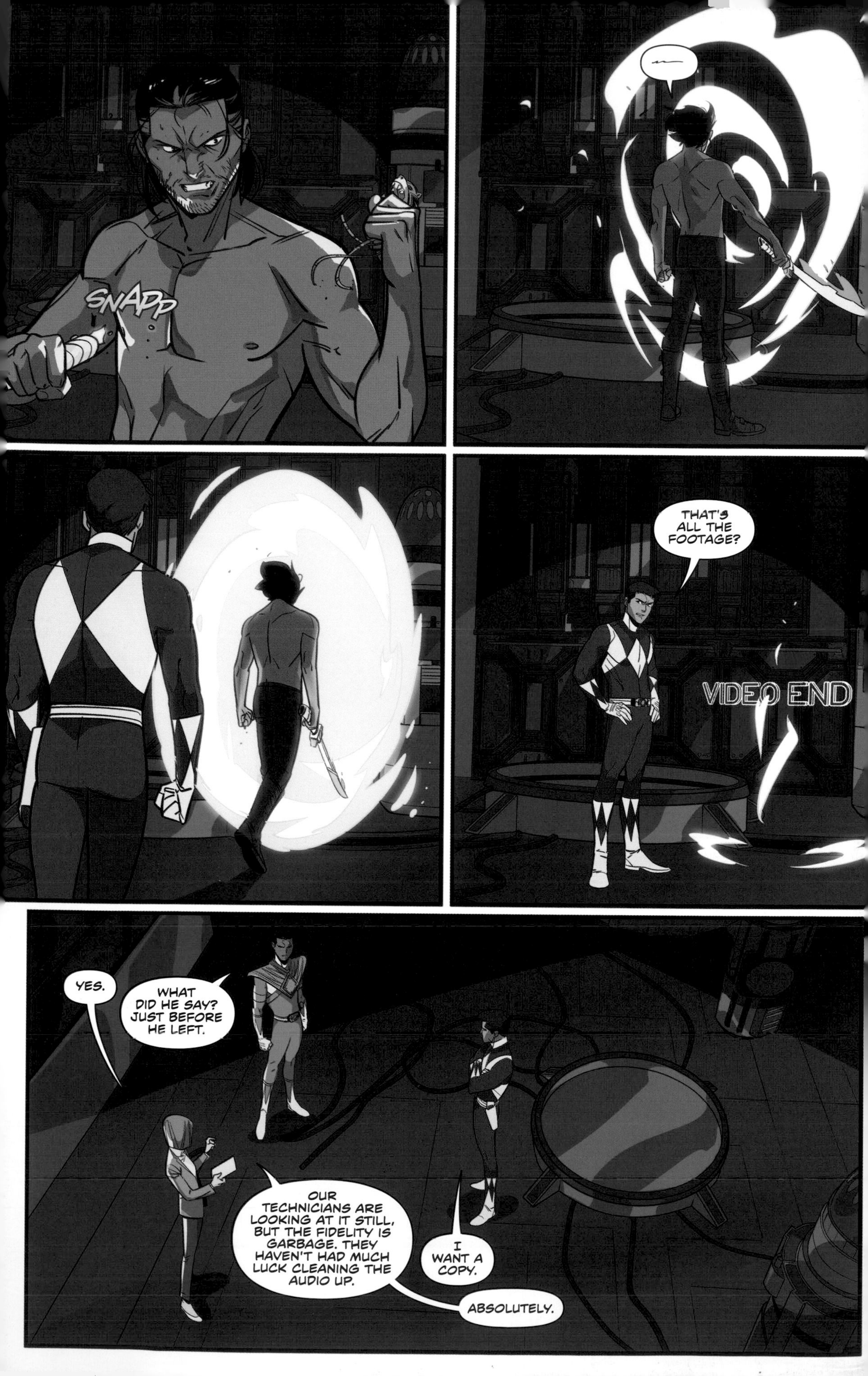
SNAPP
THAT'S ALL THE FOOTAGE?
VIDEO END
YES.
WHAT DID HE SAY? JUST BEFORE HE LEFT.
OUR TECHNICIANS ARE LOOKING AT IT STILL, BUT THE FIDELITY IS GARBAGE. THEY HAVEN'T HAD MUCH LUCK CLEANING THE AUDIO UP.
I WANT A COPY.
ABSOLUTELY.

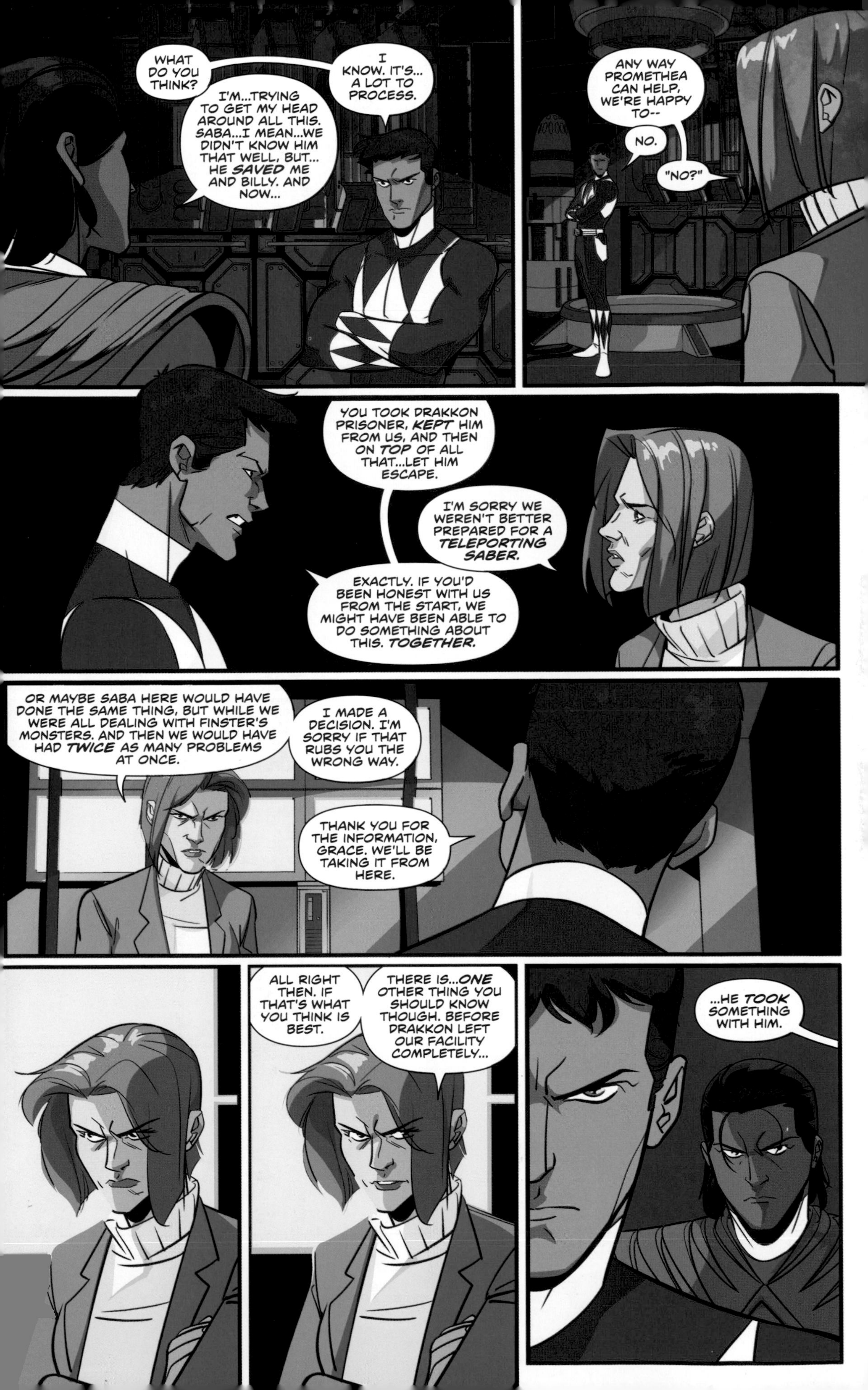
WHAT DO YOU THINK?
I KNOW. IT'S... A LOT TO PROCESS.
I'M...TRYING TO GET MY HEAD AROUND ALL THIS. SABA...I MEAN...WE DIDN'T KNOW HIM THAT WELL, BUT... HE SAVED ME AND BILLY. AND NOW...
ANY WAY PROMETHEA CAN HELP, WE'RE HAPPY TO--
NO.
"NO?"
YOU TOOK DRAKKON PRISONER, KEPT HIM FROM US, AND THEN ON TOP OF ALL THAT...LET HIM ESCAPE.
I'M SORRY WE WEREN'T BETTER PREPARED FOR A TELEPORTING SABER.
EXACTLY. IF YOU'D BEEN HONEST WITH US FROM THE START, WE MIGHT HAVE BEEN ABLE TO DO SOMETHING ABOUT THIS. TOGETHER.
OR MAYBE SABA HERE WOULD HAVE DONE THE SAME THING, BUT WHILE WE WERE ALL DEALING WITH FINSTER'S MONSTERS. AND THEN WE WOULD HAVE HAD TWICE AS MANY PROBLEMS AT ONCE.
I MADE A DECISION. I'M SORRY IF THAT RUBS YOU THE WRONG WAY.
THANK YOU FOR THE INFORMATION, GRACE. WE'LL BE TAKING IT FROM HERE.
ALL RIGHT THEN. IF THAT'S WHAT YOU THINK IS BEST.
THERE IS...ONE OTHER THING YOU SHOULD KNOW THOUGH. BEFORE DRAKKON LEFT OUR FACILITY COMPLETELY...
...HE TOOK SOMETHING WITH HIM.

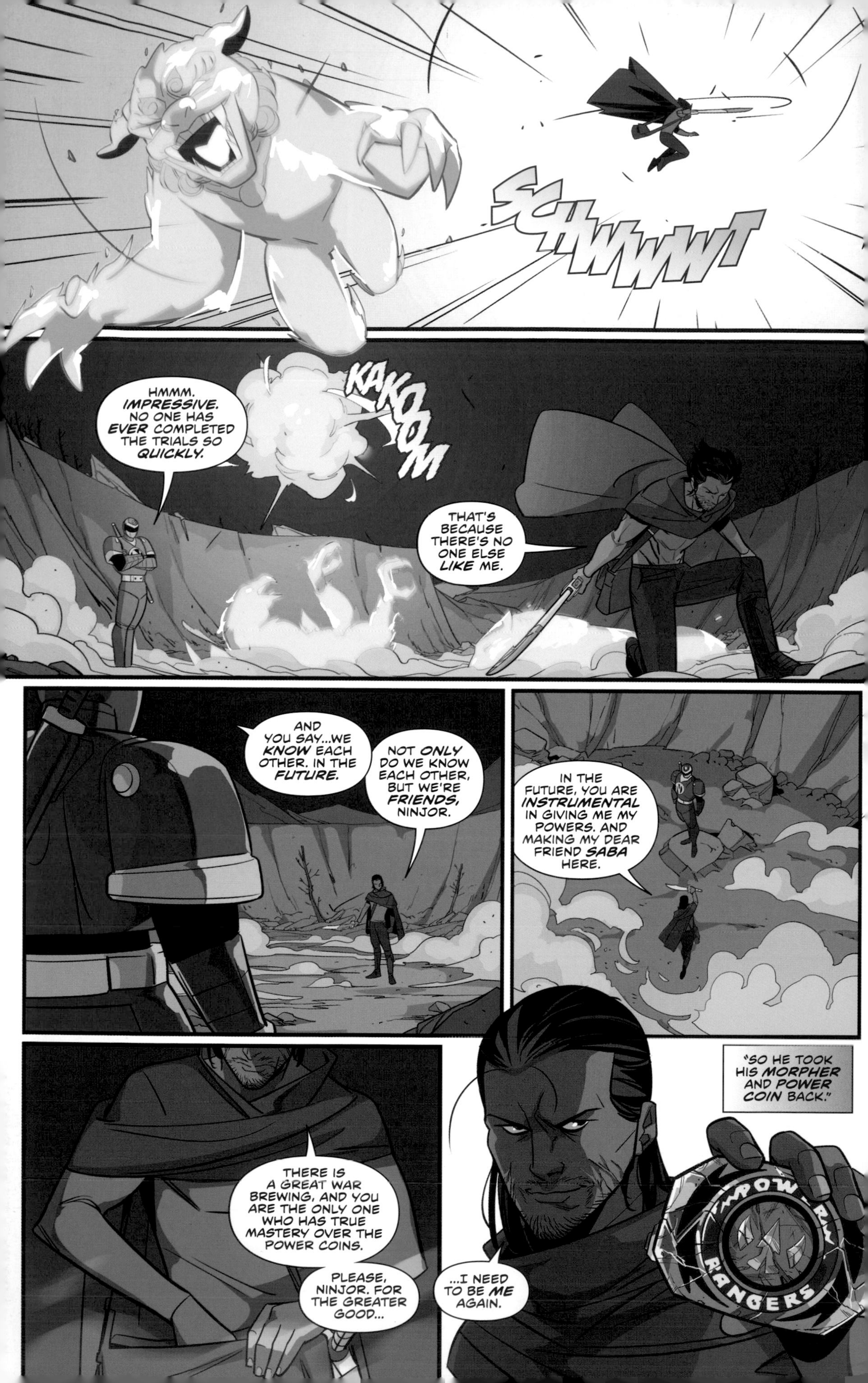
SCHWWWT
KAKOOM
HMMM. IMPRESSIVE. NO ONE HAS EVER COMPLETED THE TRIALS SO QUICKLY.
THAT'S BECAUSE THERE'S NO ONE ELSE LIKE ME.
AND YOU SAY...WE KNOW EACH OTHER. IN THE FUTURE.
NOT ONLY DO WE KNOW EACH OTHER, BUT WE'RE FRIENDS, NINJOR.
IN THE FUTURE, YOU ARE INSTRUMENTAL IN GIVING ME MY POWERS. AND MAKING MY DEAR FRIEND SABA HERE.
THERE IS A GREAT WAR BREWING, AND YOU ARE THE ONLY ONE WHO HAS TRUE MASTERY OVER THE POWER COINS.
PLEASE, NINJOR. FOR THE GREATER GOOD...
"SO HE TOOK HIS MORPHER AND POWER COIN BACK."
...I NEED TO BE ME AGAIN.
RANGERS

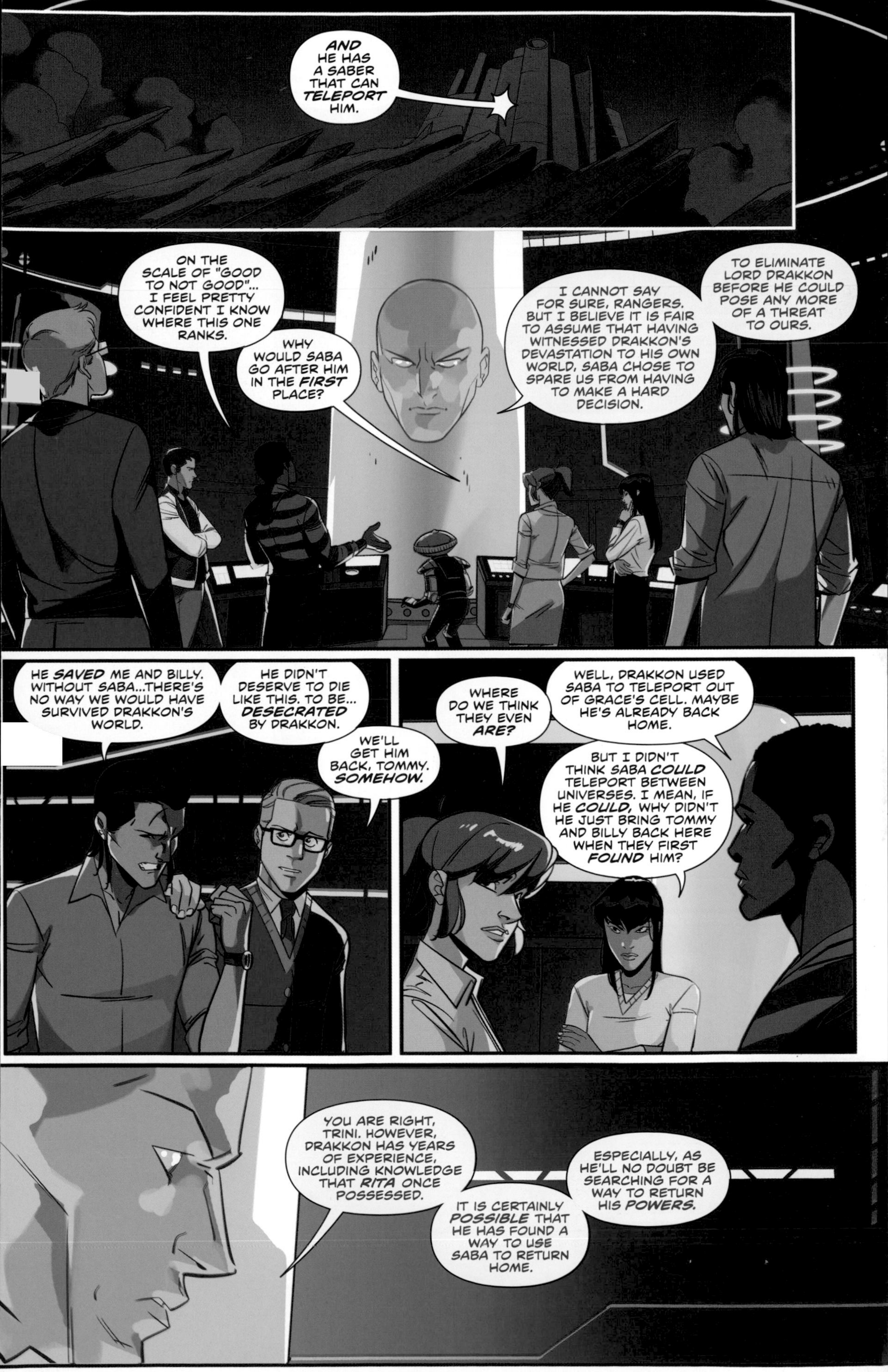
AND HE HAS A SABER THAT CAN TELEPORT HIM.
ON THE SCALE OF "GOOD TO NOT GOOD"... I FEEL PRETTY CONFIDENT I KNOW WHERE THIS ONE RANKS.
WHY WOULD SABA GO AFTER HIM IN THE FIRST PLACE?
I CANNOT SAY FOR SURE, RANGERS. BUT I BELIEVE IT IS FAIR TO ASSUME THAT HAVING WITNESSED DRAKKON'S DEVASTATION TO HIS OWN WORLD, SABA CHOSE TO SPARE US FROM HAVING TO MAKE A HARD DECISION.
TO ELIMINATE LORD DRAKKON BEFORE HE COULD POSE ANY MORE OF A THREAT TO OURS.
HE SAVED ME AND BILLY. WITHOUT SABA...THERE'S NO WAY WE WOULD HAVE SURVIVED DRAKKON'S WORLD.
HE DIDN'T DESERVE TO DIE LIKE THIS. TO BE... DESECRATED BY DRAKKON.
WE'LL GET HIM BACK, TOMMY. SOMEHOW.
WHERE DO WE THINK THEY EVEN ARE?
WELL, DRAKKON USED SABA TO TELEPORT OUT OF GRACE'S CELL. MAYBE HE'S ALREADY BACK HOME.
BUT I DIDN'T THINK SABA COULD TELEPORT BETWEEN UNIVERSES. I MEAN, IF HE COULD, WHY DIDN'T HE JUST BRING TOMMY AND BILLY BACK HERE WHEN THEY FIRST FOUND HIM?
YOU ARE RIGHT, TRINI. HOWEVER, DRAKKON HAS YEARS OF EXPERIENCE, INCLUDING KNOWLEDGE THAT RITA ONCE POSSESSED.
IT IS CERTAINLY POSSIBLE THAT HE HAS FOUND A WAY TO USE SABA TO RETURN HOME.
ESPECIALLY, AS HE'LL NO DOUBT BE SEARCHING FOR A WAY TO RETURN HIS POWERS.

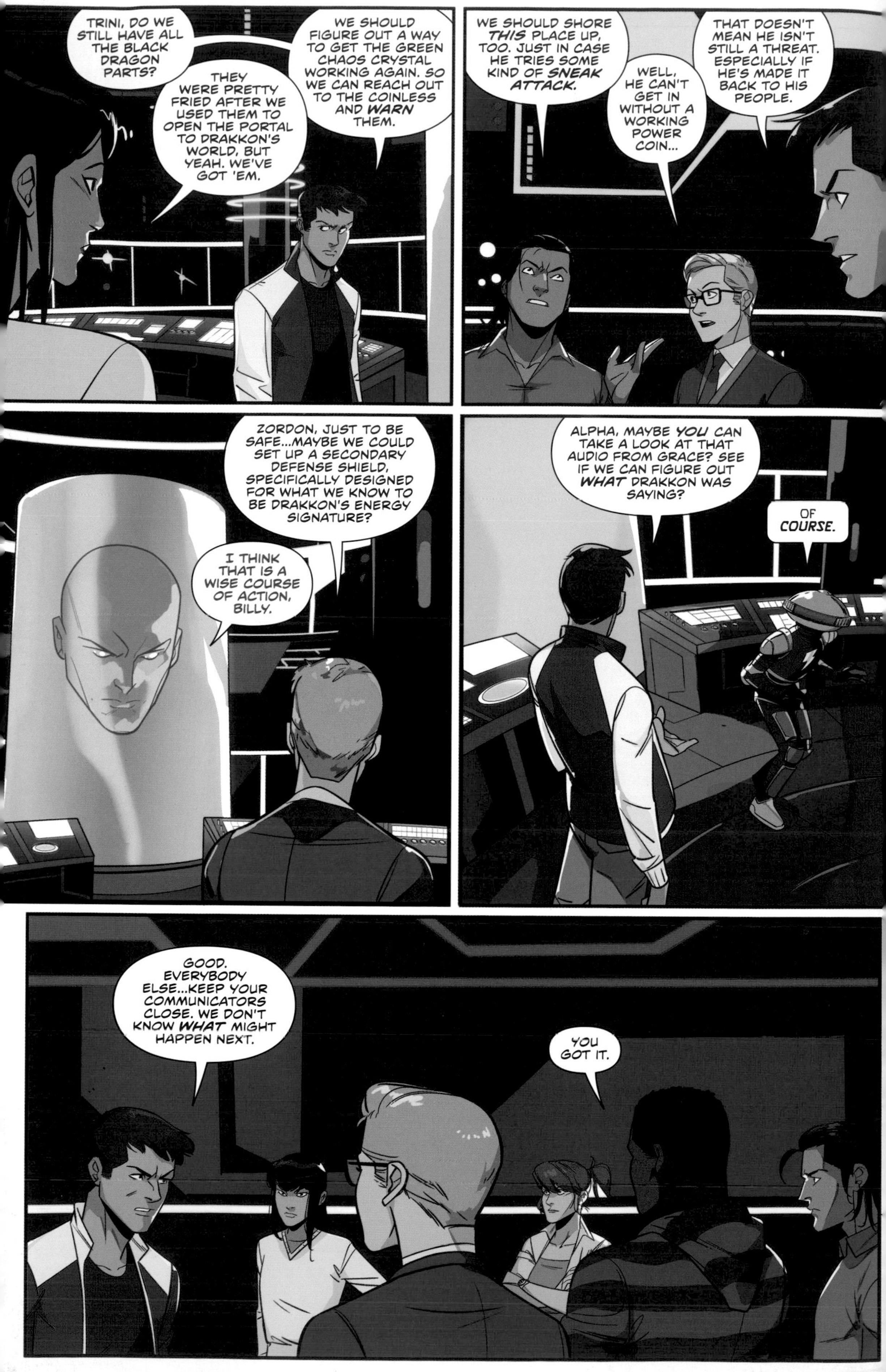
TRINI, DO WE STILL HAVE ALL THE BLACK DRAGON PARTS?
THEY WERE PRETTY FRIED AFTER WE USED THEM TO OPEN THE PORTAL TO DRAKKON'S WORLD, BUT YEAH. WE'VE GOT 'EM.
WE SHOULD FIGURE OUT A WAY TO GET THE GREEN CHAOS CRYSTAL WORKING AGAIN. SO WE CAN REACH OUT TO THE COINLESS AND WARN THEM.
WE SHOULD SHORE THIS PLACE UP, TOO. JUST IN CASE HE TRIES SOME KIND OF SNEAK ATTACK.
WELL, HE CAN'T GET IN WITHOUT A WORKING POWER COIN...
THAT DOESN'T MEAN HE ISN'T STILL A THREAT. ESPECIALLY IF HE'S MADE IT BACK TO HIS PEOPLE.
ZORDON, JUST TO BE SAFE...MAYBE WE COULD SET UP A SECONDARY DEFENSE SHIELD, SPECIFICALLY DESIGNED FOR WHAT WE KNOW TO BE DRAKKON'S ENERGY SIGNATURE?
I THINK THAT IS A WISE COURSE OF ACTION, BILLY.
ALPHA, MAYBE YOU CAN TAKE A LOOK AT THAT AUDIO FROM GRACE? SEE IF WE CAN FIGURE OUT WHAT DRAKKON WAS SAYING?
OF COURSE.
GOOD. EVERYBODY ELSE...KEEP YOUR COMMUNICATORS CLOSE. WE DON'T KNOW WHAT MIGHT HAPPEN NEXT.
YOU GOT IT.

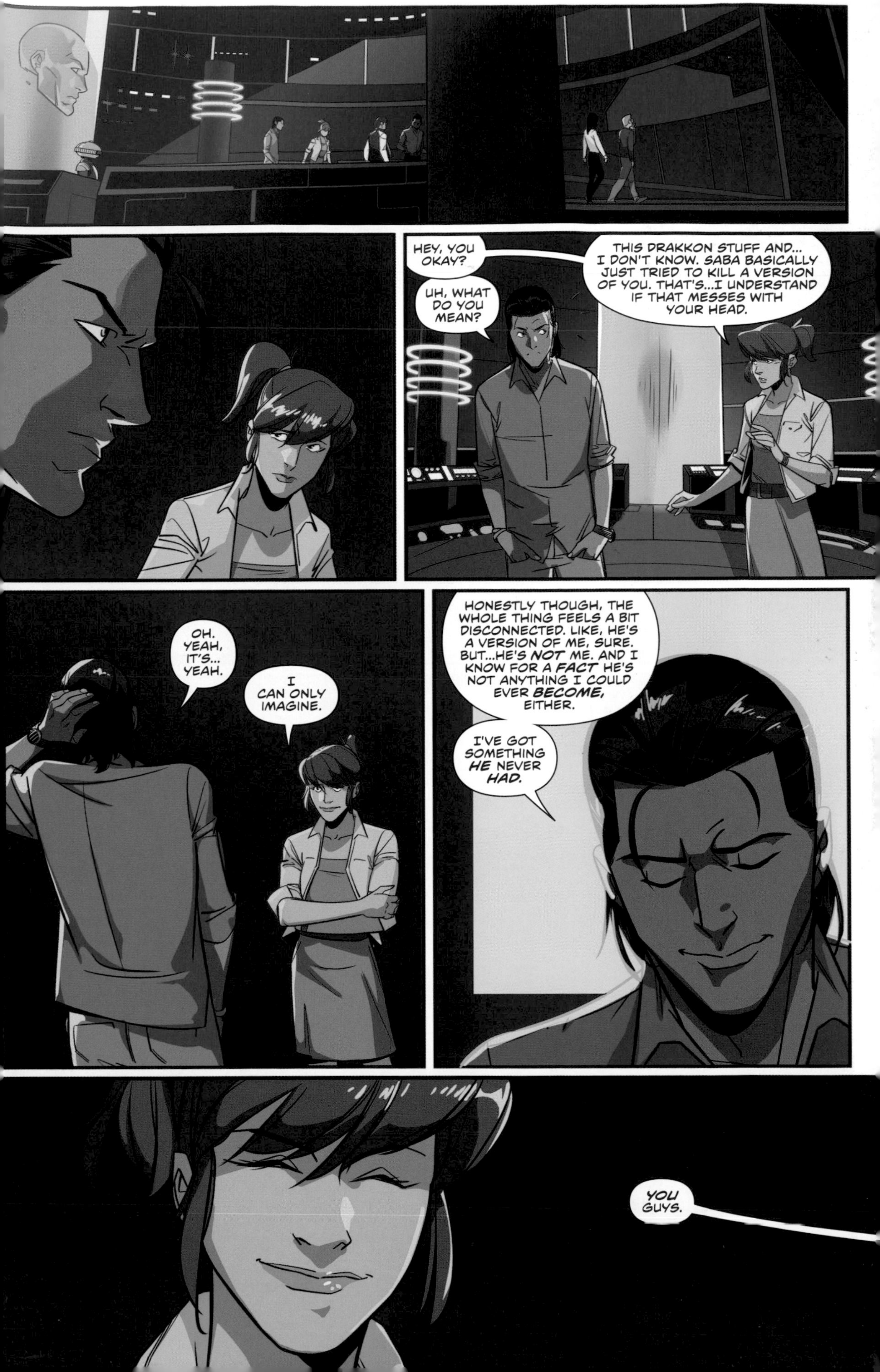
HEY, YOU OKAY?
UH, WHAT DO YOU MEAN?
THIS DRAKKON STUFF AND... I DON'T KNOW. SABA BASICALLY JUST TRIED TO KILL A VERSION OF YOU. THAT'S...I UNDERSTAND IF THAT MESSES WITH YOUR HEAD.
OH. YEAH, IT'S... YEAH.
I CAN ONLY IMAGINE.
HONESTLY THOUGH, THE WHOLE THING FEELS A BIT DISCONNECTED. LIKE, HE'S A VERSION OF ME, SURE. BUT...HE'S NOT ME. AND I KNOW FOR A FACT HE'S NOT ANYTHING I COULD EVER BECOME, EITHER.
I'VE GOT SOMETHING HE NEVER HAD.
YOU GUYS.

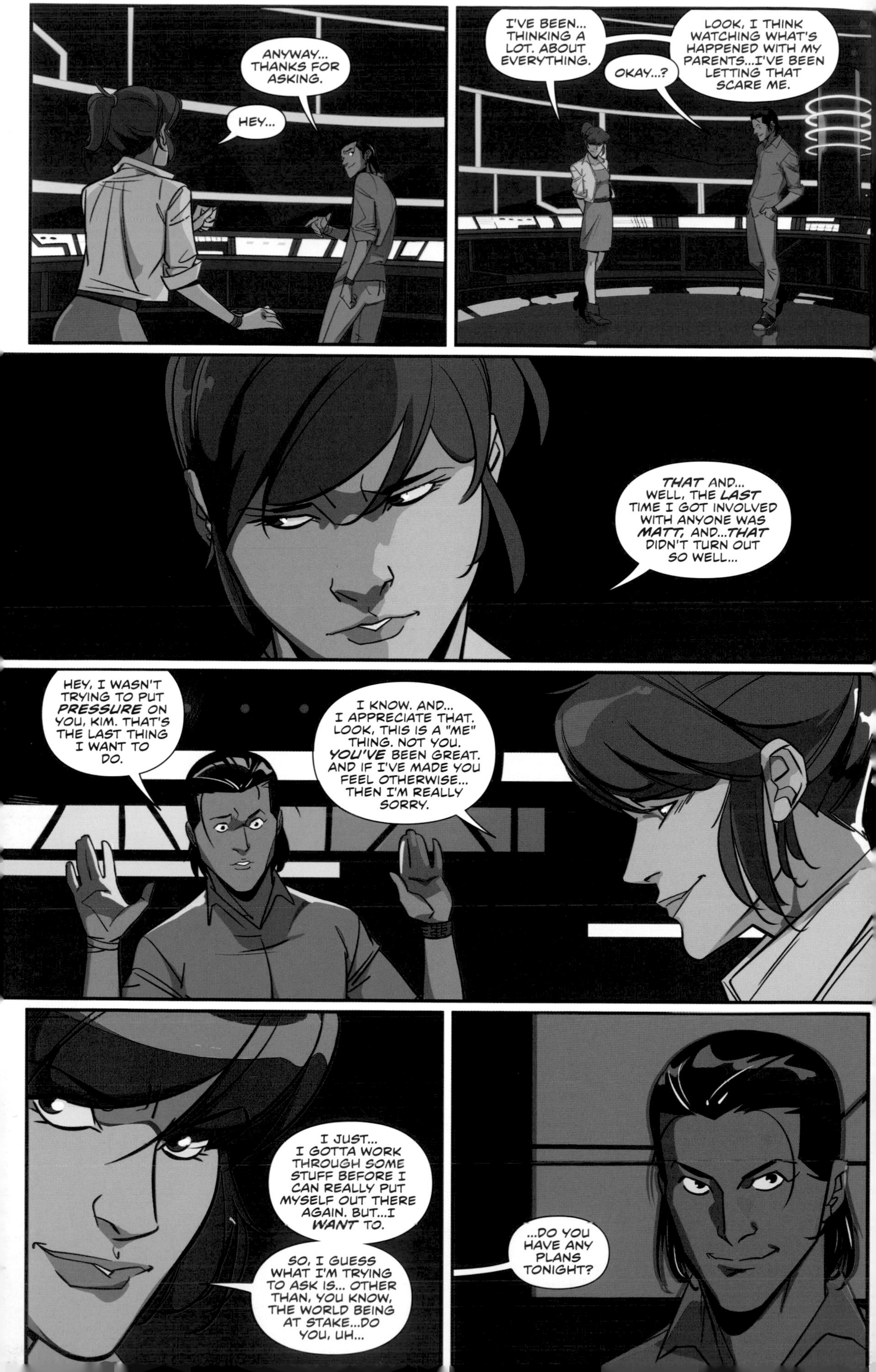
ANYWAY... THANKS FOR ASKING.
HEY...
I'VE BEEN... THINKING A LOT. ABOUT EVERYTHING.
OKAY...?
LOOK, I THINK WATCHING WHAT'S HAPPENED WITH MY PARENTS...I'VE BEEN LETTING THAT SCARE ME.
THAT AND... WELL, THE LAST TIME I GOT INVOLVED WITH ANYONE WAS MATT, AND...THAT DIDN'T TURN OUT SO WELL...
HEY, I WASN'T TRYING TO PUT PRESSURE ON YOU, KIM. THAT'S THE LAST THING I WANT TO DO.
I KNOW. AND... I APPRECIATE THAT. LOOK, THIS IS A "ME" THING. NOT YOU. YOU'VE BEEN GREAT. AND IF I'VE MADE YOU FEEL OTHERWISE... THEN I'M REALLY SORRY.
I JUST... I GOTTA WORK THROUGH SOME STUFF BEFORE I CAN REALLY PUT MYSELF OUT THERE AGAIN. BUT...I WANT TO.
SO, I GUESS WHAT I'M TRYING TO ASK IS... OTHER THAN, YOU KNOW, THE WORLD BEING AT STAKE...DO YOU, UH...
...DO YOU HAVE ANY PLANS TONIGHT?

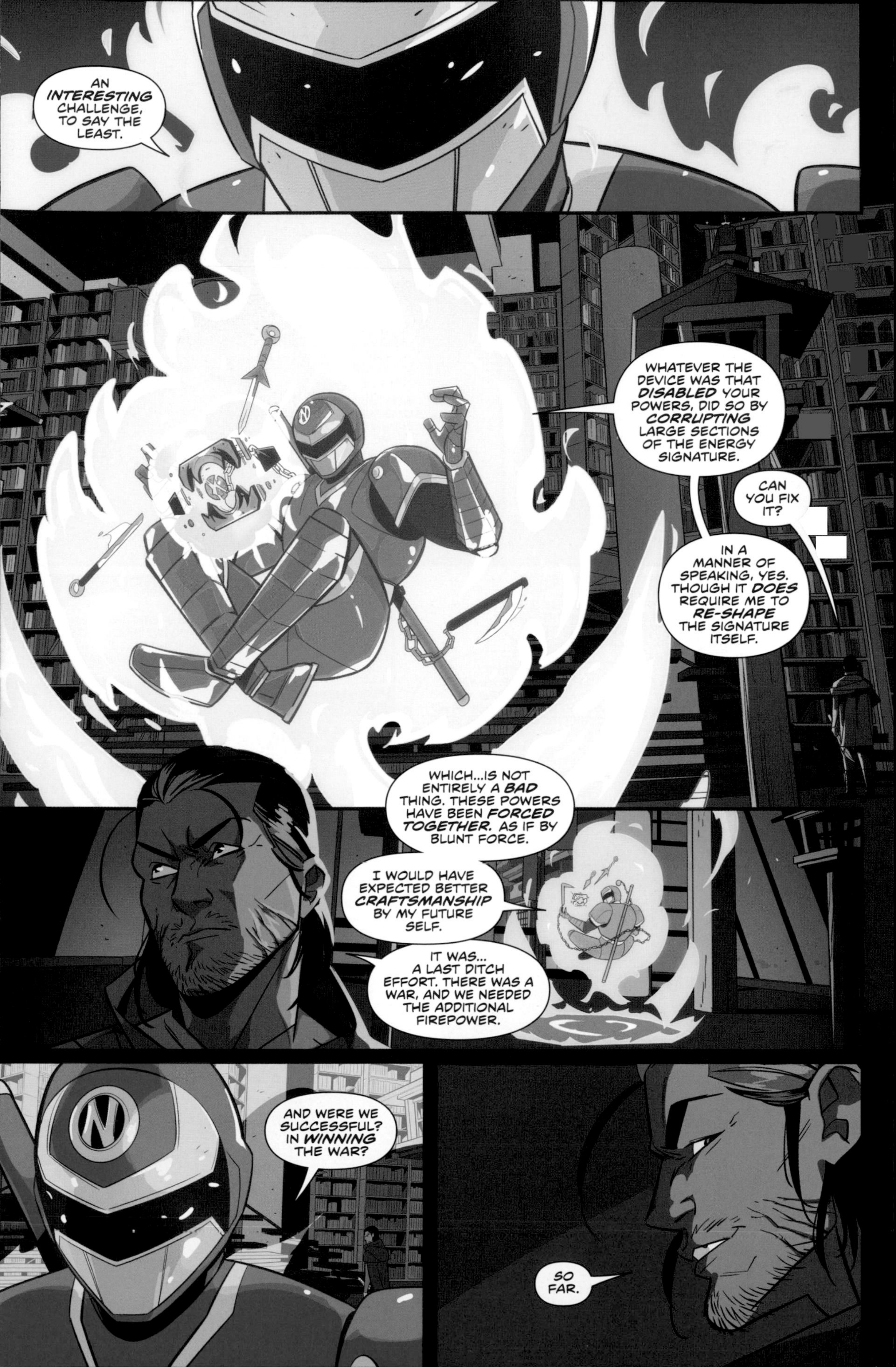
AN INTERESTING CHALLENGE, TO SAY THE LEAST.
WHATEVER THE DEVICE WAS THAT DISABLED YOUR POWERS, DID SO BY CORRUPTING LARGE SECTIONS OF THE ENERGY SIGNATURE.
CAN YOU FIX IT?
IN A MANNER OF SPEAKING, YES. THOUGH IT DOES REQUIRE ME TO RE-SHAPE THE SIGNATURE ITSELF.
WHICH...IS NOT ENTIRELY A BAD THING. THESE POWERS HAVE BEEN FORCED TOGETHER. AS IF BY BLUNT FORCE.
I WOULD HAVE EXPECTED BETTER CRAFTSMANSHIP BY MY FUTURE SELF.
IT WAS... A LAST DITCH EFFORT. THERE WAS A WAR, AND WE NEEDED THE ADDITIONAL FIREPOWER.
AND WERE WE SUCCESSFUL? IN WINNING THE WAR?
SO FAR.

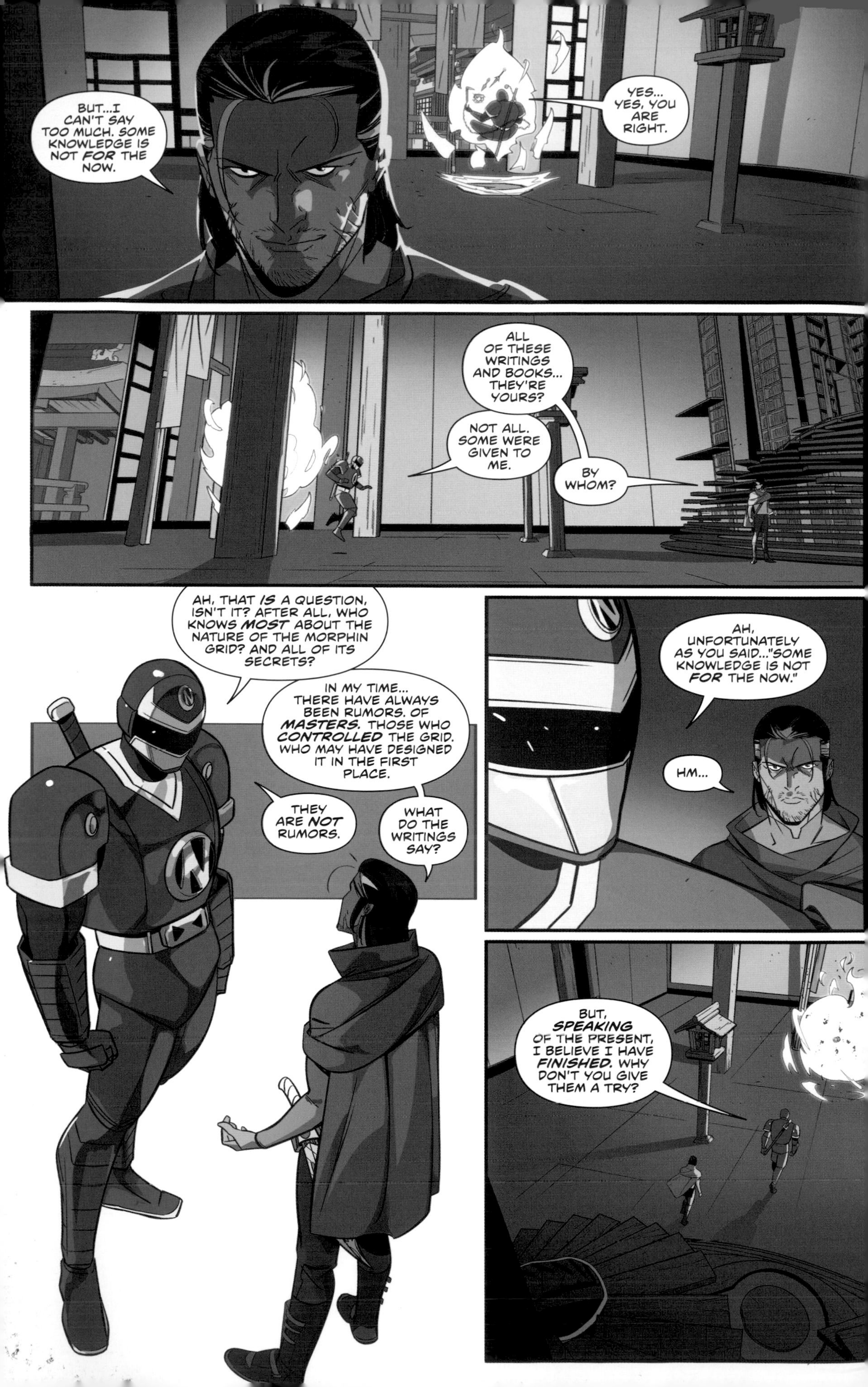
BUT...I CAN'T SAY TOO MUCH. SOME KNOWLEDGE IS NOT FOR THE NOW.
YES... YES, YOU ARE RIGHT.
ALL OF THESE WRITINGS AND BOOKS... THEY'RE YOURS?
NOT ALL. SOME WERE GIVEN TO ME.
BY WHOM?
AH, THAT IS A QUESTION, ISN'T IT? AFTER ALL, WHO KNOWS MOST ABOUT THE NATURE OF THE MORPHIN GRID? AND ALL OF ITS SECRETS?
IN MY TIME... THERE HAVE ALWAYS BEEN RUMORS. OF MASTERS. THOSE WHO CONTROLLED THE GRID. WHO MAY HAVE DESIGNED IT IN THE FIRST PLACE.
THEY ARE NOT RUMORS.
WHAT DO THE WRITINGS SAY?
AH, UNFORTUNATELY AS YOU SAID..."SOME KNOWLEDGE IS NOT FOR THE NOW."
HM...
BUT, SPEAKING OF THE PRESENT, I BELIEVE I HAVE FINISHED. WHY DON'T YOU GIVE THEM A TRY?

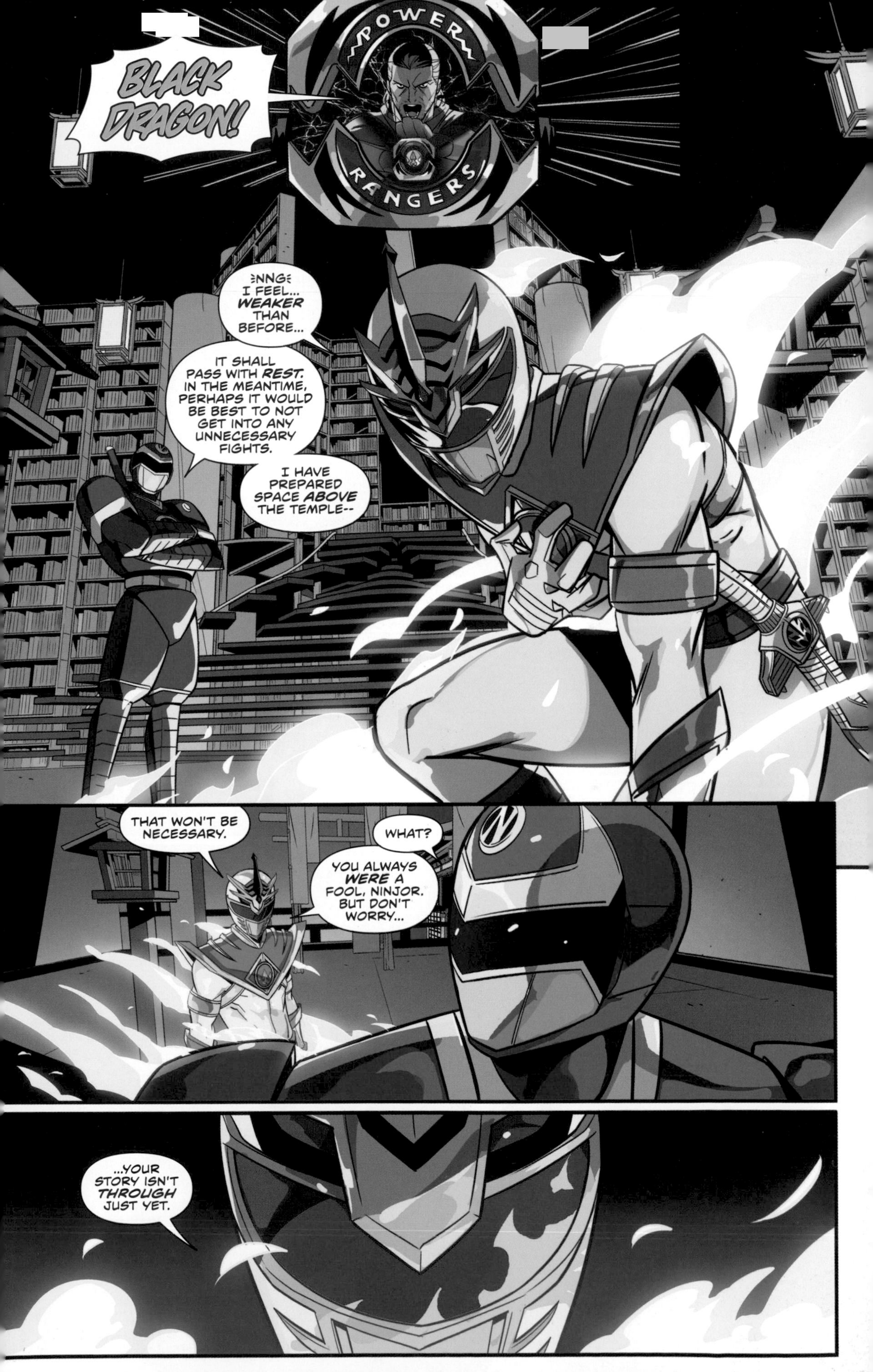

POWER RANGERS
BLACK DRAGON!
NNG I FEEL... WEAKER THAN BEFORE...
IT SHALL PASS WITH REST. IN THE MEANTIME, PERHAPS IT WOULD BE BEST TO NOT GET INTO ANY UNNECESSARY FIGHTS.
I HAVE PREPARED SPACE ABOVE THE TEMPLE--
THAT WON'T BE NECESSARY.
WHAT?
YOU ALWAYS WERE A FOOL, NINJOR. BUT DON'T WORRY...
...YOUR STORY ISN'T THROUGH JUST YET.

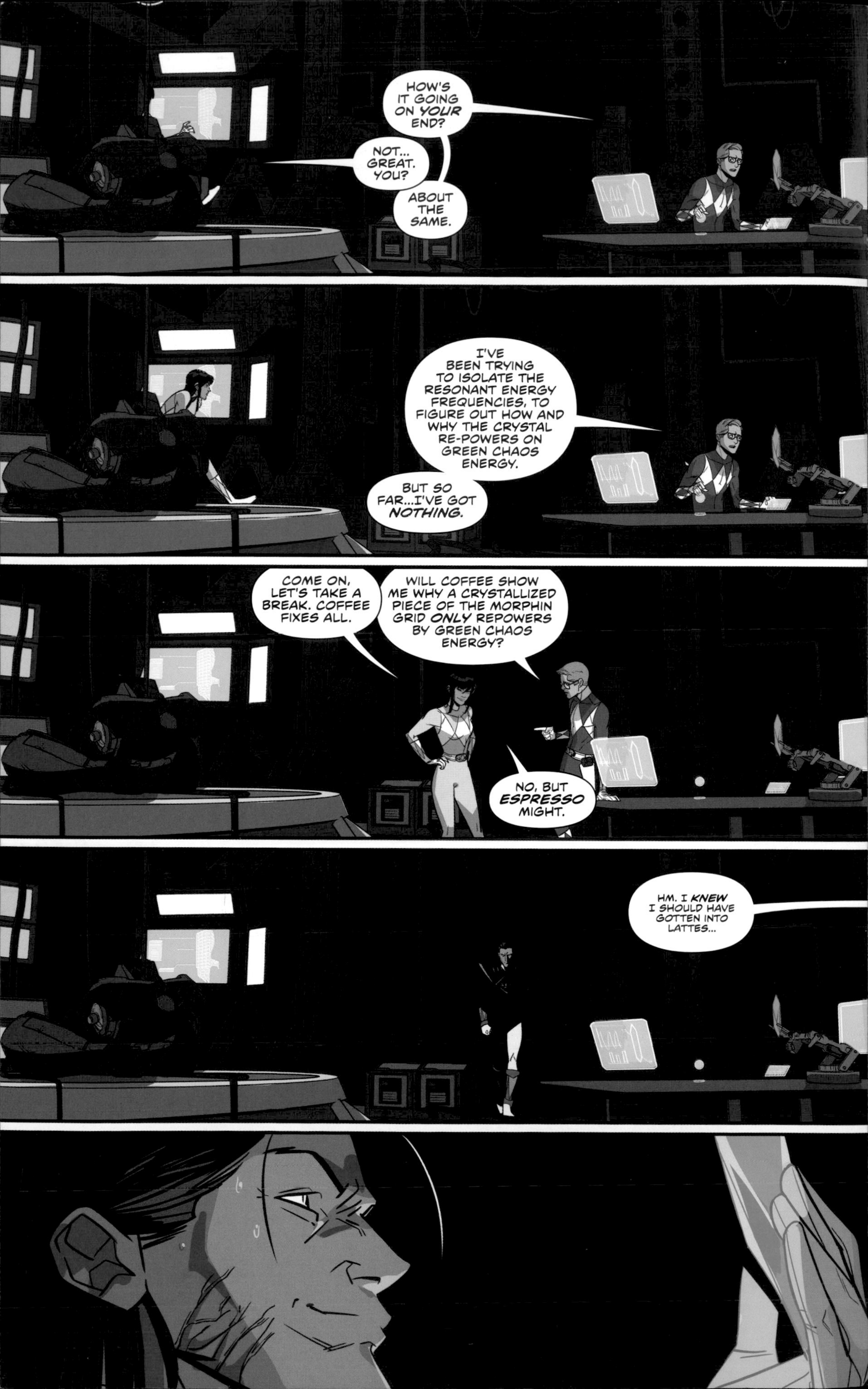
HOW'S IT GOING ON YOUR END?
NOT... GREAT. YOU?
ABOUT THE SAME.
I'VE BEEN TRYING TO ISOLATE THE RESONANT ENERGY FREQUENCIES, TO FIGURE OUT HOW AND WHY THE CRYSTAL RE-POWERS ON GREEN CHAOS ENERGY.
BUT SO FAR...I'VE GOT NOTHING.
COME ON, LET'S TAKE A BREAK. COFFEE FIXES ALL.
WILL COFFEE SHOW ME WHY A CRYSTALLIZED PIECE OF THE MORPHIN GRID ONLY REPOWERS BY GREEN CHAOS ENERGY?
NO, BUT ESPRESSO MIGHT.
HM. I KNEW I SHOULD HAVE GOTTEN INTO LATTES...

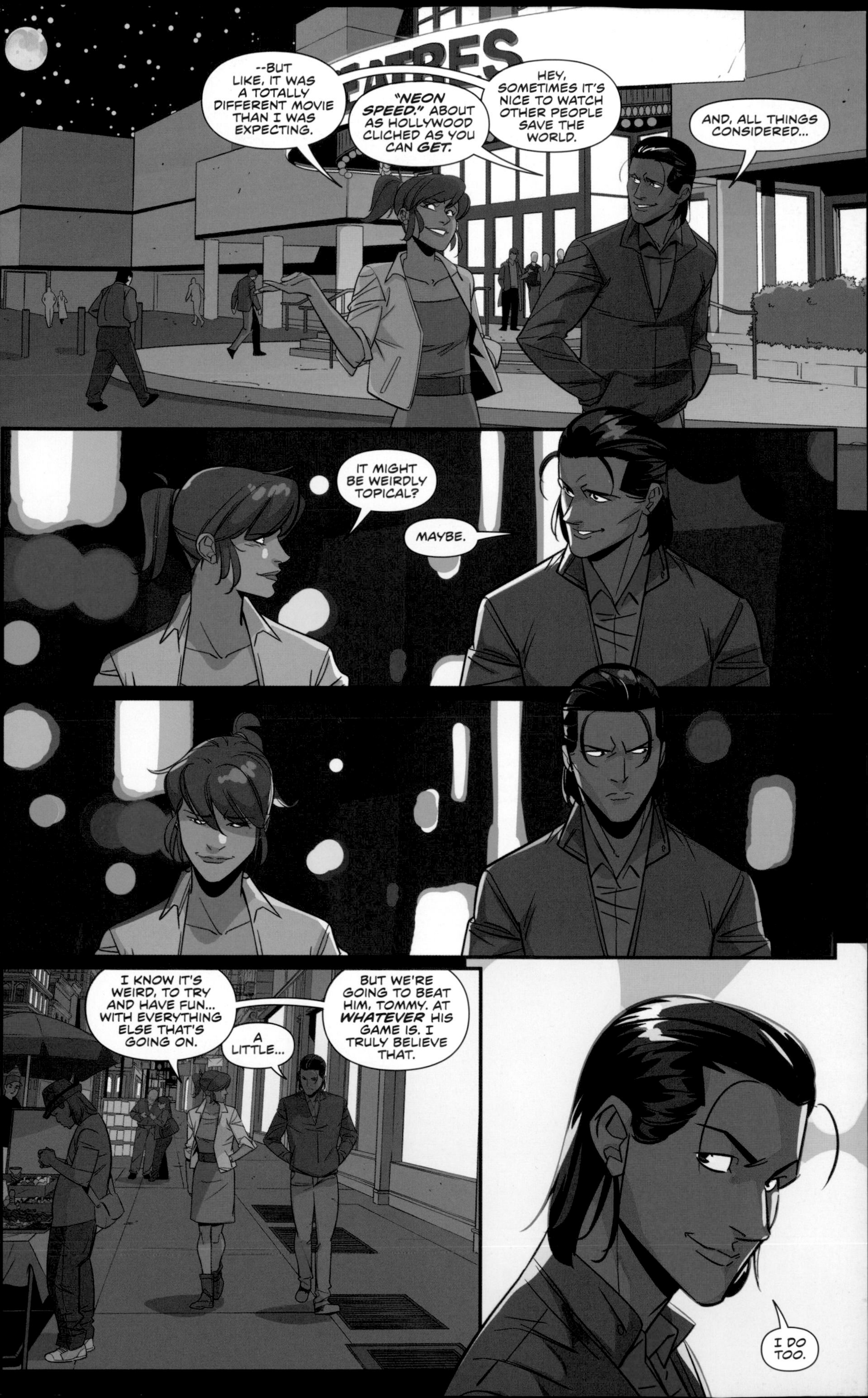
--BUT LIKE, IT WAS A TOTALLY DIFFERENT MOVIE THAN I WAS EXPECTING.
"NEON SPEED." ABOUT AS HOLLYWOOD CLICHED AS YOU CAN GET.
HEY, SOMETIMES IT'S NICE TO WATCH OTHER PEOPLE SAVE THE WORLD.
AND, ALL THINGS CONSIDERED...
IT MIGHT BE WEIRDLY TOPICAL?
MAYBE.
I KNOW IT'S WEIRD, TO TRY AND HAVE FUN... WITH EVERYTHING ELSE THAT'S GOING ON.
A LITTLE...
BUT WE'RE GOING TO BEAT HIM, TOMMY. AT WHATEVER HIS GAME IS. I TRULY BELIEVE THAT.
I DO TOO.

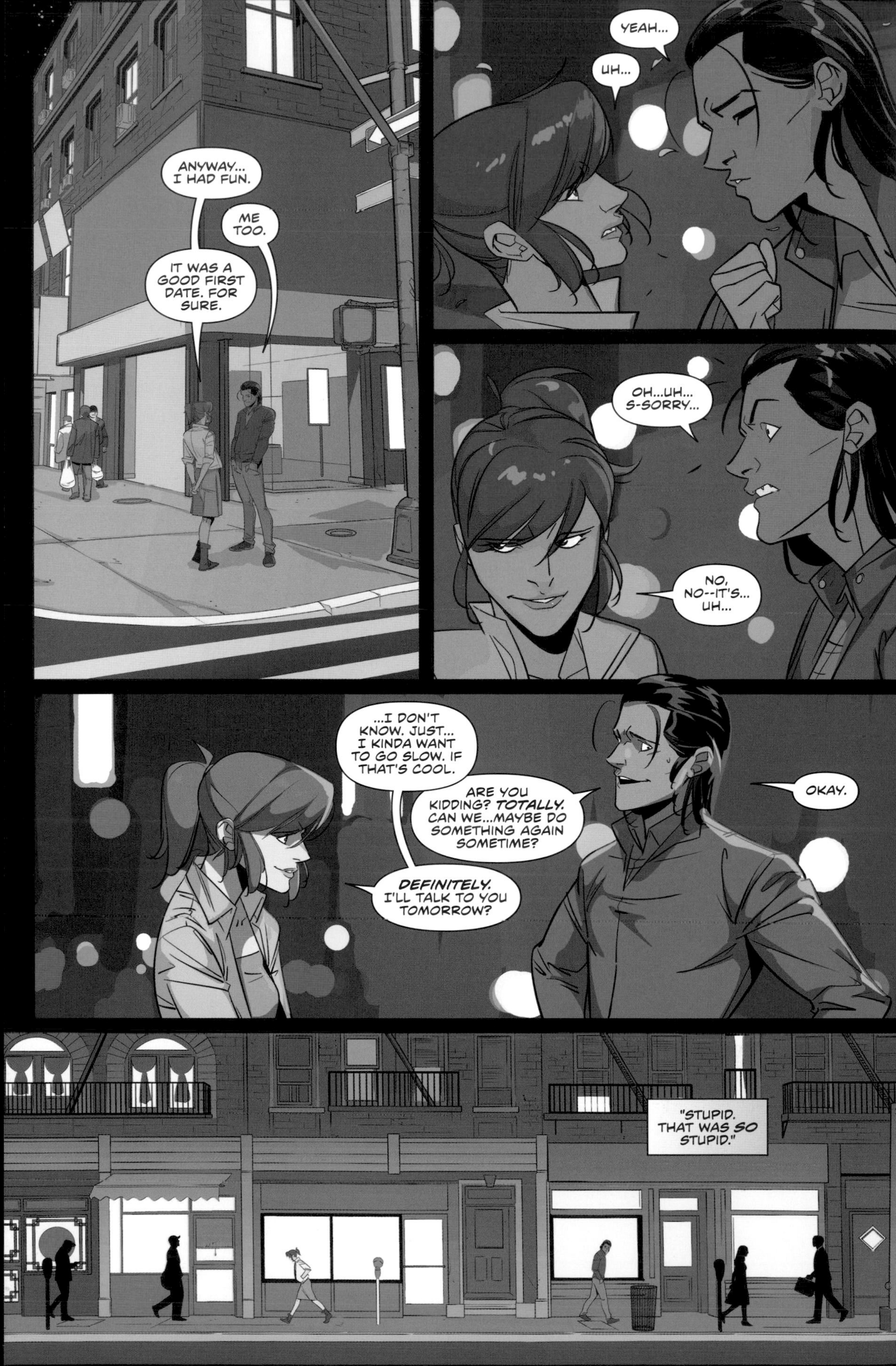
ANYWAY... I HAD FUN.
ME TOO.
IT WAS A GOOD FIRST DATE. FOR SURE.
YEAH...
UH...
OH...UH... S-SORRY...
NO, NO--IT'S... UH...
...I DON'T KNOW. JUST... I KINDA WANT TO GO SLOW. IF THAT'S COOL.
ARE YOU KIDDING? TOTALLY. CAN WE...MAYBE DO SOMETHING AGAIN SOMETIME?
DEFINITELY. I'LL TALK TO YOU TOMORROW?
OKAY.
"STUPID. THAT WAS SO STUPID."

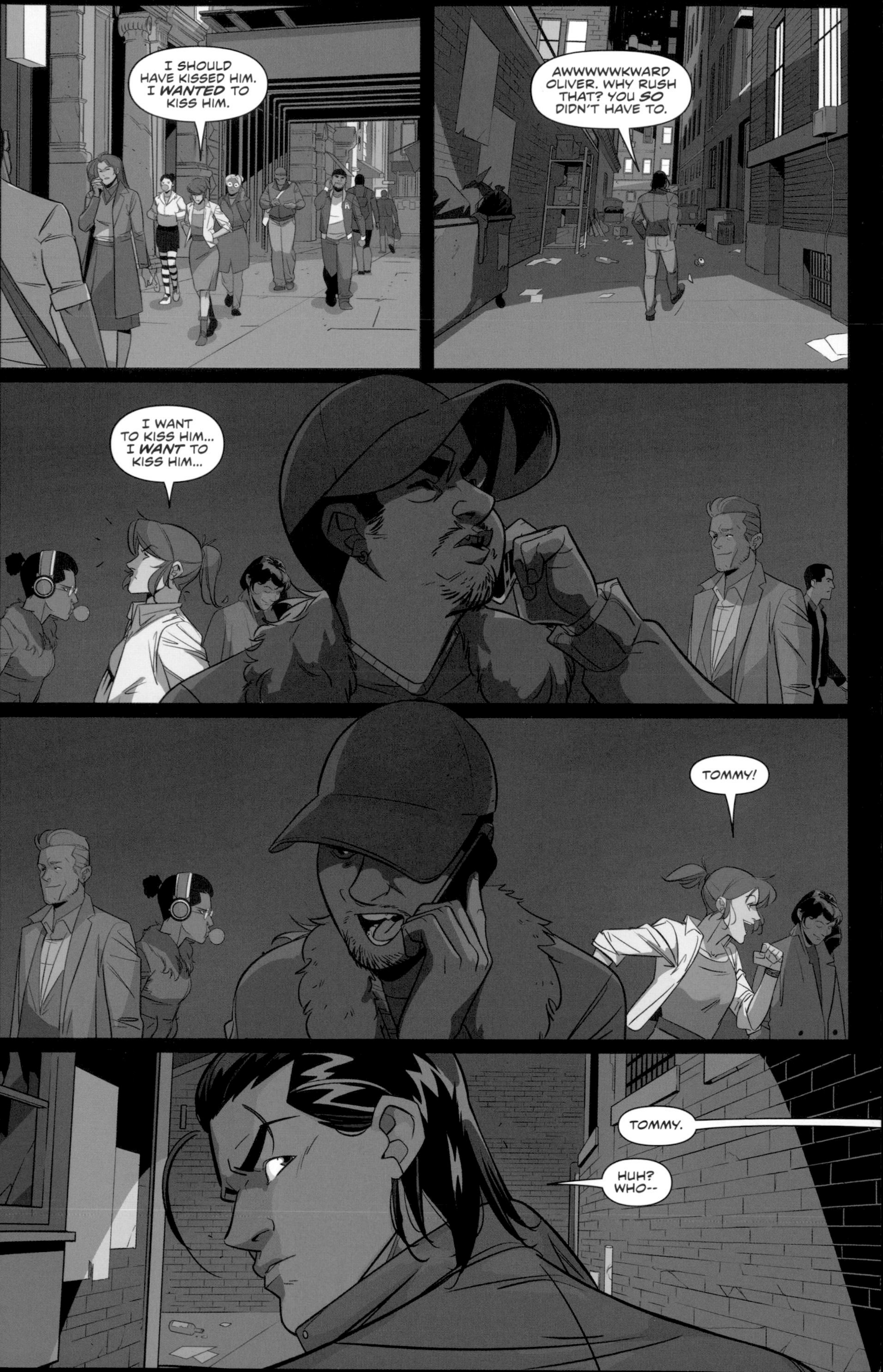
I SHOULD HAVE KISSED HIM. I *WANTED* TO KISS HIM.
AWWWWWKWARD OLIVER. WHY RUSH THAT? YOU *SO* DIDN'T HAVE TO.
I WANT TO KISS HIM... I *WANT* TO KISS HIM...
TOMMY!
TOMMY.
HUH? WHO--

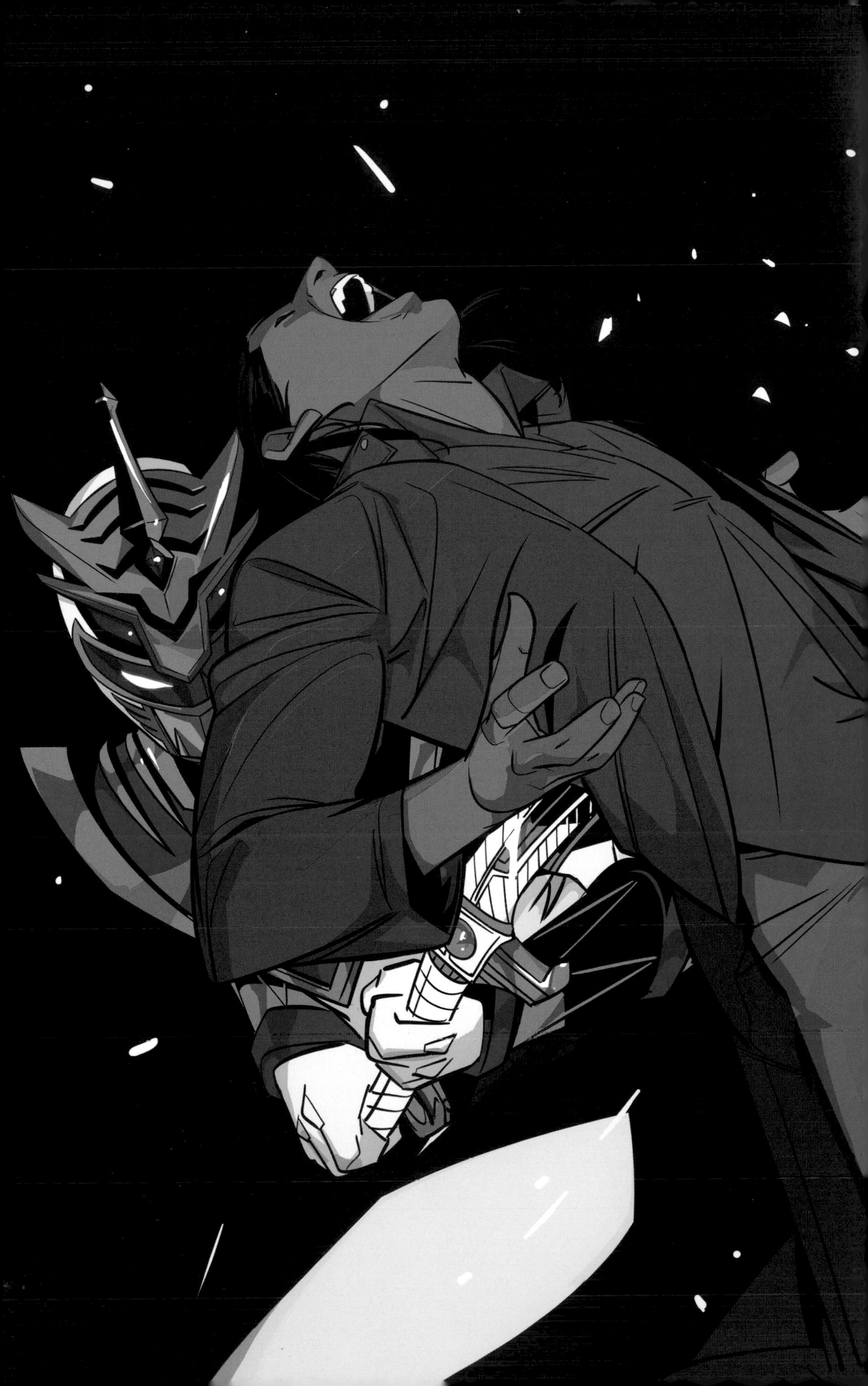

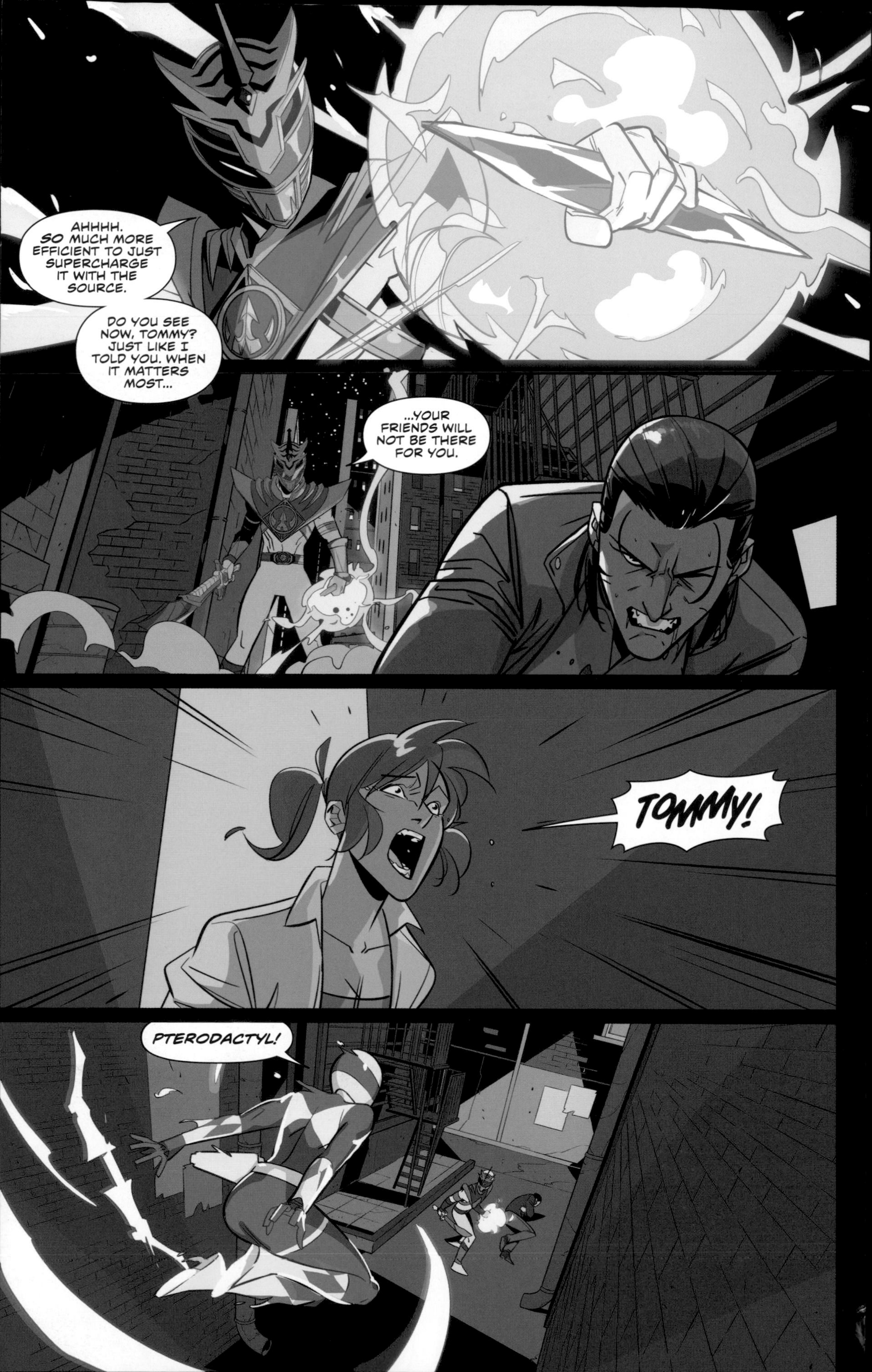
AHHHH. SO MUCH MORE EFFICIENT TO JUST SUPERCHARGE IT WITH THE SOURCE.
DO YOU SEE NOW, TOMMY? JUST LIKE I TOLD YOU. WHEN IT MATTERS MOST...
...YOUR FRIENDS WILL NOT BE THERE FOR YOU.
TOMMY!
PTERODACTYL!

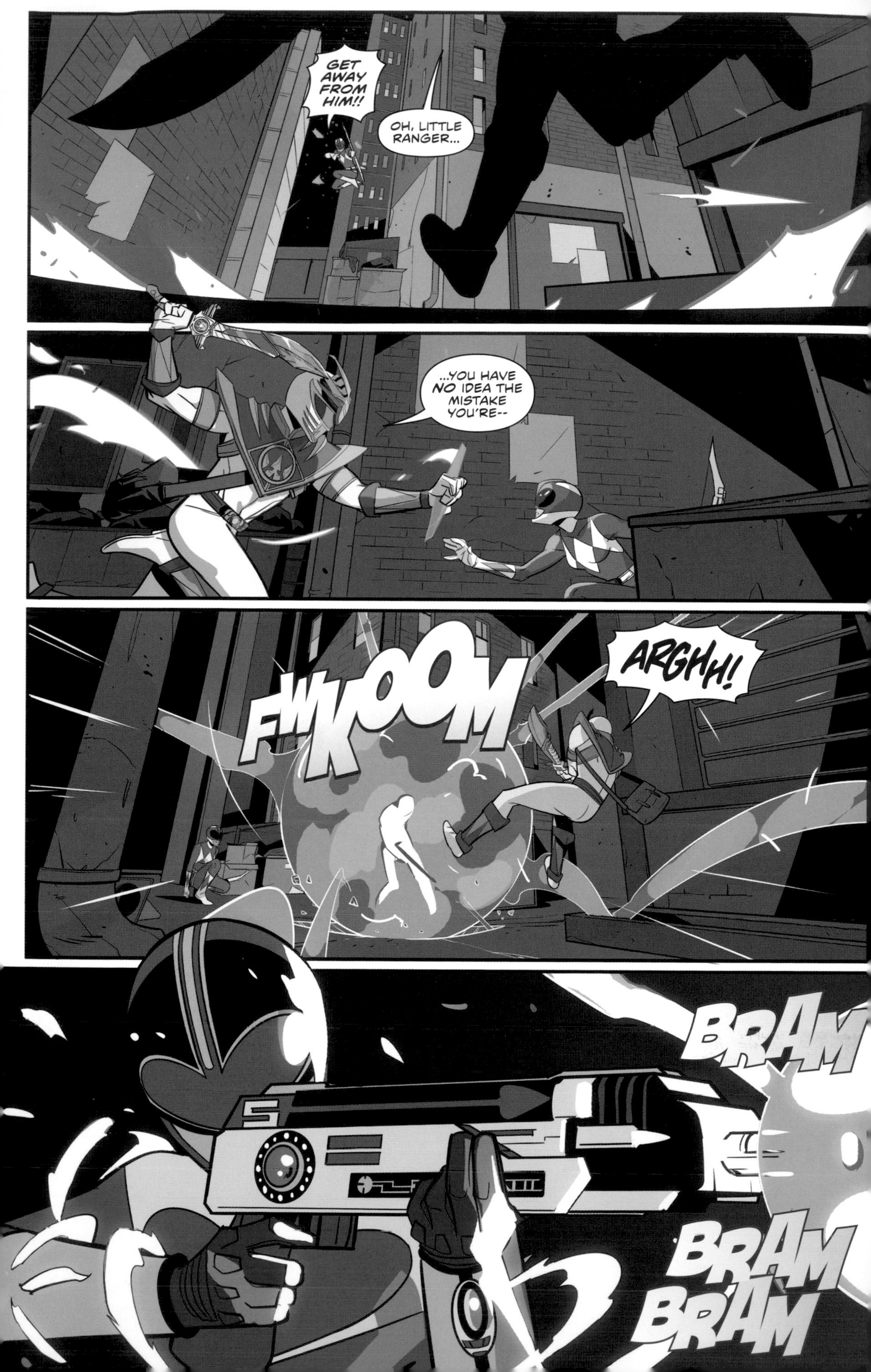
GET AWAY FROM HIM!!
OH, LITTLE RANGER...
...YOU HAVE NO IDEA THE MISTAKE YOU'RE--
FWKOOM
ARGHH!
BRAM
BRAM
BRAM

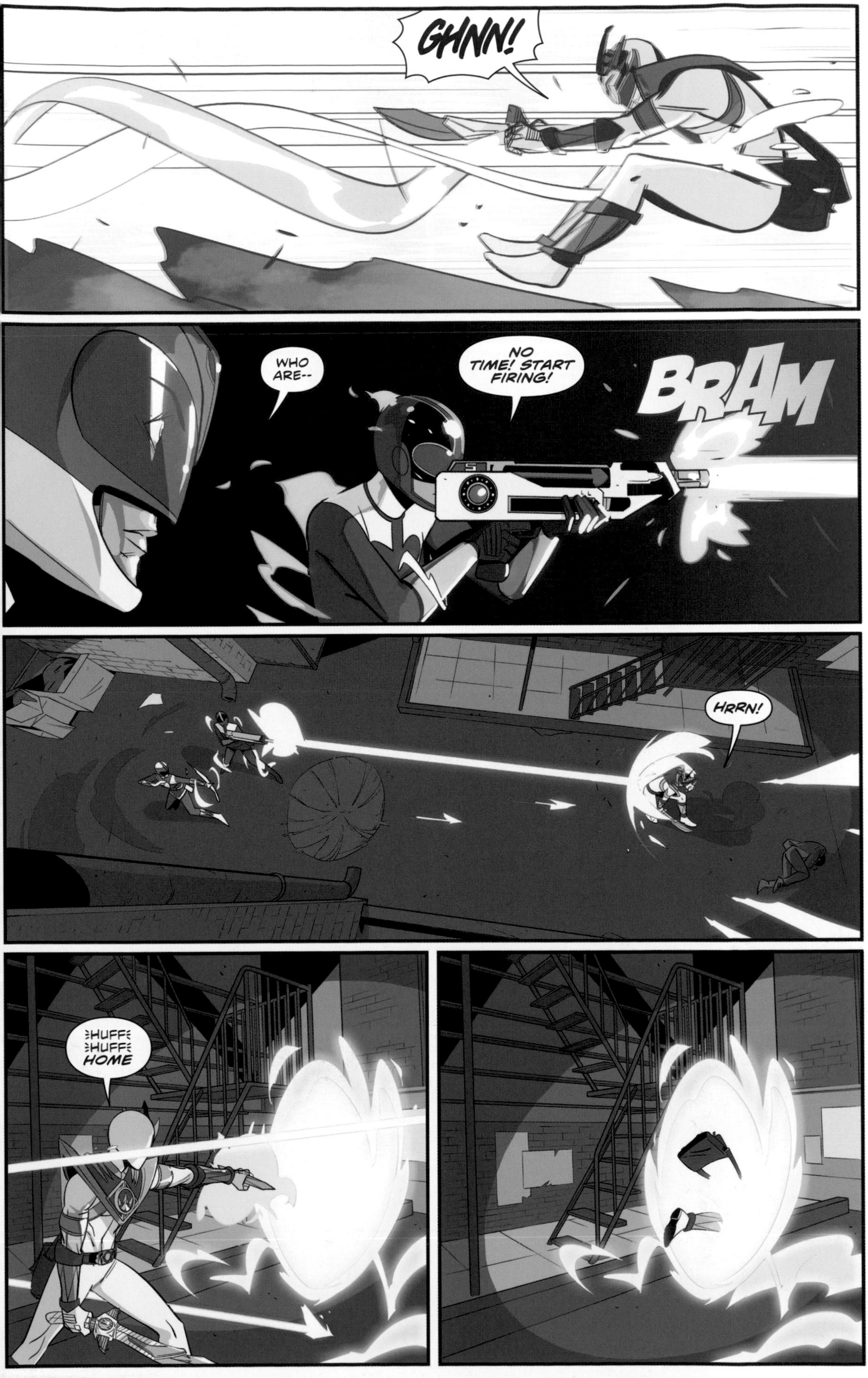
GHNN!
WHO ARE--
NO TIME! START FIRING!
BRAM
HRRN!
HUFF HUFF HOME

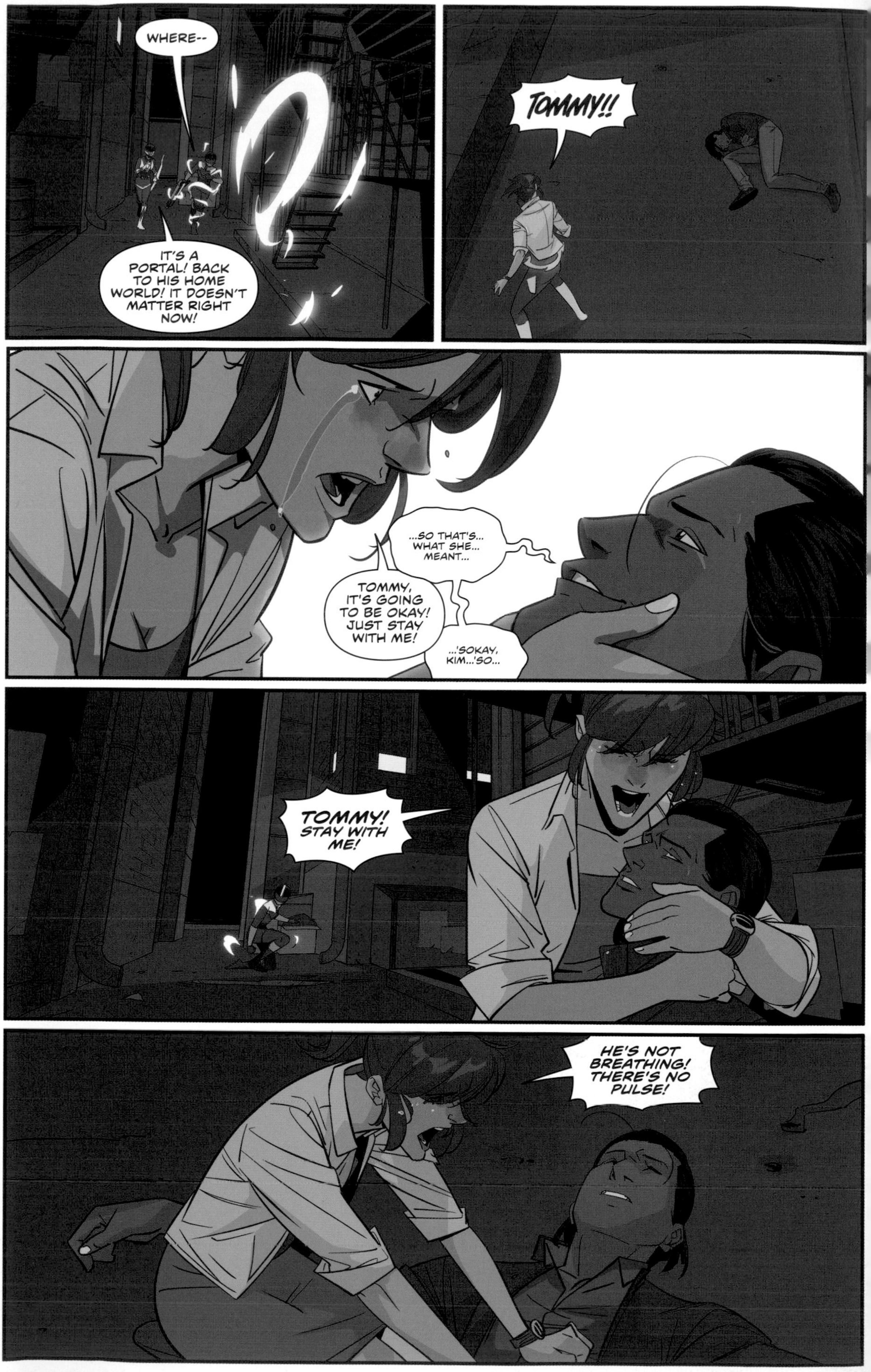
WHERE--
IT'S A PORTAL! BACK TO HIS HOME WORLD! IT DOESN'T MATTER RIGHT NOW!
TOMMY!!
...SO THAT'S... WHAT SHE... MEANT...
TOMMY, IT'S GOING TO BE OKAY! JUST STAY WITH ME!
...'SOKAY, KIM...'SO...
TOMMY! STAY WITH ME!
HE'S NOT BREATHING! THERE'S NO PULSE!

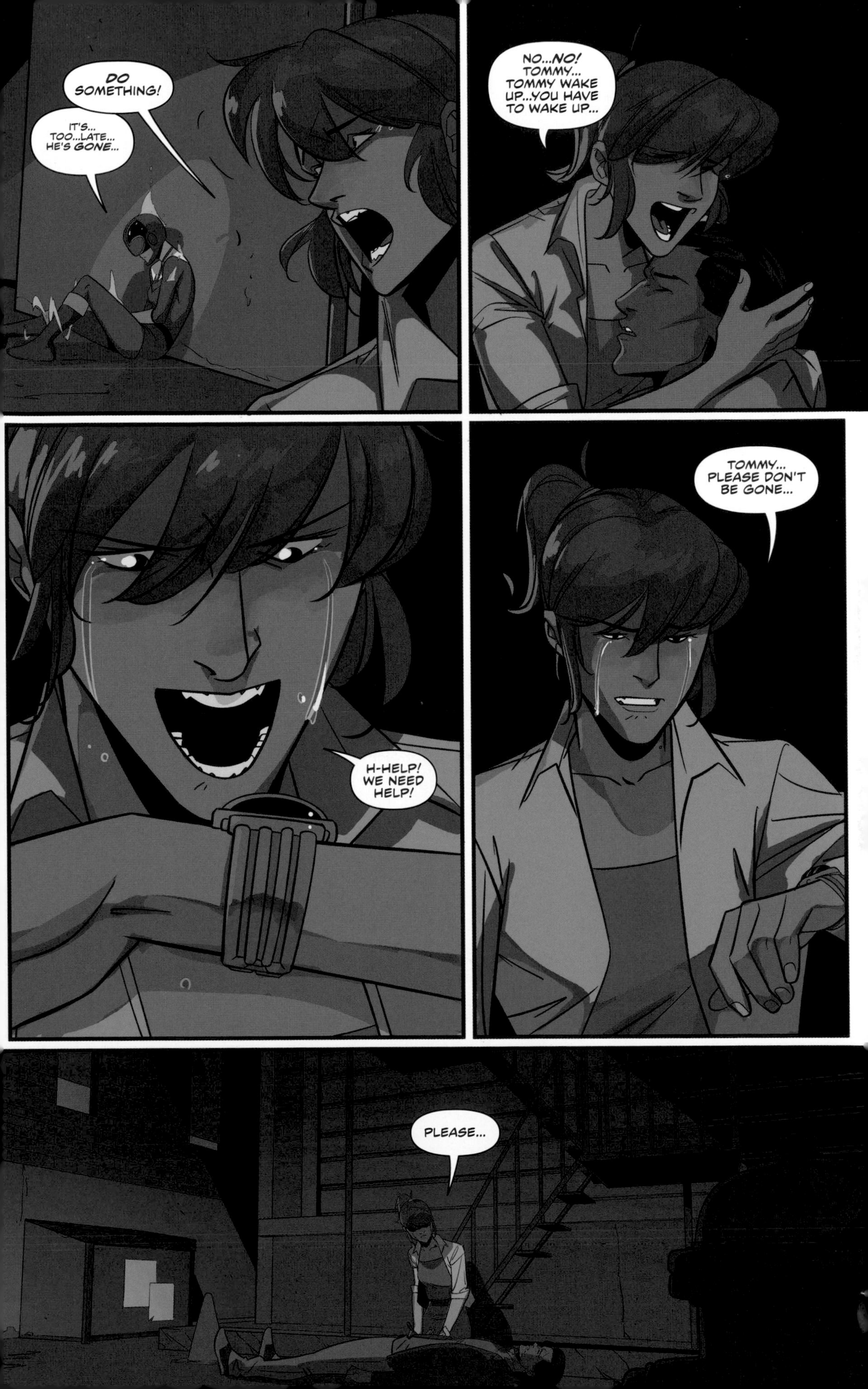
DO SOMETHING!
IT'S... TOO...LATE... HE'S GONE...
NO...NO! TOMMY... TOMMY WAKE UP...YOU HAVE TO WAKE UP...
H-HELP! WE NEED HELP!
TOMMY... PLEASE DON'T BE GONE...
PLEASE...

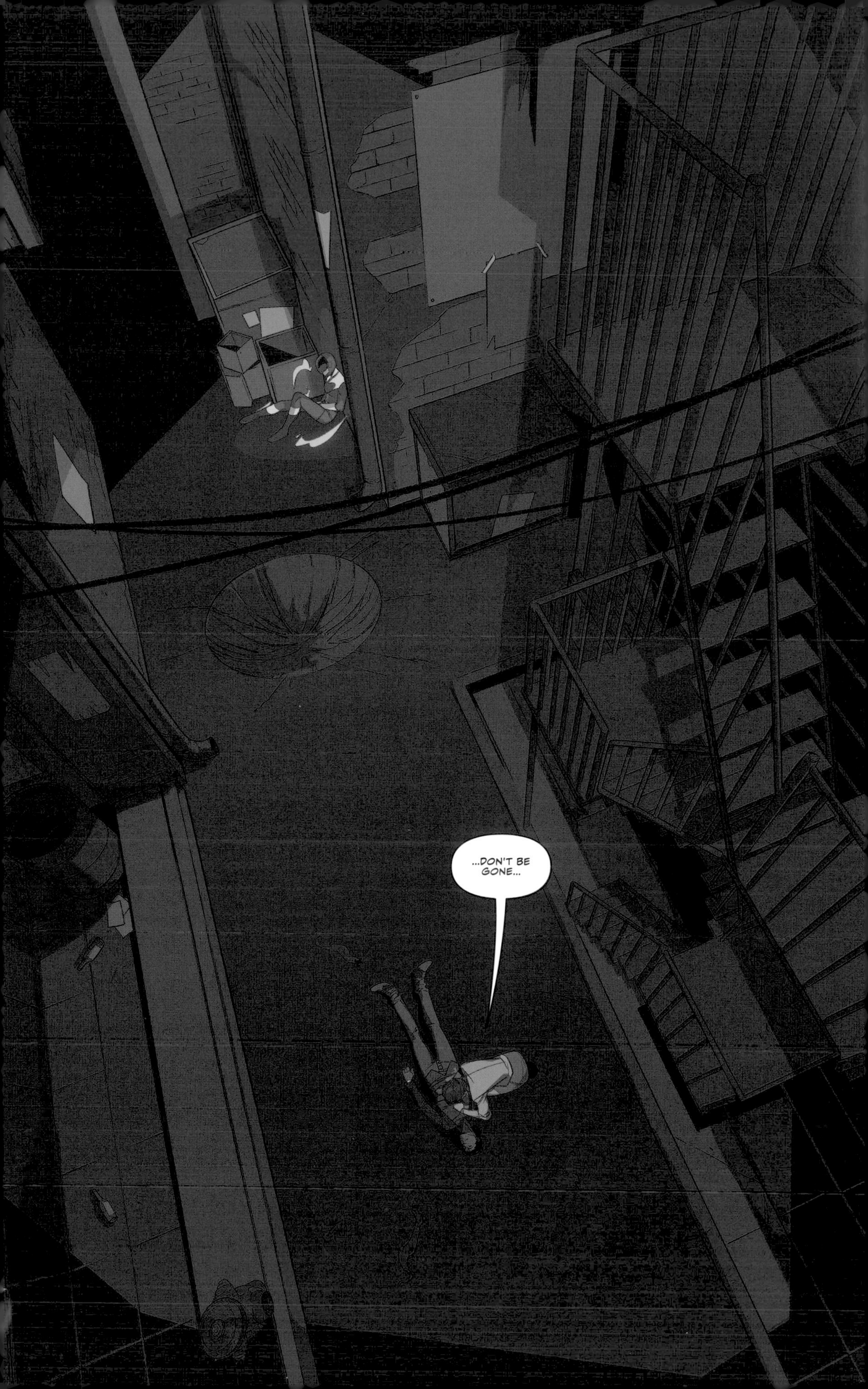
...DON'T BE GONE...

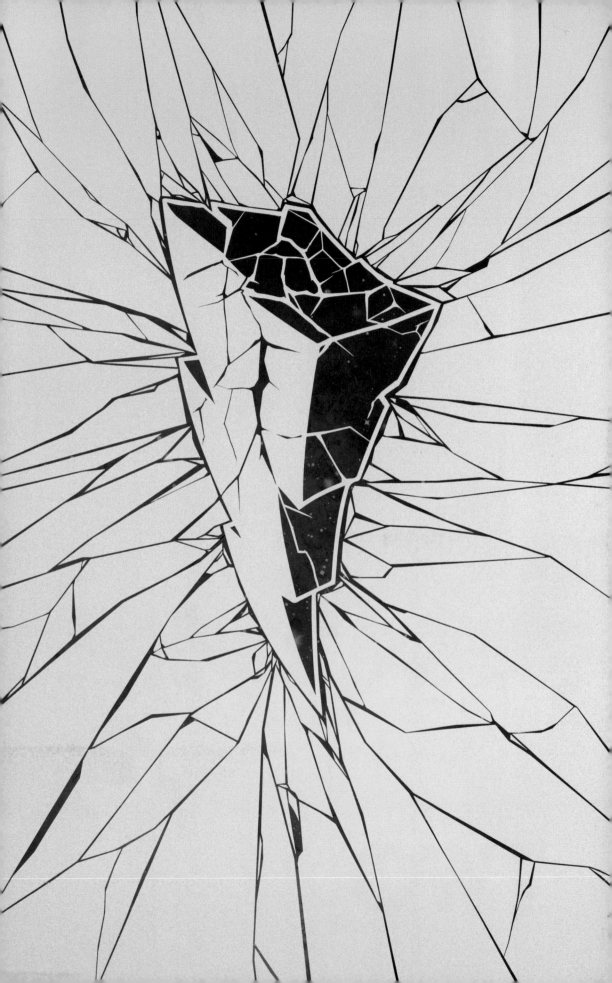

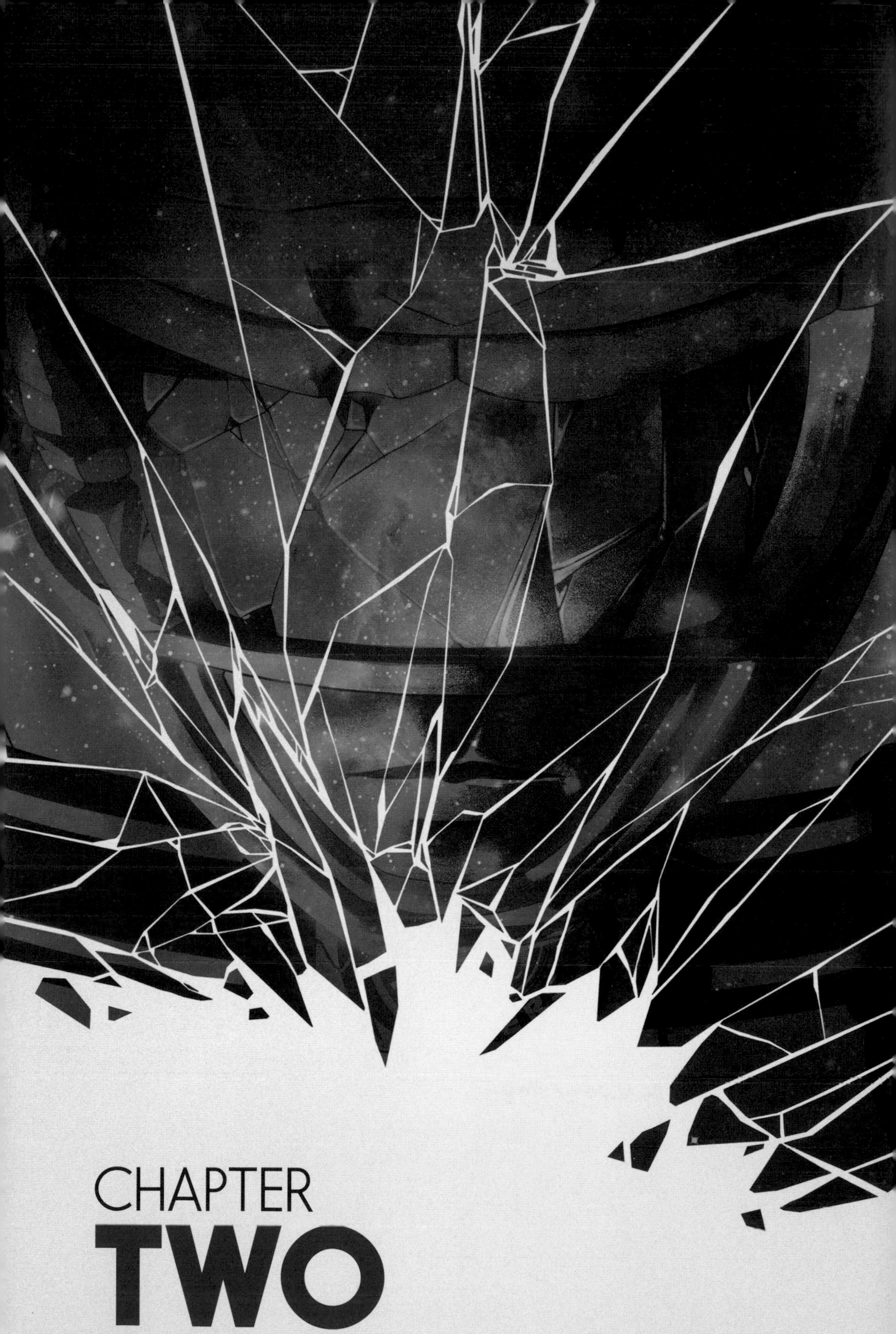

CHAPTER TWO

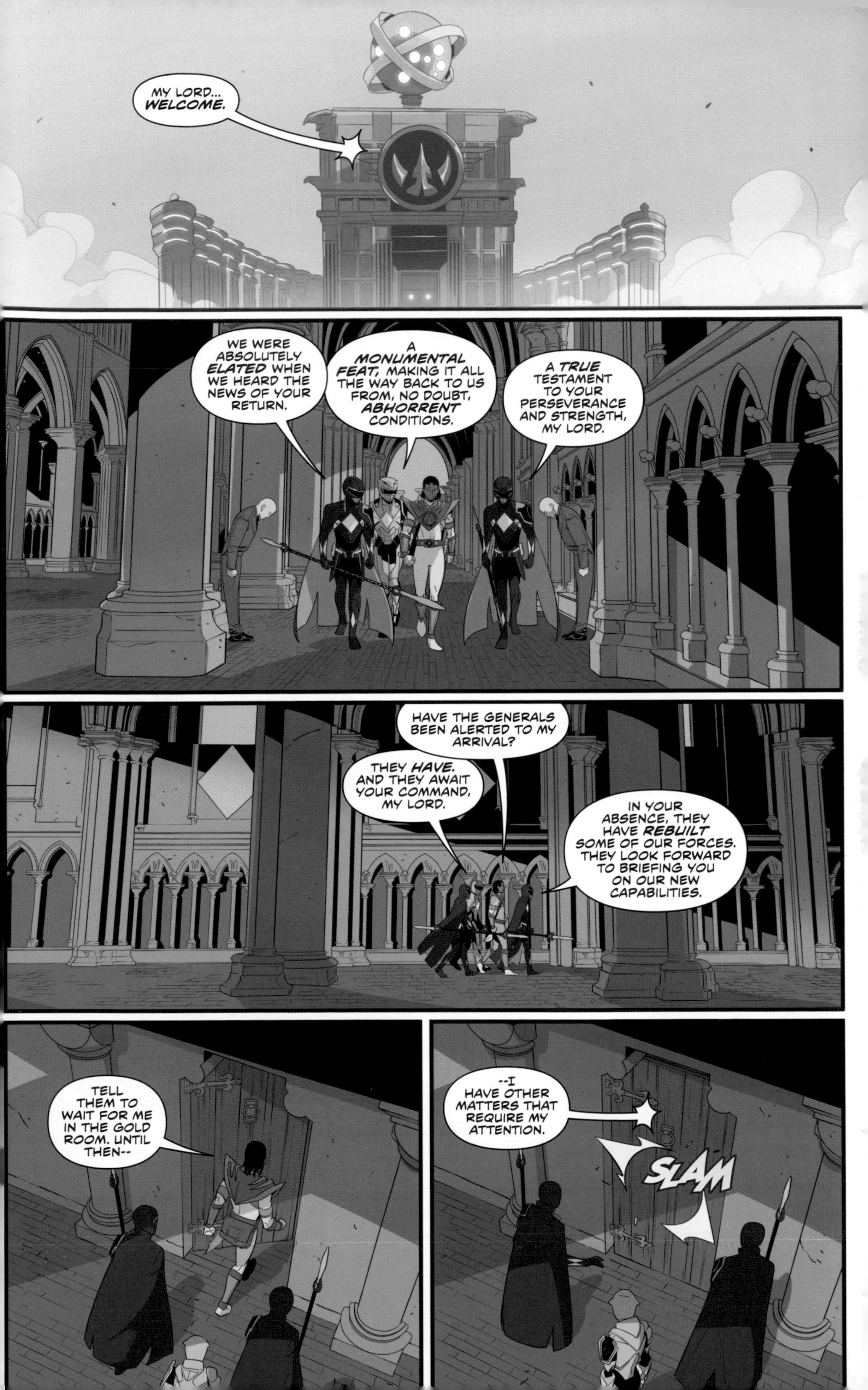
MY LORD... WELCOME.
WE WERE ABSOLUTELY ELATED WHEN WE HEARD THE NEWS OF YOUR RETURN.
A MONUMENTAL FEAT, MAKING IT ALL THE WAY BACK TO US FROM, NO DOUBT, ABHORRENT CONDITIONS.
A TRUE TESTAMENT TO YOUR PERSEVERANCE AND STRENGTH, MY LORD.
HAVE THE GENERALS BEEN ALERTED TO MY ARRIVAL?
THEY HAVE. AND THEY AWAIT YOUR COMMAND, MY LORD.
IN YOUR ABSENCE, THEY HAVE REBUILT SOME OF OUR FORCES. THEY LOOK FORWARD TO BRIEFING YOU ON OUR NEW CAPABILITIES.
TELL THEM TO WAIT FOR ME IN THE GOLD ROOM. UNTIL THEN--
--I HAVE OTHER MATTERS THAT REQUIRE MY ATTENTION.
SLAM

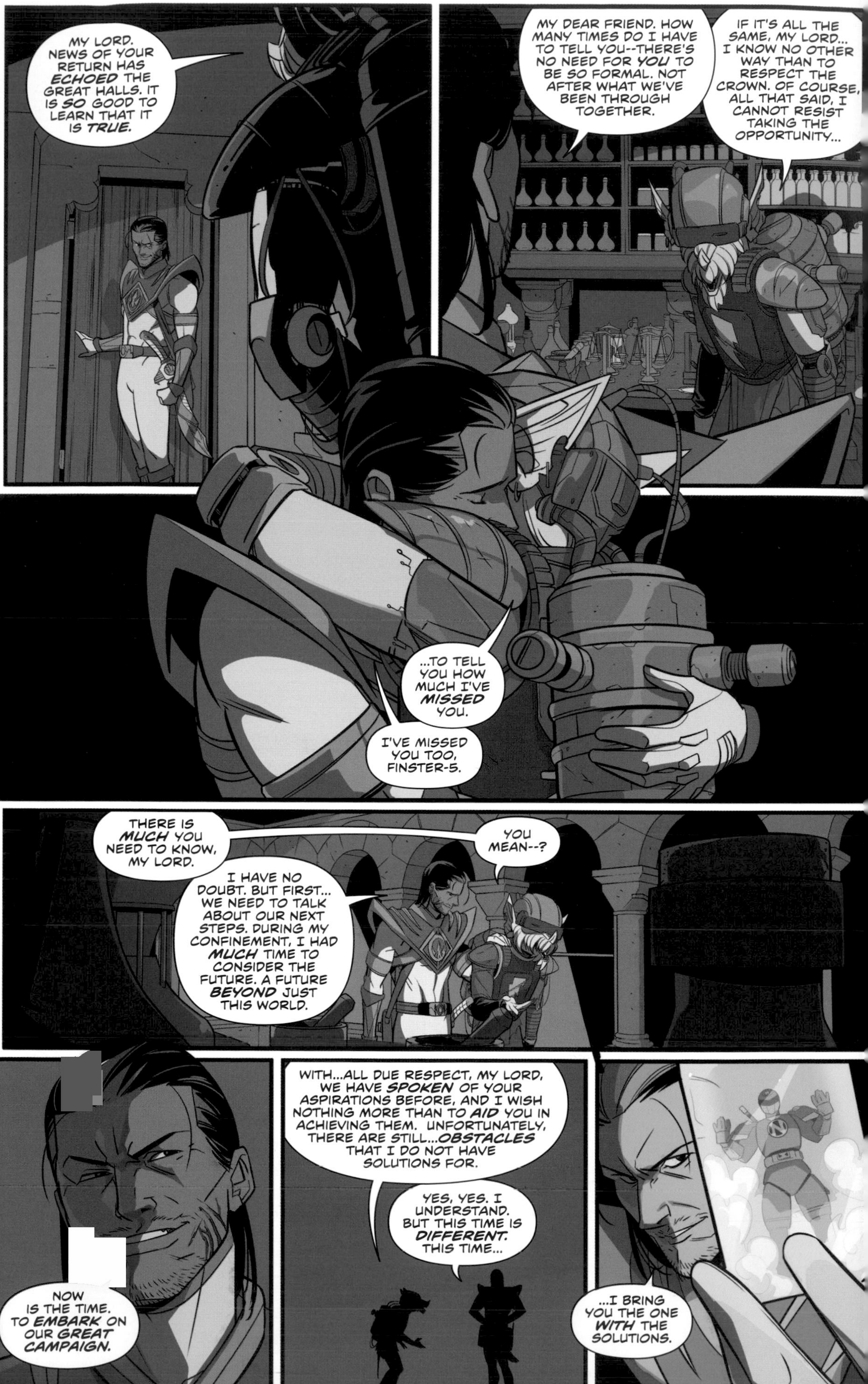
MY LORD. NEWS OF YOUR RETURN HAS ECHOED THE GREAT HALLS. IT IS SO GOOD TO LEARN THAT IT IS TRUE.
MY DEAR FRIEND. HOW MANY TIMES DO I HAVE TO TELL YOU--THERE'S NO NEED FOR YOU TO BE SO FORMAL. NOT AFTER WHAT WE'VE BEEN THROUGH TOGETHER.
IF IT'S ALL THE SAME, MY LORD... I KNOW NO OTHER WAY THAN TO RESPECT THE CROWN. OF COURSE, ALL THAT SAID, I CANNOT RESIST TAKING THE OPPORTUNITY...
...TO TELL YOU HOW MUCH I'VE MISSED YOU.
I'VE MISSED YOU TOO, FINSTER-5.
THERE IS MUCH YOU NEED TO KNOW, MY LORD.
I HAVE NO DOUBT. BUT FIRST... WE NEED TO TALK ABOUT OUR NEXT STEPS. DURING MY CONFINEMENT, I HAD MUCH TIME TO CONSIDER THE FUTURE. A FUTURE BEYOND JUST THIS WORLD.
YOU MEAN--?
NOW IS THE TIME. TO EMBARK ON OUR GREAT CAMPAIGN.
WITH...ALL DUE RESPECT, MY LORD, WE HAVE SPOKEN OF YOUR ASPIRATIONS BEFORE, AND I WISH NOTHING MORE THAN TO AID YOU IN ACHIEVING THEM. UNFORTUNATELY, THERE ARE STILL...OBSTACLES THAT I DO NOT HAVE SOLUTIONS FOR.
YES, YES. I UNDERSTAND. BUT THIS TIME IS DIFFERENT. THIS TIME...
...I BRING YOU THE ONE WITH THE SOLUTIONS.

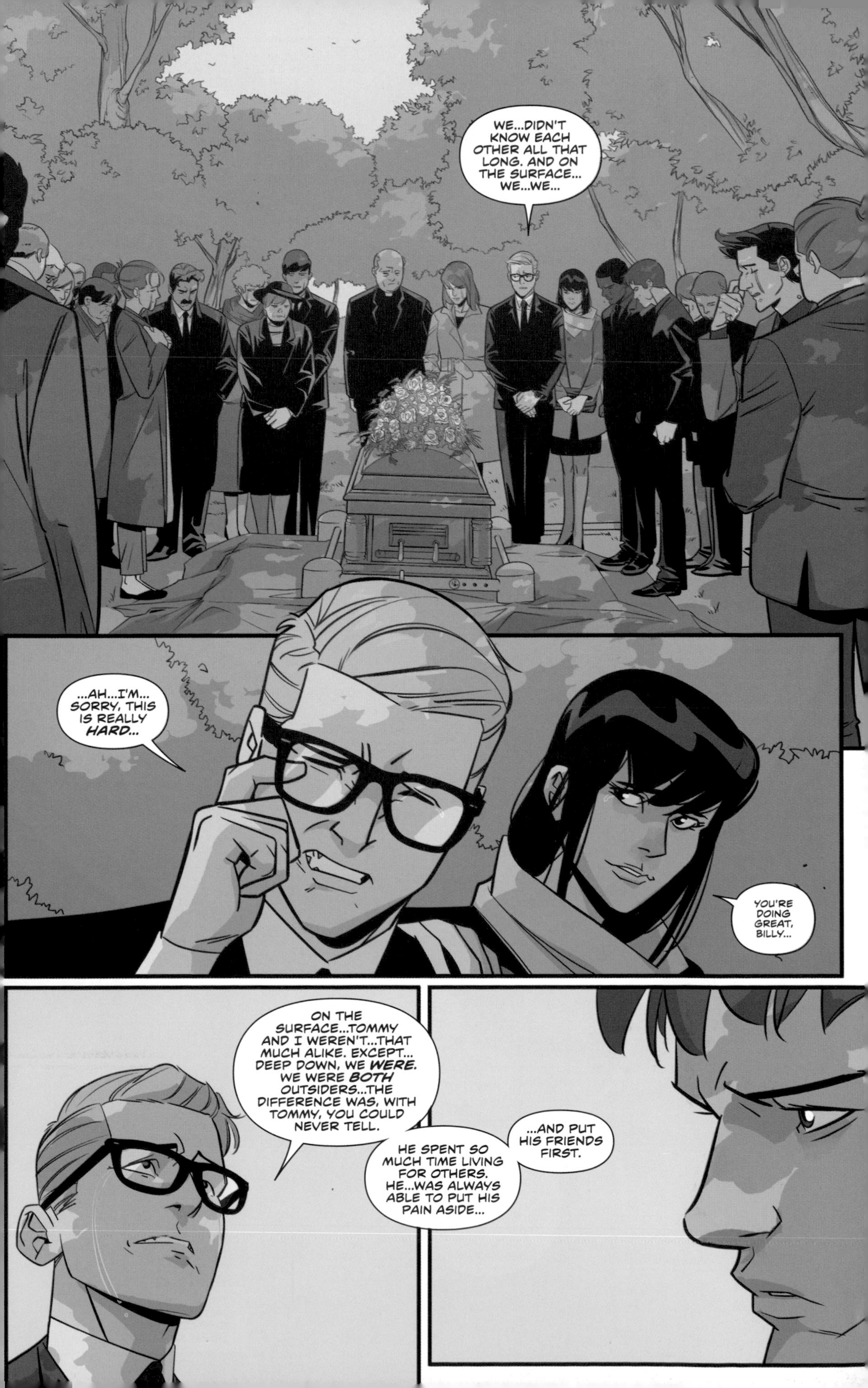
WE...DIDN'T KNOW EACH OTHER ALL THAT LONG. AND ON THE SURFACE... WE...WE...
...AH...I'M... SORRY, THIS IS REALLY *HARD*...
YOU'RE DOING GREAT, BILLY...
ON THE SURFACE...TOMMY AND I WEREN'T...THAT MUCH ALIKE. EXCEPT... DEEP DOWN, WE *WERE*. WE WERE *BOTH* OUTSIDERS...THE DIFFERENCE WAS, WITH TOMMY, YOU COULD NEVER TELL.
HE SPENT SO MUCH TIME LIVING FOR OTHERS. HE...WAS ALWAYS ABLE TO PUT HIS PAIN ASIDE...
...AND PUT HIS FRIENDS FIRST.

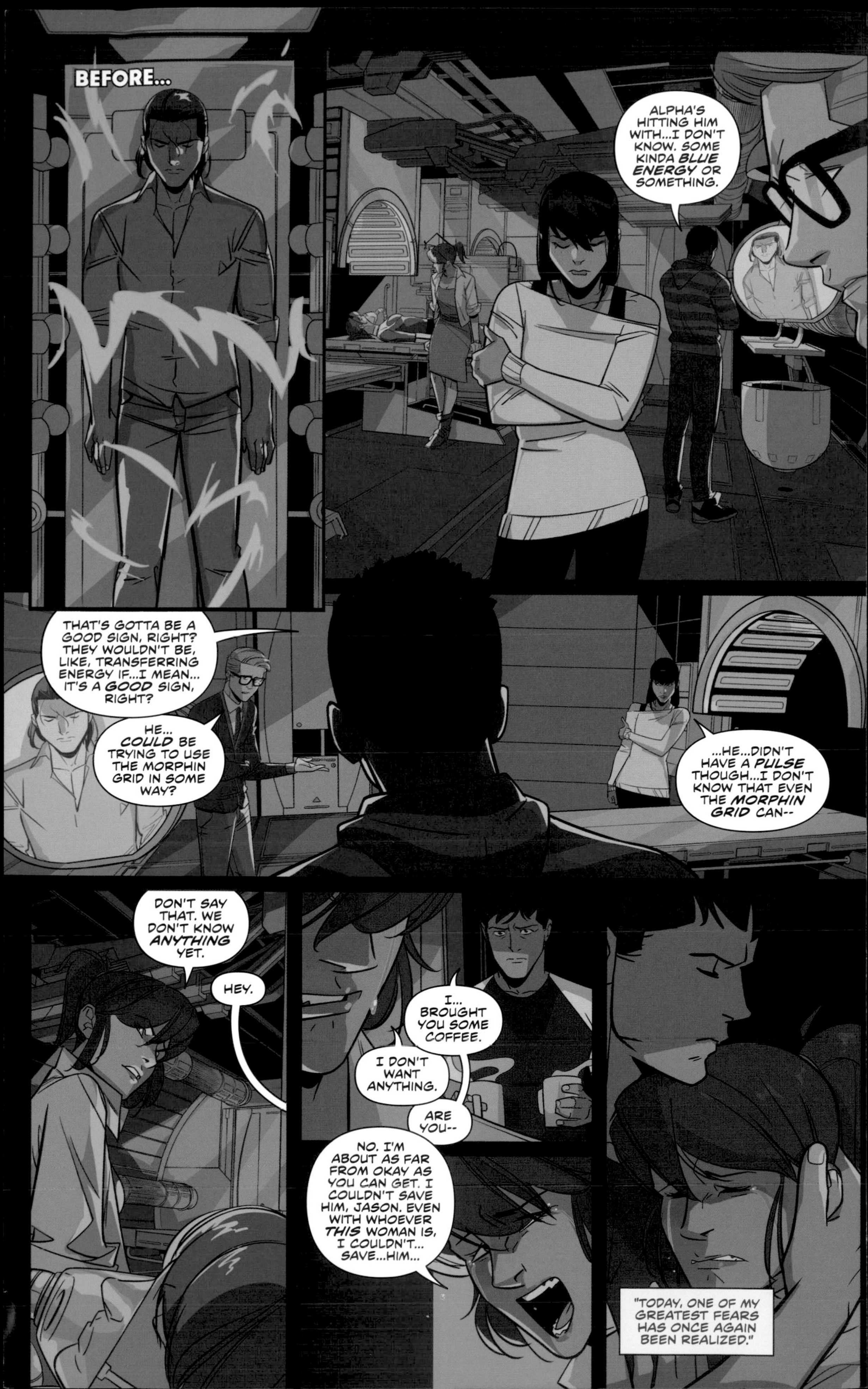
BEFORE...
ALPHA'S HITTING HIM WITH...I DON'T KNOW. SOME KINDA BLUE ENERGY OR SOMETHING.
THAT'S GOTTA BE A GOOD SIGN, RIGHT? THEY WOULDN'T BE, LIKE, TRANSFERRING ENERGY IF...I MEAN... IT'S A GOOD SIGN, RIGHT?
HE... COULD BE TRYING TO USE THE MORPHIN GRID IN SOME WAY?
...HE...DIDN'T HAVE A PULSE THOUGH...I DON'T KNOW THAT EVEN THE MORPHIN GRID CAN--
DON'T SAY THAT. WE DON'T KNOW ANYTHING YET.
HEY.
I... BROUGHT YOU SOME COFFEE.
I DON'T WANT ANYTHING.
ARE YOU--
NO. I'M ABOUT AS FAR FROM OKAY AS YOU CAN GET. I COULDN'T SAVE HIM, JASON. EVEN WITH WHOEVER THIS WOMAN IS, I COULDN'T... SAVE...HIM...
"TODAY, ONE OF MY GREATEST FEARS HAS ONCE AGAIN BEEN REALIZED."

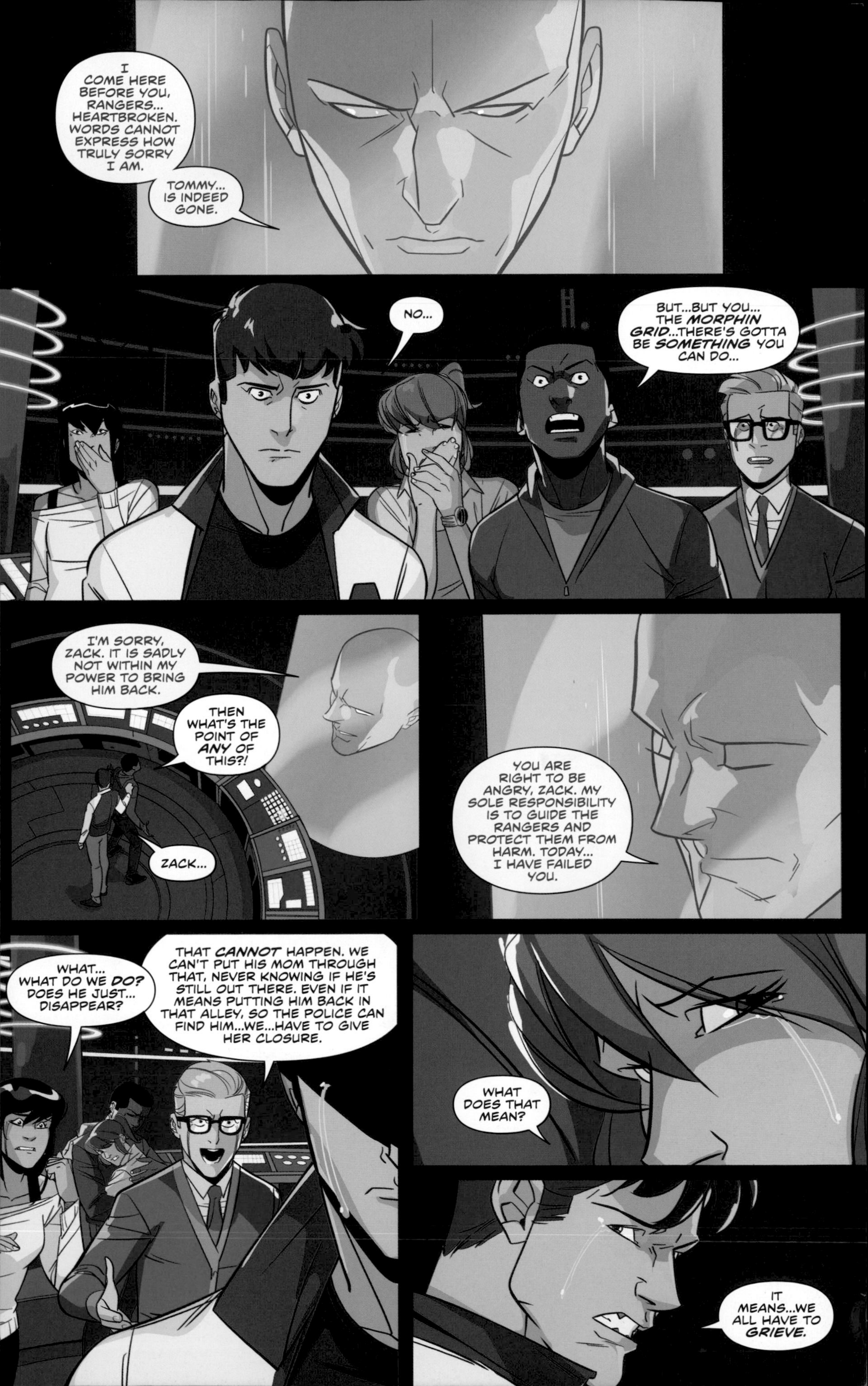
I COME HERE BEFORE YOU, RANGERS... HEARTBROKEN. WORDS CANNOT EXPRESS HOW TRULY SORRY I AM.
TOMMY... IS INDEED GONE.
NO...
BUT...BUT YOU... THE MORPHIN GRID...THERE'S GOTTA BE SOMETHING YOU CAN DO...
I'M SORRY, ZACK. IT IS SADLY NOT WITHIN MY POWER TO BRING HIM BACK.
THEN WHAT'S THE POINT OF ANY OF THIS?!
ZACK...
YOU ARE RIGHT TO BE ANGRY, ZACK. MY SOLE RESPONSIBILITY IS TO GUIDE THE RANGERS AND PROTECT THEM FROM HARM. TODAY... I HAVE FAILED YOU.
WHAT... WHAT DO WE DO? DOES HE JUST... DISAPPEAR?
THAT CANNOT HAPPEN. WE CAN'T PUT HIS MOM THROUGH THAT, NEVER KNOWING IF HE'S STILL OUT THERE. EVEN IF IT MEANS PUTTING HIM BACK IN THAT ALLEY, SO THE POLICE CAN FIND HIM...WE...HAVE TO GIVE HER CLOSURE.
WHAT DOES THAT MEAN?
IT MEANS...WE ALL HAVE TO GRIEVE.

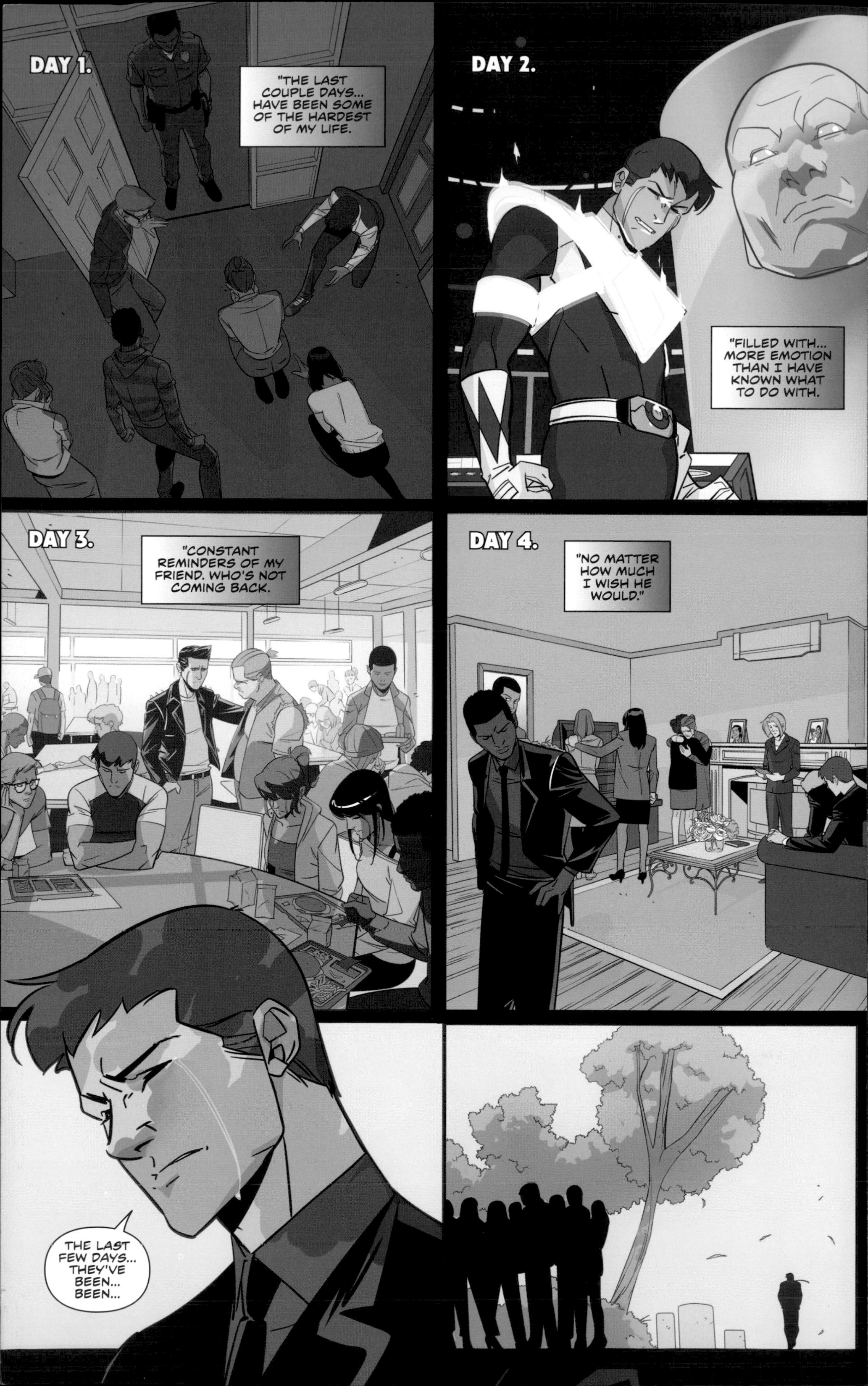
DAY 1.
"THE LAST COUPLE DAYS... HAVE BEEN SOME OF THE HARDEST OF MY LIFE.
DAY 2.
"FILLED WITH... MORE EMOTION THAN I HAVE KNOWN WHAT TO DO WITH.
DAY 3.
"CONSTANT REMINDERS OF MY FRIEND. WHO'S NOT COMING BACK.
DAY 4.
"NO MATTER HOW MUCH I WISH HE WOULD."
THE LAST FEW DAYS... THEY'VE BEEN... BEEN...

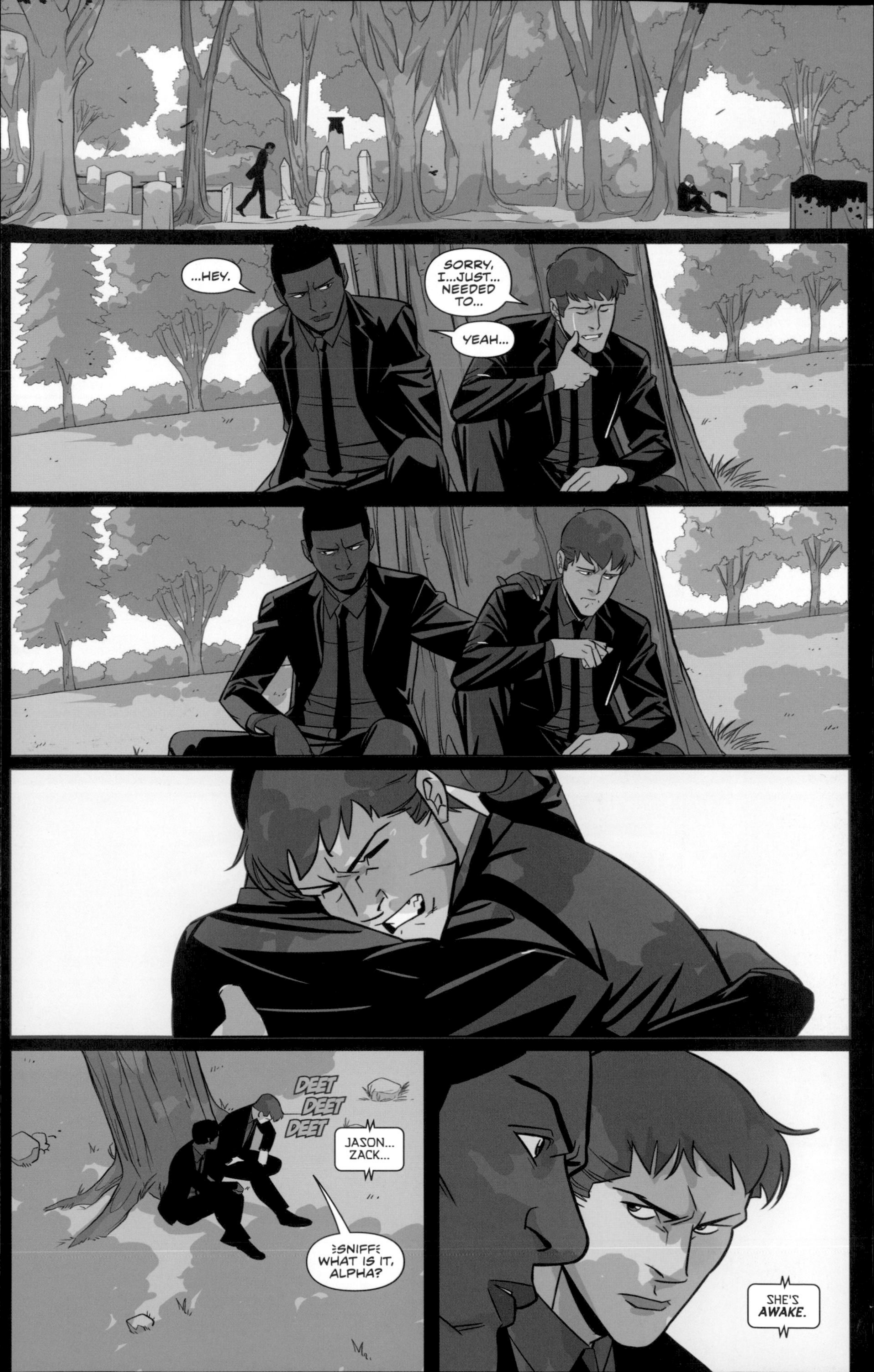
...HEY.
SORRY, I...JUST... NEEDED TO...
YEAH...
DEET DEET DEET
JASON... ZACK...
SNIFF WHAT IS IT, ALPHA?
SHE'S AWAKE.

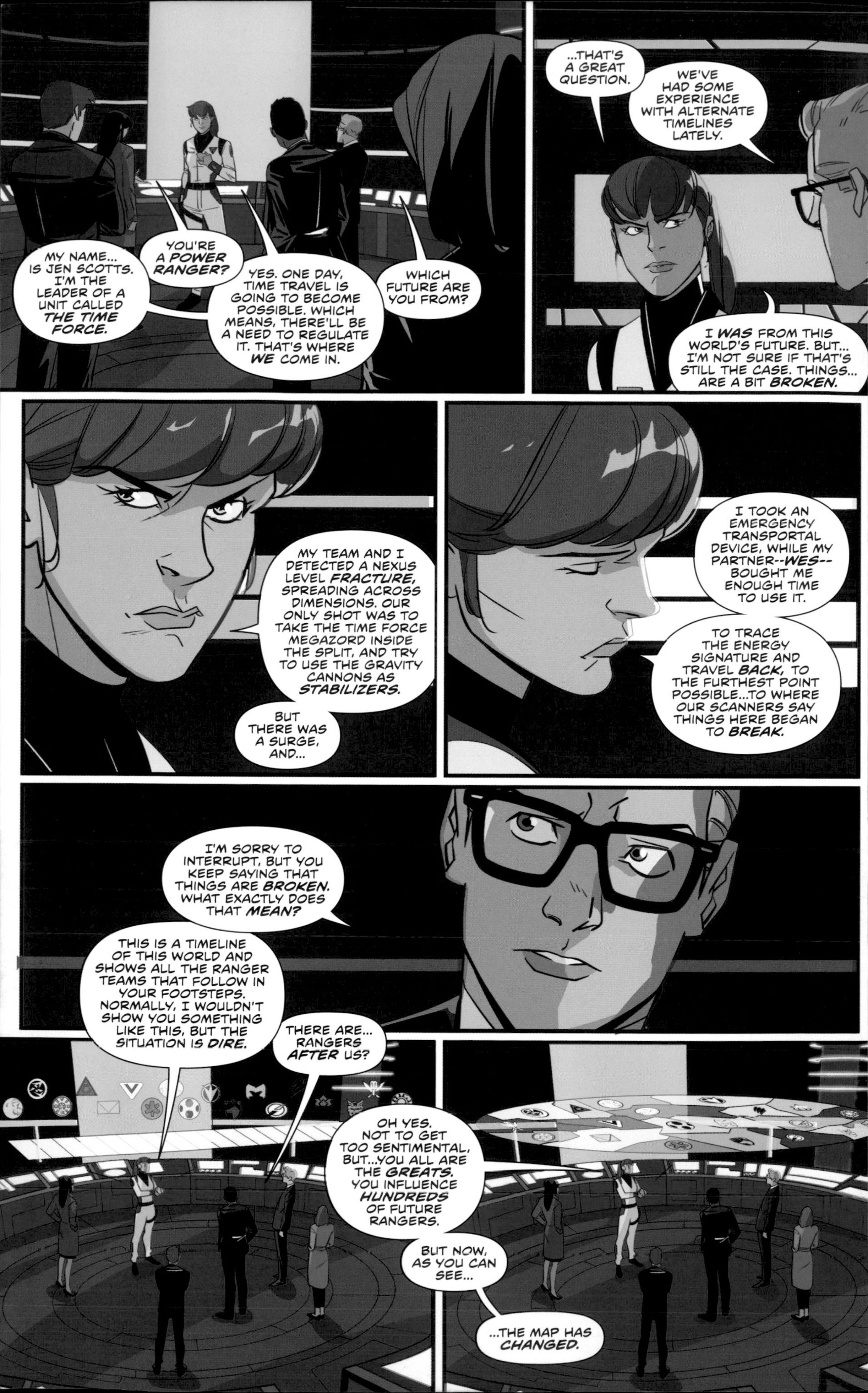
MY NAME... IS JEN SCOTTS. I'M THE LEADER OF A UNIT CALLED THE TIME FORCE.
YOU'RE A POWER RANGER?
YES. ONE DAY, TIME TRAVEL IS GOING TO BECOME POSSIBLE. WHICH MEANS, THERE'LL BE A NEED TO REGULATE IT. THAT'S WHERE WE COME IN.
WHICH FUTURE ARE YOU FROM?
...THAT'S A GREAT QUESTION.
WE'VE HAD SOME EXPERIENCE WITH ALTERNATE TIMELINES LATELY.
I WAS FROM THIS WORLD'S FUTURE. BUT... I'M NOT SURE IF THAT'S STILL THE CASE. THINGS... ARE A BIT BROKEN.
MY TEAM AND I DETECTED A NEXUS LEVEL FRACTURE, SPREADING ACROSS DIMENSIONS. OUR ONLY SHOT WAS TO TAKE THE TIME FORCE MEGAZORD INSIDE THE SPLIT, AND TRY TO USE THE GRAVITY CANNONS AS STABILIZERS.
BUT THERE WAS A SURGE, AND...
I TOOK AN EMERGENCY TRANSPORTAL DEVICE, WHILE MY PARTNER--WES--BOUGHT ME ENOUGH TIME TO USE IT.
TO TRACE THE ENERGY SIGNATURE AND TRAVEL BACK, TO THE FURTHEST POINT POSSIBLE...TO WHERE OUR SCANNERS SAY THINGS HERE BEGAN TO BREAK.
I'M SORRY TO INTERRUPT, BUT YOU KEEP SAYING THAT THINGS ARE BROKEN. WHAT EXACTLY DOES THAT MEAN?
THIS IS A TIMELINE OF THIS WORLD AND SHOWS ALL THE RANGER TEAMS THAT FOLLOW IN YOUR FOOTSTEPS. NORMALLY, I WOULDN'T SHOW YOU SOMETHING LIKE THIS, BUT THE SITUATION IS DIRE.
THERE ARE... RANGERS AFTER US?
OH YES. NOT TO GET TOO SENTIMENTAL, BUT...YOU ALL ARE THE GREATS. YOU INFLUENCE HUNDREDS OF FUTURE RANGERS.
BUT NOW, AS YOU CAN SEE...
...THE MAP HAS CHANGED.

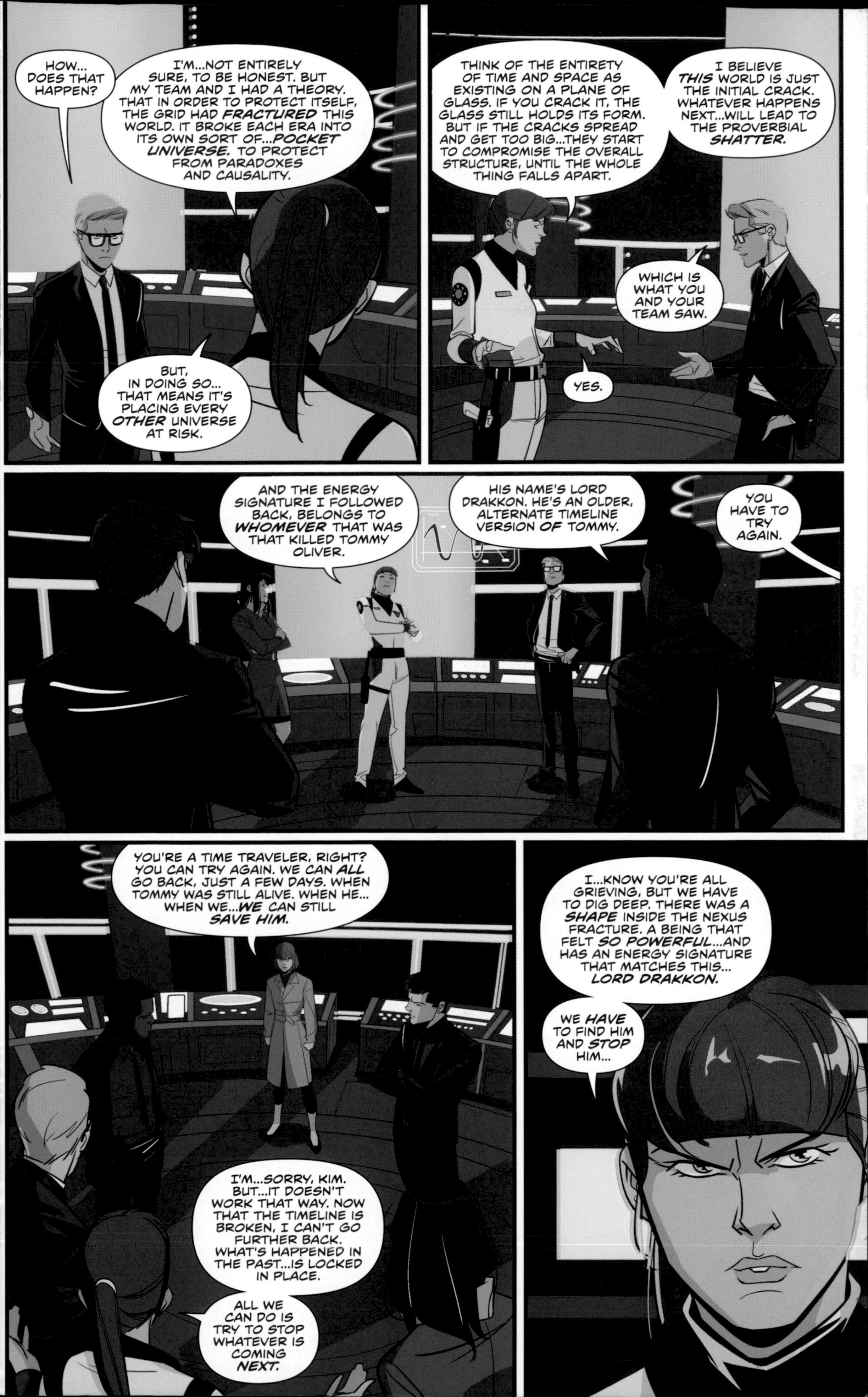
HOW... DOES THAT HAPPEN?
I'M...NOT ENTIRELY SURE, TO BE HONEST. BUT MY TEAM AND I HAD A THEORY. THAT IN ORDER TO PROTECT ITSELF, THE GRID HAD FRACTURED THIS WORLD. IT BROKE EACH ERA INTO ITS OWN SORT OF...POCKET UNIVERSE. TO PROTECT FROM PARADOXES AND CAUSALITY.
BUT, IN DOING SO... THAT MEANS IT'S PLACING EVERY OTHER UNIVERSE AT RISK.
THINK OF THE ENTIRETY OF TIME AND SPACE AS EXISTING ON A PLANE OF GLASS. IF YOU CRACK IT, THE GLASS STILL HOLDS ITS FORM. BUT IF THE CRACKS SPREAD AND GET TOO BIG...THEY START TO COMPROMISE THE OVERALL STRUCTURE, UNTIL THE WHOLE THING FALLS APART.
I BELIEVE THIS WORLD IS JUST THE INITIAL CRACK. WHATEVER HAPPENS NEXT...WILL LEAD TO THE PROVERBIAL SHATTER.
WHICH IS WHAT YOU AND YOUR TEAM SAW.
YES.
AND THE ENERGY SIGNATURE I FOLLOWED BACK, BELONGS TO WHOMEVER THAT WAS THAT KILLED TOMMY OLIVER.
HIS NAME'S LORD DRAKKON. HE'S AN OLDER, ALTERNATE TIMELINE VERSION OF TOMMY.
YOU HAVE TO TRY AGAIN.
YOU'RE A TIME TRAVELER, RIGHT? YOU CAN TRY AGAIN. WE CAN ALL GO BACK, JUST A FEW DAYS. WHEN TOMMY WAS STILL ALIVE. WHEN HE... WHEN WE...WE CAN STILL SAVE HIM.
I'M...SORRY, KIM. BUT...IT DOESN'T WORK THAT WAY. NOW THAT THE TIMELINE IS BROKEN, I CAN'T GO FURTHER BACK. WHAT'S HAPPENED IN THE PAST...IS LOCKED IN PLACE.
ALL WE CAN DO IS TRY TO STOP WHATEVER IS COMING NEXT.
I...KNOW YOU'RE ALL GRIEVING, BUT WE HAVE TO DIG DEEP. THERE WAS A SHAPE INSIDE THE NEXUS FRACTURE. A BEING THAT FELT SO POWERFUL...AND HAS AN ENERGY SIGNATURE THAT MATCHES THIS... LORD DRAKKON.
WE HAVE TO FIND HIM AND STOP HIM...

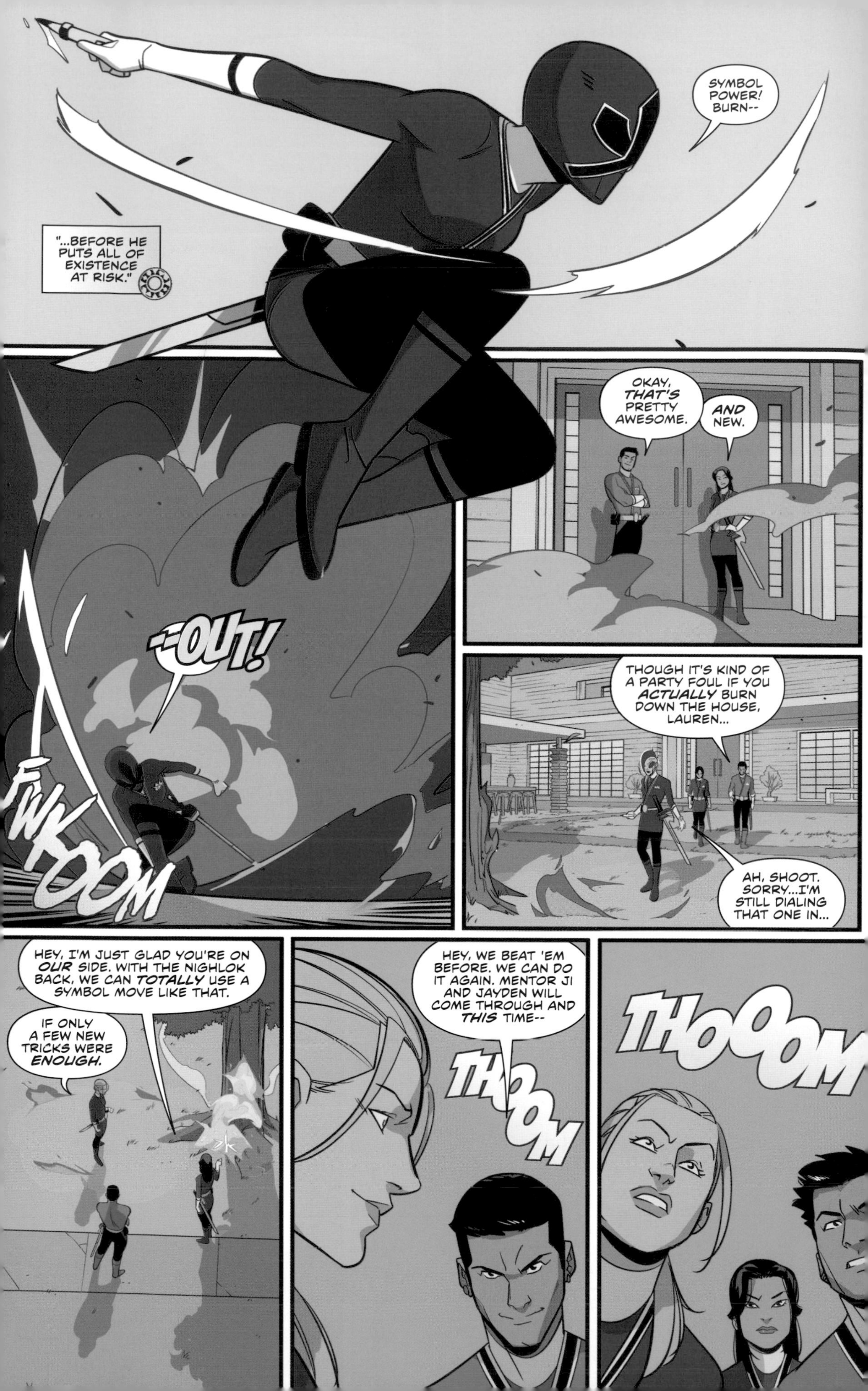

"...BEFORE HE PUTS ALL OF EXISTENCE AT RISK."
SYMBOL POWER! BURN--
--OUT!
FWKOOM
OKAY, THAT'S PRETTY AWESOME.
AND NEW.
THOUGH IT'S KIND OF A PARTY FOUL IF YOU ACTUALLY BURN DOWN THE HOUSE, LAUREN...
AH, SHOOT. SORRY...I'M STILL DIALING THAT ONE IN...
HEY, I'M JUST GLAD YOU'RE ON OUR SIDE. WITH THE NIGHLOK BACK, WE CAN TOTALLY USE A SYMBOL MOVE LIKE THAT.
IF ONLY A FEW NEW TRICKS WERE ENOUGH.
HEY, WE BEAT 'EM BEFORE. WE CAN DO IT AGAIN. MENTOR JI AND JAYDEN WILL COME THROUGH AND THIS TIME--
THOOOM
THOOOM

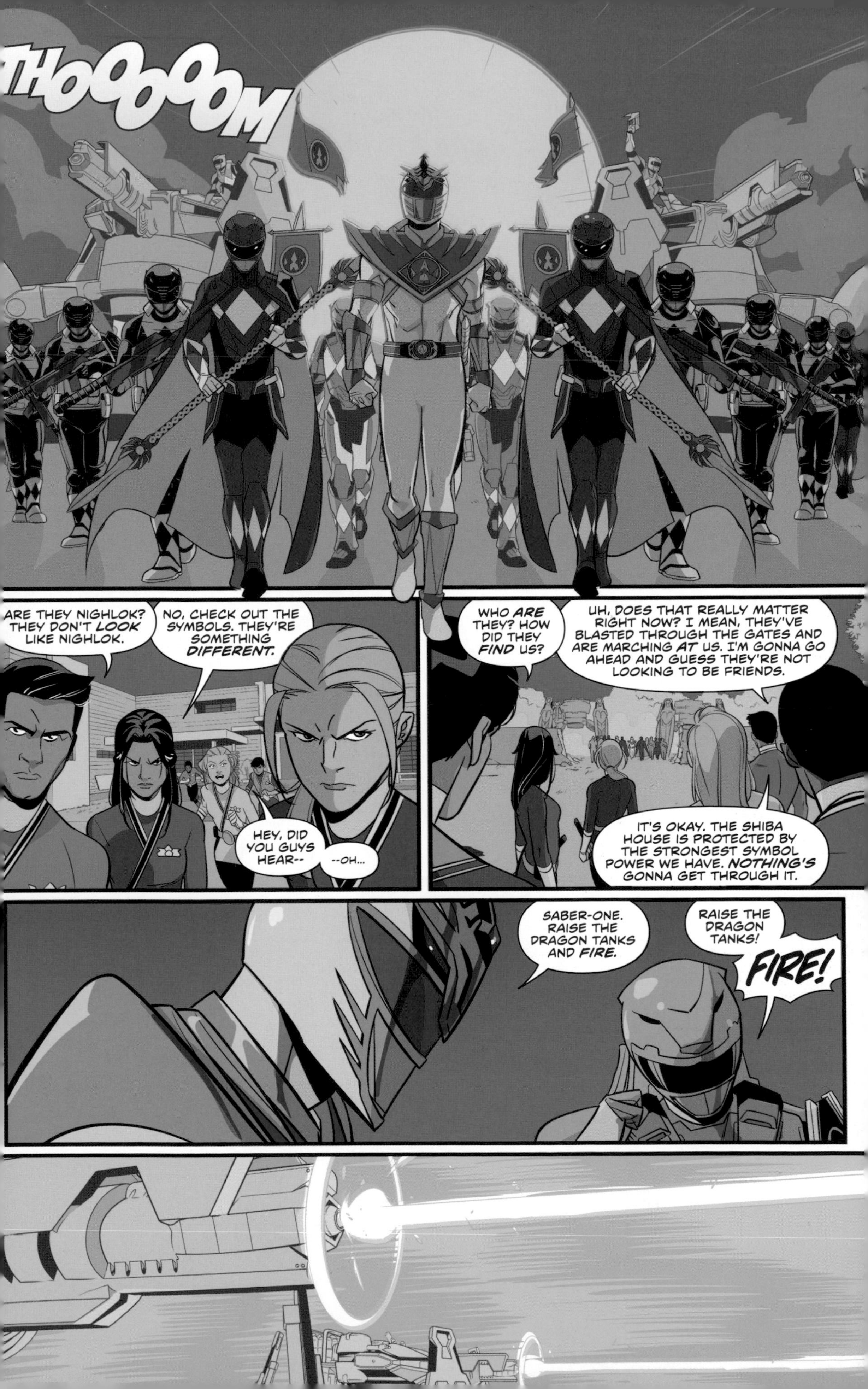
THOOOOOM
ARE THEY NIGHLOK? THEY DON'T LOOK LIKE NIGHLOK.
NO, CHECK OUT THE SYMBOLS. THEY'RE SOMETHING DIFFERENT.
HEY, DID YOU GUYS HEAR--
--OH...
WHO ARE THEY? HOW DID THEY FIND US?
UH, DOES THAT REALLY MATTER RIGHT NOW? I MEAN, THEY'VE BLASTED THROUGH THE GATES AND ARE MARCHING AT US. I'M GONNA GO AHEAD AND GUESS THEY'RE NOT LOOKING TO BE FRIENDS.
IT'S OKAY. THE SHIBA HOUSE IS PROTECTED BY THE STRONGEST SYMBOL POWER WE HAVE. NOTHING'S GONNA GET THROUGH IT.
SABER-ONE. RAISE THE DRAGON TANKS AND FIRE.
RAISE THE DRAGON TANKS!
FIRE!

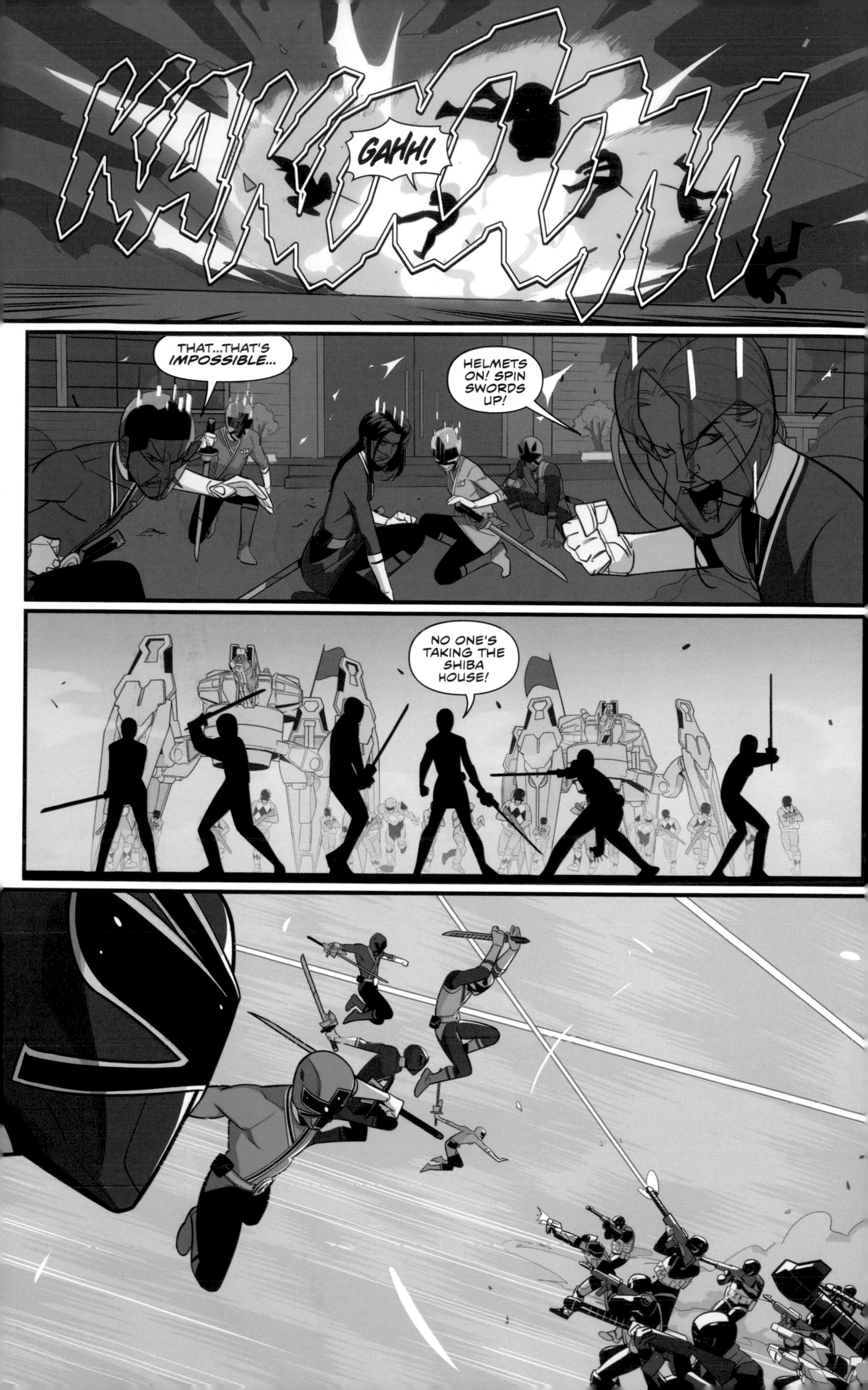
KAWOOOM
GAHH!
THAT...THAT'S IMPOSSIBLE...
HELMETS ON! SPIN SWORDS UP!
NO ONE'S TAKING THE SHIBA HOUSE!

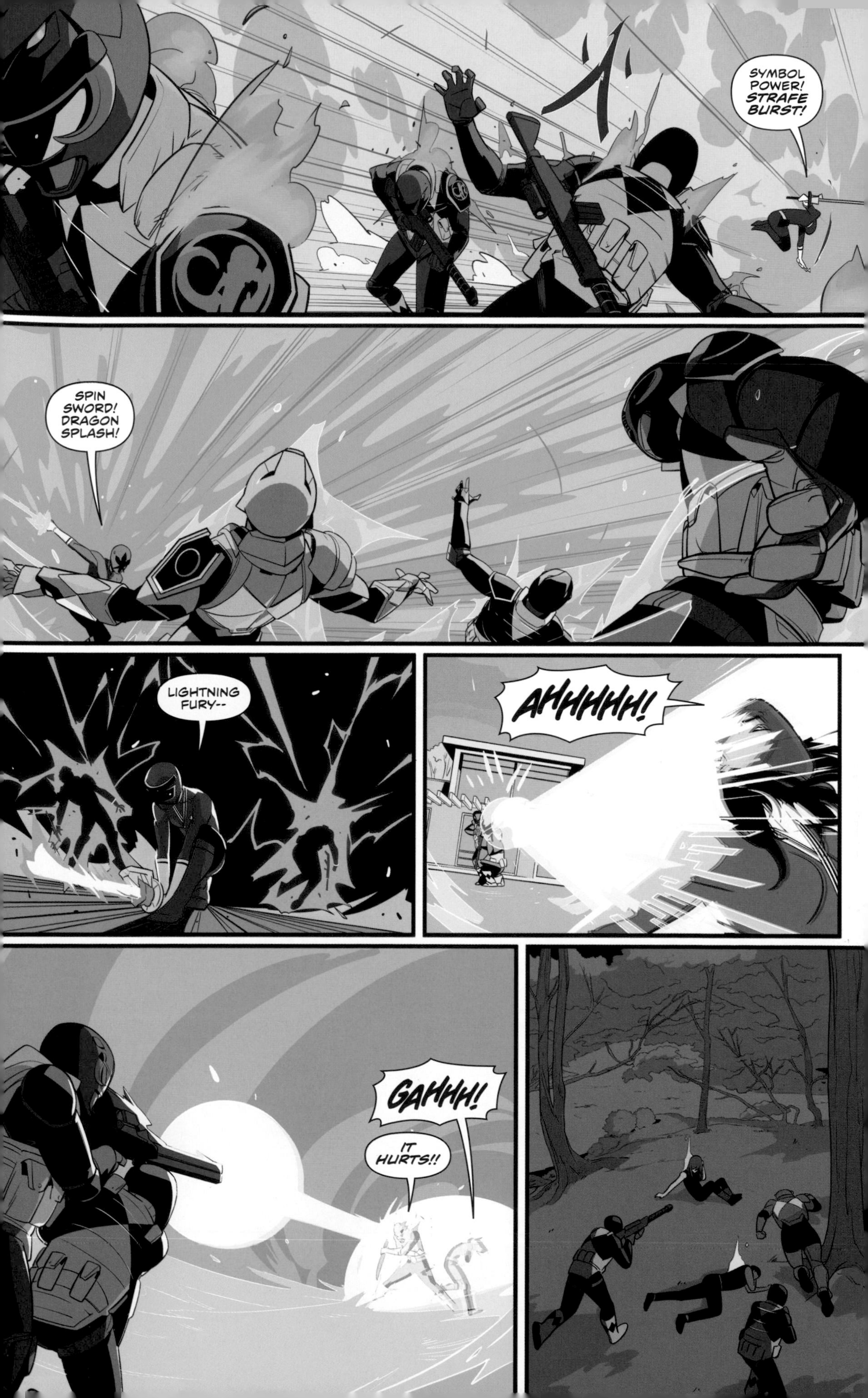
SYMBOL POWER! STRAFE BURST!
SPIN SWORD! DRAGON SPLASH!
LIGHTNING FURY--
AHHHHH!
GAHHH!
IT HURTS!!

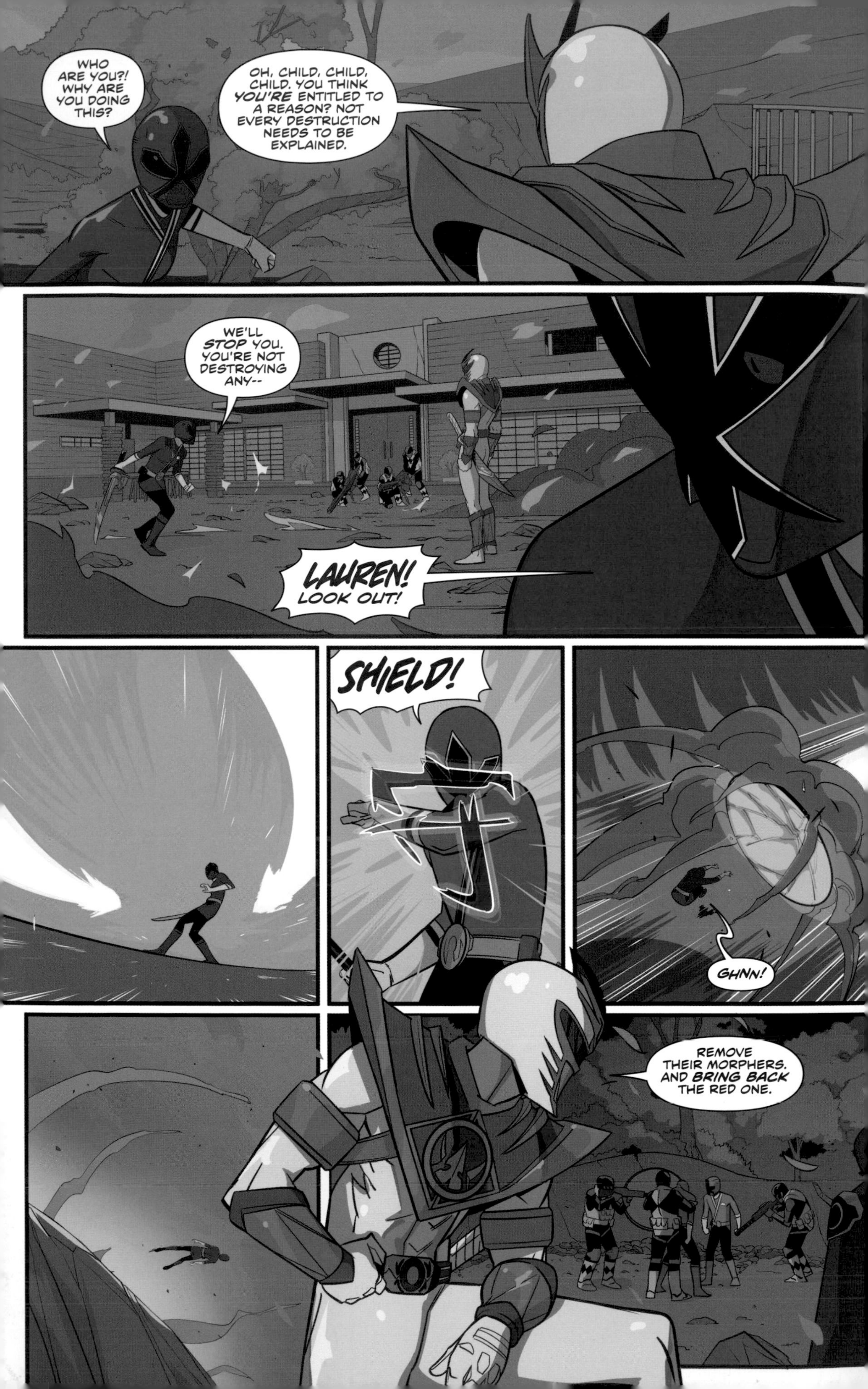
WHO ARE YOU?! WHY ARE YOU DOING THIS?
OH, CHILD, CHILD, CHILD. YOU THINK YOU'RE ENTITLED TO A REASON? NOT EVERY DESTRUCTION NEEDS TO BE EXPLAINED.
WE'LL STOP YOU. YOU'RE NOT DESTROYING ANY--
LAUREN! LOOK OUT!
SHIELD!
GHNN!
REMOVE THEIR MORPHERS. AND BRING BACK THE RED ONE.

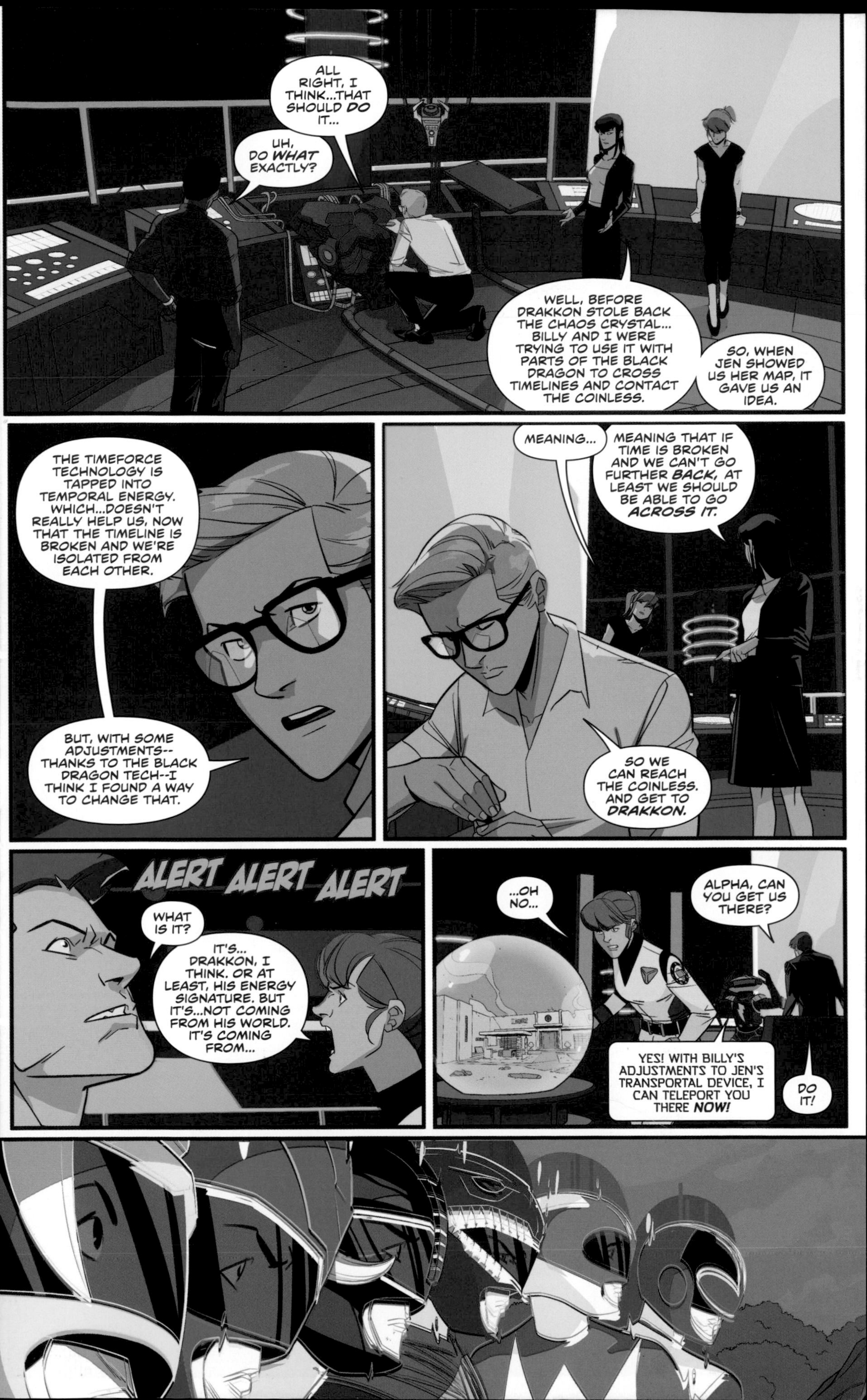
ALL RIGHT, I THINK...THAT SHOULD DO IT...
UH, DO WHAT EXACTLY?
WELL, BEFORE DRAKKON STOLE BACK THE CHAOS CRYSTAL... BILLY AND I WERE TRYING TO USE IT WITH PARTS OF THE BLACK DRAGON TO CROSS TIMELINES AND CONTACT THE COINLESS.
SO, WHEN JEN SHOWED US HER MAP, IT GAVE US AN IDEA.
THE TIMEFORCE TECHNOLOGY IS TAPPED INTO TEMPORAL ENERGY. WHICH...DOESN'T REALLY HELP US, NOW THAT THE TIMELINE IS BROKEN AND WE'RE ISOLATED FROM EACH OTHER.
BUT, WITH SOME ADJUSTMENTS-- THANKS TO THE BLACK DRAGON TECH--I THINK I FOUND A WAY TO CHANGE THAT.
MEANING...
MEANING THAT IF TIME IS BROKEN AND WE CAN'T GO FURTHER BACK, AT LEAST WE SHOULD BE ABLE TO GO ACROSS IT.
SO WE CAN REACH THE COINLESS. AND GET TO DRAKKON.
ALERT ALERT ALERT
WHAT IS IT?
IT'S... DRAKKON, I THINK. OR AT LEAST, HIS ENERGY SIGNATURE. BUT IT'S...NOT COMING FROM HIS WORLD. IT'S COMING FROM...
...OH NO...
ALPHA, CAN YOU GET US THERE?
YES! WITH BILLY'S ADJUSTMENTS TO JEN'S TRANSPORTAL DEVICE, I CAN TELEPORT YOU THERE NOW!
DO IT!

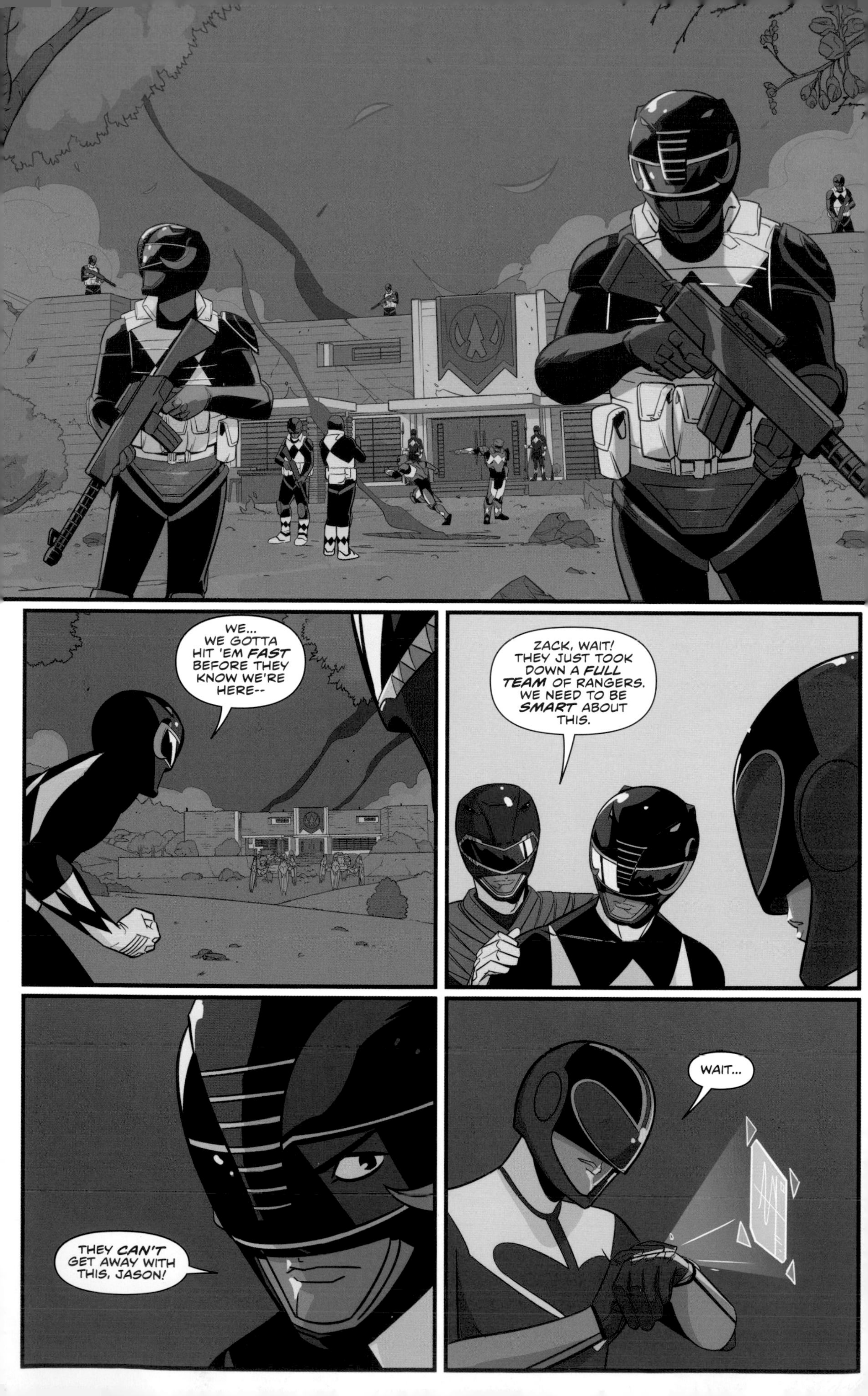
WE... WE GOTTA HIT 'EM FAST BEFORE THEY KNOW WE'RE HERE--
ZACK, WAIT! THEY JUST TOOK DOWN A FULL TEAM OF RANGERS. WE NEED TO BE SMART ABOUT THIS.
THEY CAN'T GET AWAY WITH THIS, JASON!
WAIT...

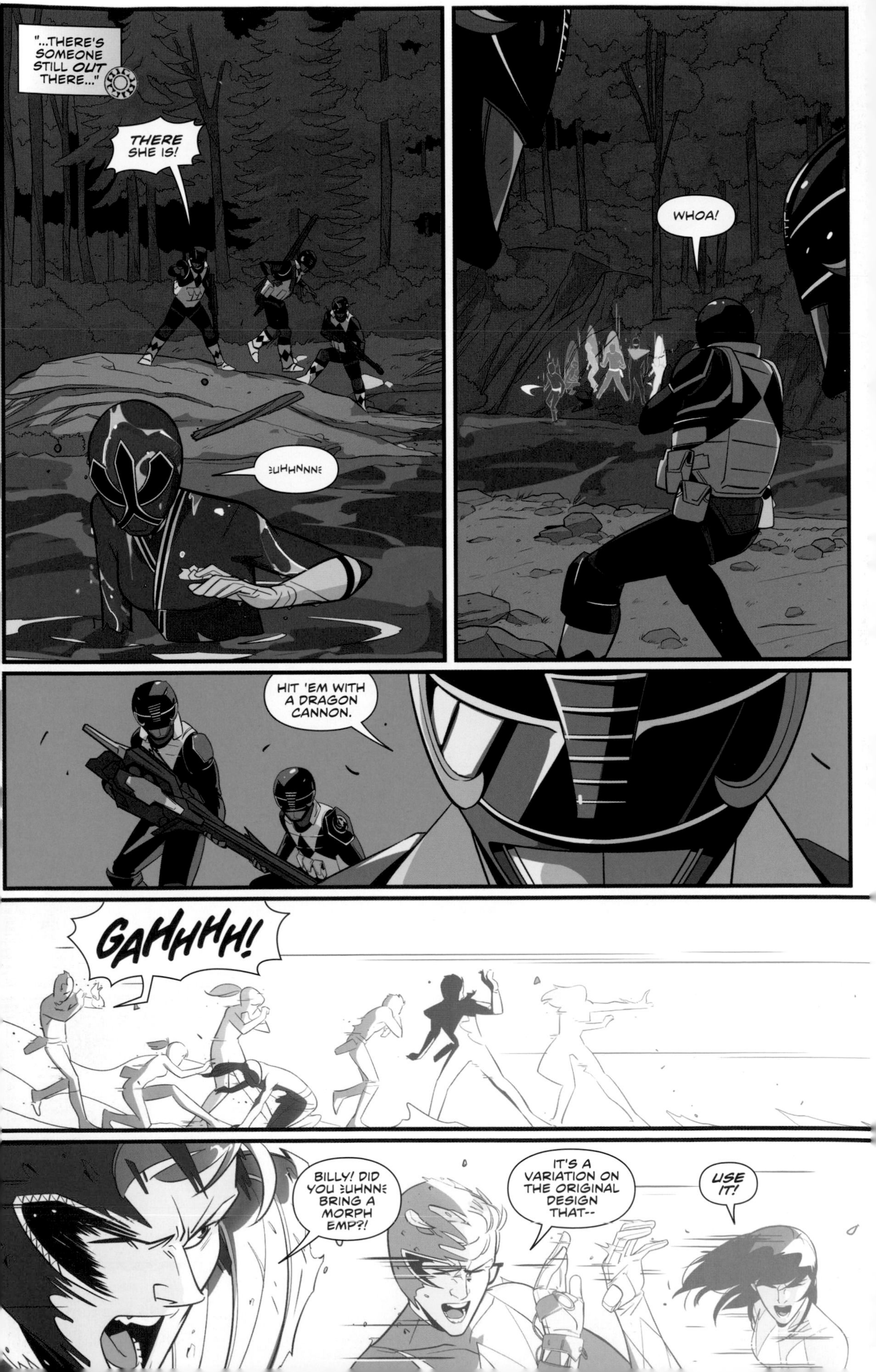
"...THERE'S SOMEONE STILL OUT THERE..."
THERE SHE IS!
UHHNNN
WHOA!
HIT 'EM WITH A DRAGON CANNON.
GAHHHH!
BILLY! DID YOU UHHN BRING A MORPH EMP?!
IT'S A VARIATION ON THE ORIGINAL DESIGN THAT--
USE IT!

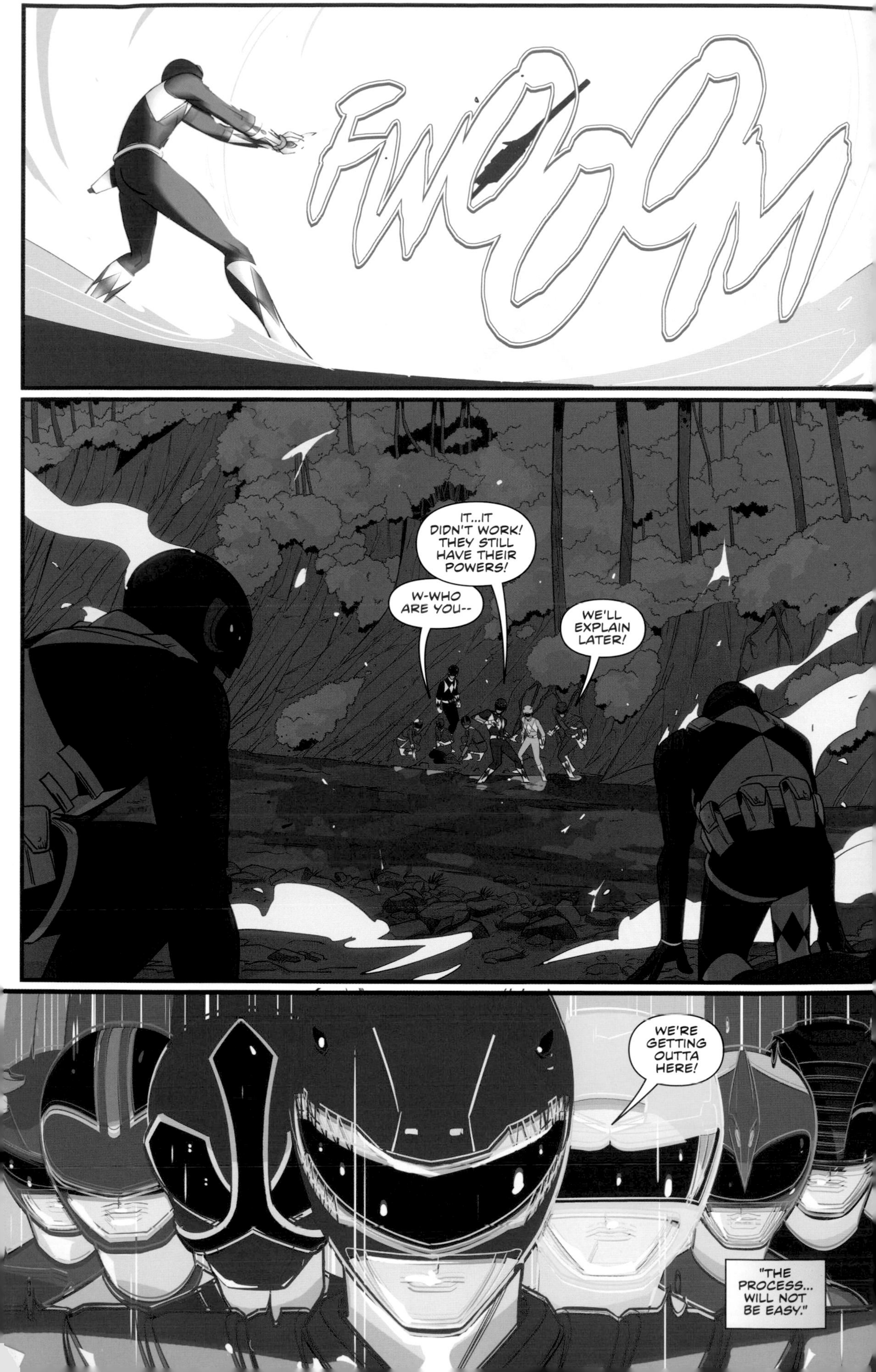
FWOOOM
IT...IT DIDN'T WORK! THEY STILL HAVE THEIR POWERS!
W-WHO ARE YOU--
WE'LL EXPLAIN LATER!
WE'RE GETTING OUTTA HERE!
"THE PROCESS... WILL NOT BE EASY."

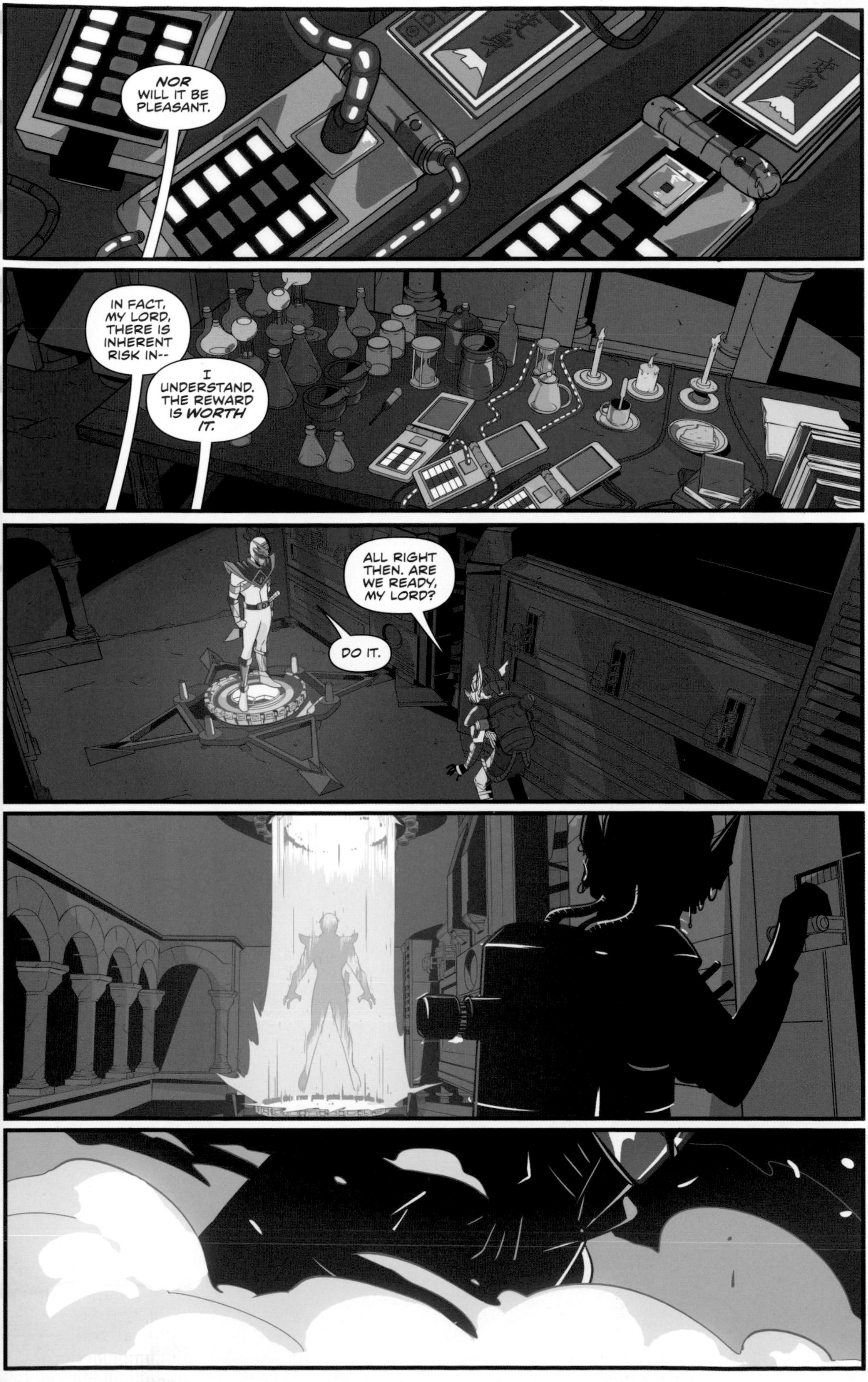
NOR WILL IT BE PLEASANT.
IN FACT, MY LORD, THERE IS INHERENT RISK IN--
I UNDERSTAND. THE REWARD IS WORTH IT.
ALL RIGHT THEN. ARE WE READY, MY LORD?
DO IT.

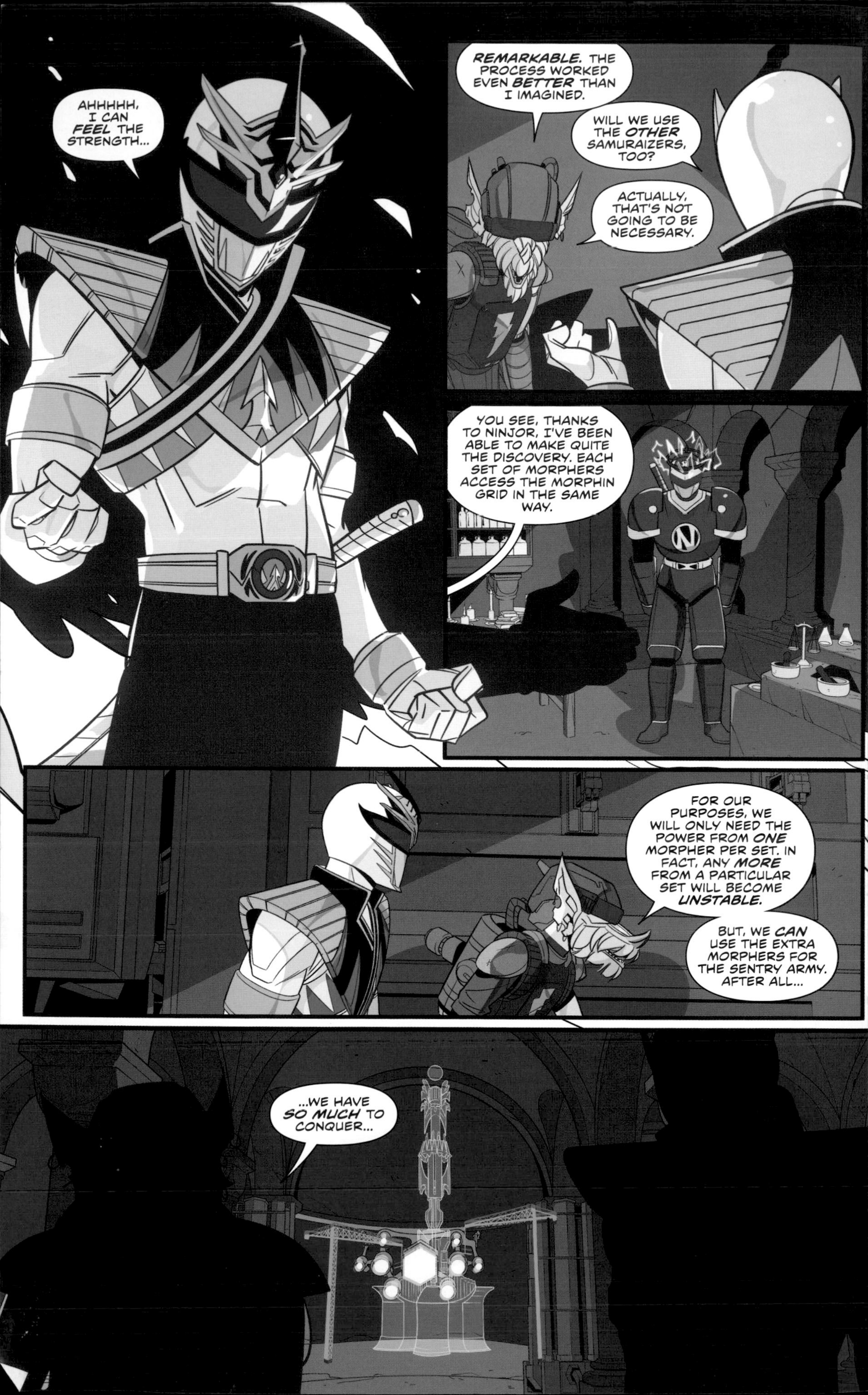
AHHHHH, I CAN FEEL THE STRENGTH...
REMARKABLE. THE PROCESS WORKED EVEN BETTER THAN I IMAGINED.
WILL WE USE THE OTHER SAMURAIZERS, TOO?
ACTUALLY, THAT'S NOT GOING TO BE NECESSARY.
YOU SEE, THANKS TO NINJOR, I'VE BEEN ABLE TO MAKE QUITE THE DISCOVERY. EACH SET OF MORPHERS ACCESS THE MORPHIN GRID IN THE SAME WAY.
FOR OUR PURPOSES, WE WILL ONLY NEED THE POWER FROM ONE MORPHER PER SET. IN FACT, ANY MORE FROM A PARTICULAR SET WILL BECOME UNSTABLE.
BUT, WE CAN USE THE EXTRA MORPHERS FOR THE SENTRY ARMY. AFTER ALL...
...WE HAVE SO MUCH TO CONQUER...

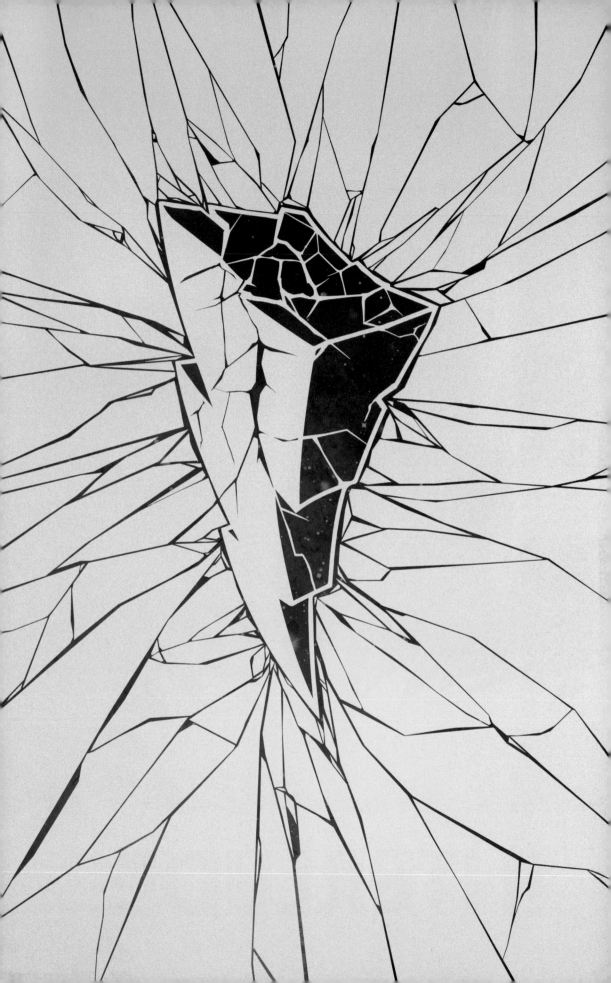

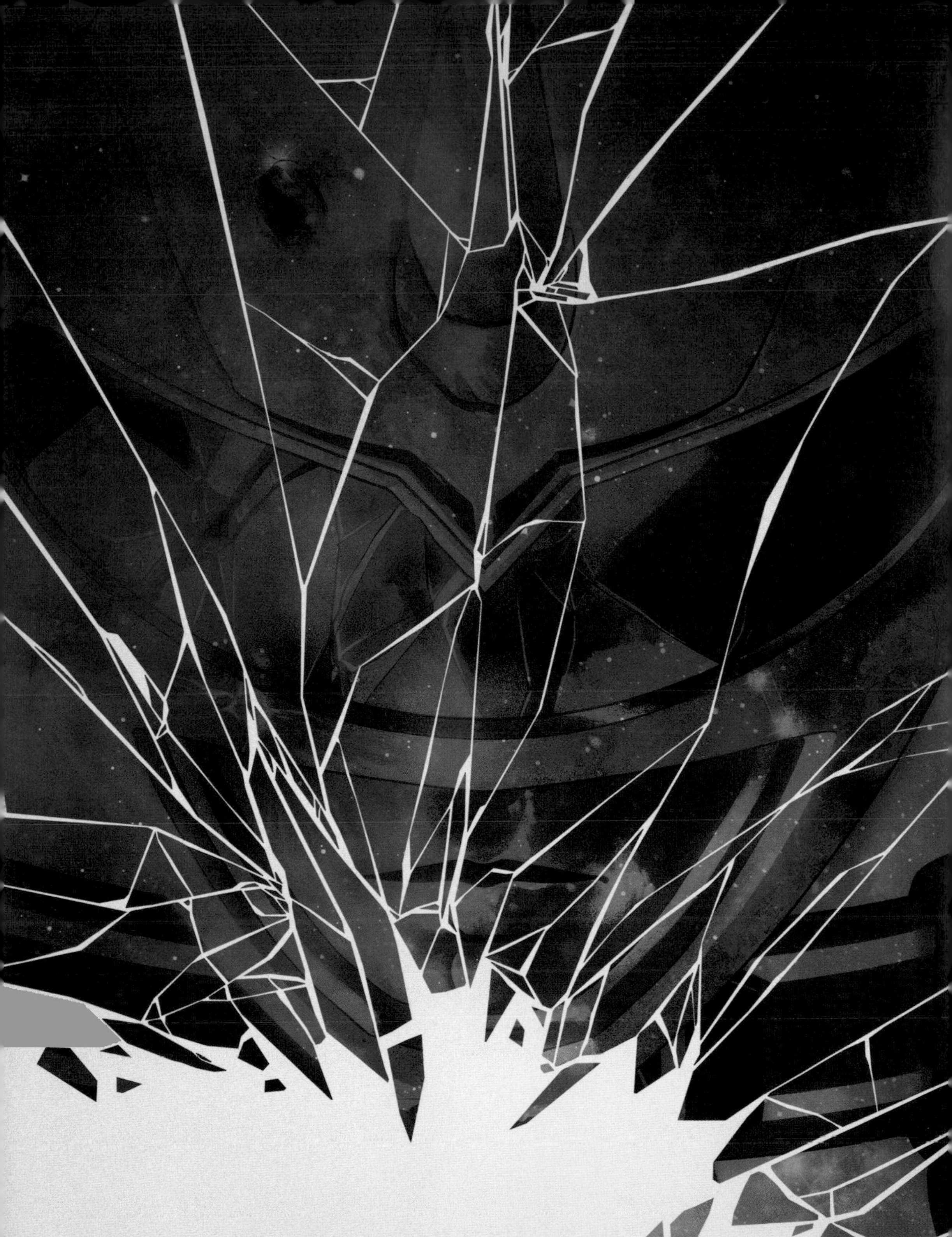

INTERLUDE

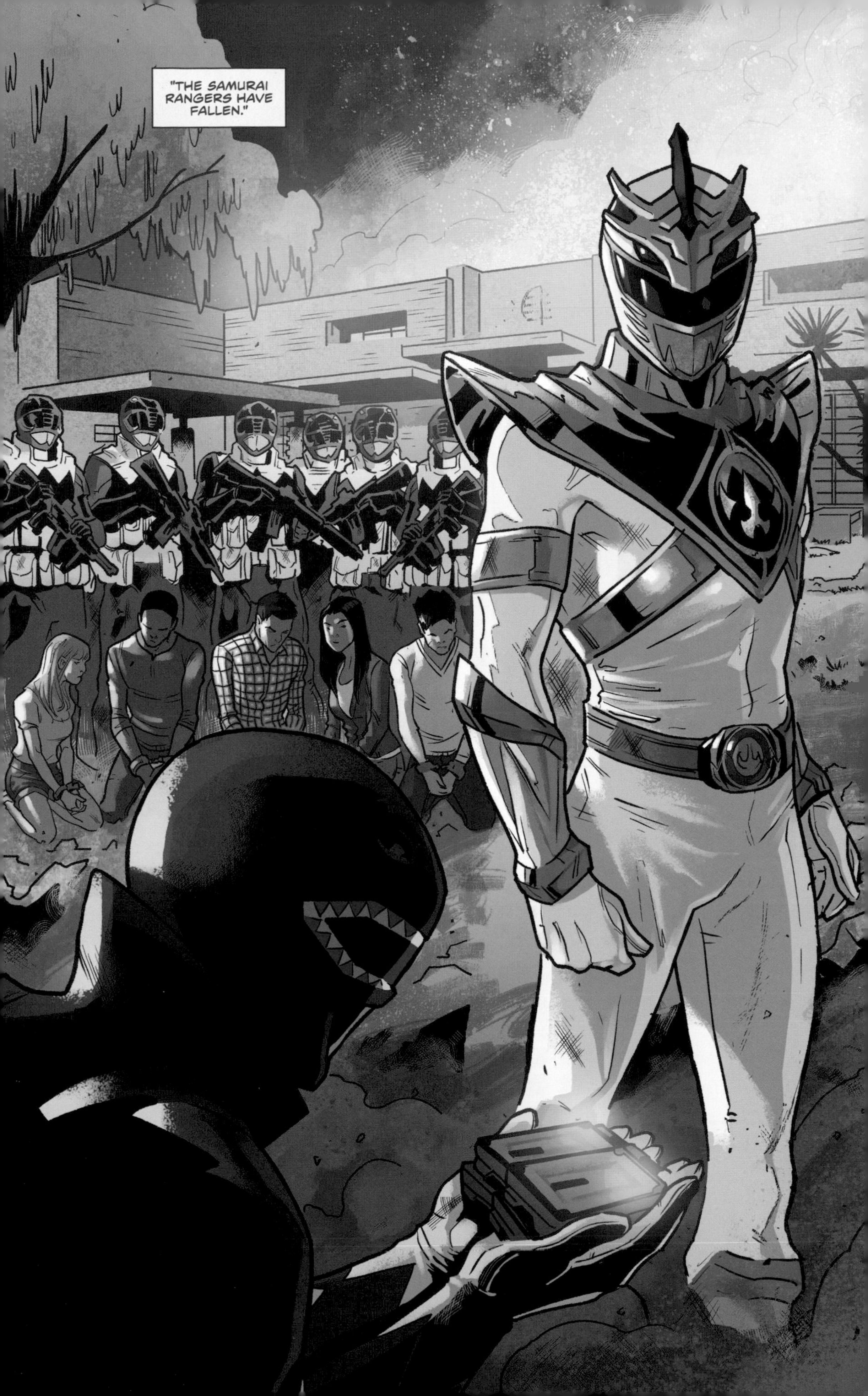
"THE SAMURAI RANGERS HAVE FALLEN."

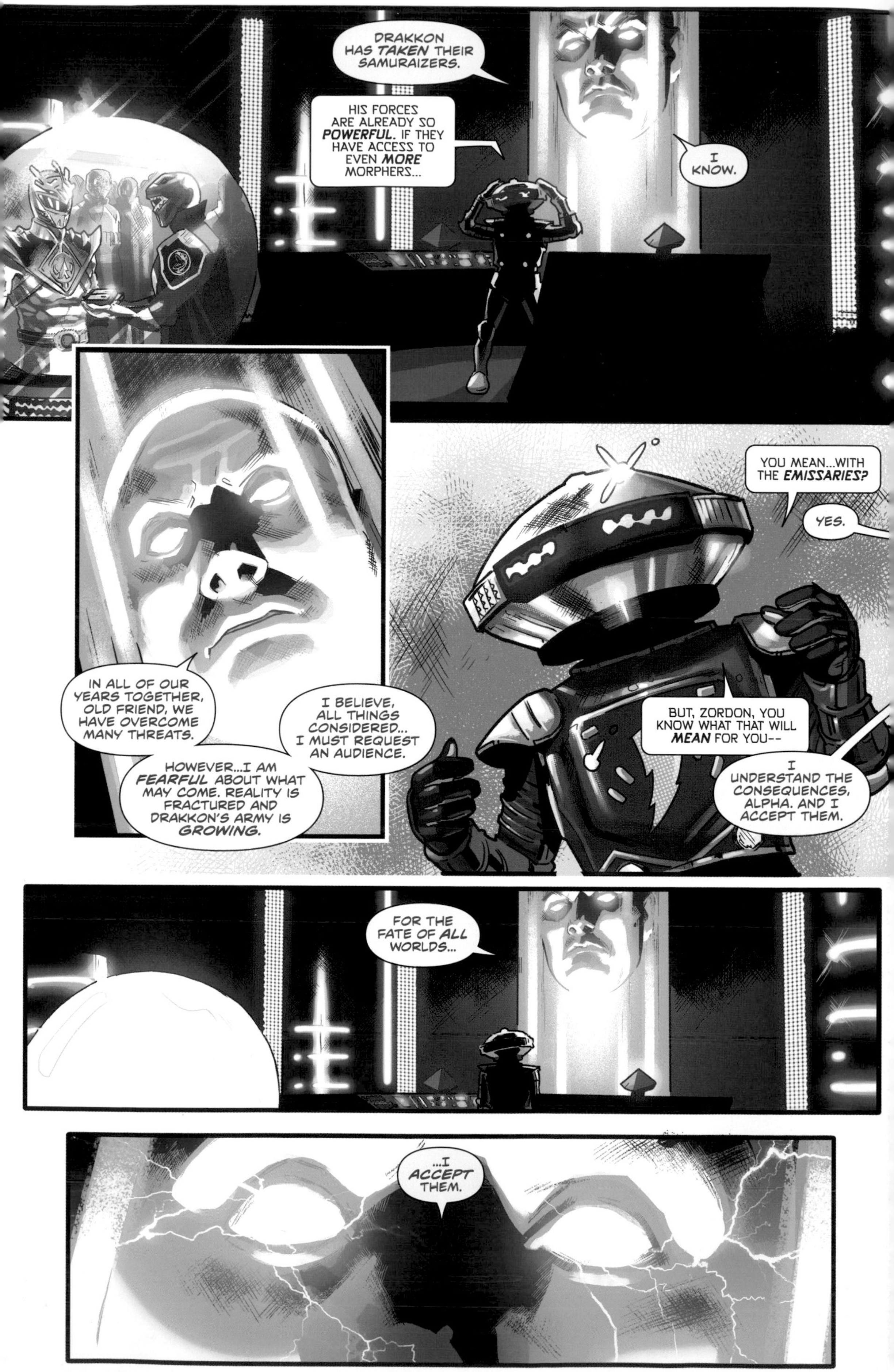
DRAKKON HAS TAKEN THEIR SAMURAIZERS.
HIS FORCES ARE ALREADY SO POWERFUL. IF THEY HAVE ACCESS TO EVEN MORE MORPHERS...
I KNOW.
IN ALL OF OUR YEARS TOGETHER, OLD FRIEND, WE HAVE OVERCOME MANY THREATS.
HOWEVER...I AM FEARFUL ABOUT WHAT MAY COME. REALITY IS FRACTURED AND DRAKKON'S ARMY IS GROWING.
I BELIEVE, ALL THINGS CONSIDERED... I MUST REQUEST AN AUDIENCE.
YOU MEAN...WITH THE EMISSARIES?
YES.
BUT, ZORDON, YOU KNOW WHAT THAT WILL MEAN FOR YOU--
I UNDERSTAND THE CONSEQUENCES, ALPHA. AND I ACCEPT THEM.
FOR THE FATE OF ALL WORLDS...
...I ACCEPT THEM.

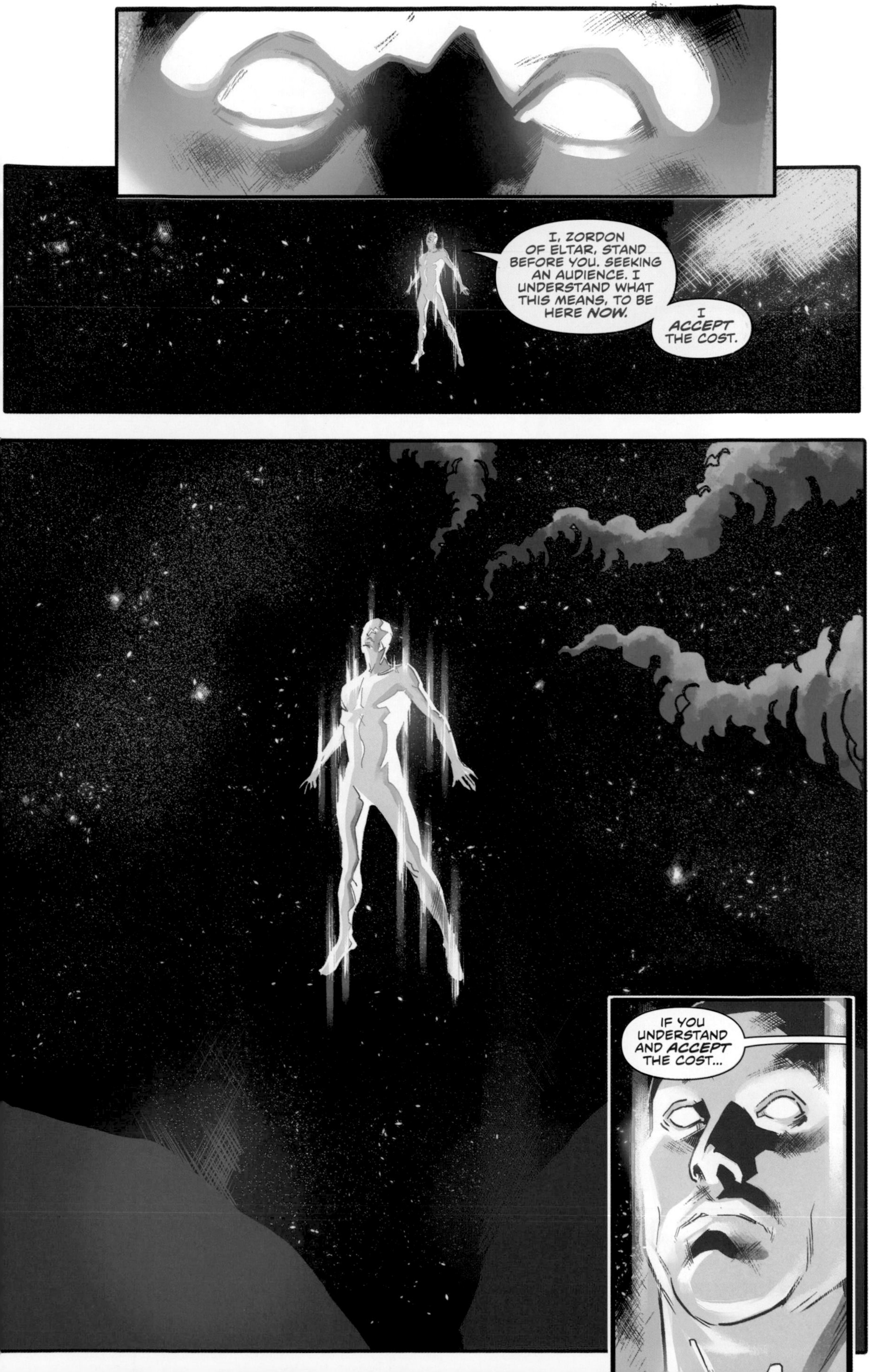
I, ZORDON OF ELTAR, STAND BEFORE YOU. SEEKING AN AUDIENCE. I UNDERSTAND WHAT THIS MEANS, TO BE HERE *NOW*.
I *ACCEPT* THE COST.
IF YOU UNDERSTAND AND *ACCEPT* THE COST...

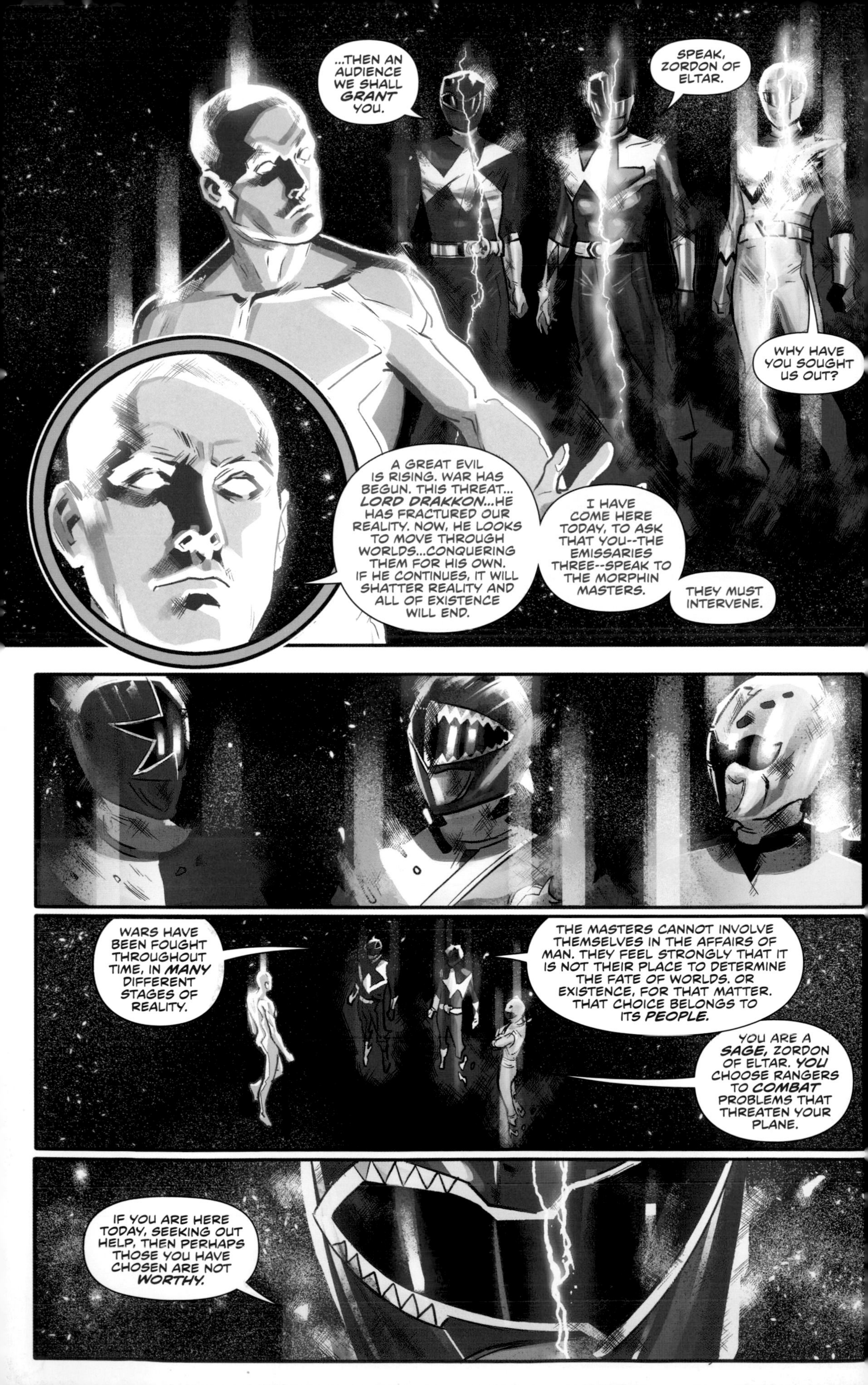
...THEN AN AUDIENCE WE SHALL GRANT YOU.
SPEAK, ZORDON OF ELTAR.
WHY HAVE YOU SOUGHT US OUT?
A GREAT EVIL IS RISING. WAR HAS BEGUN. THIS THREAT... LORD DRAKKON...HE HAS FRACTURED OUR REALITY. NOW, HE LOOKS TO MOVE THROUGH WORLDS...CONQUERING THEM FOR HIS OWN. IF HE CONTINUES, IT WILL SHATTER REALITY AND ALL OF EXISTENCE WILL END.
I HAVE COME HERE TODAY, TO ASK THAT YOU--THE EMISSARIES THREE--SPEAK TO THE MORPHIN MASTERS.
THEY MUST INTERVENE.
WARS HAVE BEEN FOUGHT THROUGHOUT TIME, IN MANY DIFFERENT STAGES OF REALITY.
THE MASTERS CANNOT INVOLVE THEMSELVES IN THE AFFAIRS OF MAN. THEY FEEL STRONGLY THAT IT IS NOT THEIR PLACE TO DETERMINE THE FATE OF WORLDS. OR EXISTENCE, FOR THAT MATTER. THAT CHOICE BELONGS TO ITS PEOPLE.
YOU ARE A SAGE, ZORDON OF ELTAR. YOU CHOOSE RANGERS TO COMBAT PROBLEMS THAT THREATEN YOUR PLANE.
IF YOU ARE HERE TODAY, SEEKING OUT HELP, THEN PERHAPS THOSE YOU HAVE CHOSEN ARE NOT WORTHY.

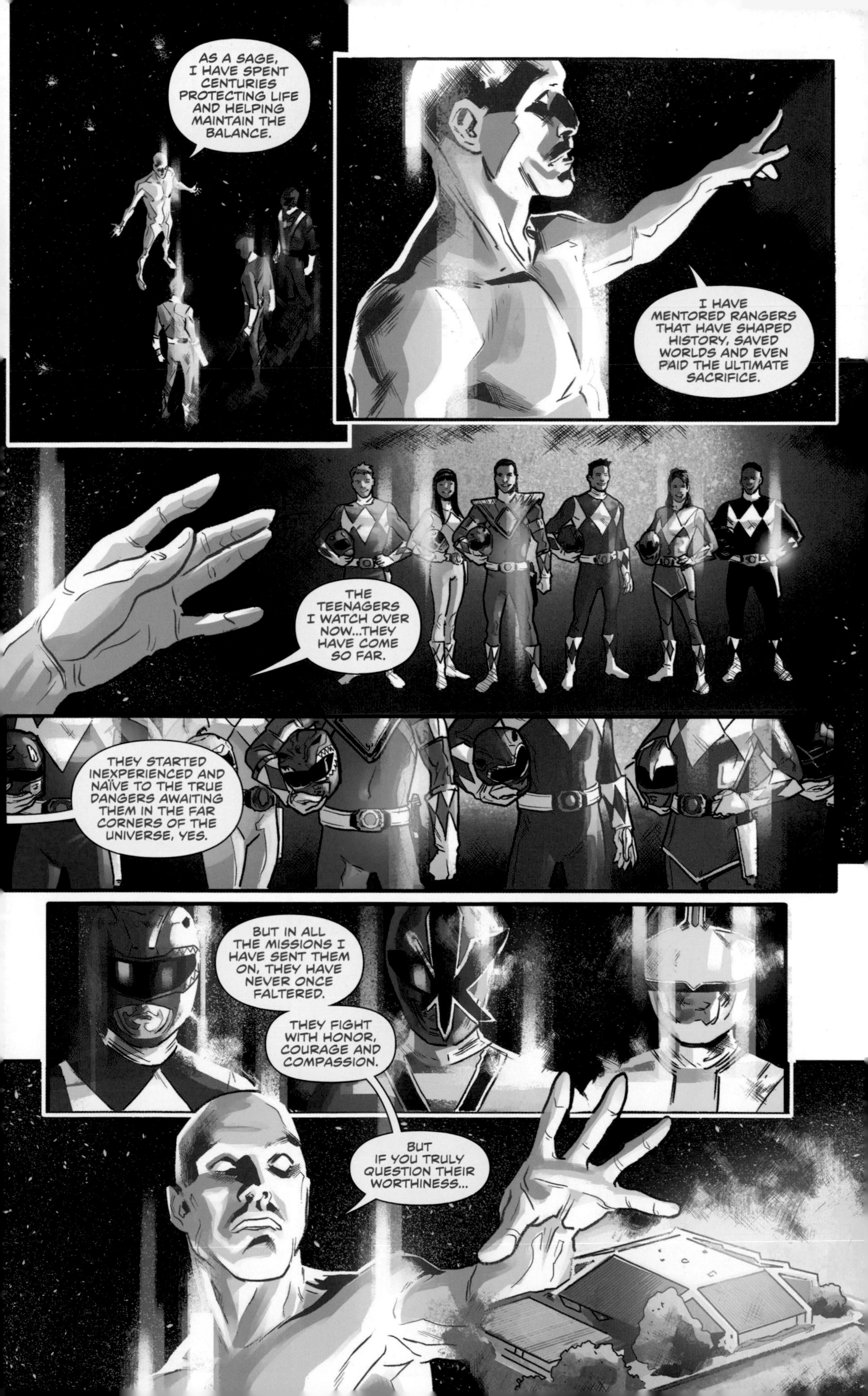
AS A SAGE, I HAVE SPENT CENTURIES PROTECTING LIFE AND HELPING MAINTAIN THE BALANCE.
I HAVE MENTORED RANGERS THAT HAVE SHAPED HISTORY, SAVED WORLDS AND EVEN PAID THE ULTIMATE SACRIFICE.
THE TEENAGERS I WATCH OVER NOW...THEY HAVE COME SO FAR.
THEY STARTED INEXPERIENCED AND NAÏVE TO THE TRUE DANGERS AWAITING THEM IN THE FAR CORNERS OF THE UNIVERSE, YES.
BUT IN ALL THE MISSIONS I HAVE SENT THEM ON, THEY HAVE NEVER ONCE FALTERED.
THEY FIGHT WITH HONOR, COURAGE AND COMPASSION.
BUT IF YOU TRULY QUESTION THEIR WORTHINESS...

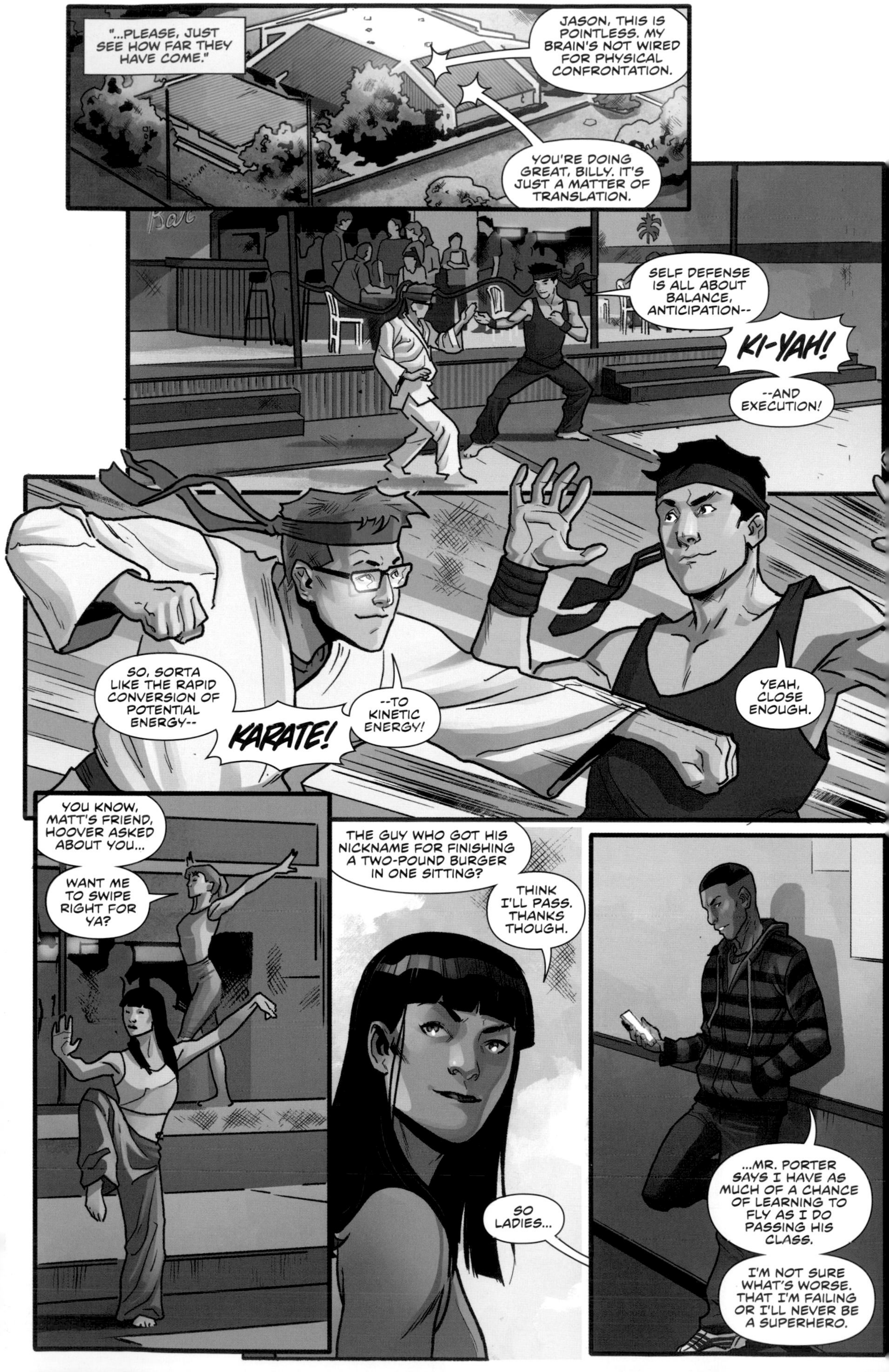
"...PLEASE, JUST SEE HOW FAR THEY HAVE COME."
JASON, THIS IS POINTLESS. MY BRAIN'S NOT WIRED FOR PHYSICAL CONFRONTATION.
YOU'RE DOING GREAT, BILLY. IT'S JUST A MATTER OF TRANSLATION.
SELF DEFENSE IS ALL ABOUT BALANCE, ANTICIPATION--
KI-YAH!
--AND EXECUTION!
SO, SORTA LIKE THE RAPID CONVERSION OF POTENTIAL ENERGY--
KARATE!
--TO KINETIC ENERGY!
YEAH, CLOSE ENOUGH.
YOU KNOW, MATT'S FRIEND, HOOVER ASKED ABOUT YOU...
WANT ME TO SWIPE RIGHT FOR YA?
THE GUY WHO GOT HIS NICKNAME FOR FINISHING A TWO-POUND BURGER IN ONE SITTING?
THINK I'LL PASS. THANKS THOUGH.
SO LADIES...
...MR. PORTER SAYS I HAVE AS MUCH OF A CHANCE OF LEARNING TO FLY AS I DO PASSING HIS CLASS.
I'M NOT SURE WHAT'S WORSE. THAT I'M FAILING OR I'LL NEVER BE A SUPERHERO.

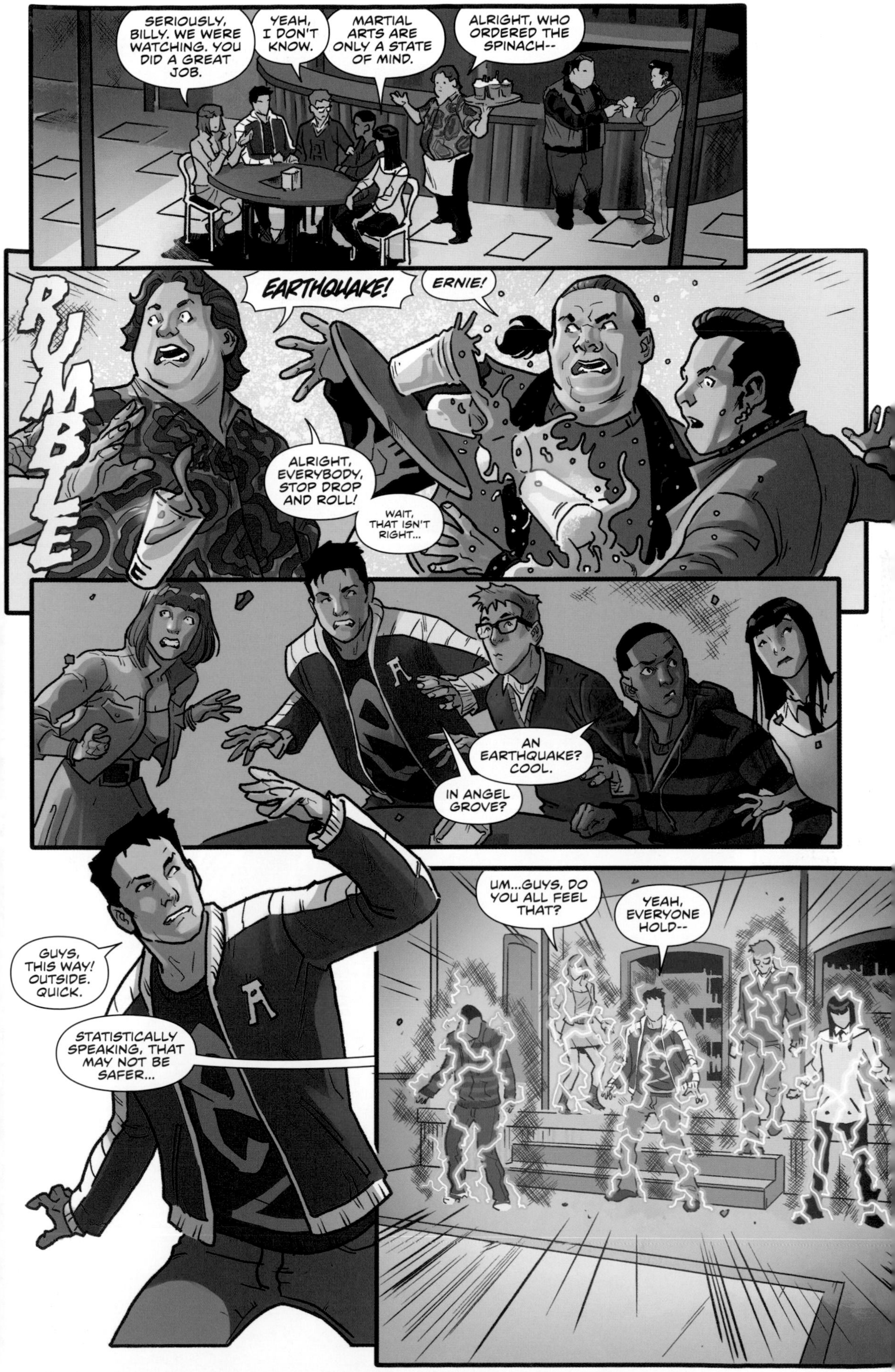
SERIOUSLY, BILLY. WE WERE WATCHING. YOU DID A GREAT JOB.
YEAH, I DON'T KNOW.
MARTIAL ARTS ARE ONLY A STATE OF MIND.
ALRIGHT, WHO ORDERED THE SPINACH--
RUMBLE
EARTHQUAKE!
ERNIE!
ALRIGHT, EVERYBODY, STOP DROP AND ROLL!
WAIT, THAT ISN'T RIGHT...
AN EARTHQUAKE? COOL.
IN ANGEL GROVE?
GUYS, THIS WAY! OUTSIDE. QUICK.
STATISTICALLY SPEAKING, THAT MAY NOT BE SAFER...
UM...GUYS, DO YOU ALL FEEL THAT?
YEAH, EVERYONE HOLD--

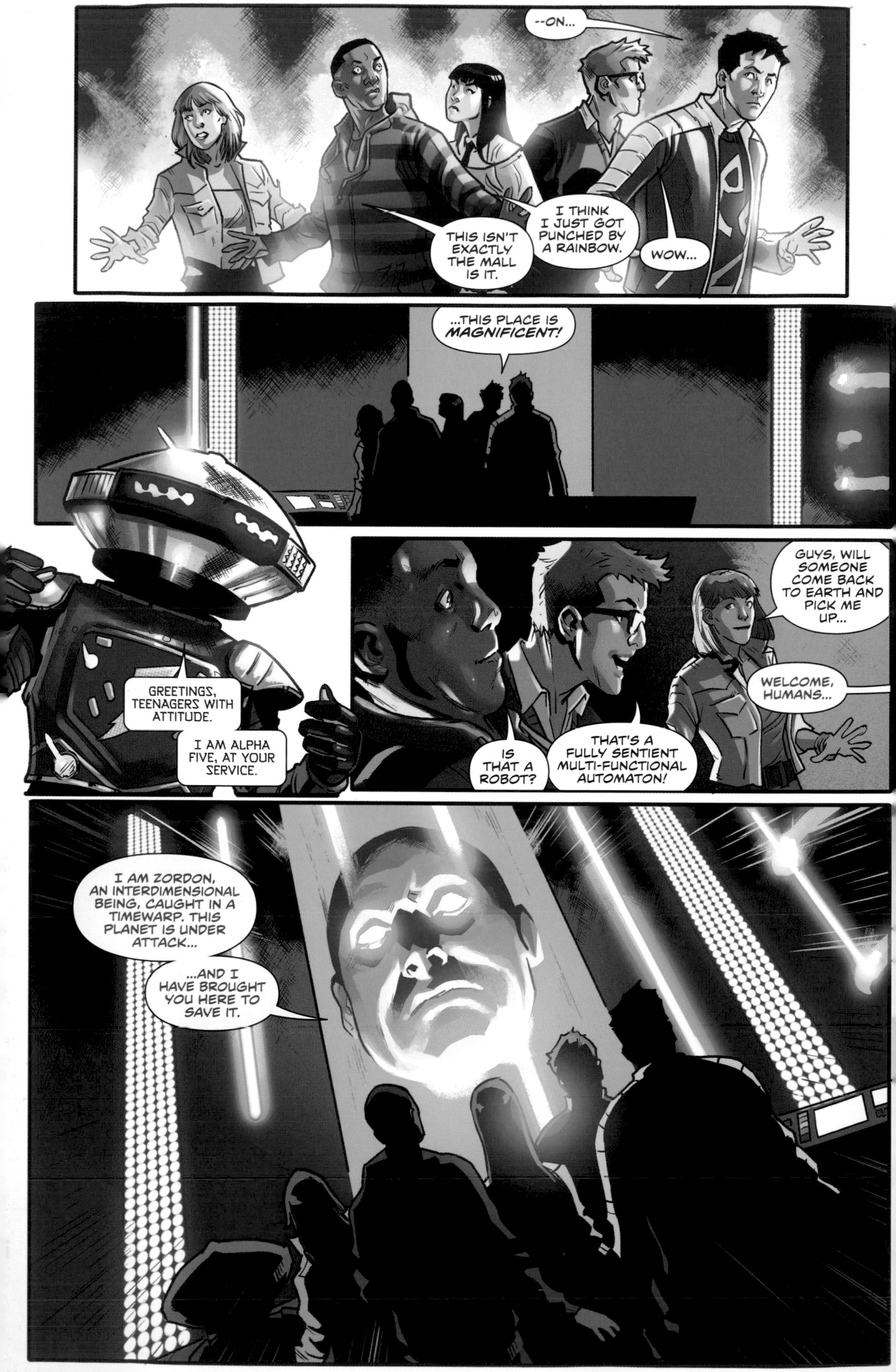
--ON...
WOW...
I THINK I JUST GOT PUNCHED BY A RAINBOW.
THIS ISN'T EXACTLY THE MALL IS IT.
...THIS PLACE IS *MAGNIFICENT!*
GUYS, WILL SOMEONE COME BACK TO EARTH AND PICK ME UP...
WELCOME, HUMANS...
GREETINGS, TEENAGERS WITH ATTITUDE.
I AM ALPHA FIVE, AT YOUR SERVICE.
IS THAT A ROBOT?
THAT'S A FULLY SENTIENT MULTI-FUNCTIONAL AUTOMATON!
I AM ZORDON, AN INTERDIMENSIONAL BEING, CAUGHT IN A TIMEWARP. THIS PLANET IS UNDER ATTACK...
...AND I HAVE BROUGHT YOU HERE TO SAVE IT.

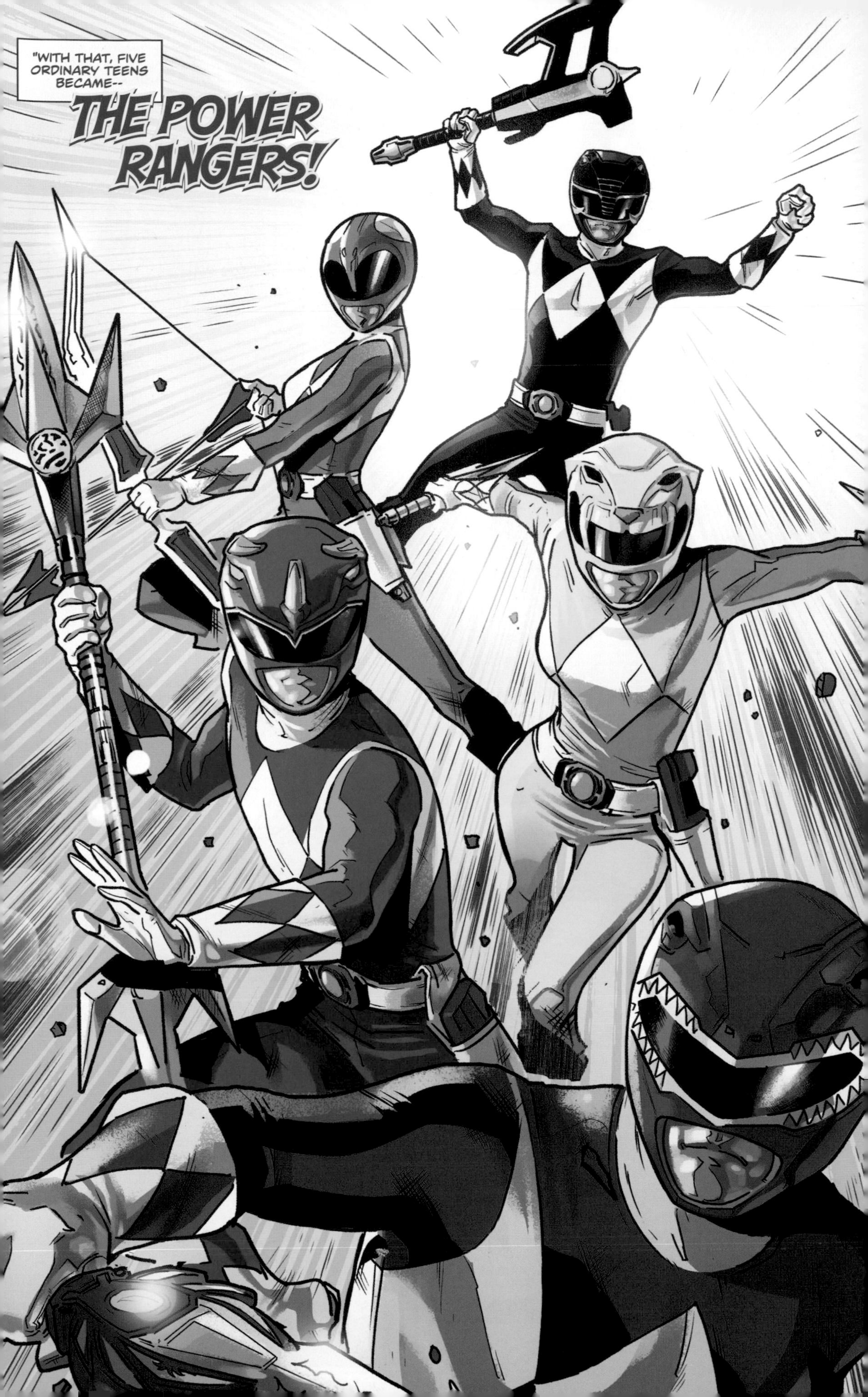
"WITH THAT, FIVE ORDINARY TEENS BECAME--
THE POWER RANGERS!

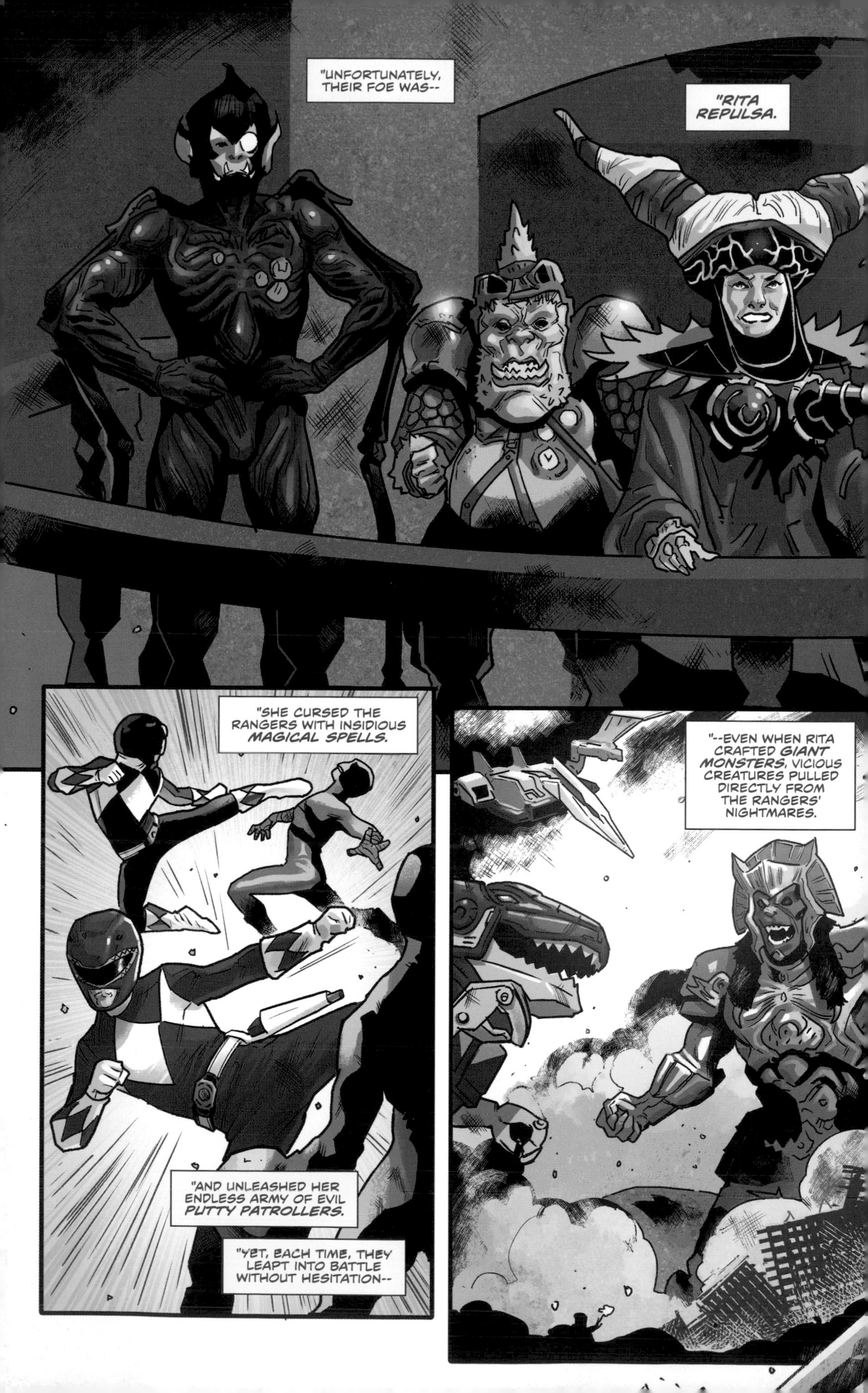
"UNFORTUNATELY, THEIR FOE WAS--
"RITA REPULSA.
"SHE CURSED THE RANGERS WITH INSIDIOUS MAGICAL SPELLS.
"AND UNLEASHED HER ENDLESS ARMY OF EVIL PUTTY PATROLLERS.
"YET, EACH TIME, THEY LEAPT INTO BATTLE WITHOUT HESITATION--
"--EVEN WHEN RITA CRAFTED GIANT MONSTERS, VICIOUS CREATURES PULLED DIRECTLY FROM THE RANGERS' NIGHTMARES.

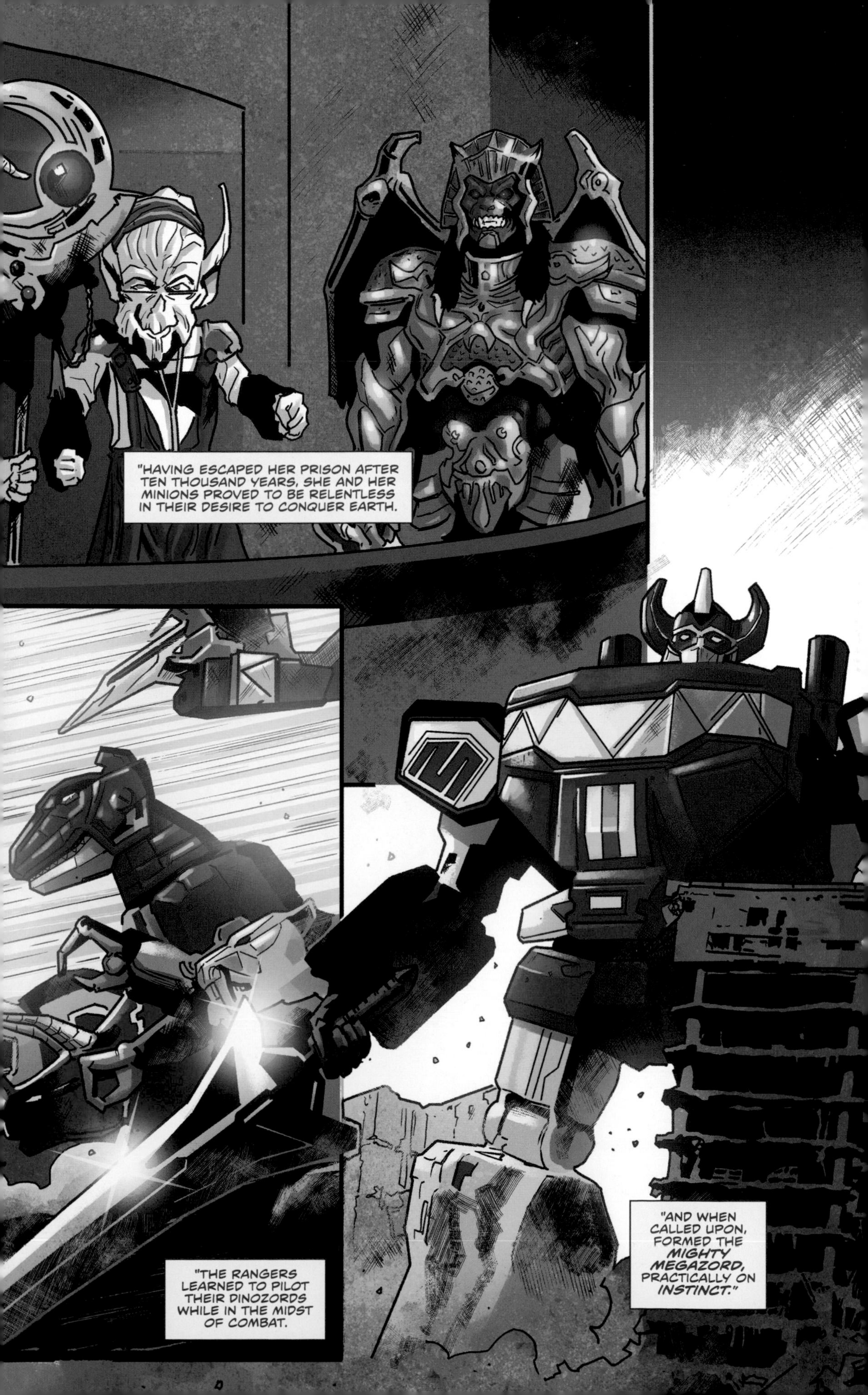
"HAVING ESCAPED HER PRISON AFTER TEN THOUSAND YEARS, SHE AND HER MINIONS PROVED TO BE RELENTLESS IN THEIR DESIRE TO CONQUER EARTH.
"THE RANGERS LEARNED TO PILOT THEIR DINOZORDS WHILE IN THE MIDST OF COMBAT.
"AND WHEN CALLED UPON, FORMED THE *MIGHTY MEGAZORD,* PRACTICALLY ON *INSTINCT.*"

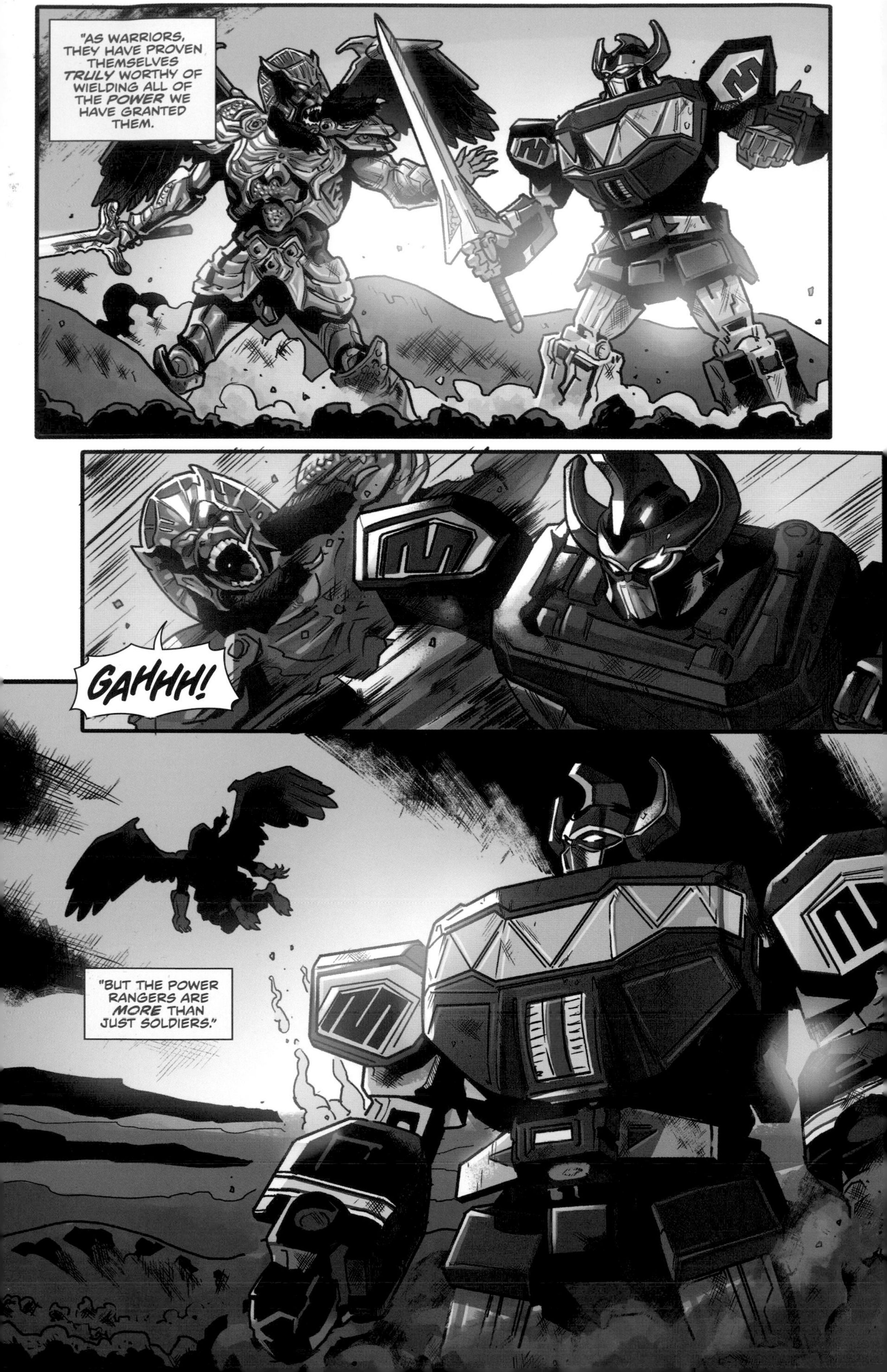
"AS WARRIORS, THEY HAVE PROVEN THEMSELVES *TRULY* WORTHY OF WIELDING ALL OF THE *POWER* WE HAVE GRANTED THEM.
GAHHH!
"BUT THE POWER RANGERS ARE *MORE* THAN JUST SOLDIERS."

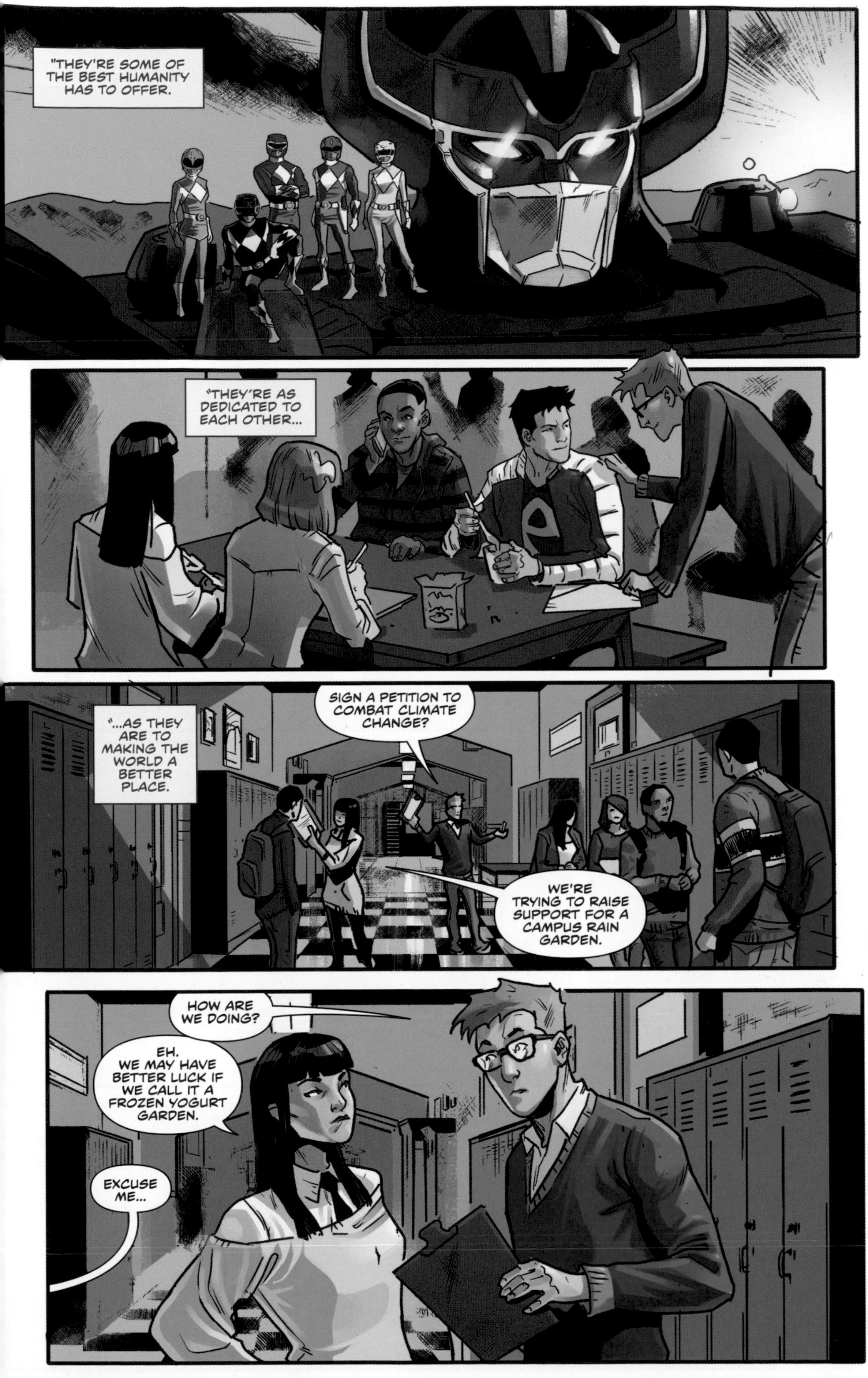
"THEY'RE SOME OF THE BEST HUMANITY HAS TO OFFER.
"THEY'RE AS DEDICATED TO EACH OTHER...
"...AS THEY ARE TO MAKING THE WORLD A BETTER PLACE.
SIGN A PETITION TO COMBAT CLIMATE CHANGE?
WE'RE TRYING TO RAISE SUPPORT FOR A CAMPUS RAIN GARDEN.
HOW ARE WE DOING?
EH. WE MAY HAVE BETTER LUCK IF WE CALL IT A FROZEN YOGURT GARDEN.
EXCUSE ME...

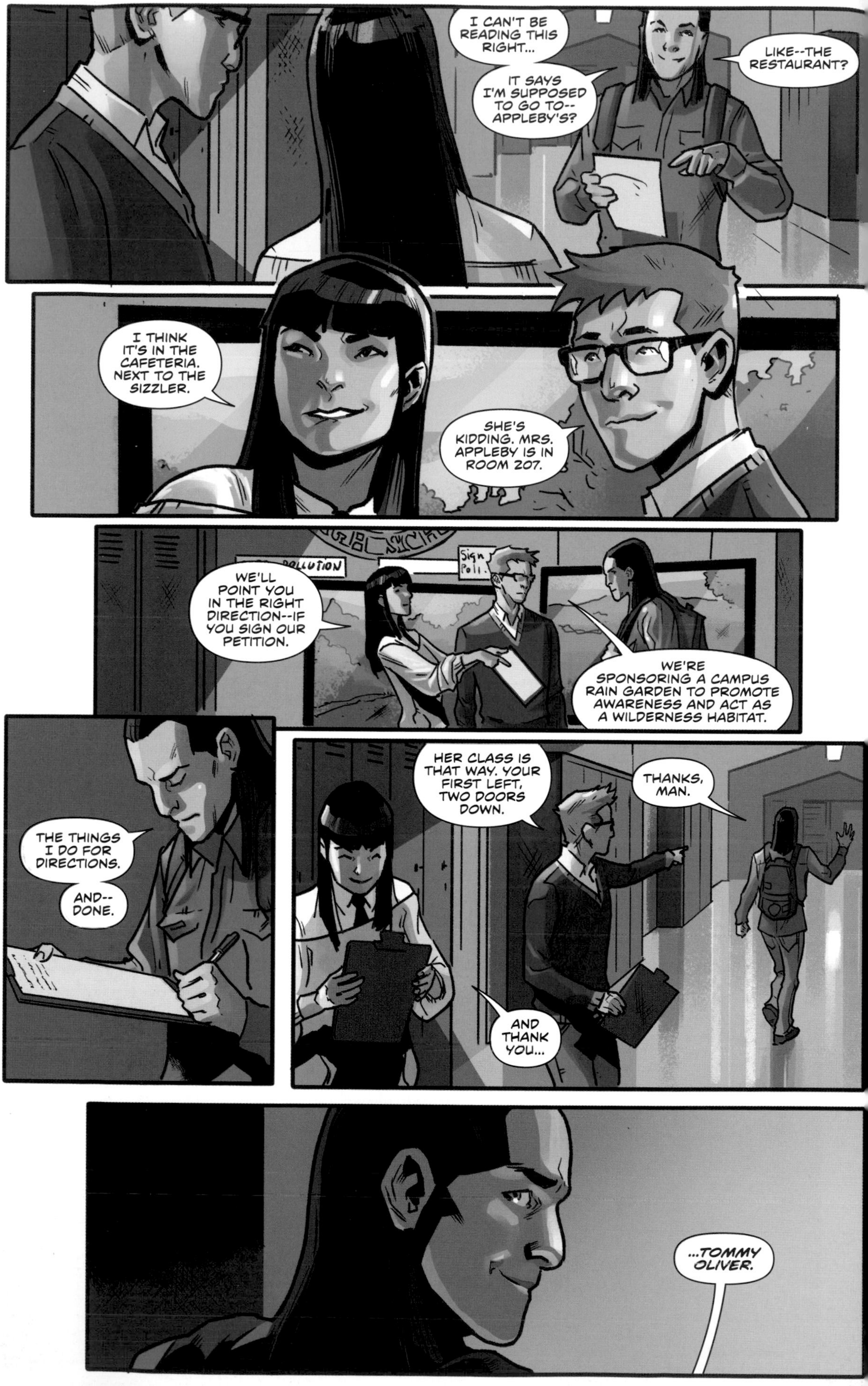
I CAN'T BE READING THIS RIGHT...
IT SAYS I'M SUPPOSED TO GO TO-- APPLEBY'S?
LIKE--THE RESTAURANT?
I THINK IT'S IN THE CAFETERIA. NEXT TO THE SIZZLER.
SHE'S KIDDING. MRS. APPLEBY IS IN ROOM 207.
POLLUTION
Sign Poli.
WE'LL POINT YOU IN THE RIGHT DIRECTION--IF YOU SIGN OUR PETITION.
WE'RE SPONSORING A CAMPUS RAIN GARDEN TO PROMOTE AWARENESS AND ACT AS A WILDERNESS HABITAT.
THE THINGS I DO FOR DIRECTIONS.
AND-- DONE.
HER CLASS IS THAT WAY. YOUR FIRST LEFT, TWO DOORS DOWN.
THANKS, MAN.
AND THANK YOU...
...TOMMY OLIVER.

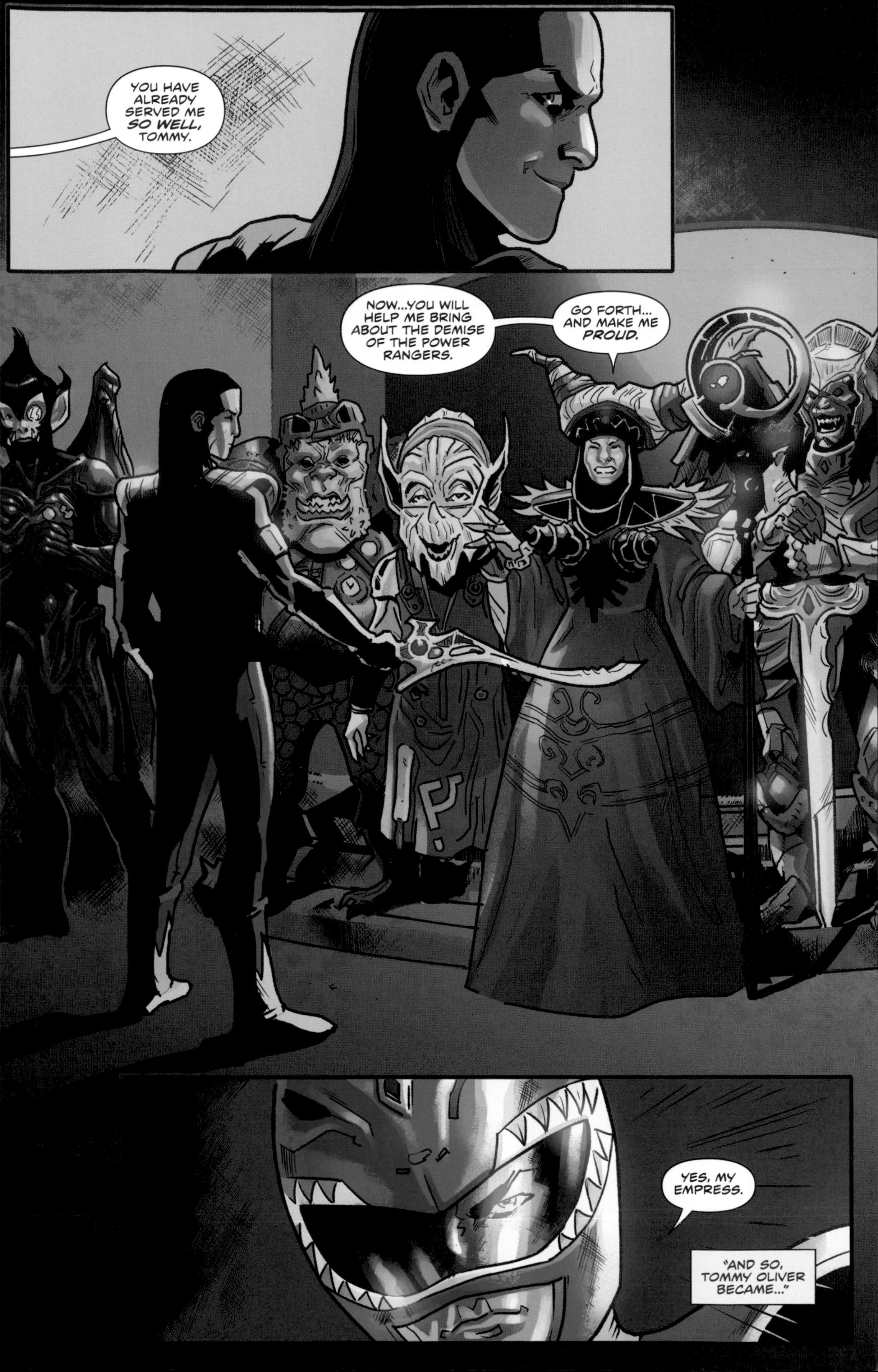
YOU HAVE ALREADY SERVED ME SO WELL, TOMMY.
NOW...YOU WILL HELP ME BRING ABOUT THE DEMISE OF THE POWER RANGERS.
GO FORTH... AND MAKE ME PROUD.
YES, MY EMPRESS.
"AND SO, TOMMY OLIVER BECAME..."

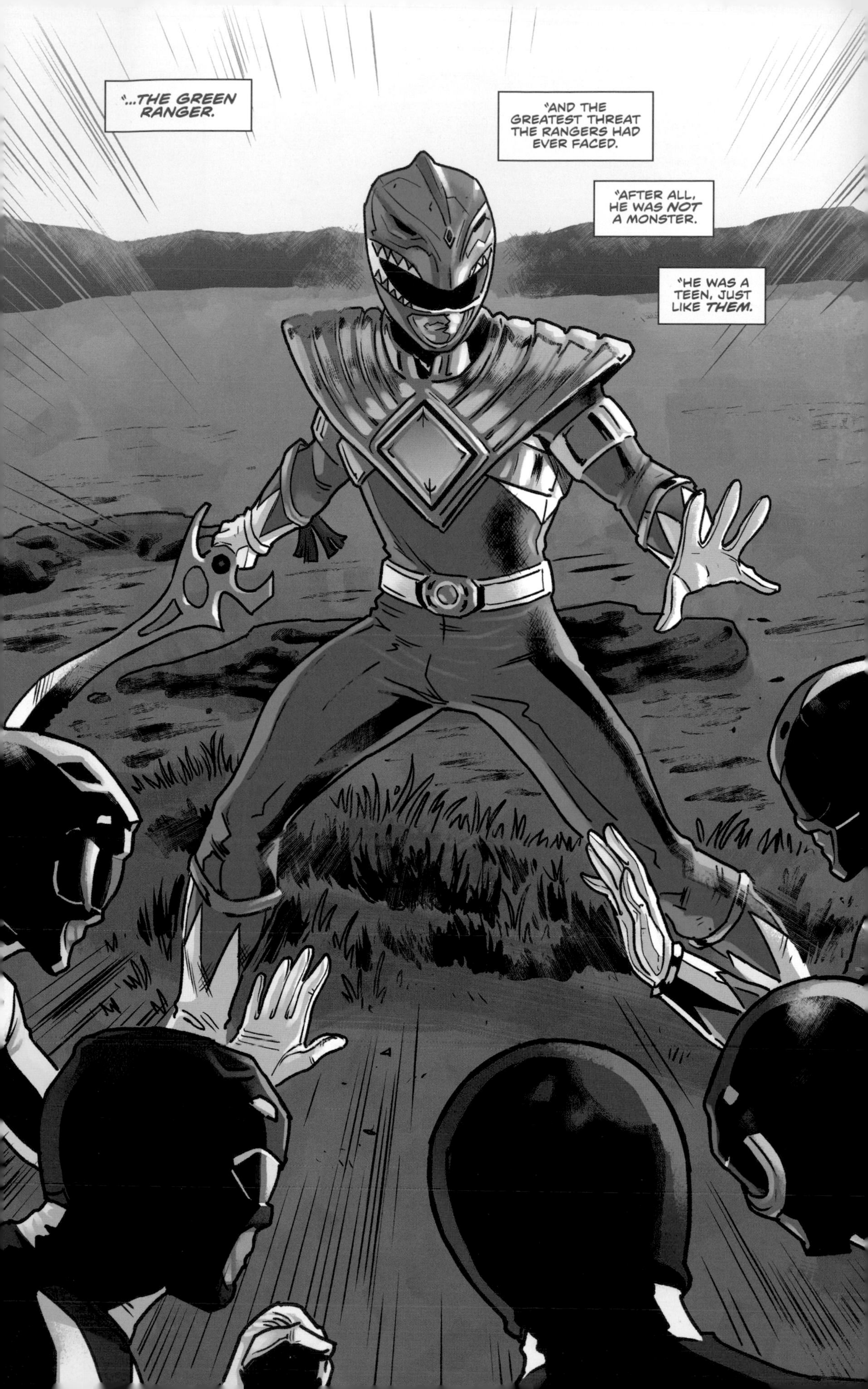
"...THE GREEN RANGER.
"AND THE GREATEST THREAT THE RANGERS HAD EVER FACED.
"AFTER ALL, HE WAS *NOT* A MONSTER.
"HE WAS A TEEN, JUST LIKE *THEM*.

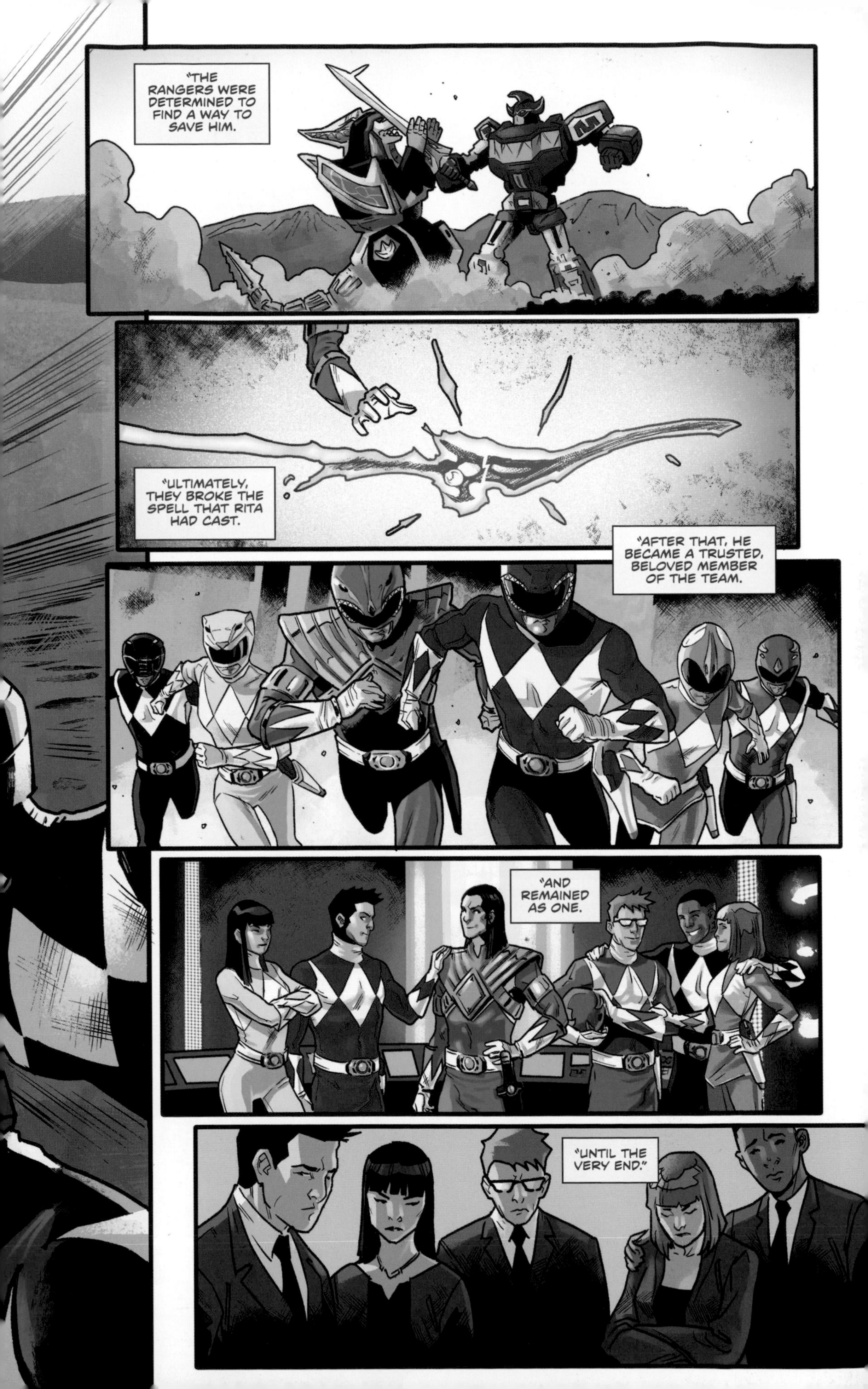
"THE RANGERS WERE DETERMINED TO FIND A WAY TO SAVE HIM.
"ULTIMATELY, THEY BROKE THE SPELL THAT RITA HAD CAST.
"AFTER THAT, HE BECAME A TRUSTED, BELOVED MEMBER OF THE TEAM.
"AND REMAINED AS ONE.
"UNTIL THE VERY END."

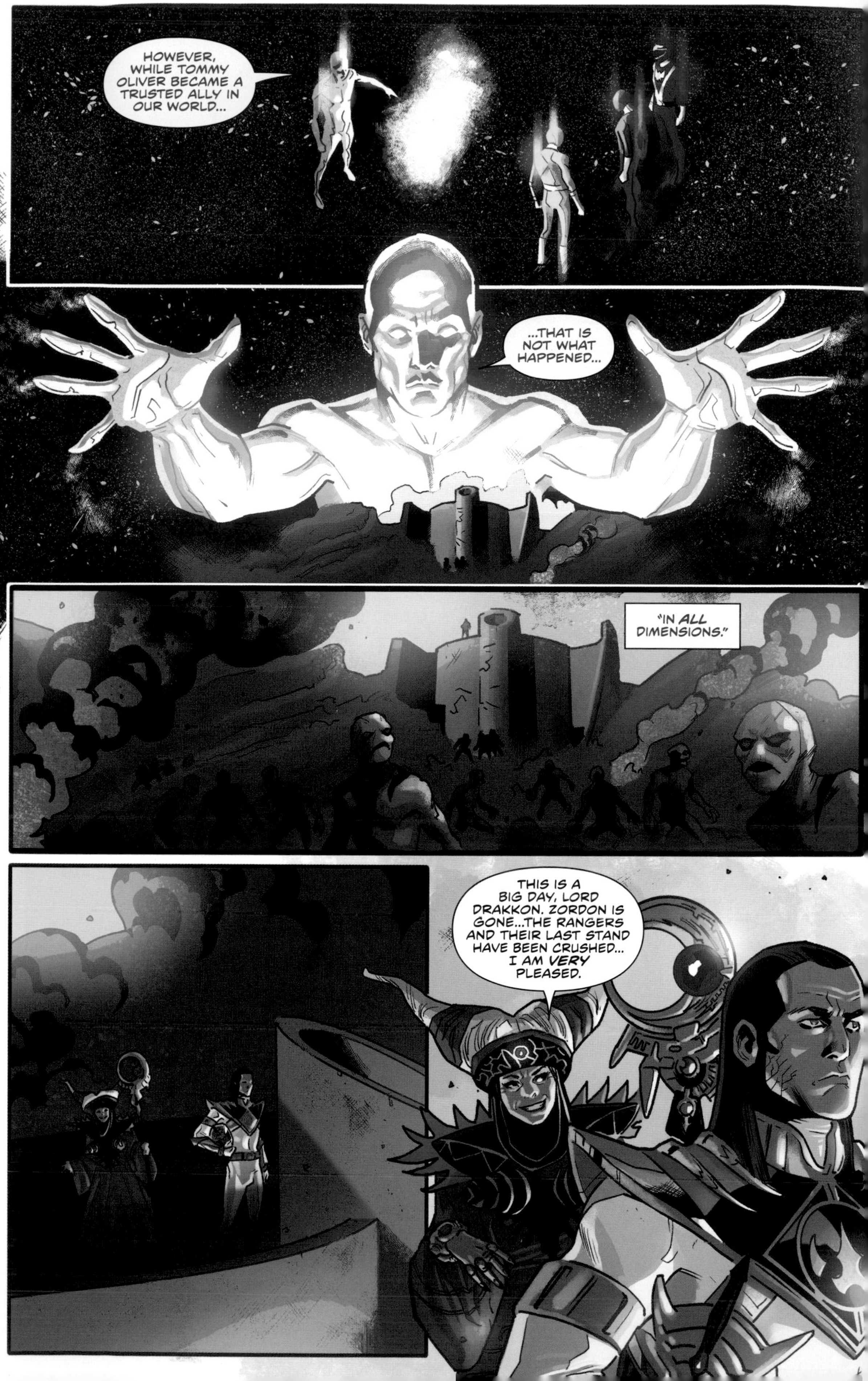
HOWEVER, WHILE TOMMY OLIVER BECAME A TRUSTED ALLY IN OUR WORLD...
...THAT IS NOT WHAT HAPPENED...
"IN *ALL* DIMENSIONS."
THIS IS A BIG DAY, LORD DRAKKON. ZORDON IS GONE...THE RANGERS AND THEIR LAST STAND HAVE BEEN CRUSHED... I AM *VERY* PLEASED.

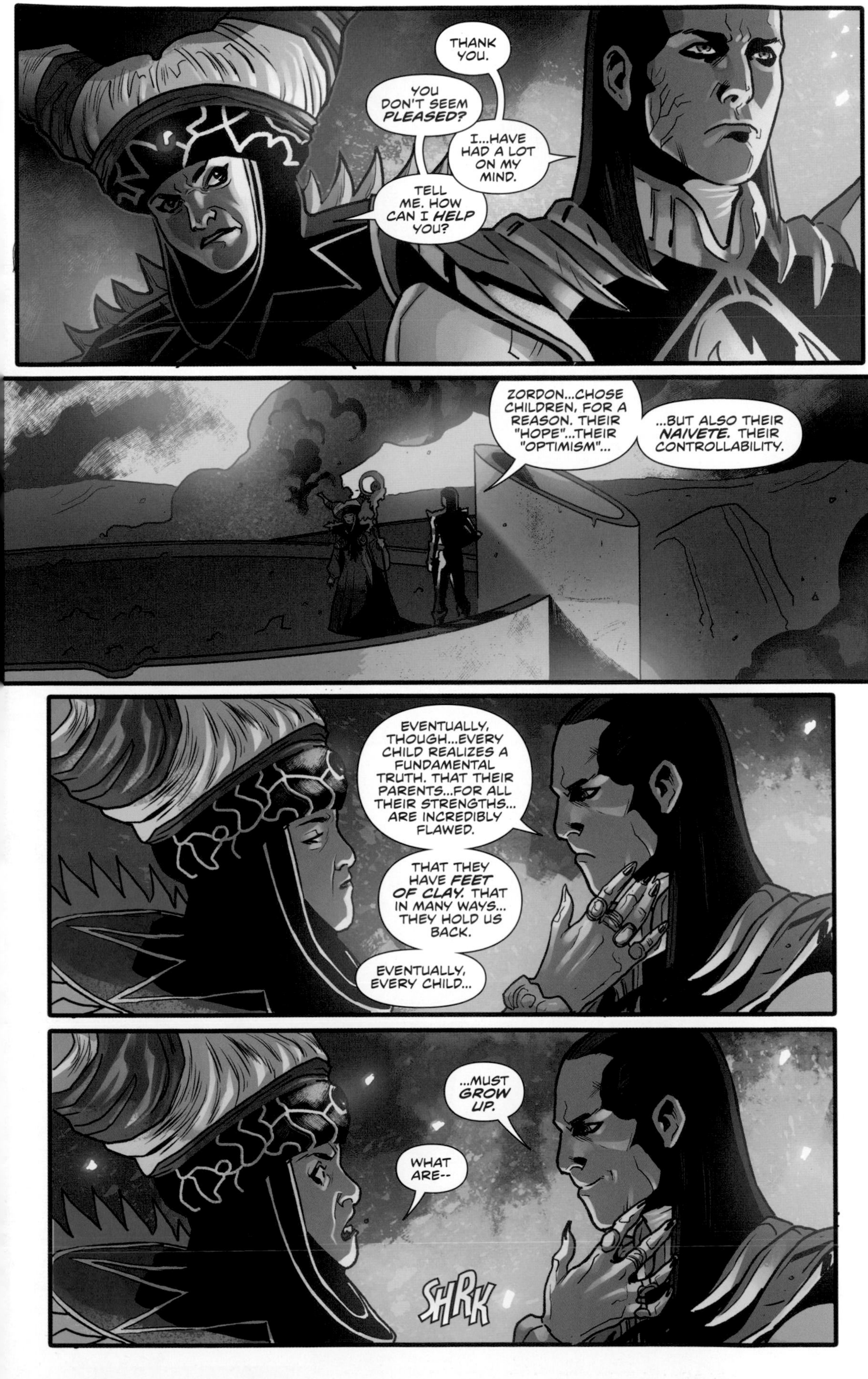
THANK YOU.
YOU DON'T SEEM PLEASED?
I...HAVE HAD A LOT ON MY MIND.
TELL ME. HOW CAN I HELP YOU?
ZORDON...CHOSE CHILDREN, FOR A REASON. THEIR "HOPE"...THEIR "OPTIMISM"...
...BUT ALSO THEIR NAIVETE. THEIR CONTROLLABILITY.
EVENTUALLY, THOUGH...EVERY CHILD REALIZES A FUNDAMENTAL TRUTH. THAT THEIR PARENTS...FOR ALL THEIR STRENGTHS... ARE INCREDIBLY FLAWED.
THAT THEY HAVE FEET OF CLAY. THAT IN MANY WAYS... THEY HOLD US BACK.
EVENTUALLY, EVERY CHILD...
...MUST GROW UP.
WHAT ARE--
SHRK

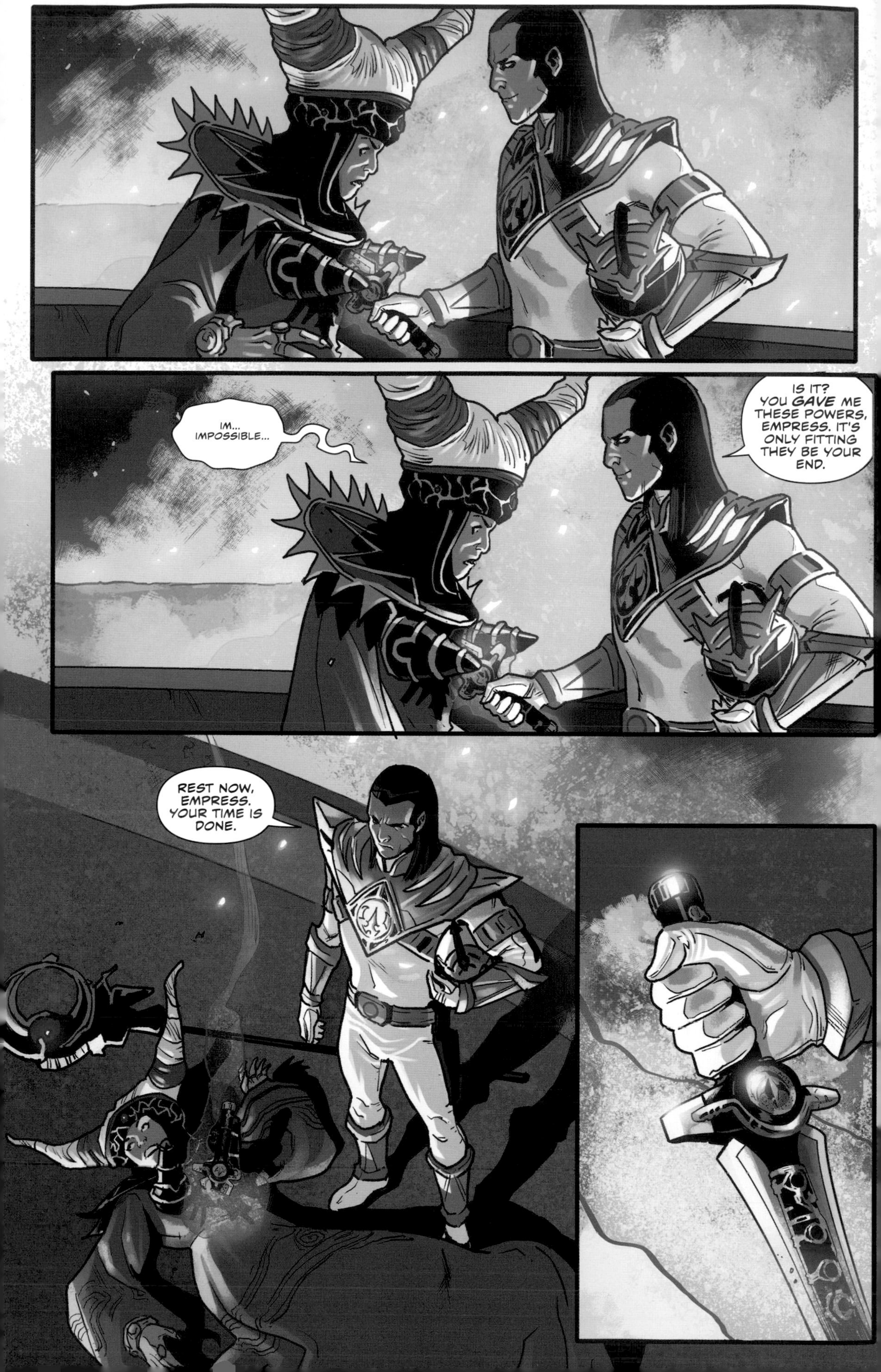
IM... IMPOSSIBLE...
IS IT? YOU GAVE ME THESE POWERS, EMPRESS. IT'S ONLY FITTING THEY BE YOUR END.
REST NOW, EMPRESS. YOUR TIME IS DONE.

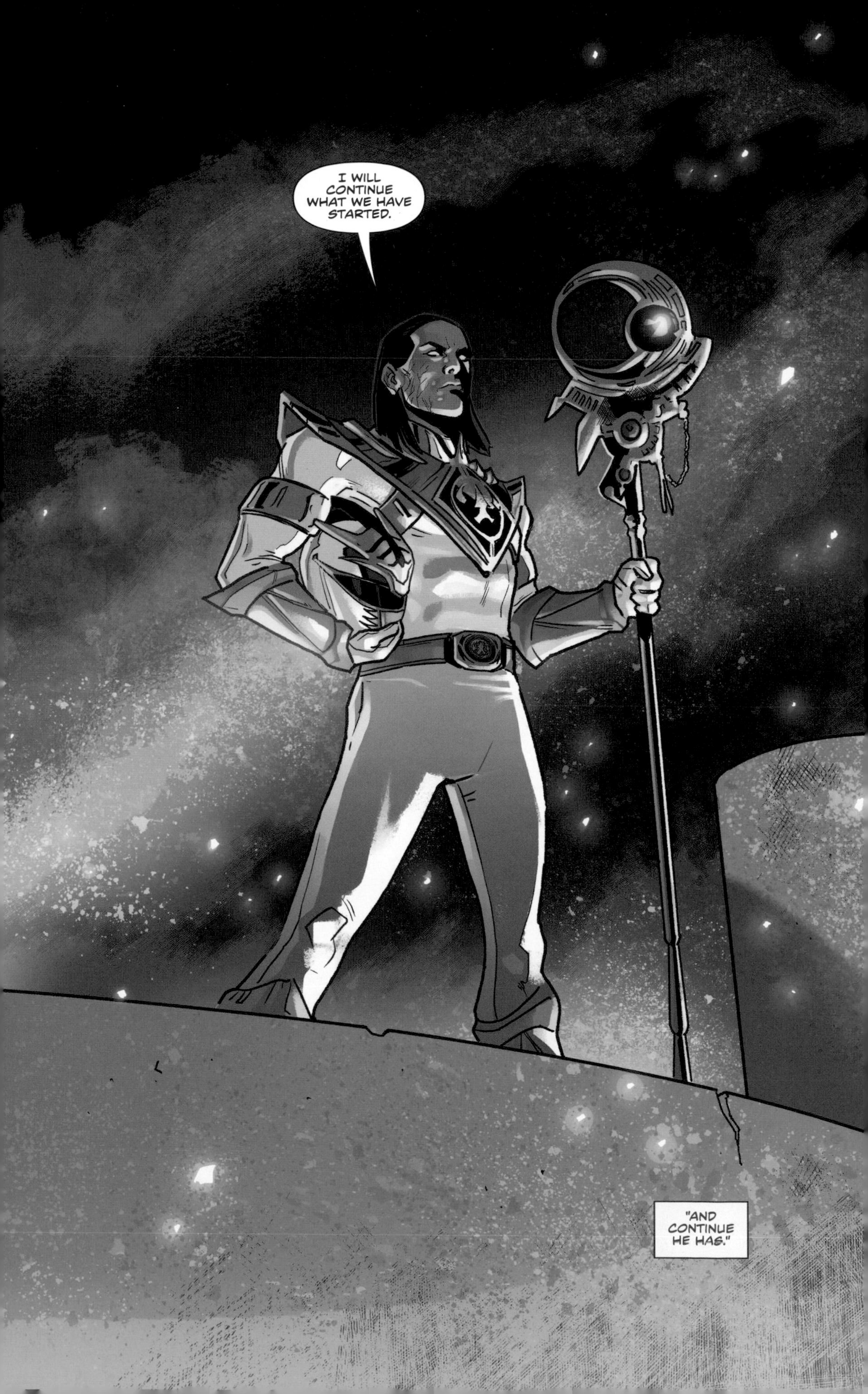
I WILL CONTINUE WHAT WE HAVE STARTED.
"AND CONTINUE HE HAS."

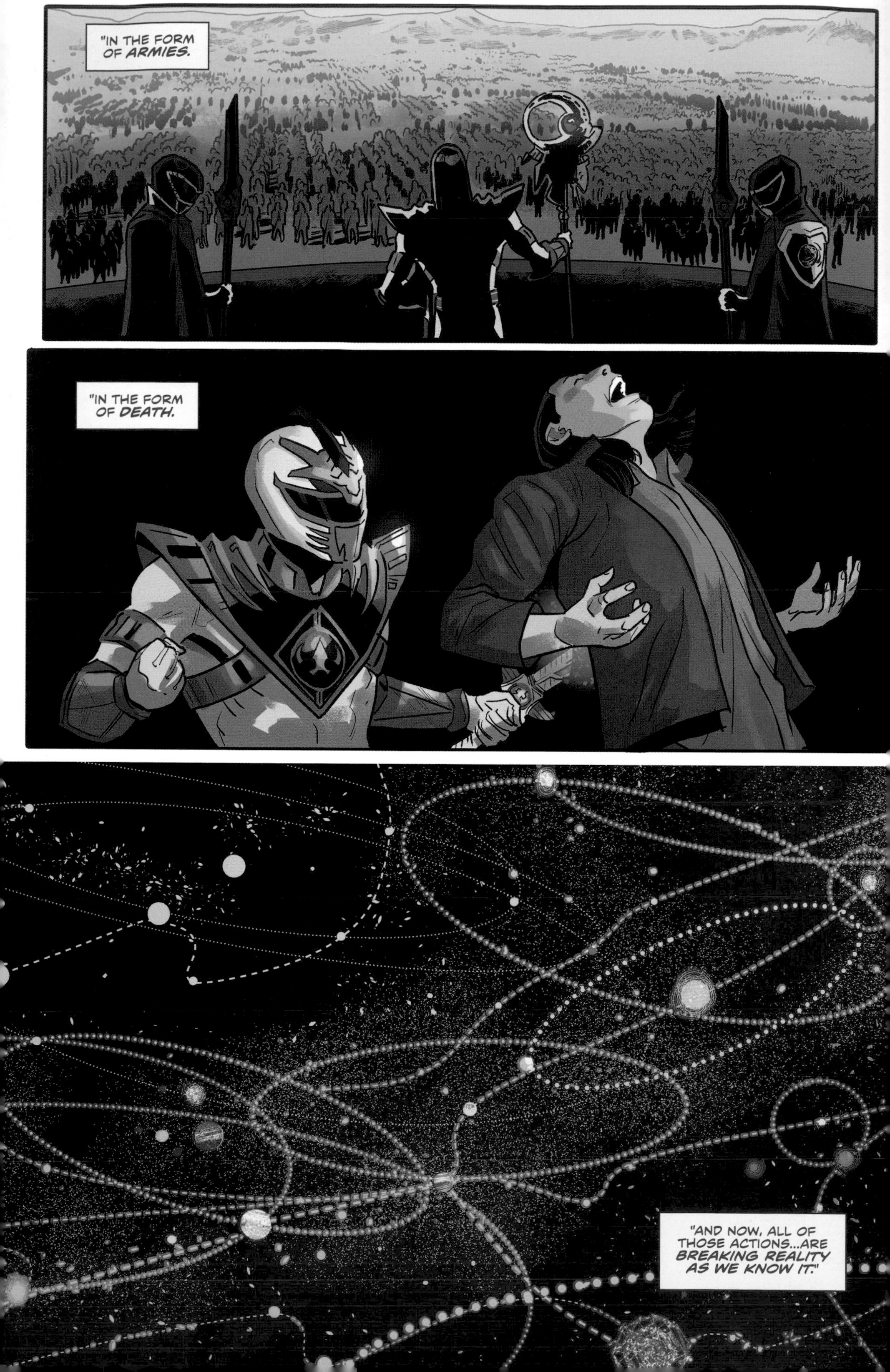
"IN THE FORM OF ARMIES.
"IN THE FORM OF DEATH.
"AND NOW, ALL OF THOSE ACTIONS...ARE BREAKING REALITY AS WE KNOW IT."

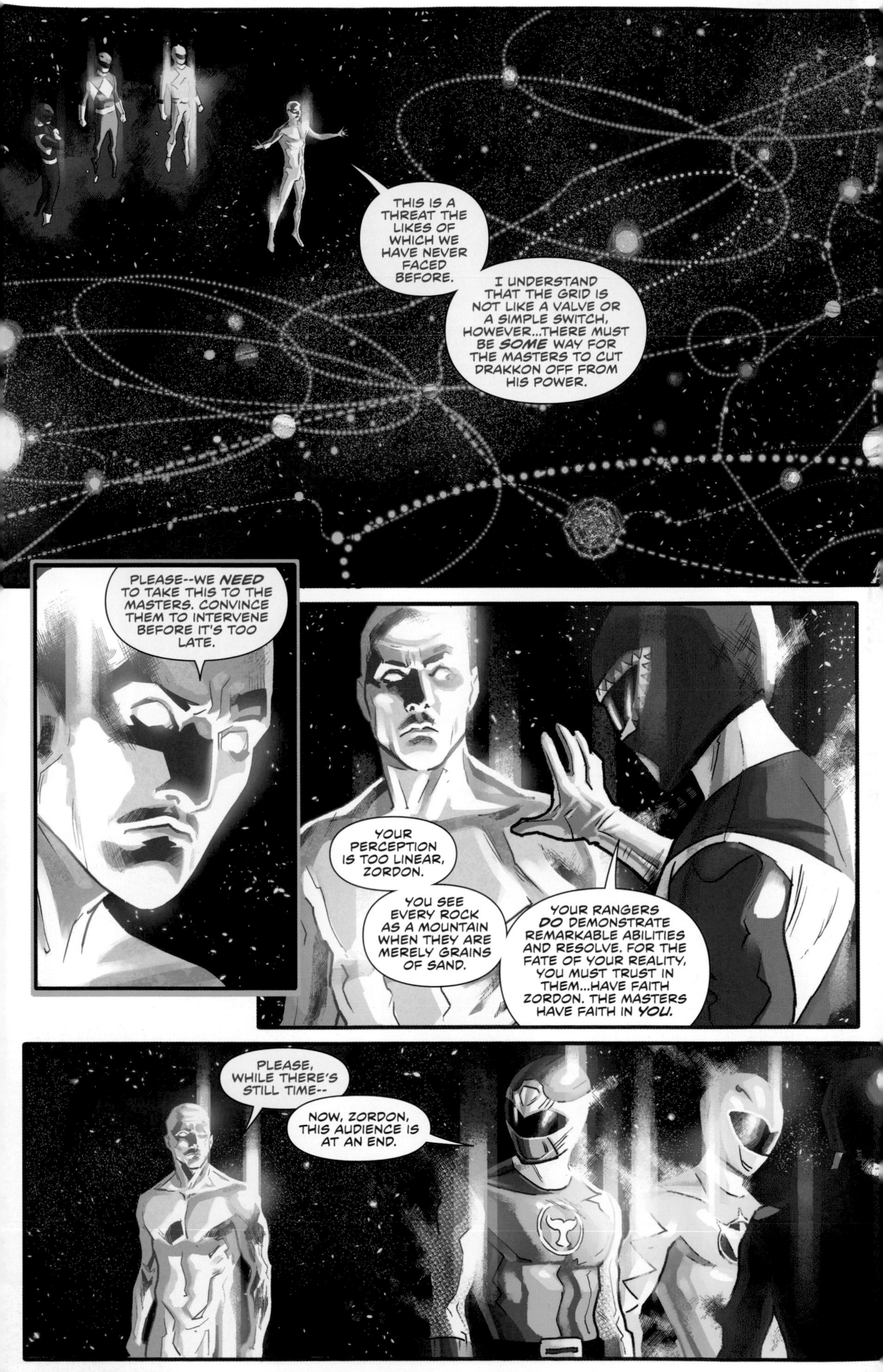
THIS IS A THREAT THE LIKES OF WHICH WE HAVE NEVER FACED BEFORE.
I UNDERSTAND THAT THE GRID IS NOT LIKE A VALVE OR A SIMPLE SWITCH, HOWEVER...THERE MUST BE SOME WAY FOR THE MASTERS TO CUT DRAKKON OFF FROM HIS POWER.
PLEASE--WE NEED TO TAKE THIS TO THE MASTERS. CONVINCE THEM TO INTERVENE BEFORE IT'S TOO LATE.
YOUR PERCEPTION IS TOO LINEAR, ZORDON.
YOU SEE EVERY ROCK AS A MOUNTAIN WHEN THEY ARE MERELY GRAINS OF SAND.
YOUR RANGERS DO DEMONSTRATE REMARKABLE ABILITIES AND RESOLVE. FOR THE FATE OF YOUR REALITY, YOU MUST TRUST IN THEM...HAVE FAITH ZORDON. THE MASTERS HAVE FAITH IN YOU.
PLEASE, WHILE THERE'S STILL TIME--
NOW, ZORDON, THIS AUDIENCE IS AT AN END.

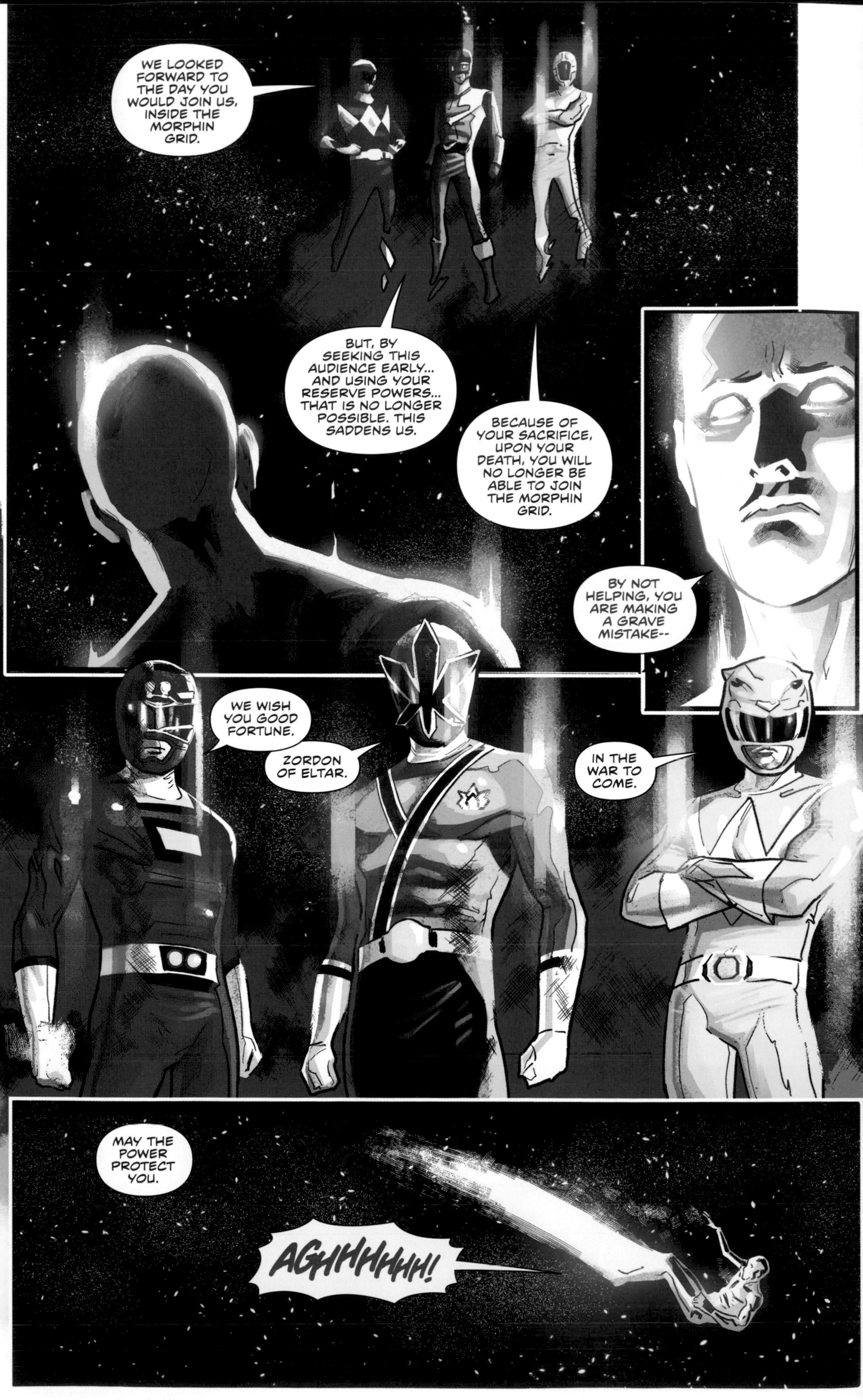
WE LOOKED FORWARD TO THE DAY YOU WOULD JOIN US, INSIDE THE MORPHIN GRID.
BUT, BY SEEKING THIS AUDIENCE EARLY... AND USING YOUR RESERVE POWERS... THAT IS NO LONGER POSSIBLE. THIS SADDENS US.
BECAUSE OF YOUR SACRIFICE, UPON YOUR DEATH, YOU WILL NO LONGER BE ABLE TO JOIN THE MORPHIN GRID.
BY NOT HELPING, YOU ARE MAKING A GRAVE MISTAKE--
WE WISH YOU GOOD FORTUNE.
ZORDON OF ELTAR.
IN THE WAR TO COME.
MAY THE POWER PROTECT YOU.
AGHHHHHH!

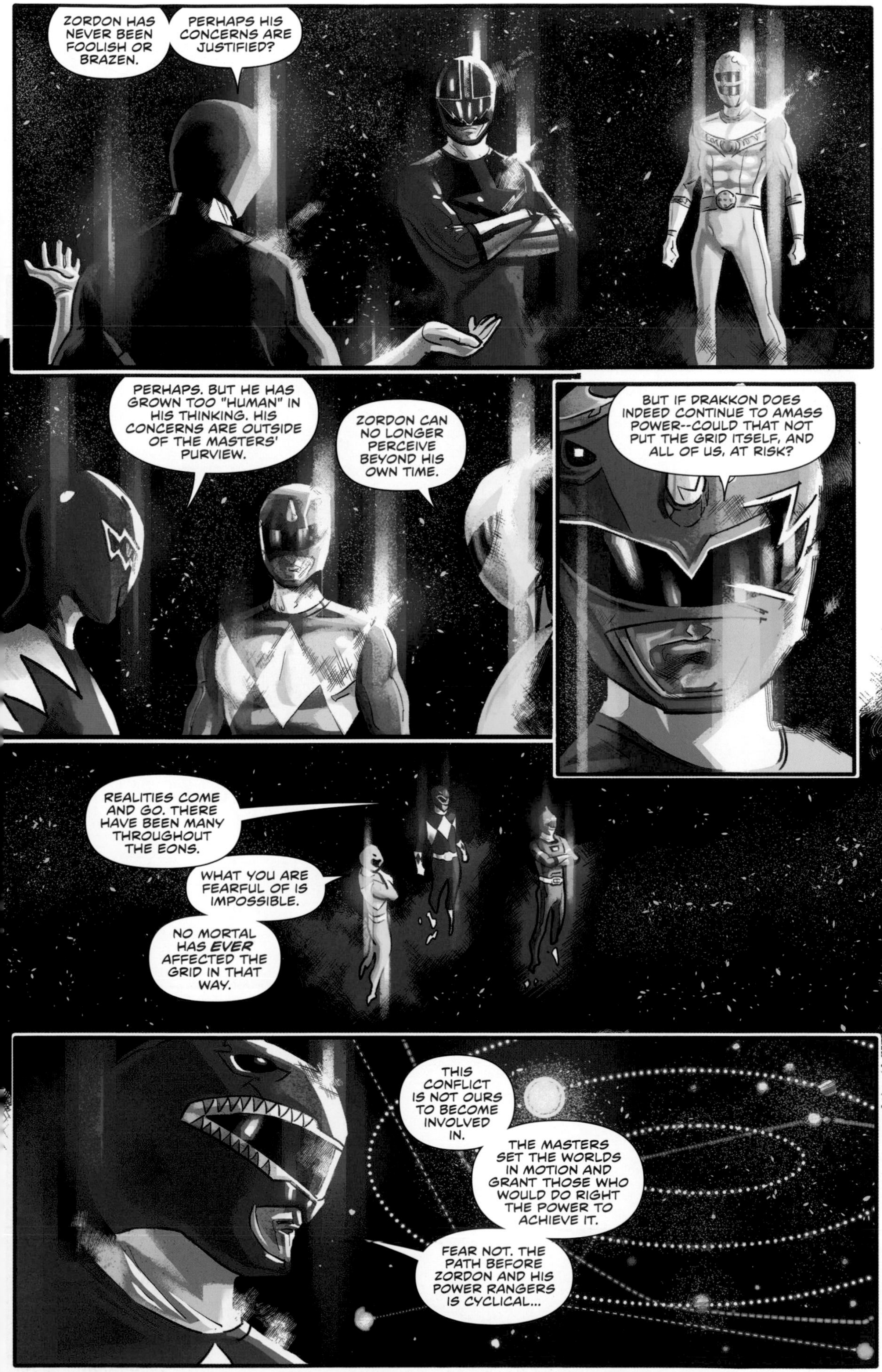

ZORDON HAS NEVER BEEN FOOLISH OR BRAZEN.
PERHAPS HIS CONCERNS ARE JUSTIFIED?
PERHAPS. BUT HE HAS GROWN TOO "HUMAN" IN HIS THINKING. HIS CONCERNS ARE OUTSIDE OF THE MASTERS' PURVIEW.
ZORDON CAN NO LONGER PERCEIVE BEYOND HIS OWN TIME.
BUT IF DRAKKON DOES INDEED CONTINUE TO AMASS POWER--COULD THAT NOT PUT THE GRID ITSELF, AND ALL OF US, AT RISK?
REALITIES COME AND GO. THERE HAVE BEEN MANY THROUGHOUT THE EONS.
WHAT YOU ARE FEARFUL OF IS IMPOSSIBLE.
NO MORTAL HAS *EVER* AFFECTED THE GRID IN THAT WAY.
THIS CONFLICT IS NOT OURS TO BECOME INVOLVED IN.
THE MASTERS SET THE WORLDS IN MOTION AND GRANT THOSE WHO WOULD DO RIGHT THE POWER TO ACHIEVE IT.
FEAR NOT. THE PATH BEFORE ZORDON AND HIS POWER RANGERS IS CYCLICAL...

"....WITH THE STRUGGLE BETWEEN ORDER AND CHAOS RISING AND FALLING LIKE THE TIDE.

"UNENDING, UNRELENTING...

"...AND UNBREAKABLE."

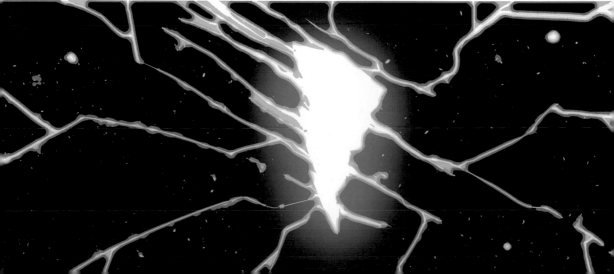

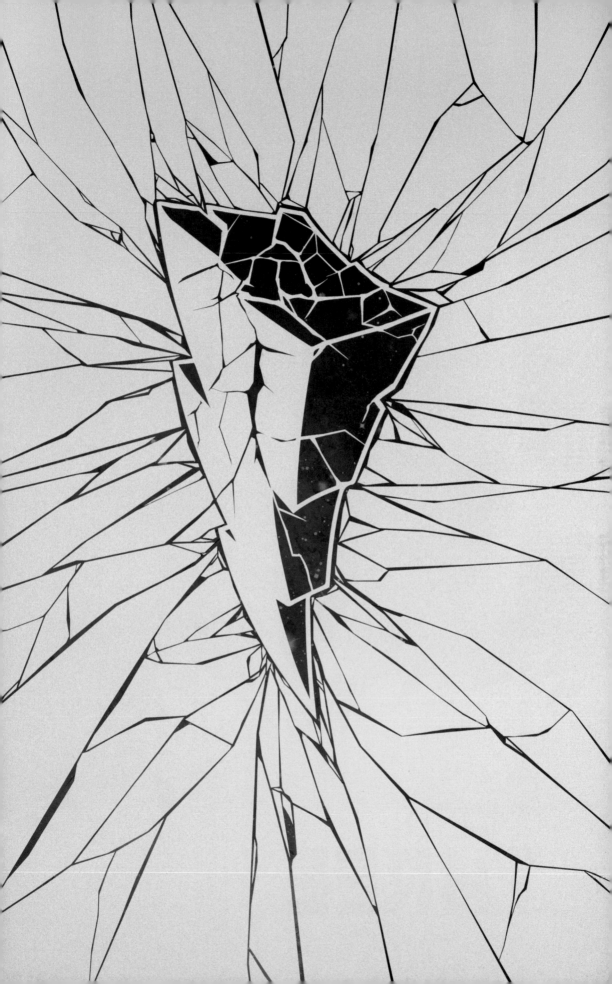

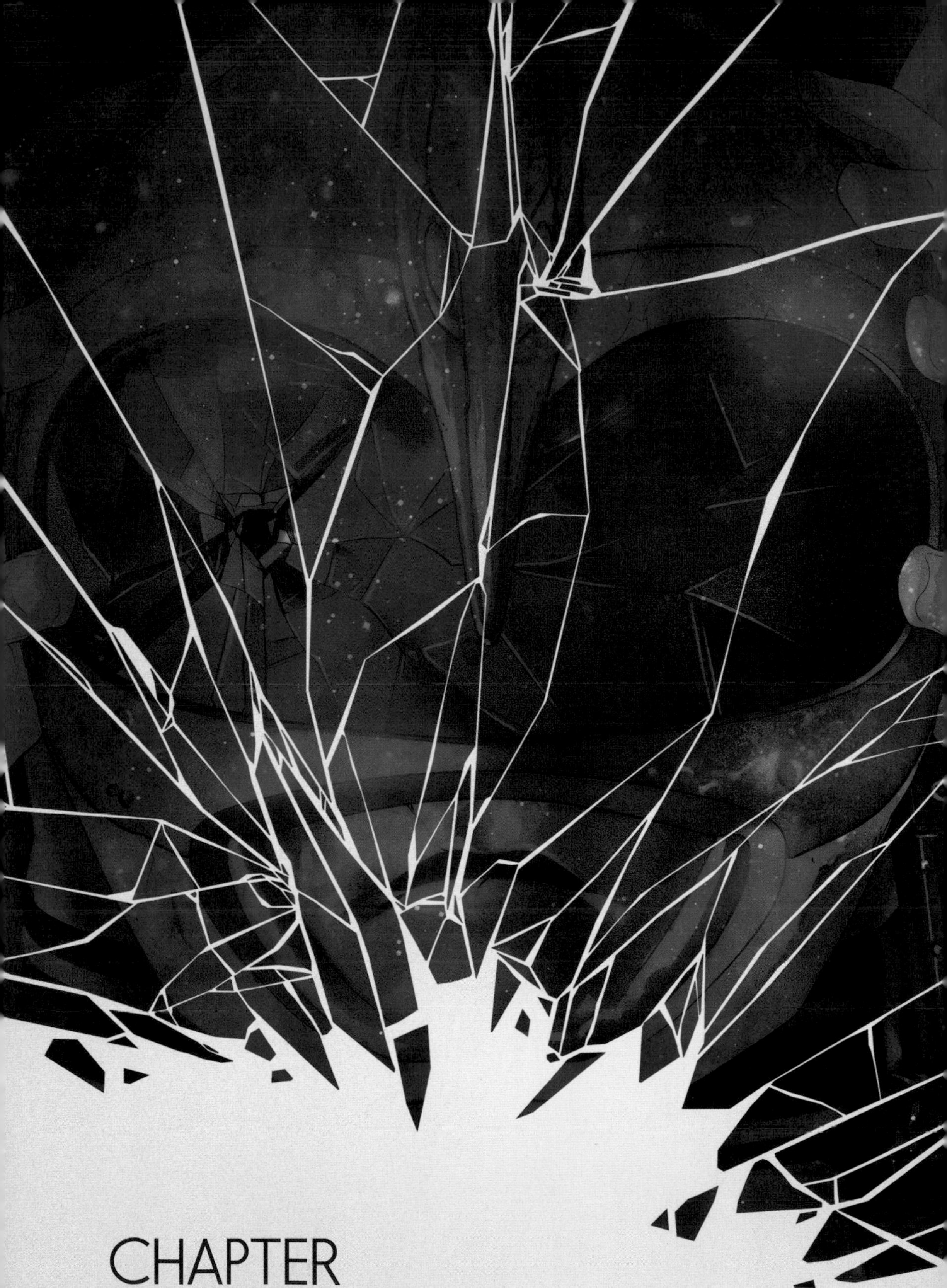

CHAPTER THREE

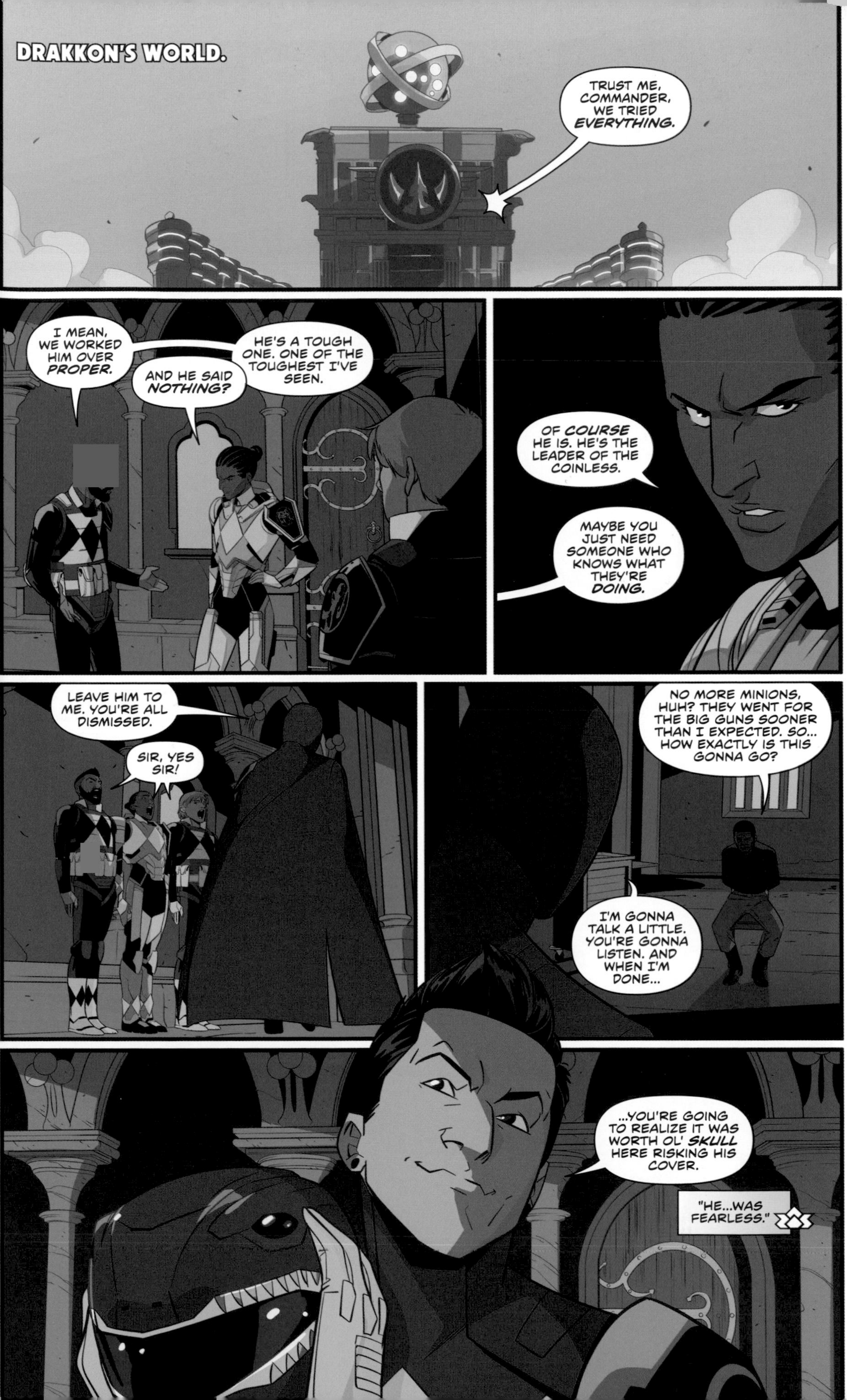
DRAKKON'S WORLD.
TRUST ME, COMMANDER, WE TRIED EVERYTHING.
I MEAN, WE WORKED HIM OVER PROPER.
AND HE SAID NOTHING?
HE'S A TOUGH ONE. ONE OF THE TOUGHEST I'VE SEEN.
OF COURSE HE IS. HE'S THE LEADER OF THE COINLESS.
MAYBE YOU JUST NEED SOMEONE WHO KNOWS WHAT THEY'RE DOING.
LEAVE HIM TO ME. YOU'RE ALL DISMISSED.
SIR, YES SIR!
NO MORE MINIONS, HUH? THEY WENT FOR THE BIG GUNS SOONER THAN I EXPECTED. SO... HOW EXACTLY IS THIS GONNA GO?
I'M GONNA TALK A LITTLE. YOU'RE GONNA LISTEN. AND WHEN I'M DONE...
...YOU'RE GOING TO REALIZE IT WAS WORTH OL' SKULL HERE RISKING HIS COVER.
"HE...WAS FEARLESS."

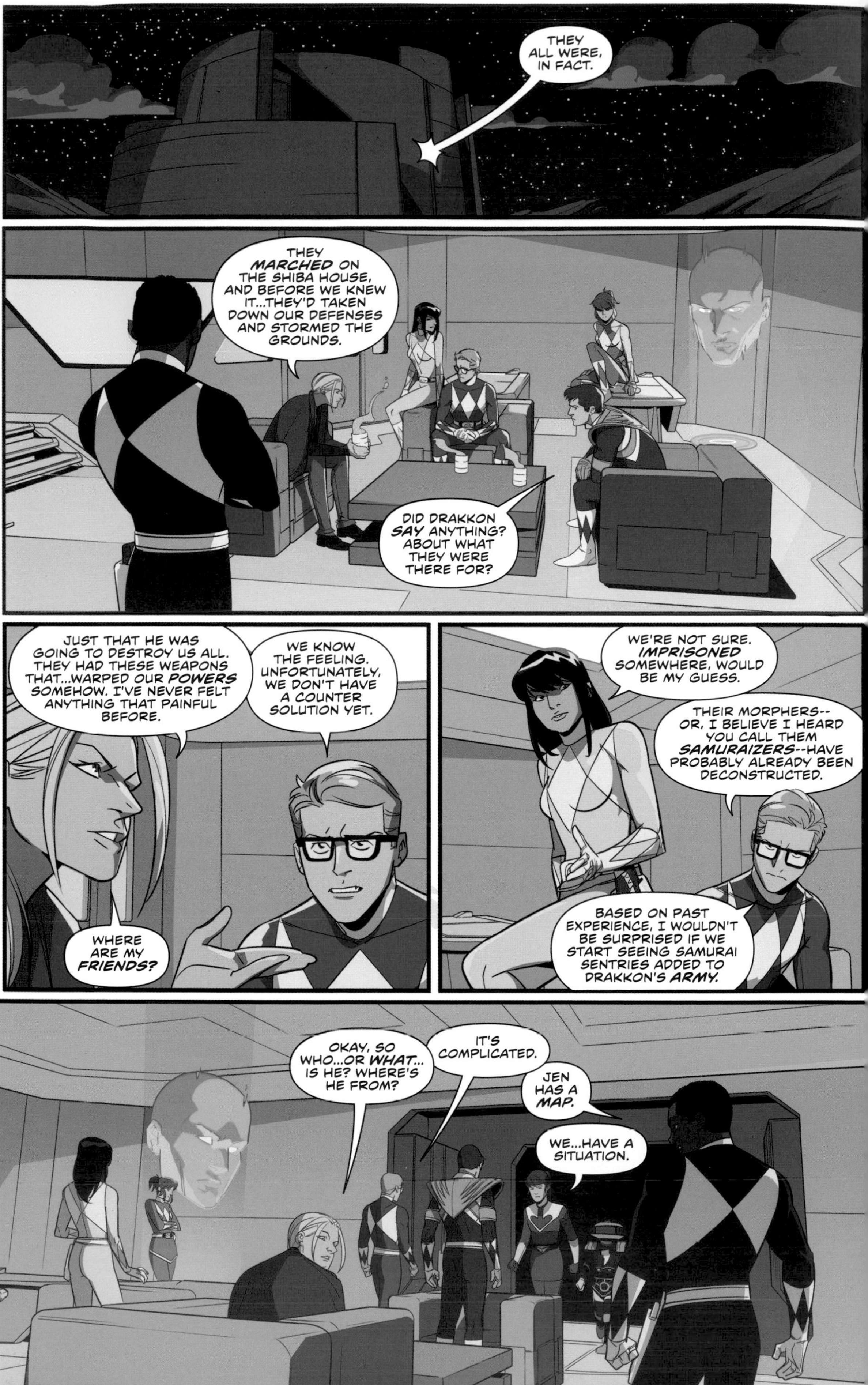
THEY ALL WERE, IN FACT.
THEY MARCHED ON THE SHIBA HOUSE, AND BEFORE WE KNEW IT...THEY'D TAKEN DOWN OUR DEFENSES AND STORMED THE GROUNDS.
DID DRAKKON SAY ANYTHING? ABOUT WHAT THEY WERE THERE FOR?
JUST THAT HE WAS GOING TO DESTROY US ALL. THEY HAD THESE WEAPONS THAT...WARPED OUR POWERS SOMEHOW. I'VE NEVER FELT ANYTHING THAT PAINFUL BEFORE.
WE KNOW THE FEELING. UNFORTUNATELY, WE DON'T HAVE A COUNTER SOLUTION YET.
WHERE ARE MY FRIENDS?
WE'RE NOT SURE. IMPRISONED SOMEWHERE, WOULD BE MY GUESS.
THEIR MORPHERS--OR, I BELIEVE I HEARD YOU CALL THEM SAMURAIZERS--HAVE PROBABLY ALREADY BEEN DECONSTRUCTED.
BASED ON PAST EXPERIENCE, I WOULDN'T BE SURPRISED IF WE START SEEING SAMURAI SENTRIES ADDED TO DRAKKON'S ARMY.
OKAY, SO WHO...OR WHAT... IS HE? WHERE'S HE FROM?
IT'S COMPLICATED.
JEN HAS A MAP.
WE...HAVE A SITUATION.

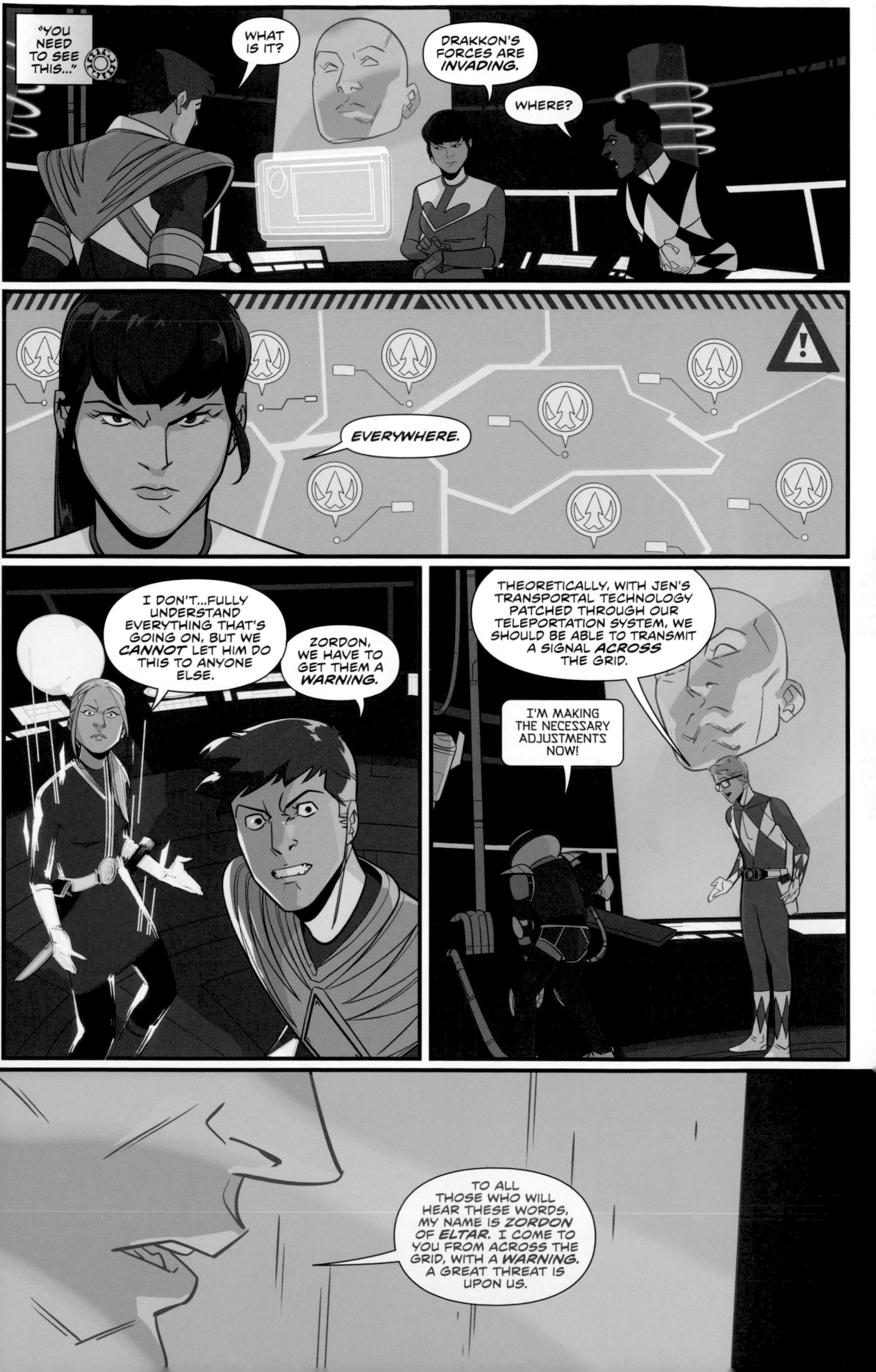
"YOU NEED TO SEE THIS..."
WHAT IS IT?
DRAKKON'S FORCES ARE *INVADING.*
WHERE?
EVERYWHERE.
I DON'T...FULLY UNDERSTAND EVERYTHING THAT'S GOING ON, BUT WE *CANNOT* LET HIM DO THIS TO ANYONE ELSE.
ZORDON, WE HAVE TO GET THEM A *WARNING.*
THEORETICALLY, WITH JEN'S TRANSPORTAL TECHNOLOGY PATCHED THROUGH OUR TELEPORTATION SYSTEM, WE SHOULD BE ABLE TO TRANSMIT A SIGNAL *ACROSS* THE GRID.
I'M MAKING THE NECESSARY ADJUSTMENTS NOW!
TO ALL THOSE WHO WILL HEAR THESE WORDS, MY NAME IS *ZORDON OF ELTAR.* I COME TO YOU FROM ACROSS THE GRID, WITH A *WARNING.* A GREAT THREAT IS UPON US.

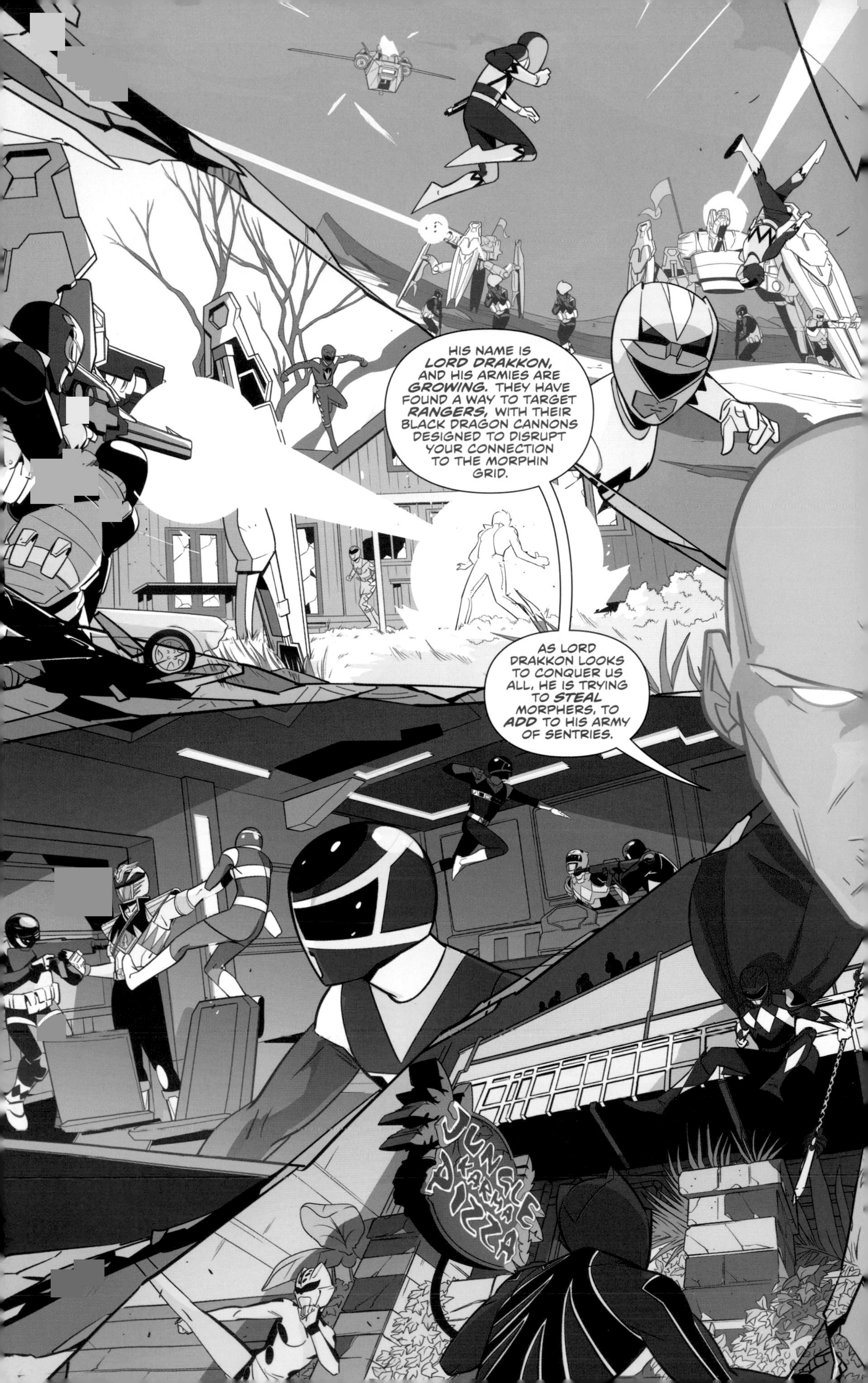
HIS NAME IS LORD DRAKKON, AND HIS ARMIES ARE GROWING. THEY HAVE FOUND A WAY TO TARGET RANGERS, WITH THEIR BLACK DRAGON CANNONS DESIGNED TO DISRUPT YOUR CONNECTION TO THE MORPHIN GRID.
AS LORD DRAKKON LOOKS TO CONQUER US ALL, HE IS TRYING TO STEAL MORPHERS, TO ADD TO HIS ARMY OF SENTRIES.
JUNGLE KARMA PIZZA

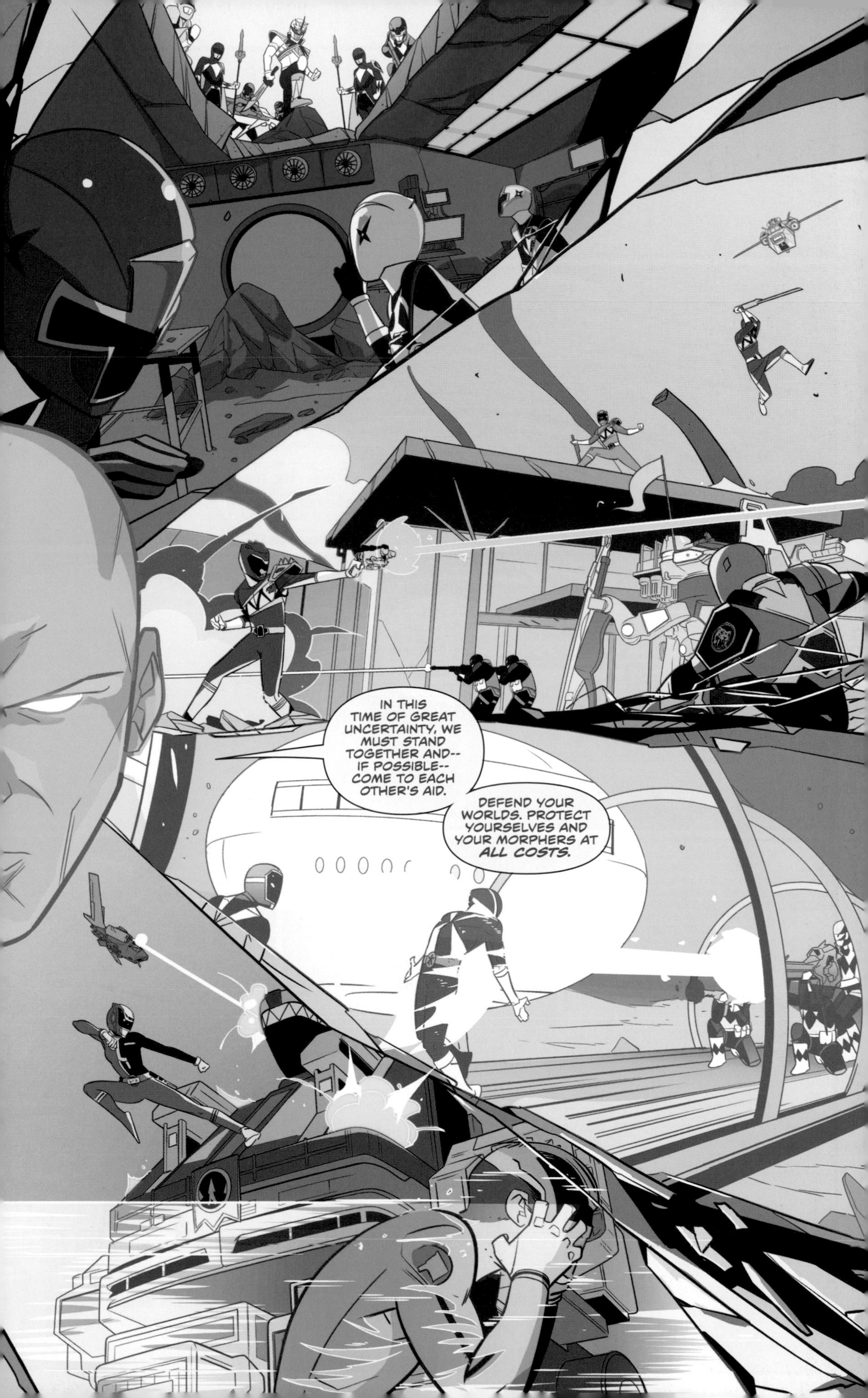
IN THIS TIME OF GREAT UNCERTAINTY, WE MUST STAND TOGETHER AND--IF POSSIBLE--COME TO EACH OTHER'S AID.
DEFEND YOUR WORLDS. PROTECT YOURSELVES AND YOUR MORPHERS AT ***ALL COSTS.***

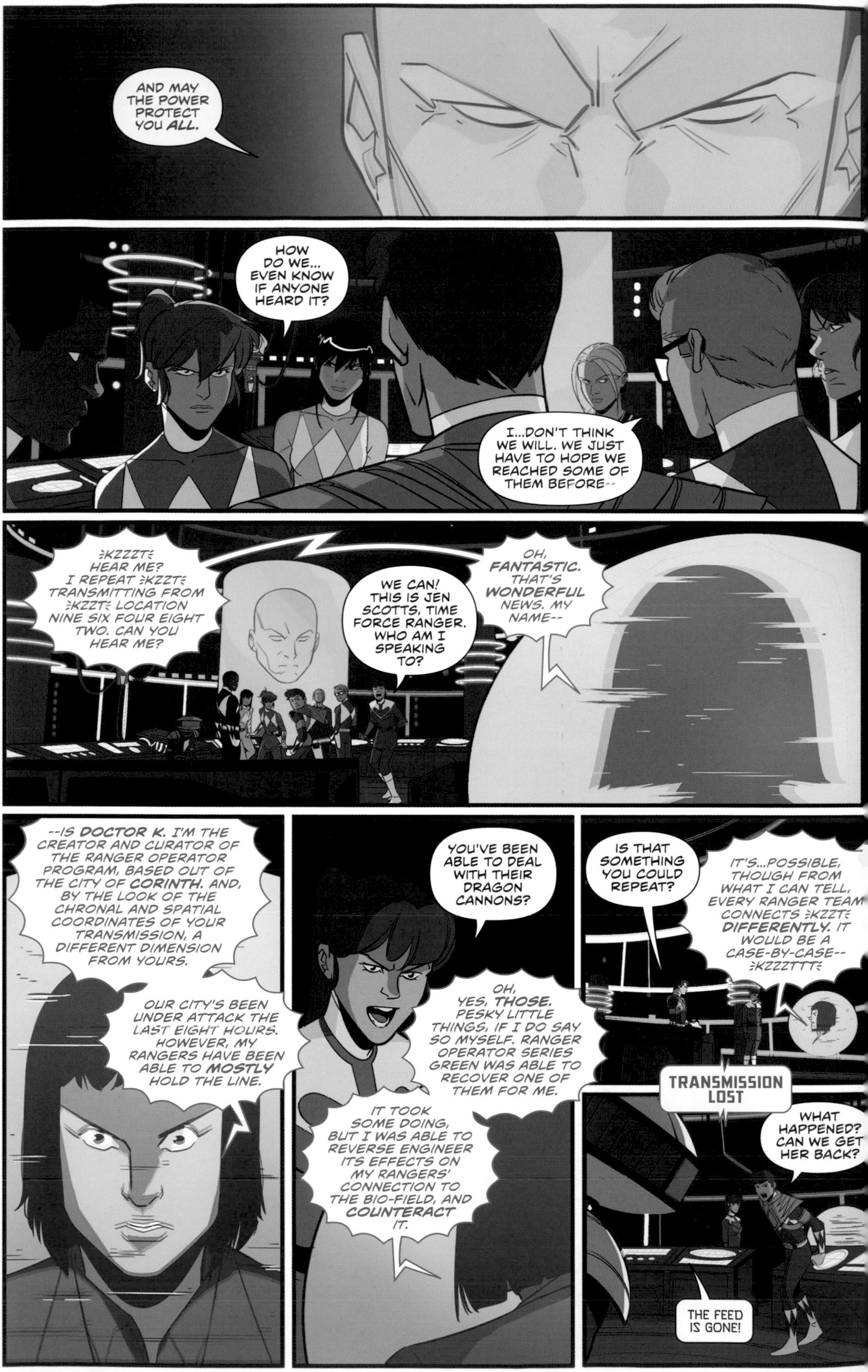
AND MAY THE POWER PROTECT YOU ALL.
HOW DO WE... EVEN KNOW IF ANYONE HEARD IT?
I...DON'T THINK WE WILL. WE JUST HAVE TO HOPE WE REACHED SOME OF THEM BEFORE--
ƸKZZZTƷ HEAR ME? I REPEAT ƸKZZTƷ TRANSMITTING FROM ƸKZZTƷ LOCATION NINE SIX FOUR EIGHT TWO. CAN YOU HEAR ME?
WE CAN! THIS IS JEN SCOTTS, TIME FORCE RANGER. WHO AM I SPEAKING TO?
OH, FANTASTIC. THAT'S WONDERFUL NEWS. MY NAME--
--IS DOCTOR K. I'M THE CREATOR AND CURATOR OF THE RANGER OPERATOR PROGRAM, BASED OUT OF THE CITY OF CORINTH. AND, BY THE LOOK OF THE CHRONAL AND SPATIAL COORDINATES OF YOUR TRANSMISSION, A DIFFERENT DIMENSION FROM YOURS.
OUR CITY'S BEEN UNDER ATTACK THE LAST EIGHT HOURS. HOWEVER, MY RANGERS HAVE BEEN ABLE TO MOSTLY HOLD THE LINE.
YOU'VE BEEN ABLE TO DEAL WITH THEIR DRAGON CANNONS?
OH, YES, THOSE. PESKY LITTLE THINGS, IF I DO SAY SO MYSELF. RANGER OPERATOR SERIES GREEN WAS ABLE TO RECOVER ONE OF THEM FOR ME.
IT TOOK SOME DOING, BUT I WAS ABLE TO REVERSE ENGINEER ITS EFFECTS ON MY RANGERS' CONNECTION TO THE BIO-FIELD, AND COUNTERACT IT.
IS THAT SOMETHING YOU COULD REPEAT?
IT'S...POSSIBLE, THOUGH FROM WHAT I CAN TELL, EVERY RANGER TEAM CONNECTS ƸKZZTƷ DIFFERENTLY. IT WOULD BE A CASE-BY-CASE-- ƸKZZZTTTƷ
TRANSMISSION LOST
WHAT HAPPENED? CAN WE GET HER BACK?
THE FEED IS GONE!

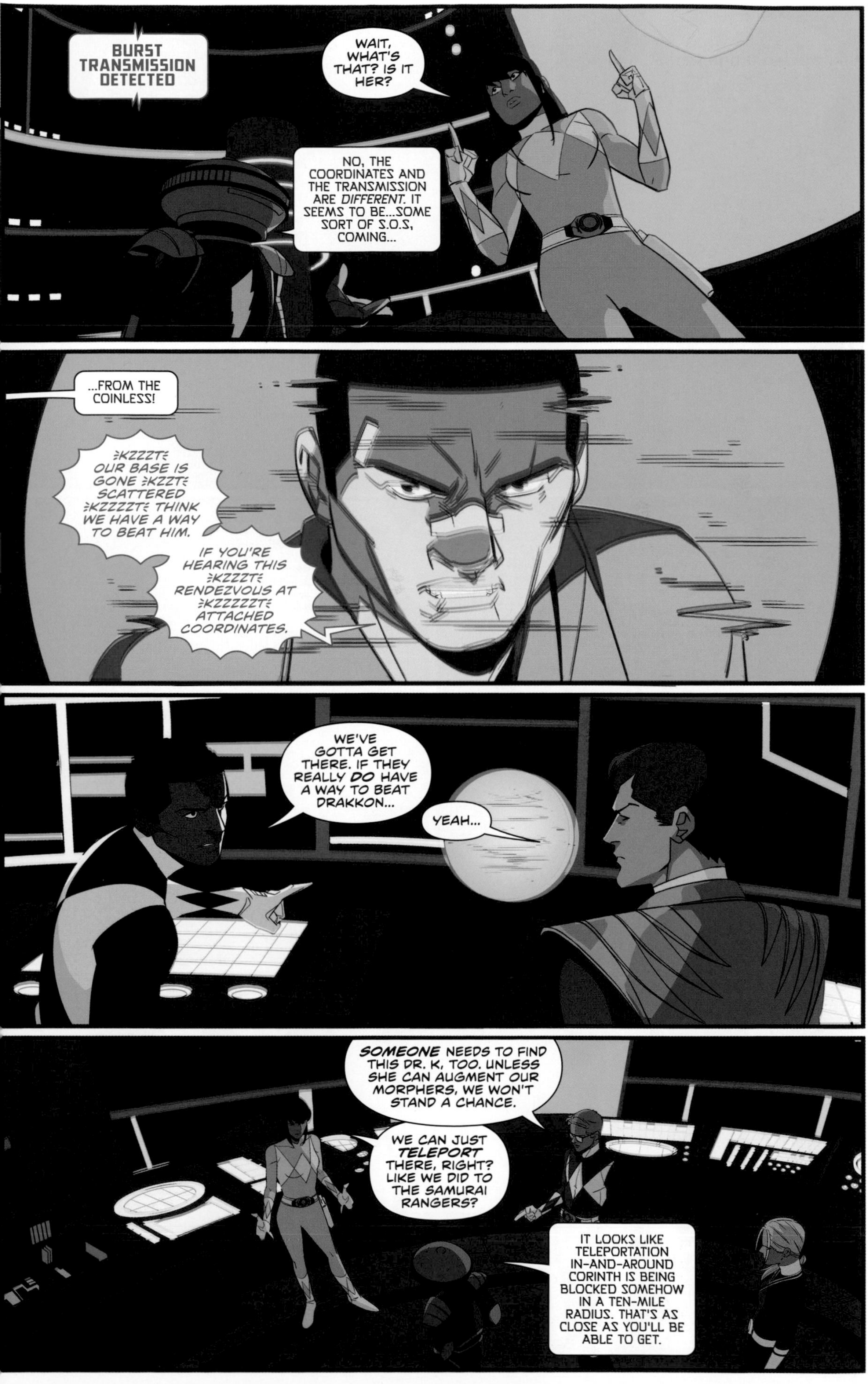
BURST TRANSMISSION DETECTED
WAIT, WHAT'S THAT? IS IT HER?
NO, THE COORDINATES AND THE TRANSMISSION ARE *DIFFERENT*. IT SEEMS TO BE...SOME SORT OF S.O.S, COMING...
...FROM THE COINLESS!
KZZZT OUR BASE IS GONE *KZZT* SCATTERED *KZZZZT* THINK WE HAVE A WAY TO BEAT HIM.
IF YOU'RE HEARING THIS *KZZZT* RENDEZVOUS AT *KZZZZZT* ATTACHED COORDINATES.
WE'VE GOTTA GET THERE. IF THEY REALLY *DO* HAVE A WAY TO BEAT DRAKKON...
YEAH...
SOMEONE NEEDS TO FIND THIS DR. K, TOO. UNLESS SHE CAN AUGMENT OUR MORPHERS, WE WON'T STAND A CHANCE.
WE CAN JUST *TELEPORT* THERE, RIGHT? LIKE WE DID TO THE SAMURAI RANGERS?
IT LOOKS LIKE TELEPORTATION IN-AND-AROUND CORINTH IS BEING BLOCKED SOMEHOW IN A TEN-MILE RADIUS. THAT'S AS CLOSE AS YOU'LL BE ABLE TO GET.

WHAT ABOUT THESE OTHER RANGERS? THEY'RE ALL UNDER *ATTACK*. WE HAVE TO FIGURE OUT SOME WAY TO *HELP* THEM.

ALL RIGHT, HERE'S WHAT WE'RE GOING TO DO. BILLY, ZACK, AND TRINI-- YOU THREE HEAD TO THE COORDINATES THAT THE COINLESS SENT, IN DRAKKON'S WORLD. FIND OUT WHAT THEY KNOW AND WHAT IT MIGHT TAKE TO EXECUTE.

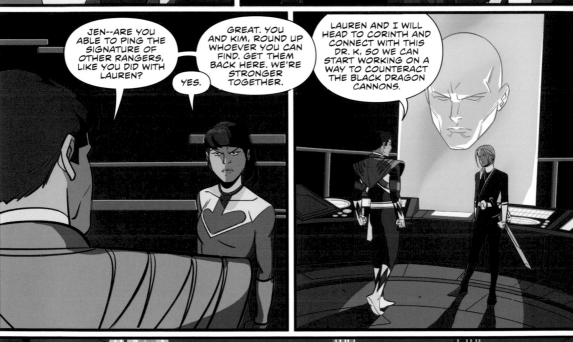

JEN--ARE YOU ABLE TO PING THE SIGNATURE OF OTHER RANGERS, LIKE YOU DID WITH LAUREN?

YES.

GREAT. YOU AND KIM, ROUND UP WHOEVER YOU CAN FIND. GET THEM BACK HERE. WE'RE STRONGER TOGETHER.

LAUREN AND I WILL HEAD TO CORINTH AND CONNECT WITH THIS DR. K, SO WE CAN START WORKING ON A WAY TO COUNTERACT THE BLACK DRAGON CANNONS.

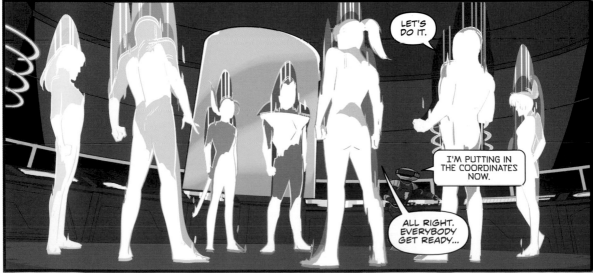

LET'S DO IT.

I'M PUTTING IN THE COORDINATES NOW.

ALL RIGHT. EVERYBODY GET READY...

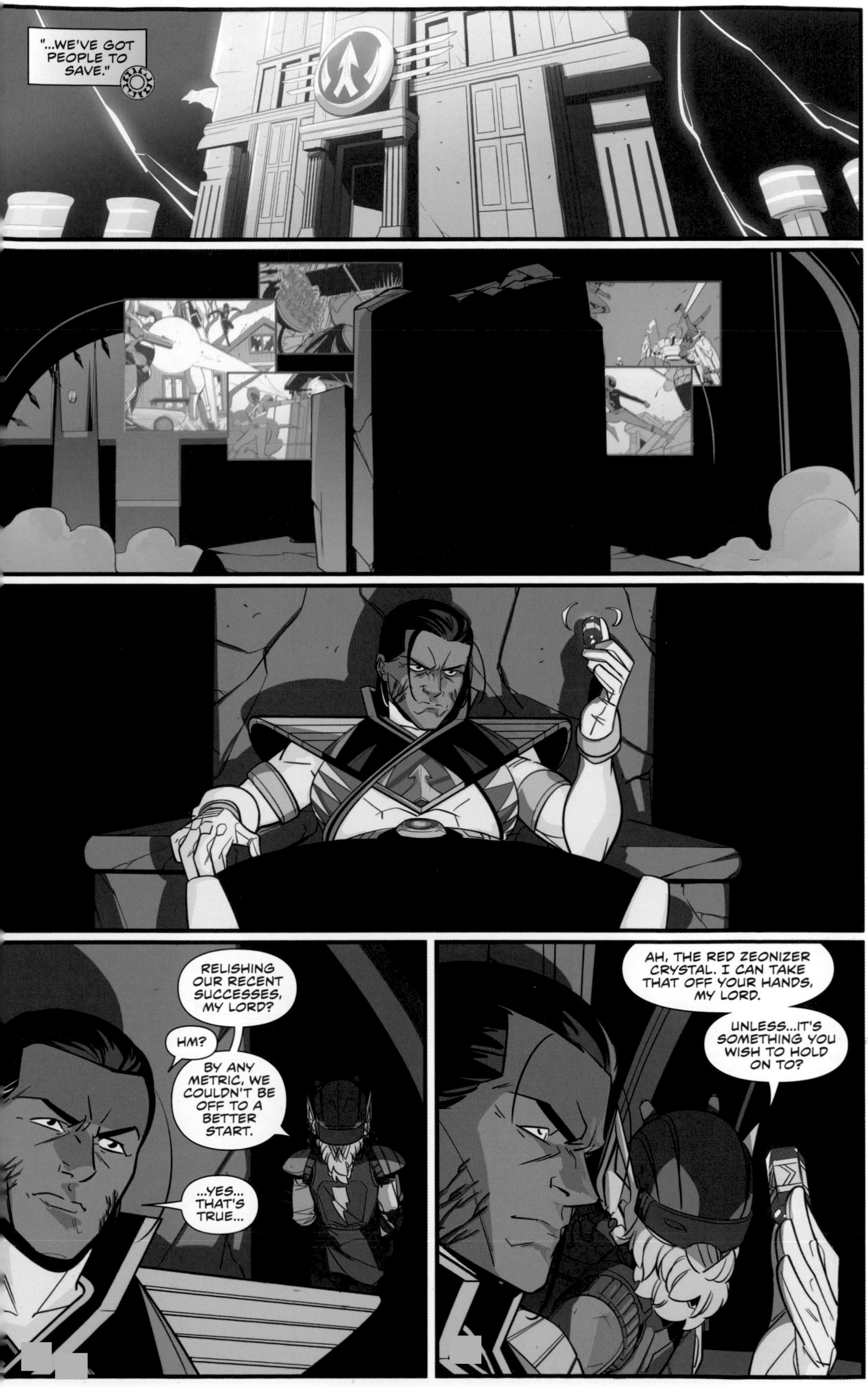
"...WE'VE GOT PEOPLE TO SAVE."
RELISHING OUR RECENT SUCCESSES, MY LORD?
HM?
BY ANY METRIC, WE COULDN'T BE OFF TO A BETTER START.
...YES... THAT'S TRUE...
AH, THE RED ZEONIZER CRYSTAL. I CAN TAKE THAT OFF YOUR HANDS, MY LORD.
UNLESS...IT'S SOMETHING YOU WISH TO HOLD ON TO?

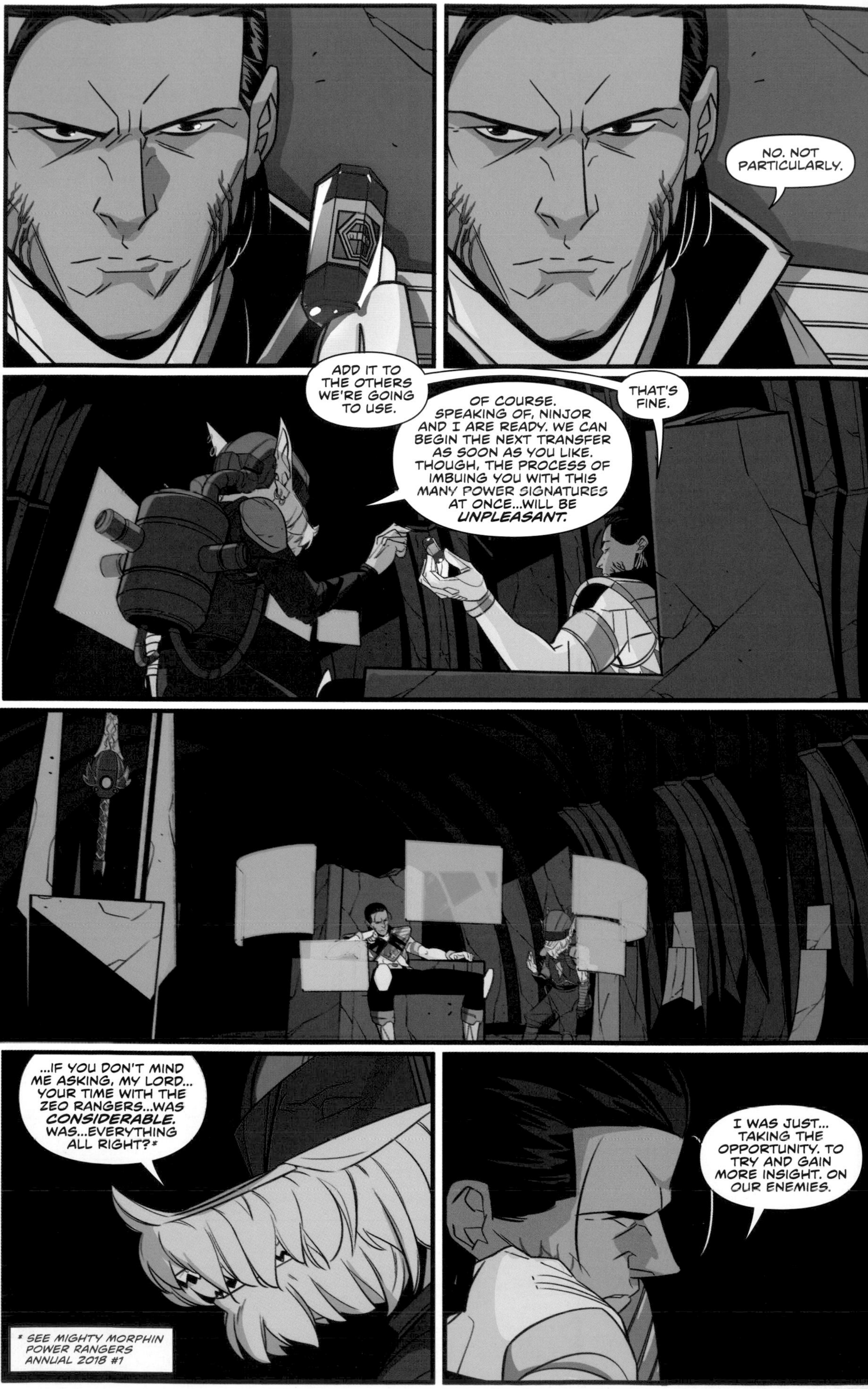
NO. NOT PARTICULARLY.
ADD IT TO THE OTHERS WE'RE GOING TO USE.
OF COURSE. SPEAKING OF, NINJOR AND I ARE READY. WE CAN BEGIN THE NEXT TRANSFER AS SOON AS YOU LIKE. THOUGH, THE PROCESS OF IMBUING YOU WITH THIS MANY POWER SIGNATURES AT ONCE...WILL BE *UNPLEASANT.*
THAT'S FINE.
...IF YOU DON'T MIND ME ASKING, MY LORD... YOUR TIME WITH THE ZEO RANGERS...WAS *CONSIDERABLE.* WAS...EVERYTHING ALL RIGHT?*
* SEE MIGHTY MORPHIN POWER RANGERS ANNUAL 2018 #1
I WAS JUST... TAKING THE OPPORTUNITY. TO TRY AND GAIN MORE INSIGHT. ON OUR ENEMIES.

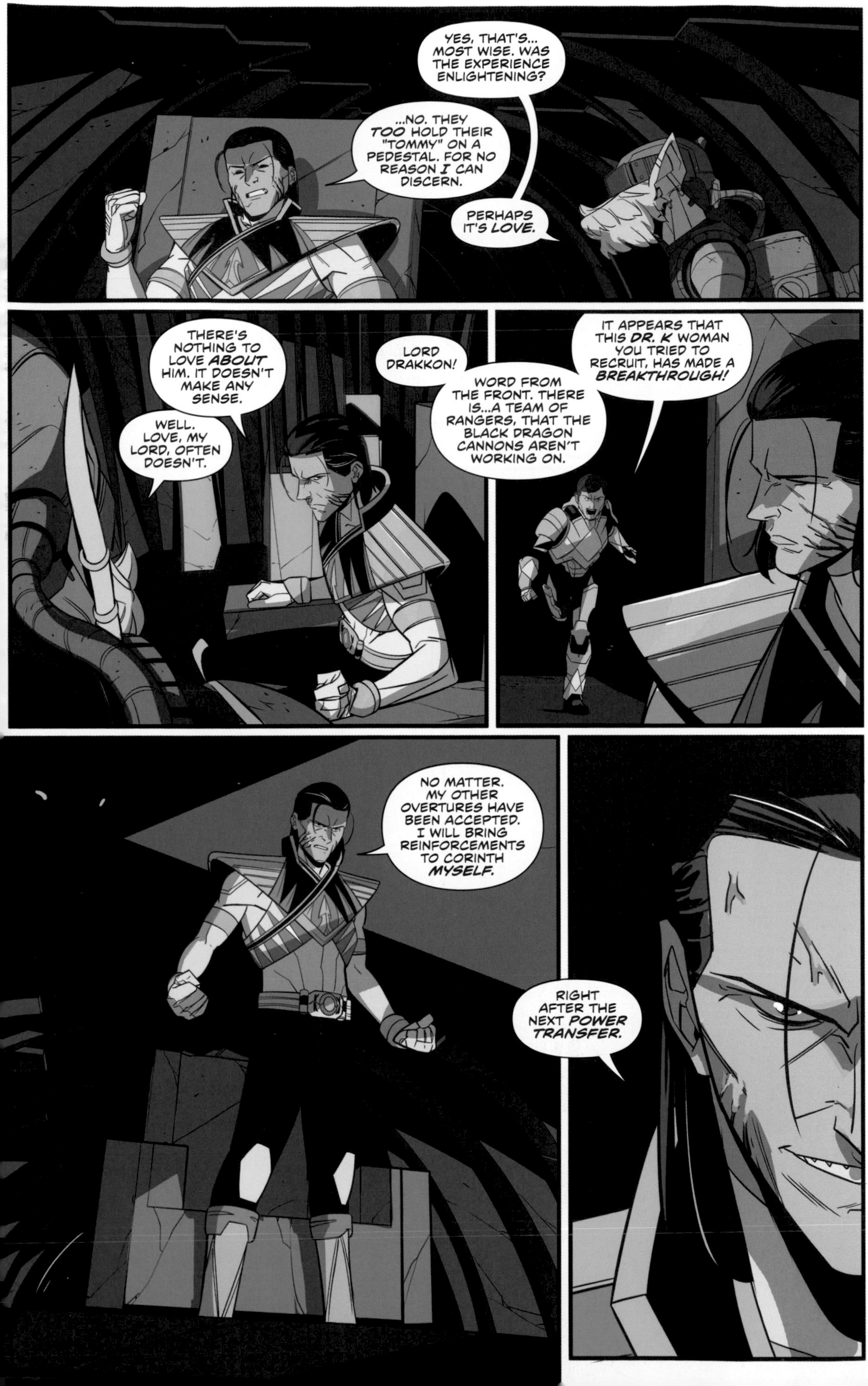
YES, THAT'S... MOST WISE. WAS THE EXPERIENCE ENLIGHTENING?
...NO. THEY TOO HOLD THEIR "TOMMY" ON A PEDESTAL. FOR NO REASON I CAN DISCERN.
PERHAPS IT'S LOVE.
THERE'S NOTHING TO LOVE ABOUT HIM. IT DOESN'T MAKE ANY SENSE.
WELL. LOVE, MY LORD, OFTEN DOESN'T.
LORD DRAKKON!
WORD FROM THE FRONT. THERE IS...A TEAM OF RANGERS, THAT THE BLACK DRAGON CANNONS AREN'T WORKING ON.
IT APPEARS THAT THIS DR. K WOMAN YOU TRIED TO RECRUIT, HAS MADE A BREAKTHROUGH!
NO MATTER. MY OTHER OVERTURES HAVE BEEN ACCEPTED. I WILL BRING REINFORCEMENTS TO CORINTH MYSELF.
RIGHT AFTER THE NEXT POWER TRANSFER.

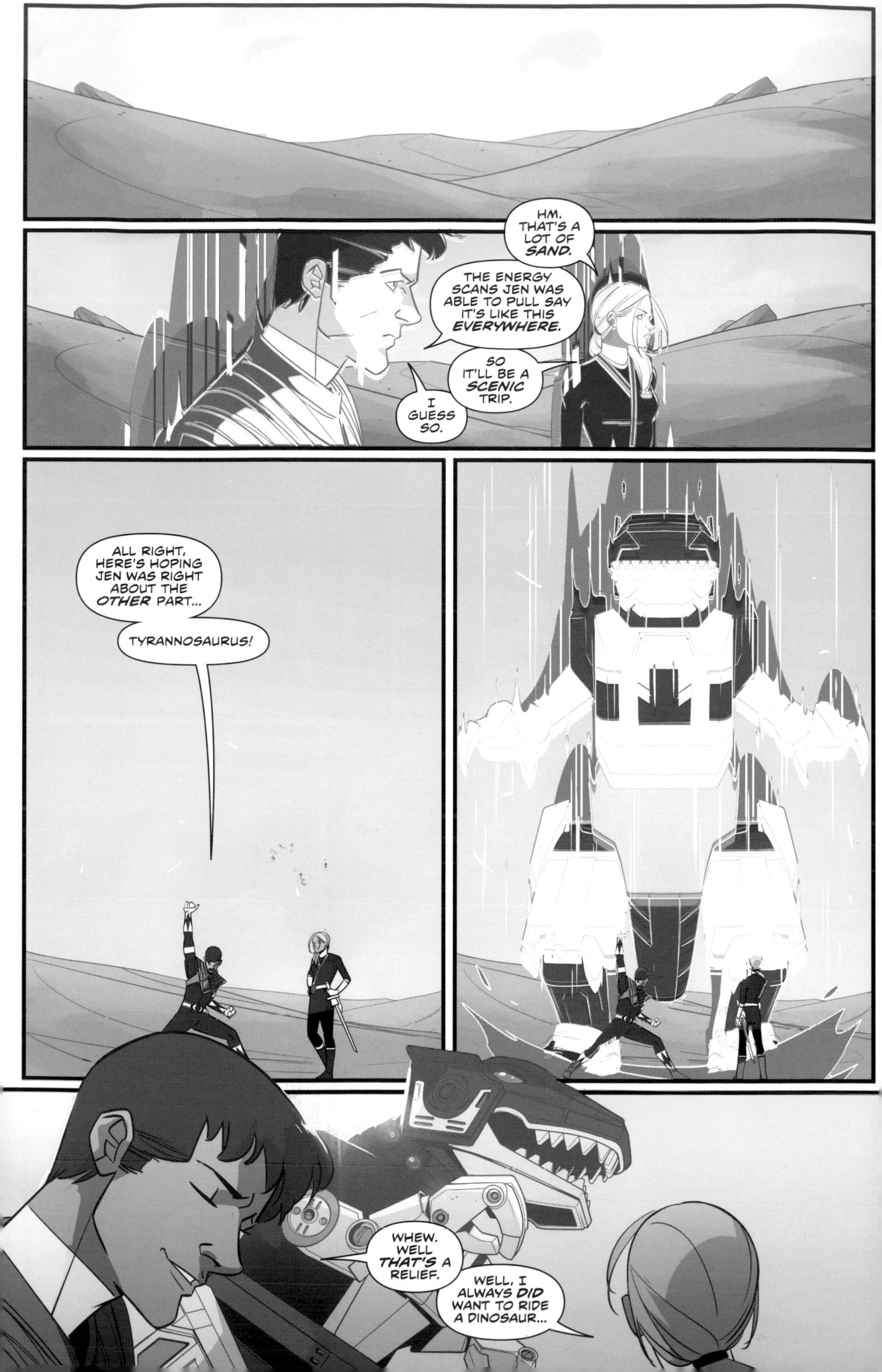
HM. THAT'S A LOT OF SAND.
THE ENERGY SCANS JEN WAS ABLE TO PULL SAY IT'S LIKE THIS EVERYWHERE.
SO IT'LL BE A SCENIC TRIP.
I GUESS SO.
ALL RIGHT, HERE'S HOPING JEN WAS RIGHT ABOUT THE OTHER PART...
TYRANNOSAURUS!
WHEW. WELL THAT'S A RELIEF.
WELL, I ALWAYS DID WANT TO RIDE A DINOSAUR...

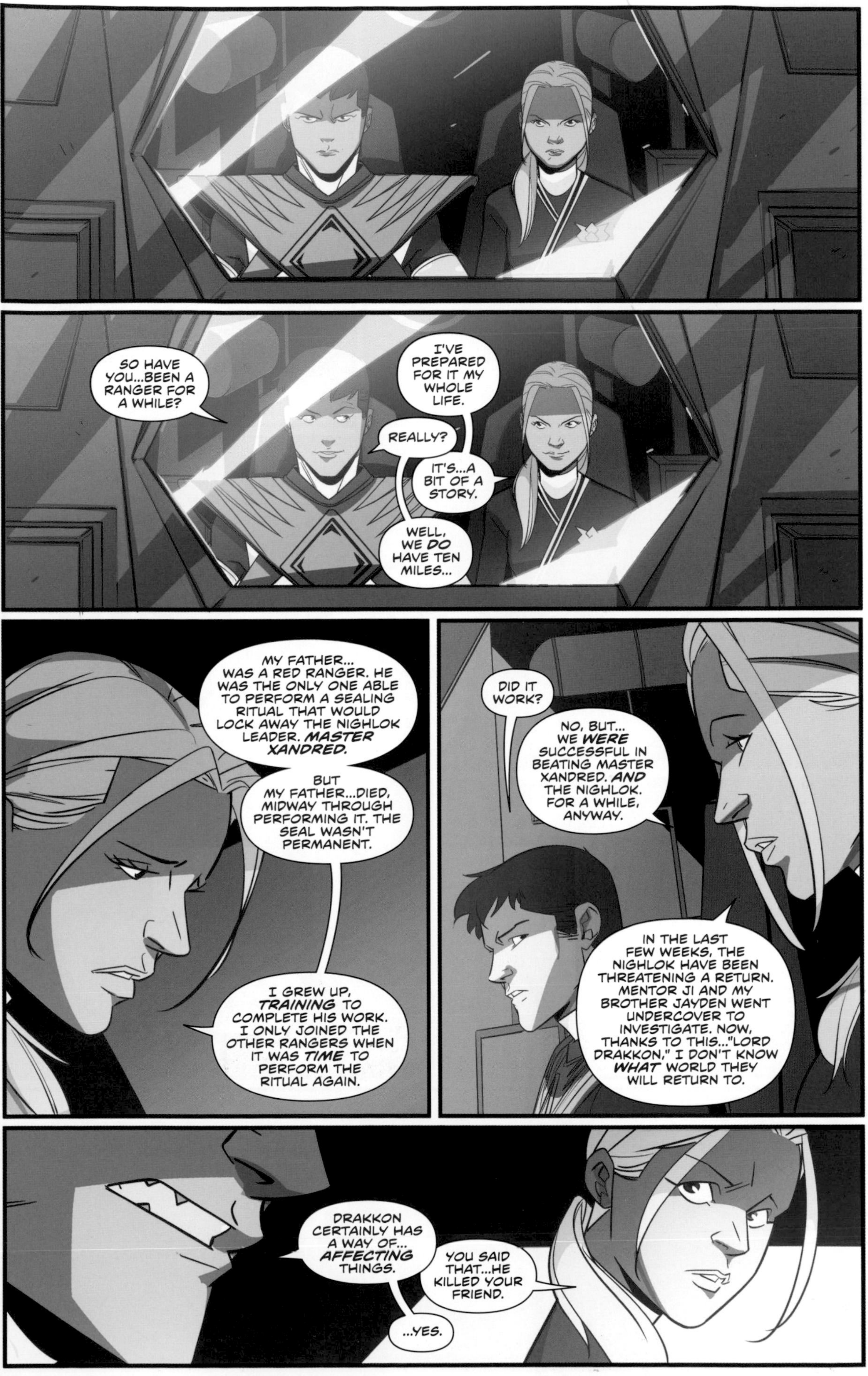
SO HAVE YOU...BEEN A RANGER FOR A WHILE?
I'VE PREPARED FOR IT MY WHOLE LIFE.
REALLY?
IT'S...A BIT OF A STORY.
WELL, WE DO HAVE TEN MILES...
MY FATHER... WAS A RED RANGER. HE WAS THE ONLY ONE ABLE TO PERFORM A SEALING RITUAL THAT WOULD LOCK AWAY THE NIGHLOK LEADER. MASTER XANDRED.
BUT MY FATHER...DIED, MIDWAY THROUGH PERFORMING IT. THE SEAL WASN'T PERMANENT.
I GREW UP, TRAINING TO COMPLETE HIS WORK. I ONLY JOINED THE OTHER RANGERS WHEN IT WAS TIME TO PERFORM THE RITUAL AGAIN.
DID IT WORK?
NO, BUT... WE WERE SUCCESSFUL IN BEATING MASTER XANDRED. AND THE NIGHLOK. FOR A WHILE, ANYWAY.
IN THE LAST FEW WEEKS, THE NIGHLOK HAVE BEEN THREATENING A RETURN. MENTOR JI AND MY BROTHER JAYDEN WENT UNDERCOVER TO INVESTIGATE. NOW, THANKS TO THIS..."LORD DRAKKON," I DON'T KNOW WHAT WORLD THEY WILL RETURN TO.
DRAKKON CERTAINLY HAS A WAY OF... AFFECTING THINGS.
YOU SAID THAT...HE KILLED YOUR FRIEND.
...YES.

I'M SORRY. I'M SURE THAT'S INCREDIBLY PAINFUL. YOU'RE BLAMING YOURSELF, AREN'T YOU?

IT'S...KIND OF WHAT I DO.

I UNDERSTAND.

WE...DON'T KNOW FOR SURE WHAT DRAKKON *DID* WITH THE OTHER SAMURAI RANGERS. IF THEY'RE STILL ALIVE, WE *WILL* FIND THEM.

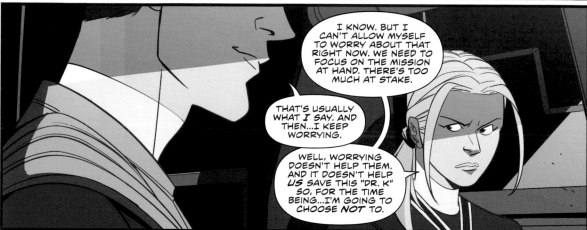

I KNOW. BUT I CAN'T ALLOW MYSELF TO WORRY ABOUT THAT RIGHT NOW. WE NEED TO FOCUS ON THE MISSION AT HAND. THERE'S TOO MUCH AT STAKE.

THAT'S USUALLY WHAT *I* SAY. AND THEN...I KEEP WORRYING.

WELL, WORRYING DOESN'T HELP THEM. AND IT DOESN'T HELP *US* SAVE THIS "DR. K" SO, FOR THE TIME BEING...I'M GOING TO CHOOSE *NOT* TO.

HEY, I FIGHT DEMONS FOR *A LIVING.* LITERALLY.

...RIGHT...

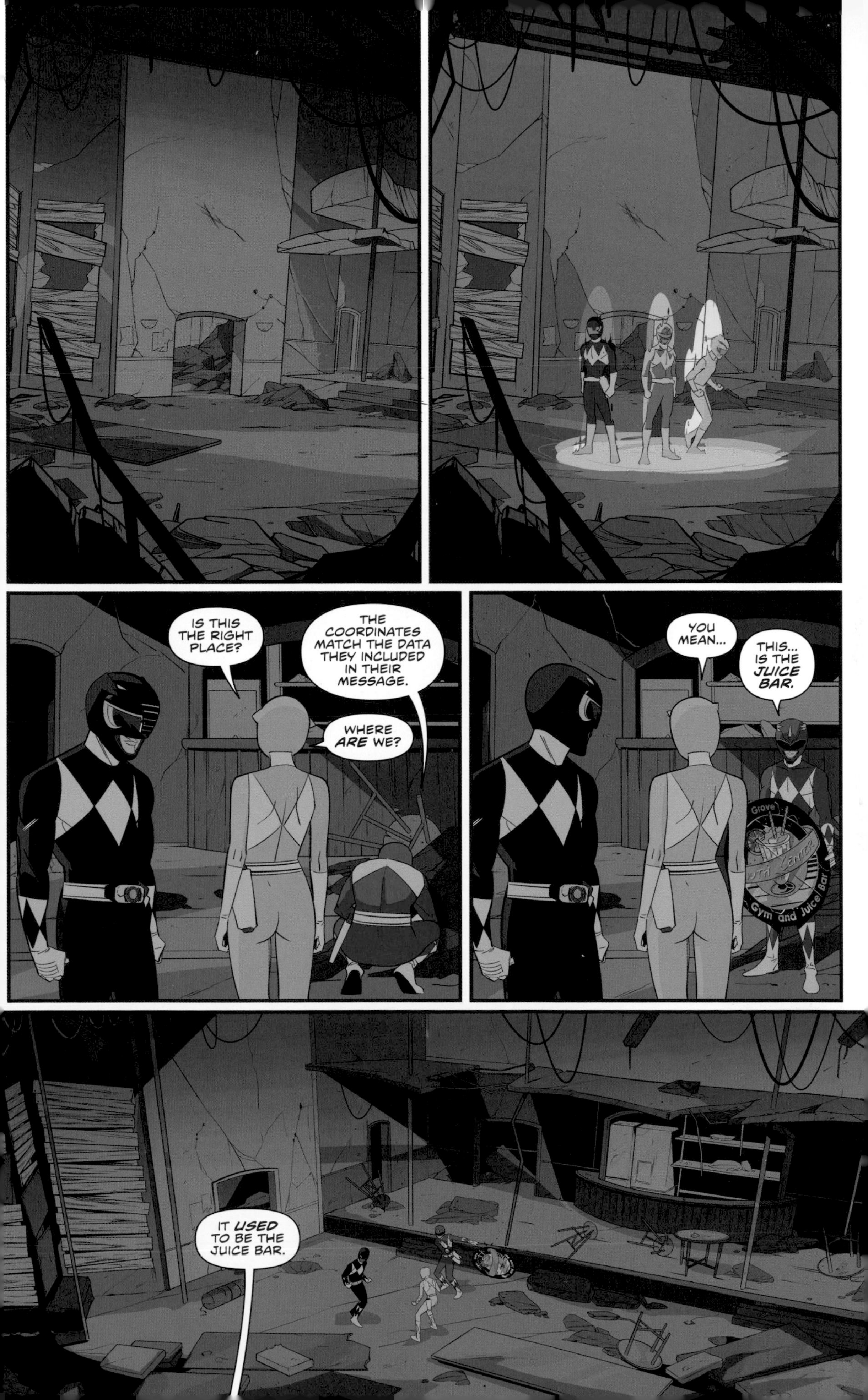
IS THIS THE RIGHT PLACE?
THE COORDINATES MATCH THE DATA THEY INCLUDED IN THEIR MESSAGE.
WHERE ARE WE?
YOU MEAN...
THIS... IS THE JUICE BAR.
Grove
Gym and Juice Bar
IT USED TO BE THE JUICE BAR.

THEY KEPT IT STANDING THOUGH. AS A REMINDER. A... WEIRD SORT OF TROPHY.

YOU'RE *OKAY*.

YES.

WHERE...IS EVERYBODY ELSE?

THIS IS ALL OF US THAT ARE LEFT. AFTER YOU GUYS WENT BACK TO YOUR WORLD, THE WAR KEPT ON. SCORPINA LED THE CHARGE. OUR BASES WERE WIPED OUT. WE LOST...ALMOST EVERYONE.

BUT... THANKS TO SKULL HERE, WE STILL HAVE A CHANCE.

I'VE BEEN UNDERCOVER IN DRAKKON'S ARMY FOR YEARS. I... PLAYED THE RIGHT POLITICS. GOT PROMOTED TO ONE OF HIS RED SENTRIES. I'VE... SEEN THINGS. THE INNER WORKINGS OF THE THRONE ROOM. HIS OPERATION.

NOW, THEY HAVE NINJOR. *YOUR* NINJOR.

WHAT'S A "NINJOR?"

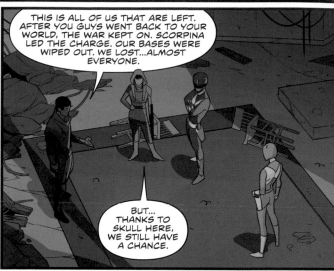

THEY HAVEN'T MET HIM YET.

...RIGHT...

NINJOR IS THE ONE WHO CREATED THE POWER COINS. NOW, DRAKKON HAS HIM UNDER SOME KIND OF SPELL. *HELPING* THEM. BUT IF WE CAN SAVE NINJOR...

...WE CAN BEAT DRAKKON.

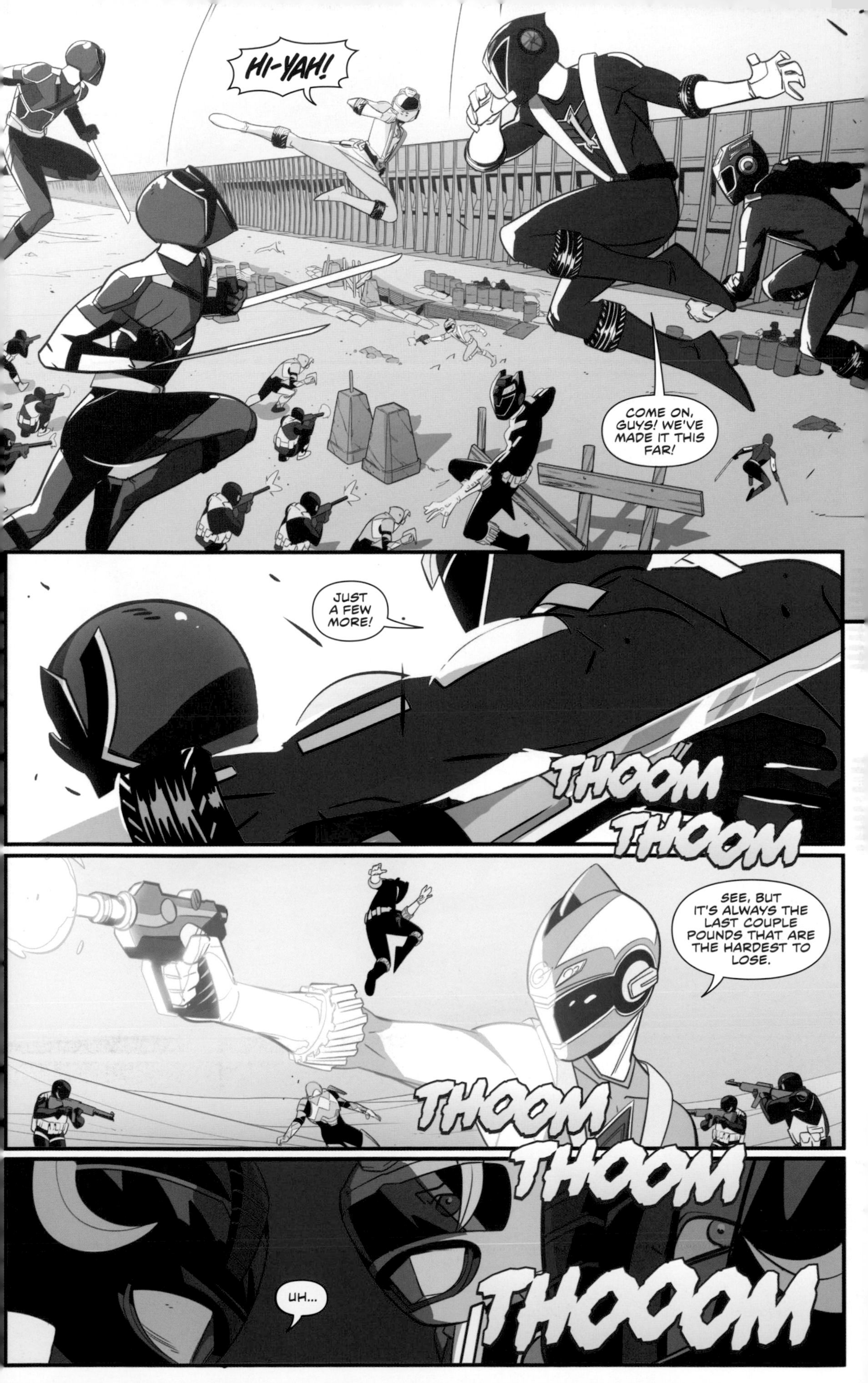
HI-YAH!
COME ON, GUYS! WE'VE MADE IT THIS FAR!
JUST A FEW MORE!
THOOM
THOOM
SEE, BUT IT'S ALWAYS THE LAST COUPLE POUNDS THAT ARE THE HARDEST TO LOSE.
THOOM
THOOM
UH...
THOOOM

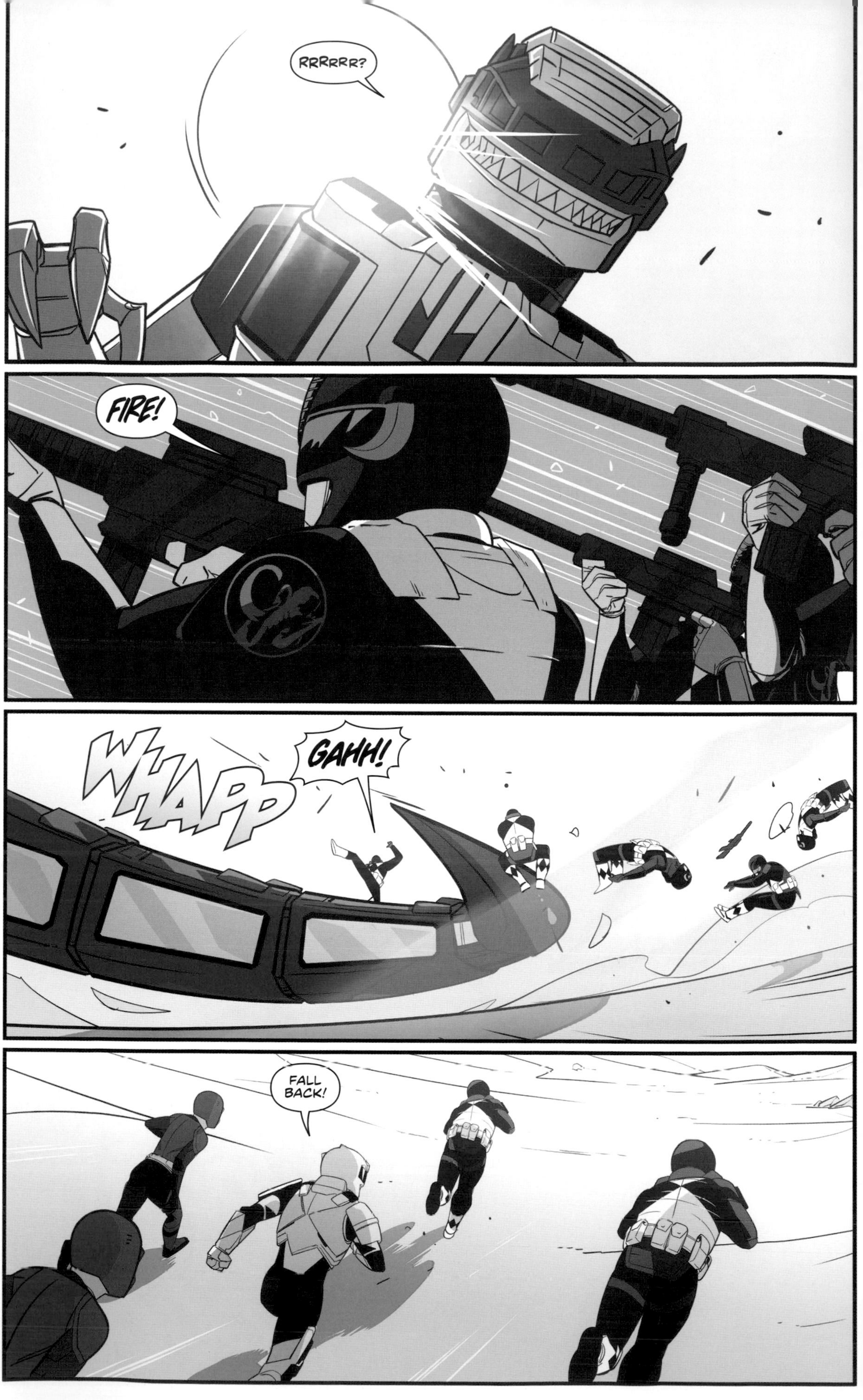
RRRRRR?
FIRE!
WHAPP
GAHH!
FALL BACK!

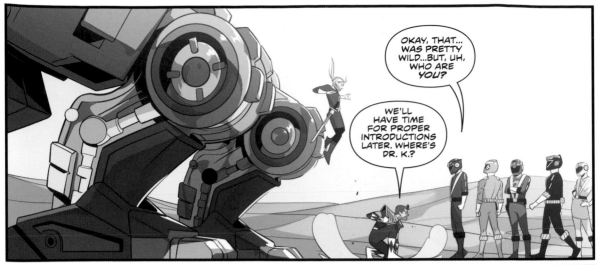

OKAY, THAT... WAS PRETTY WILD...BUT, UH, WHO ARE *YOU?*

WE'LL HAVE TIME FOR PROPER INTRODUCTIONS LATER. WHERE'S DR. K.?

THAT WOULD BE *ME.*

AGAIN, YOU *SHOULDN'T* BE OUT HERE--

BUT I NEEDED TO TAKE READINGS *MYSELF.*

DR. K., WE'RE HERE TO BRING YOU BACK TO OUR DIMENSION, SO WE CAN START--

UH, THAT MAY BE A PROBLEM...

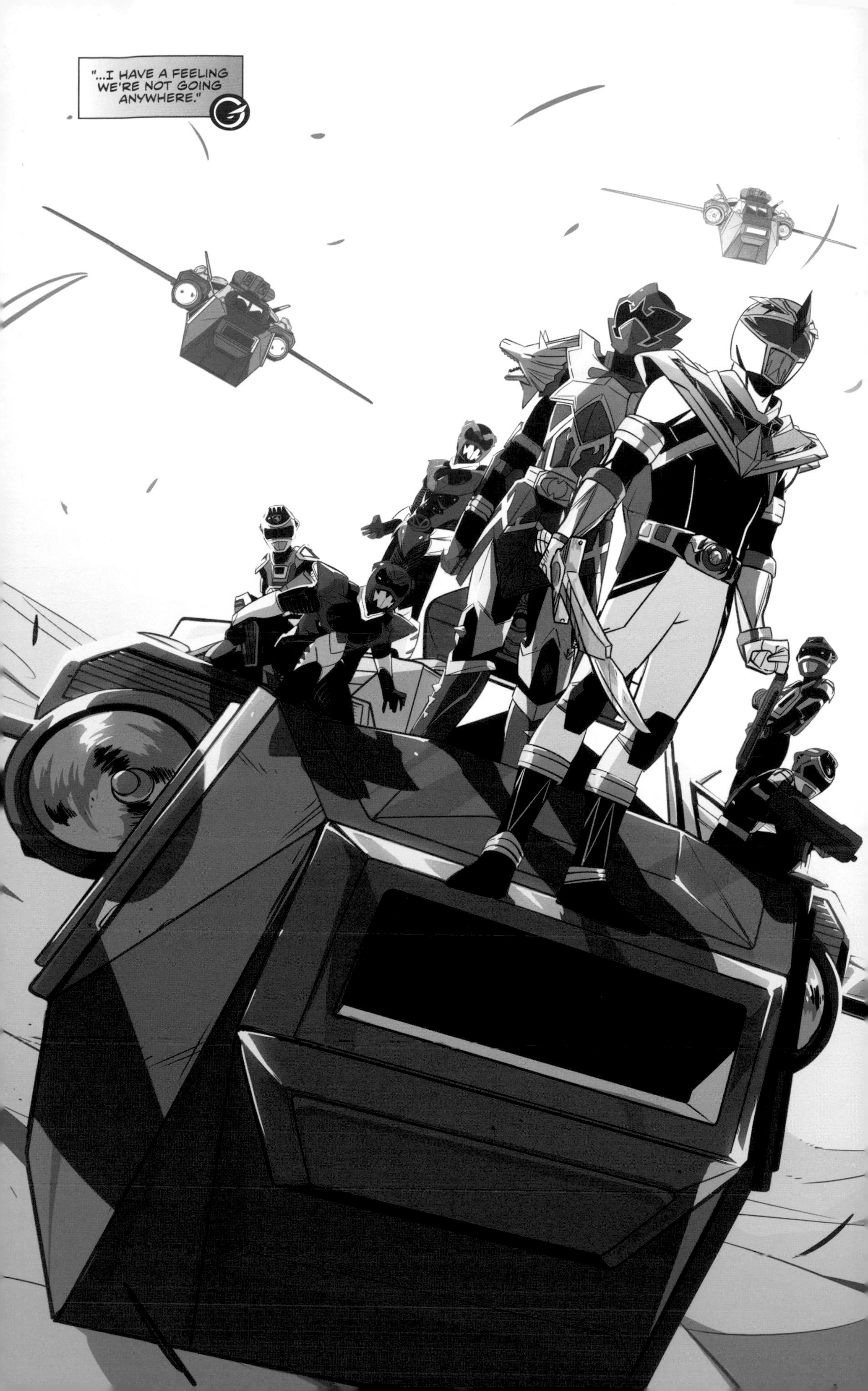
"...I HAVE A FEELING WE'RE NOT GOING ANYWHERE."

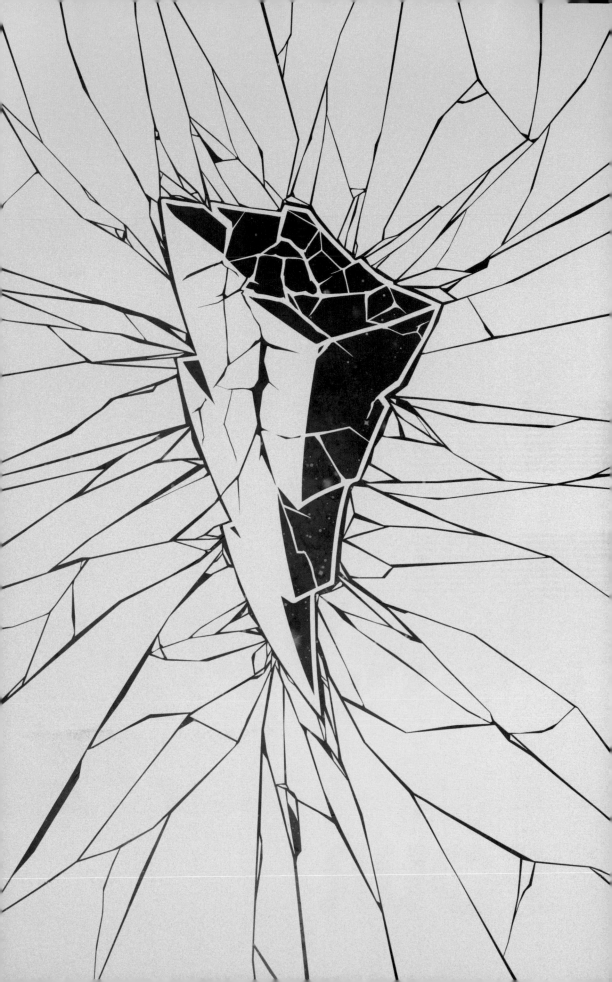

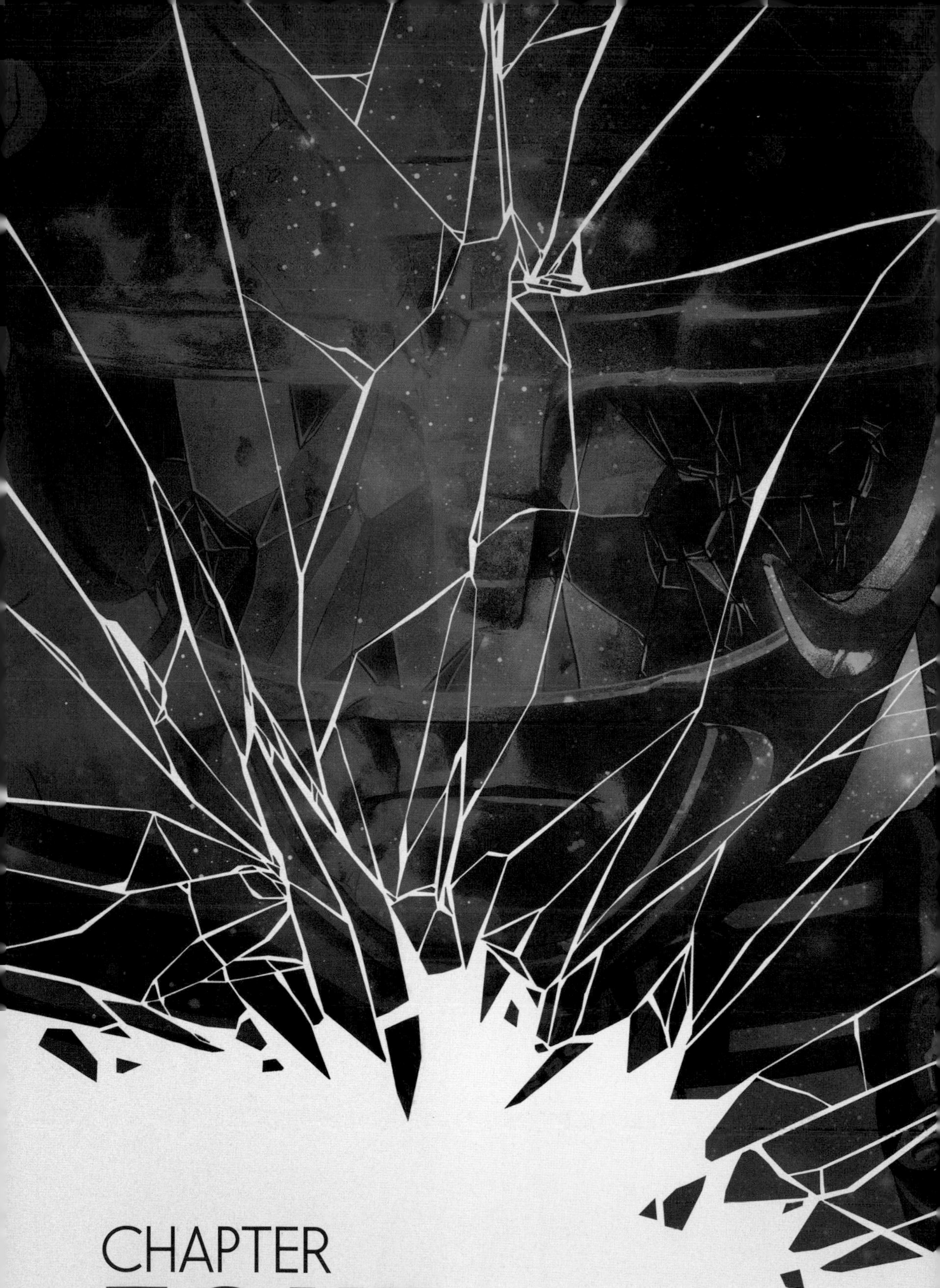

CHAPTER
FOUR

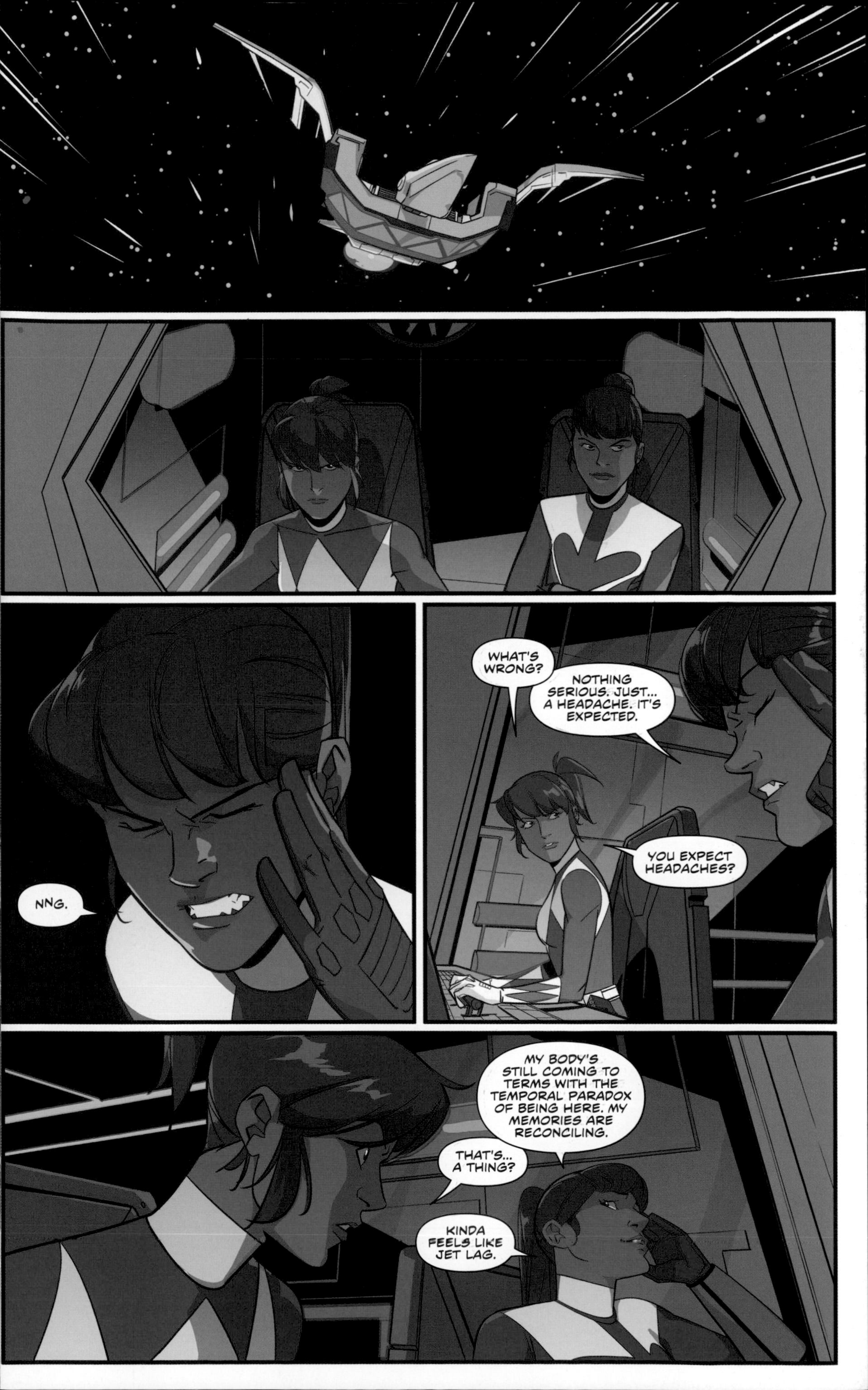
NNG.
WHAT'S WRONG?
NOTHING SERIOUS. JUST... A HEADACHE. IT'S EXPECTED.
YOU EXPECT HEADACHES?
MY BODY'S STILL COMING TO TERMS WITH THE TEMPORAL PARADOX OF BEING HERE. MY MEMORIES ARE RECONCILING.
THAT'S... A THING?
KINDA FEELS LIKE JET LAG.

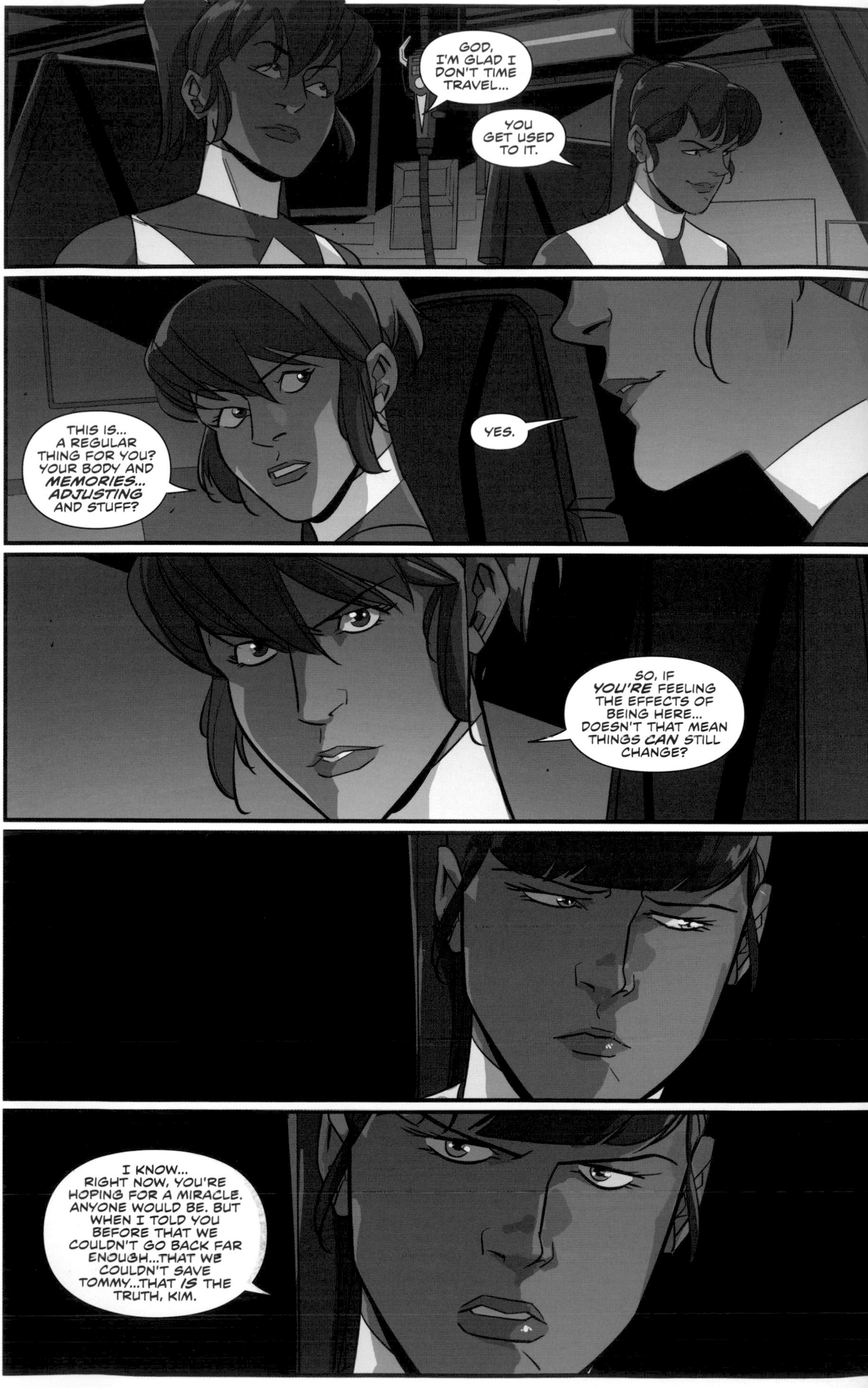
GOD, I'M GLAD I DON'T TIME TRAVEL...
YOU GET USED TO IT.
THIS IS... A REGULAR THING FOR YOU? YOUR BODY AND MEMORIES... ADJUSTING AND STUFF?
YES.
SO, IF YOU'RE FEELING THE EFFECTS OF BEING HERE... DOESN'T THAT MEAN THINGS CAN STILL CHANGE?
I KNOW... RIGHT NOW, YOU'RE HOPING FOR A MIRACLE. ANYONE WOULD BE. BUT WHEN I TOLD YOU BEFORE THAT WE COULDN'T GO BACK FAR ENOUGH...THAT WE COULDN'T SAVE TOMMY...THAT IS THE TRUTH, KIM.

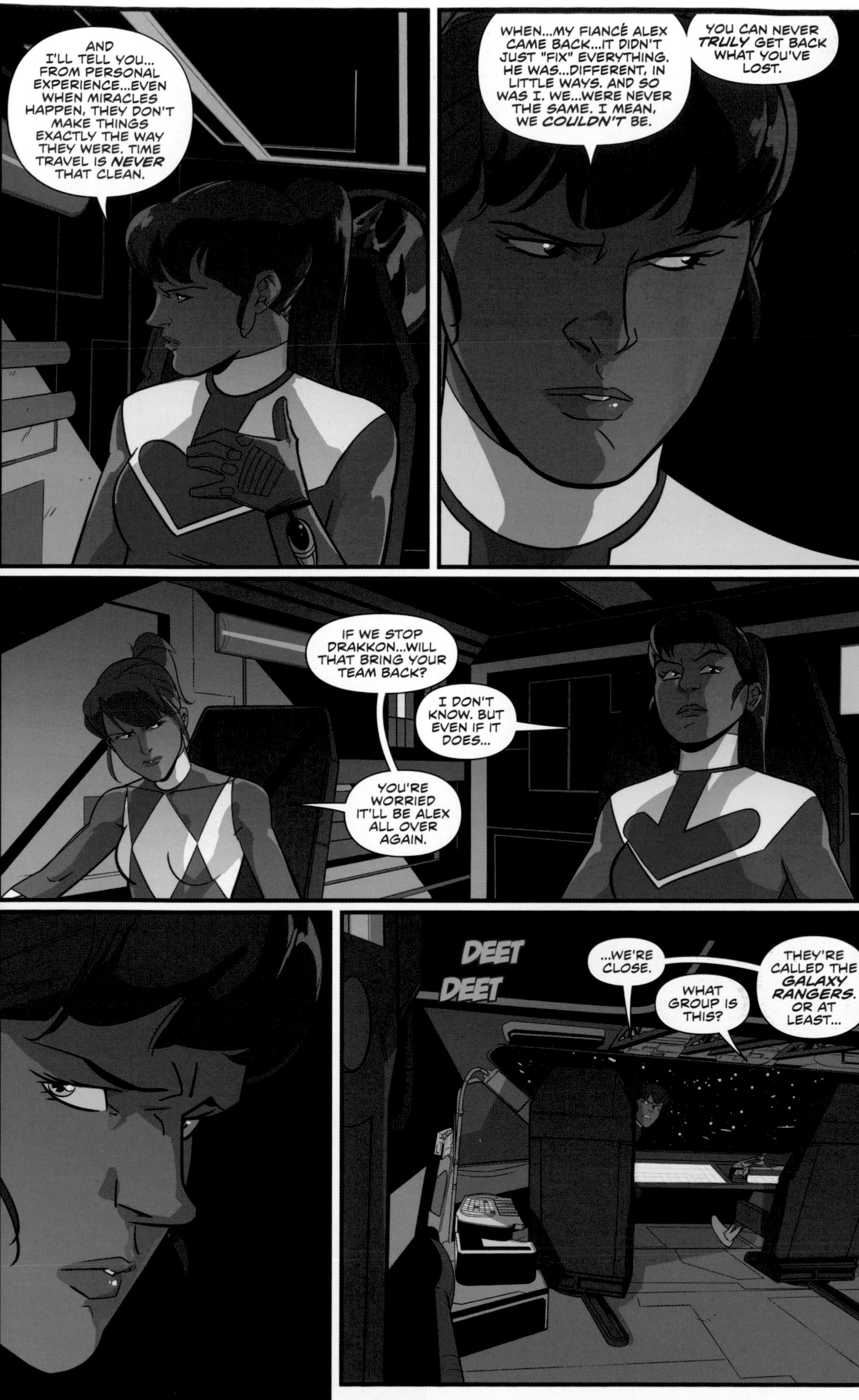
AND I'LL TELL YOU... FROM PERSONAL EXPERIENCE...EVEN WHEN MIRACLES HAPPEN, THEY DON'T MAKE THINGS EXACTLY THE WAY THEY WERE. TIME TRAVEL IS NEVER THAT CLEAN.
WHEN...MY FIANCÉ ALEX CAME BACK...IT DIDN'T JUST "FIX" EVERYTHING. HE WAS...DIFFERENT, IN LITTLE WAYS. AND SO WAS I. WE...WERE NEVER THE SAME. I MEAN, WE COULDN'T BE.
YOU CAN NEVER TRULY GET BACK WHAT YOU'VE LOST.
IF WE STOP DRAKKON...WILL THAT BRING YOUR TEAM BACK?
I DON'T KNOW. BUT EVEN IF IT DOES...
YOU'RE WORRIED IT'LL BE ALEX ALL OVER AGAIN.
DEET
DEET
...WE'RE CLOSE.
WHAT GROUP IS THIS?
THEY'RE CALLED THE GALAXY RANGERS. OR AT LEAST...

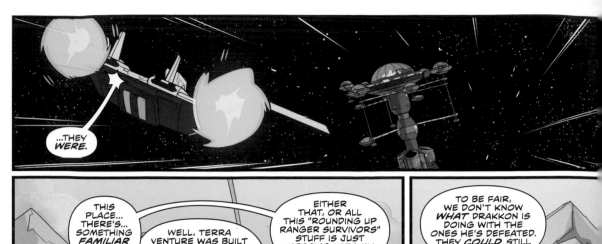

...THEY *WERE.*

THIS PLACE... THERE'S... SOMETHING *FAMILIAR* ABOUT IT ALL...

WELL, TERRA VENTURE WAS BUILT WITH A VARIETY OF ENVIRONMENTS, EACH HOUSED IN A DIFFERENT DOME. THEY ALL HAD TO BE BASED ON *SOMETHING.* YOU'VE PROBABLY BEEN SOMEWHERE *SIMILAR.*

EITHER THAT, OR ALL THIS "ROUNDING UP RANGER SURVIVORS" STUFF IS JUST MESSING WITH MY HEAD.

TO BE FAIR, WE DON'T KNOW *WHAT* DRAKKON IS DOING WITH THE ONES HE'S DEFEATED. THEY *COULD* STILL BE ALIVE.

THERE! UP IN THE MOUNTAINS.

HUH.

WHAT *NOW?*

THIS... ISN'T THE PINK RANGER I WAS EXPECTING.

HER NAME IS *KARONE,* BUT SHE USED TO BE KNOWN AS *ASTRONEMA.* SHE WAS ONE OF THE GREATEST THREATS THE UNIVERSE HAD EVER SEEN.

AND NOW SHE'S A *RANGER?*

I GUESS THIS IS FURTHER IN HER TIMELINE THAN I THOUGHT. SHE'S ALREADY BEEN REFORMED. ANOTHER LITTLE QUIRK OF TIME TRAVEL.

HEY, HOW'S IT GOING OUT THERE?

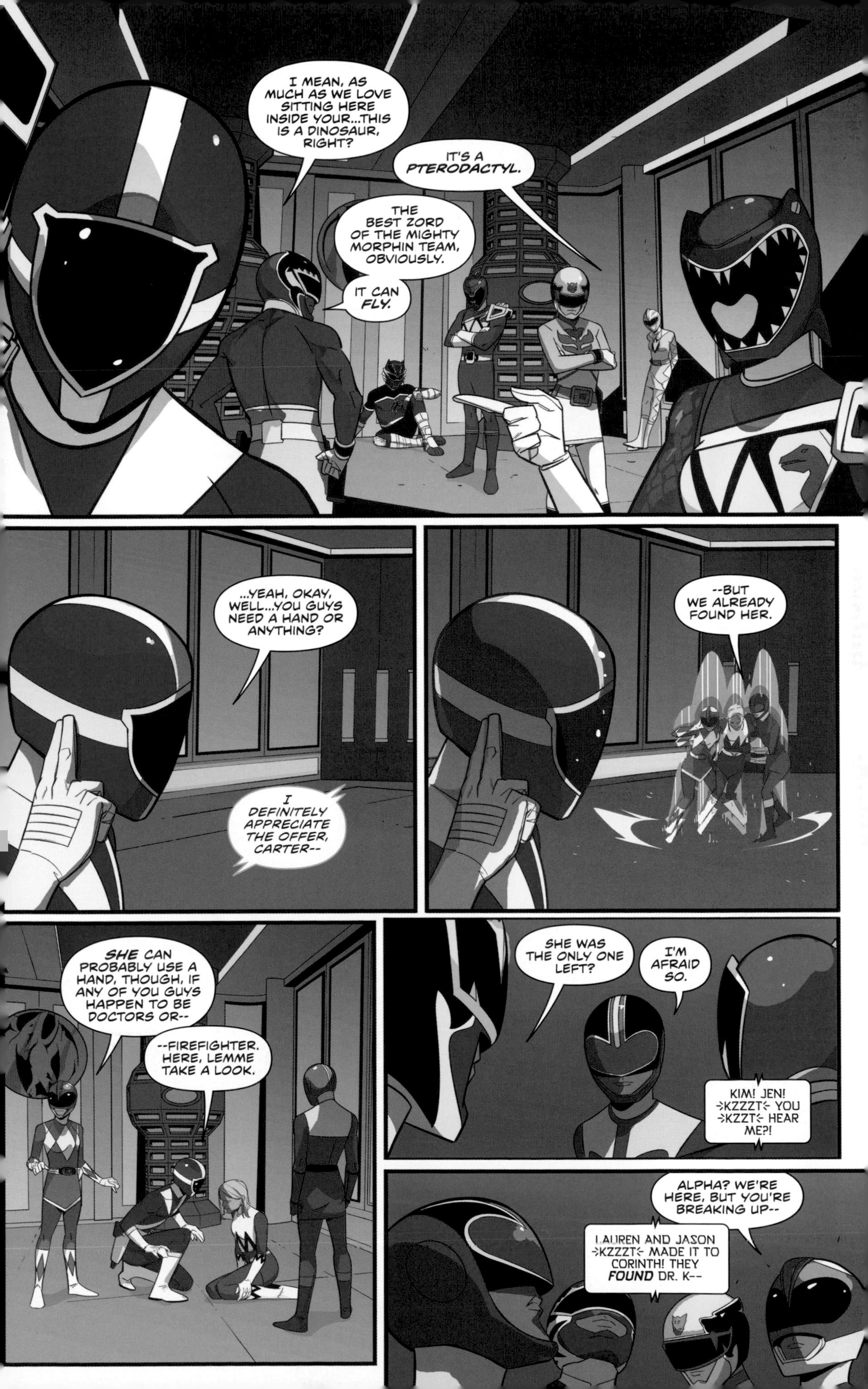
I MEAN, AS MUCH AS WE LOVE SITTING HERE INSIDE YOUR...THIS IS A DINOSAUR, RIGHT?
IT'S A PTERODACTYL.
THE BEST ZORD OF THE MIGHTY MORPHIN TEAM, OBVIOUSLY.
IT CAN FLY.
...YEAH, OKAY, WELL...YOU GUYS NEED A HAND OR ANYTHING?
I DEFINITELY APPRECIATE THE OFFER, CARTER--
--BUT WE ALREADY FOUND HER.
SHE CAN PROBABLY USE A HAND, THOUGH, IF ANY OF YOU GUYS HAPPEN TO BE DOCTORS OR--
--FIREFIGHTER. HERE, LEMME TAKE A LOOK.
SHE WAS THE ONLY ONE LEFT?
I'M AFRAID SO.
KIM! JEN! ›KZZZT‹ YOU ›KZZT‹ HEAR ME?!
ALPHA? WE'RE HERE, BUT YOU'RE BREAKING UP--
LAUREN AND JASON ›KZZZT‹ MADE IT TO CORINTH! THEY FOUND DR. K--

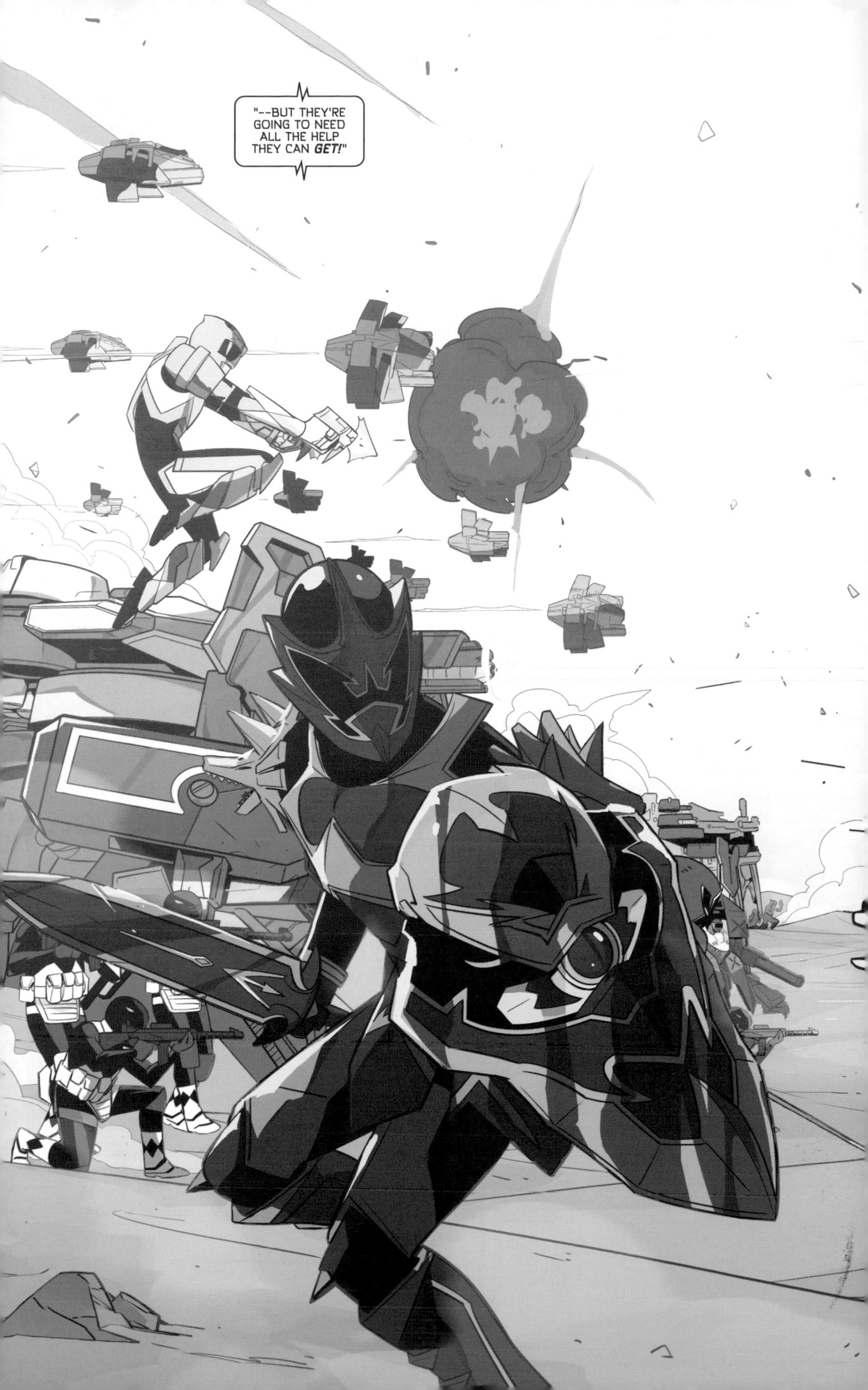
"--BUT THEY'RE GOING TO NEED ALL THE HELP THEY CAN *GET!*"

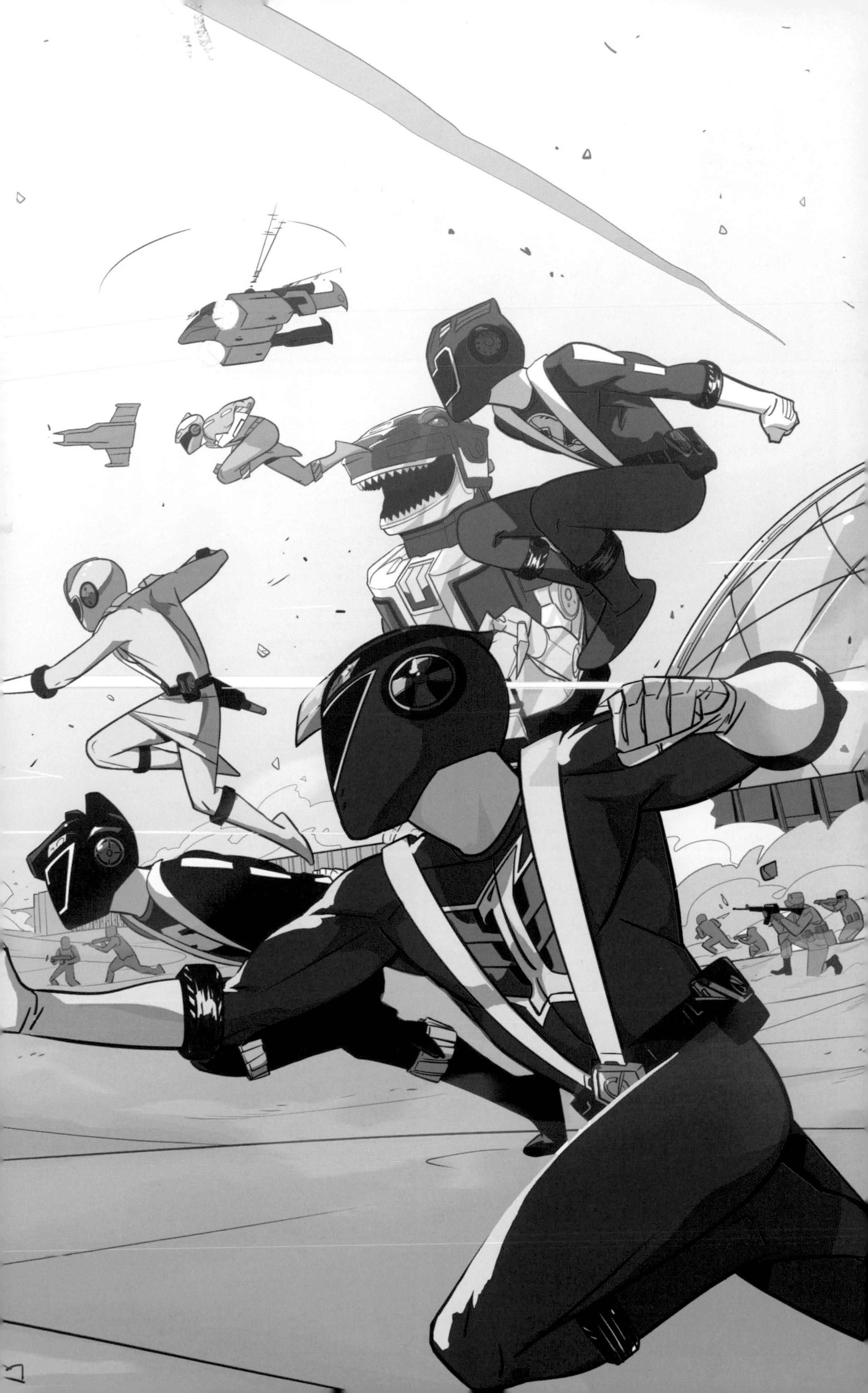

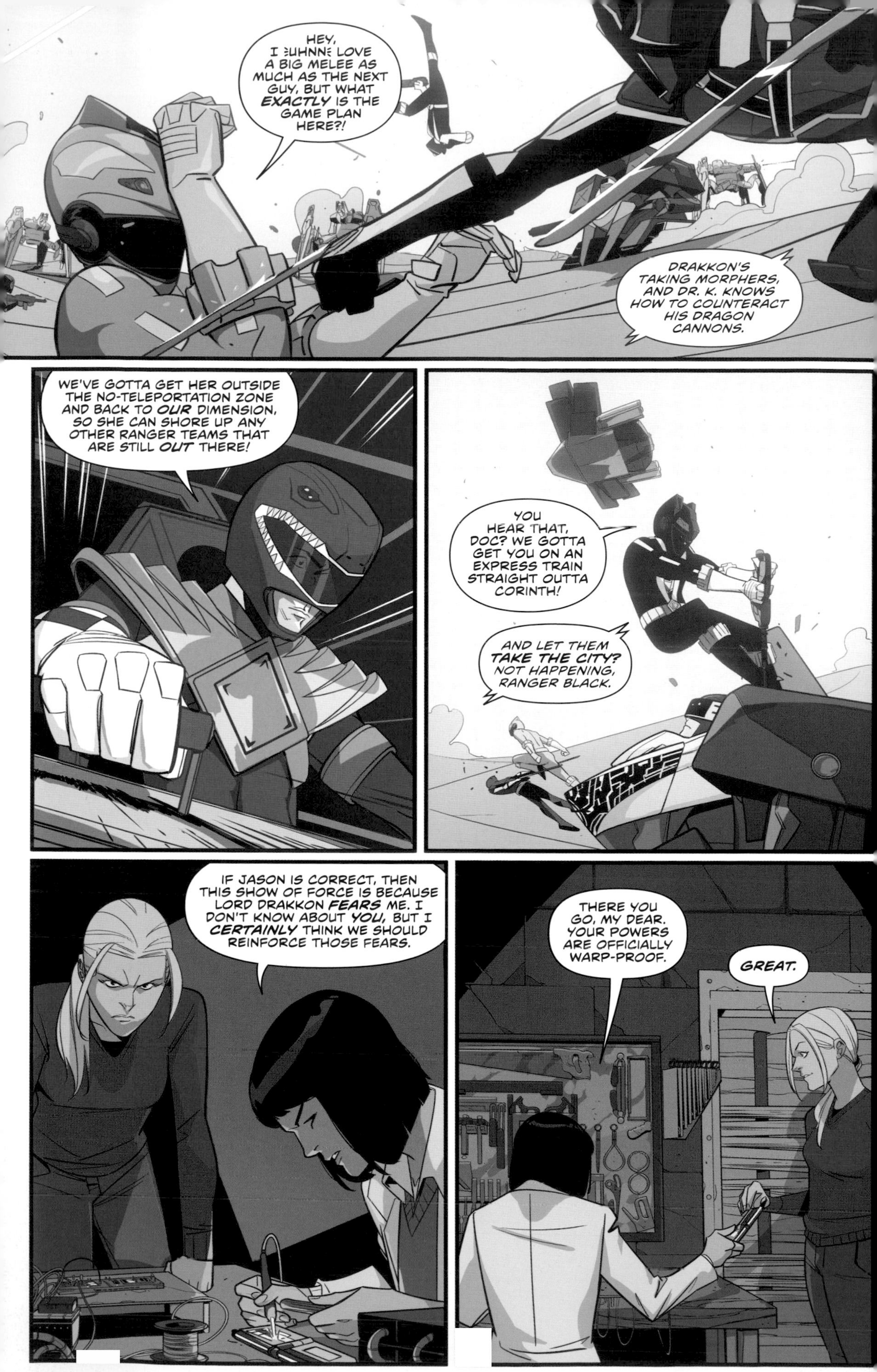
HEY, I UHNN LOVE A BIG MELEE AS MUCH AS THE NEXT GUY, BUT WHAT EXACTLY IS THE GAME PLAN HERE?!
DRAKKON'S TAKING MORPHERS, AND DR. K. KNOWS HOW TO COUNTERACT HIS DRAGON CANNONS.
WE'VE GOTTA GET HER OUTSIDE THE NO-TELEPORTATION ZONE AND BACK TO OUR DIMENSION, SO SHE CAN SHORE UP ANY OTHER RANGER TEAMS THAT ARE STILL OUT THERE!
YOU HEAR THAT, DOC? WE GOTTA GET YOU ON AN EXPRESS TRAIN STRAIGHT OUTTA CORINTH!
AND LET THEM TAKE THE CITY? NOT HAPPENING, RANGER BLACK.
IF JASON IS CORRECT, THEN THIS SHOW OF FORCE IS BECAUSE LORD DRAKKON FEARS ME. I DON'T KNOW ABOUT YOU, BUT I CERTAINLY THINK WE SHOULD REINFORCE THOSE FEARS.
THERE YOU GO, MY DEAR. YOUR POWERS ARE OFFICIALLY WARP-PROOF.
GREAT.

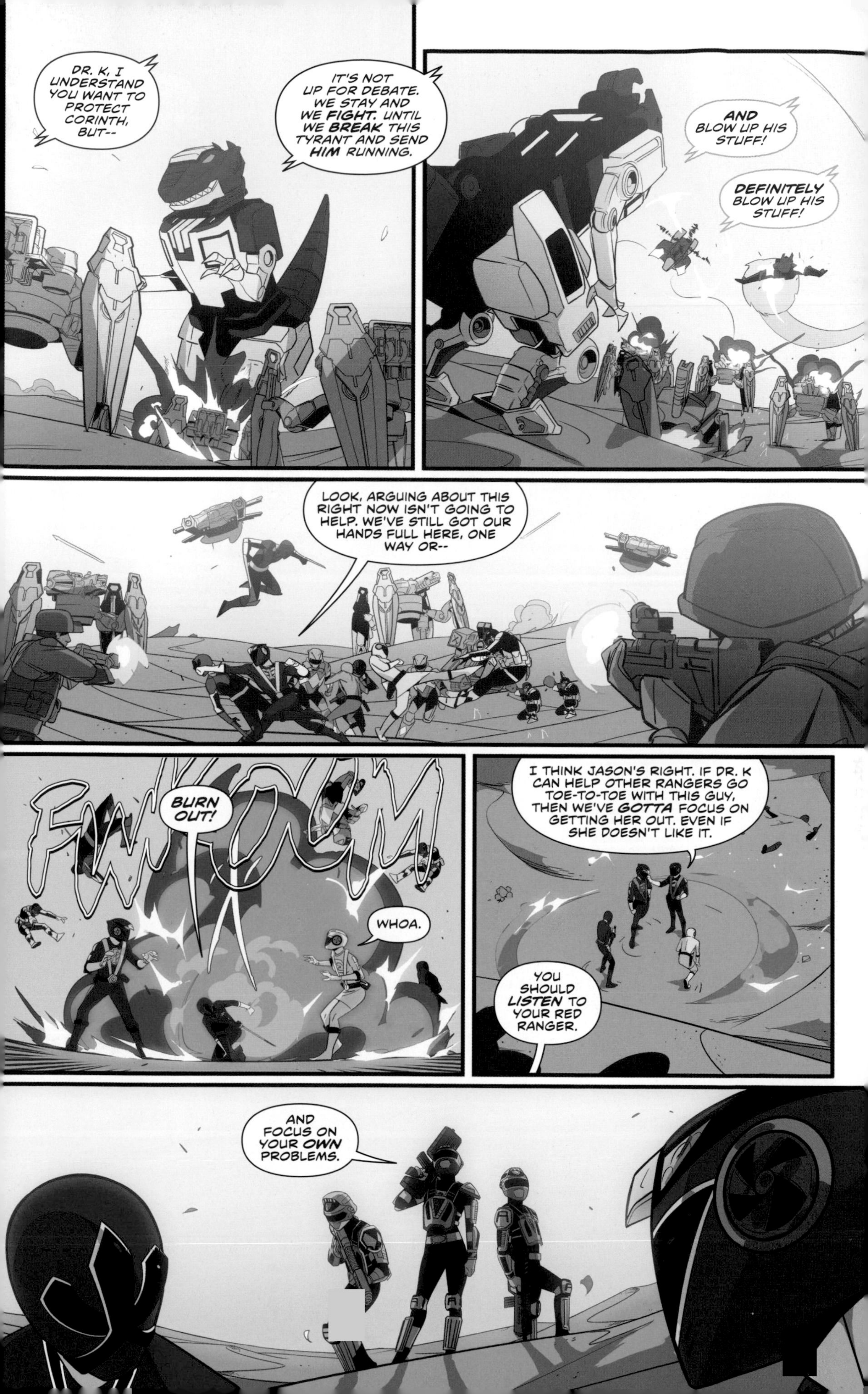
DR. K, I UNDERSTAND YOU WANT TO PROTECT CORINTH, BUT--
IT'S NOT UP FOR DEBATE. WE STAY AND WE FIGHT. UNTIL WE BREAK THIS TYRANT AND SEND HIM RUNNING.
AND BLOW UP HIS STUFF!
DEFINITELY BLOW UP HIS STUFF!
LOOK, ARGUING ABOUT THIS RIGHT NOW ISN'T GOING TO HELP. WE'VE STILL GOT OUR HANDS FULL HERE, ONE WAY OR--
FWOOM
BURN OUT!
WHOA.
I THINK JASON'S RIGHT. IF DR. K CAN HELP OTHER RANGERS GO TOE-TO-TOE WITH THIS GUY, THEN WE'VE GOTTA FOCUS ON GETTING HER OUT. EVEN IF SHE DOESN'T LIKE IT.
YOU SHOULD LISTEN TO YOUR RED RANGER.
AND FOCUS ON YOUR OWN PROBLEMS.

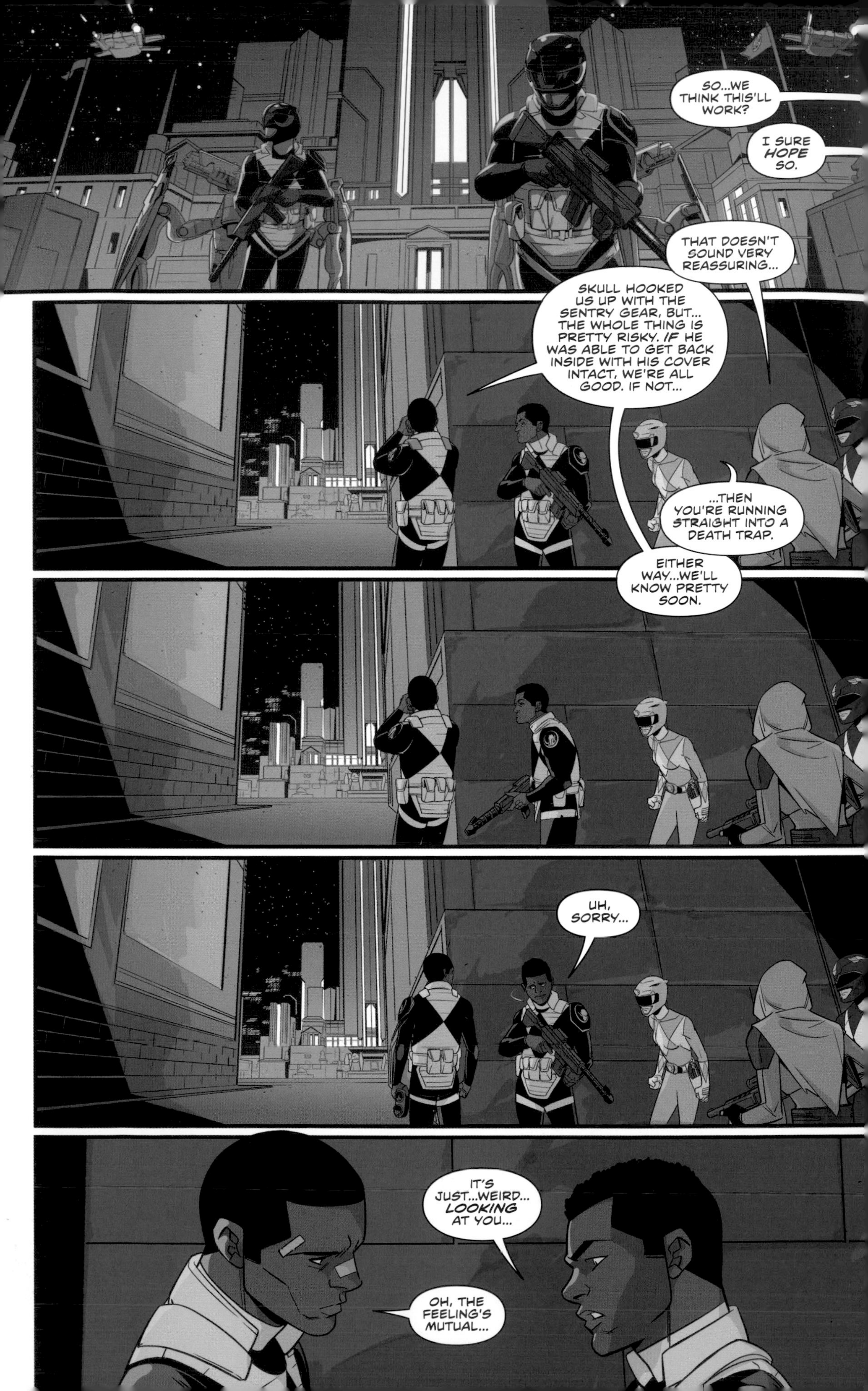
SO...WE THINK THIS'LL WORK?
I SURE *HOPE* SO.
THAT DOESN'T SOUND VERY REASSURING...
SKULL HOOKED US UP WITH THE SENTRY GEAR, BUT... THE WHOLE THING IS PRETTY RISKY. *IF* HE WAS ABLE TO GET BACK INSIDE WITH HIS COVER INTACT, WE'RE ALL GOOD. IF NOT...
...THEN YOU'RE RUNNING STRAIGHT INTO A DEATH TRAP.
EITHER WAY...WE'LL KNOW PRETTY SOON.
UH, SORRY...
IT'S JUST...WEIRD... *LOOKING* AT YOU...
OH, THE FEELING'S MUTUAL...

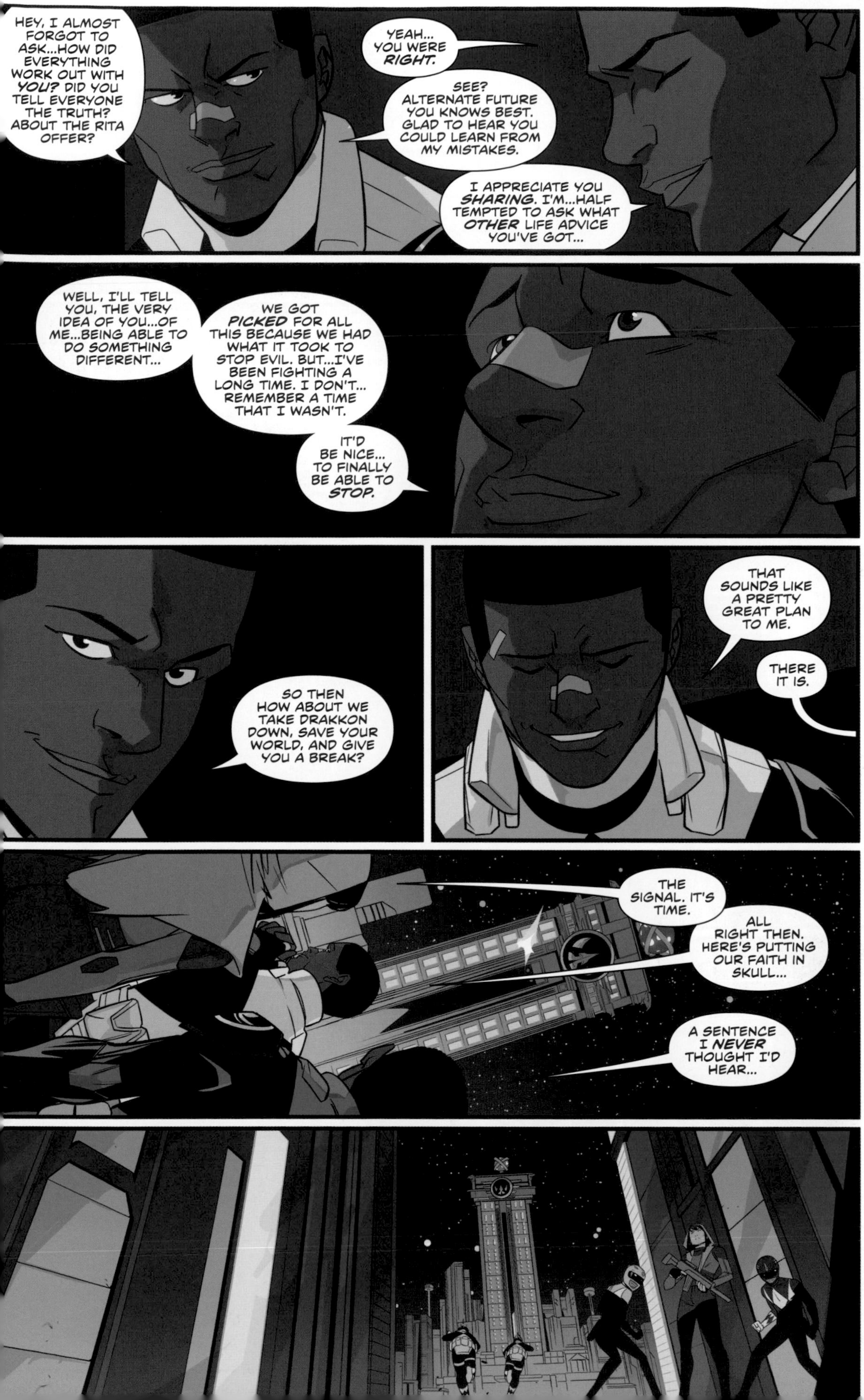
HEY, I ALMOST FORGOT TO ASK...HOW DID EVERYTHING WORK OUT WITH YOU? DID YOU TELL EVERYONE THE TRUTH? ABOUT THE RITA OFFER?
YEAH... YOU WERE RIGHT.
SEE? ALTERNATE FUTURE YOU KNOWS BEST. GLAD TO HEAR YOU COULD LEARN FROM MY MISTAKES.
I APPRECIATE YOU SHARING. I'M...HALF TEMPTED TO ASK WHAT OTHER LIFE ADVICE YOU'VE GOT...
WELL, I'LL TELL YOU, THE VERY IDEA OF YOU...OF ME...BEING ABLE TO DO SOMETHING DIFFERENT...
WE GOT PICKED FOR ALL THIS BECAUSE WE HAD WHAT IT TOOK TO STOP EVIL. BUT...I'VE BEEN FIGHTING A LONG TIME. I DON'T... REMEMBER A TIME THAT I WASN'T.
IT'D BE NICE... TO FINALLY BE ABLE TO STOP.
SO THEN HOW ABOUT WE TAKE DRAKKON DOWN, SAVE YOUR WORLD, AND GIVE YOU A BREAK?
THAT SOUNDS LIKE A PRETTY GREAT PLAN TO ME.
THERE IT IS.
THE SIGNAL. IT'S TIME.
ALL RIGHT THEN. HERE'S PUTTING OUR FAITH IN SKULL...
A SENTENCE I NEVER THOUGHT I'D HEAR...

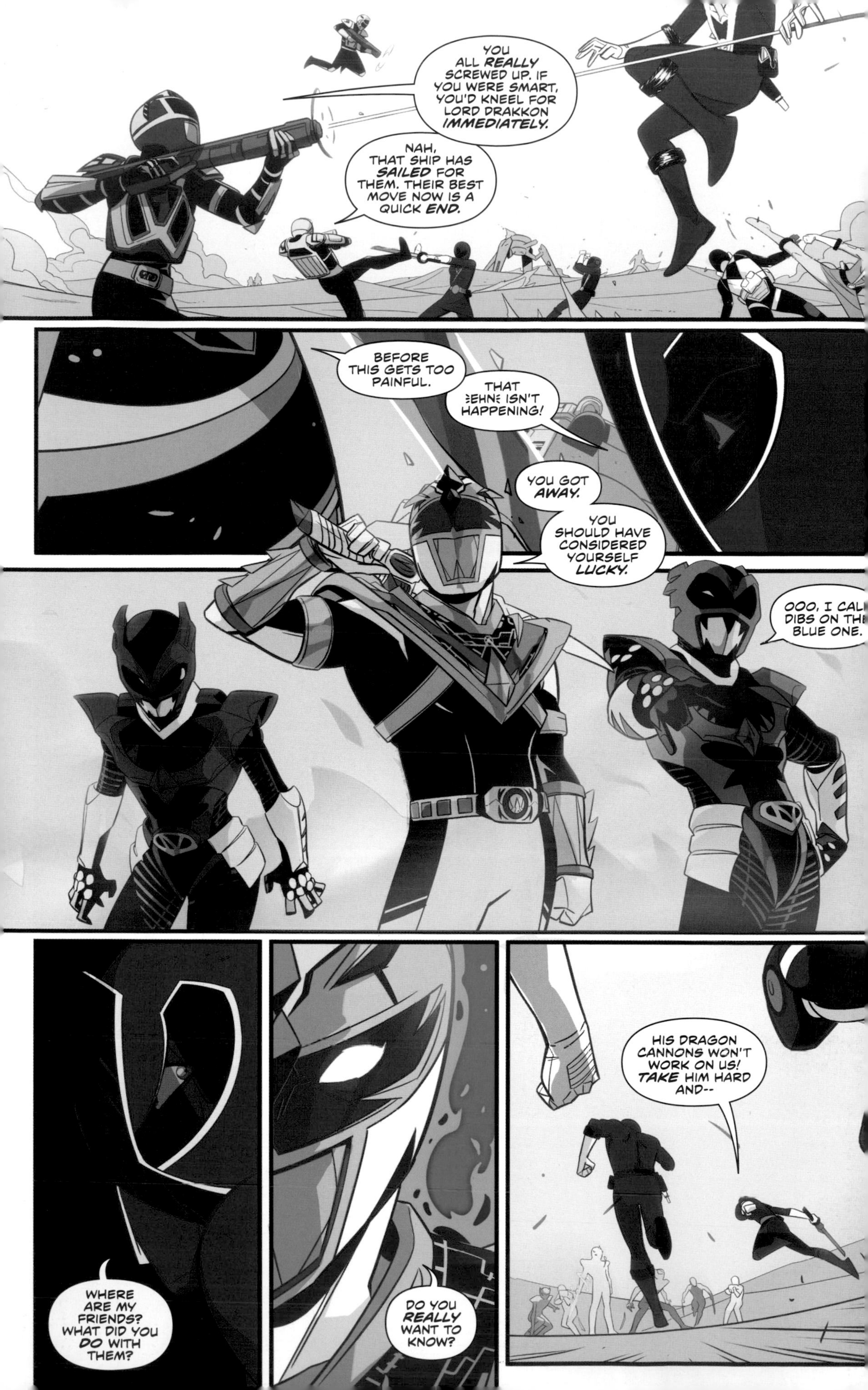

YOU ALL REALLY SCREWED UP. IF YOU WERE SMART, YOU'D KNEEL FOR LORD DRAKKON IMMEDIATELY.
NAH, THAT SHIP HAS SAILED FOR THEM. THEIR BEST MOVE NOW IS A QUICK END.
BEFORE THIS GETS TOO PAINFUL.
THAT EHN ISN'T HAPPENING!
YOU GOT AWAY.
YOU SHOULD HAVE CONSIDERED YOURSELF LUCKY.
OOO, I CAL DIBS ON TH BLUE ONE.
WHERE ARE MY FRIENDS? WHAT DID YOU DO WITH THEM?
DO YOU REALLY WANT TO KNOW?
HIS DRAGON CANNONS WON'T WORK ON US! TAKE HIM HARD AND--

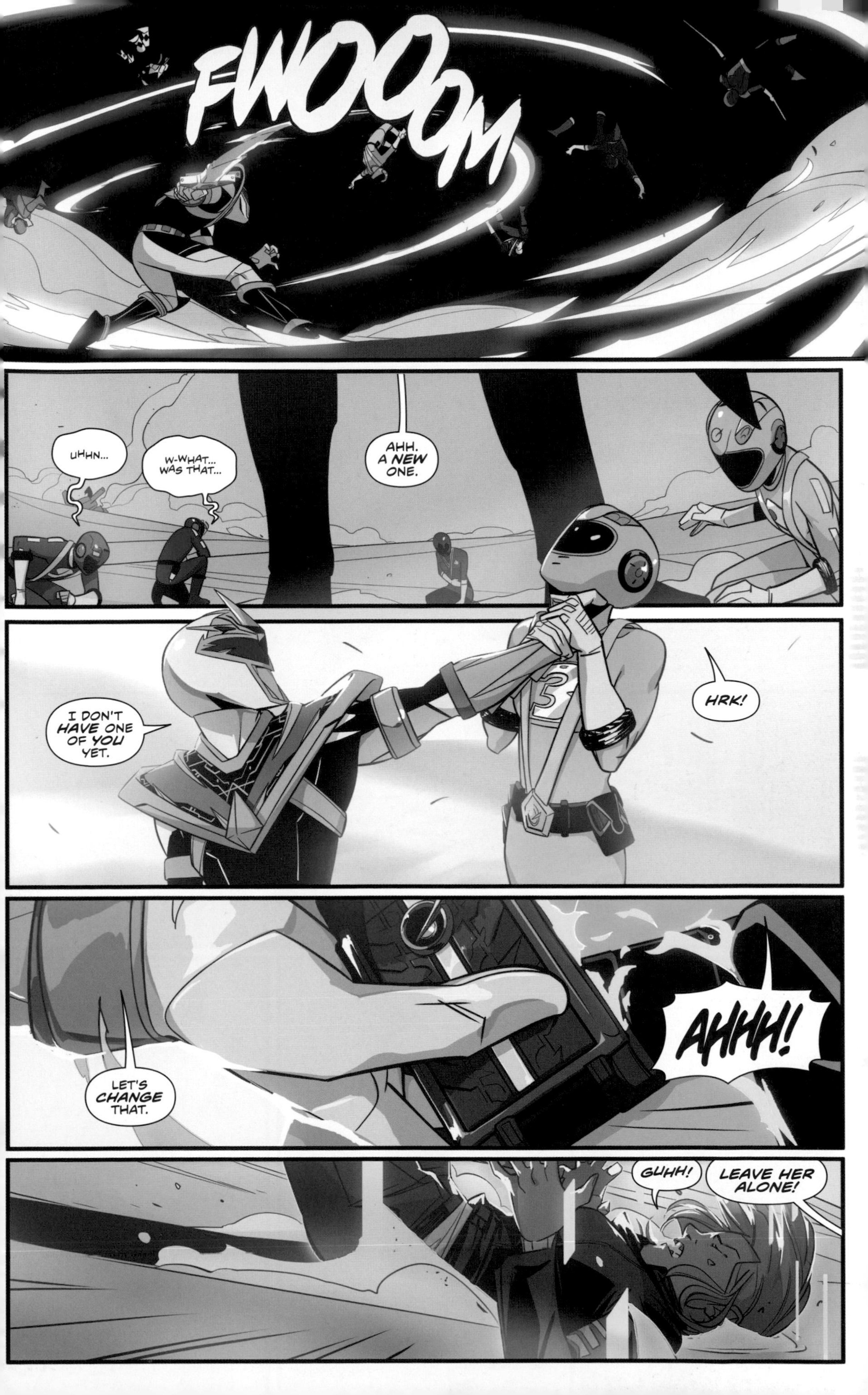
FWOOOM
UHHN...
W-WHAT... WAS THAT...
AHH. A NEW ONE.
I DON'T HAVE ONE OF YOU YET.
HRK!
LET'S CHANGE THAT.
AHHH!
GUHH!
LEAVE HER ALONE!

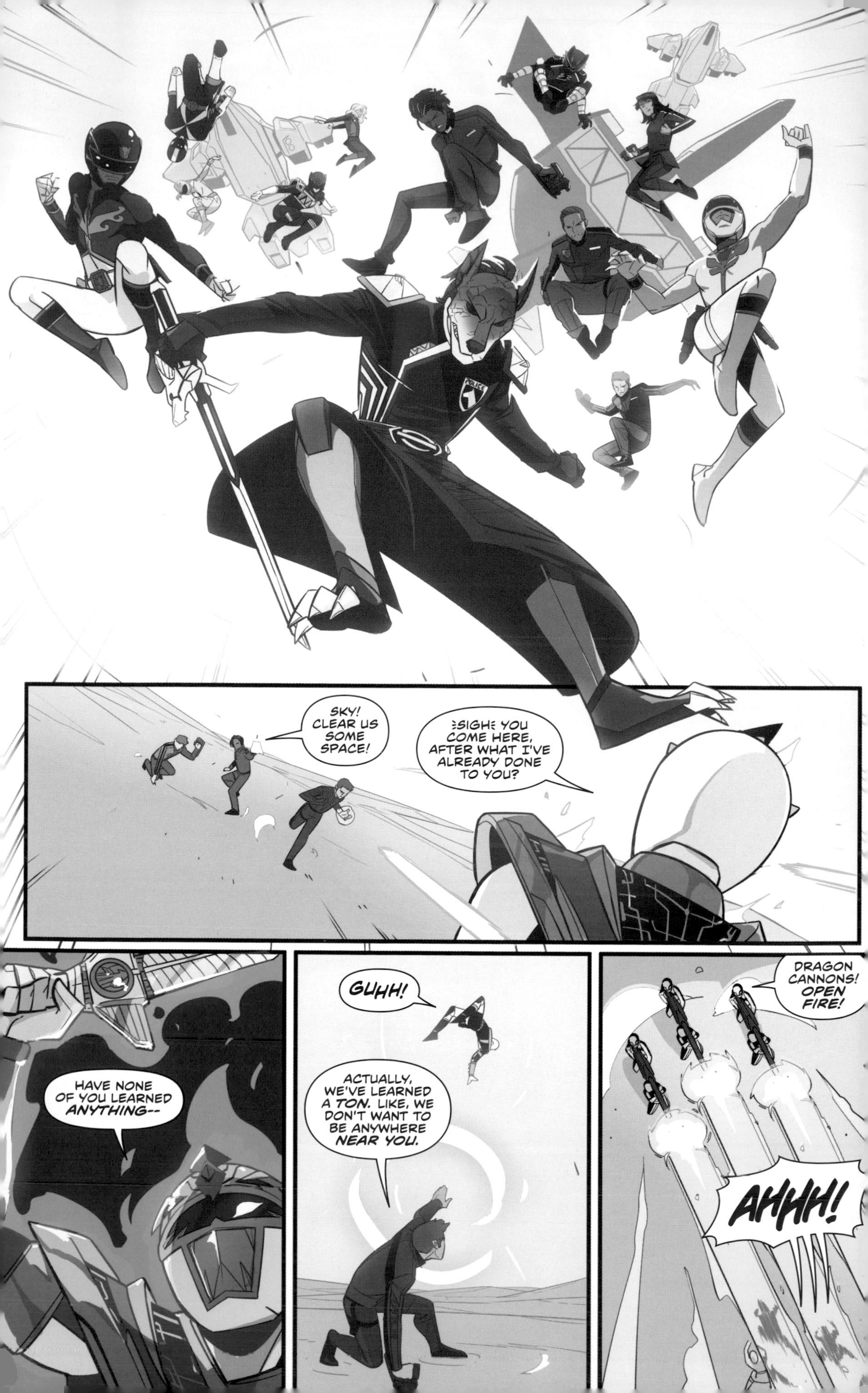
SKY! CLEAR US SOME SPACE!
SIGH YOU COME HERE, AFTER WHAT I'VE ALREADY DONE TO YOU?
HAVE NONE OF YOU LEARNED ANYTHING--
GUHH!
ACTUALLY, WE'VE LEARNED A TON. LIKE, WE DON'T WANT TO BE ANYWHERE NEAR YOU.
DRAGON CANNONS! OPEN FIRE!
AHHH!

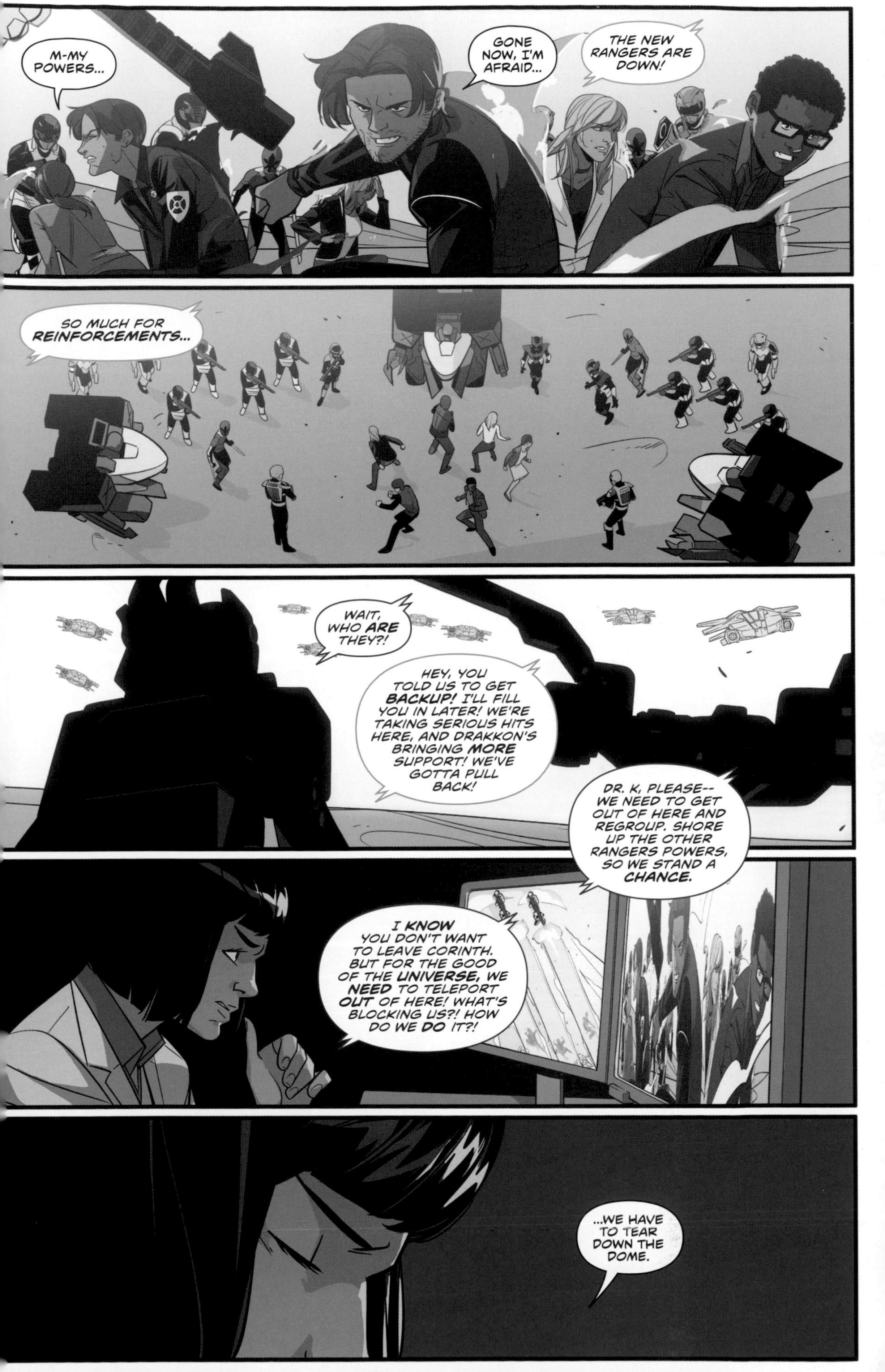
M-MY POWERS...
GONE NOW, I'M AFRAID...
THE NEW RANGERS ARE DOWN!
SO MUCH FOR REINFORCEMENTS...
WAIT, WHO ARE THEY?!
HEY, YOU TOLD US TO GET BACKUP! I'LL FILL YOU IN LATER! WE'RE TAKING SERIOUS HITS HERE, AND DRAKKON'S BRINGING MORE SUPPORT! WE'VE GOTTA PULL BACK!
DR. K, PLEASE-- WE NEED TO GET OUT OF HERE AND REGROUP. SHORE UP THE OTHER RANGERS POWERS, SO WE STAND A CHANCE.
I KNOW YOU DON'T WANT TO LEAVE CORINTH. BUT FOR THE GOOD OF THE UNIVERSE, WE NEED TO TELEPORT OUT OF HERE! WHAT'S BLOCKING US?! HOW DO WE DO IT?!
...WE HAVE TO TEAR DOWN THE DOME.

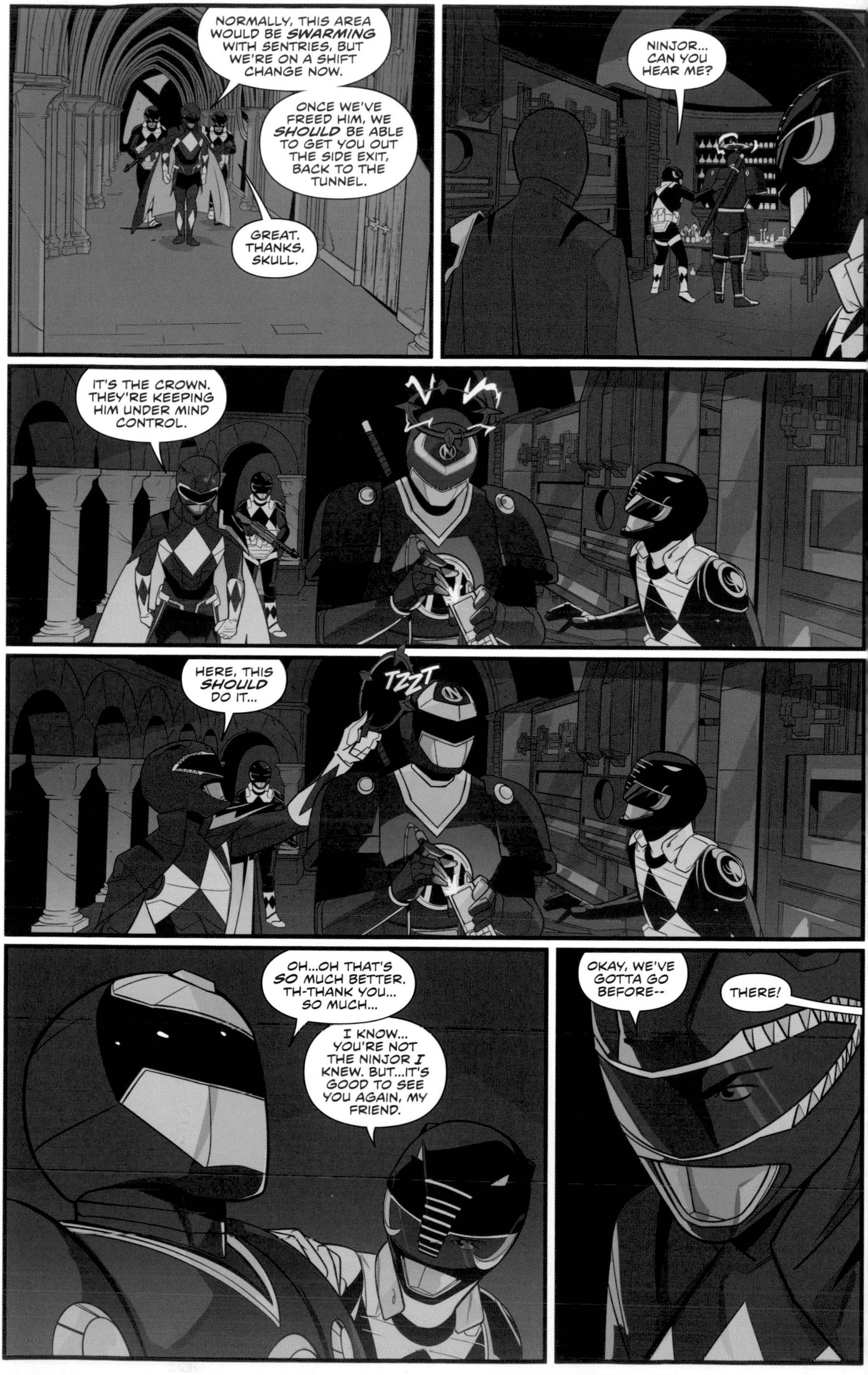
NORMALLY, THIS AREA WOULD BE SWARMING WITH SENTRIES, BUT WE'RE ON A SHIFT CHANGE NOW.
ONCE WE'VE FREED HIM, WE SHOULD BE ABLE TO GET YOU OUT THE SIDE EXIT, BACK TO THE TUNNEL.
GREAT. THANKS, SKULL.
NINJOR... CAN YOU HEAR ME?
IT'S THE CROWN. THEY'RE KEEPING HIM UNDER MIND CONTROL.
HERE, THIS SHOULD DO IT...
TZZT
OH...OH THAT'S SO MUCH BETTER. TH-THANK YOU... SO MUCH...
I KNOW... YOU'RE NOT THE NINJOR I KNEW. BUT...IT'S GOOD TO SEE YOU AGAIN, MY FRIEND.
OKAY, WE'VE GOTTA GO BEFORE--
THERE!

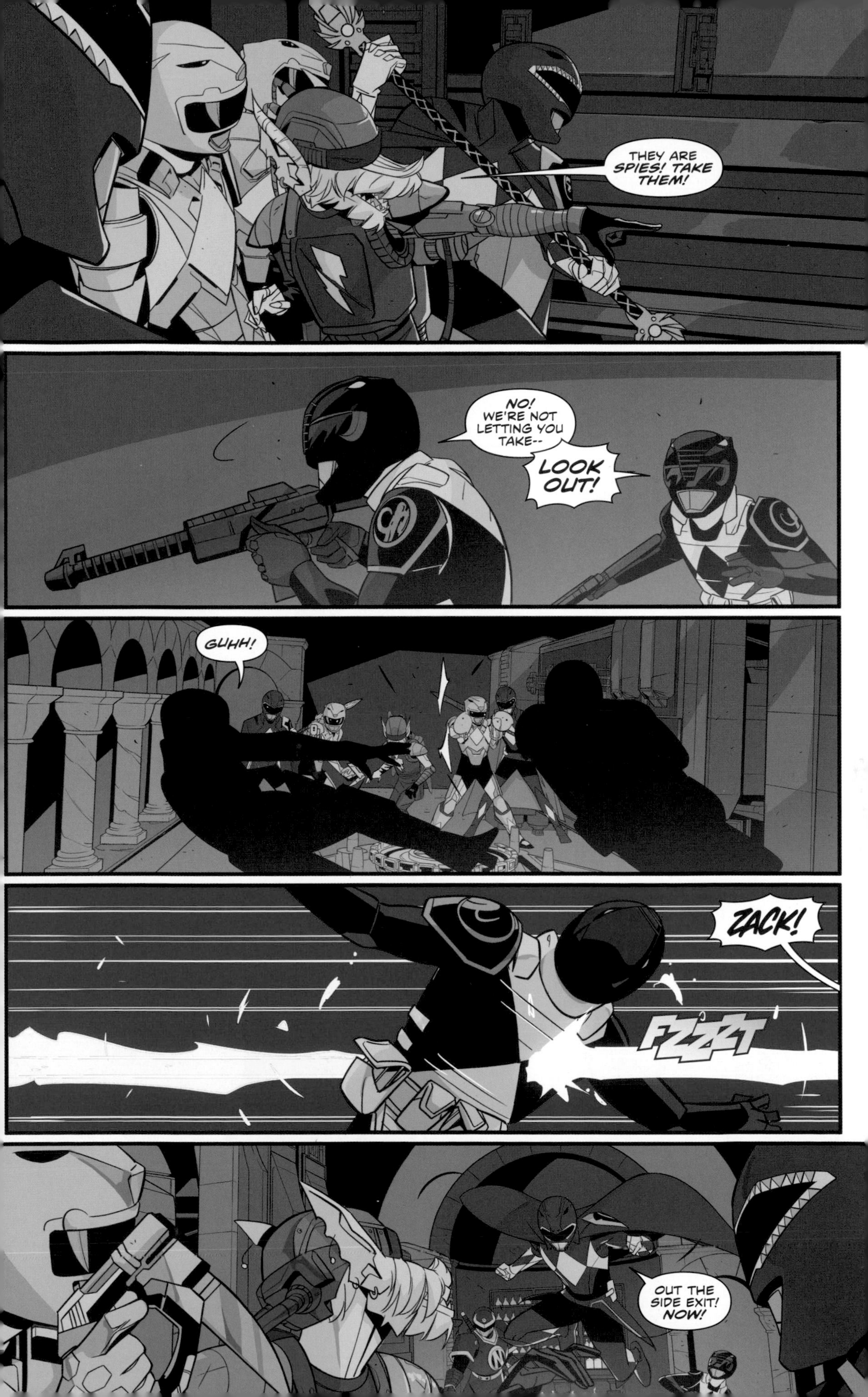
THEY ARE SPIES! TAKE THEM!
NO! WE'RE NOT LETTING YOU TAKE--
LOOK OUT!
GUHH!
ZACK!
FZZZT
OUT THE SIDE EXIT! NOW!

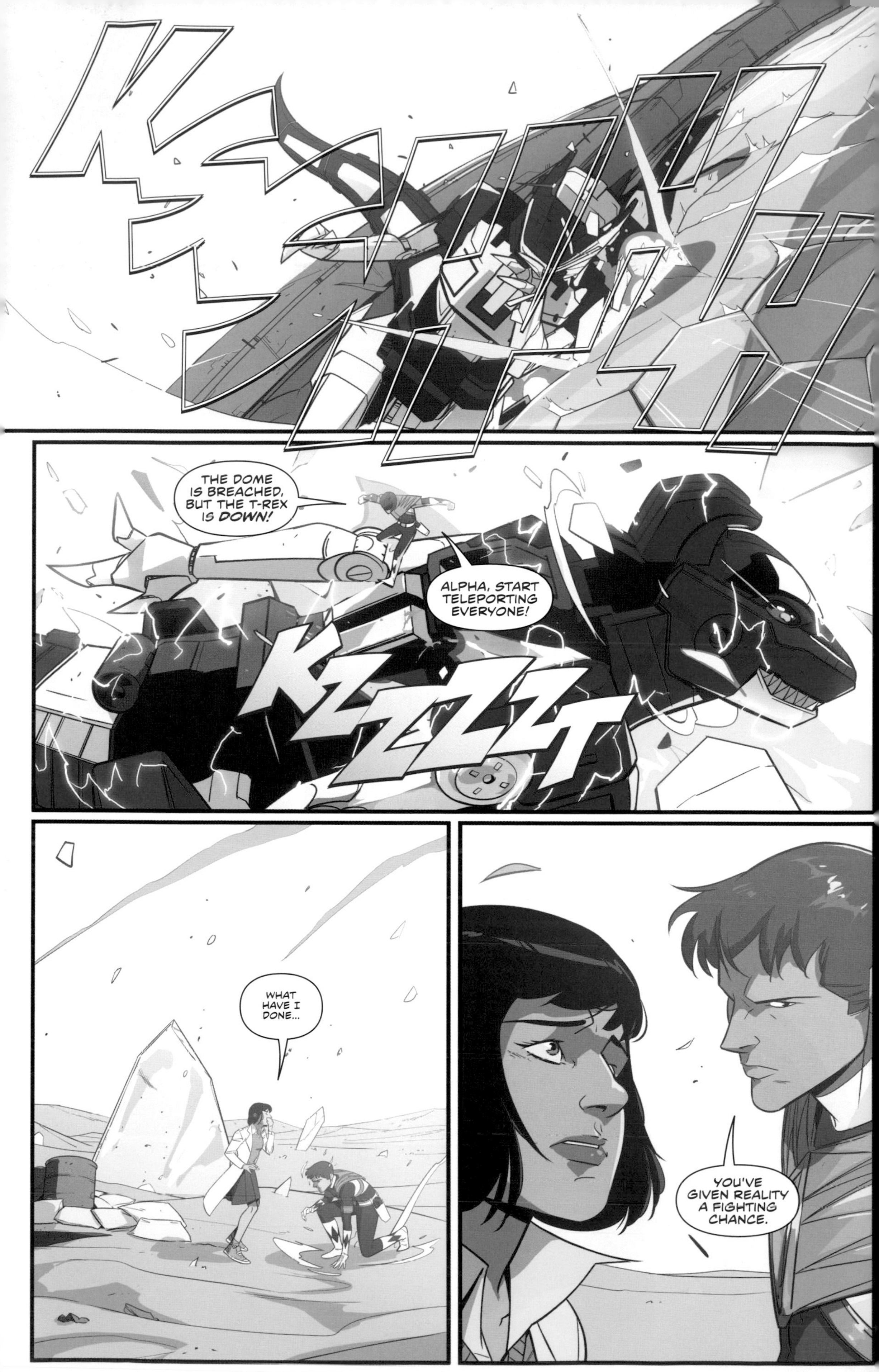
KZZOOOSSSHH
THE DOME IS BREACHED, BUT THE T-REX IS *DOWN!*
ALPHA, START TELEPORTING EVERYONE!
KZZZZT
WHAT HAVE I DONE...
YOU'VE GIVEN REALITY A FIGHTING CHANCE.

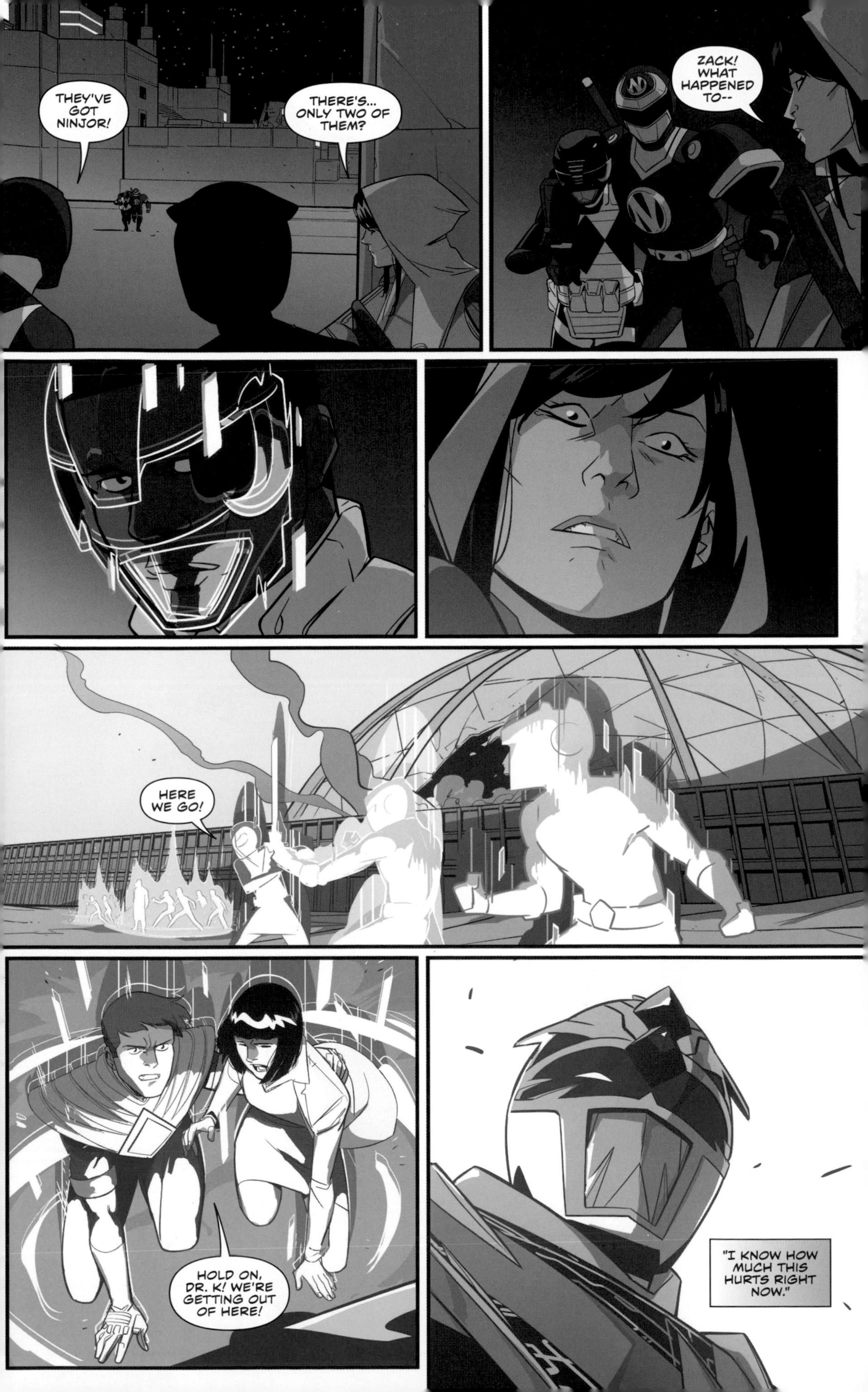
THEY'VE GOT NINJOR!
THERE'S... ONLY TWO OF THEM?
ZACK! WHAT HAPPENED TO--
HERE WE GO!
HOLD ON, DR. K! WE'RE GETTING OUT OF HERE!
"I KNOW HOW MUCH THIS HURTS RIGHT NOW."

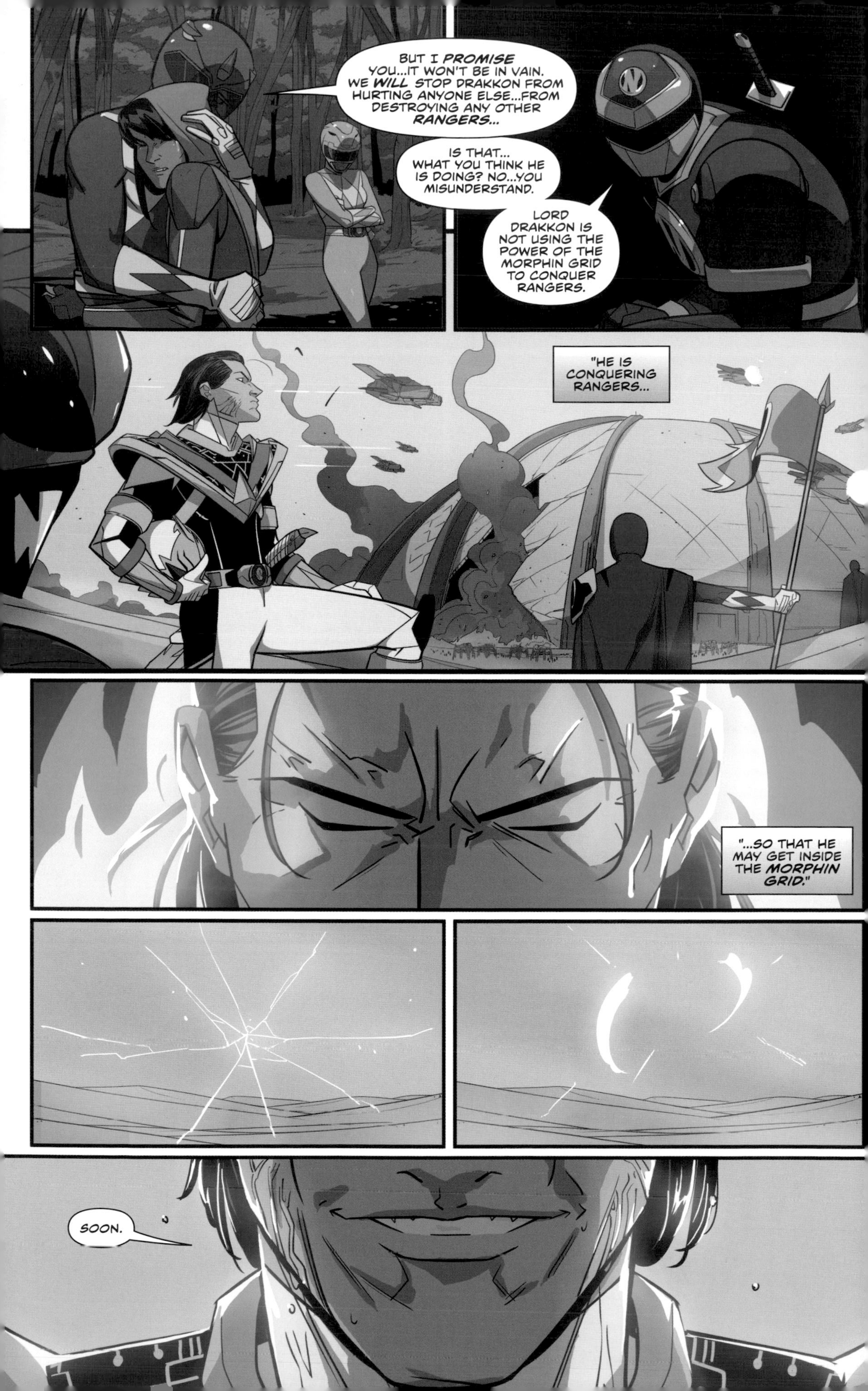
BUT I *PROMISE* YOU...IT WON'T BE IN VAIN. WE *WILL* STOP DRAKKON FROM HURTING ANYONE ELSE...FROM DESTROYING ANY OTHER *RANGERS...*
IS THAT... WHAT YOU THINK HE IS DOING? NO...YOU MISUNDERSTAND.
LORD DRAKKON IS NOT USING THE POWER OF THE MORPHIN GRID TO CONQUER RANGERS.
"HE IS CONQUERING RANGERS...
"...SO THAT HE MAY GET INSIDE THE *MORPHIN GRID.*"
SOON.

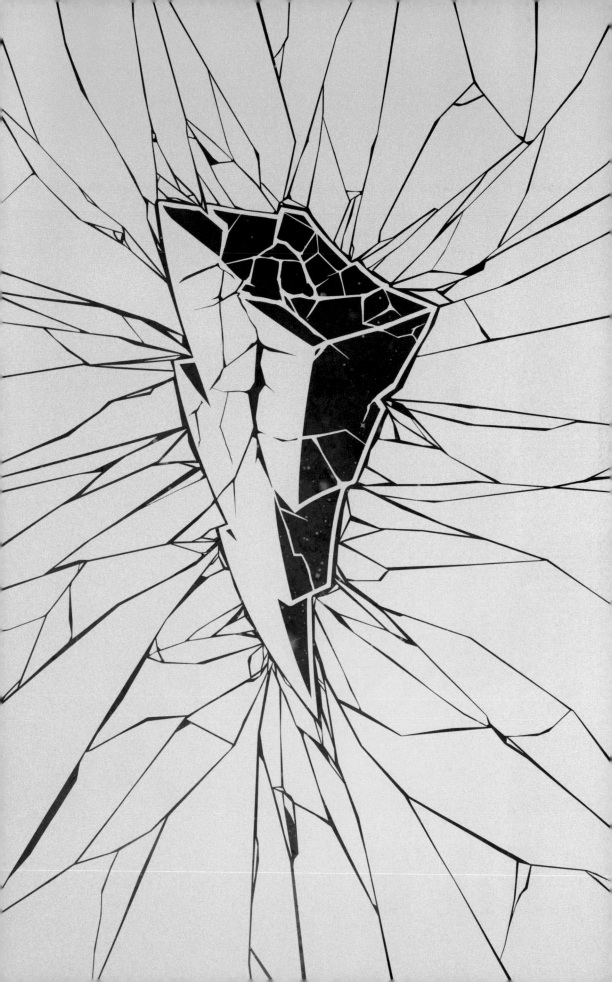

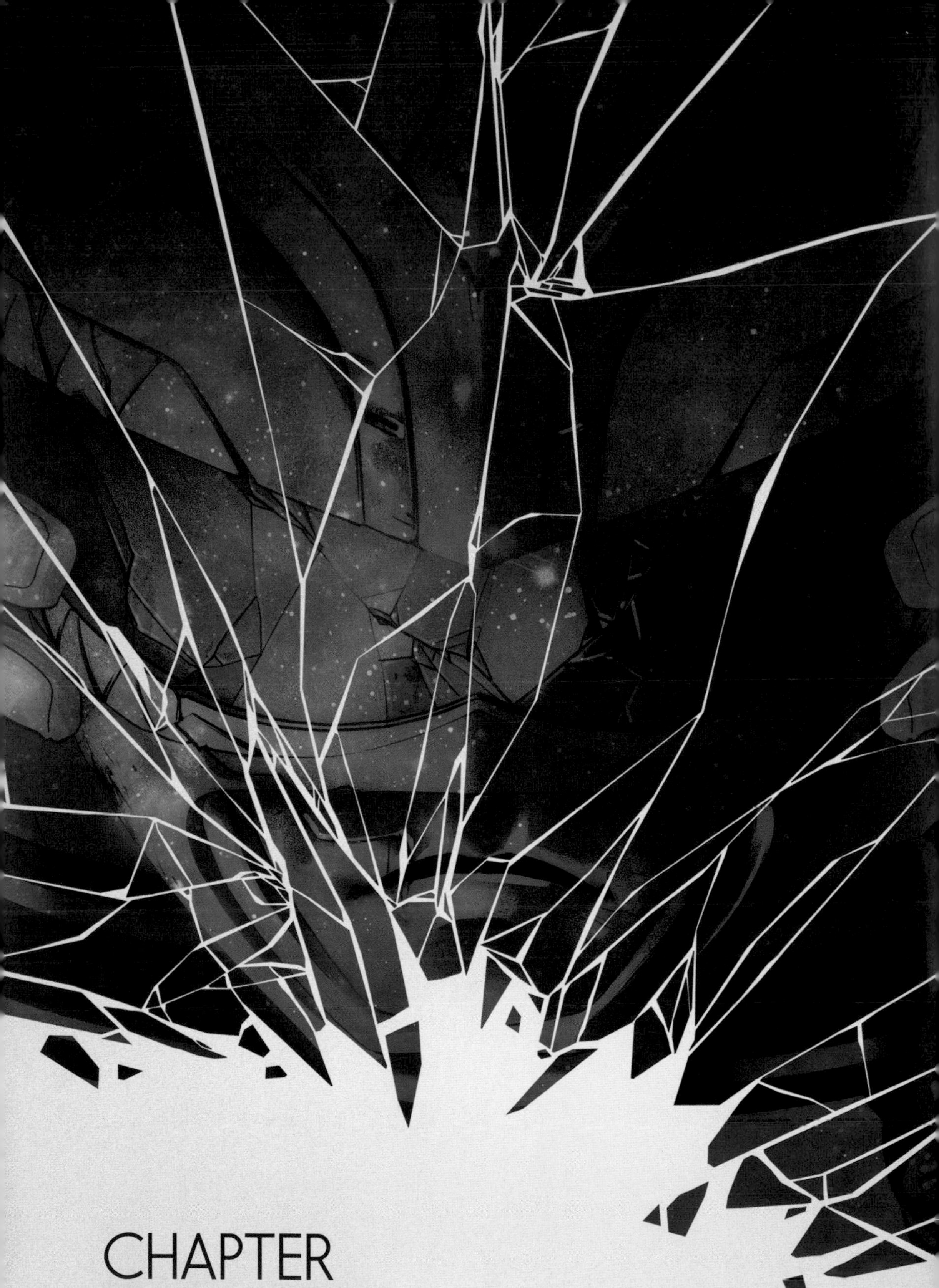

CHAPTER FIVE

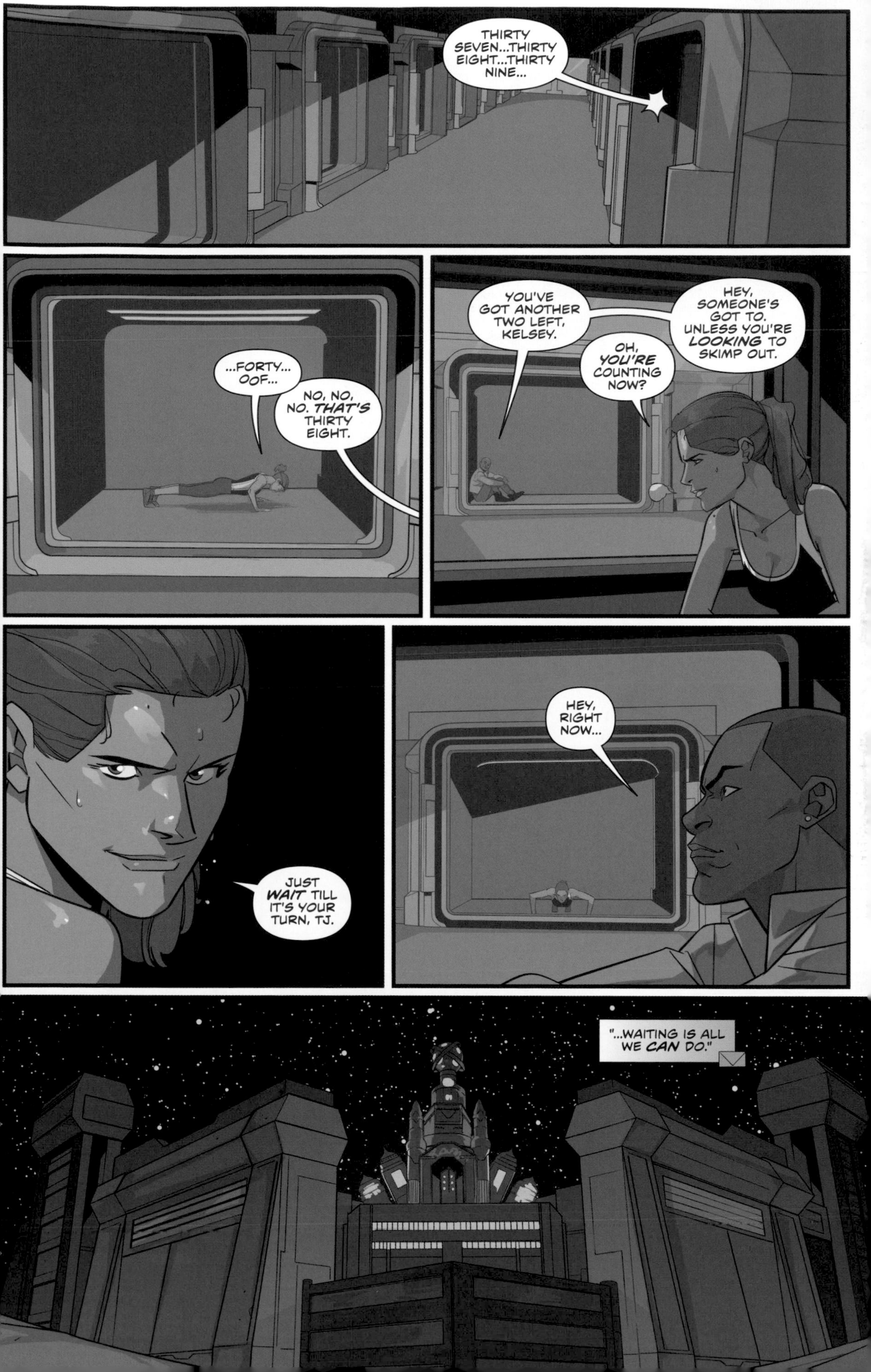
THIRTY SEVEN...THIRTY EIGHT...THIRTY NINE...
...FORTY... OOF...
NO, NO, NO. THAT'S THIRTY EIGHT.
YOU'VE GOT ANOTHER TWO LEFT, KELSEY.
OH, YOU'RE COUNTING NOW?
HEY, SOMEONE'S GOT TO. UNLESS YOU'RE LOOKING TO SKIMP OUT.
JUST WAIT TILL IT'S YOUR TURN, TJ.
HEY, RIGHT NOW...
"...WAITING IS ALL WE CAN DO."

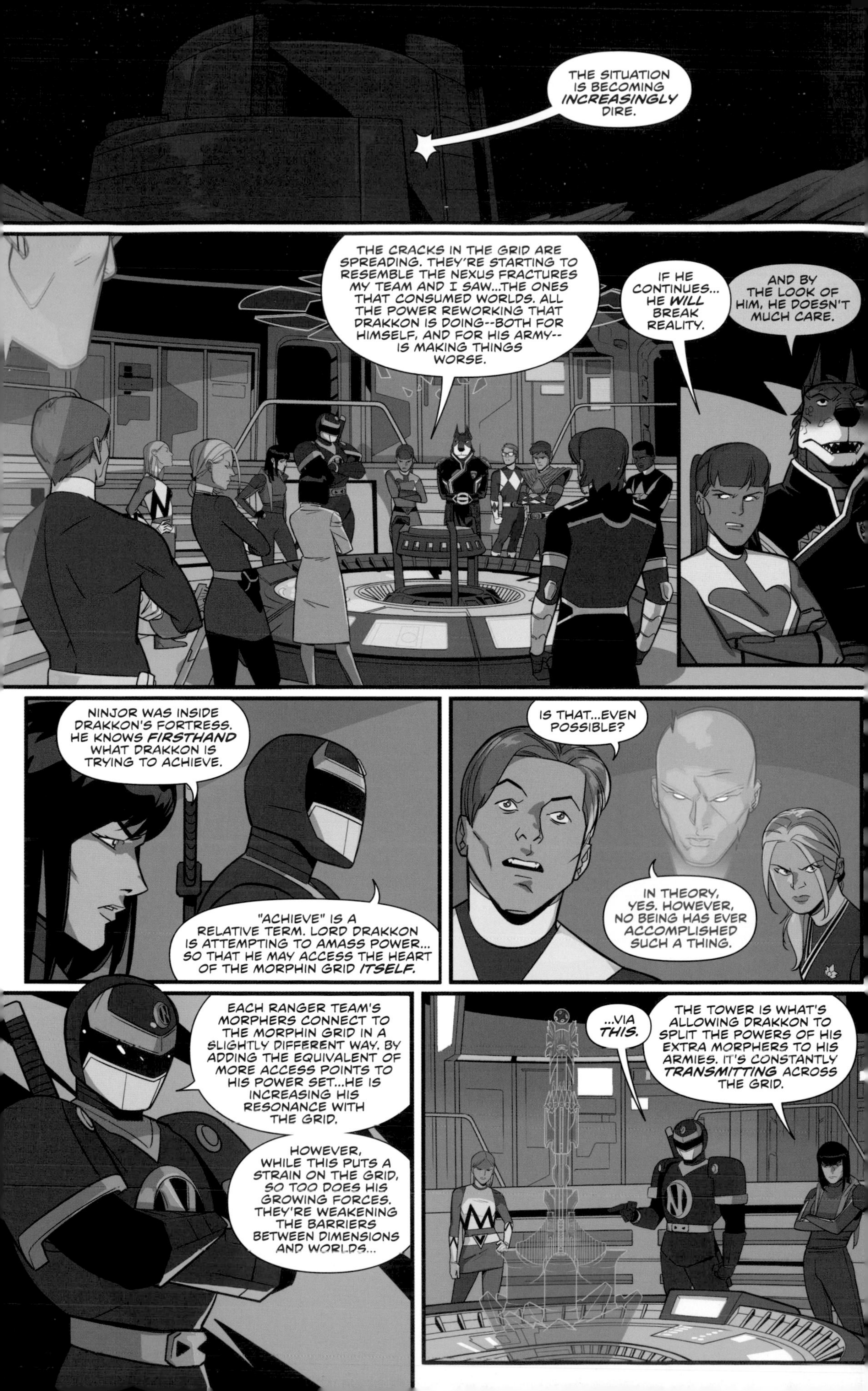
THE SITUATION IS BECOMING *INCREASINGLY* DIRE.
THE CRACKS IN THE GRID ARE SPREADING. THEY'RE STARTING TO RESEMBLE THE NEXUS FRACTURES MY TEAM AND I SAW...THE ONES THAT CONSUMED WORLDS. ALL THE POWER REWORKING THAT DRAKKON IS DOING--BOTH FOR HIMSELF, AND FOR HIS ARMY--IS MAKING THINGS WORSE.
IF HE CONTINUES... HE *WILL* BREAK REALITY.
AND BY THE LOOK OF HIM, HE DOESN'T MUCH CARE.
NINJOR WAS INSIDE DRAKKON'S FORTRESS. HE KNOWS *FIRSTHAND* WHAT DRAKKON IS TRYING TO ACHIEVE.
"ACHIEVE" IS A RELATIVE TERM. LORD DRAKKON IS ATTEMPTING TO AMASS POWER... SO THAT HE MAY ACCESS THE HEART OF THE MORPHIN GRID *ITSELF.*
IS THAT...EVEN POSSIBLE?
IN THEORY, YES. HOWEVER, NO BEING HAS EVER ACCOMPLISHED SUCH A THING.
EACH RANGER TEAM'S MORPHERS CONNECT TO THE MORPHIN GRID IN A SLIGHTLY DIFFERENT WAY. BY ADDING THE EQUIVALENT OF MORE ACCESS POINTS TO HIS POWER SET...HE IS INCREASING HIS RESONANCE WITH THE GRID.
HOWEVER, WHILE THIS PUTS A STRAIN ON THE GRID, SO TOO DOES HIS GROWING FORCES. THEY'RE WEAKENING THE BARRIERS BETWEEN DIMENSIONS AND WORLDS...
...VIA *THIS.*
THE TOWER IS WHAT'S ALLOWING DRAKKON TO SPLIT THE POWERS OF HIS EXTRA MORPHERS TO HIS ARMIES. IT'S CONSTANTLY *TRANSMITTING* ACROSS THE GRID.

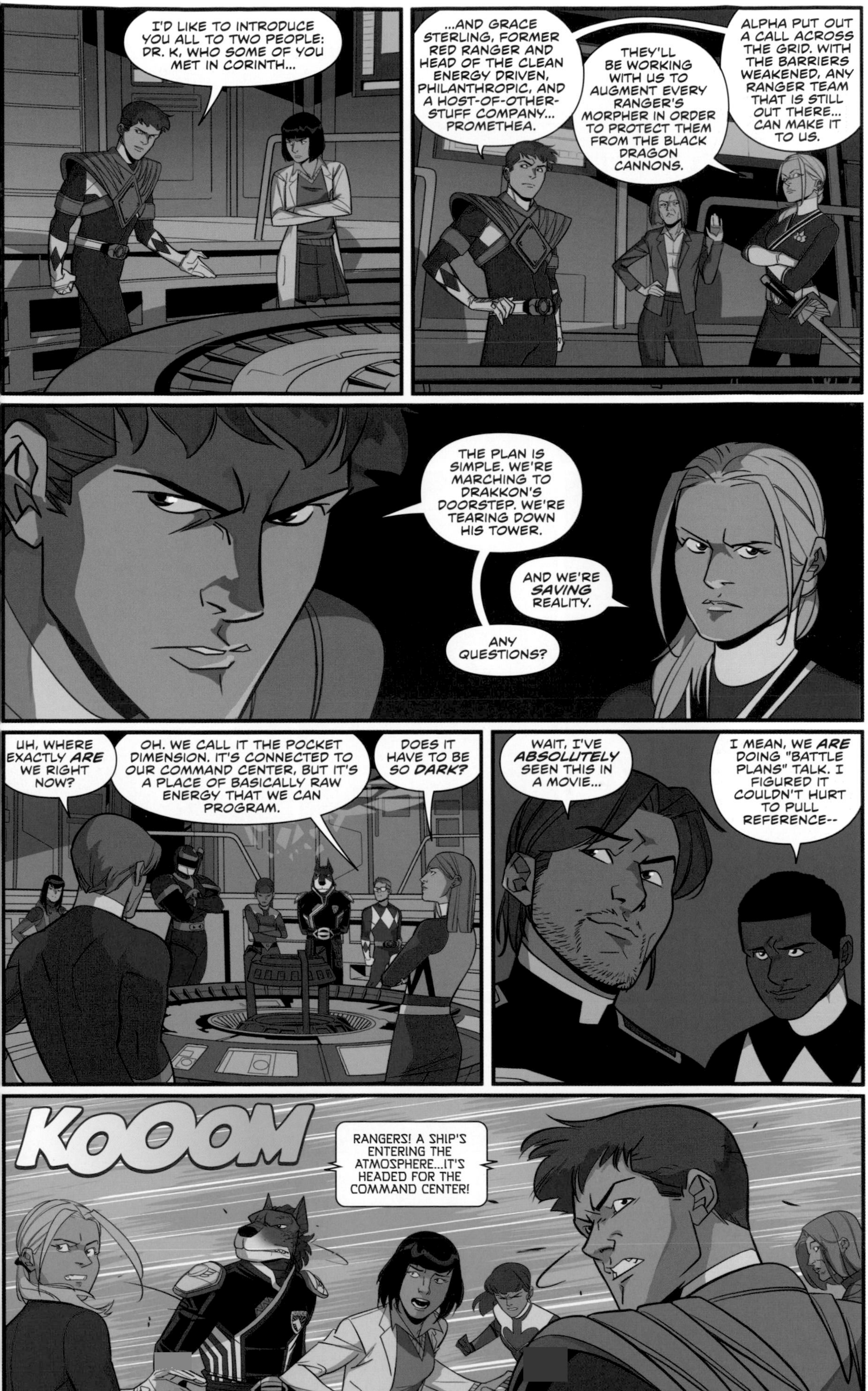

I'D LIKE TO INTRODUCE YOU ALL TO TWO PEOPLE: DR. K, WHO SOME OF YOU MET IN CORINTH...
...AND GRACE STERLING, FORMER RED RANGER AND HEAD OF THE CLEAN ENERGY DRIVEN, PHILANTHROPIC, AND A HOST-OF-OTHER-STUFF COMPANY... PROMETHEA.
THEY'LL BE WORKING WITH US TO AUGMENT EVERY RANGER'S MORPHER IN ORDER TO PROTECT THEM FROM THE BLACK DRAGON CANNONS.
ALPHA PUT OUT A CALL ACROSS THE GRID. WITH THE BARRIERS WEAKENED, ANY RANGER TEAM THAT IS STILL OUT THERE... CAN MAKE IT TO US.
THE PLAN IS SIMPLE. WE'RE MARCHING TO DRAKKON'S DOORSTEP. WE'RE TEARING DOWN HIS TOWER.
AND WE'RE SAVING REALITY.
ANY QUESTIONS?
UH, WHERE EXACTLY ARE WE RIGHT NOW?
OH. WE CALL IT THE POCKET DIMENSION. IT'S CONNECTED TO OUR COMMAND CENTER, BUT IT'S A PLACE OF BASICALLY RAW ENERGY THAT WE CAN PROGRAM.
DOES IT HAVE TO BE SO DARK?
WAIT, I'VE ABSOLUTELY SEEN THIS IN A MOVIE...
I MEAN, WE ARE DOING "BATTLE PLANS" TALK. I FIGURED IT COULDN'T HURT TO PULL REFERENCE--
KOOOM
RANGERS! A SHIP'S ENTERING THE ATMOSPHERE...IT'S HEADED FOR THE COMMAND CENTER!

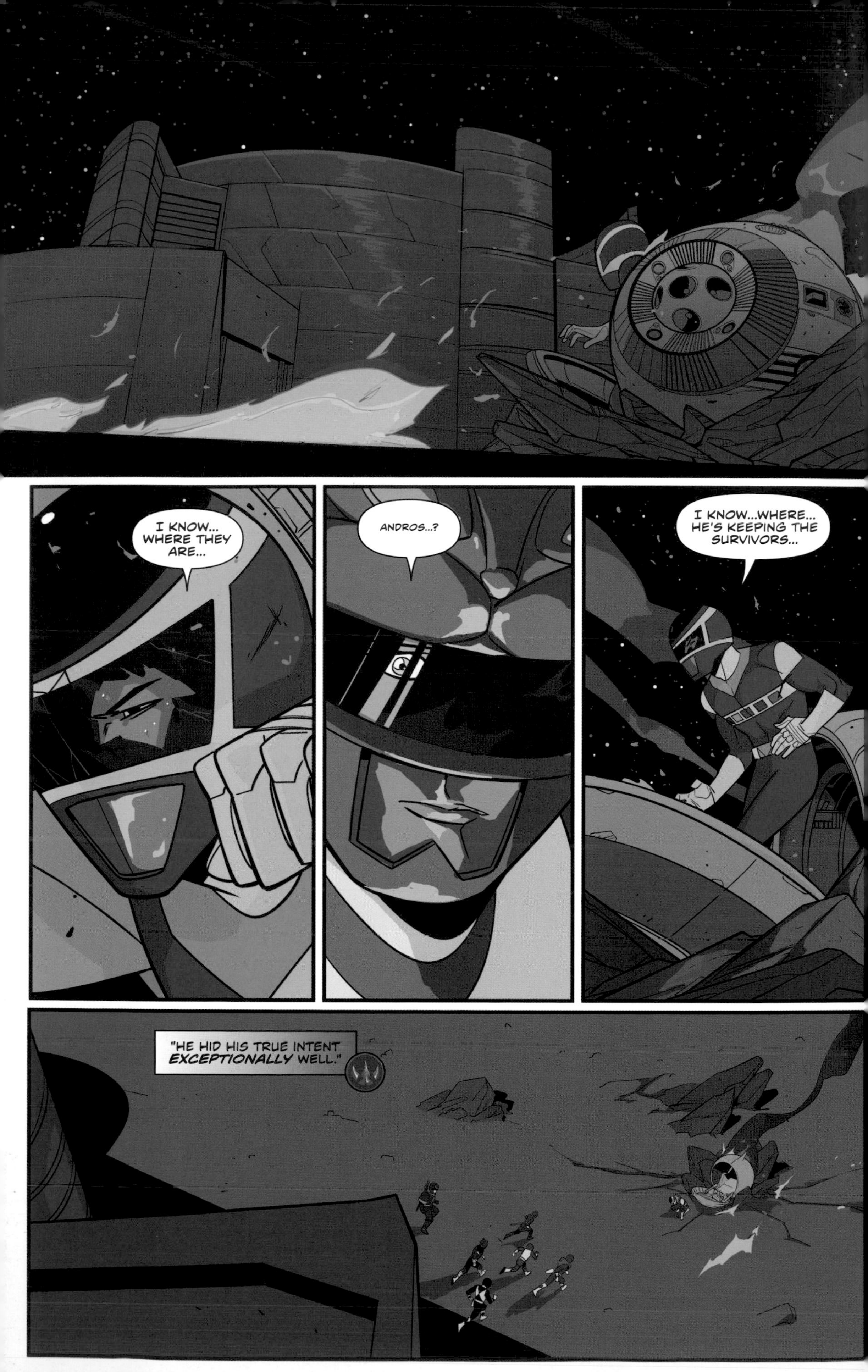
I KNOW... WHERE THEY ARE...
ANDROS...?
I KNOW...WHERE... HE'S KEEPING THE SURVIVORS...
"HE HID HIS TRUE INTENT *EXCEPTIONALLY* WELL."

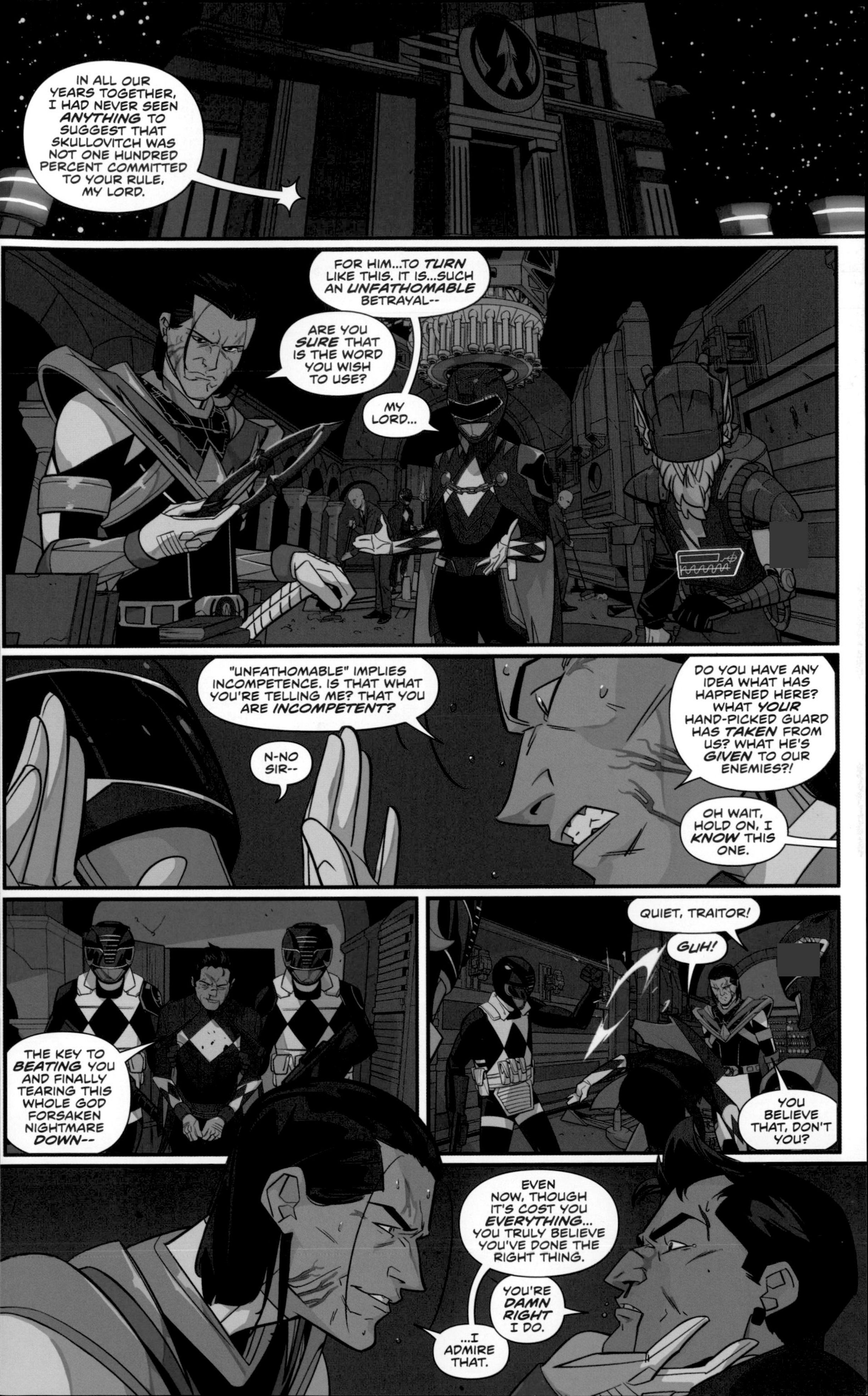
IN ALL OUR YEARS TOGETHER, I HAD NEVER SEEN ANYTHING TO SUGGEST THAT SKULLOVITCH WAS NOT ONE HUNDRED PERCENT COMMITTED TO YOUR RULE, MY LORD.
FOR HIM...TO TURN LIKE THIS. IT IS...SUCH AN UNFATHOMABLE BETRAYAL--
ARE YOU SURE THAT IS THE WORD YOU WISH TO USE?
MY LORD...
"UNFATHOMABLE" IMPLIES INCOMPETENCE. IS THAT WHAT YOU'RE TELLING ME? THAT YOU ARE INCOMPETENT?
N-NO SIR--
DO YOU HAVE ANY IDEA WHAT HAS HAPPENED HERE? WHAT YOUR HAND-PICKED GUARD HAS TAKEN FROM US? WHAT HE'S GIVEN TO OUR ENEMIES?!
OH WAIT, HOLD ON, I KNOW THIS ONE.
THE KEY TO BEATING YOU AND FINALLY TEARING THIS WHOLE GOD FORSAKEN NIGHTMARE DOWN--
QUIET, TRAITOR!
GUH!
YOU BELIEVE THAT, DON'T YOU?
EVEN NOW, THOUGH IT'S COST YOU EVERYTHING... YOU TRULY BELIEVE YOU'VE DONE THE RIGHT THING.
YOU'RE DAMN RIGHT I DO.
...I ADMIRE THAT.

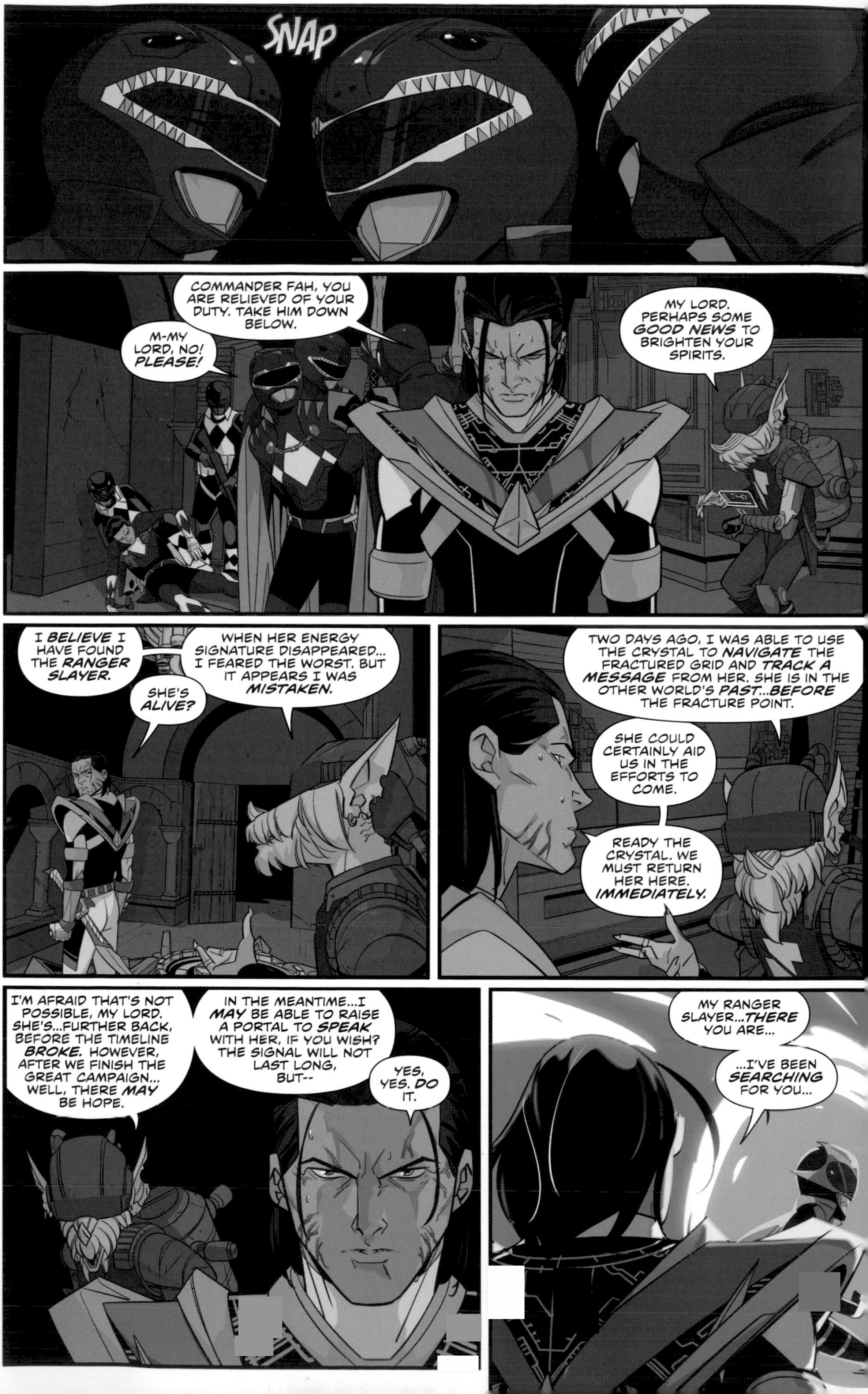
SNAP
M-MY LORD, NO! PLEASE!
COMMANDER FAH, YOU ARE RELIEVED OF YOUR DUTY. TAKE HIM DOWN BELOW.
MY LORD. PERHAPS SOME GOOD NEWS TO BRIGHTEN YOUR SPIRITS.
I BELIEVE I HAVE FOUND THE RANGER SLAYER.
SHE'S ALIVE?
WHEN HER ENERGY SIGNATURE DISAPPEARED... I FEARED THE WORST. BUT IT APPEARS I WAS MISTAKEN.
TWO DAYS AGO, I WAS ABLE TO USE THE CRYSTAL TO NAVIGATE THE FRACTURED GRID AND TRACK A MESSAGE FROM HER. SHE IS IN THE OTHER WORLD'S PAST...BEFORE THE FRACTURE POINT.
SHE COULD CERTAINLY AID US IN THE EFFORTS TO COME.
READY THE CRYSTAL. WE MUST RETURN HER HERE. IMMEDIATELY.
I'M AFRAID THAT'S NOT POSSIBLE, MY LORD. SHE'S...FURTHER BACK, BEFORE THE TIMELINE BROKE. HOWEVER, AFTER WE FINISH THE GREAT CAMPAIGN... WELL, THERE MAY BE HOPE.
IN THE MEANTIME...I MAY BE ABLE TO RAISE A PORTAL TO SPEAK WITH HER, IF YOU WISH? THE SIGNAL WILL NOT LAST LONG, BUT--
YES, YES. DO IT.
MY RANGER SLAYER...THERE YOU ARE...
...I'VE BEEN SEARCHING FOR YOU...

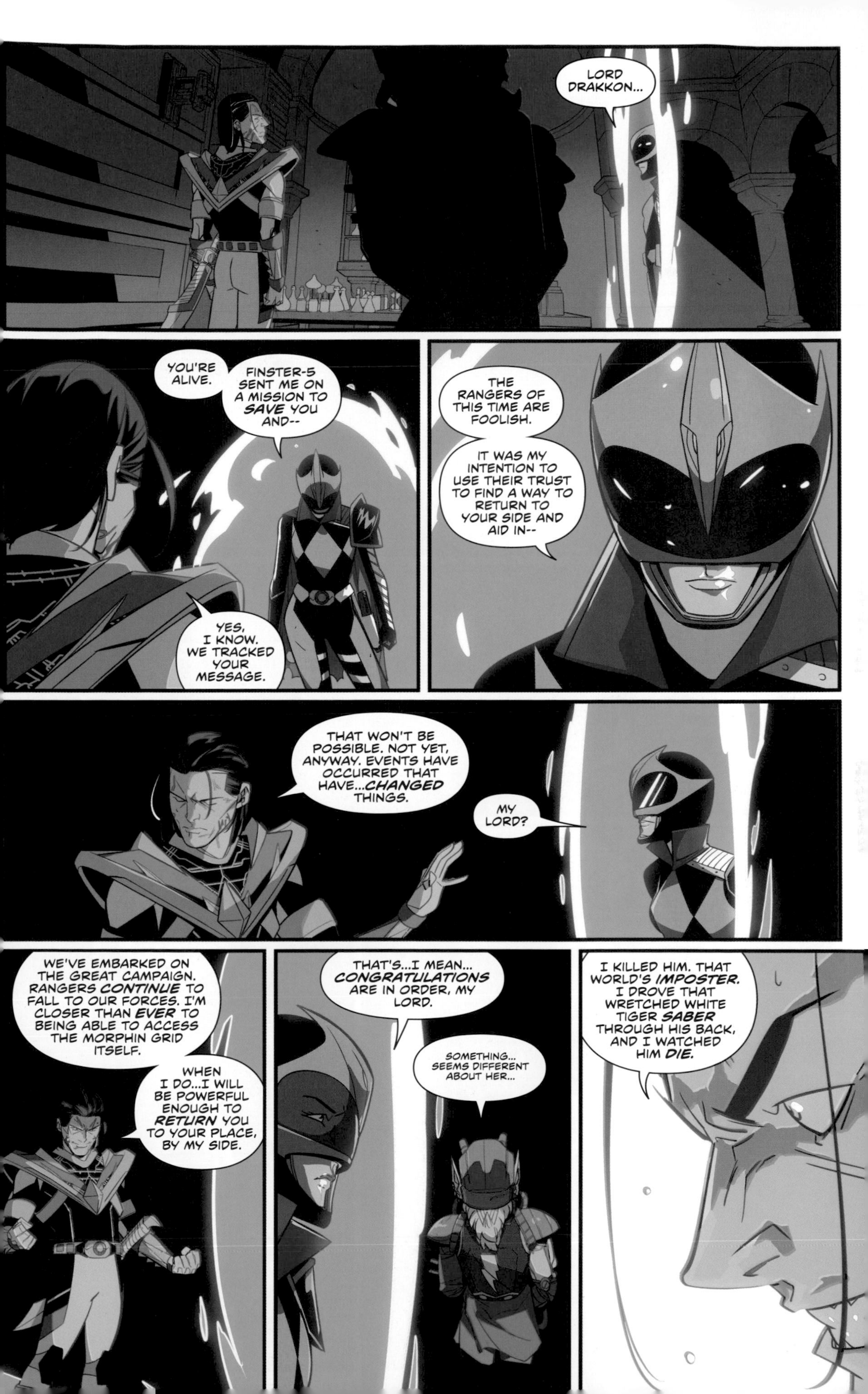

LORD DRAKKON...
YOU'RE ALIVE.
FINSTER-5 SENT ME ON A MISSION TO SAVE YOU AND--
YES, I KNOW. WE TRACKED YOUR MESSAGE.
THE RANGERS OF THIS TIME ARE FOOLISH.
IT WAS MY INTENTION TO USE THEIR TRUST TO FIND A WAY TO RETURN TO YOUR SIDE AND AID IN--
THAT WON'T BE POSSIBLE. NOT YET, ANYWAY. EVENTS HAVE OCCURRED THAT HAVE...CHANGED THINGS.
MY LORD?
WE'VE EMBARKED ON THE GREAT CAMPAIGN. RANGERS CONTINUE TO FALL TO OUR FORCES. I'M CLOSER THAN EVER TO BEING ABLE TO ACCESS THE MORPHIN GRID ITSELF.
WHEN I DO...I WILL BE POWERFUL ENOUGH TO RETURN YOU TO YOUR PLACE, BY MY SIDE.
THAT'S...I MEAN... CONGRATULATIONS ARE IN ORDER, MY LORD.
SOMETHING... SEEMS DIFFERENT ABOUT HER...
I KILLED HIM. THAT WORLD'S IMPOSTER. I DROVE THAT WRETCHED WHITE TIGER SABER THROUGH HIS BACK, AND I WATCHED HIM DIE.

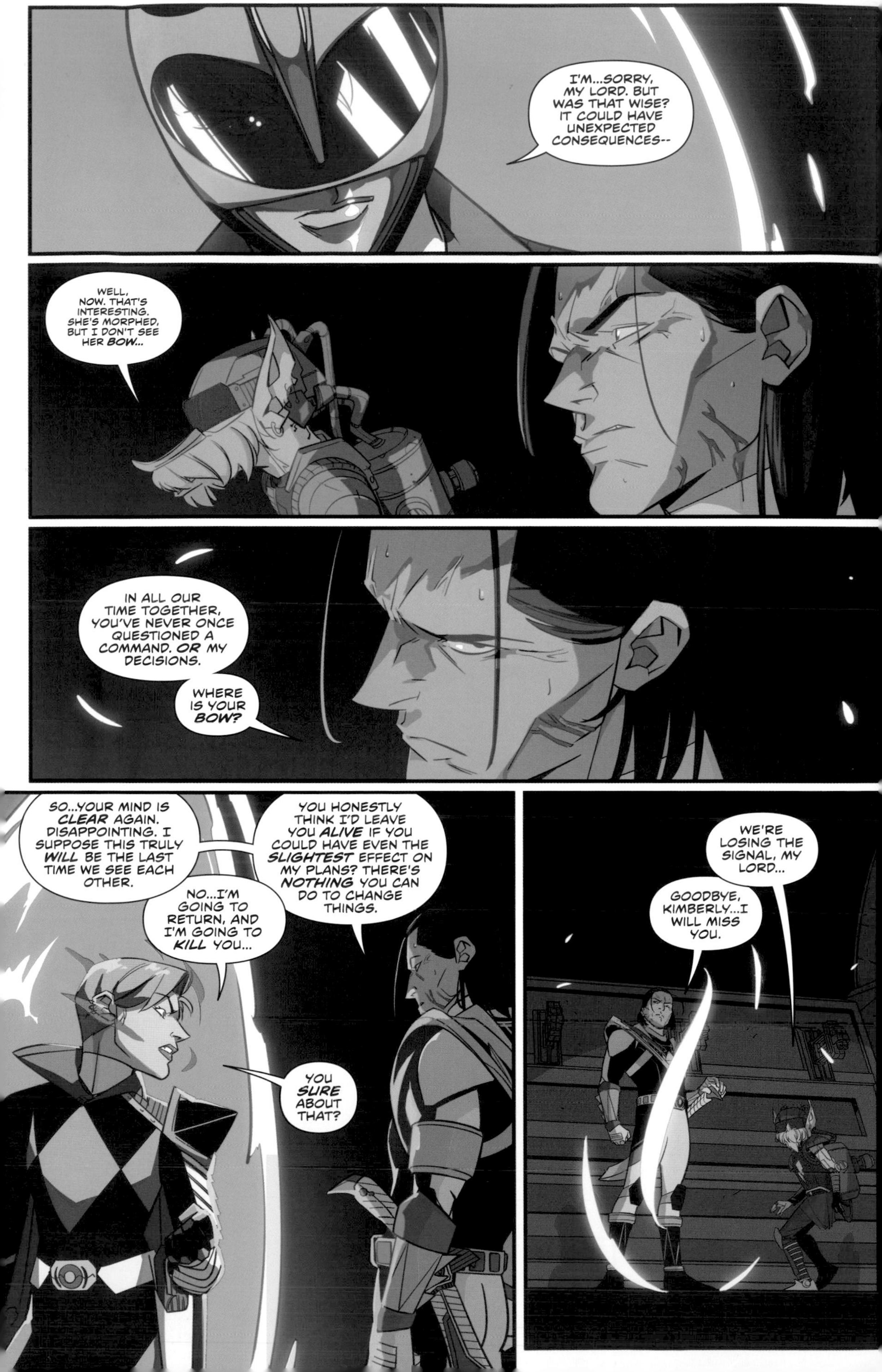
I'M...SORRY, MY LORD. BUT WAS THAT WISE? IT COULD HAVE UNEXPECTED CONSEQUENCES--
WELL, NOW. THAT'S INTERESTING. SHE'S MORPHED, BUT I DON'T SEE HER BOW...
IN ALL OUR TIME TOGETHER, YOU'VE NEVER ONCE QUESTIONED A COMMAND. OR MY DECISIONS.
WHERE IS YOUR BOW?
SO...YOUR MIND IS CLEAR AGAIN. DISAPPOINTING. I SUPPOSE THIS TRULY WILL BE THE LAST TIME WE SEE EACH OTHER.
NO...I'M GOING TO RETURN, AND I'M GOING TO KILL YOU...
YOU HONESTLY THINK I'D LEAVE YOU ALIVE IF YOU COULD HAVE EVEN THE SLIGHTEST EFFECT ON MY PLANS? THERE'S NOTHING YOU CAN DO TO CHANGE THINGS.
YOU SURE ABOUT THAT?
WE'RE LOSING THE SIGNAL, MY LORD...
GOODBYE, KIMBERLY...I WILL MISS YOU.

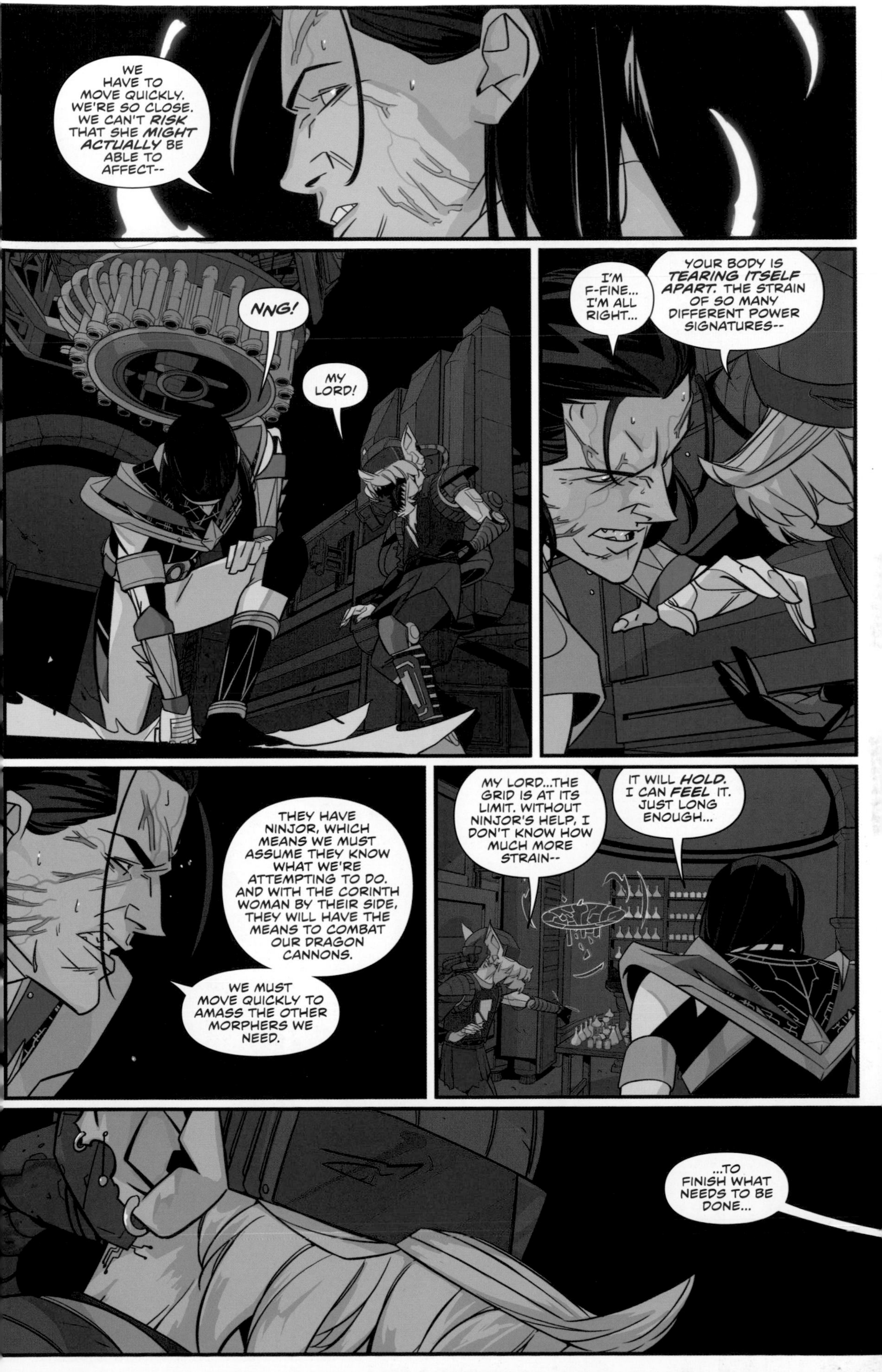

WE HAVE TO MOVE QUICKLY. WE'RE SO CLOSE. WE CAN'T RISK THAT SHE MIGHT ACTUALLY BE ABLE TO AFFECT--
NNG!
MY LORD!
I'M F-FINE... I'M ALL RIGHT...
YOUR BODY IS TEARING ITSELF APART. THE STRAIN OF SO MANY DIFFERENT POWER SIGNATURES--
THEY HAVE NINJOR, WHICH MEANS WE MUST ASSUME THEY KNOW WHAT WE'RE ATTEMPTING TO DO. AND WITH THE CORINTH WOMAN BY THEIR SIDE, THEY WILL HAVE THE MEANS TO COMBAT OUR DRAGON CANNONS.
WE MUST MOVE QUICKLY TO AMASS THE OTHER MORPHERS WE NEED.
MY LORD...THE GRID IS AT ITS LIMIT. WITHOUT NINJOR'S HELP, I DON'T KNOW HOW MUCH MORE STRAIN--
IT WILL HOLD. I CAN FEEL IT. JUST LONG ENOUGH...
...TO FINISH WHAT NEEDS TO BE DONE...

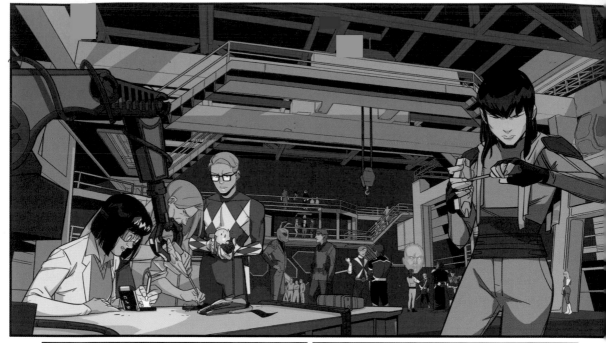

MY TEAM...HAD BEEN WAITING ON A CONTACT, WHO HAD INTEL ON *ASTRONEMA'S* LOCATION.

BUT THEN...OUR SHIP WAS *BOARDED.* BY THIS "LORD DRAKKON."

THEY...FELL, ONE BY ONE. BUT...TJ...IS *STILL ALIVE.* DRAKKON *TOOK* HIM, FOR SOME REASON. AS THE BARRIERS BETWEEN DIMENSIONS WEAKENED, I WAS ABLE TO TRACK HIS LOCATION-- DRAKKON IS HOLDING HIM, AND THE *OTHER* RANGERS HE *CAPTURED,* ON THE *MOON.*

WE MUST GET THEM BACK...

...HE'S THE ONLY FAMILY I HAVE *LEFT.*

YOU HAVEN'T SPOKEN TO HIM YET, HAVE YOU?

WHAT?

YOUR BROTHER.

I...DON'T KNOW WHAT I WOULD SAY. I...DON'T KNOW HOW TO TELL HIM WHO I AM.

WELL, YOU MAY JUST HAVE TO WING IT.

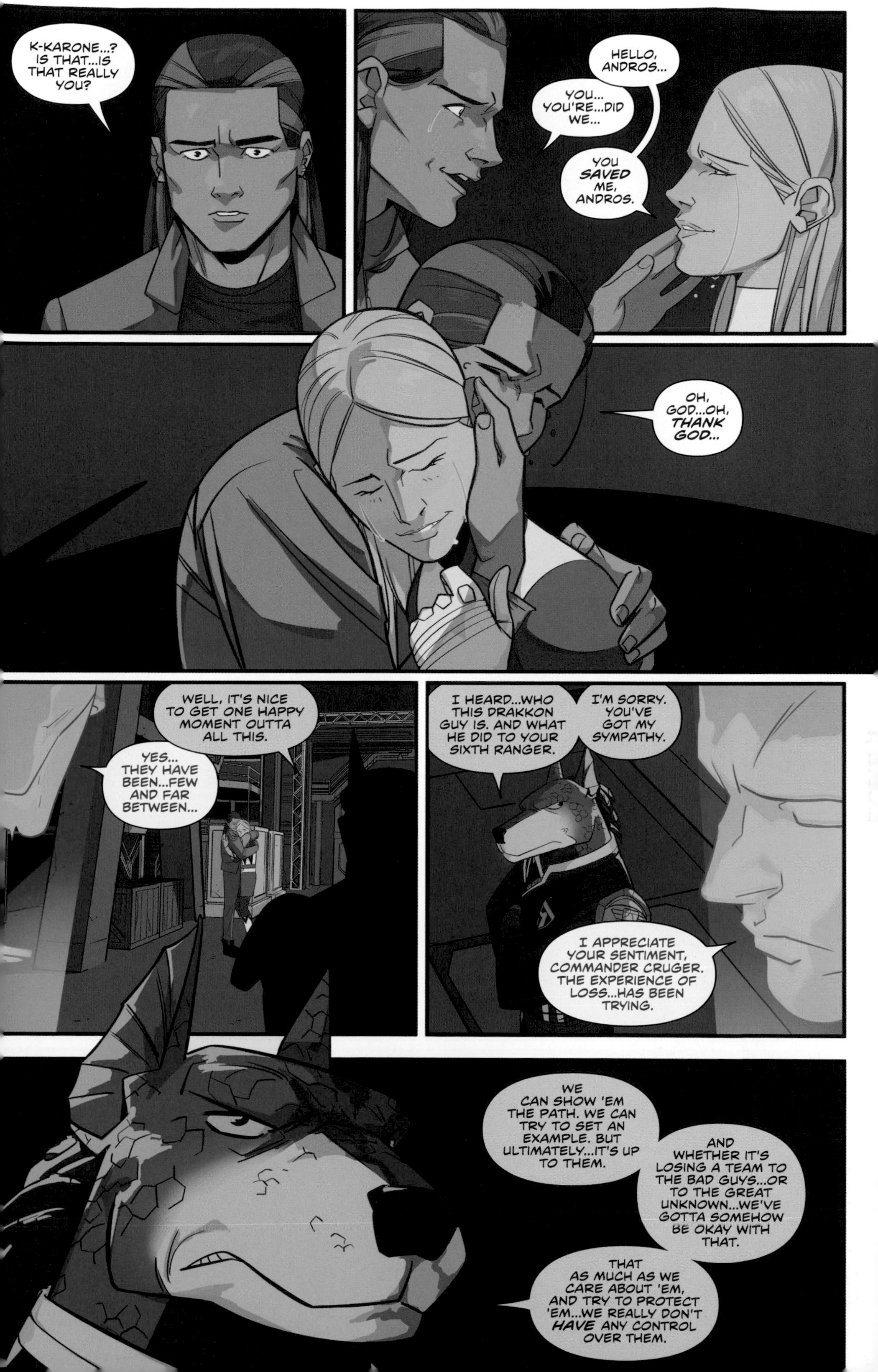
K-KARONE...? IS THAT...IS THAT REALLY YOU?
HELLO, ANDROS...
YOU... YOU'RE...DID WE...
YOU SAVED ME, ANDROS.
OH, GOD...OH, THANK GOD...
WELL, IT'S NICE TO GET ONE HAPPY MOMENT OUTTA ALL THIS.
YES... THEY HAVE BEEN...FEW AND FAR BETWEEN...
I HEARD...WHO THIS DRAKKON GUY IS. AND WHAT HE DID TO YOUR SIXTH RANGER.
I'M SORRY. YOU'VE GOT MY SYMPATHY.
I APPRECIATE YOUR SENTIMENT, COMMANDER CRUGER. THE EXPERIENCE OF LOSS...HAS BEEN TRYING.
WE CAN SHOW 'EM THE PATH. WE CAN TRY TO SET AN EXAMPLE. BUT ULTIMATELY...IT'S UP TO THEM.
AND WHETHER IT'S LOSING A TEAM TO THE BAD GUYS...OR TO THE GREAT UNKNOWN...WE'VE GOTTA SOMEHOW BE OKAY WITH THAT.
THAT AS MUCH AS WE CARE ABOUT 'EM, AND TRY TO PROTECT 'EM...WE REALLY DON'T HAVE ANY CONTROL OVER THEM.

...NO, COMMANDER. WE DO NOT.

BUT SOMETIMES, IF WE'RE LUCKY...I BELIEVE THEY LEARN AND GROW THE MOST...

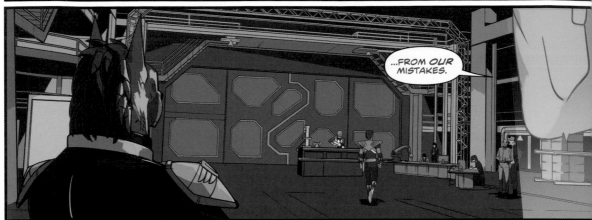

...FROM *OUR* MISTAKES.

I WASN'T SURE IF YOU'D COME.

REALITY'S AT RISK. SEEMED PRETTY IMPORTANT. ALTHOUGH...

...I WASN'T SURE YOU WOULD *CALL.*

LIKE YOU SAID...REALITY'S AT RISK.

AND...WELL... ZORDON SAID SOMETHING TO ME. BEFORE EVERYTHING WITH SABA.

THAT ONE DAY I MIGHT KNOW WHAT IT'S *LIKE* TO MAKE THE WRONG DECISION, FOR THE RIGHT REASONS. I DIDN'T REALLY UNDERSTAND WHAT HE MEANT.

BUT I THINK...I DO NOW.

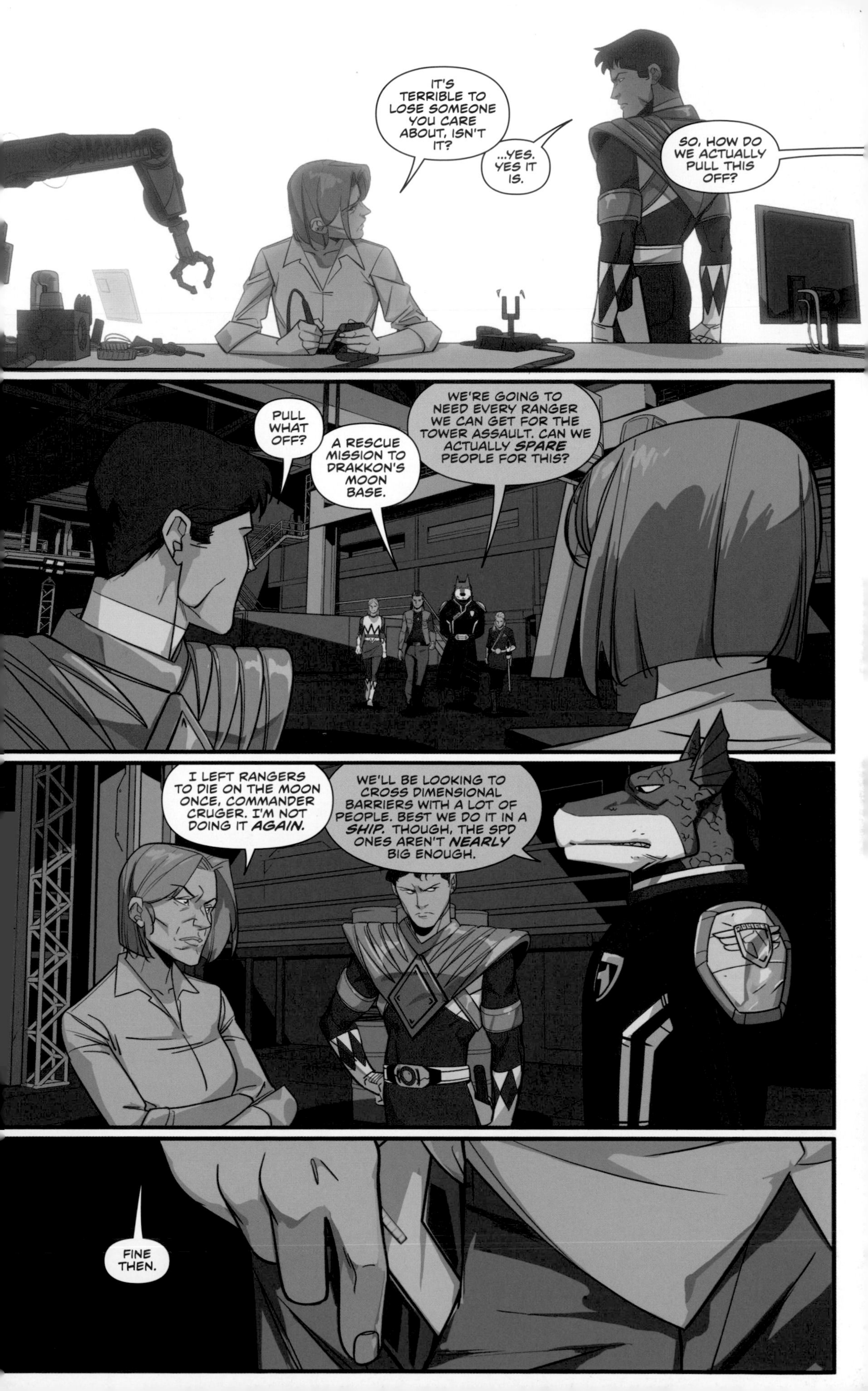
IT'S TERRIBLE TO LOSE SOMEONE YOU CARE ABOUT, ISN'T IT?
...YES. YES IT IS.
SO, HOW DO WE ACTUALLY PULL THIS OFF?
PULL WHAT OFF?
A RESCUE MISSION TO DRAKKON'S MOON BASE.
WE'RE GOING TO NEED EVERY RANGER WE CAN GET FOR THE TOWER ASSAULT. CAN WE ACTUALLY SPARE PEOPLE FOR THIS?
I LEFT RANGERS TO DIE ON THE MOON ONCE, COMMANDER CRUGER. I'M NOT DOING IT AGAIN.
WE'LL BE LOOKING TO CROSS DIMENSIONAL BARRIERS WITH A LOT OF PEOPLE. BEST WE DO IT IN A SHIP. THOUGH, THE SPD ONES AREN'T NEARLY BIG ENOUGH.
FINE THEN.

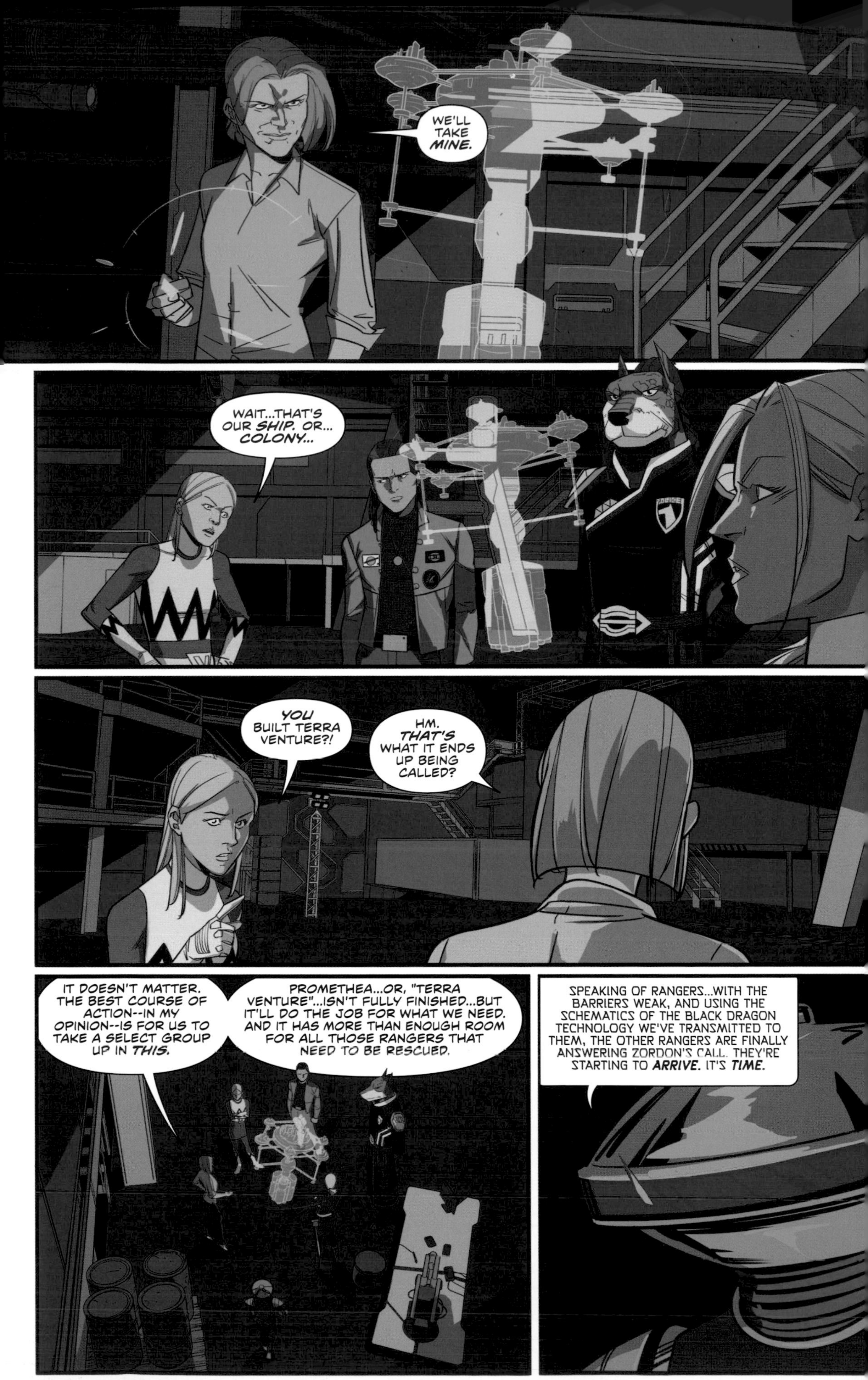
WE'LL TAKE MINE.
WAIT...THAT'S OUR SHIP. OR... COLONY...
YOU BUILT TERRA VENTURE?!
HM. THAT'S WHAT IT ENDS UP BEING CALLED?
IT DOESN'T MATTER. THE BEST COURSE OF ACTION--IN MY OPINION--IS FOR US TO TAKE A SELECT GROUP UP IN THIS.
PROMETHEA...OR, "TERRA VENTURE"...ISN'T FULLY FINISHED...BUT IT'LL DO THE JOB FOR WHAT WE NEED. AND IT HAS MORE THAN ENOUGH ROOM FOR ALL THOSE RANGERS THAT NEED TO BE RESCUED.
SPEAKING OF RANGERS...WITH THE BARRIERS WEAK, AND USING THE SCHEMATICS OF THE BLACK DRAGON TECHNOLOGY WE'VE TRANSMITTED TO THEM, THE OTHER RANGERS ARE FINALLY ANSWERING ZORDON'S CALL. THEY'RE STARTING TO ARRIVE. IT'S TIME.

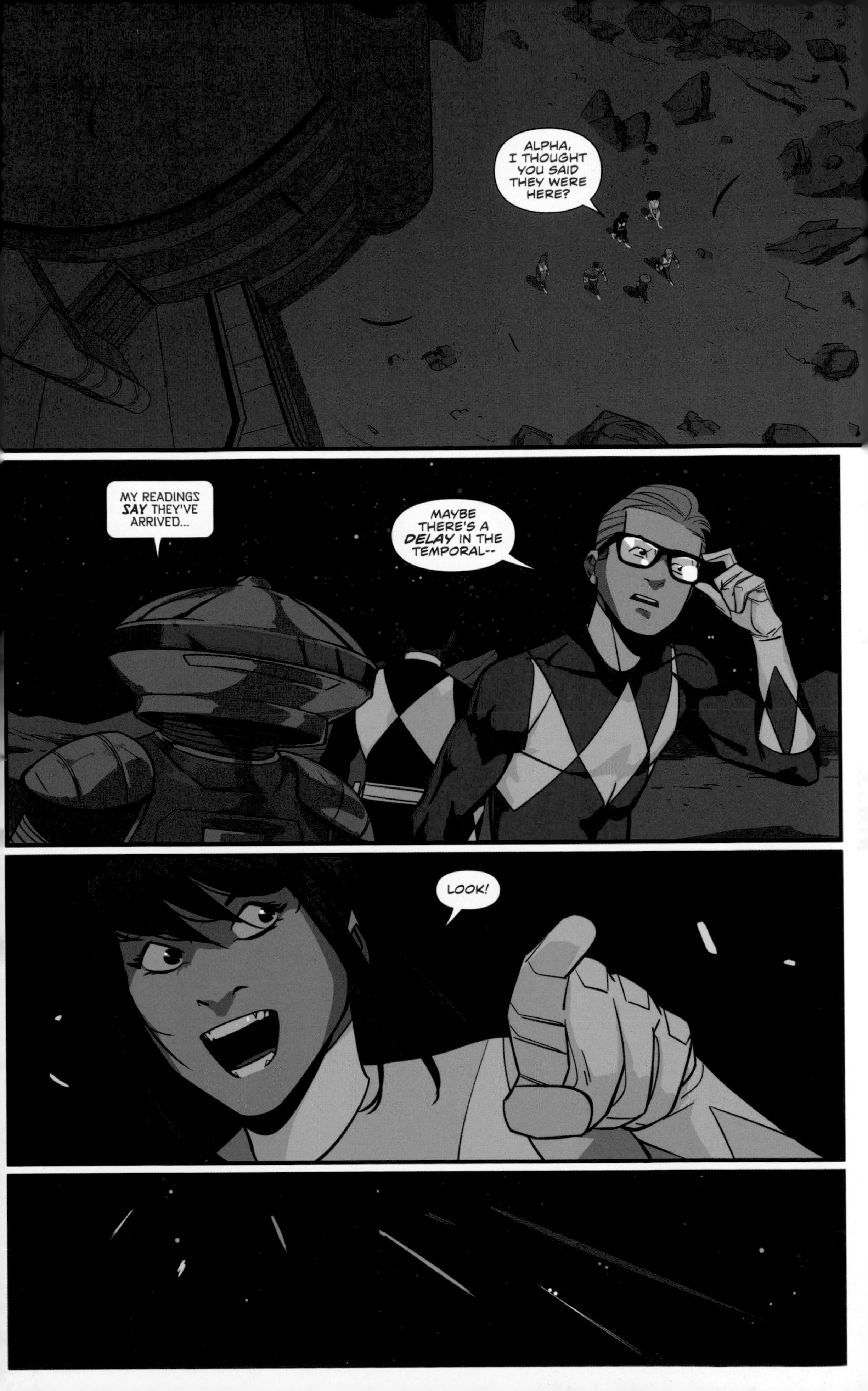
ALPHA, I THOUGHT YOU SAID THEY WERE HERE?
MY READINGS **SAY** THEY'VE ARRIVED...
MAYBE THERE'S A **DELAY** IN THE TEMPORAL--
LOOK!

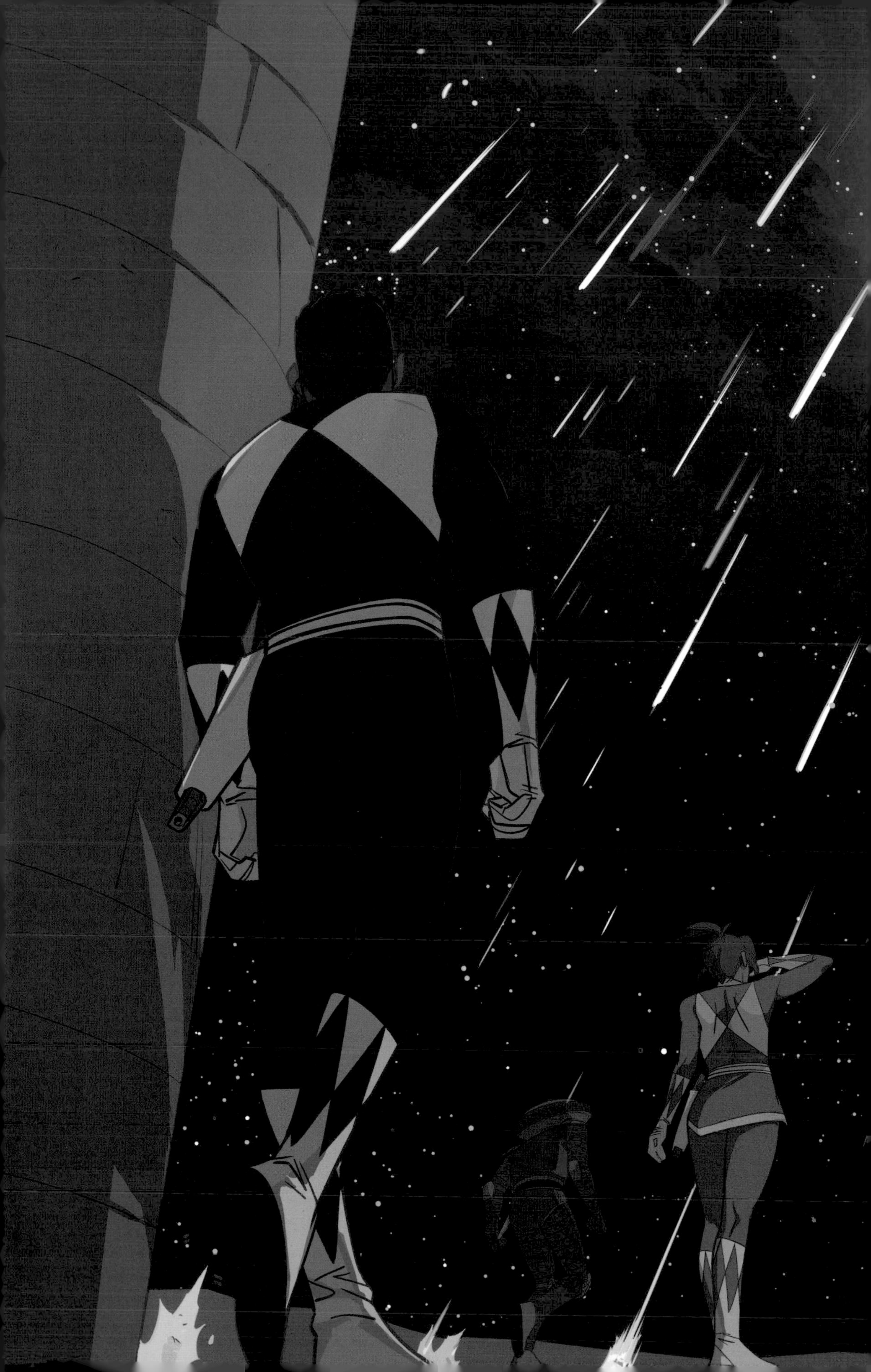

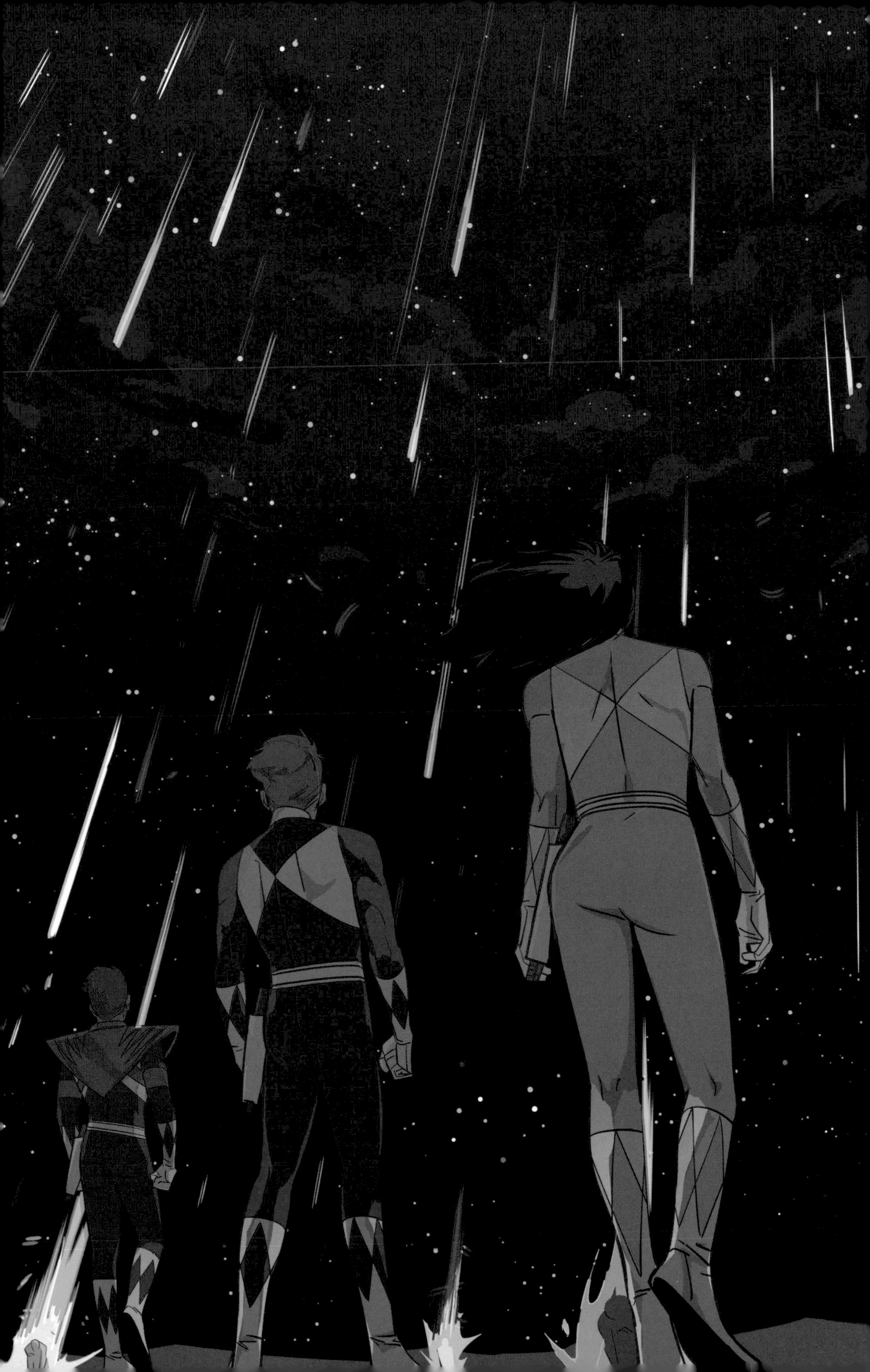

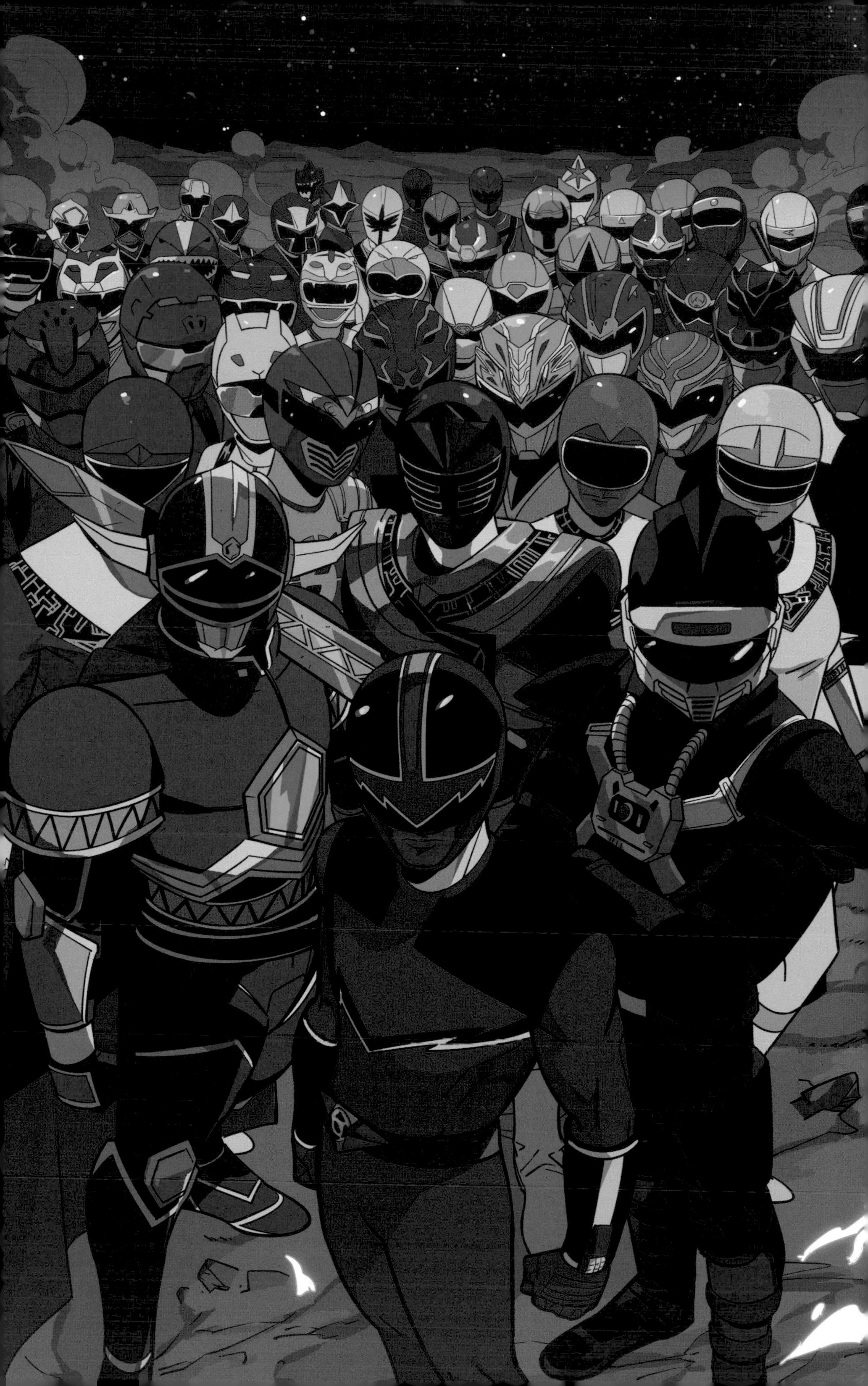

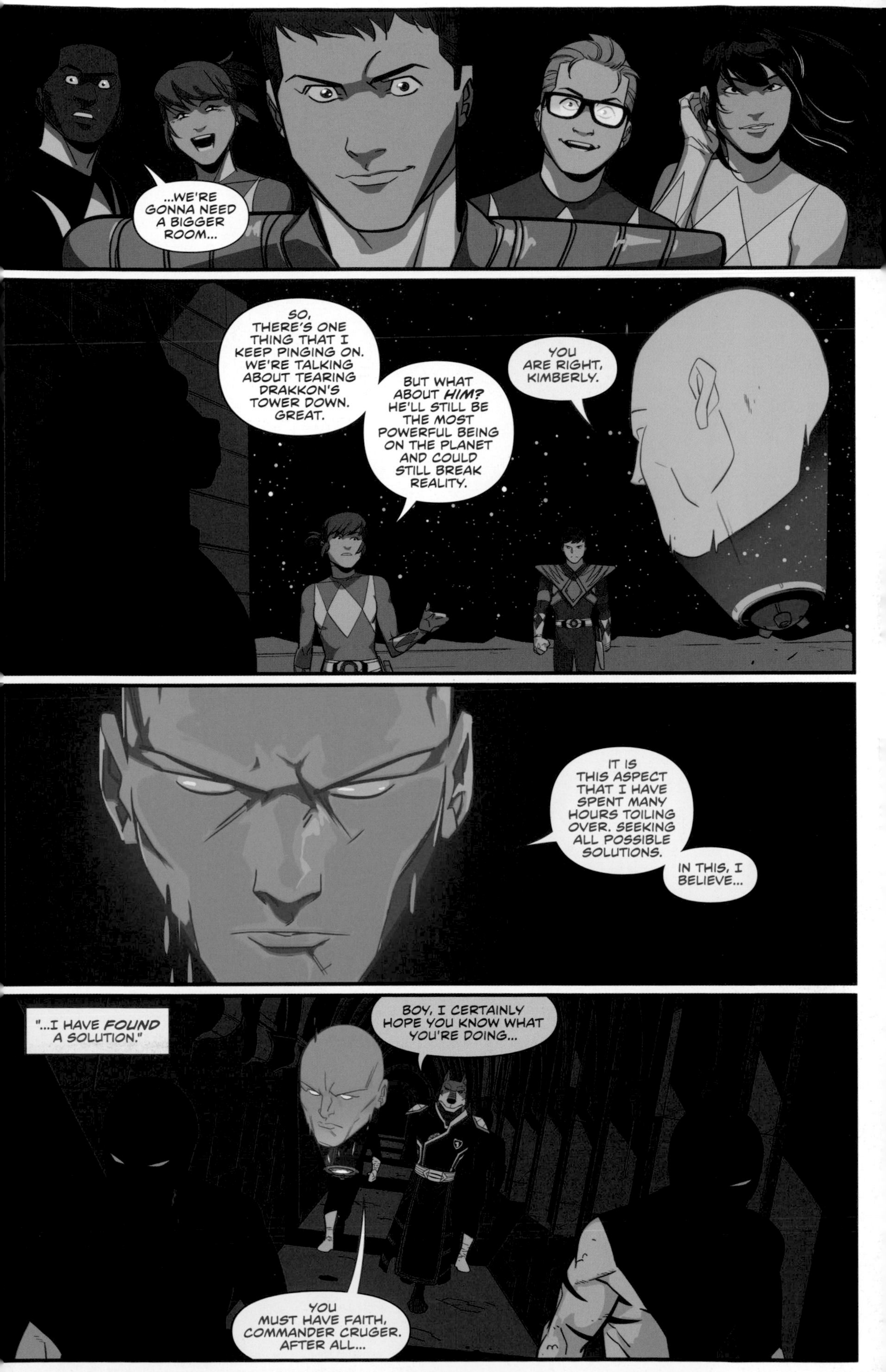
...WE'RE GONNA NEED A BIGGER ROOM...
SO, THERE'S ONE THING THAT I KEEP PINGING ON. WE'RE TALKING ABOUT TEARING DRAKKON'S TOWER DOWN. GREAT.
BUT WHAT ABOUT *HIM?* HE'LL STILL BE THE MOST POWERFUL BEING ON THE PLANET AND COULD STILL BREAK REALITY.
YOU ARE RIGHT, KIMBERLY.
IT IS THIS ASPECT THAT I HAVE SPENT MANY HOURS TOILING OVER. SEEKING ALL POSSIBLE SOLUTIONS.
IN THIS, I BELIEVE...
"...I HAVE *FOUND* A SOLUTION."
BOY, I CERTAINLY HOPE YOU KNOW WHAT YOU'RE DOING...
YOU MUST HAVE FAITH, COMMANDER CRUGER. AFTER ALL...

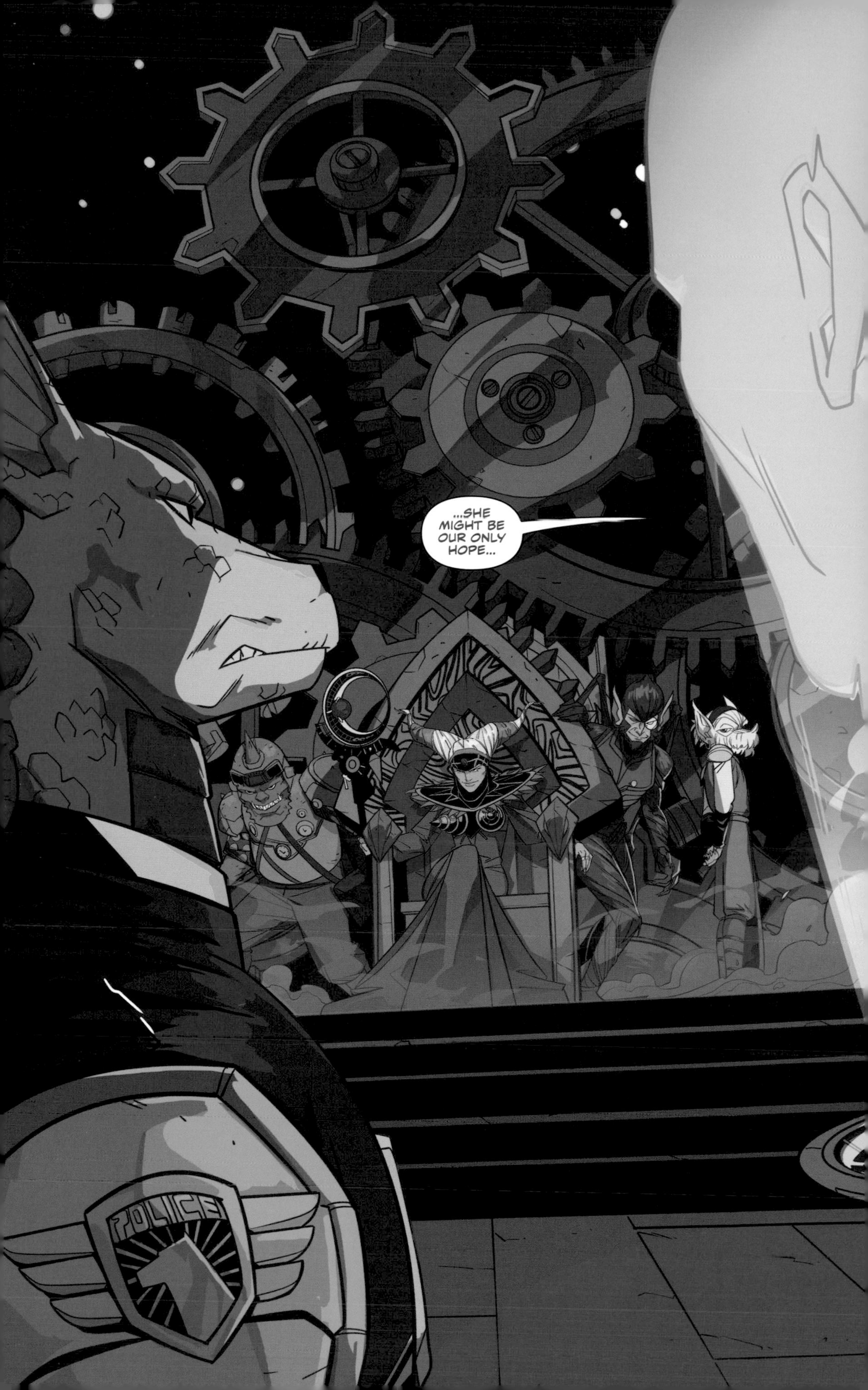
...SHE MIGHT BE OUR ONLY HOPE...
POLICE

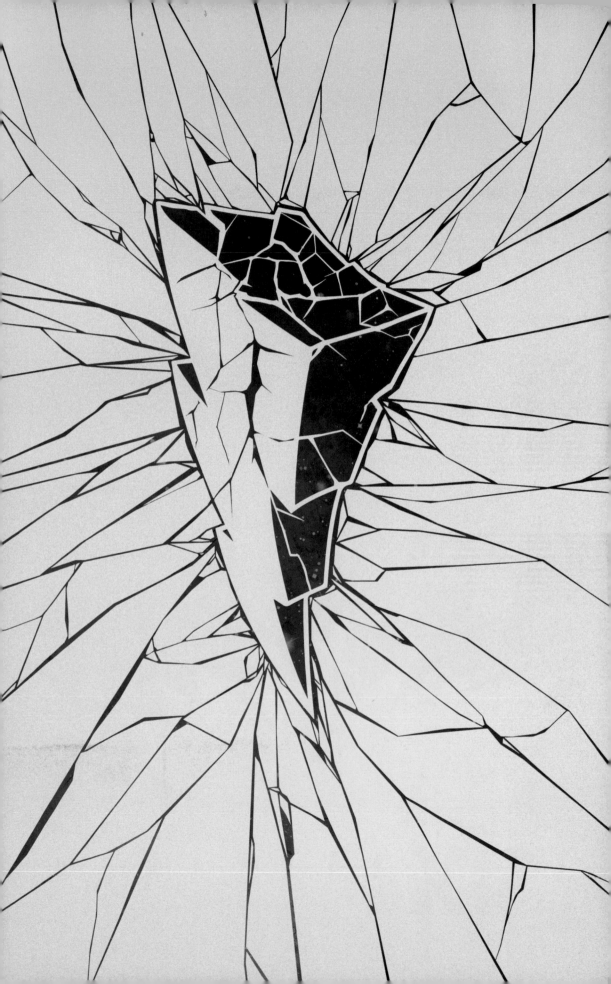

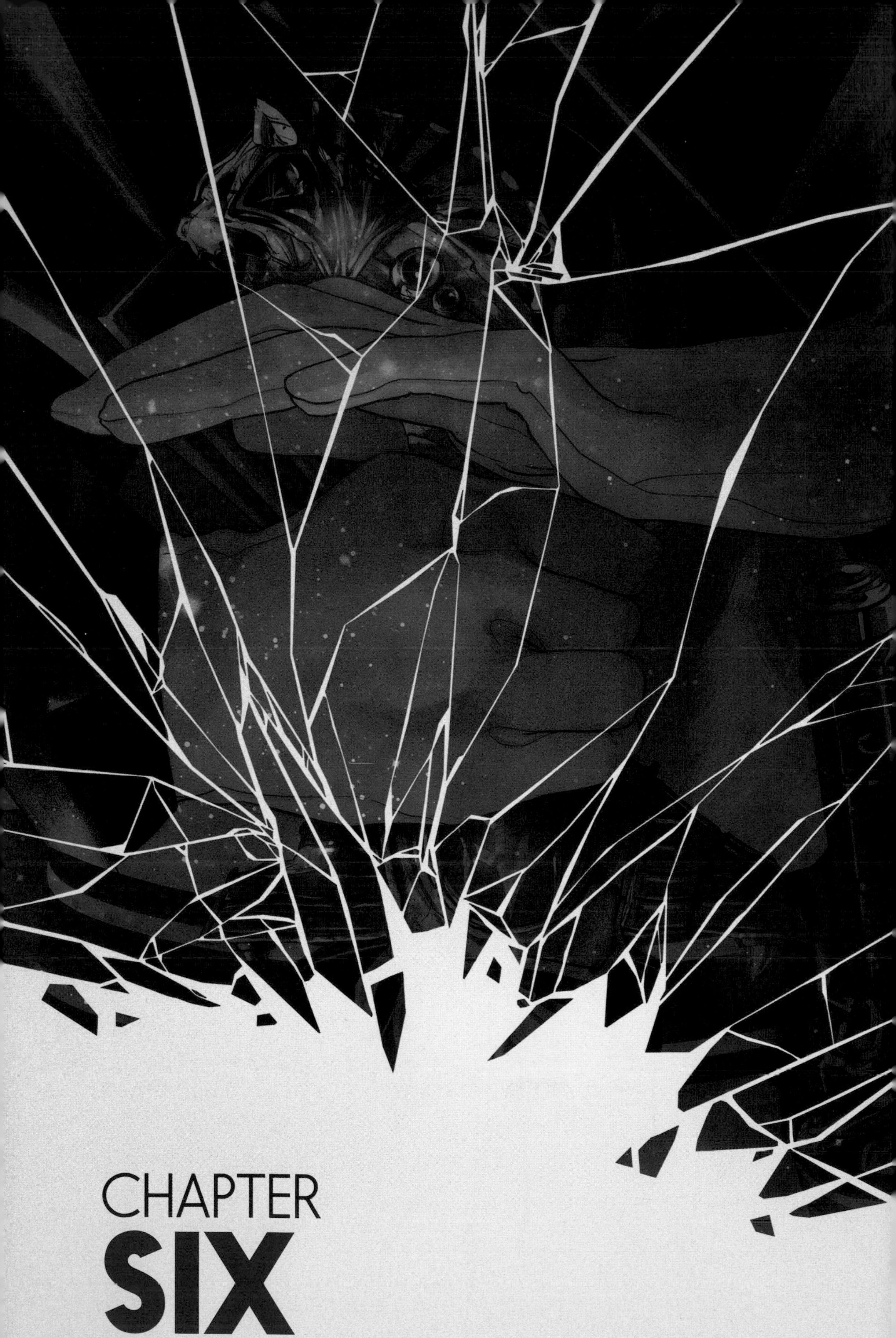

CHAPTER SIX

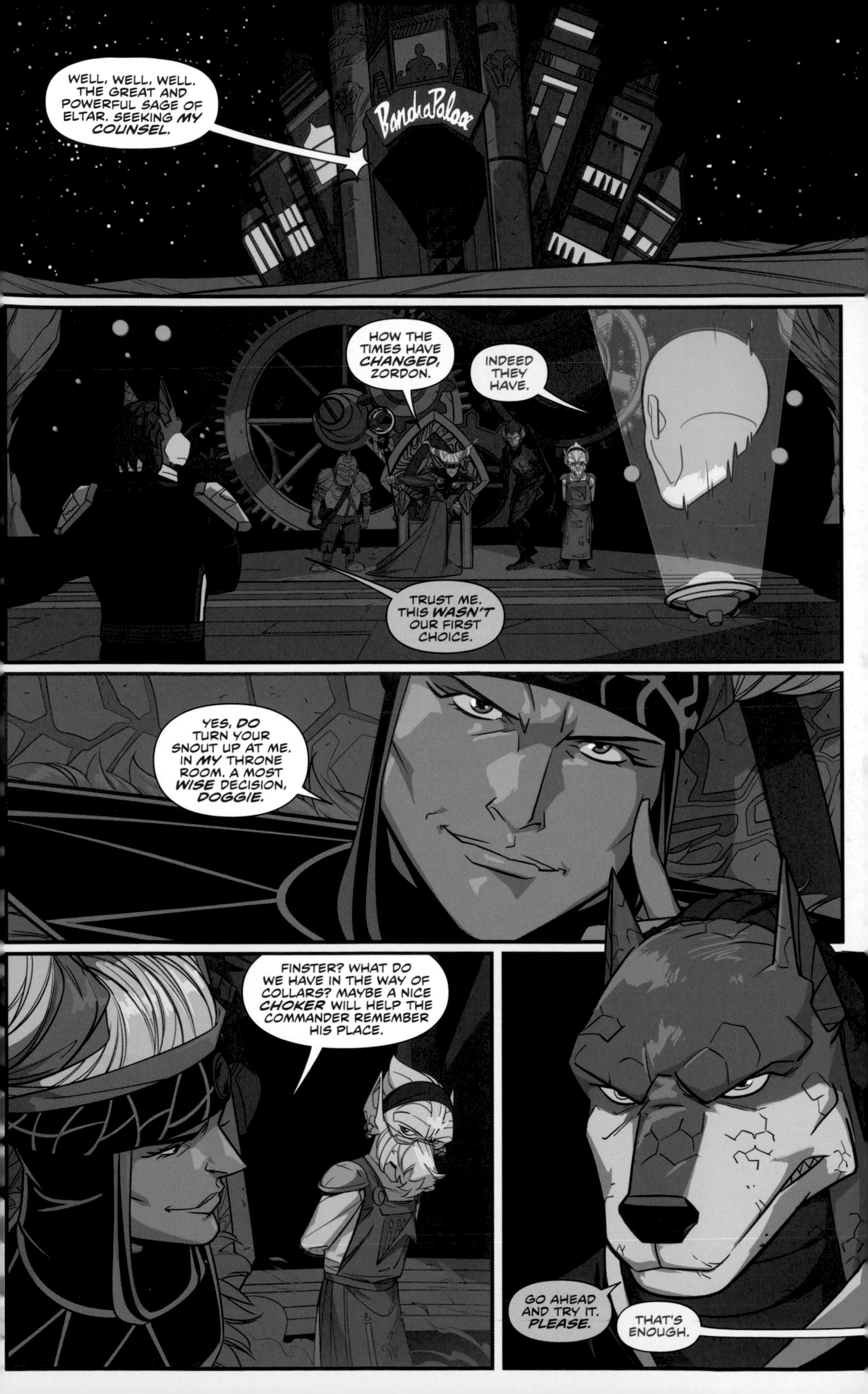
WELL, WELL, WELL. THE GREAT AND POWERFUL SAGE OF ELTAR. SEEKING *MY COUNSEL.*
HOW THE TIMES HAVE *CHANGED,* ZORDON.
INDEED THEY HAVE.
TRUST ME. THIS *WASN'T* OUR FIRST CHOICE.
YES, *DO* TURN YOUR SNOUT UP AT ME. IN *MY* THRONE ROOM. A MOST *WISE* DECISION, *DOGGIE.*
FINSTER? WHAT DO WE HAVE IN THE WAY OF COLLARS? MAYBE A NICE *CHOKER* WILL HELP THE COMMANDER REMEMBER HIS PLACE.
GO AHEAD AND TRY IT. *PLEASE.*
THAT'S ENOUGH.

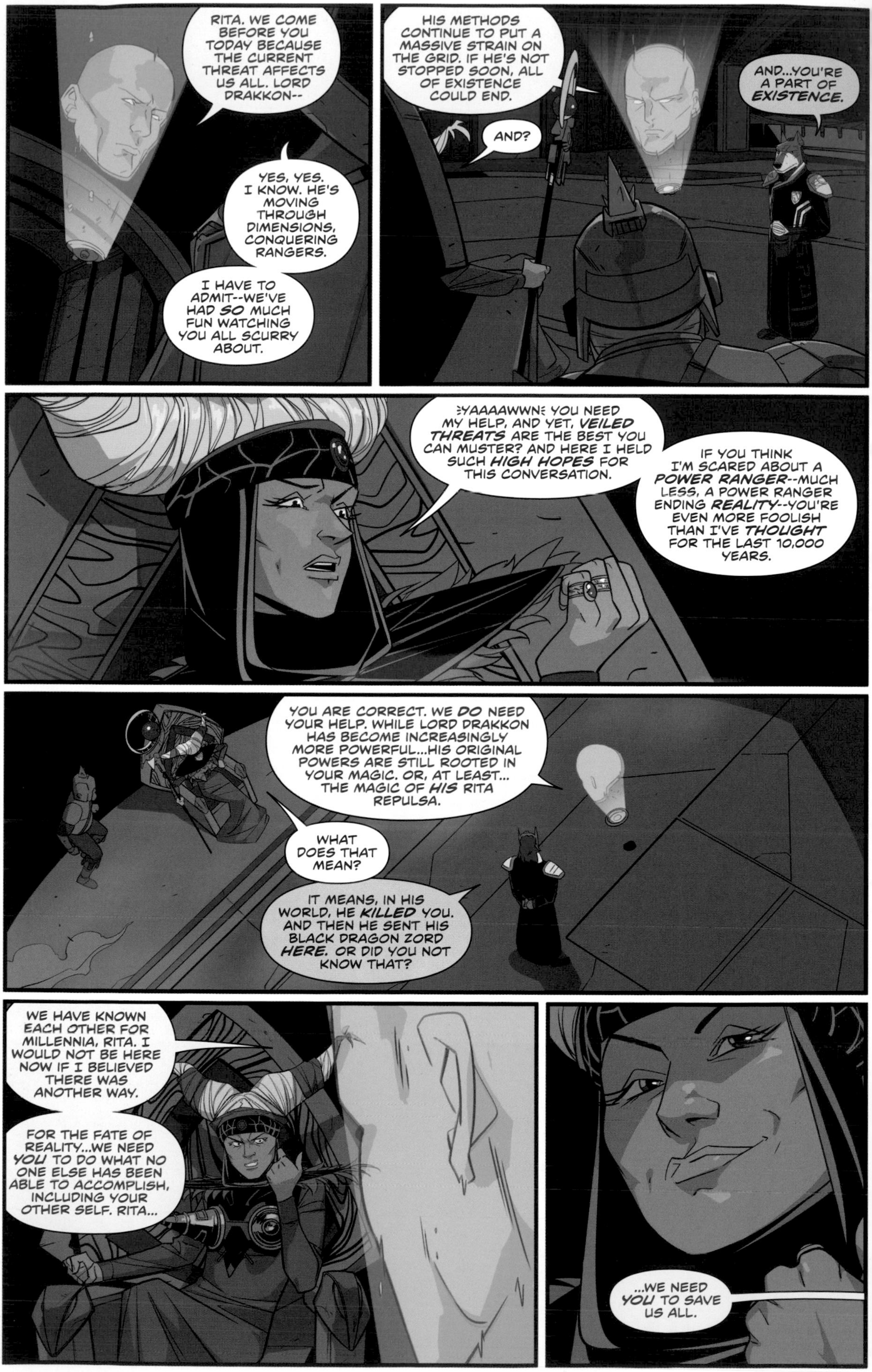
RITA. WE COME BEFORE YOU TODAY BECAUSE THE CURRENT THREAT AFFECTS US ALL. LORD DRAKKON--
YES, YES. I KNOW. HE'S MOVING THROUGH DIMENSIONS, CONQUERING RANGERS.
I HAVE TO ADMIT--WE'VE HAD SO MUCH FUN WATCHING YOU ALL SCURRY ABOUT.
HIS METHODS CONTINUE TO PUT A MASSIVE STRAIN ON THE GRID. IF HE'S NOT STOPPED SOON, ALL OF EXISTENCE COULD END.
AND?
AND...YOU'RE A PART OF EXISTENCE.
ƎYAAAAWWNE YOU NEED MY HELP, AND YET, VEILED THREATS ARE THE BEST YOU CAN MUSTER? AND HERE I HELD SUCH HIGH HOPES FOR THIS CONVERSATION.
IF YOU THINK I'M SCARED ABOUT A POWER RANGER--MUCH LESS, A POWER RANGER ENDING REALITY--YOU'RE EVEN MORE FOOLISH THAN I'VE THOUGHT FOR THE LAST 10,000 YEARS.
YOU ARE CORRECT. WE DO NEED YOUR HELP. WHILE LORD DRAKKON HAS BECOME INCREASINGLY MORE POWERFUL...HIS ORIGINAL POWERS ARE STILL ROOTED IN YOUR MAGIC. OR, AT LEAST... THE MAGIC OF HIS RITA REPULSA.
WHAT DOES THAT MEAN?
IT MEANS, IN HIS WORLD, HE KILLED YOU. AND THEN HE SENT HIS BLACK DRAGON ZORD HERE. OR DID YOU NOT KNOW THAT?
WE HAVE KNOWN EACH OTHER FOR MILLENNIA, RITA. I WOULD NOT BE HERE NOW IF I BELIEVED THERE WAS ANOTHER WAY.
FOR THE FATE OF REALITY...WE NEED YOU TO DO WHAT NO ONE ELSE HAS BEEN ABLE TO ACCOMPLISH, INCLUDING YOUR OTHER SELF. RITA...
...WE NEED YOU TO SAVE US ALL.

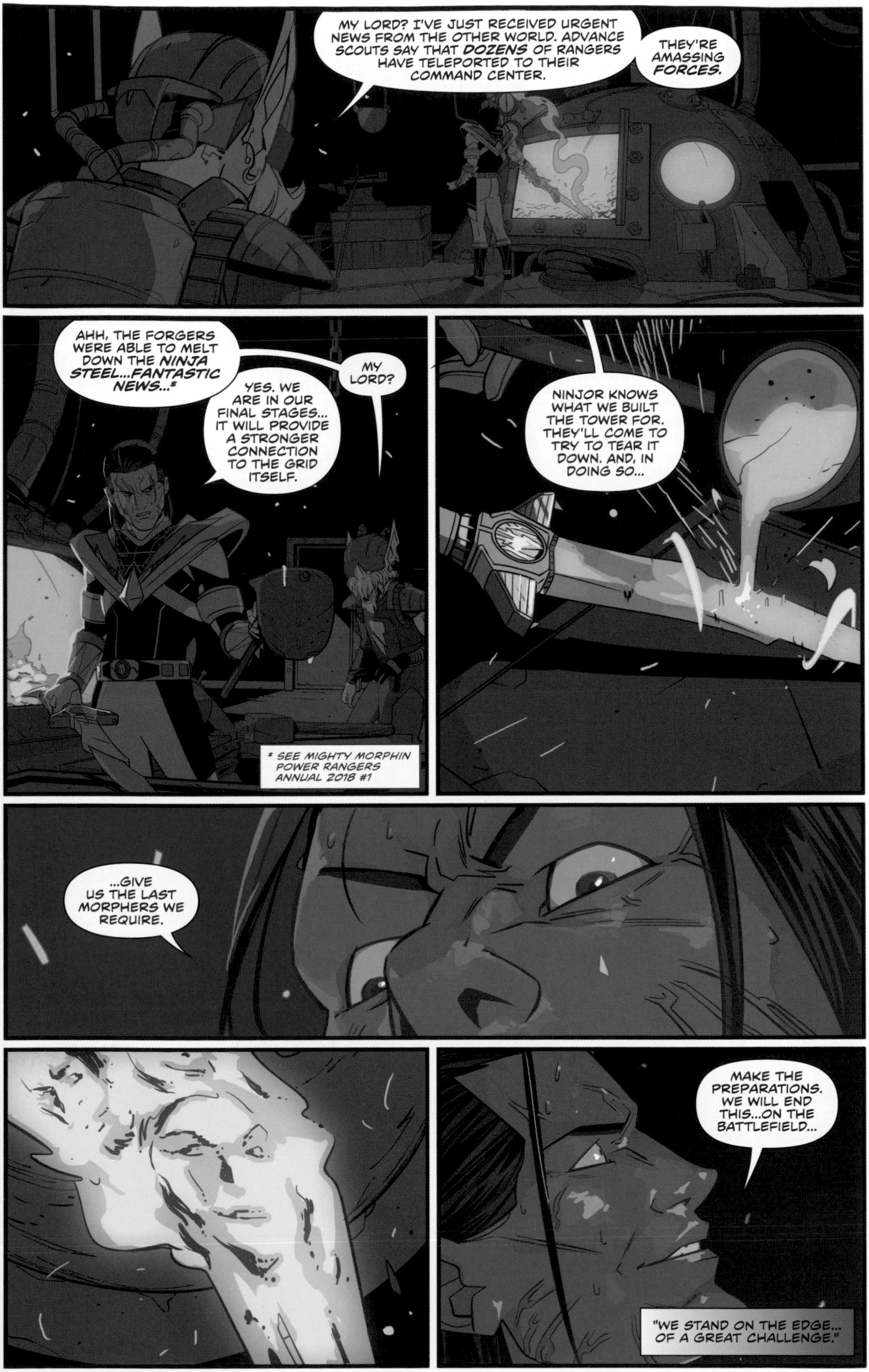
MY LORD? I'VE JUST RECEIVED URGENT NEWS FROM THE OTHER WORLD. ADVANCE SCOUTS SAY THAT **DOZENS** OF RANGERS HAVE TELEPORTED TO THEIR COMMAND CENTER.
THEY'RE AMASSING **FORCES.**
AHH, THE FORGERS WERE ABLE TO MELT DOWN THE **NINJA STEEL...FANTASTIC NEWS...***
MY LORD?
YES. WE ARE IN OUR FINAL STAGES... IT WILL PROVIDE A STRONGER CONNECTION TO THE GRID ITSELF.
* SEE MIGHTY MORPHIN POWER RANGERS ANNUAL 2018 #1
NINJOR KNOWS WHAT WE BUILT THE TOWER FOR. THEY'LL COME TO TRY TO TEAR IT DOWN. AND, IN DOING SO...
...GIVE US THE LAST MORPHERS WE REQUIRE.
MAKE THE PREPARATIONS. WE WILL END THIS...ON THE BATTLEFIELD...
"WE STAND ON THE EDGE... OF A GREAT CHALLENGE."

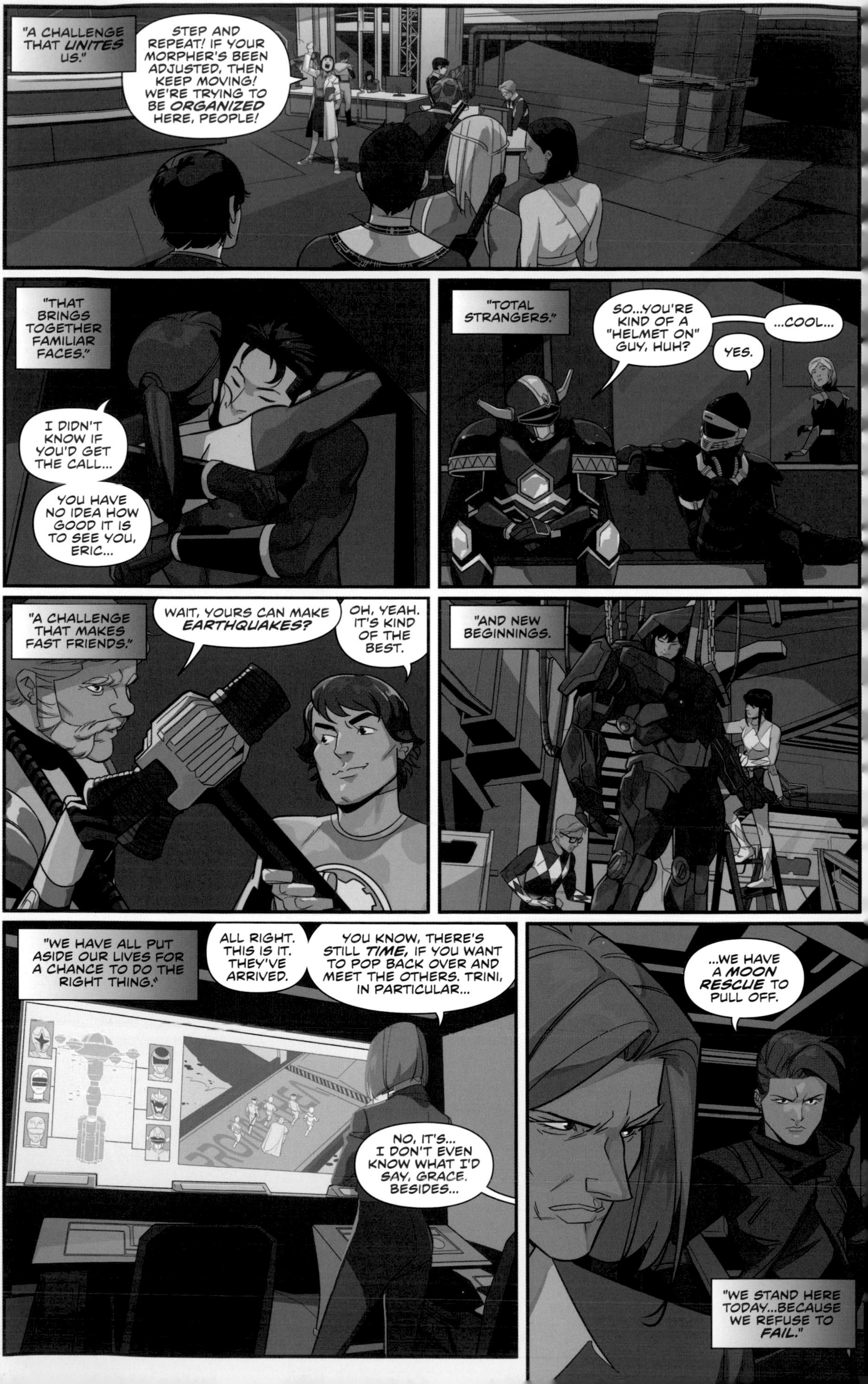
"A CHALLENGE THAT UNITES US."
STEP AND REPEAT! IF YOUR MORPHER'S BEEN ADJUSTED, THEN KEEP MOVING! WE'RE TRYING TO BE ORGANIZED HERE, PEOPLE!
"THAT BRINGS TOGETHER FAMILIAR FACES."
I DIDN'T KNOW IF YOU'D GET THE CALL...
YOU HAVE NO IDEA HOW GOOD IT IS TO SEE YOU, ERIC...
"TOTAL STRANGERS."
SO...YOU'RE KIND OF A "HELMET ON" GUY, HUH?
YES.
...COOL...
"A CHALLENGE THAT MAKES FAST FRIENDS."
WAIT, YOURS CAN MAKE EARTHQUAKES?
OH, YEAH. IT'S KIND OF THE BEST.
"AND NEW BEGINNINGS.
"WE HAVE ALL PUT ASIDE OUR LIVES FOR A CHANCE TO DO THE RIGHT THING."
ALL RIGHT. THIS IS IT. THEY'VE ARRIVED.
YOU KNOW, THERE'S STILL TIME, IF YOU WANT TO POP BACK OVER AND MEET THE OTHERS. TRINI, IN PARTICULAR...
NO, IT'S... I DON'T EVEN KNOW WHAT I'D SAY, GRACE. BESIDES...
...WE HAVE A MOON RESCUE TO PULL OFF.
"WE STAND HERE TODAY...BECAUSE WE REFUSE TO FAIL."

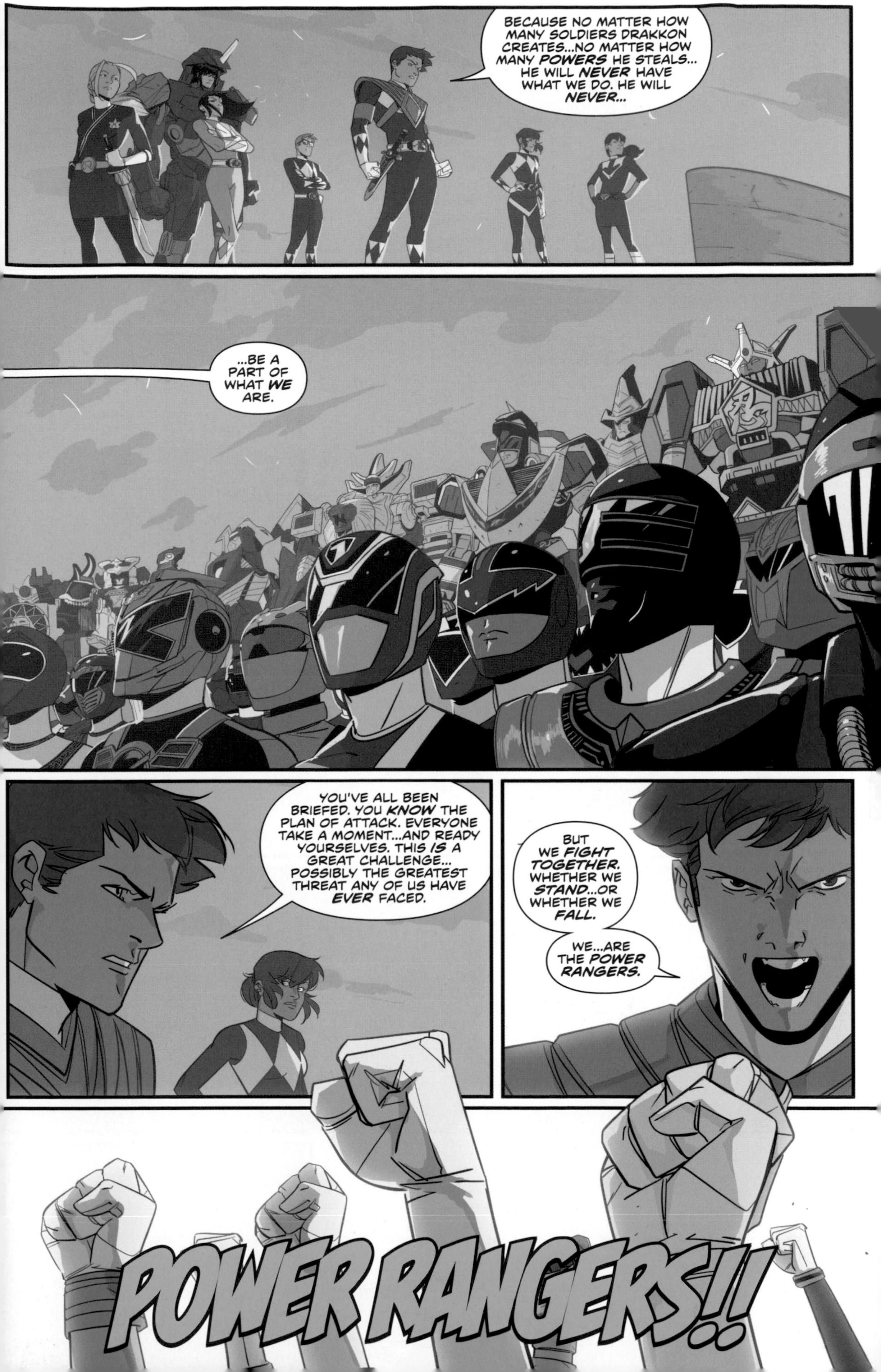
BECAUSE NO MATTER HOW MANY SOLDIERS DRAKKON CREATES...NO MATTER HOW MANY *POWERS* HE STEALS... HE WILL *NEVER* HAVE WHAT WE DO. HE WILL *NEVER*...
...BE A PART OF WHAT *WE* ARE.
YOU'VE ALL BEEN BRIEFED. YOU *KNOW* THE PLAN OF ATTACK. EVERYONE TAKE A MOMENT...AND READY YOURSELVES. THIS *IS* A GREAT CHALLENGE... POSSIBLY THE GREATEST THREAT ANY OF US HAVE *EVER* FACED.
BUT WE *FIGHT TOGETHER*. WHETHER WE *STAND*...OR WHETHER WE *FALL*.
WE...ARE THE *POWER RANGERS*.
POWER RANGERS!!

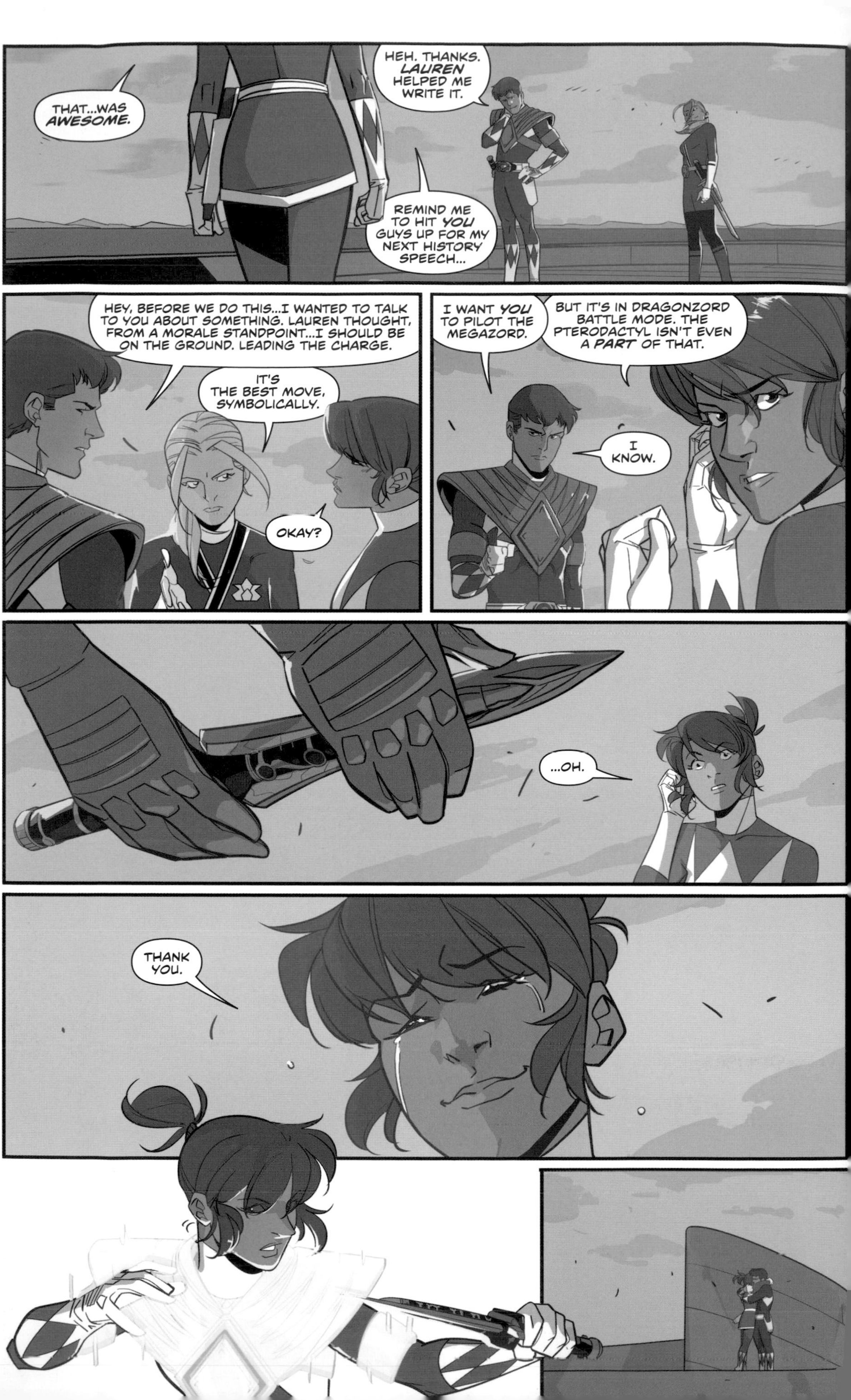
THAT...WAS AWESOME.
HEH. THANKS. LAUREN HELPED ME WRITE IT.
REMIND ME TO HIT YOU GUYS UP FOR MY NEXT HISTORY SPEECH...
HEY, BEFORE WE DO THIS...I WANTED TO TALK TO YOU ABOUT SOMETHING. LAUREN THOUGHT, FROM A MORALE STANDPOINT...I SHOULD BE ON THE GROUND. LEADING THE CHARGE.
IT'S THE BEST MOVE, SYMBOLICALLY.
OKAY?
I WANT YOU TO PILOT THE MEGAZORD.
BUT IT'S IN DRAGONZORD BATTLE MODE. THE PTERODACTYL ISN'T EVEN A PART OF THAT.
I KNOW.
...OH.
THANK YOU.

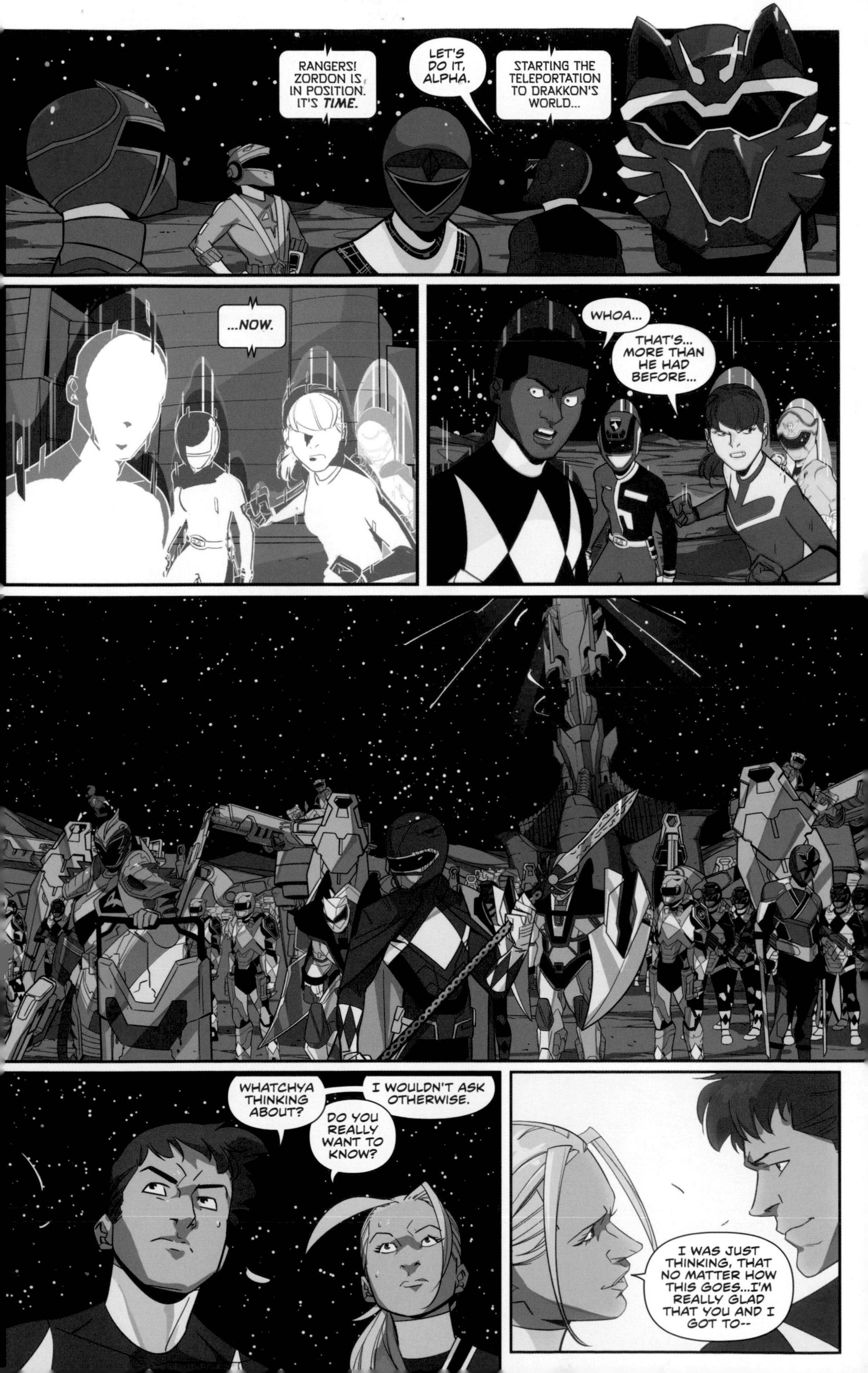
RANGERS! ZORDON IS IN POSITION. IT'S *TIME.*
LET'S DO IT, ALPHA.
STARTING THE TELEPORTATION TO DRAKKON'S WORLD...
...*NOW.*
WHOA...
THAT'S... MORE THAN HE HAD BEFORE...
WHATCHYA THINKING ABOUT?
DO YOU REALLY WANT TO KNOW?
I WOULDN'T ASK OTHERWISE.
I WAS JUST THINKING, THAT NO MATTER HOW THIS GOES...I'M REALLY GLAD THAT YOU AND I GOT TO--

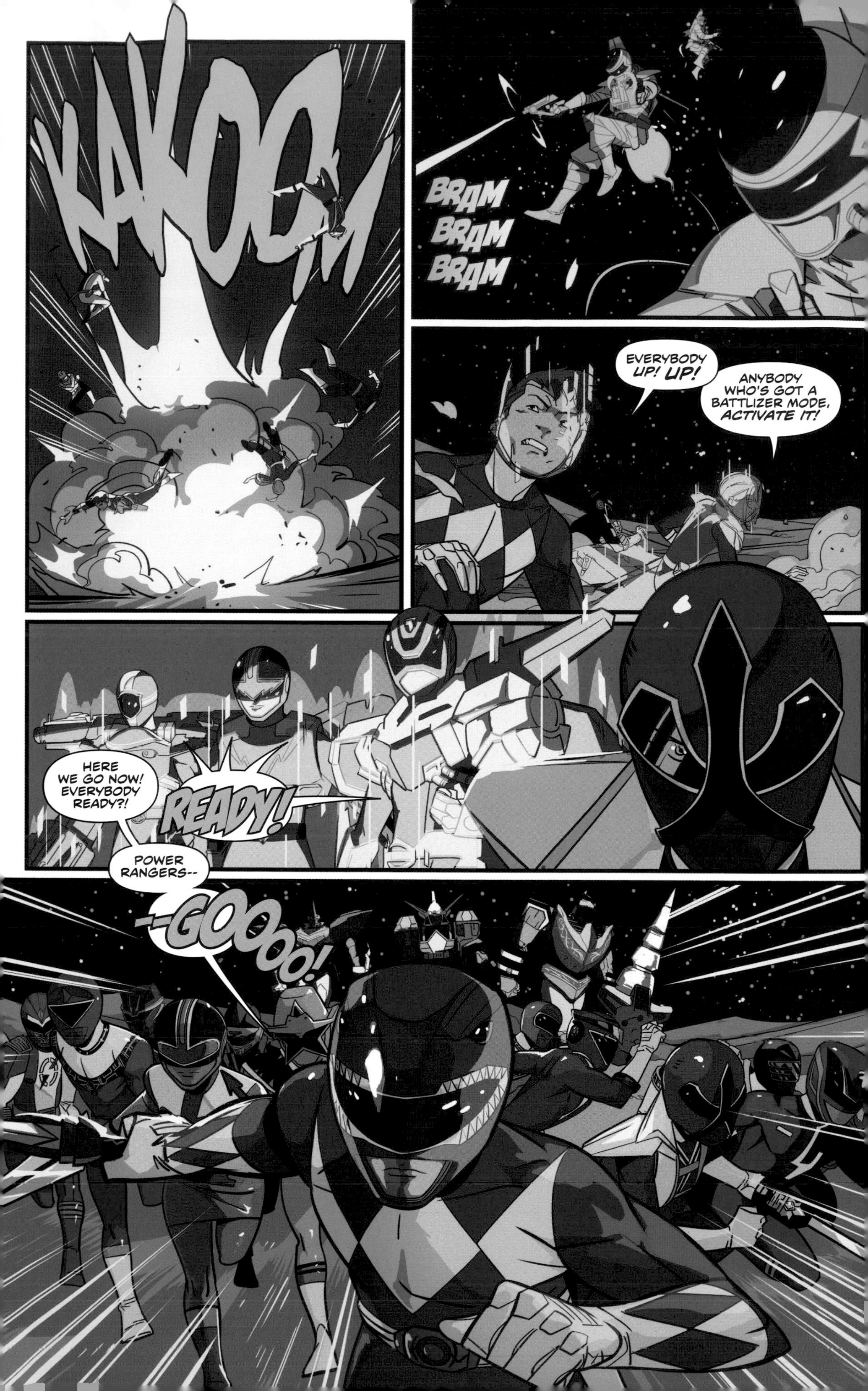
KAKOOM
BRAM
BRAM
BRAM
EVERYBODY UP! UP!
ANYBODY WHO'S GOT A BATTLIZER MODE, ACTIVATE IT!
HERE WE GO NOW! EVERYBODY READY?!
READY!
POWER RANGERS--
--GOOOO!

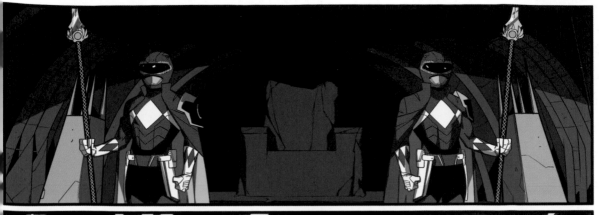

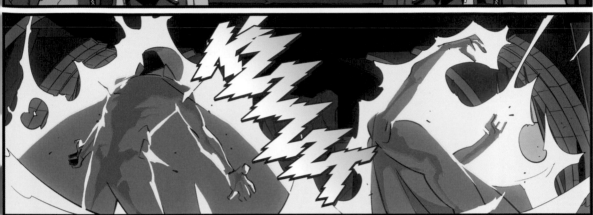

WALK ME THROUGH WHY WE'VE GOTTA DO THIS *HERE*?

MAGIC...ENERGY... THEY ALL WORK ON THE SAME PRINCIPLE. THEIR *INTERACTION* WITH THE WORLD.

THE MORE SOMEONE RETURNS TO A PLACE, THE MORE IT TAKES ON AN AURA. AND HERE...

...IS THE CENTER OF DRAKKON'S.

I *RECOGNIZE* THAT SIGNATURE. THE WIZARD OF DECEPTION. THE *COST* FOR SOMETHING LIKE THAT...

YES. I KNOW. BUT, LIKE YOU SAID...

...ONLY *I* CAN SAVE US ALL.

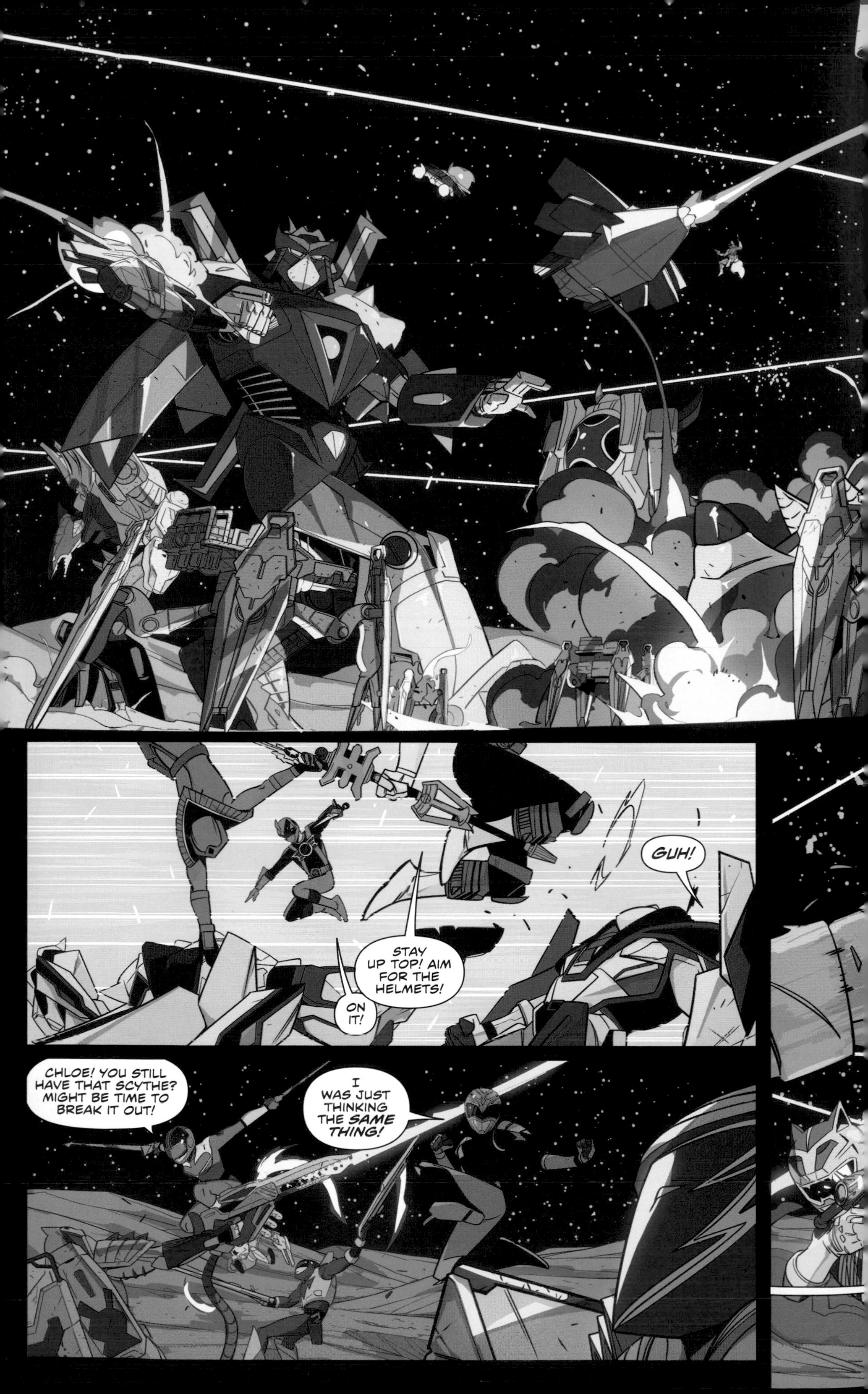
GUH!
STAY UP TOP! AIM FOR THE HELMETS!
ON IT!
CHLOE! YOU STILL HAVE THAT SCYTHE? MIGHT BE TIME TO BREAK IT OUT!
I WAS JUST THINKING THE SAME THING!

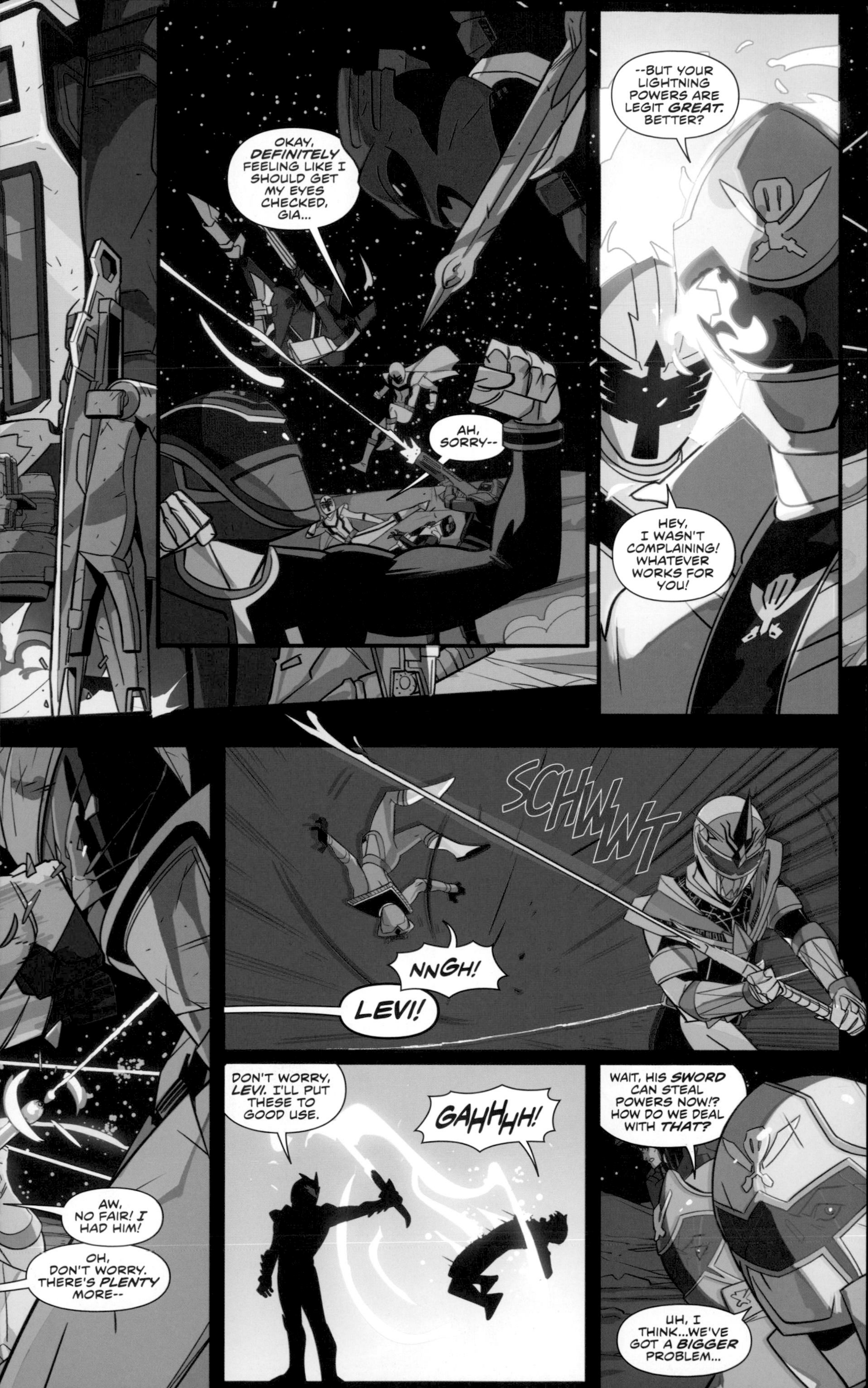
OKAY, DEFINITELY FEELING LIKE I SHOULD GET MY EYES CHECKED, GIA...
AH, SORRY--
--BUT YOUR LIGHTNING POWERS ARE LEGIT GREAT. BETTER?
HEY, I WASN'T COMPLAINING! WHATEVER WORKS FOR YOU!
SCHWWT
NNGH!
LEVI!
AW, NO FAIR! I HAD HIM!
OH, DON'T WORRY. THERE'S PLENTY MORE--
DON'T WORRY, LEVI. I'LL PUT THESE TO GOOD USE.
GAHHHH!
WAIT, HIS SWORD CAN STEAL POWERS NOW!? HOW DO WE DEAL WITH THAT?
UH, I THINK...WE'VE GOT A BIGGER PROBLEM...

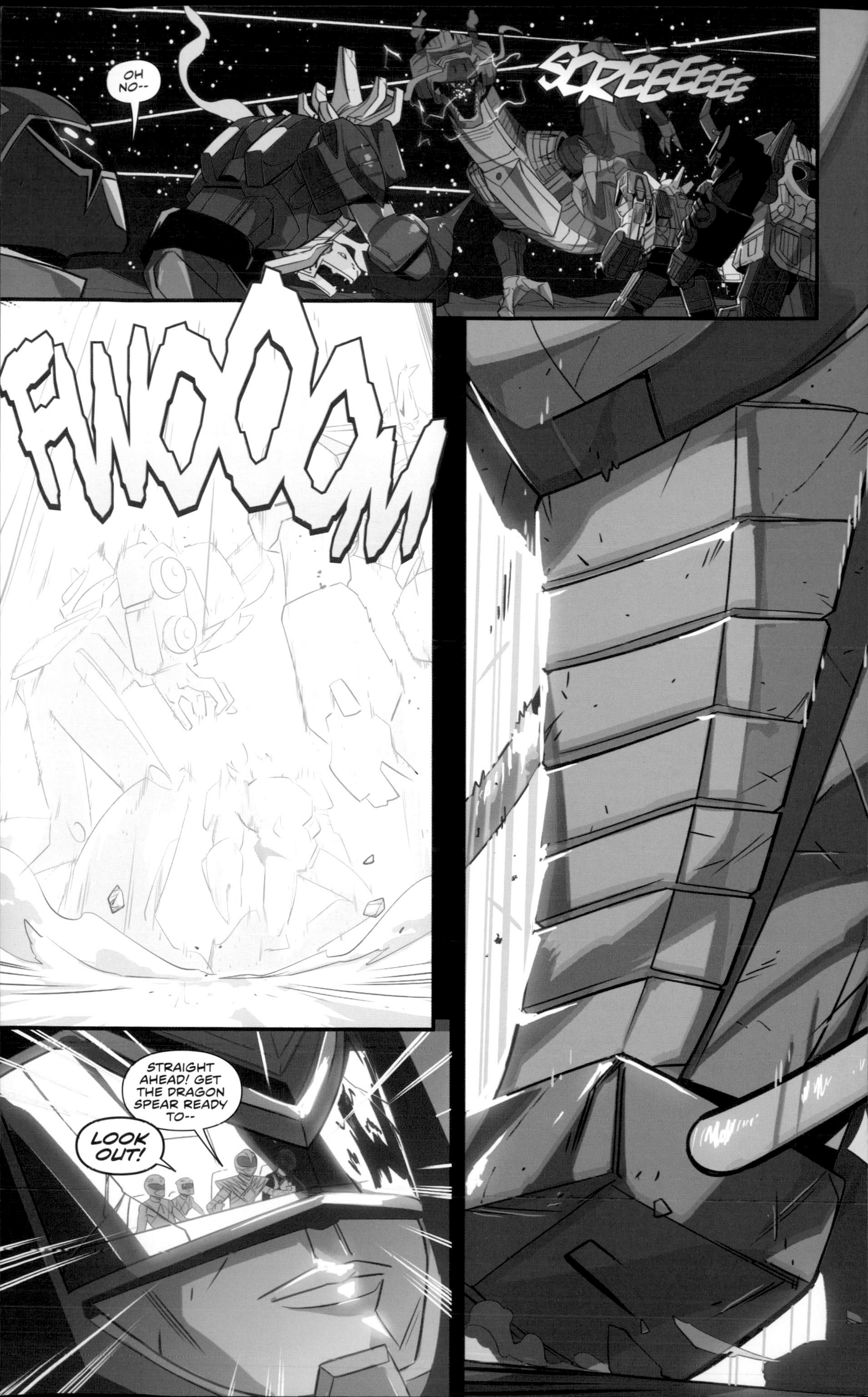
OH NO--
SCREEEEEEE
FWOOOM
STRAIGHT AHEAD! GET THE DRAGON SPEAR READY TO--
LOOK OUT!

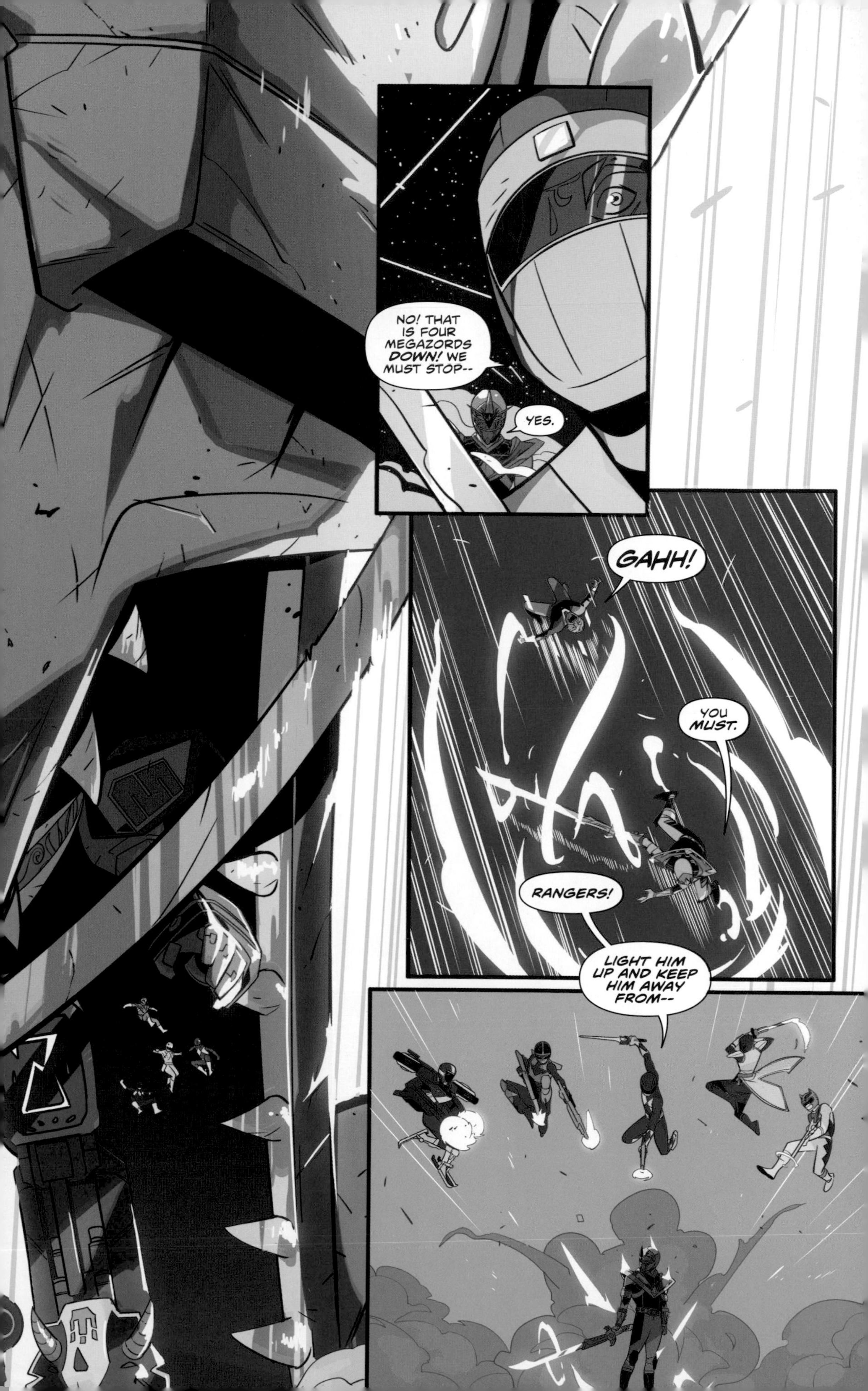
NO! THAT IS FOUR MEGAZORDS DOWN! WE MUST STOP--
YES.
GAHH!
YOU MUST.
RANGERS!
LIGHT HIM UP AND KEEP HIM AWAY FROM--

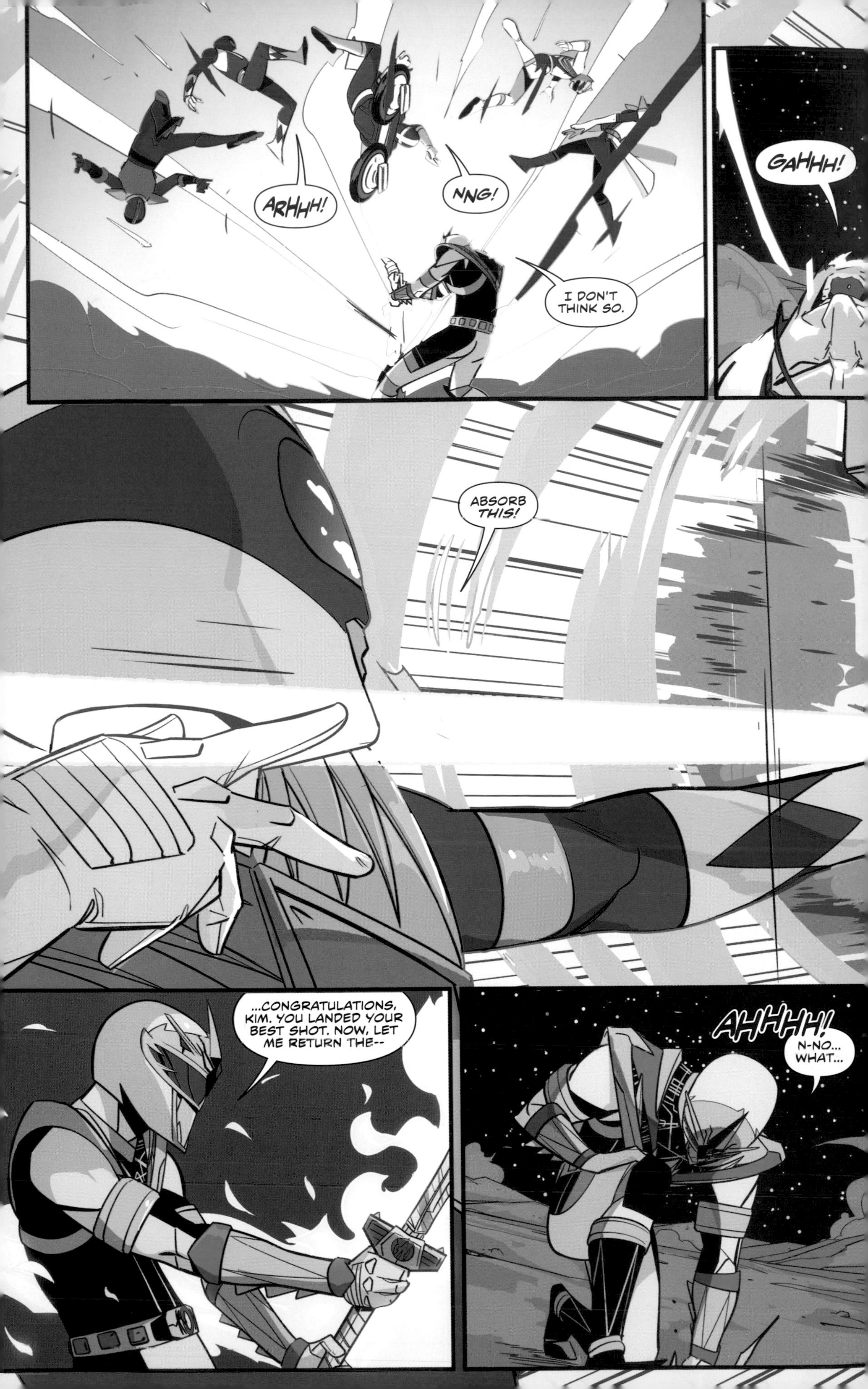
ARHHH!
NNG!
I DON'T THINK SO.
GAHHH!
ABSORB THIS!
...CONGRATULATIONS, KIM. YOU LANDED YOUR BEST SHOT. NOW, LET ME RETURN THE--
AHHHH!
N-NO... WHAT...

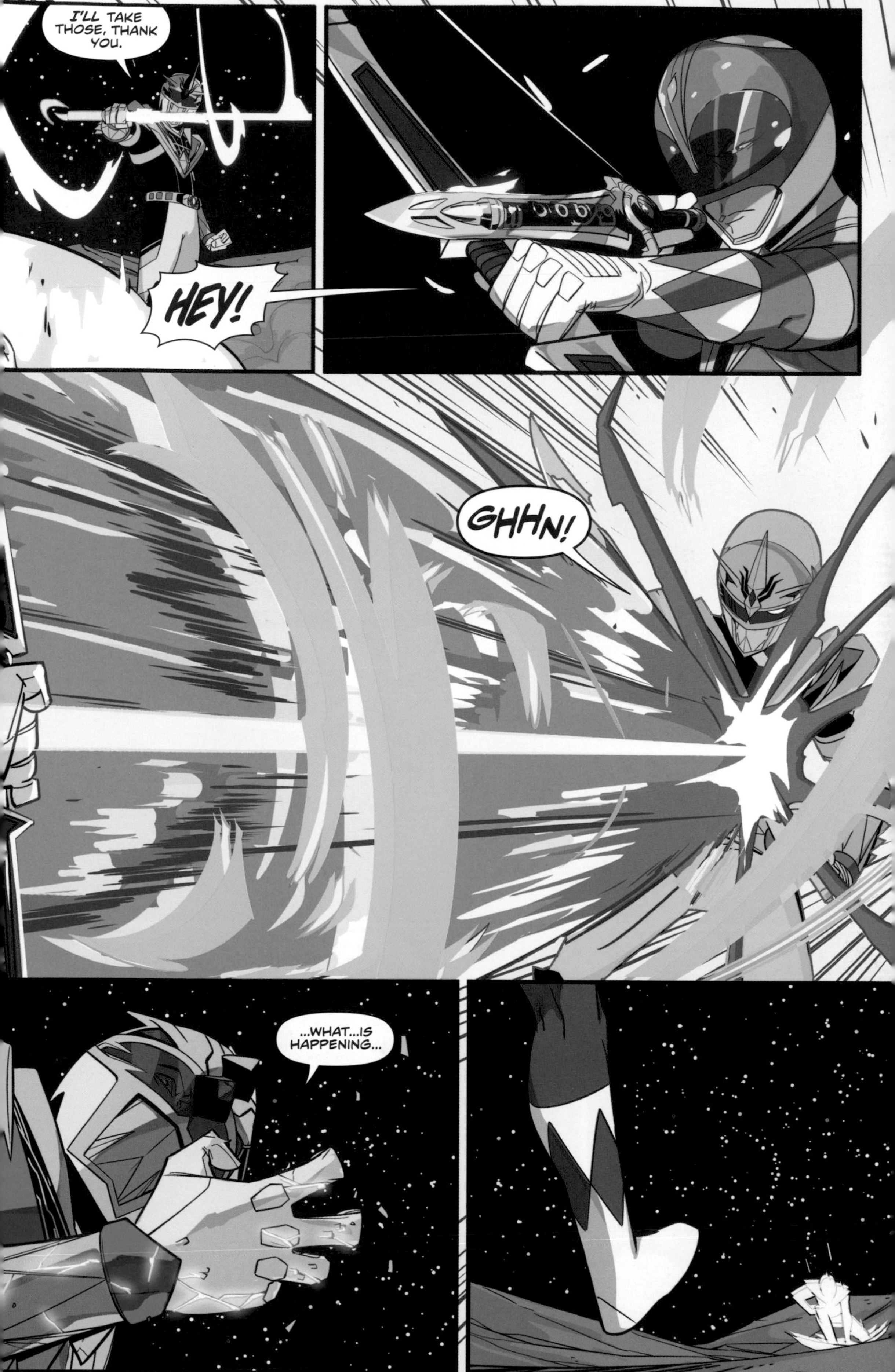
I'LL TAKE THOSE, THANK YOU.
HEY!
GHHN!
...WHAT...IS HAPPENING...

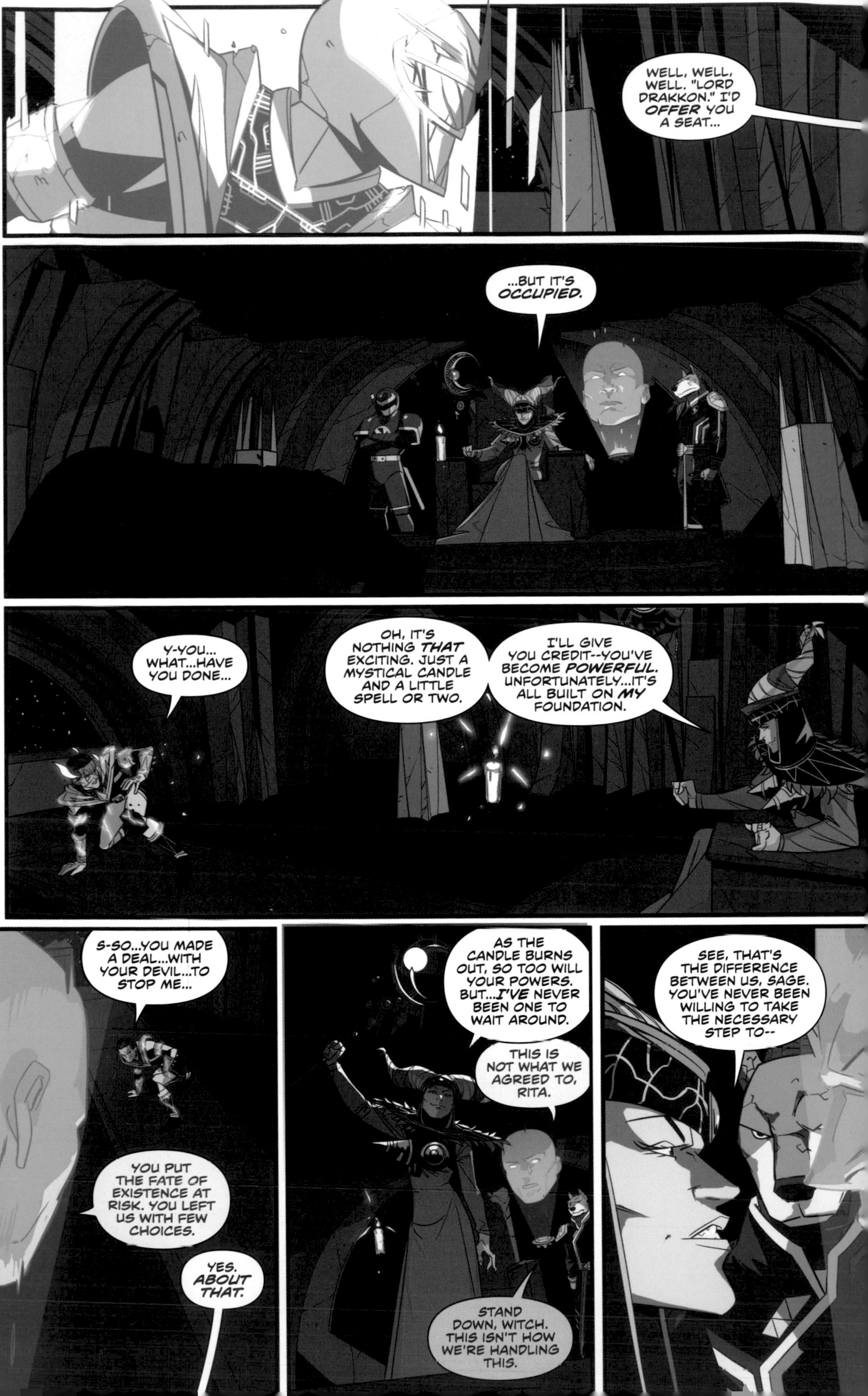

WELL, WELL, WELL. "LORD DRAKKON." I'D OFFER YOU A SEAT...
...BUT IT'S OCCUPIED.
Y-YOU... WHAT...HAVE YOU DONE...
OH, IT'S NOTHING THAT EXCITING. JUST A MYSTICAL CANDLE AND A LITTLE SPELL OR TWO.
I'LL GIVE YOU CREDIT--YOU'VE BECOME POWERFUL. UNFORTUNATELY...IT'S ALL BUILT ON MY FOUNDATION.
S-SO...YOU MADE A DEAL...WITH YOUR DEVIL...TO STOP ME...
YOU PUT THE FATE OF EXISTENCE AT RISK. YOU LEFT US WITH FEW CHOICES.
YES. ABOUT THAT.
AS THE CANDLE BURNS OUT, SO TOO WILL YOUR POWERS. BUT...I'VE NEVER BEEN ONE TO WAIT AROUND.
THIS IS NOT WHAT WE AGREED TO, RITA.
STAND DOWN, WITCH. THIS ISN'T HOW WE'RE HANDLING THIS.
SEE, THAT'S THE DIFFERENCE BETWEEN US, SAGE. YOU'VE NEVER BEEN WILLING TO TAKE THE NECESSARY STEP TO--

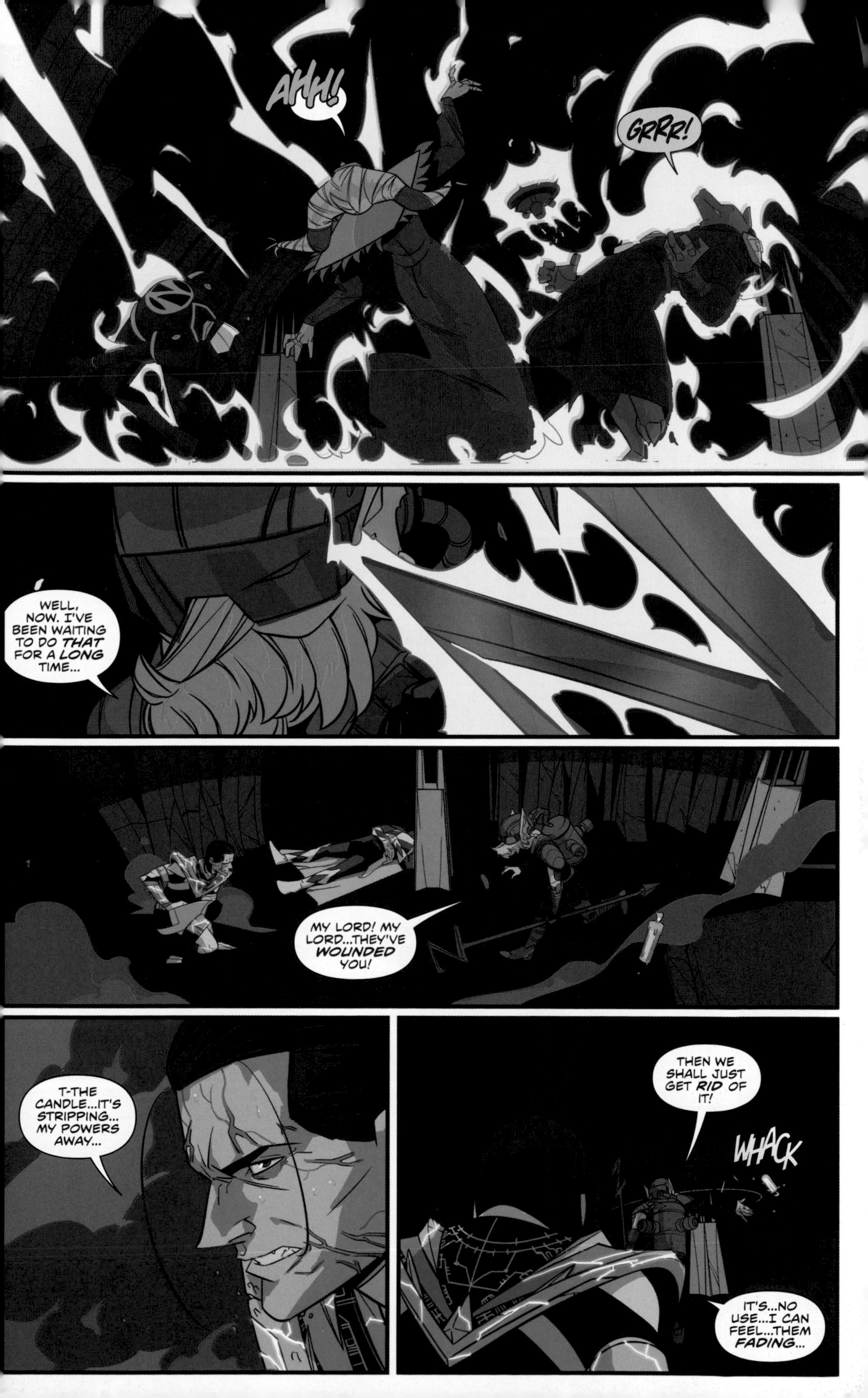
AHH!
GRRR!
WELL, NOW. I'VE BEEN WAITING TO DO THAT FOR A LONG TIME...
MY LORD! MY LORD...THEY'VE WOUNDED YOU!
T-THE CANDLE...IT'S STRIPPING... MY POWERS AWAY...
THEN WE SHALL JUST GET RID OF IT!
WHACK
IT'S...NO USE...I CAN FEEL...THEM FADING...

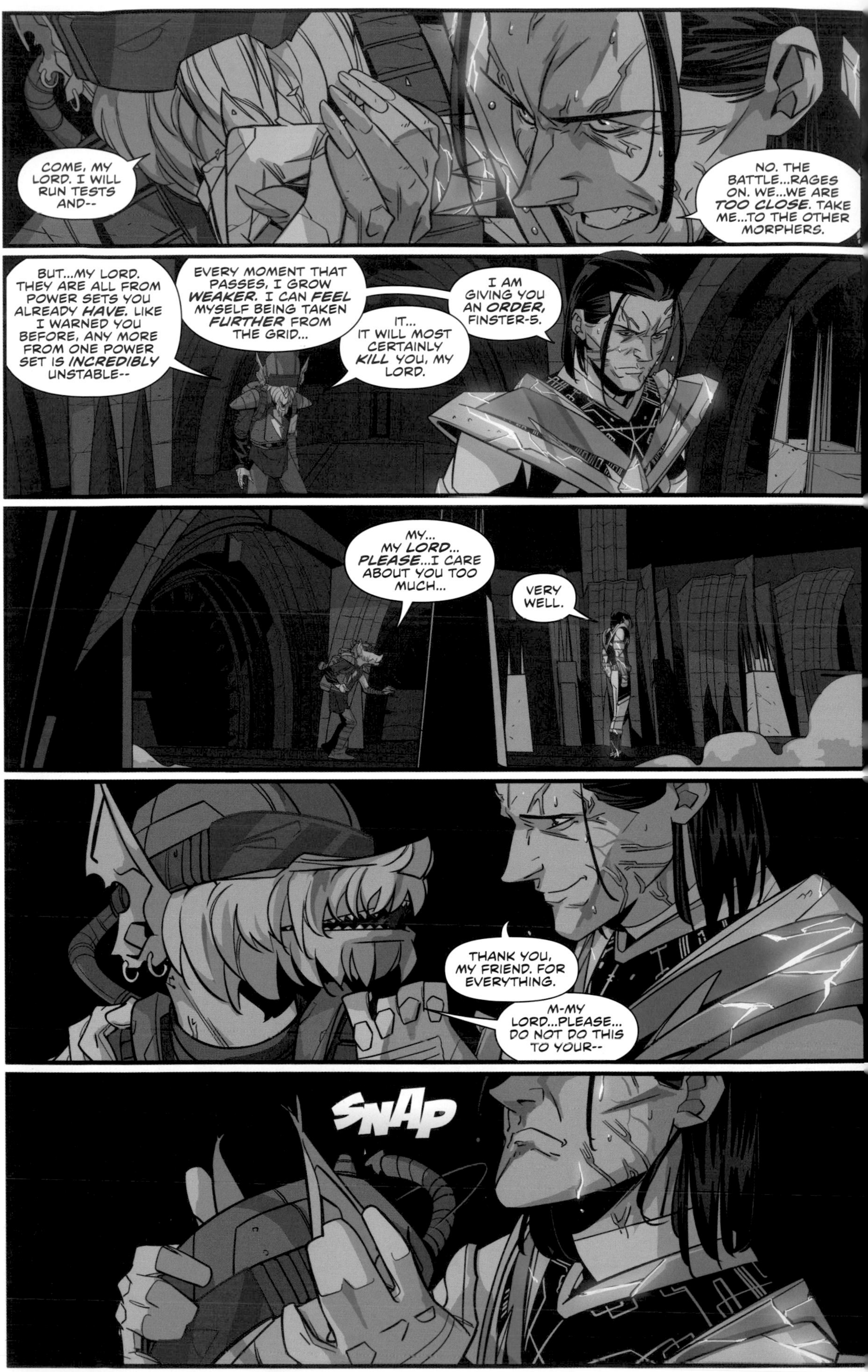
COME, MY LORD. I WILL RUN TESTS AND--
NO. THE BATTLE...RAGES ON. WE...WE ARE TOO CLOSE. TAKE ME...TO THE OTHER MORPHERS.
BUT...MY LORD. THEY ARE ALL FROM POWER SETS YOU ALREADY HAVE. LIKE I WARNED YOU BEFORE, ANY MORE FROM ONE POWER SET IS INCREDIBLY UNSTABLE--
EVERY MOMENT THAT PASSES, I GROW WEAKER. I CAN FEEL MYSELF BEING TAKEN FURTHER FROM THE GRID...
IT... IT WILL MOST CERTAINLY KILL YOU, MY LORD.
I AM GIVING YOU AN ORDER, FINSTER-5.
MY... MY LORD... PLEASE...I CARE ABOUT YOU TOO MUCH...
VERY WELL.
THANK YOU, MY FRIEND. FOR EVERYTHING.
M-MY LORD...PLEASE... DO NOT DO THIS TO YOUR--
SNAP

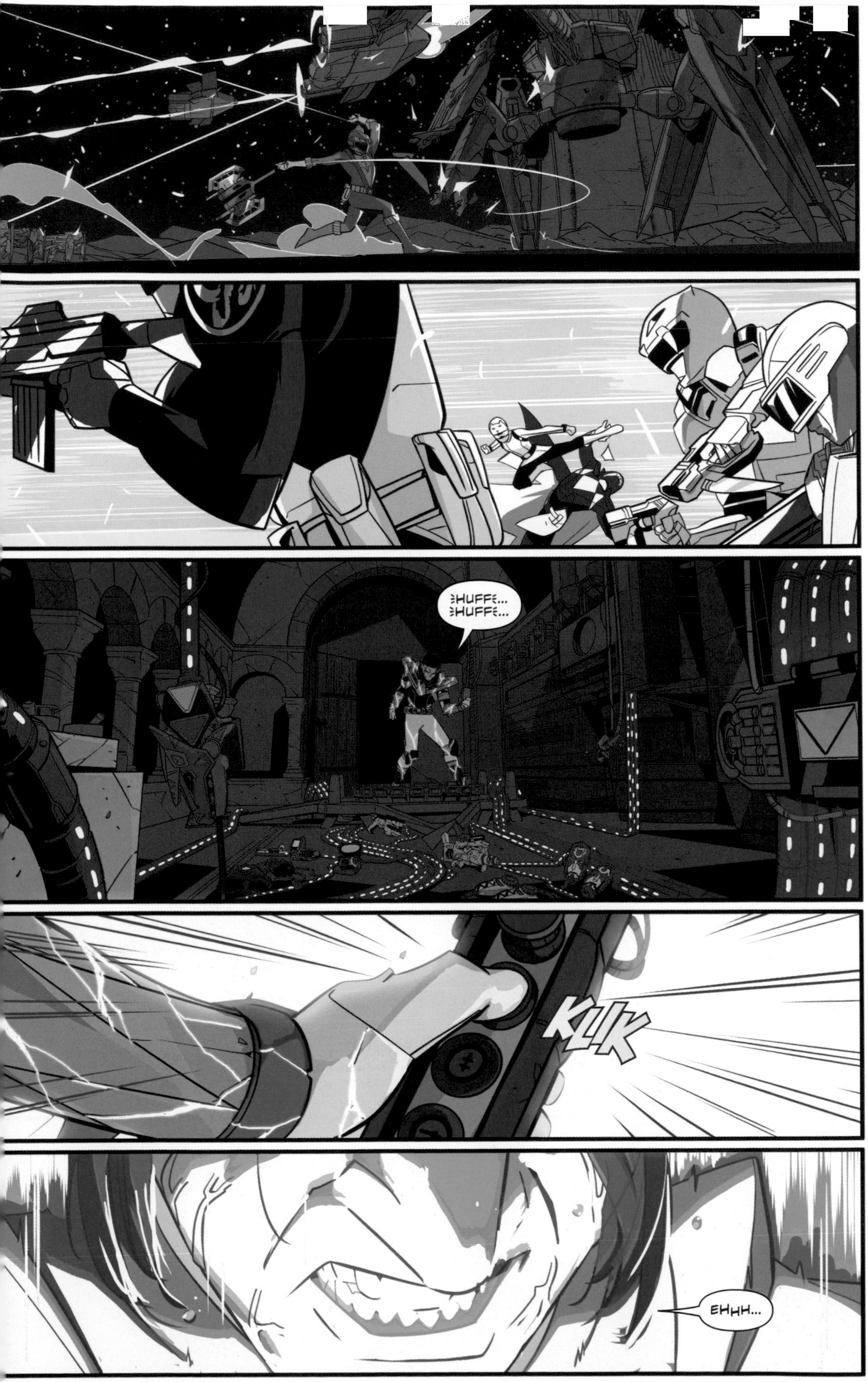
HUFF... HUFF...
KLIK
EHHH...

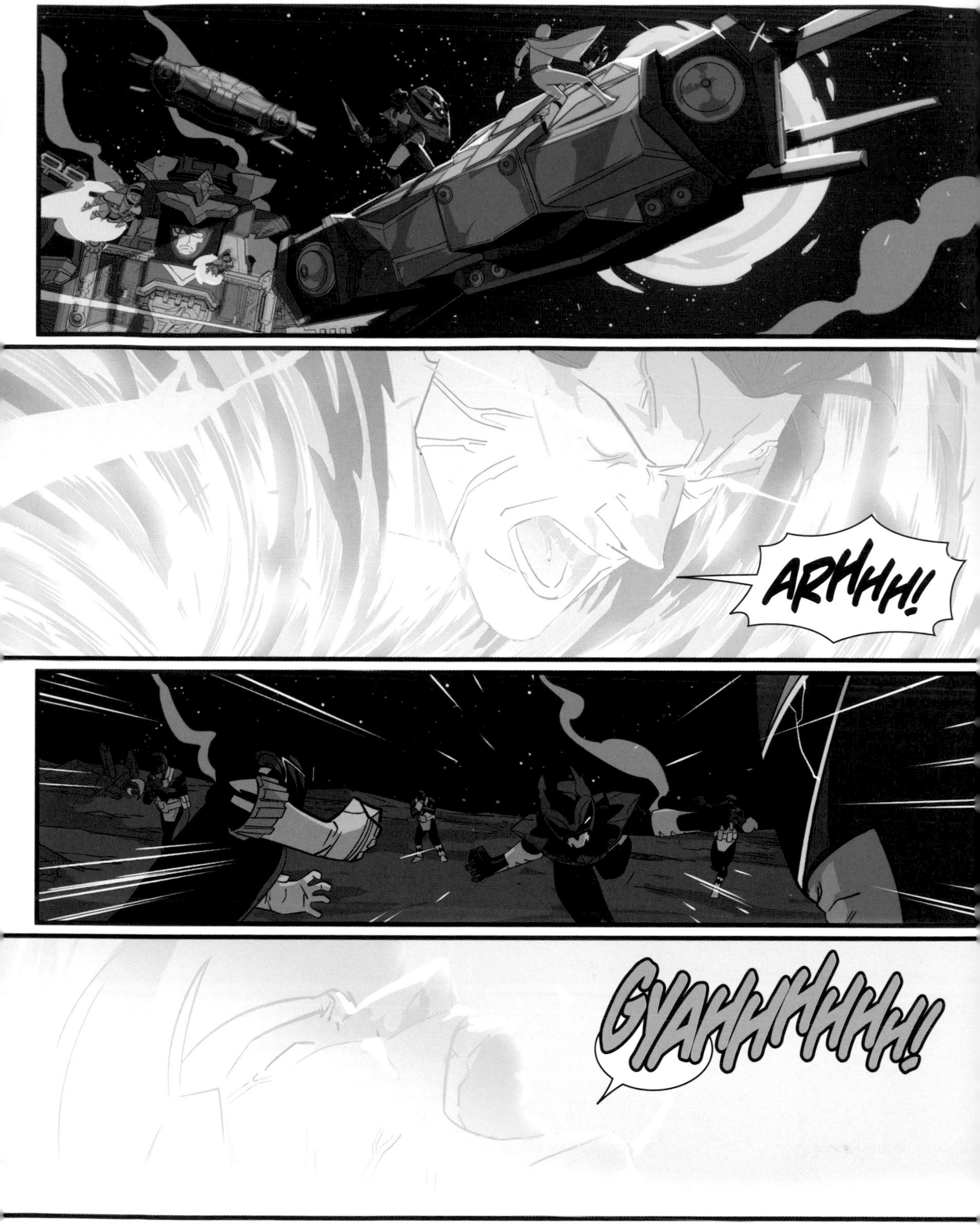
ARHHH!
GYAHHHHHH!

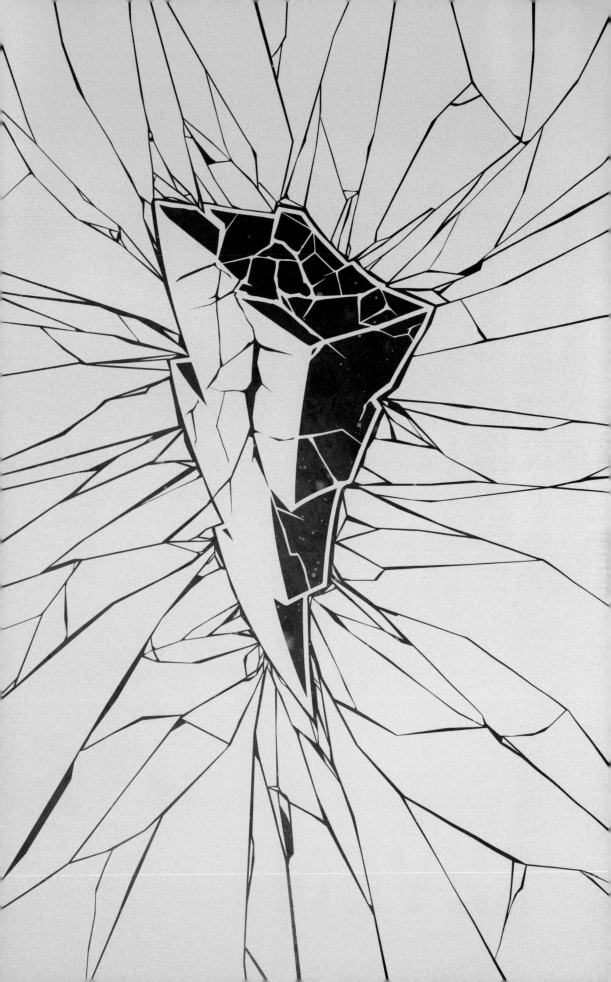

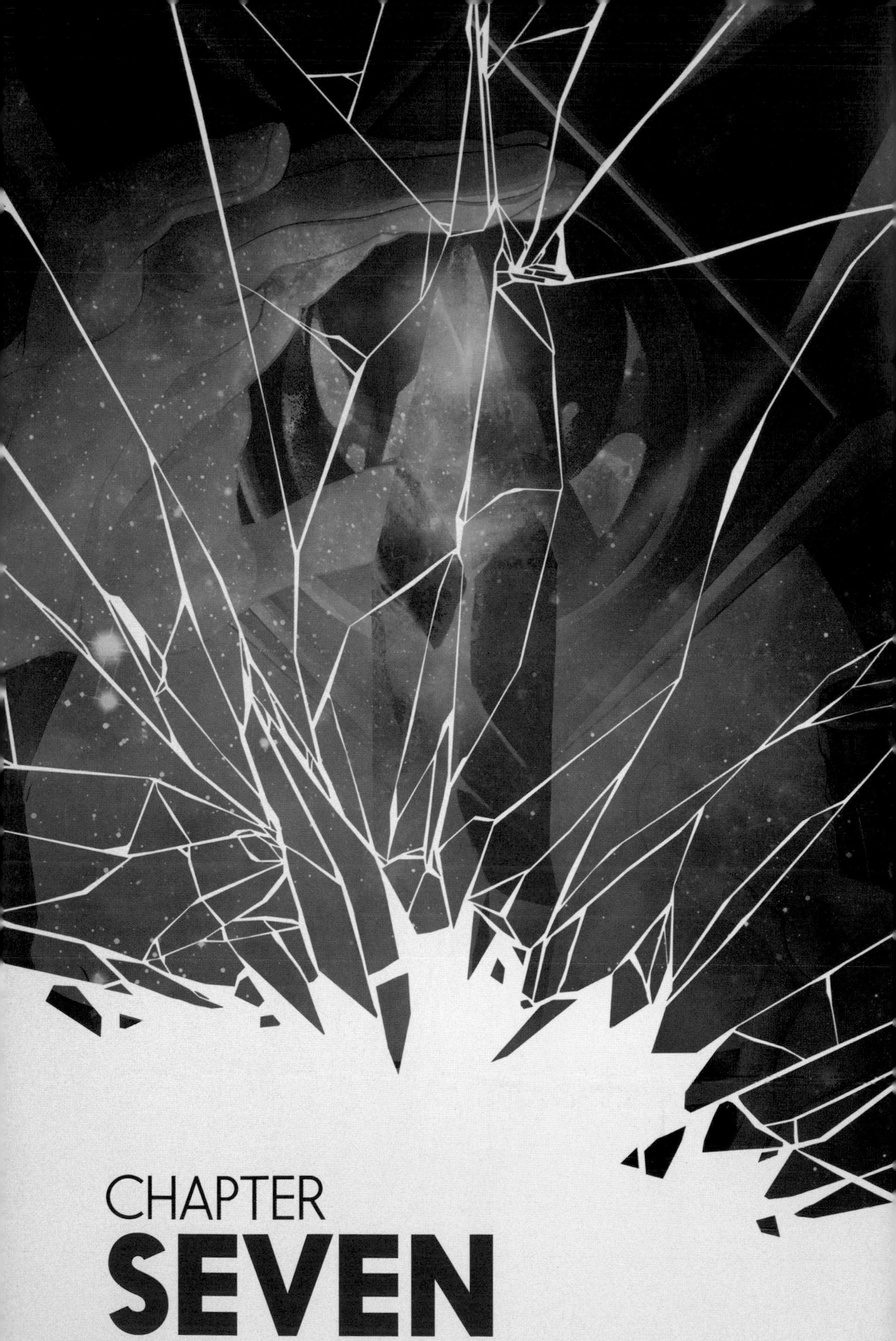

CHAPTER **SEVEN**

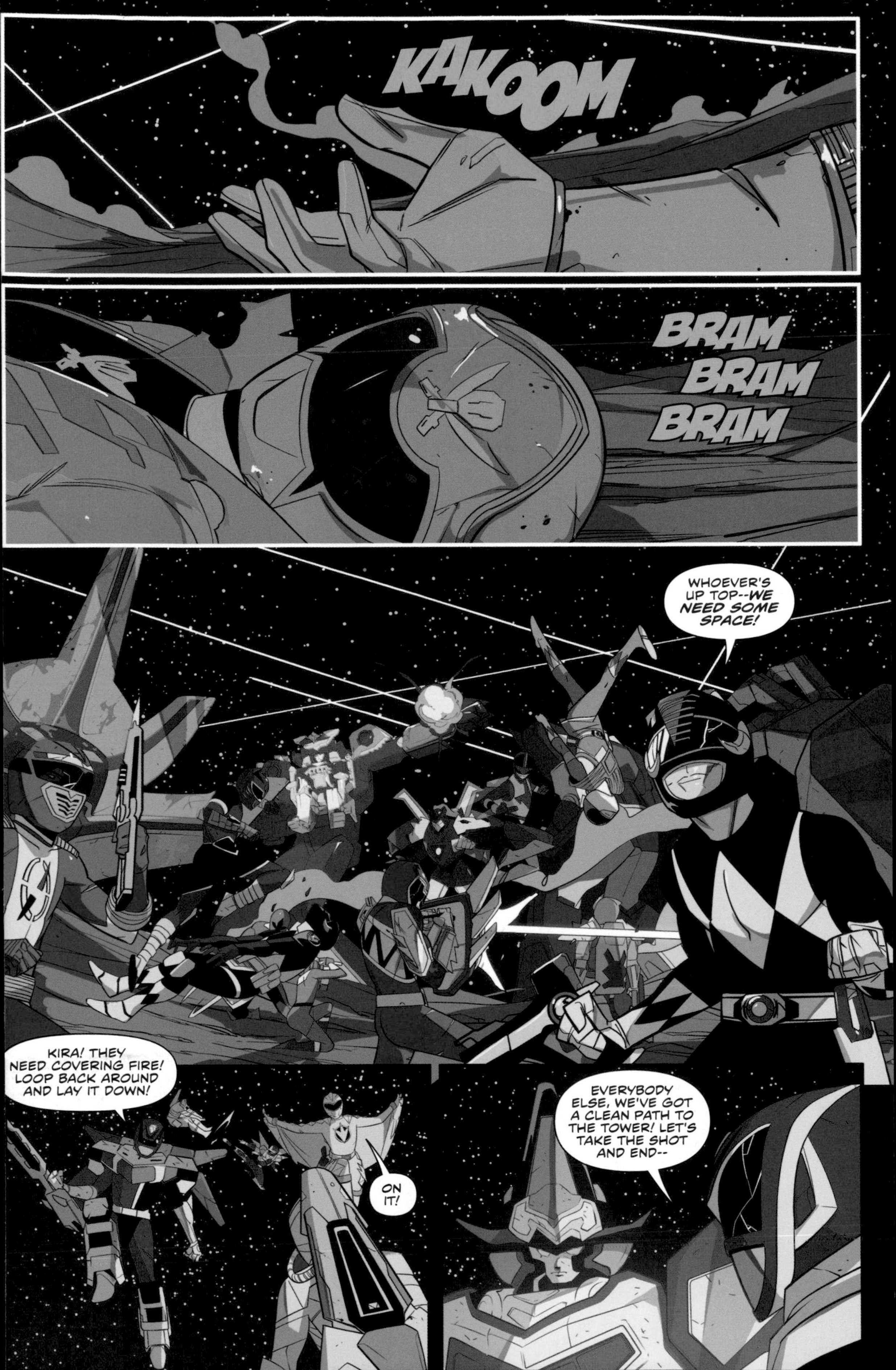
KAKOOM
BRAM
BRAM
BRAM
WHOEVER'S UP TOP--WE NEED SOME SPACE!
KIRA! THEY NEED COVERING FIRE! LOOP BACK AROUND AND LAY IT DOWN!
ON IT!
EVERYBODY ELSE, WE'VE GOT A CLEAN PATH TO THE TOWER! LET'S TAKE THE SHOT AND END--

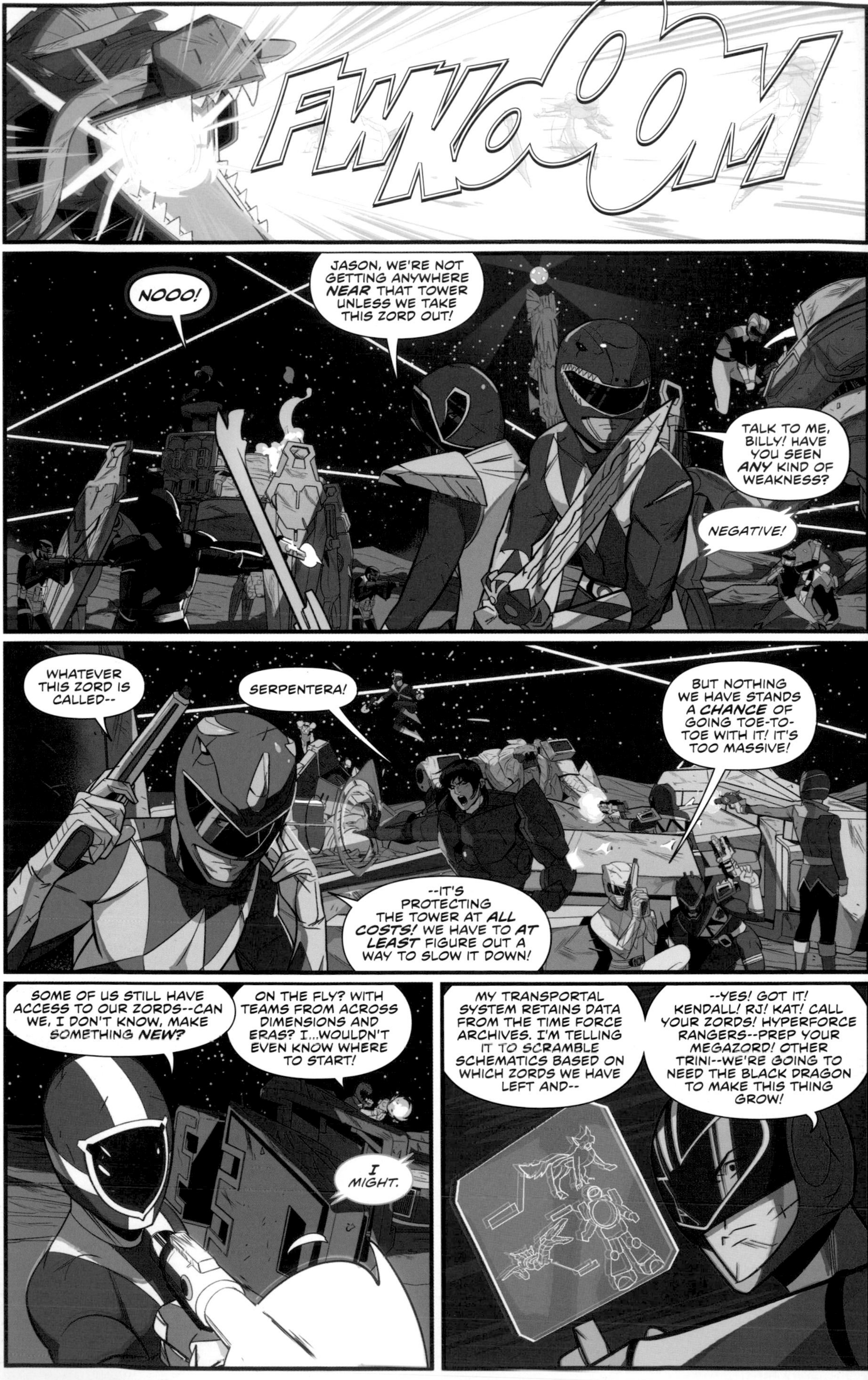
FWKOOOM
NOOO!
JASON, WE'RE NOT GETTING ANYWHERE NEAR THAT TOWER UNLESS WE TAKE THIS ZORD OUT!
TALK TO ME, BILLY! HAVE YOU SEEN ANY KIND OF WEAKNESS?
NEGATIVE!
WHATEVER THIS ZORD IS CALLED--
SERPENTERA!
--IT'S PROTECTING THE TOWER AT ALL COSTS! WE HAVE TO AT LEAST FIGURE OUT A WAY TO SLOW IT DOWN!
BUT NOTHING WE HAVE STANDS A CHANCE OF GOING TOE-TO-TOE WITH IT! IT'S TOO MASSIVE!
SOME OF US STILL HAVE ACCESS TO OUR ZORDS--CAN WE, I DON'T KNOW, MAKE SOMETHING NEW?
ON THE FLY? WITH TEAMS FROM ACROSS DIMENSIONS AND ERAS? I...WOULDN'T EVEN KNOW WHERE TO START!
I MIGHT.
MY TRANSPORTAL SYSTEM RETAINS DATA FROM THE TIME FORCE ARCHIVES. I'M TELLING IT TO SCRAMBLE SCHEMATICS BASED ON WHICH ZORDS WE HAVE LEFT AND--
--YES! GOT IT! KENDALL! RJ! KAT! CALL YOUR ZORDS! HYPERFORCE RANGERS--PREP YOUR MEGAZORD! OTHER TRINI--WE'RE GOING TO NEED THE BLACK DRAGON TO MAKE THIS THING GROW!

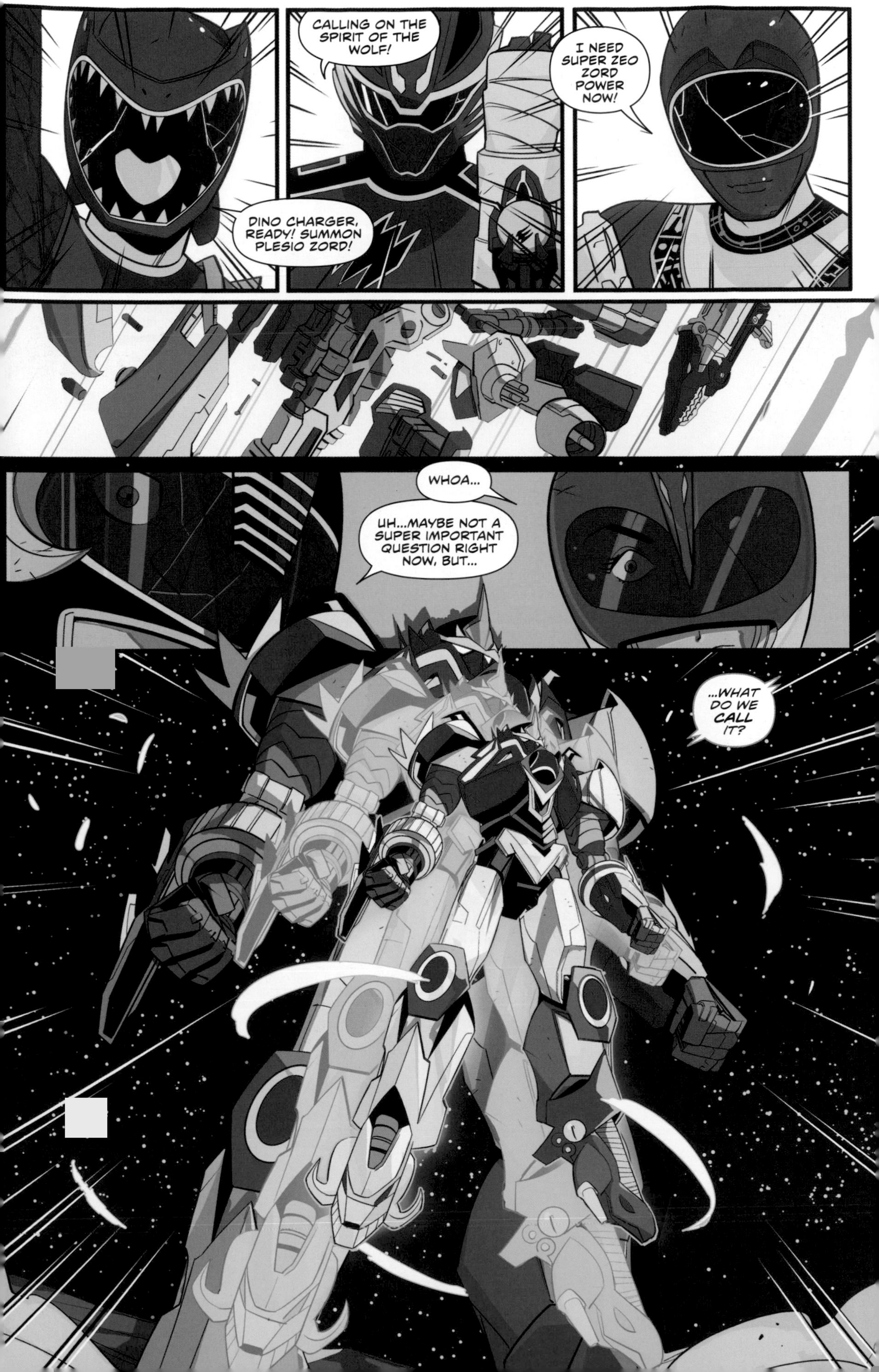
DINO CHARGER, READY! SUMMON PLESIO ZORD!
CALLING ON THE SPIRIT OF THE WOLF!
I NEED SUPER ZEO ZORD POWER NOW!
WHOA...
UH...MAYBE NOT A SUPER IMPORTANT QUESTION RIGHT NOW, BUT...
...WHAT DO WE CALL IT?

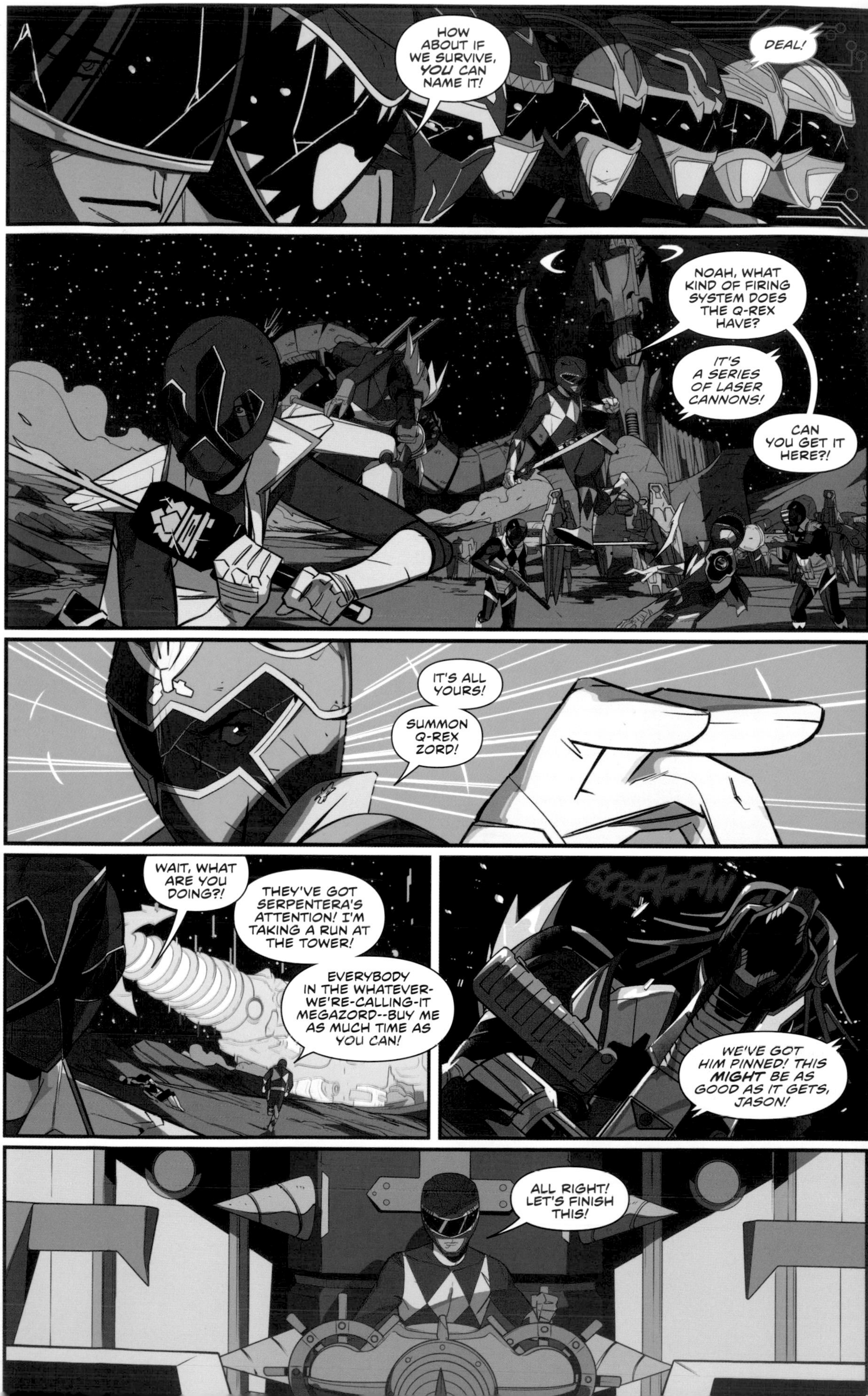
HOW ABOUT IF WE SURVIVE, *YOU* CAN NAME IT!
DEAL!
NOAH, WHAT KIND OF FIRING SYSTEM DOES THE Q-REX HAVE?
IT'S A SERIES OF LASER CANNONS!
CAN YOU GET IT HERE?!
IT'S ALL YOURS!
SUMMON Q-REX ZORD!
WAIT, WHAT ARE YOU DOING?!
THEY'VE GOT SERPENTERA'S ATTENTION! I'M TAKING A RUN AT THE TOWER!
EVERYBODY IN THE WHATEVER-WE'RE-CALLING-IT MEGAZORD--BUY ME AS MUCH TIME AS YOU CAN!
WE'VE GOT HIM PINNED! THIS **MIGHT** BE AS GOOD AS IT GETS, JASON!
ALL RIGHT! LET'S FINISH THIS!

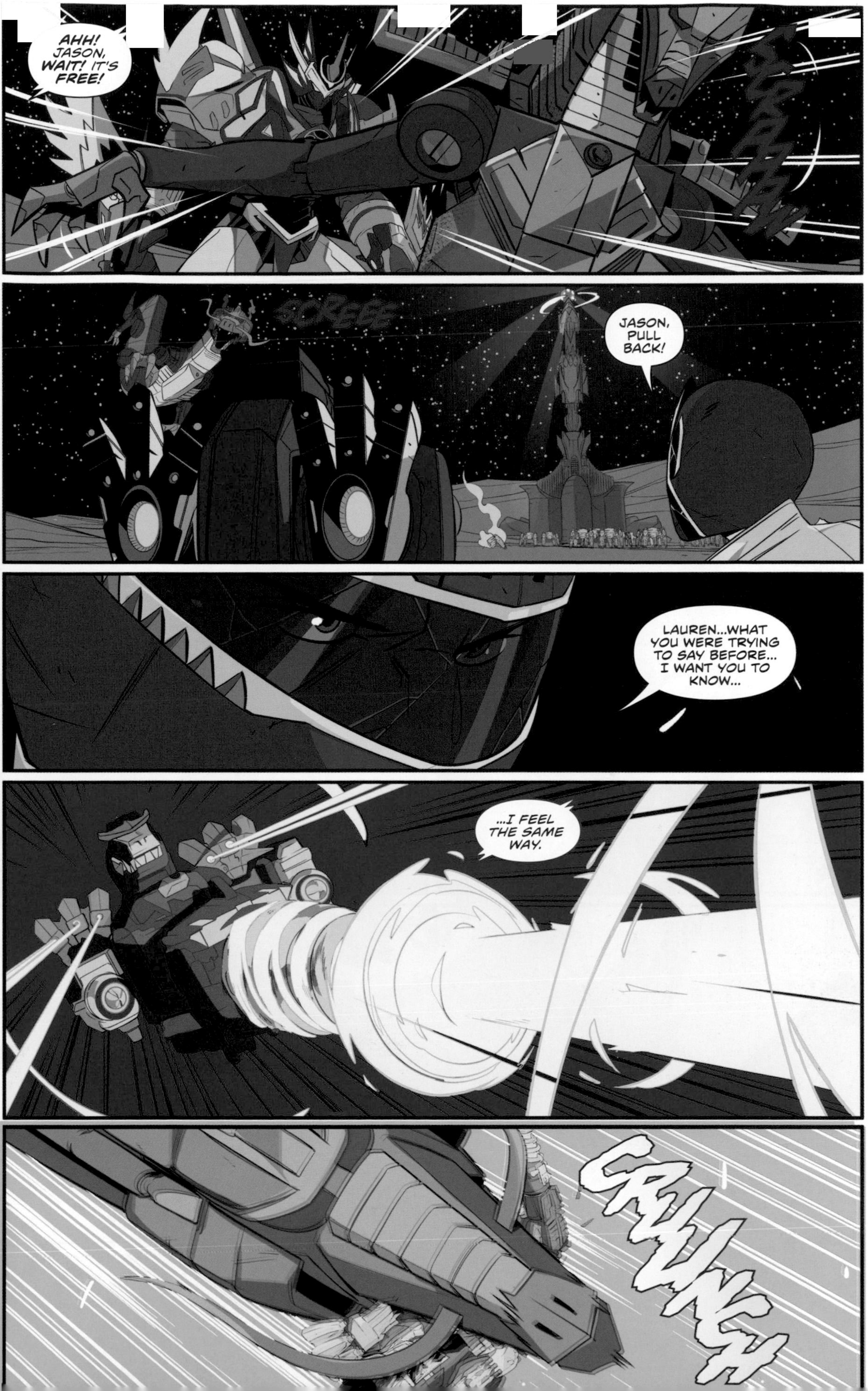
AHH! JASON, WAIT! IT'S FREE!
SCREEE
JASON, PULL BACK!
LAUREN...WHAT YOU WERE TRYING TO SAY BEFORE... I WANT YOU TO KNOW...
...I FEEL THE SAME WAY.
CRUNCH

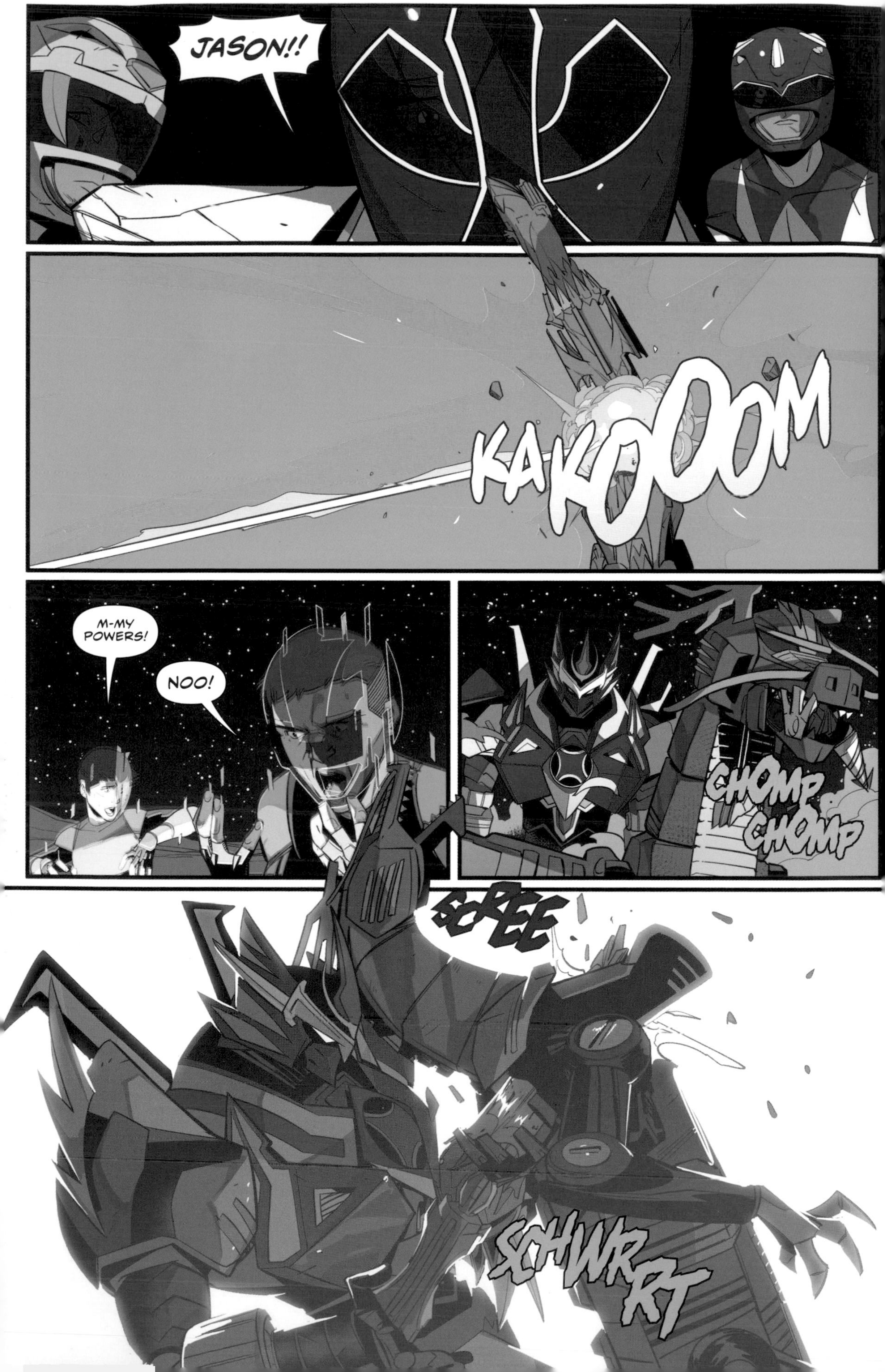
JASON!!
KAKOOOOM
M-MY POWERS!
NOO!
CHOMP CHOMP
SCREE
SCHWRRT

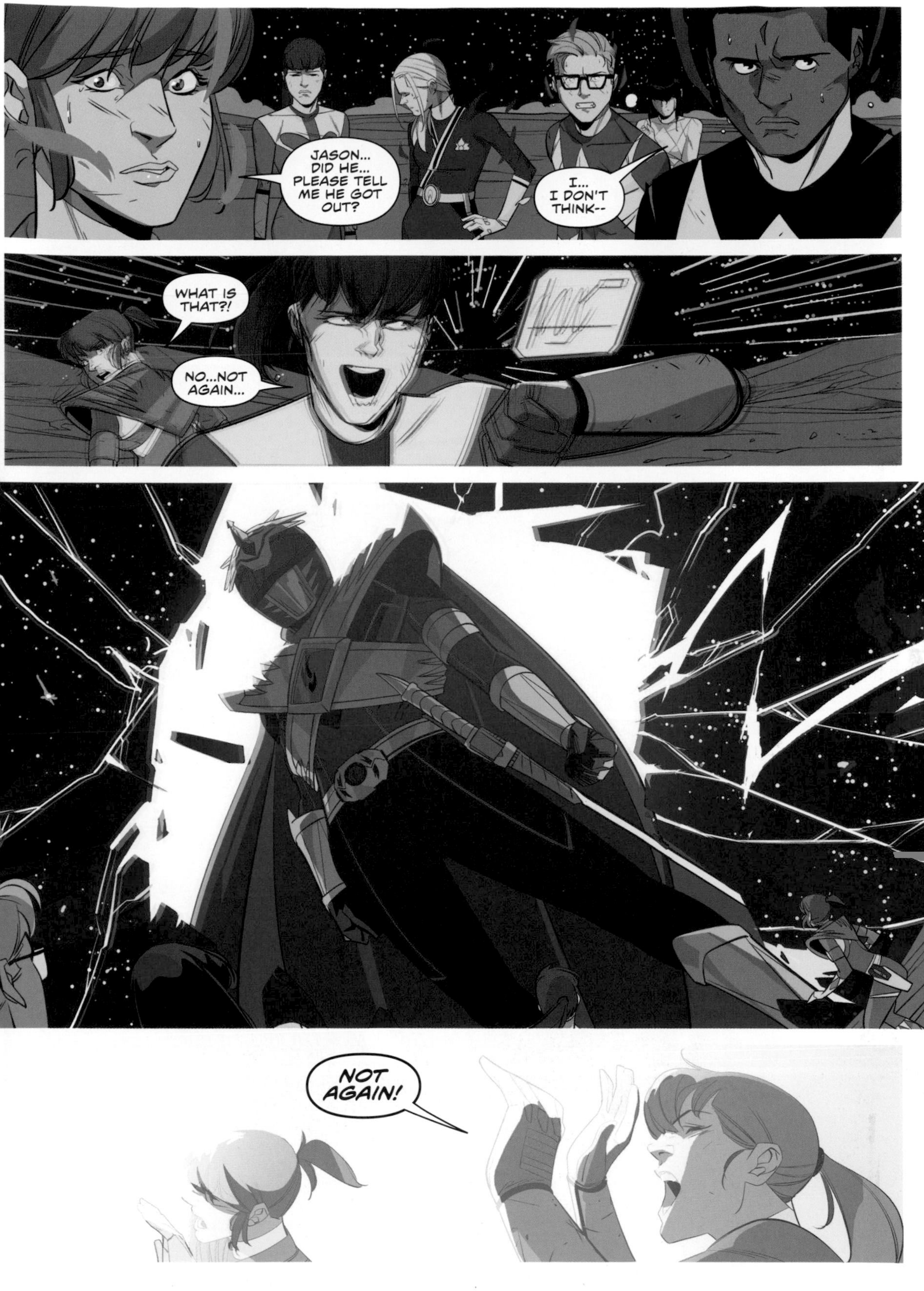
JASON... DID HE... PLEASE TELL ME HE GOT OUT?
I... I DON'T THINK--
WHAT IS THAT?!
NO...NOT AGAIN...
NOT AGAIN!

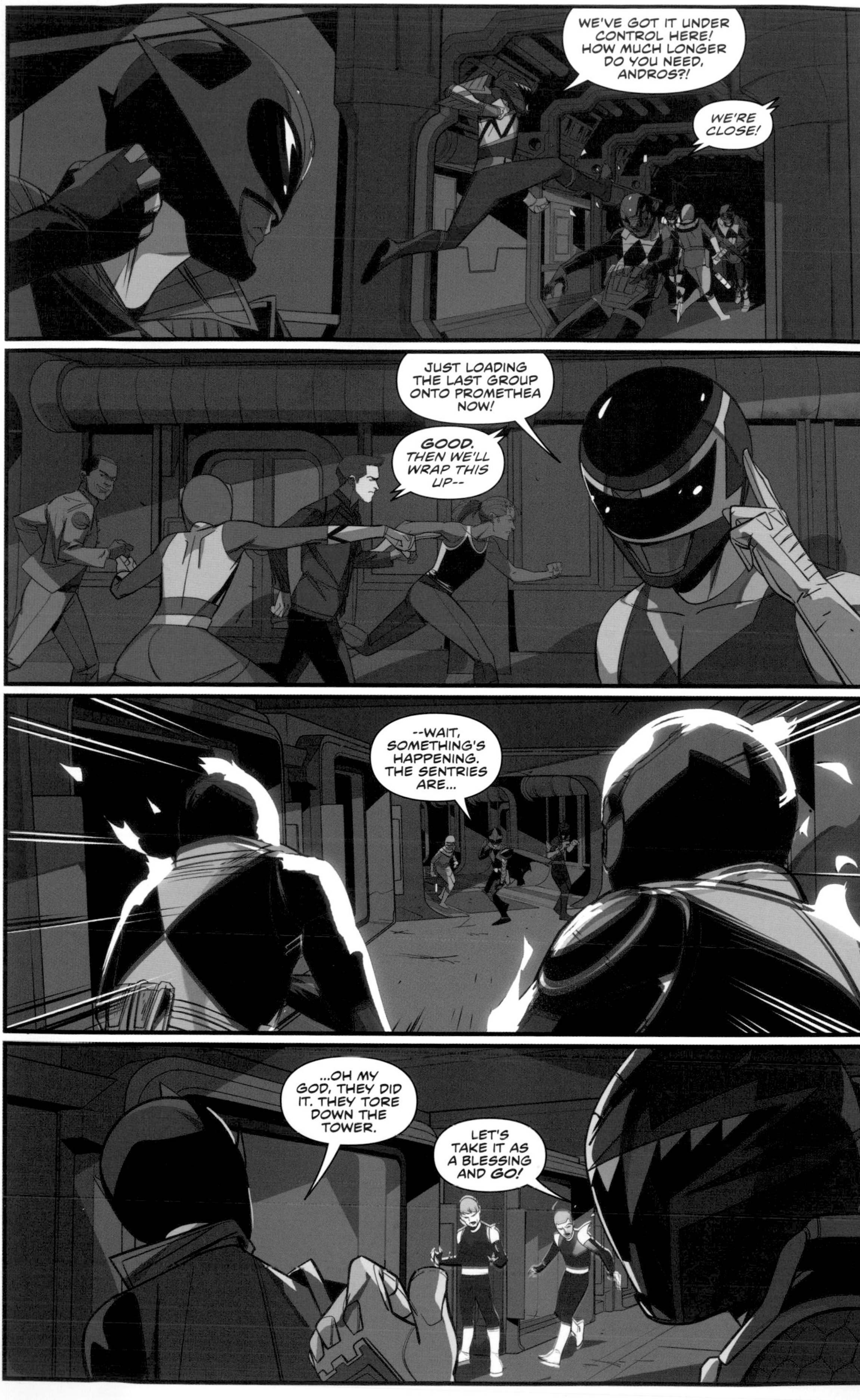
WE'VE GOT IT UNDER CONTROL HERE! HOW MUCH LONGER DO YOU NEED, ANDROS?!
WE'RE CLOSE!
JUST LOADING THE LAST GROUP ONTO PROMETHEA NOW!
GOOD. THEN WE'LL WRAP THIS UP--
--WAIT, SOMETHING'S HAPPENING. THE SENTRIES ARE...
...OH MY GOD, THEY DID IT. THEY TORE DOWN THE TOWER.
LET'S TAKE IT AS A BLESSING AND GO!

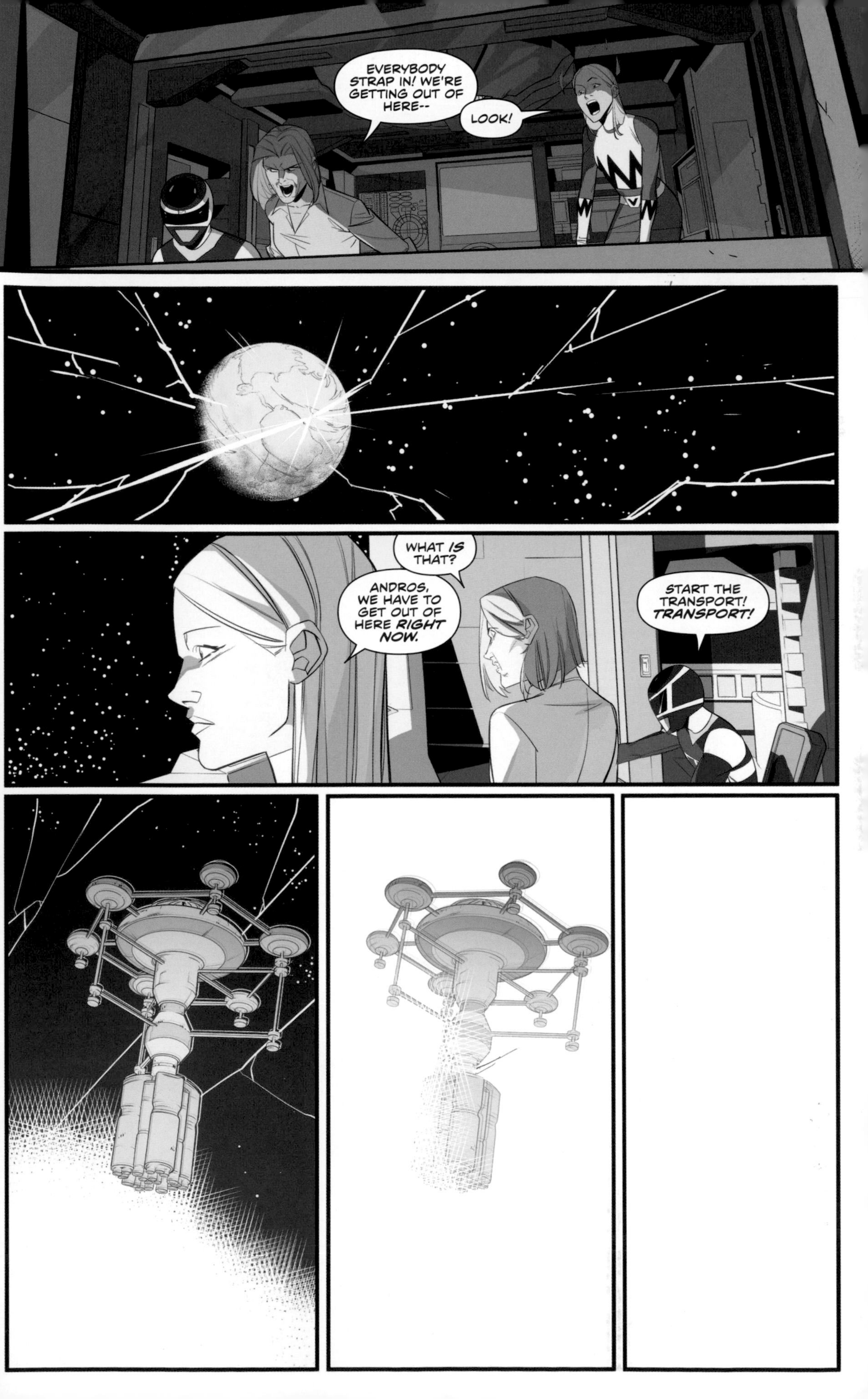
EVERYBODY STRAP IN! WE'RE GETTING OUT OF HERE--
LOOK!
WHAT *IS* THAT?
ANDROS, WE HAVE TO GET OUT OF HERE *RIGHT NOW.*
START THE TRANSPORT! *TRANSPORT!*

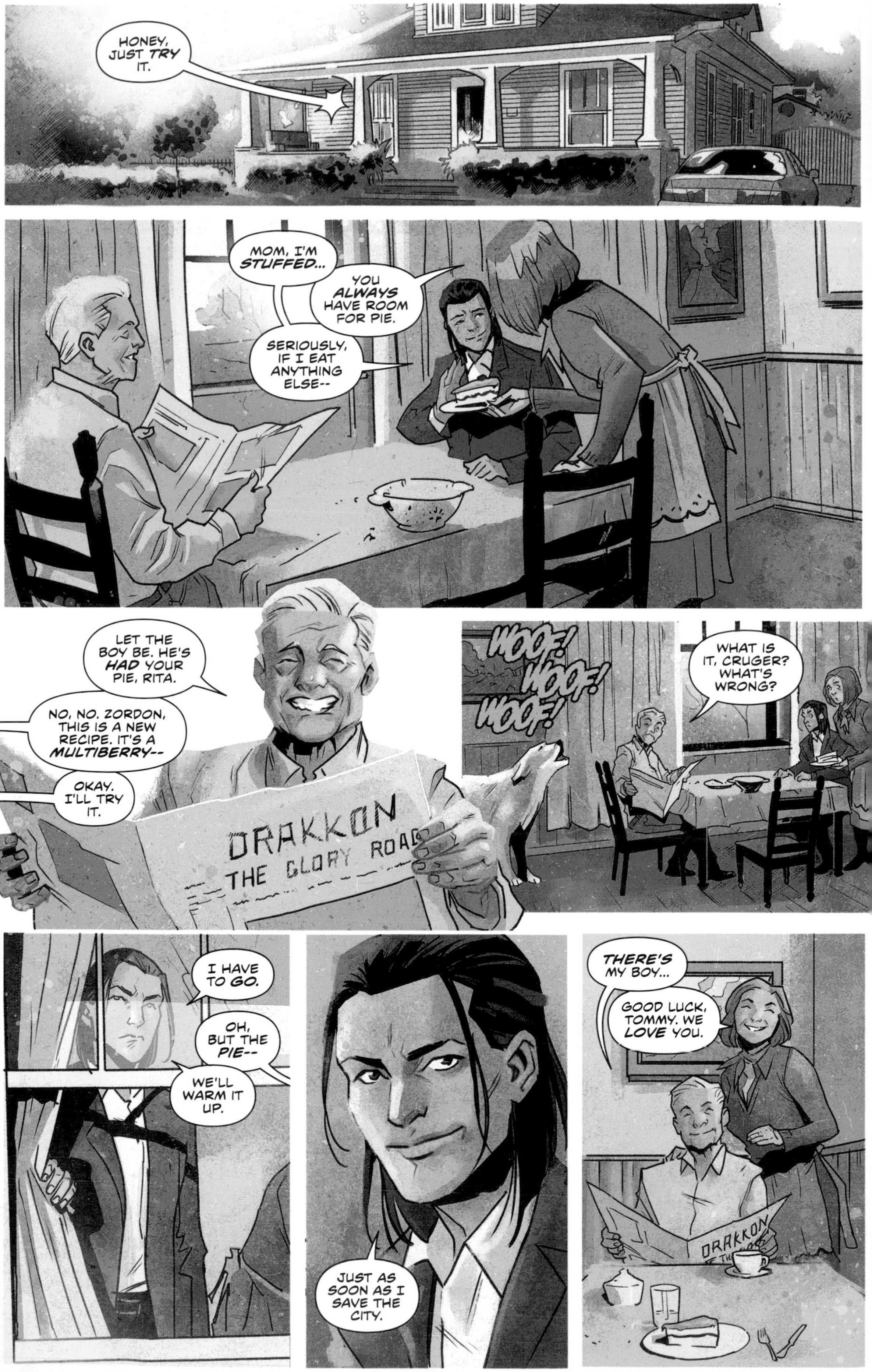

HONEY, JUST TRY IT.
MOM, I'M STUFFED...
YOU ALWAYS HAVE ROOM FOR PIE.
SERIOUSLY, IF I EAT ANYTHING ELSE--
LET THE BOY BE. HE'S HAD YOUR PIE, RITA.
NO, NO. ZORDON, THIS IS A NEW RECIPE. IT'S A MULTIBERRY--
OKAY. I'LL TRY IT.
DRAKKON THE GLORY ROAD
WOOF! WOOF! WOOF!
WHAT IS IT, CRUGER? WHAT'S WRONG?
I HAVE TO GO.
OH, BUT THE PIE--
WE'LL WARM IT UP.
JUST AS SOON AS I SAVE THE CITY.
THERE'S MY BOY...
GOOD LUCK, TOMMY. WE LOVE YOU.
DRAKKON

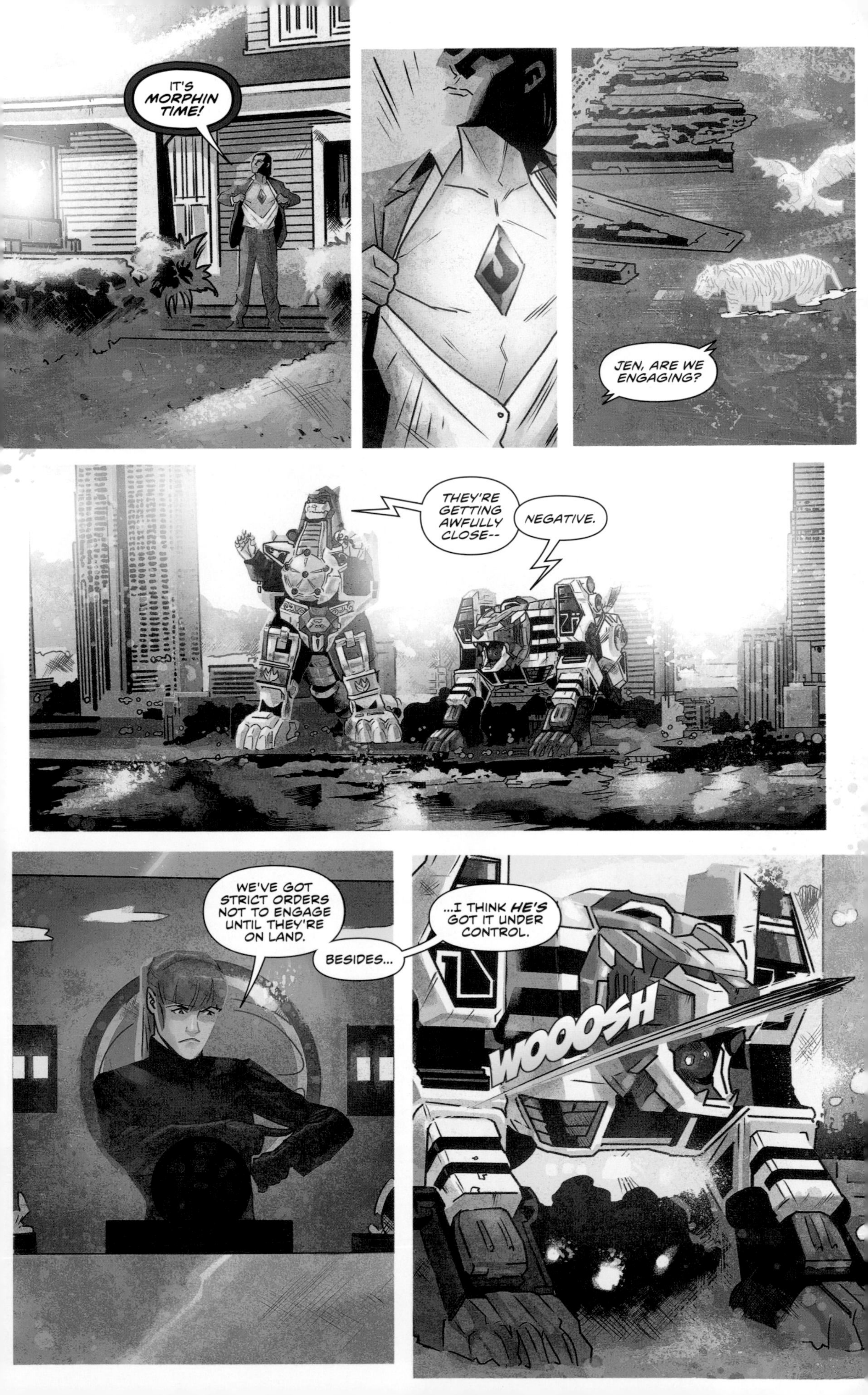
IT'S MORPHIN TIME!
JEN, ARE WE ENGAGING?
THEY'RE GETTING AWFULLY CLOSE--
NEGATIVE.
WE'VE GOT STRICT ORDERS NOT TO ENGAGE UNTIL THEY'RE ON LAND.
BESIDES...
...I THINK HE'S GOT IT UNDER CONTROL.
WOOOSH

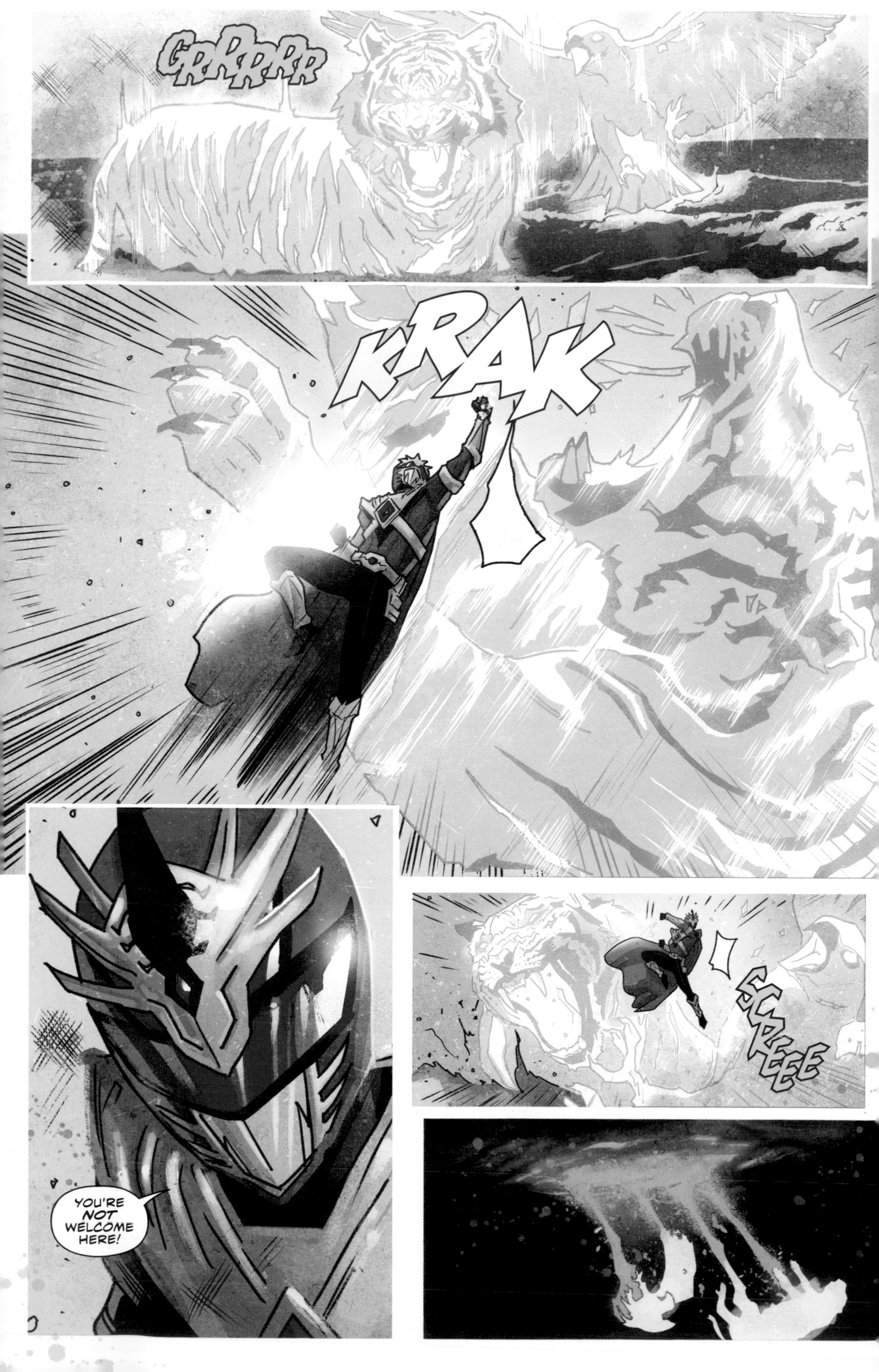
GRRRRRR
KRAK
SCREEE
YOU'RE NOT WELCOME HERE!

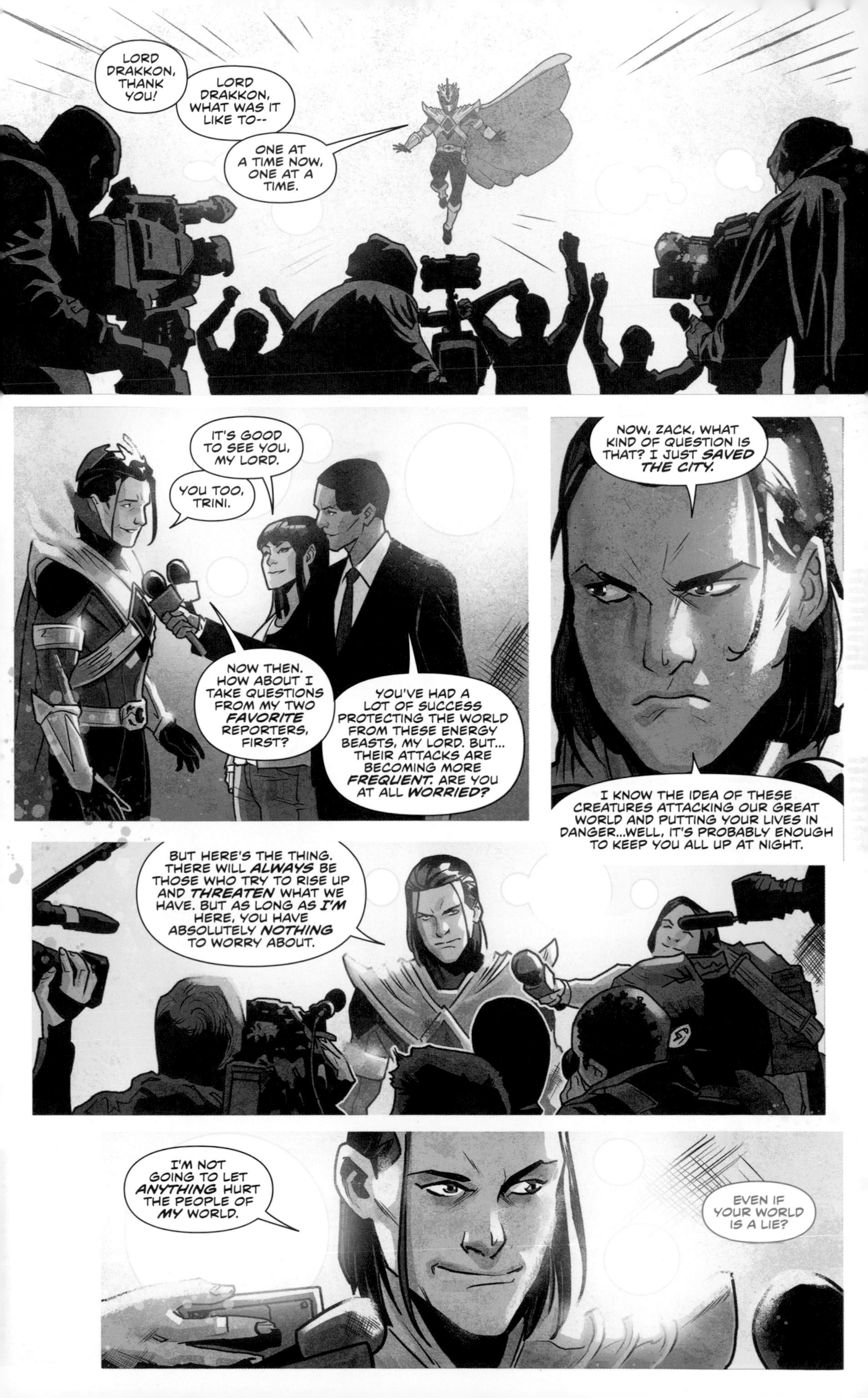
LORD DRAKKON, THANK YOU!
LORD DRAKKON, WHAT WAS IT LIKE TO--
ONE AT A TIME NOW, ONE AT A TIME.
IT'S GOOD TO SEE YOU, MY LORD.
YOU TOO, TRINI.
NOW THEN. HOW ABOUT I TAKE QUESTIONS FROM MY TWO FAVORITE REPORTERS, FIRST?
YOU'VE HAD A LOT OF SUCCESS PROTECTING THE WORLD FROM THESE ENERGY BEASTS, MY LORD. BUT... THEIR ATTACKS ARE BECOMING MORE FREQUENT. ARE YOU AT ALL WORRIED?
NOW, ZACK, WHAT KIND OF QUESTION IS THAT? I JUST SAVED THE CITY.
I KNOW THE IDEA OF THESE CREATURES ATTACKING OUR GREAT WORLD AND PUTTING YOUR LIVES IN DANGER...WELL, IT'S PROBABLY ENOUGH TO KEEP YOU ALL UP AT NIGHT.
BUT HERE'S THE THING. THERE WILL ALWAYS BE THOSE WHO TRY TO RISE UP AND THREATEN WHAT WE HAVE. BUT AS LONG AS I'M HERE, YOU HAVE ABSOLUTELY NOTHING TO WORRY ABOUT.
I'M NOT GOING TO LET ANYTHING HURT THE PEOPLE OF MY WORLD.
EVEN IF YOUR WORLD IS A LIE?

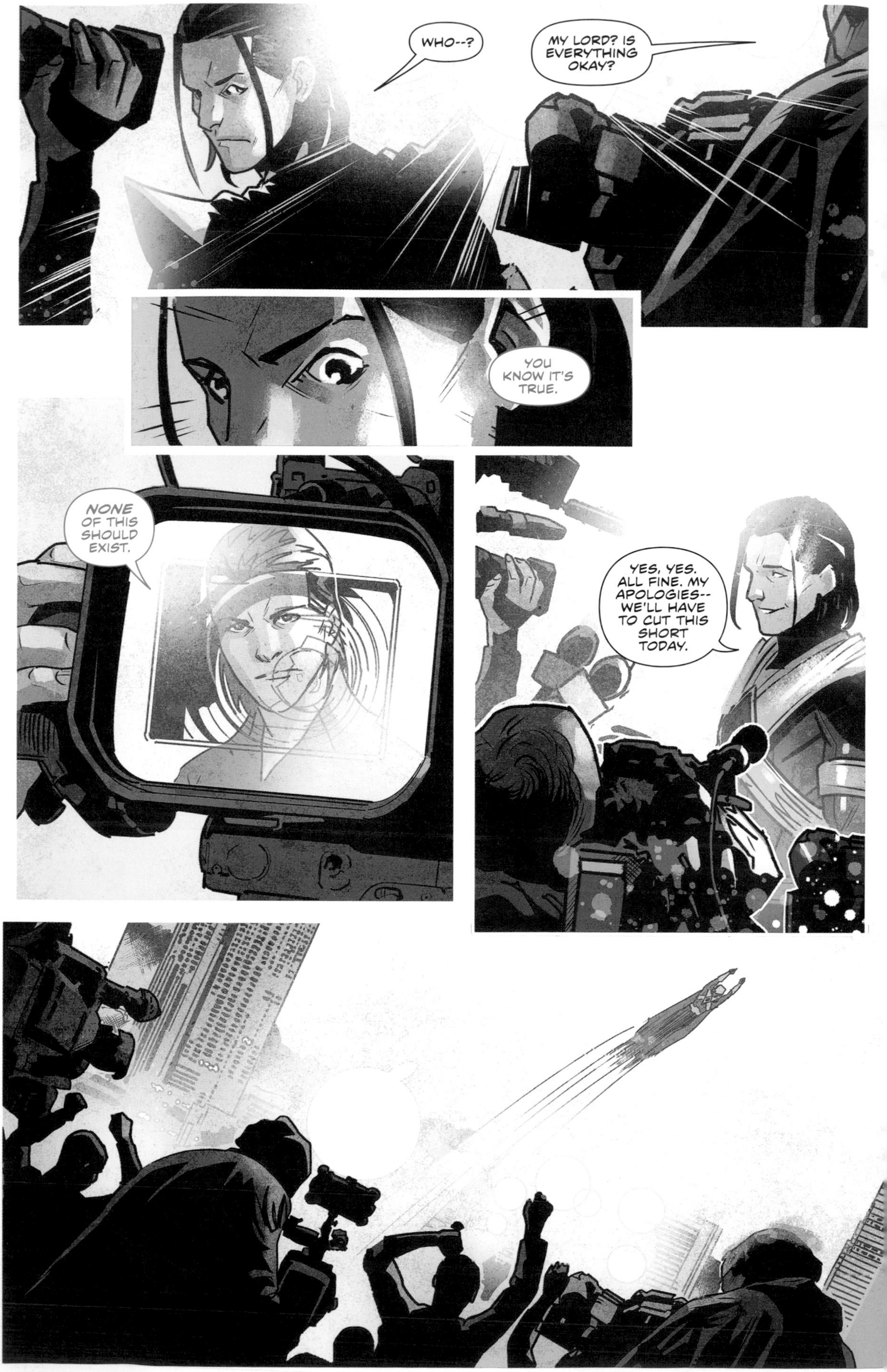
WHO--?
MY LORD? IS EVERYTHING OKAY?
YOU KNOW IT'S TRUE.
NONE OF THIS SHOULD EXIST.
YES, YES. ALL FINE. MY APOLOGIES-- WE'LL HAVE TO CUT THIS SHORT TODAY.

MY LORD. WELCOME *HOME*. AND, AS ALWAYS, *CONGRATULATIONS*. NEWS OF YOUR SUCCESS AGAINST THE ENERGY BEASTS IS ON *ALL* THE NEWS STATIONS.

THANK YOU, FINSTER. IT'S GOOD TO BE BACK.

HOW'S IT GOING, BILLY?

THE THROTTLE'S STILL STICKING A LITTLE BIT. BUT THE NITROUS OXIDE ADDITIONS ARE WORKING *GREAT*. I THINK YOU'RE GOING TO LOVE IT.

I CAN'T WAIT.

THERE ARE SEVERAL MATTERS OF THE DAY THAT REQUIRE YOUR ATTENTION, SIR.

THE METRO CITY GALA HAS REQUESTED YOUR ATTENDANCE, AND THE DRAKKON ACADEMY IS PRACTICING ON THE *LAWN* THIS AFTERNOON.

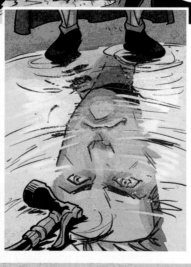

MY LORD?

...YES...THE DRAKKON ACADEMY. I SHOULD SAY *HELLO*.

--WHICH IS WHY THE MOST IMPORTANT THING IS THAT YOU MAINTAIN *FOCUS*.

REMEMBER, AS A PART OF THE DRAKKON ACADEMY, YOU'RE PREPARING TO SERVE OUR LORD AND CARRY HIS MESSAGE ACROSS THE LANDS--

LORD DRAKKON!

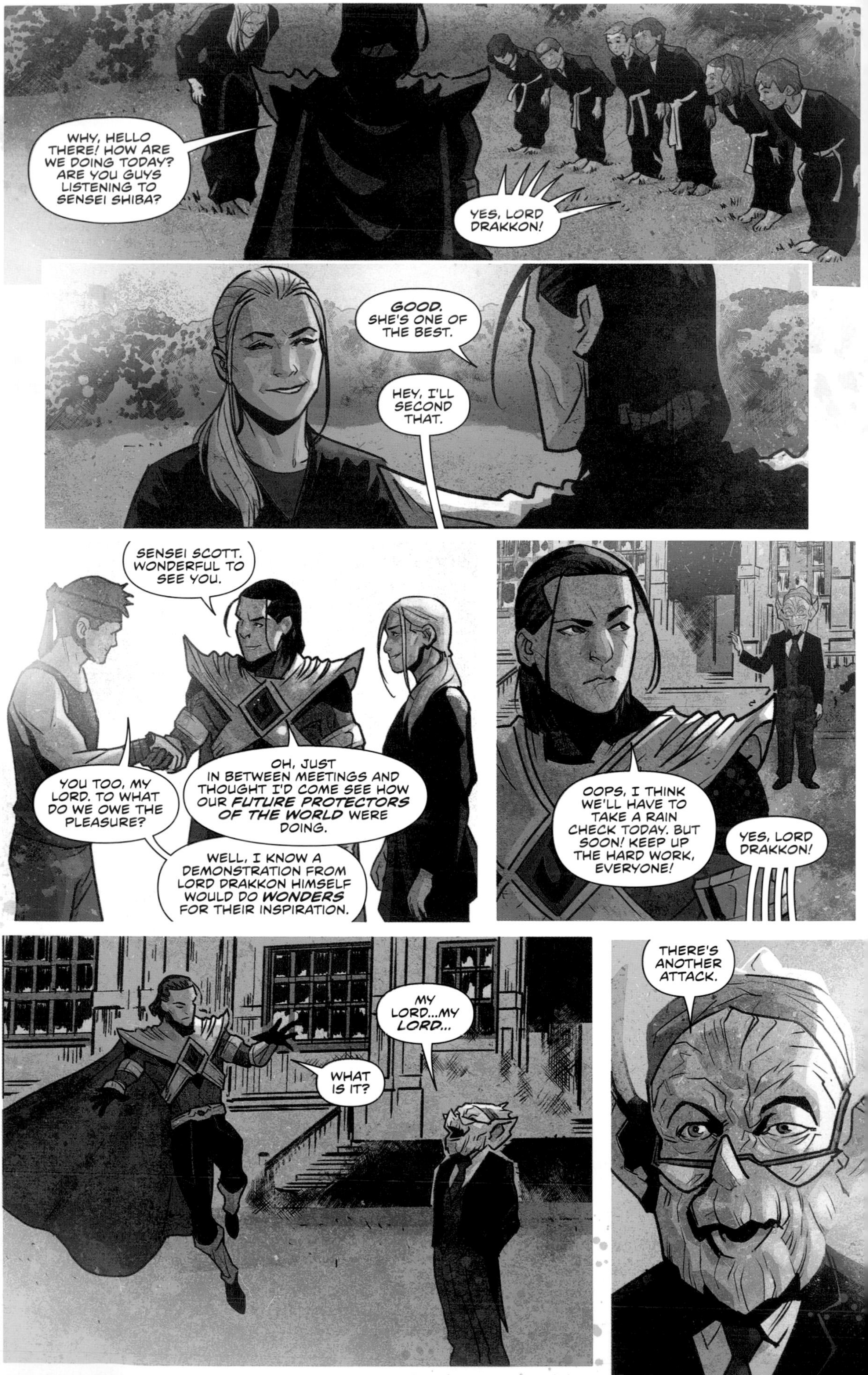
WHY, HELLO THERE! HOW ARE WE DOING TODAY? ARE YOU GUYS LISTENING TO SENSEI SHIBA?
YES, LORD DRAKKON!
GOOD. SHE'S ONE OF THE BEST.
HEY, I'LL SECOND THAT.
SENSEI SCOTT. WONDERFUL TO SEE YOU.
YOU TOO, MY LORD. TO WHAT DO WE OWE THE PLEASURE?
OH, JUST IN BETWEEN MEETINGS AND THOUGHT I'D COME SEE HOW OUR FUTURE PROTECTORS OF THE WORLD WERE DOING.
WELL, I KNOW A DEMONSTRATION FROM LORD DRAKKON HIMSELF WOULD DO WONDERS FOR THEIR INSPIRATION.
OOPS, I THINK WE'LL HAVE TO TAKE A RAIN CHECK TODAY. BUT SOON! KEEP UP THE HARD WORK, EVERYONE!
YES, LORD DRAKKON!
MY LORD...MY LORD...
WHAT IS IT?
THERE'S ANOTHER ATTACK.

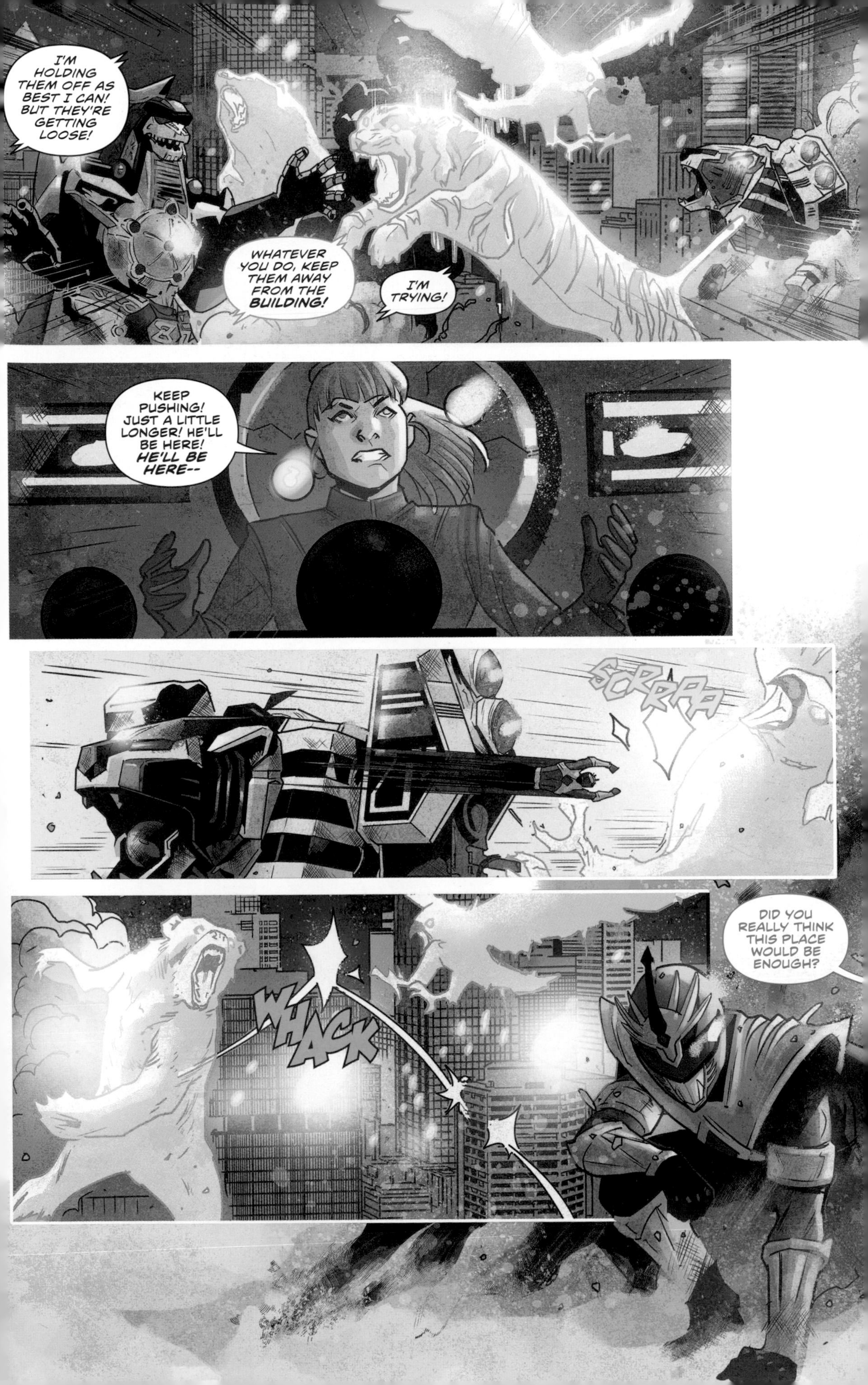
I'M HOLDING THEM OFF AS BEST I CAN! BUT THEY'RE GETTING LOOSE!
WHATEVER YOU DO, KEEP THEM AWAY FROM THE BUILDING!
I'M TRYING!
KEEP PUSHING! JUST A LITTLE LONGER! HE'LL BE HERE! HE'LL BE HERE--
SCRRAA
WHACK
DID YOU REALLY THINK THIS PLACE WOULD BE ENOUGH?

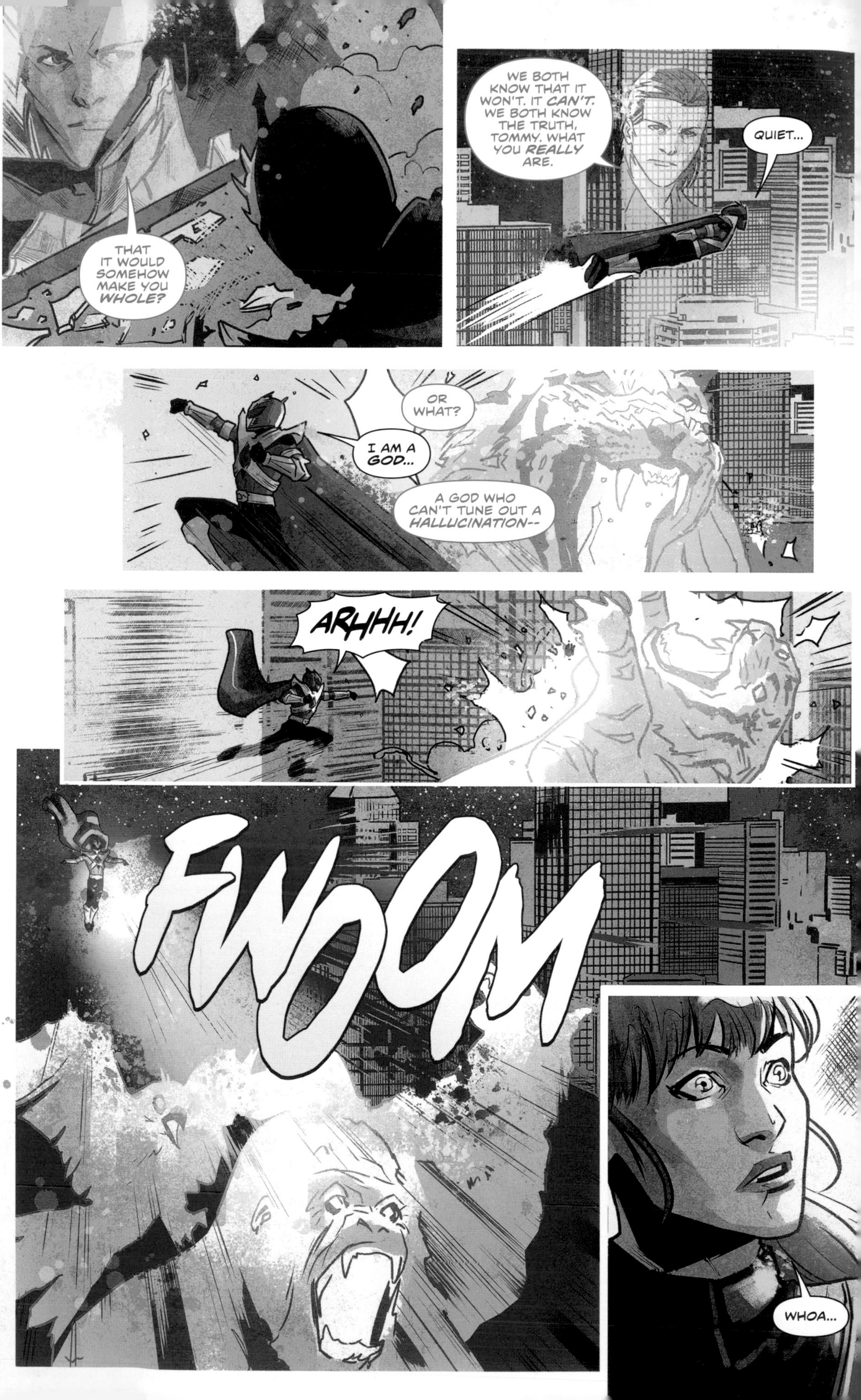
THAT IT WOULD SOMEHOW MAKE YOU WHOLE?
WE BOTH KNOW THAT IT WON'T. IT CAN'T. WE BOTH KNOW THE TRUTH, TOMMY. WHAT YOU REALLY ARE.
QUIET...
OR WHAT?
I AM A GOD...
A GOD WHO CAN'T TUNE OUT A HALLUCINATION--
ARHHH!
FWOOM
WHOA...

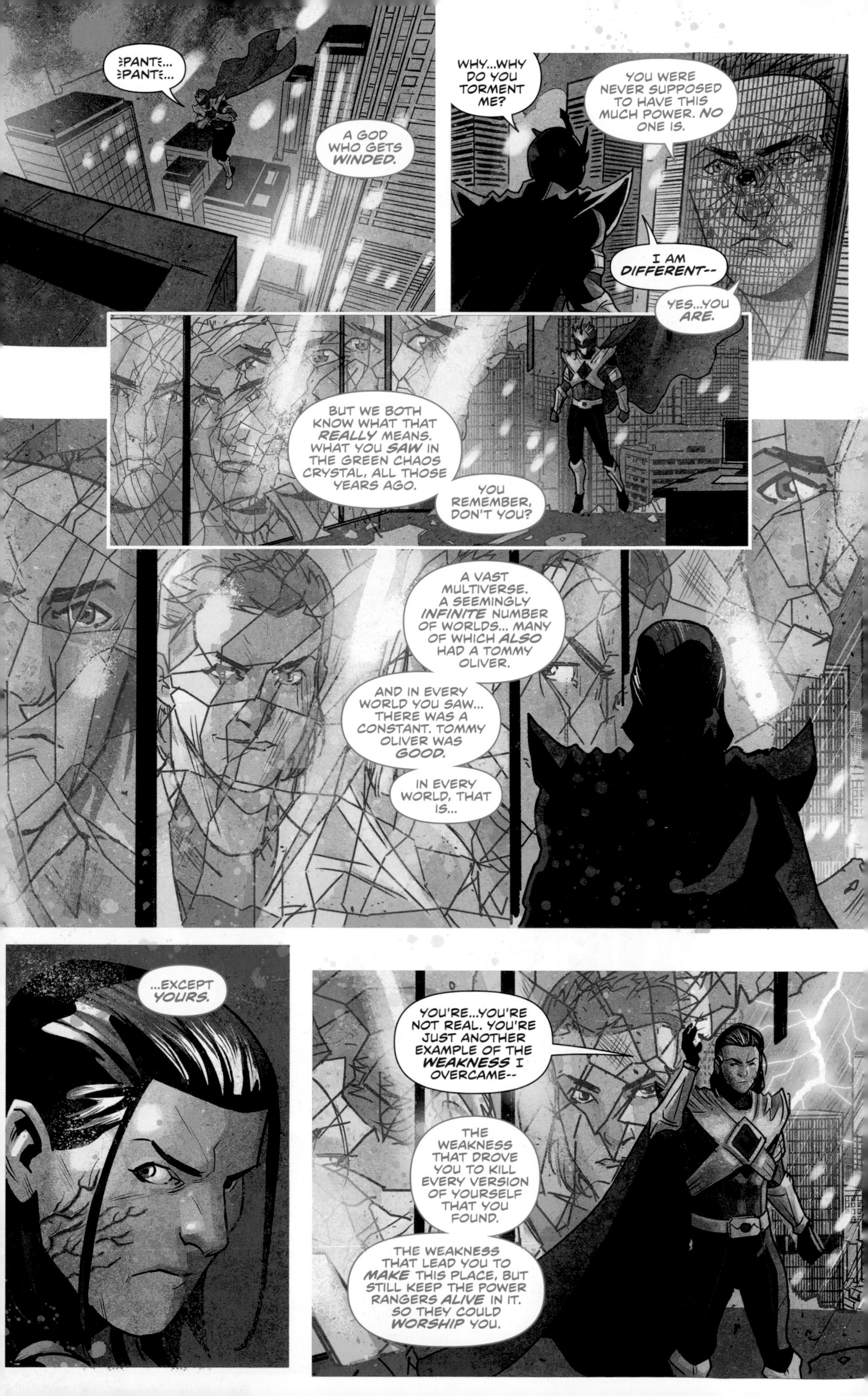
PANT...
PANT...
A GOD WHO GETS *WINDED.*
WHY...WHY DO YOU TORMENT ME?
YOU WERE NEVER SUPPOSED TO HAVE THIS MUCH POWER. *NO* ONE IS.
I AM *DIFFERENT--*
YES...YOU *ARE.*
BUT WE BOTH KNOW WHAT THAT *REALLY* MEANS. WHAT YOU *SAW* IN THE GREEN CHAOS CRYSTAL, ALL THOSE YEARS AGO.
YOU REMEMBER, DON'T YOU?
A VAST MULTIVERSE. A SEEMINGLY *INFINITE* NUMBER OF WORLDS... MANY OF WHICH *ALSO* HAD A TOMMY OLIVER.
AND IN EVERY WORLD YOU SAW... THERE WAS A CONSTANT. TOMMY OLIVER WAS *GOOD.*
IN EVERY WORLD, THAT IS...
...EXCEPT *YOURS.*
YOU'RE...YOU'RE NOT REAL. YOU'RE JUST ANOTHER EXAMPLE OF THE *WEAKNESS* I OVERCAME--
THE WEAKNESS THAT DROVE YOU TO KILL EVERY VERSION OF YOURSELF THAT YOU FOUND.
THE WEAKNESS THAT LEAD YOU TO *MAKE* THIS PLACE, BUT STILL KEEP THE POWER RANGERS *ALIVE* IN IT. SO THEY COULD *WORSHIP* YOU.

THE WEAKNESS... THAT WON'T LET YOU BE HONEST WITH YOURSELF.

NO.... YOU'RE NOT REAL...

THAT IN ALL OF EXISTENCE--

--YOU WERE THE FLAWED ONE.

YOU'RE NOT REAL!

THIS ISN'T REAL!

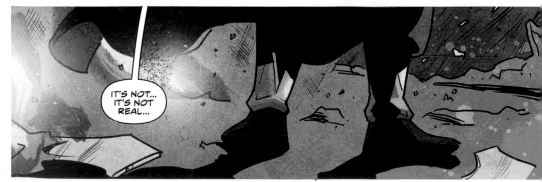

IT'S NOT... IT'S NOT REAL...

HE HAS LOST CONTROL.

THE BARRIERS ARE WEAK.

NOW IS OUR BEST CHANCE.

FOCUS.

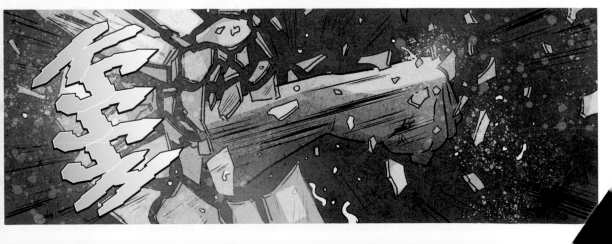

--IT JUST WOULD HAVE BEEN NICE TO HAVE A HEADS UP THAT HE MIGHT COME BY.

I MEAN, THEY *ARE* HIS GROUNDS. WE SHOULD PROBABLY FIGURE THERE'S ALWAYS A *CHANCE* OF HIM SHOWING--

--UP...

ALL RIGHT, THAT'S IT FOR ME. I'LL SEE YOU GUYS TOMORROW.

HAVE A GOOD NIGHT, JEN.

WHAT... THE...

"--BUT LORD DRAKKON MADE A POINT TO ASSURE EVERYONE THAT THE ENERGY BEASTS WOULD BE STOPPED."

EH, TOO MUCH PASSIVE VOICE. HERE, LET ME TAKE A--

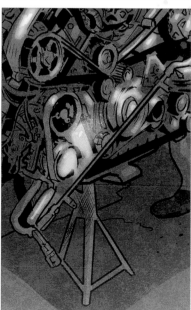

OH...

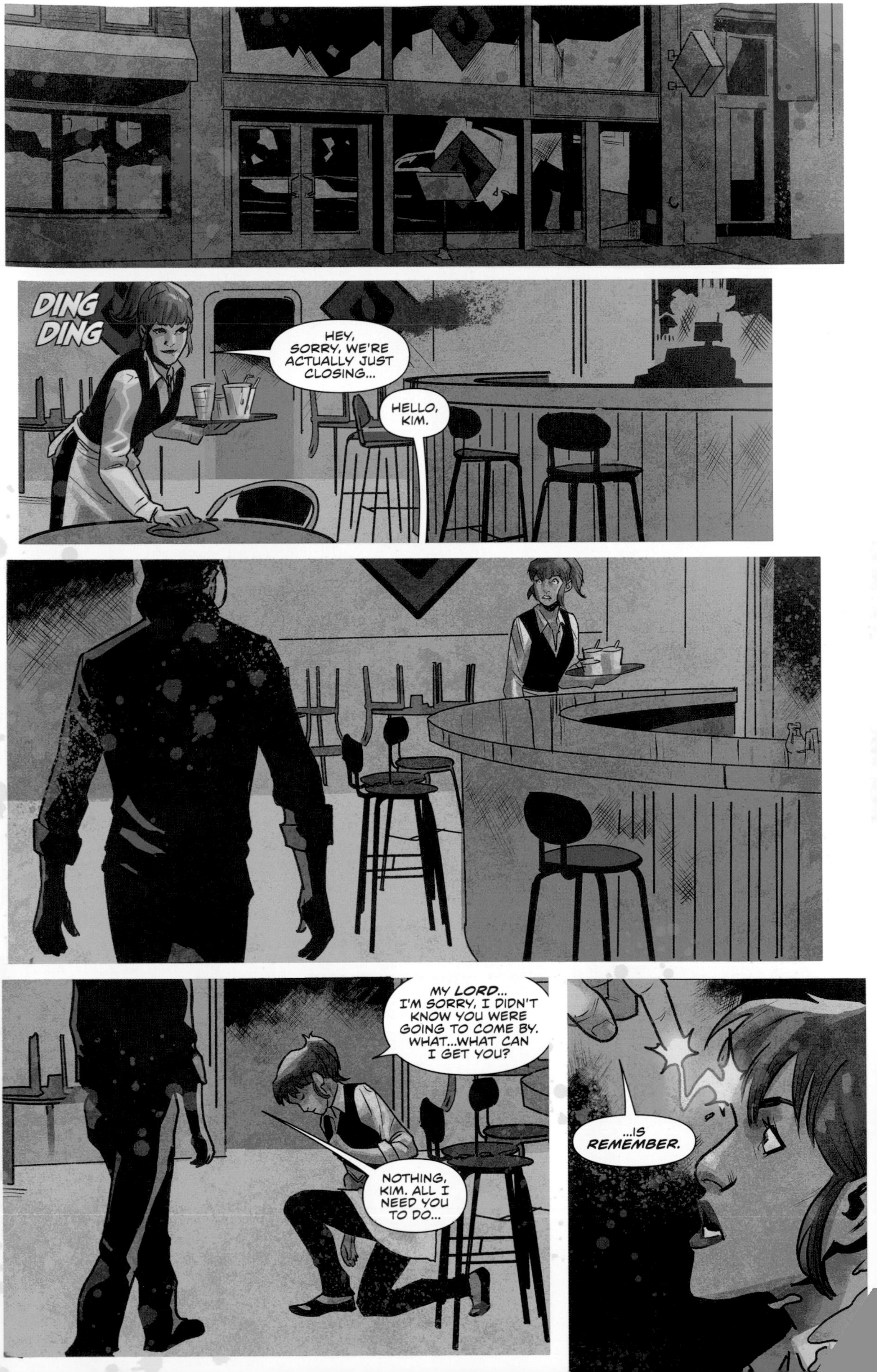
DING DING
HEY, SORRY, WE'RE ACTUALLY JUST CLOSING...
HELLO, KIM.
MY LORD... I'M SORRY, I DIDN'T KNOW YOU WERE GOING TO COME BY. WHAT...WHAT CAN I GET YOU?
NOTHING, KIM. ALL I NEED YOU TO DO...
...IS REMEMBER.

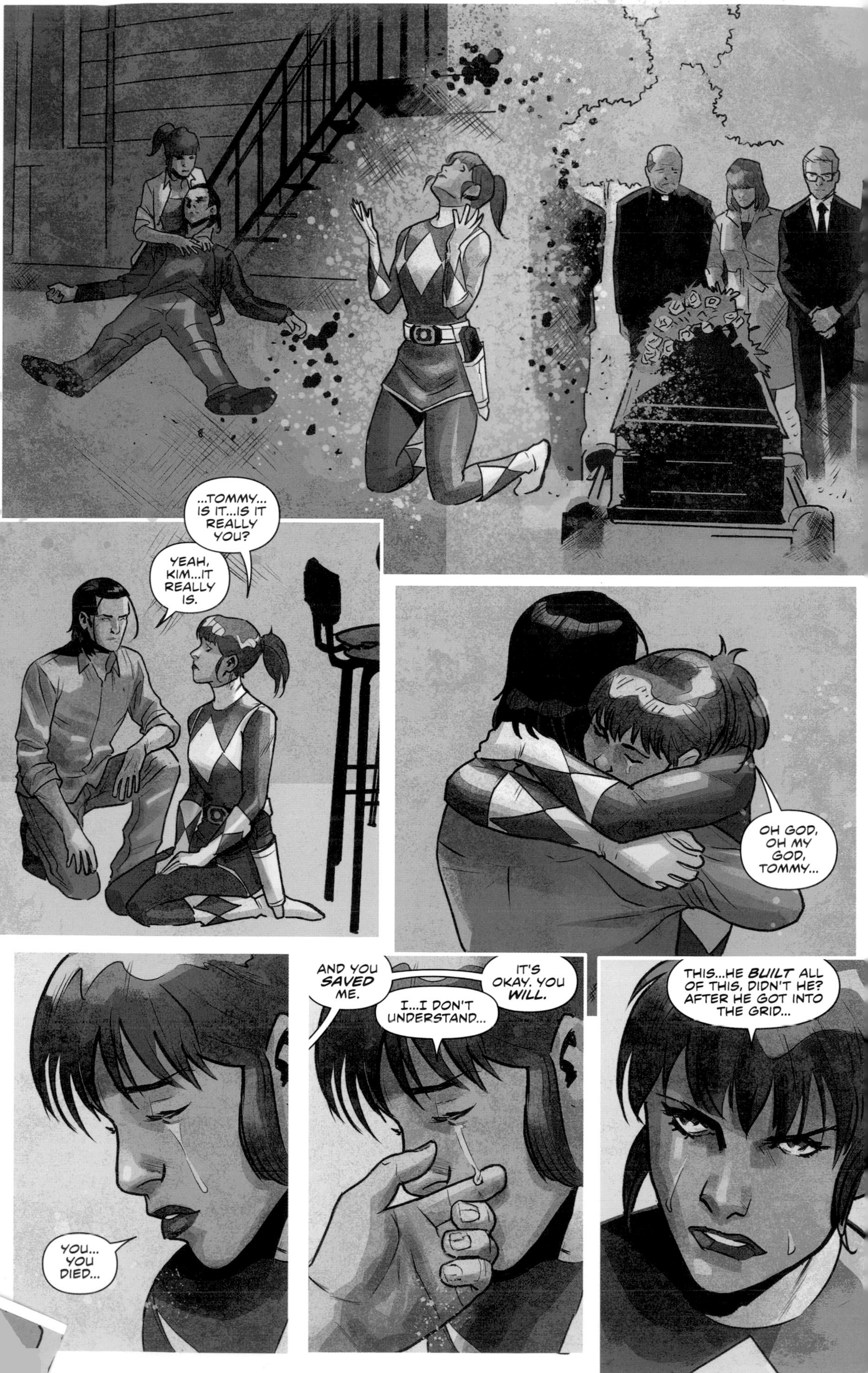
...TOMMY... IS IT...IS IT REALLY YOU?
YEAH, KIM...IT REALLY IS.
OH GOD, OH MY GOD, TOMMY...
YOU... YOU DIED...
AND YOU *SAVED* ME.
I...I DON'T UNDERSTAND...
IT'S OKAY. YOU *WILL*.
THIS...HE *BUILT* ALL OF THIS, DIDN'T HE? AFTER HE GOT INTO THE GRID...

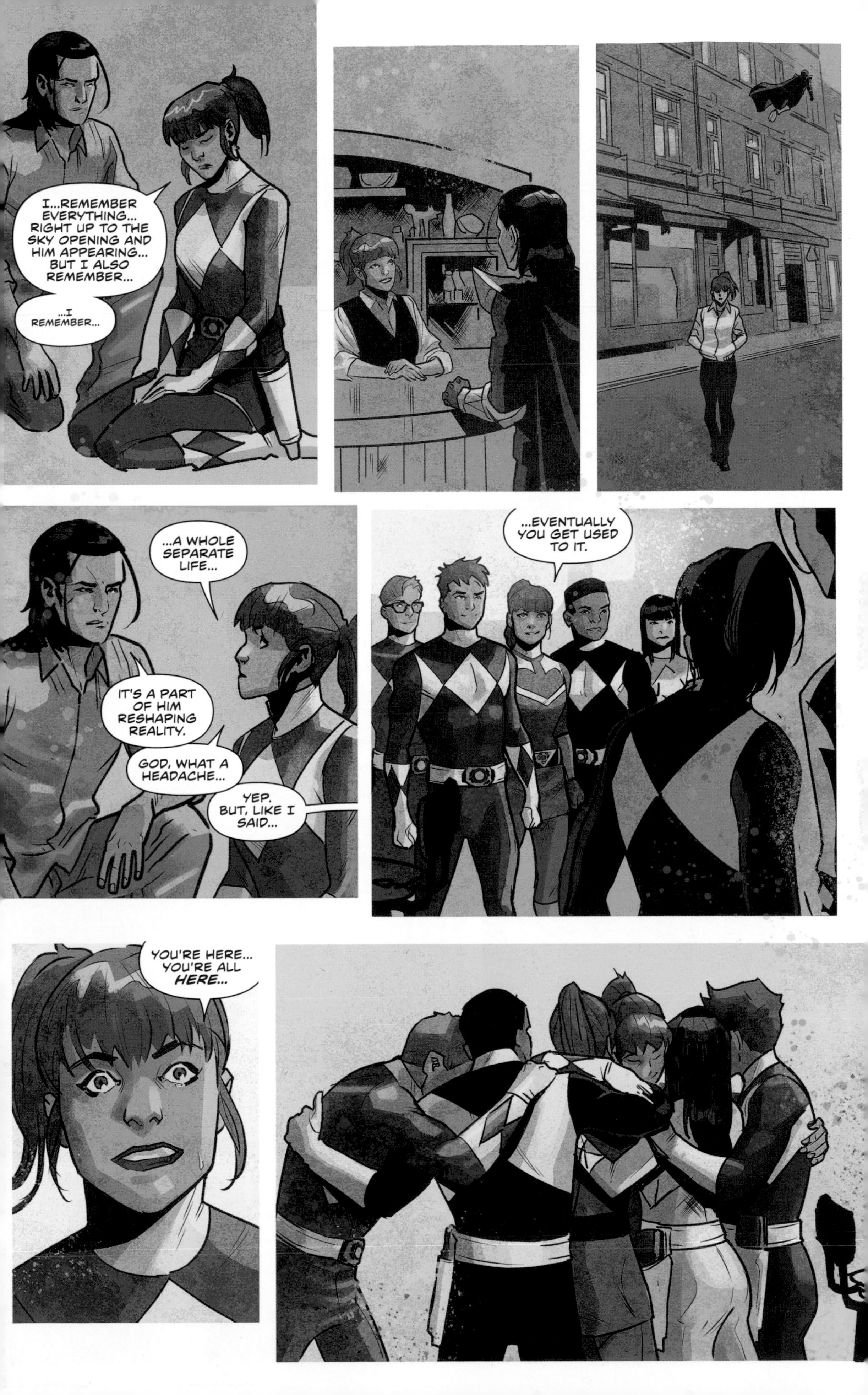
I...REMEMBER EVERYTHING... RIGHT UP TO THE SKY OPENING AND HIM APPEARING... BUT I ALSO REMEMBER...
...I REMEMBER...
...A WHOLE SEPARATE LIFE...
IT'S A PART OF HIM RESHAPING REALITY.
GOD, WHAT A HEADACHE...
YEP. BUT, LIKE I SAID...
...EVENTUALLY YOU GET USED TO IT.
YOU'RE HERE... YOU'RE ALL *HERE*...

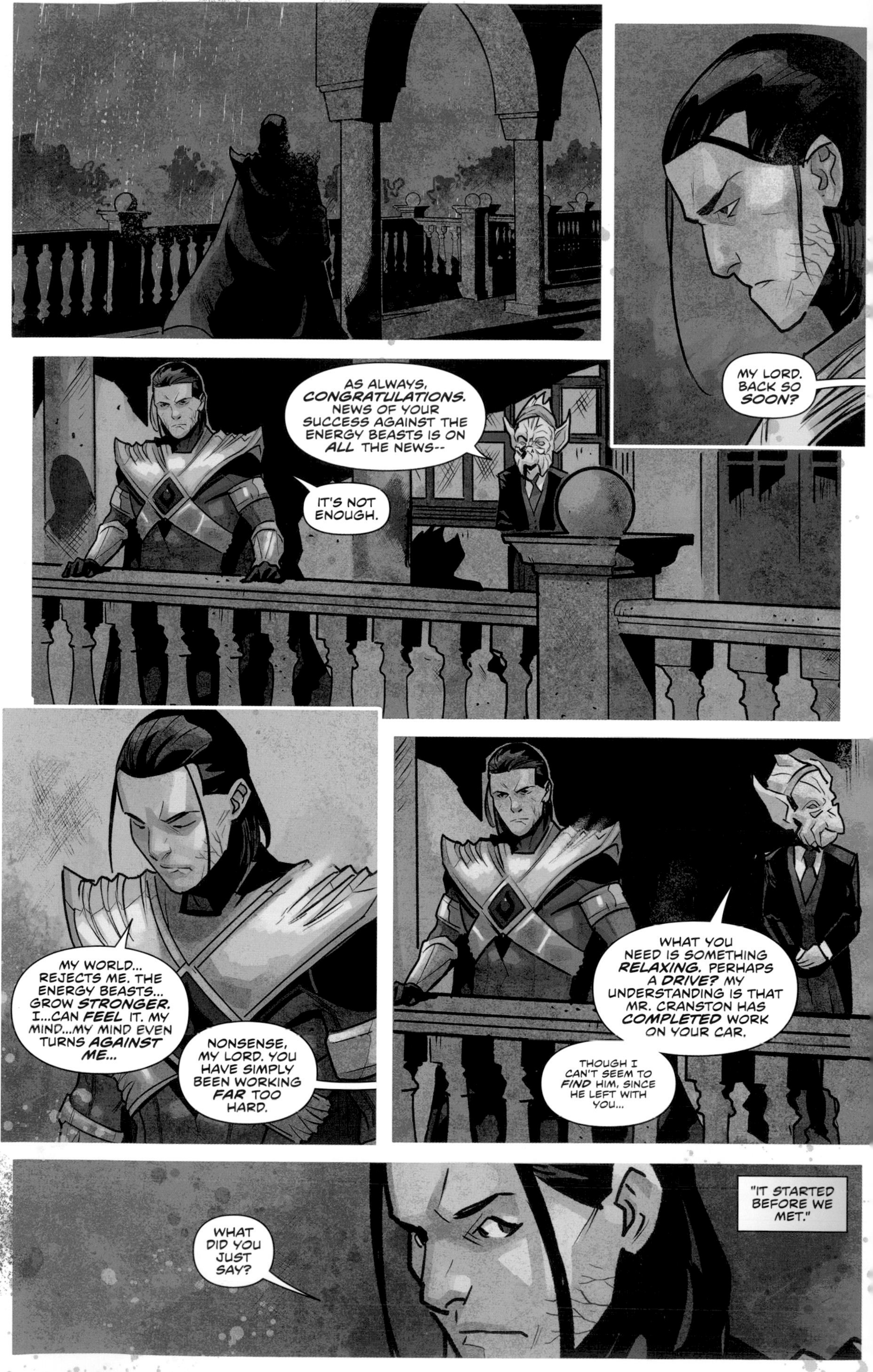
MY LORD. BACK SO SOON?
AS ALWAYS, CONGRATULATIONS. NEWS OF YOUR SUCCESS AGAINST THE ENERGY BEASTS IS ON ALL THE NEWS--
IT'S NOT ENOUGH.
MY WORLD... REJECTS ME. THE ENERGY BEASTS... GROW STRONGER. I...CAN FEEL IT. MY MIND...MY MIND EVEN TURNS AGAINST ME...
NONSENSE, MY LORD. YOU HAVE SIMPLY BEEN WORKING FAR TOO HARD.
WHAT YOU NEED IS SOMETHING RELAXING. PERHAPS A DRIVE? MY UNDERSTANDING IS THAT MR. CRANSTON HAS COMPLETED WORK ON YOUR CAR.
THOUGH I CAN'T SEEM TO FIND HIM, SINCE HE LEFT WITH YOU...
"IT STARTED BEFORE WE MET."
WHAT DID YOU JUST SAY?

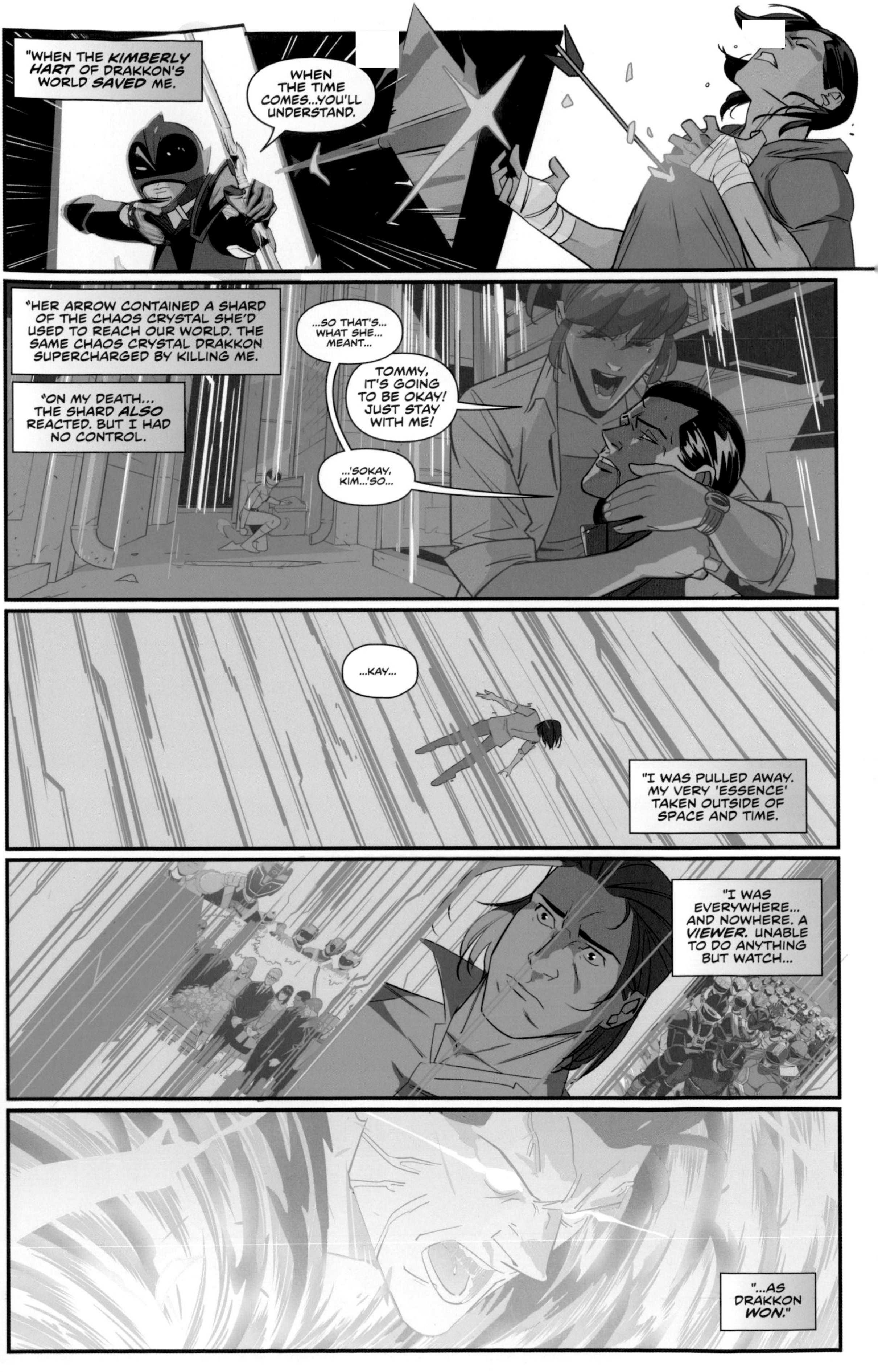
"WHEN THE KIMBERLY HART OF DRAKKON'S WORLD SAVED ME.
WHEN THE TIME COMES...YOU'LL UNDERSTAND.
"HER ARROW CONTAINED A SHARD OF THE CHAOS CRYSTAL SHE'D USED TO REACH OUR WORLD. THE SAME CHAOS CRYSTAL DRAKKON SUPERCHARGED BY KILLING ME.
"ON MY DEATH... THE SHARD ALSO REACTED. BUT I HAD NO CONTROL.
...SO THAT'S... WHAT SHE... MEANT...
TOMMY, IT'S GOING TO BE OKAY! JUST STAY WITH ME!
...'SOKAY, KIM...'SO...
...KAY...
"I WAS PULLED AWAY. MY VERY 'ESSENCE' TAKEN OUTSIDE OF SPACE AND TIME.
"I WAS EVERYWHERE... AND NOWHERE. A VIEWER. UNABLE TO DO ANYTHING BUT WATCH...
"...AS DRAKKON WON."

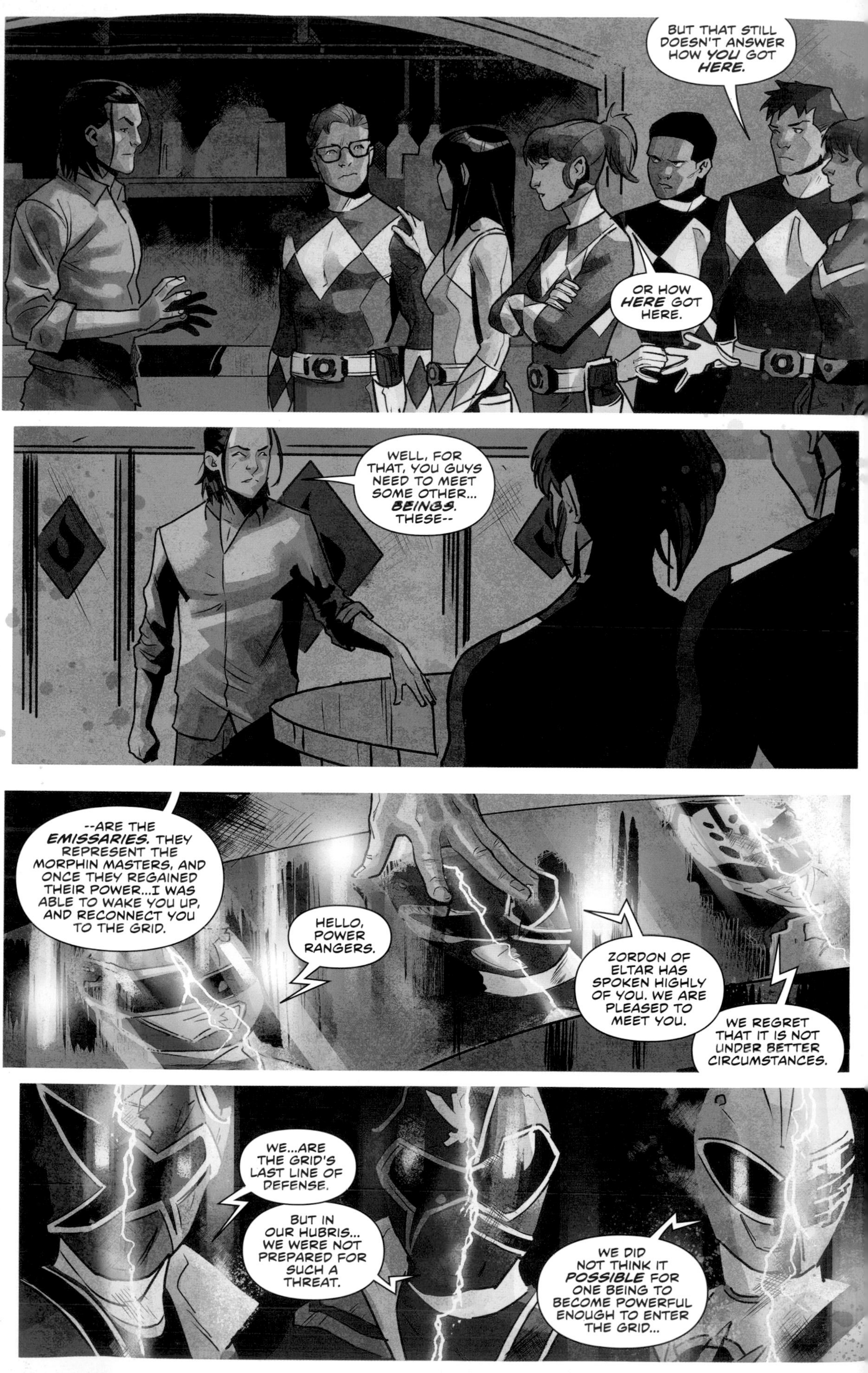
BUT THAT STILL DOESN'T ANSWER HOW YOU GOT HERE.
OR HOW HERE GOT HERE.
WELL, FOR THAT, YOU GUYS NEED TO MEET SOME OTHER... BEINGS. THESE--
--ARE THE EMISSARIES. THEY REPRESENT THE MORPHIN MASTERS, AND ONCE THEY REGAINED THEIR POWER...I WAS ABLE TO WAKE YOU UP, AND RECONNECT YOU TO THE GRID.
HELLO, POWER RANGERS.
ZORDON OF ELTAR HAS SPOKEN HIGHLY OF YOU. WE ARE PLEASED TO MEET YOU.
WE REGRET THAT IT IS NOT UNDER BETTER CIRCUMSTANCES.
WE...ARE THE GRID'S LAST LINE OF DEFENSE.
BUT IN OUR HUBRIS... WE WERE NOT PREPARED FOR SUCH A THREAT.
WE DID NOT THINK IT POSSIBLE FOR ONE BEING TO BECOME POWERFUL ENOUGH TO ENTER THE GRID...

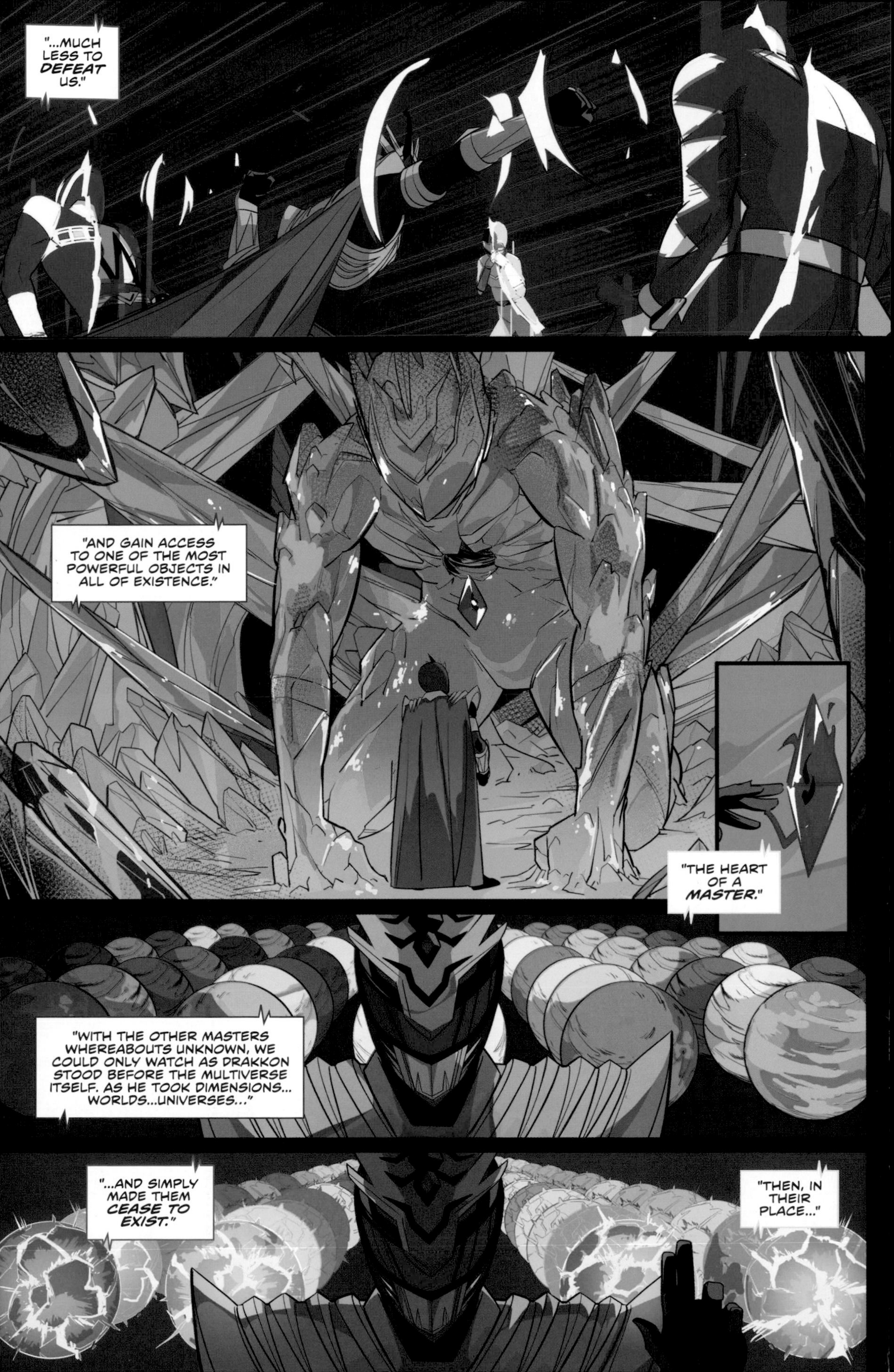
"...MUCH LESS TO DEFEAT US."
"AND GAIN ACCESS TO ONE OF THE MOST POWERFUL OBJECTS IN ALL OF EXISTENCE."
"THE HEART OF A MASTER."
"WITH THE OTHER MASTERS WHEREABOUTS UNKNOWN, WE COULD ONLY WATCH AS DRAKKON STOOD BEFORE THE MULTIVERSE ITSELF. AS HE TOOK DIMENSIONS... WORLDS...UNIVERSES..."
"...AND SIMPLY MADE THEM CEASE TO EXIST."
"THEN, IN THEIR PLACE..."

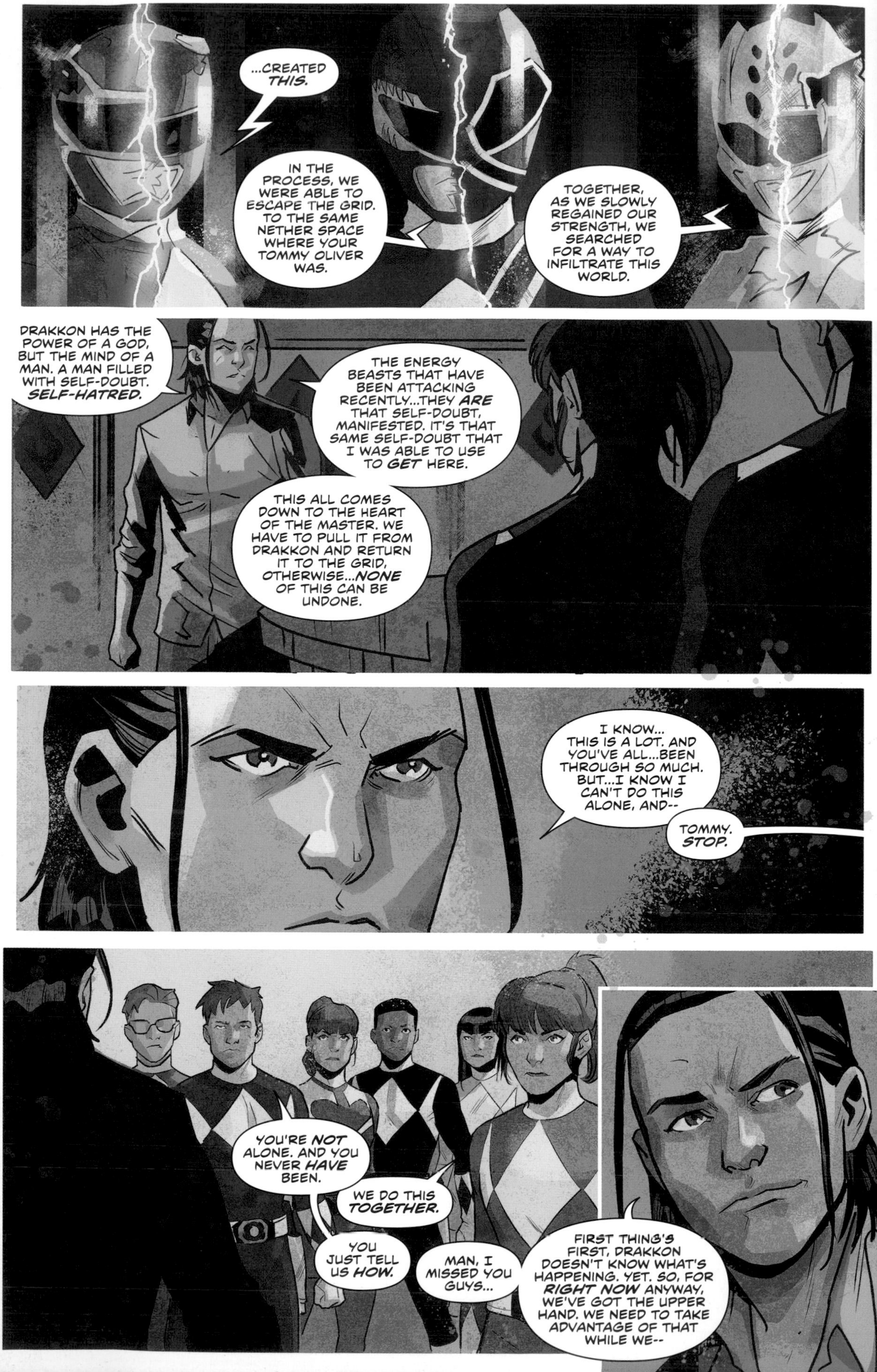
...CREATED THIS.
IN THE PROCESS, WE WERE ABLE TO ESCAPE THE GRID. TO THE SAME NETHER SPACE WHERE YOUR TOMMY OLIVER WAS.
TOGETHER, AS WE SLOWLY REGAINED OUR STRENGTH, WE SEARCHED FOR A WAY TO INFILTRATE THIS WORLD.
DRAKKON HAS THE POWER OF A GOD, BUT THE MIND OF A MAN. A MAN FILLED WITH SELF-DOUBT. SELF-HATRED.
THE ENERGY BEASTS THAT HAVE BEEN ATTACKING RECENTLY...THEY ARE THAT SELF-DOUBT, MANIFESTED. IT'S THAT SAME SELF-DOUBT THAT I WAS ABLE TO USE TO GET HERE.
THIS ALL COMES DOWN TO THE HEART OF THE MASTER. WE HAVE TO PULL IT FROM DRAKKON AND RETURN IT TO THE GRID, OTHERWISE...NONE OF THIS CAN BE UNDONE.
I KNOW... THIS IS A LOT. AND YOU'VE ALL...BEEN THROUGH SO MUCH. BUT...I KNOW I CAN'T DO THIS ALONE, AND--
TOMMY. STOP.
YOU'RE NOT ALONE. AND YOU NEVER HAVE BEEN.
WE DO THIS TOGETHER.
YOU JUST TELL US HOW.
MAN, I MISSED YOU GUYS...
FIRST THING'S FIRST, DRAKKON DOESN'T KNOW WHAT'S HAPPENING. YET. SO, FOR RIGHT NOW ANYWAY, WE'VE GOT THE UPPER HAND. WE NEED TO TAKE ADVANTAGE OF THAT WHILE WE--

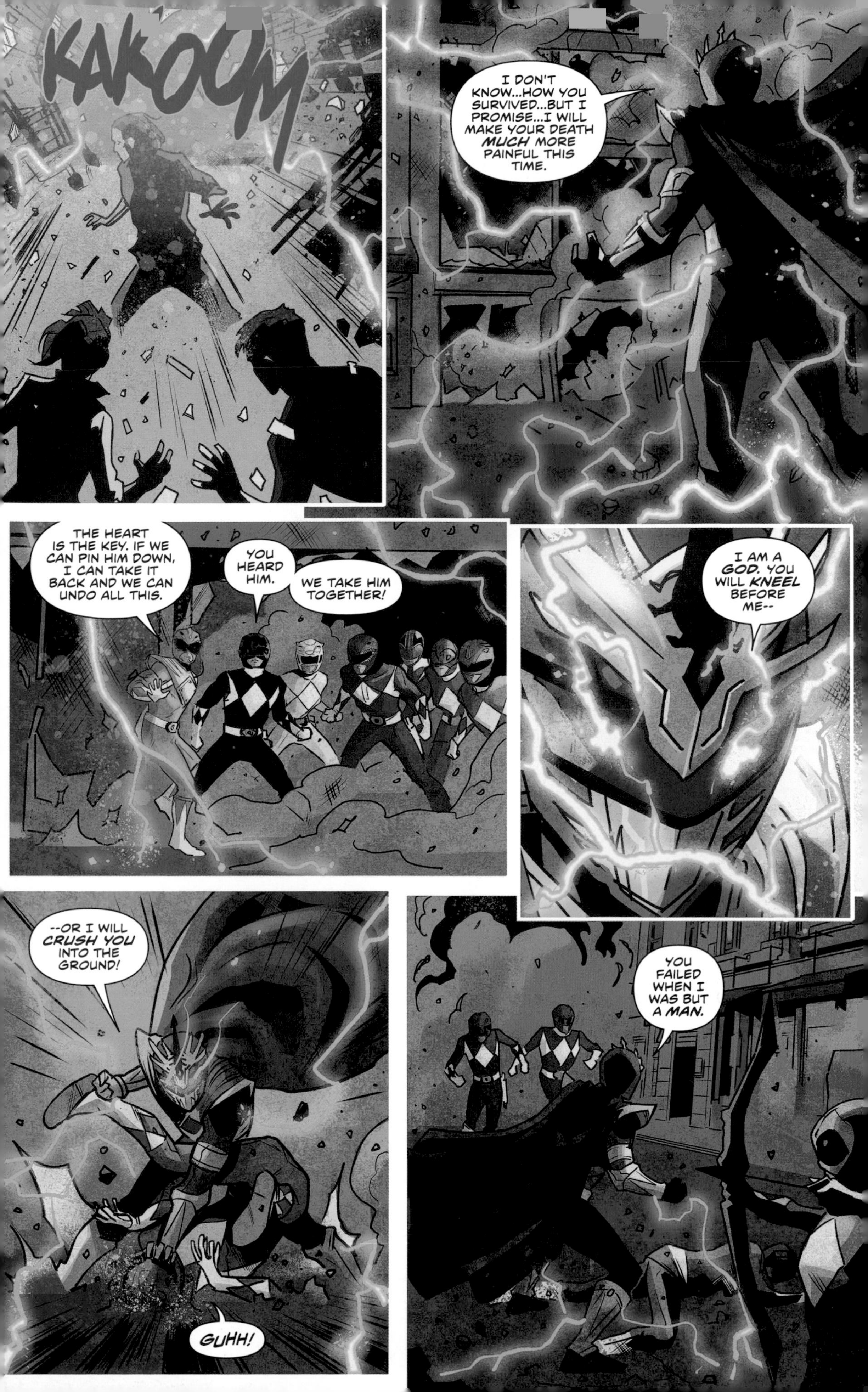
KAKOOM
I DON'T KNOW...HOW YOU SURVIVED...BUT I PROMISE...I WILL MAKE YOUR DEATH MUCH MORE PAINFUL THIS TIME.
THE HEART IS THE KEY. IF WE CAN PIN HIM DOWN, I CAN TAKE IT BACK AND WE CAN UNDO ALL THIS.
YOU HEARD HIM.
WE TAKE HIM TOGETHER!
I AM A GOD. YOU WILL KNEEL BEFORE ME--
--OR I WILL CRUSH YOU INTO THE GROUND!
GUHH!
YOU FAILED WHEN I WAS BUT A MAN.

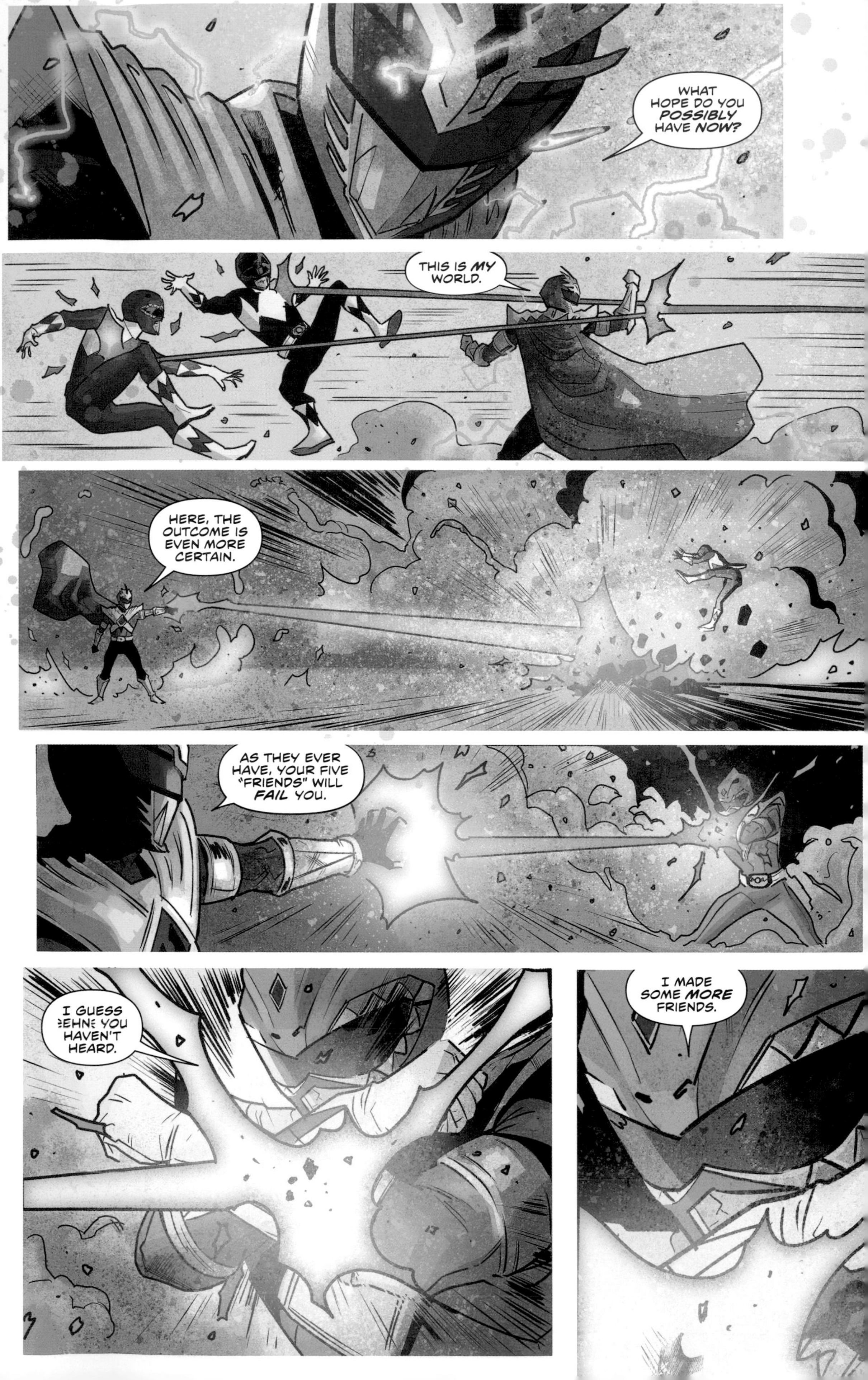
WHAT HOPE DO YOU *POSSIBLY* HAVE *NOW?*
THIS IS *MY* WORLD.
HERE, THE OUTCOME IS EVEN MORE CERTAIN.
AS THEY EVER HAVE, YOUR FIVE "FRIENDS" WILL *FAIL* YOU.
I GUESS ƎEHNƐ YOU HAVEN'T HEARD.
I MADE SOME *MORE* FRIENDS.

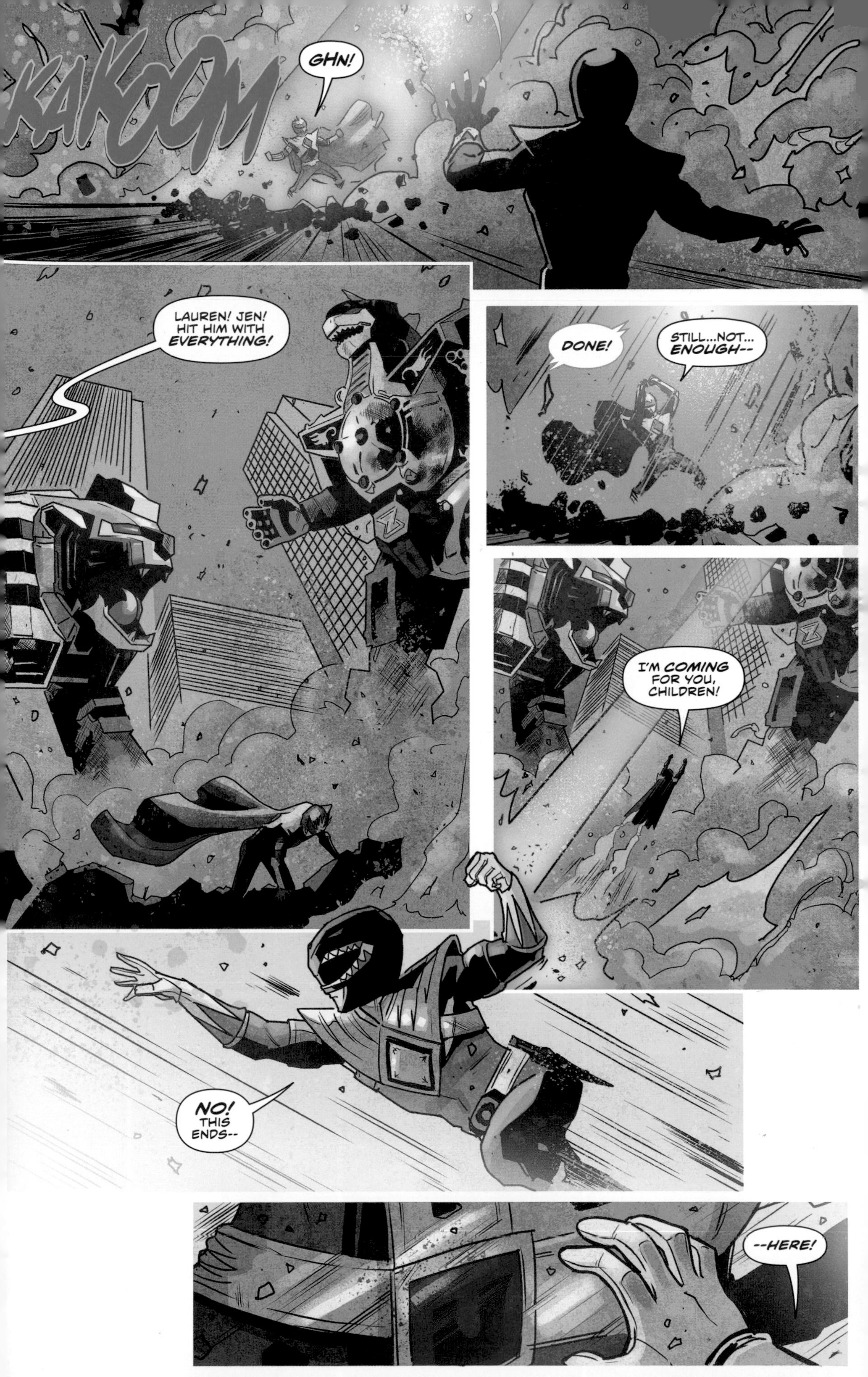
KAKOOM
GHN!
LAUREN! JEN! HIT HIM WITH EVERYTHING!
DONE!
STILL...NOT... ENOUGH--
I'M COMING FOR YOU, CHILDREN!
NO! THIS ENDS--
--HERE!

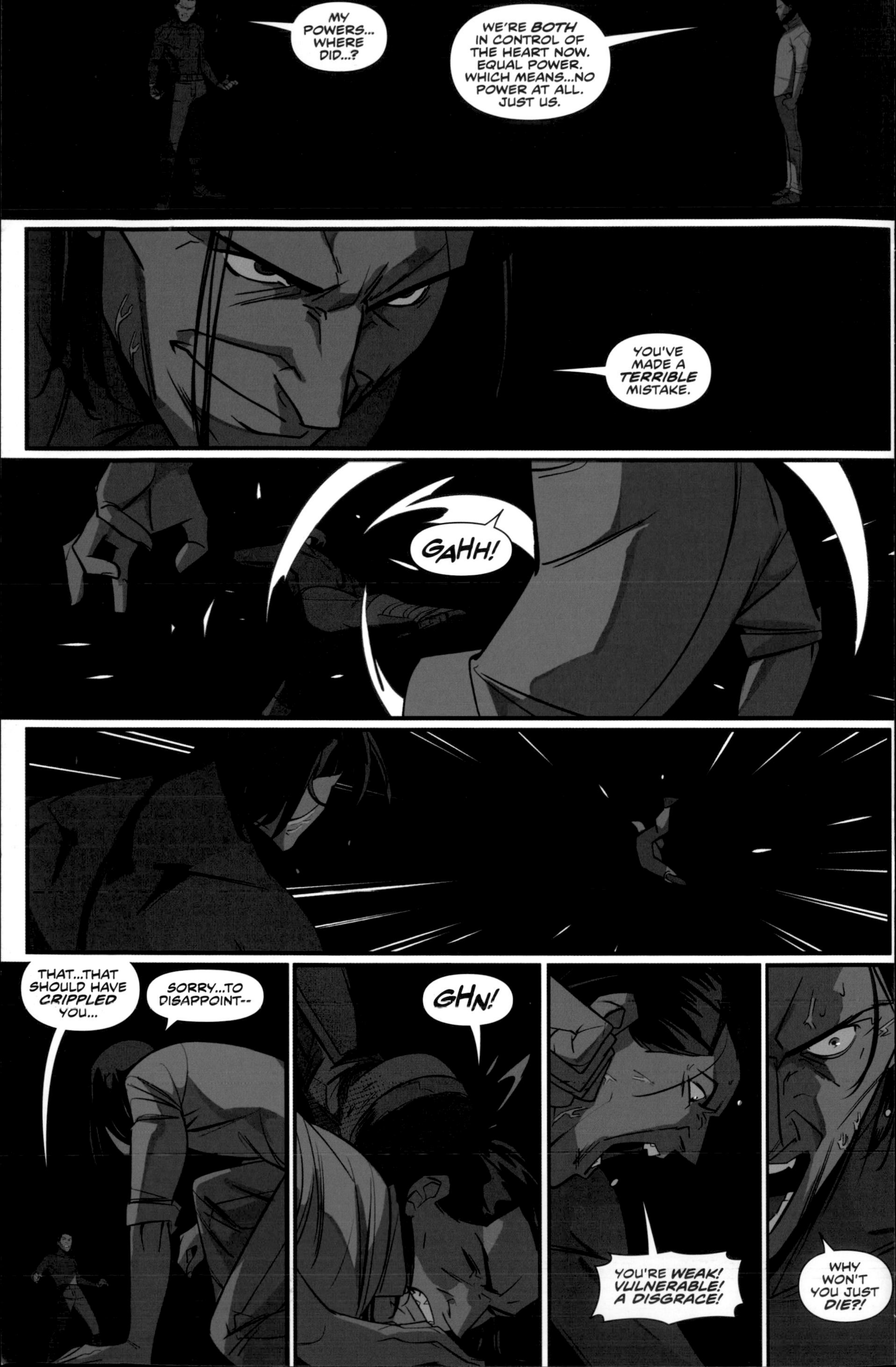
MY POWERS... WHERE DID...?
WE'RE BOTH IN CONTROL OF THE HEART NOW. EQUAL POWER. WHICH MEANS...NO POWER AT ALL. JUST US.
YOU'VE MADE A TERRIBLE MISTAKE.
GAHH!
THAT...THAT SHOULD HAVE CRIPPLED YOU...
SORRY...TO DISAPPOINT--
GHN!
YOU'RE WEAK! VULNERABLE! A DISGRACE!
WHY WON'T YOU JUST DIE?!

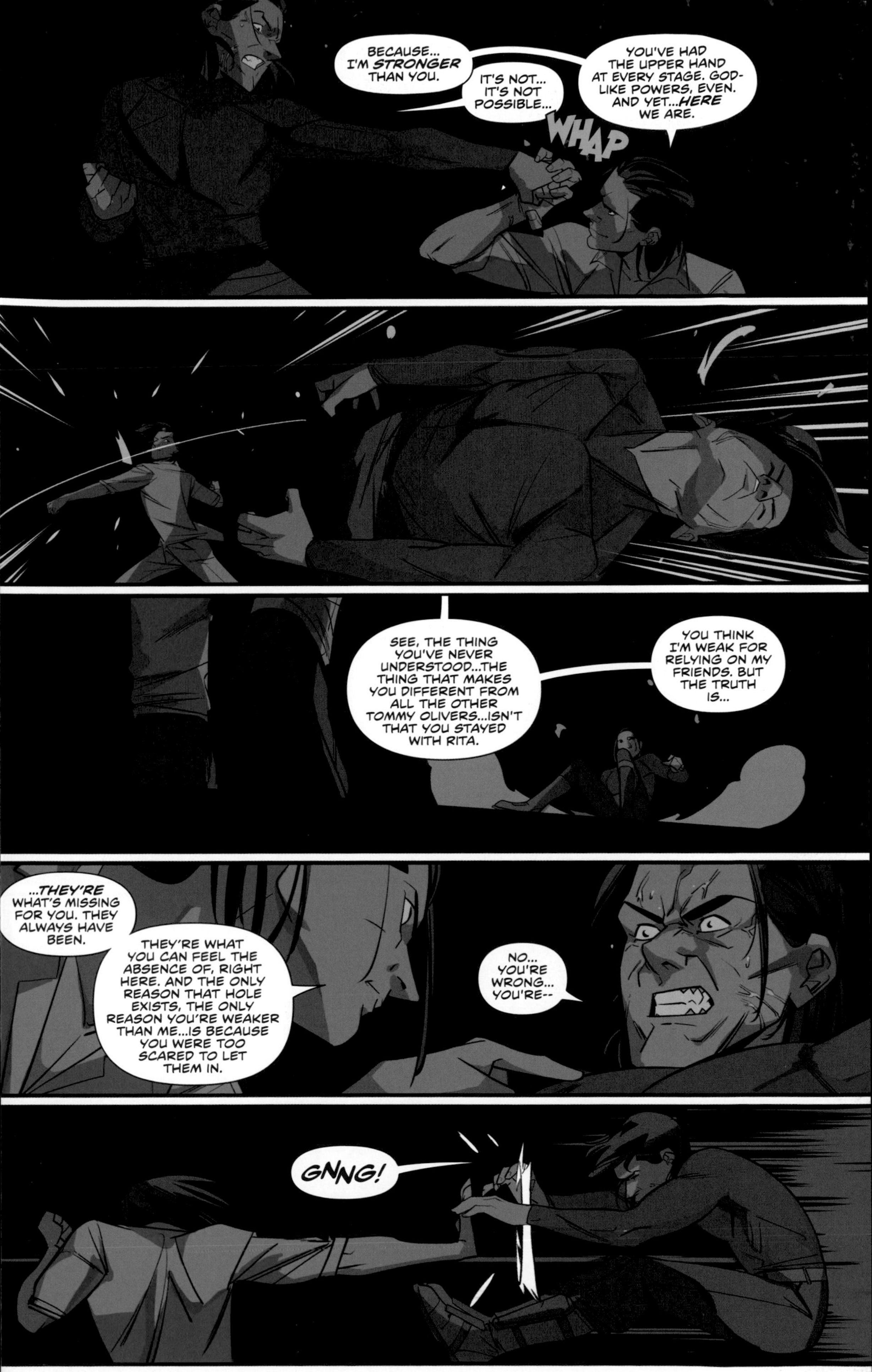
BECAUSE... I'M STRONGER THAN YOU.
IT'S NOT... IT'S NOT POSSIBLE...
YOU'VE HAD THE UPPER HAND AT EVERY STAGE. GOD-LIKE POWERS, EVEN. AND YET...HERE WE ARE.
WHAP
SEE, THE THING YOU'VE NEVER UNDERSTOOD...THE THING THAT MAKES YOU DIFFERENT FROM ALL THE OTHER TOMMY OLIVERS...ISN'T THAT YOU STAYED WITH RITA.
YOU THINK I'M WEAK FOR RELYING ON MY FRIENDS. BUT THE TRUTH IS...
...THEY'RE WHAT'S MISSING FOR YOU. THEY ALWAYS HAVE BEEN.
THEY'RE WHAT YOU CAN FEEL THE ABSENCE OF, RIGHT HERE. AND THE ONLY REASON THAT HOLE EXISTS, THE ONLY REASON YOU'RE WEAKER THAN ME...IS BECAUSE YOU WERE TOO SCARED TO LET THEM IN.
NO... YOU'RE WRONG... YOU'RE--
GNNG!

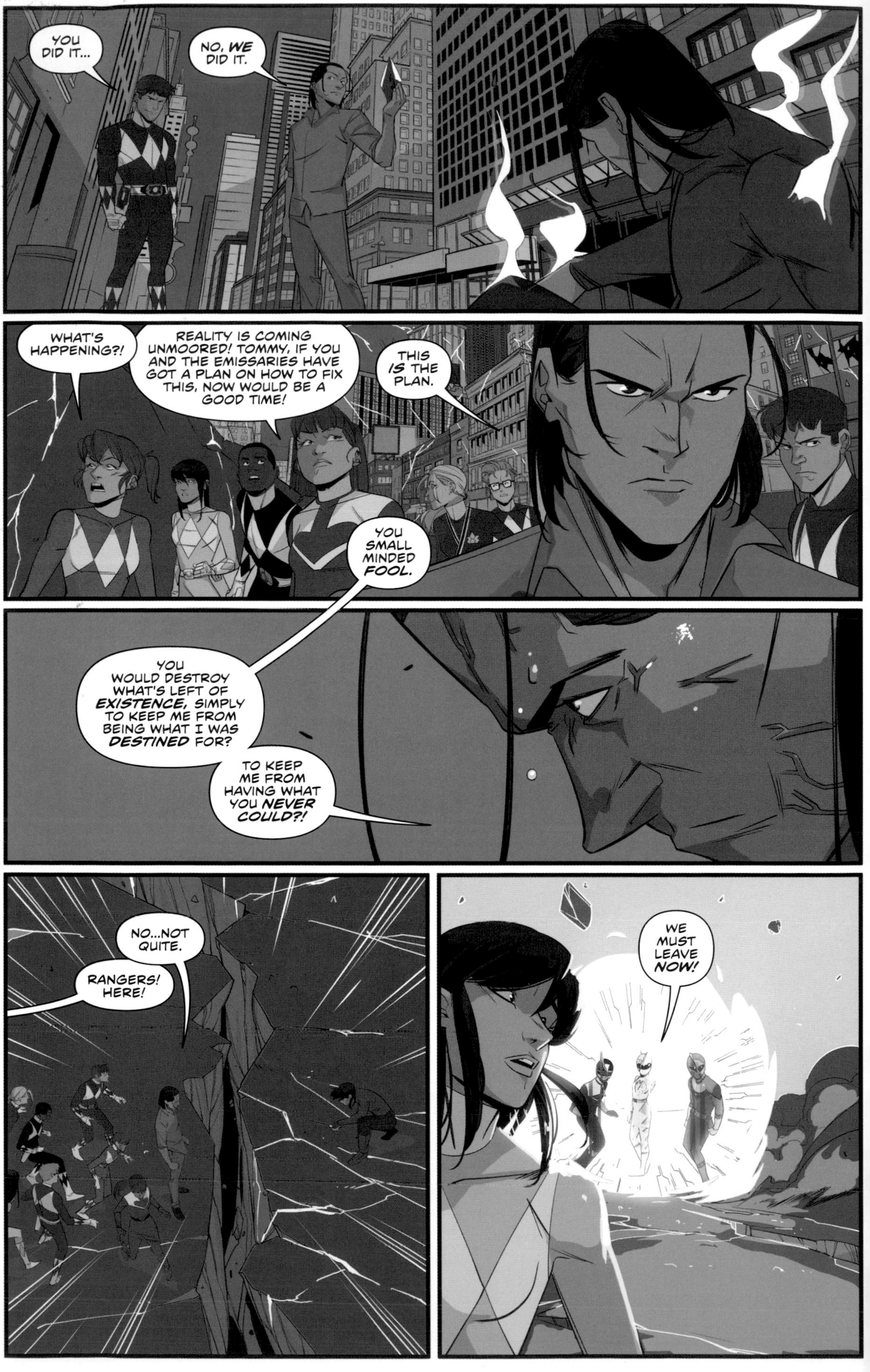
YOU DID IT...
NO, WE DID IT.
WHAT'S HAPPENING?!
REALITY IS COMING UNMOORED! TOMMY, IF YOU AND THE EMISSARIES HAVE GOT A PLAN ON HOW TO FIX THIS, NOW WOULD BE A GOOD TIME!
THIS IS THE PLAN.
YOU SMALL MINDED FOOL.
YOU WOULD DESTROY WHAT'S LEFT OF EXISTENCE, SIMPLY TO KEEP ME FROM BEING WHAT I WAS DESTINED FOR?
TO KEEP ME FROM HAVING WHAT YOU NEVER COULD?!
NO...NOT QUITE.
RANGERS! HERE!
WE MUST LEAVE NOW!

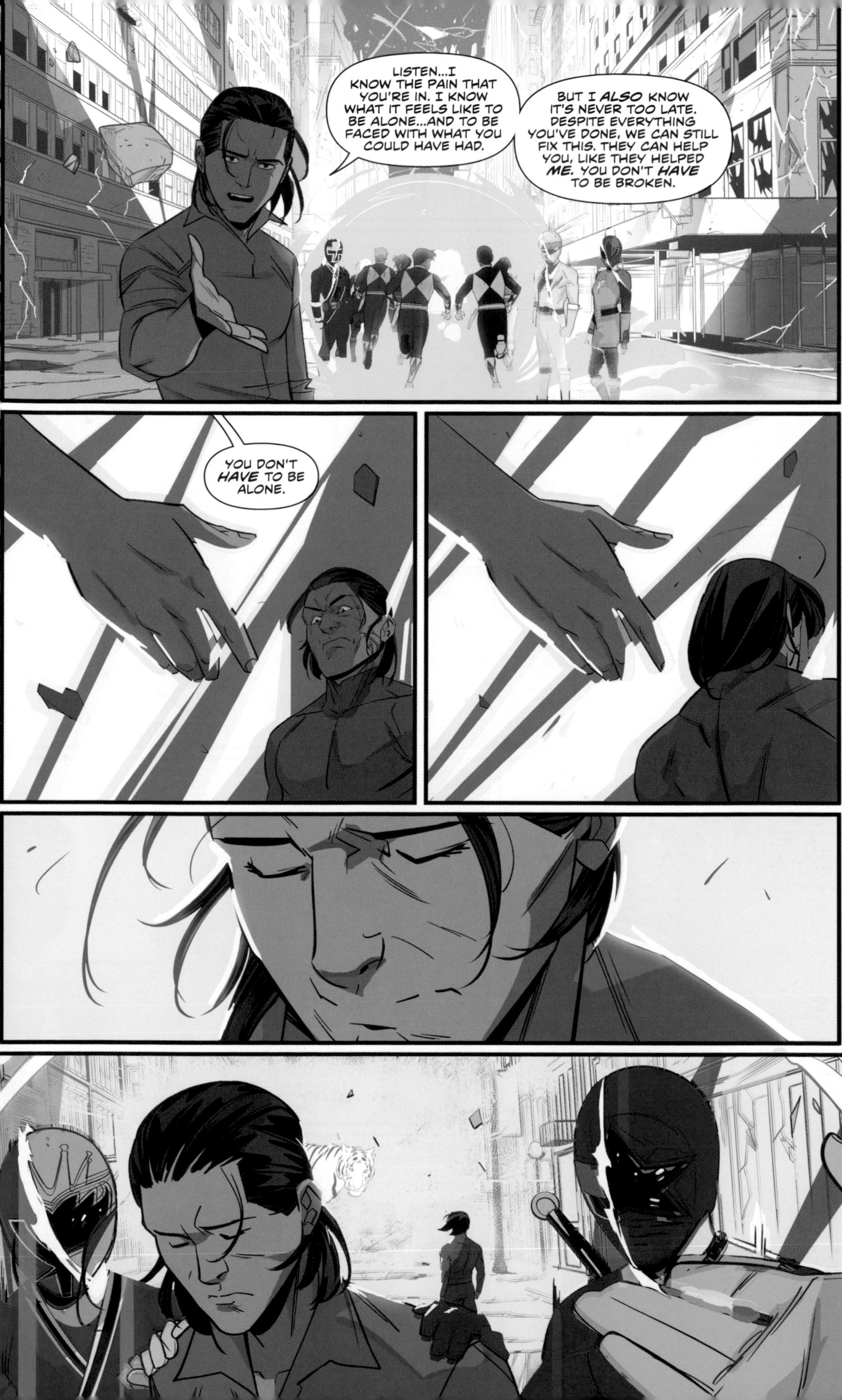
LISTEN...I KNOW THE PAIN THAT YOU'RE IN. I KNOW WHAT IT FEELS LIKE TO BE ALONE...AND TO BE FACED WITH WHAT YOU COULD HAVE HAD.
BUT I ALSO KNOW IT'S NEVER TOO LATE. DESPITE EVERYTHING YOU'VE DONE, WE CAN STILL FIX THIS. THEY CAN HELP YOU, LIKE THEY HELPED ME. YOU DON'T HAVE TO BE BROKEN.
YOU DON'T HAVE TO BE ALONE.

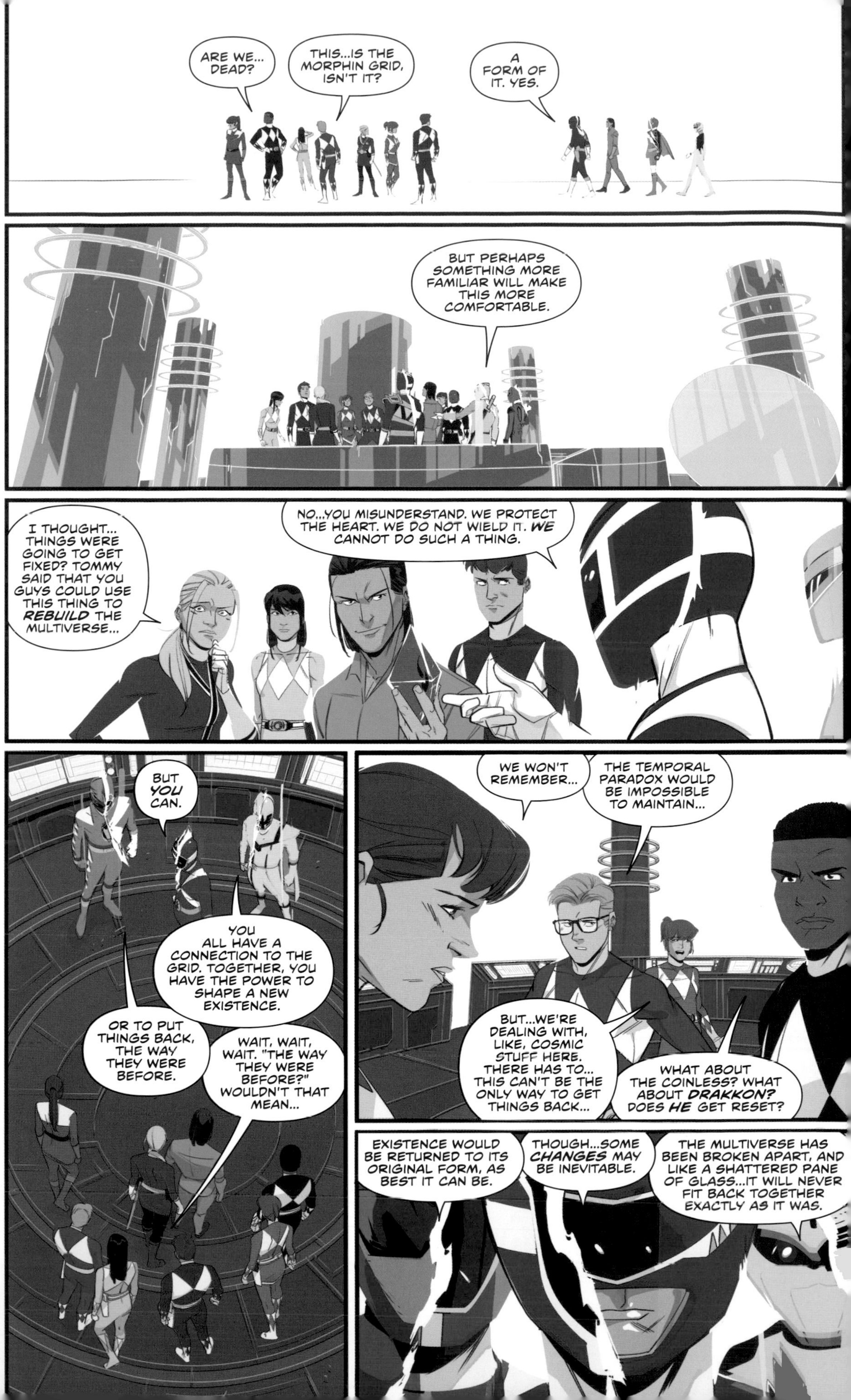
ARE WE... DEAD?
THIS...IS THE MORPHIN GRID, ISN'T IT?
A FORM OF IT. YES.
BUT PERHAPS SOMETHING MORE FAMILIAR WILL MAKE THIS MORE COMFORTABLE.
I THOUGHT... THINGS WERE GOING TO GET FIXED? TOMMY SAID THAT YOU GUYS COULD USE THIS THING TO REBUILD THE MULTIVERSE...
NO...YOU MISUNDERSTAND. WE PROTECT THE HEART. WE DO NOT WIELD IT. WE CANNOT DO SUCH A THING.
BUT YOU CAN.
YOU ALL HAVE A CONNECTION TO THE GRID. TOGETHER, YOU HAVE THE POWER TO SHAPE A NEW EXISTENCE.
OR TO PUT THINGS BACK, THE WAY THEY WERE BEFORE.
WAIT, WAIT, WAIT. "THE WAY THEY WERE BEFORE?" WOULDN'T THAT MEAN...
WE WON'T REMEMBER...
THE TEMPORAL PARADOX WOULD BE IMPOSSIBLE TO MAINTAIN...
BUT...WE'RE DEALING WITH, LIKE, COSMIC STUFF HERE. THERE HAS TO... THIS CAN'T BE THE ONLY WAY TO GET THINGS BACK...
WHAT ABOUT THE COINLESS? WHAT ABOUT DRAKKON? DOES HE GET RESET?
EXISTENCE WOULD BE RETURNED TO ITS ORIGINAL FORM, AS BEST IT CAN BE.
THOUGH...SOME CHANGES MAY BE INEVITABLE.
THE MULTIVERSE HAS BEEN BROKEN APART, AND LIKE A SHATTERED PANE OF GLASS...IT WILL NEVER FIT BACK TOGETHER EXACTLY AS IT WAS.

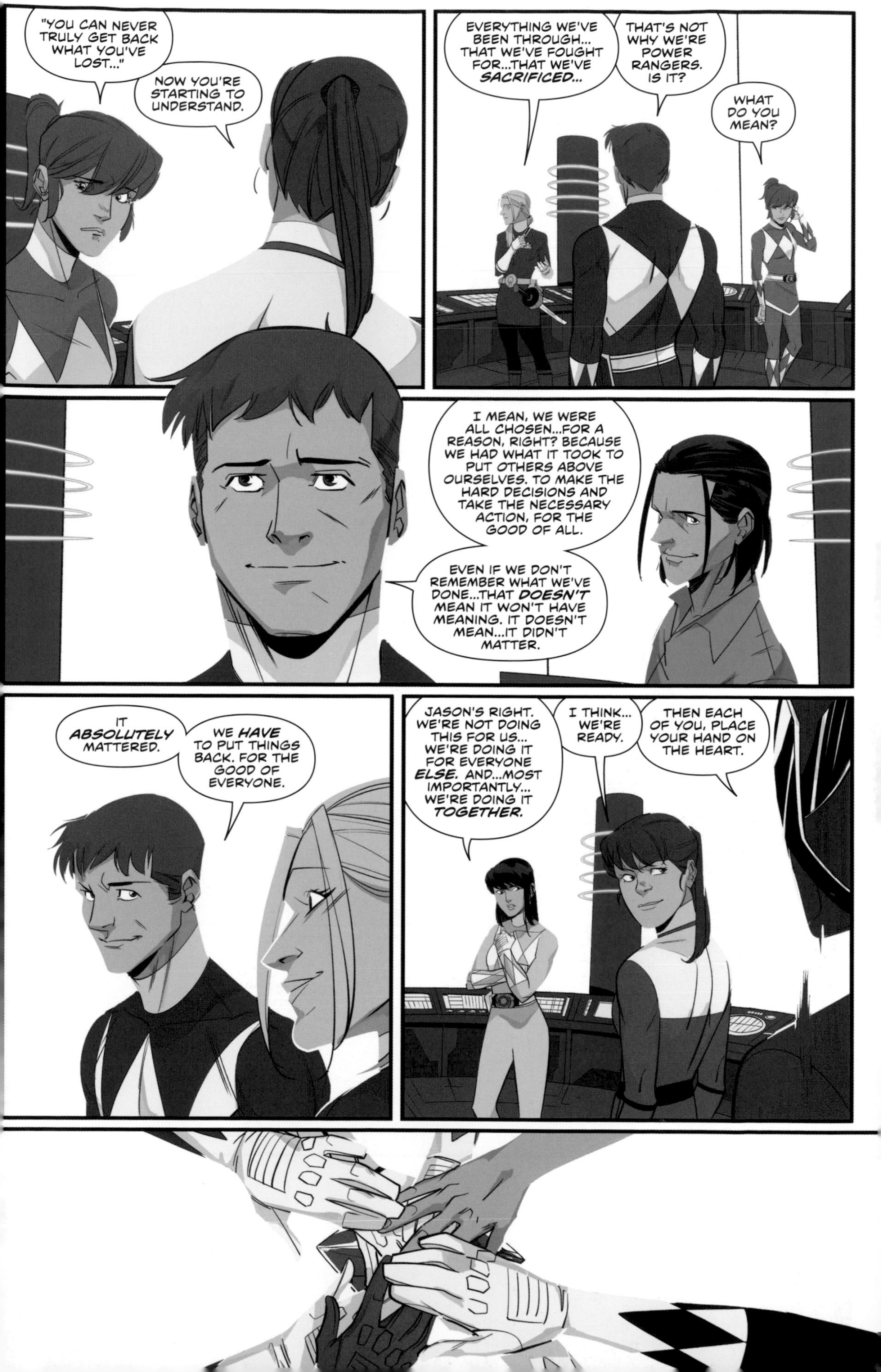
"YOU CAN NEVER TRULY GET BACK WHAT YOU'VE LOST..."
NOW YOU'RE STARTING TO UNDERSTAND.
EVERYTHING WE'VE BEEN THROUGH... THAT WE'VE FOUGHT FOR...THAT WE'VE SACRIFICED...
THAT'S NOT WHY WE'RE POWER RANGERS. IS IT?
WHAT DO YOU MEAN?
I MEAN, WE WERE ALL CHOSEN...FOR A REASON, RIGHT? BECAUSE WE HAD WHAT IT TOOK TO PUT OTHERS ABOVE OURSELVES. TO MAKE THE HARD DECISIONS AND TAKE THE NECESSARY ACTION, FOR THE GOOD OF ALL.
EVEN IF WE DON'T REMEMBER WHAT WE'VE DONE...THAT DOESN'T MEAN IT WON'T HAVE MEANING. IT DOESN'T MEAN...IT DIDN'T MATTER.
IT ABSOLUTELY MATTERED.
WE HAVE TO PUT THINGS BACK. FOR THE GOOD OF EVERYONE.
JASON'S RIGHT. WE'RE NOT DOING THIS FOR US... WE'RE DOING IT FOR EVERYONE ELSE. AND...MOST IMPORTANTLY... WE'RE DOING IT TOGETHER.
I THINK... WE'RE READY.
THEN EACH OF YOU, PLACE YOUR HAND ON THE HEART.

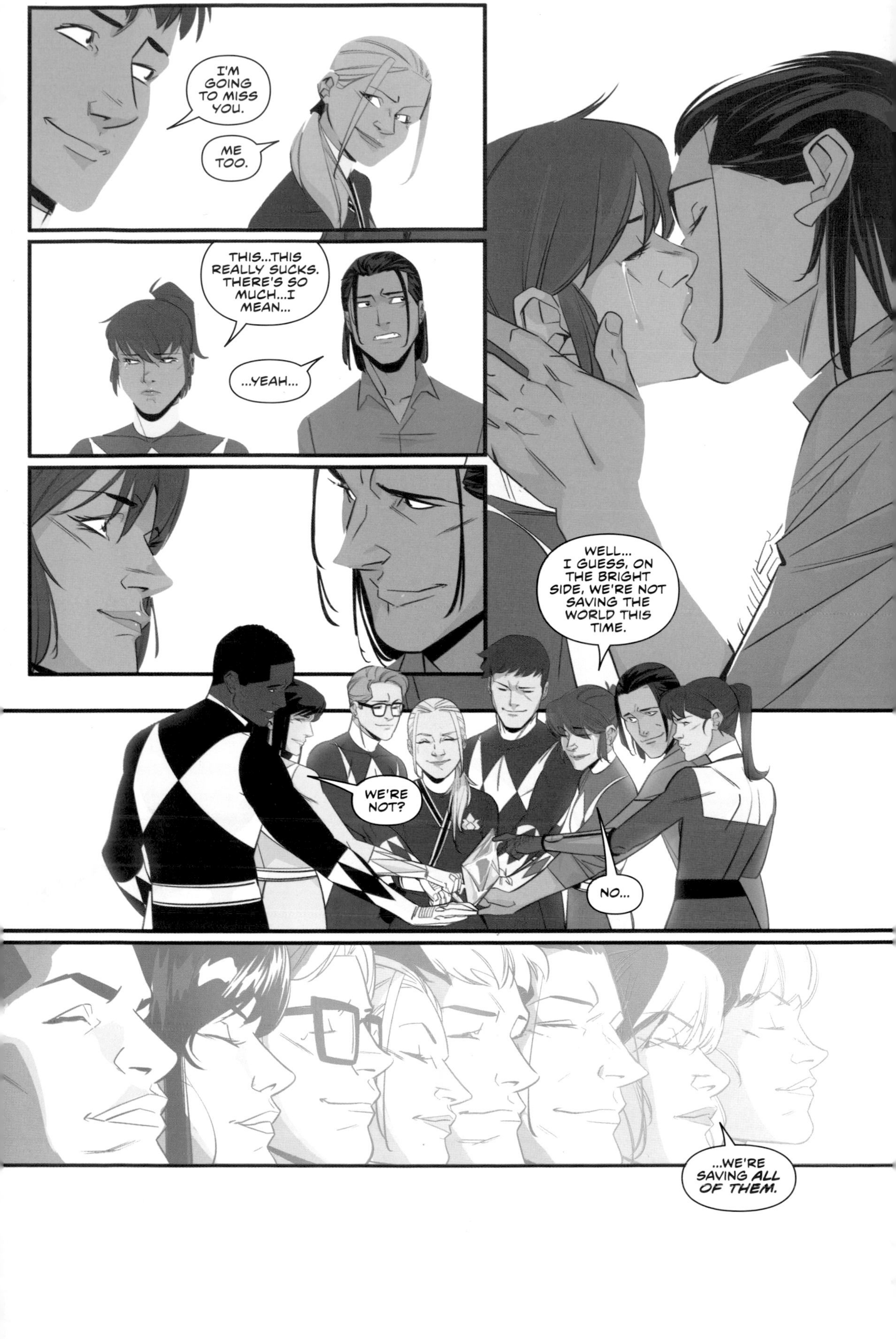
I'M GOING TO MISS YOU.
ME TOO.
THIS...THIS REALLY SUCKS. THERE'S SO MUCH...I MEAN...
...YEAH...
WELL... I GUESS, ON THE BRIGHT SIDE, WE'RE NOT SAVING THE WORLD THIS TIME.
WE'RE NOT?
NO...
...WE'RE SAVING *ALL OF THEM.*
THE END

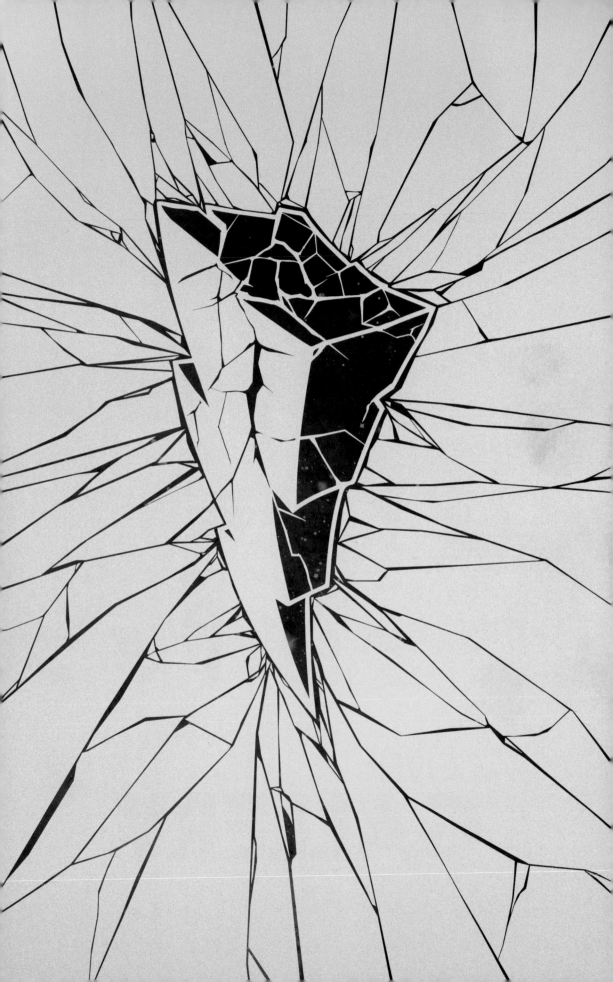

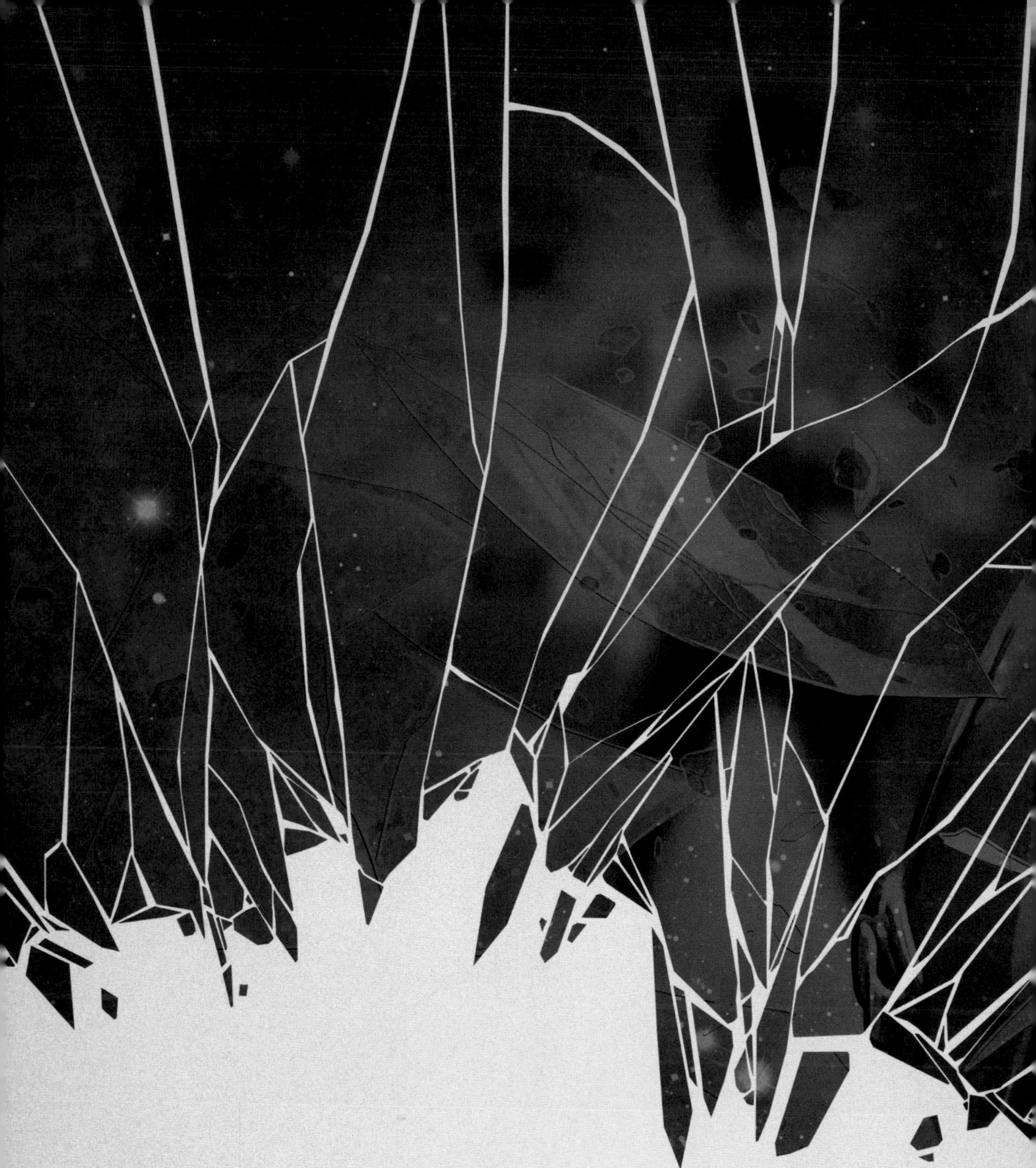

COVER GALLERY

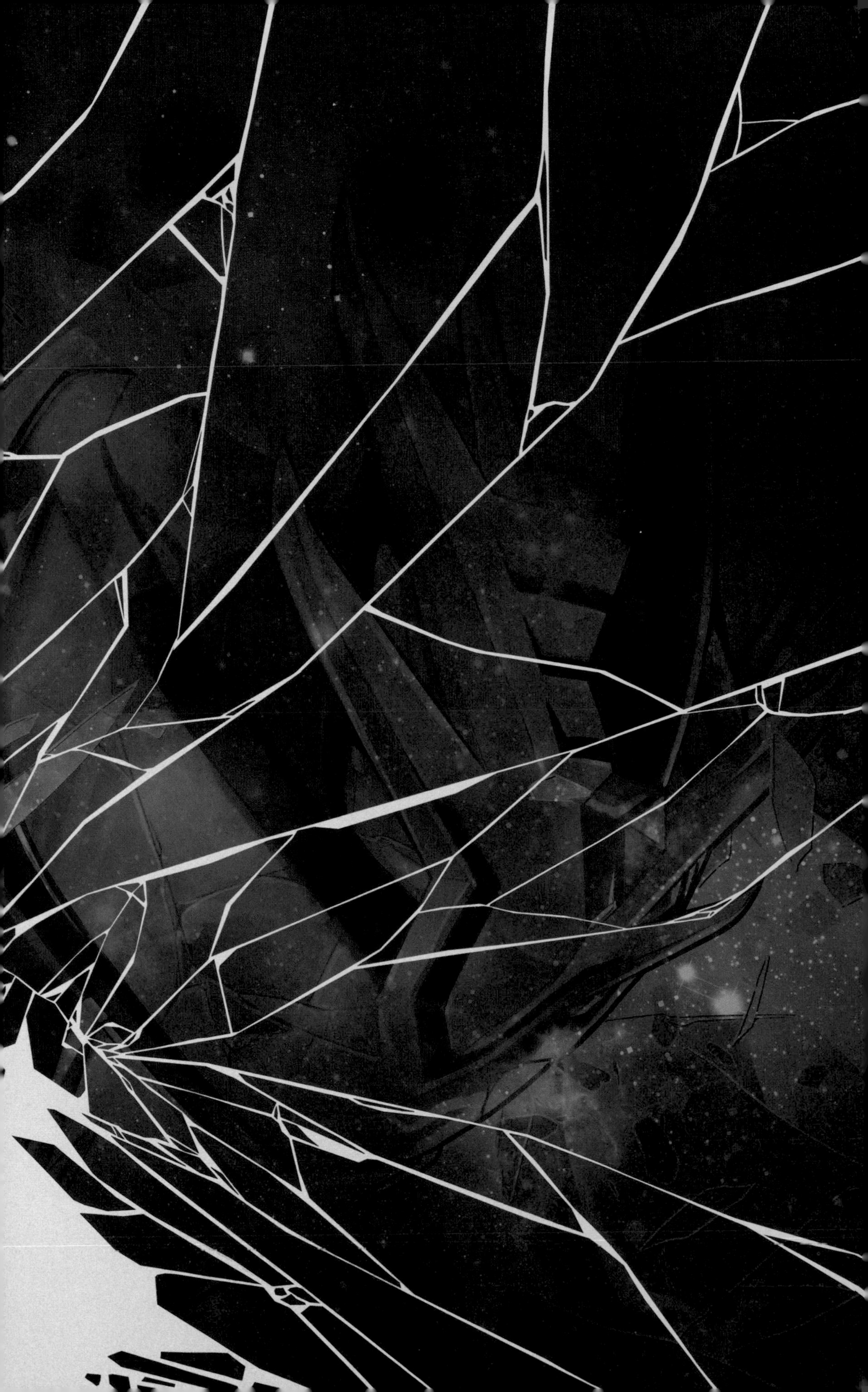

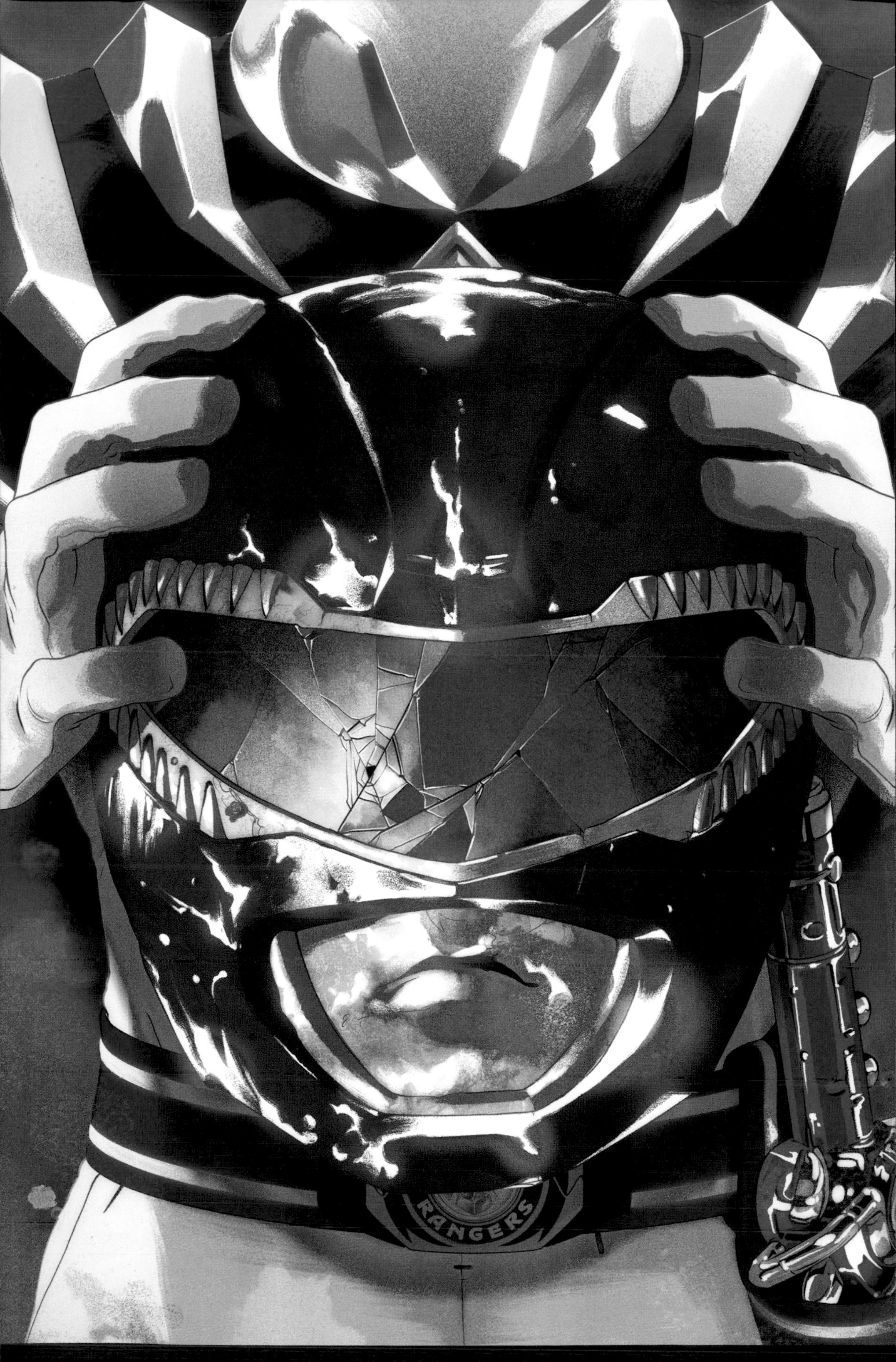
RANGERS

GOÑI MONTES | ISSUE TWENTY-FIVE COVER

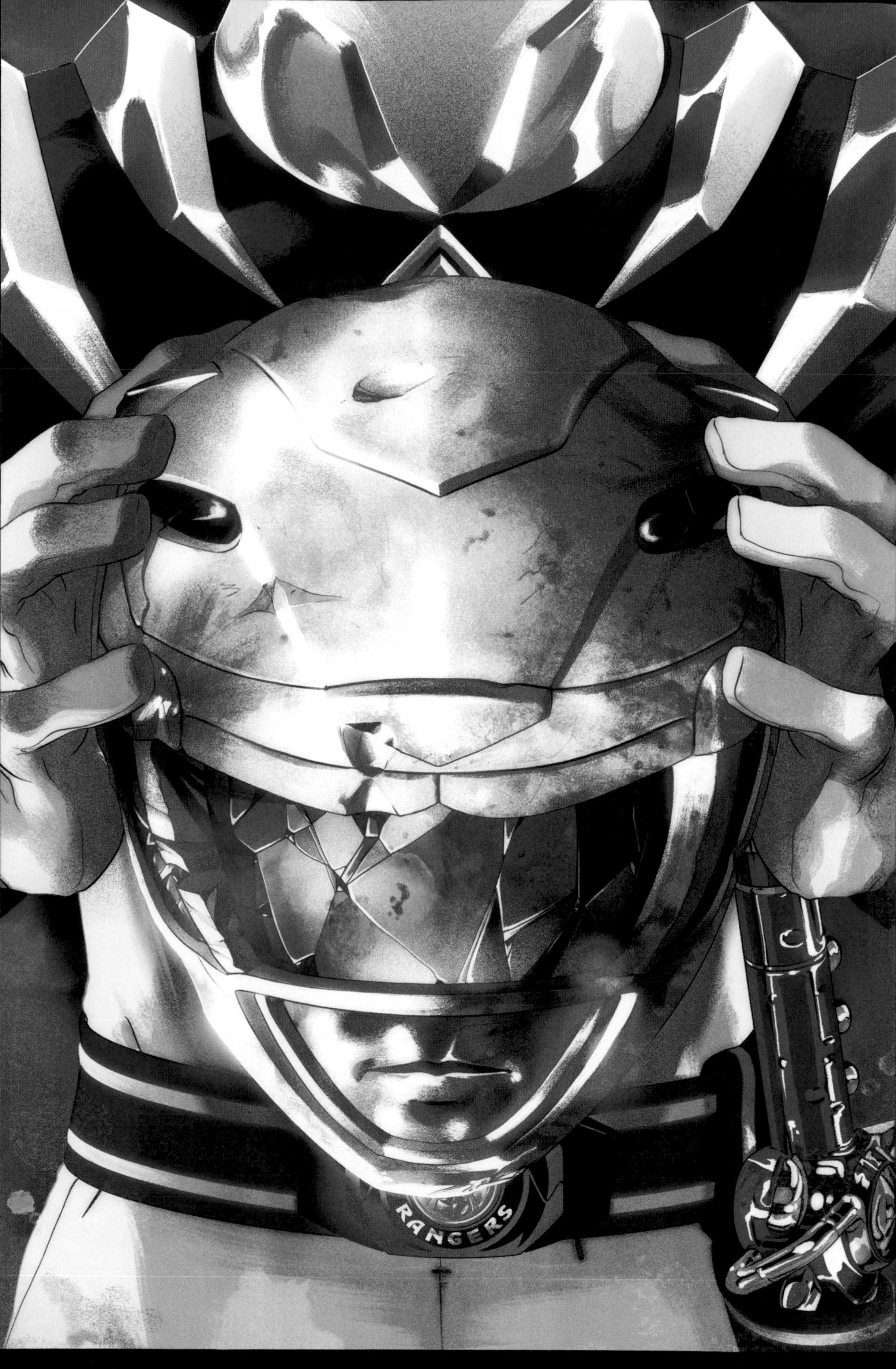
RANGERS

GOÑI MONTES ISSUE TWENTY-FIVE COVER

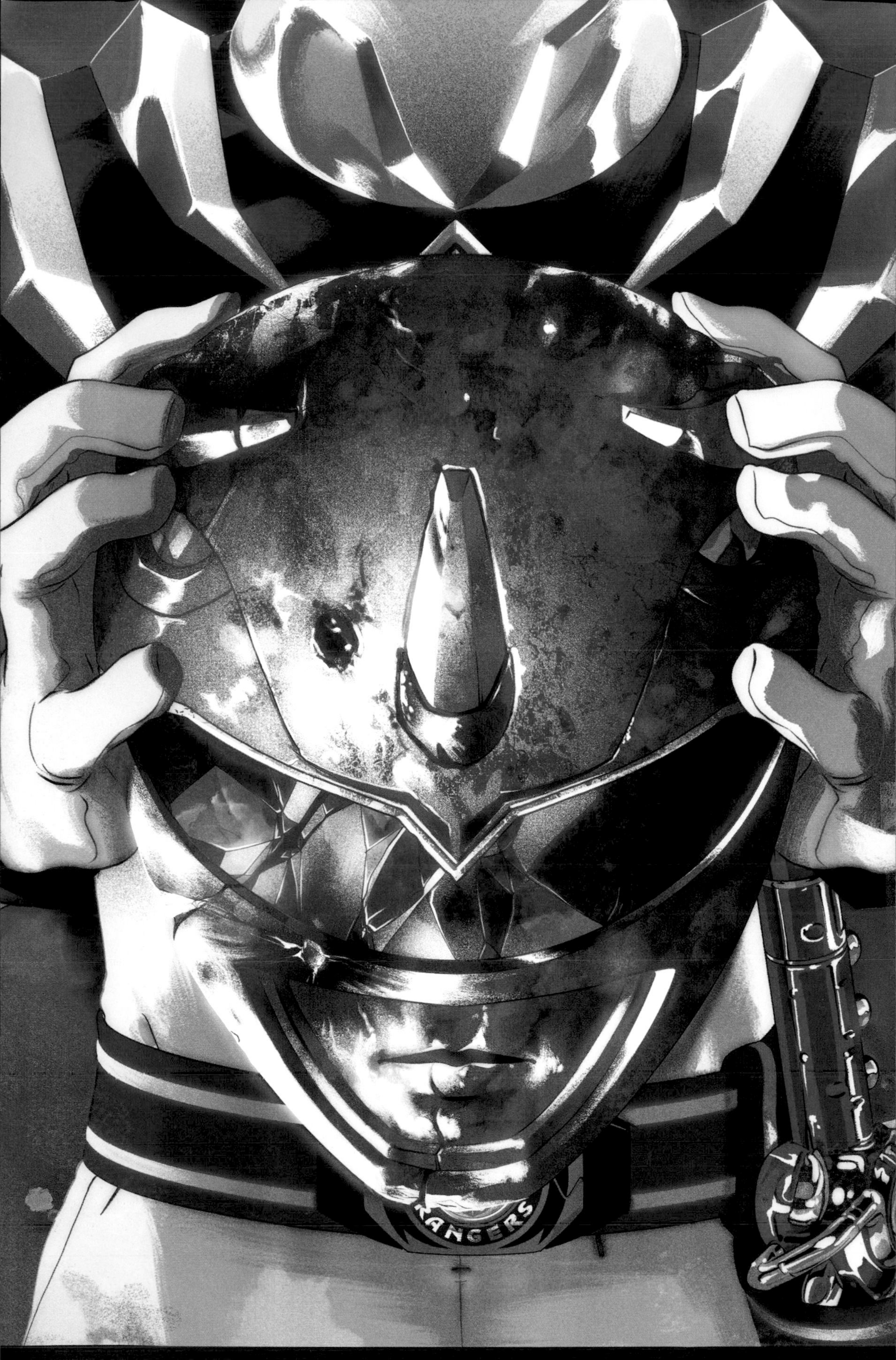
RANGERS

GOÑI MONTES ISSUE TWENTY-FIVE COVER

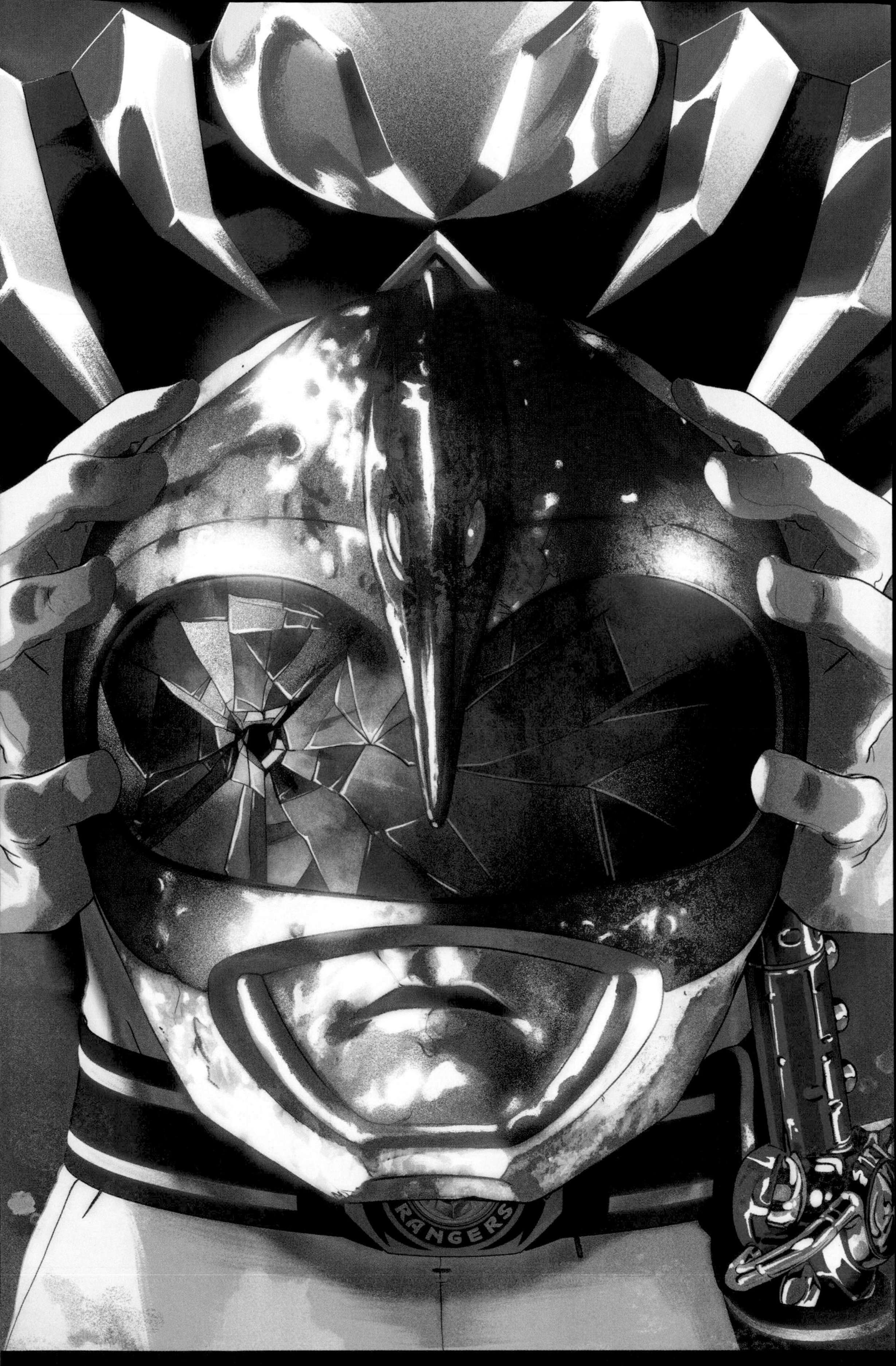
RANGERS

GOÑI MONTES ISSUE TWENTY-FIVE COVER

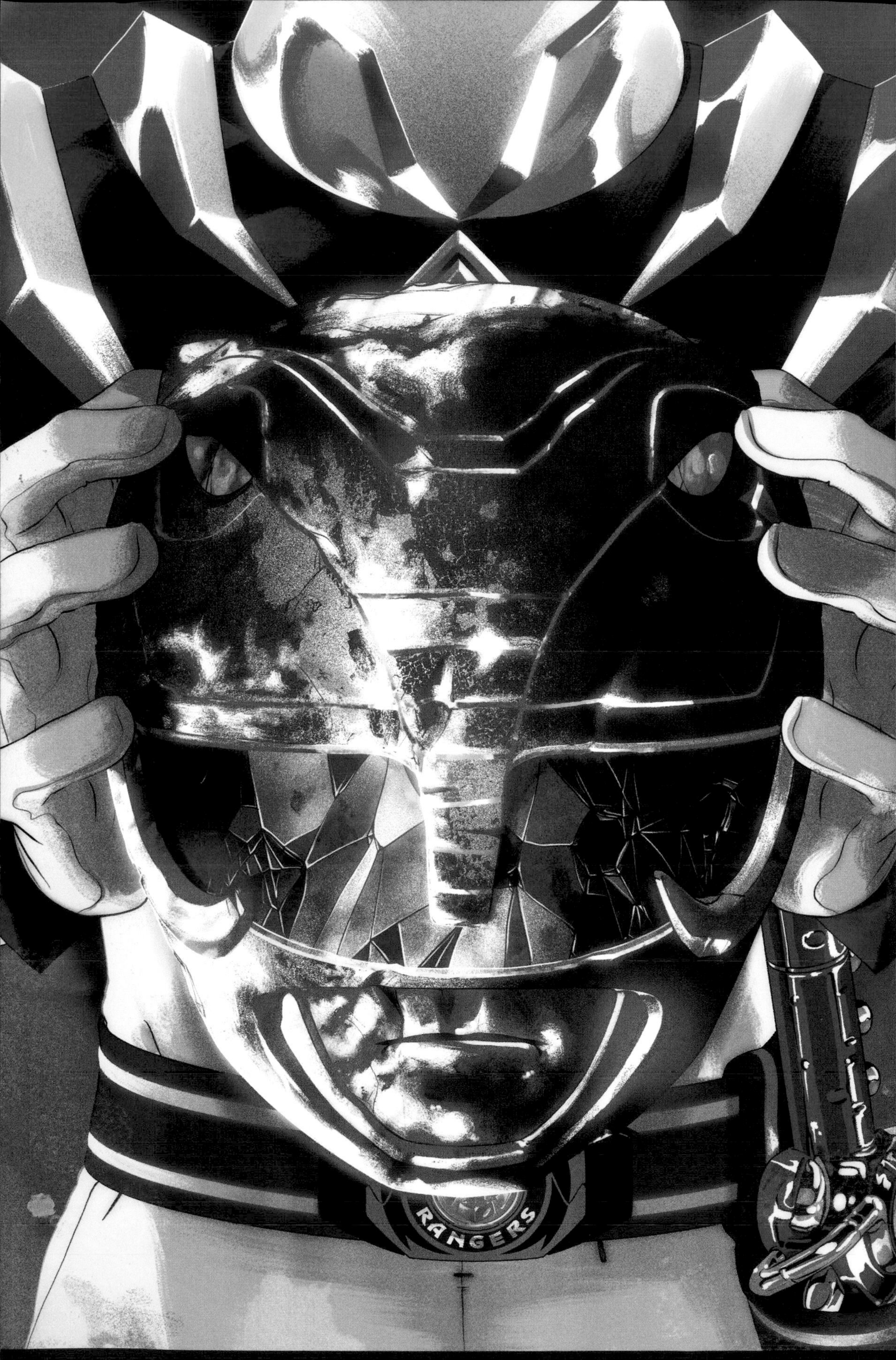
RANGERS

GOÑI MONTES | ISSUE TWENTY-FIVE COVER

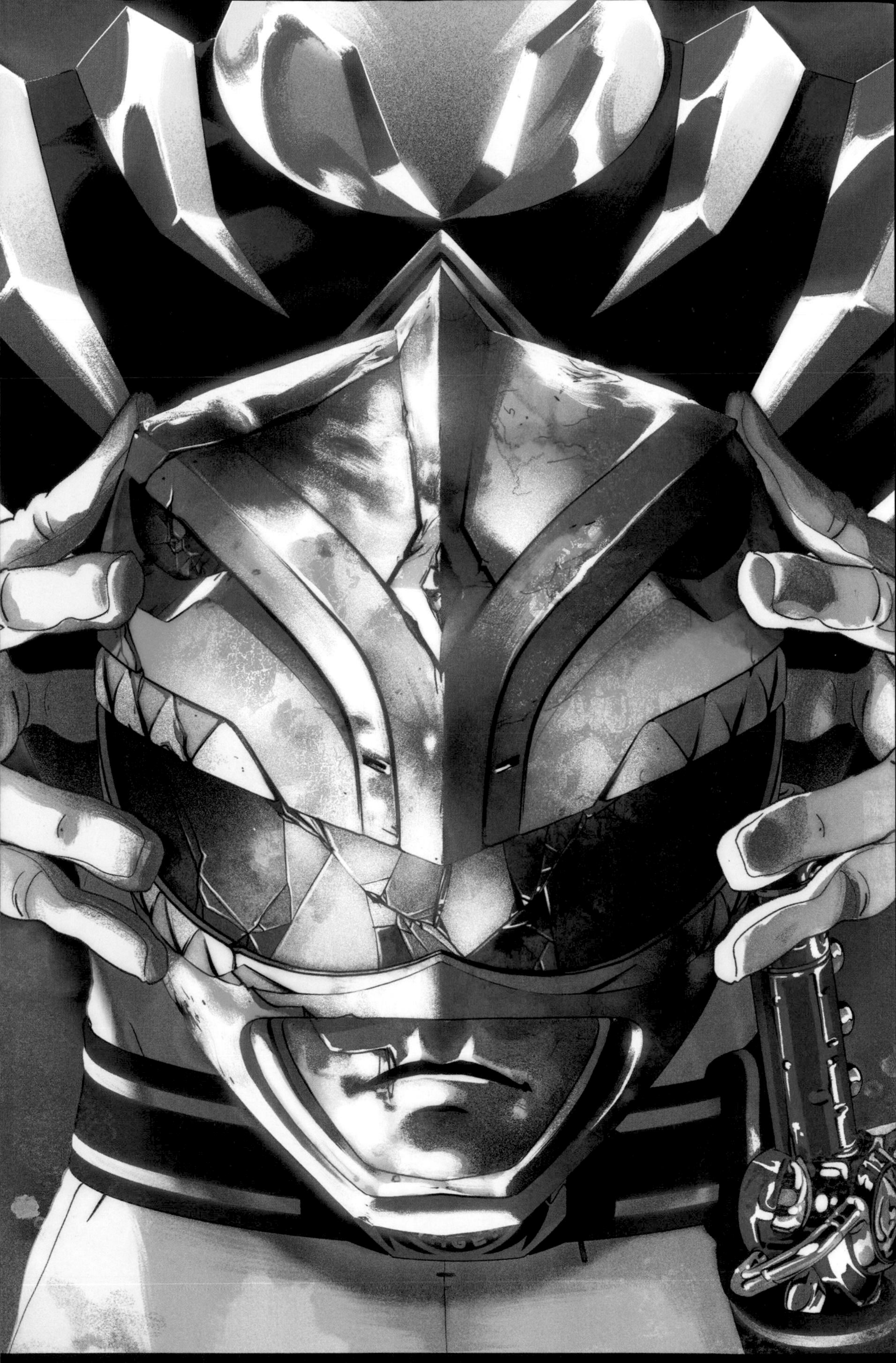

GOÑI MONTES ISSUE TWENTY-FIVE COVER

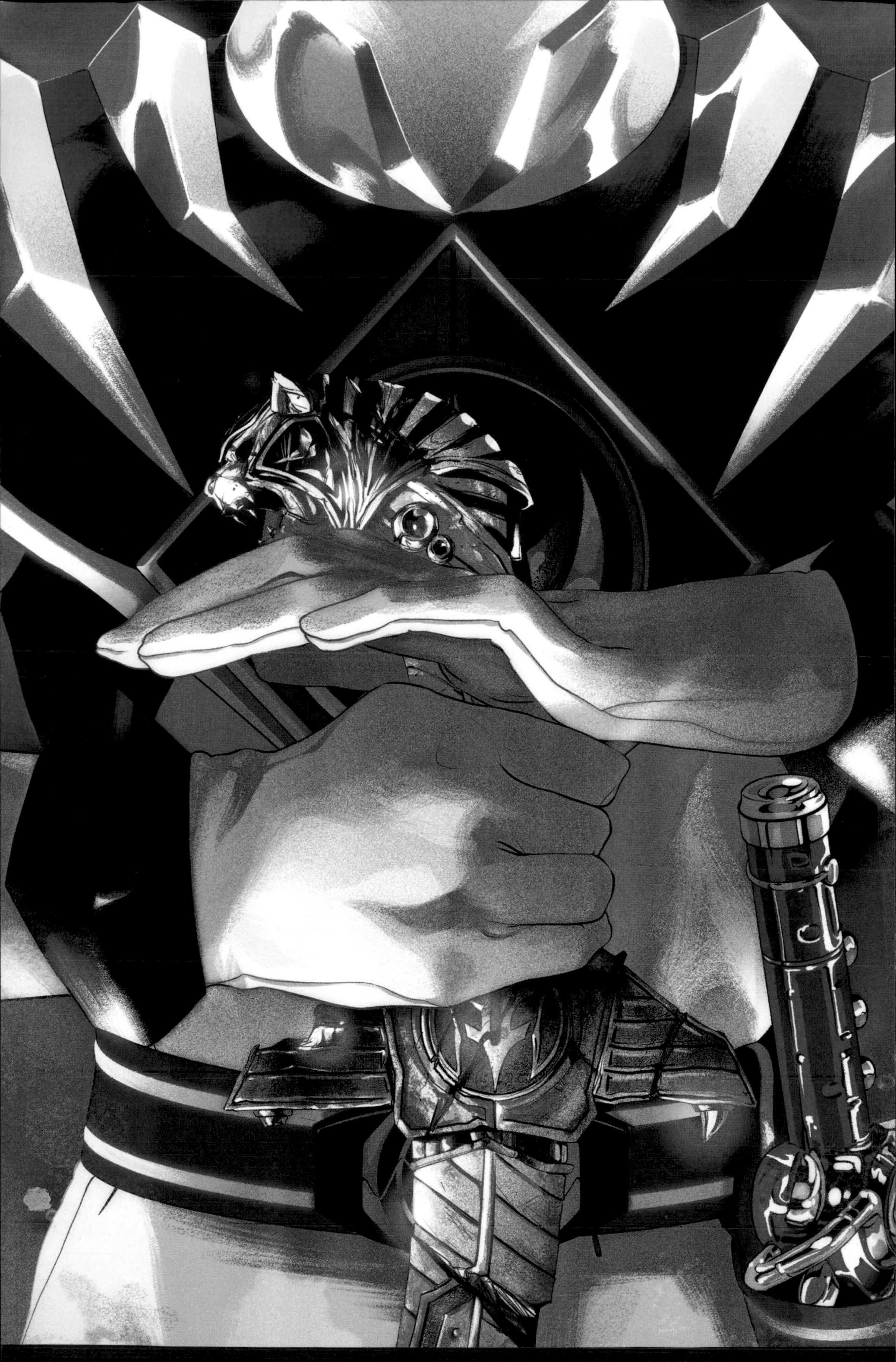

GOÑI MONTES | ISSUE TWENTY-FIVE COVER

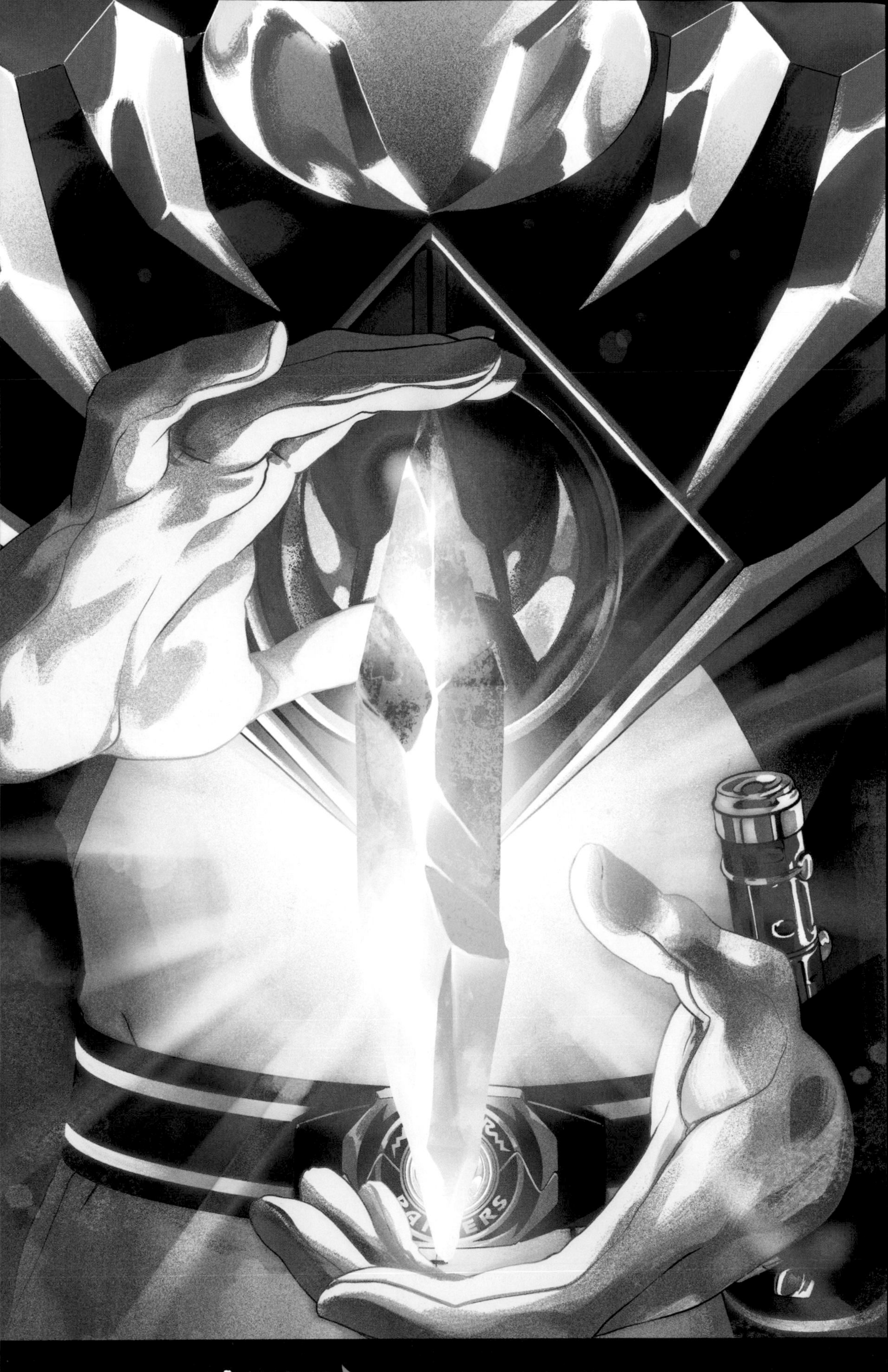

GOÑI MONTES | ISSUE TWENTY-FIVE ONE PER STORE COVER

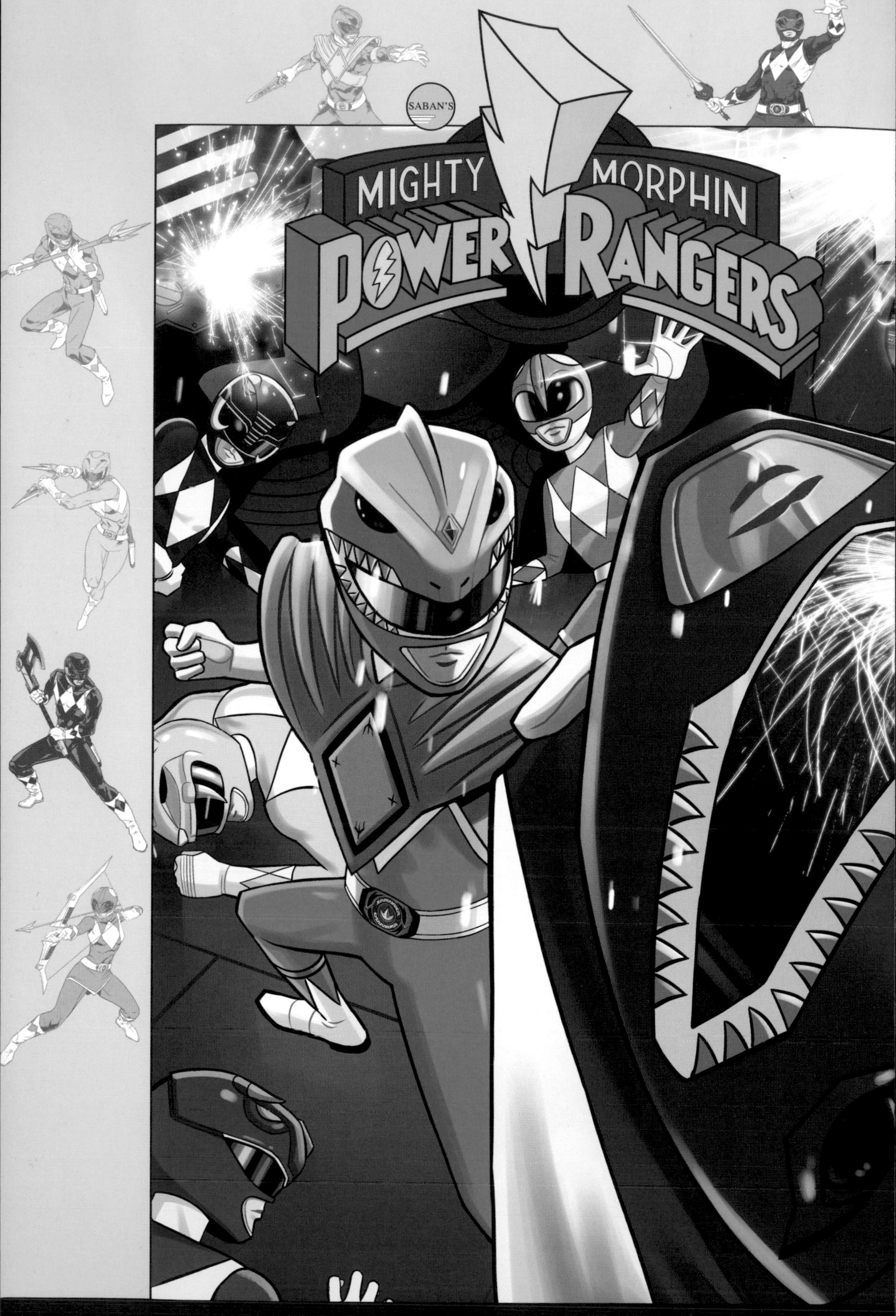
SABAN'S
MIGHTY MORPHIN
POWER RANGERS

JORDAN GIBSON ISSUE TWENTY-FIVE SUBSCRIPTION COVER

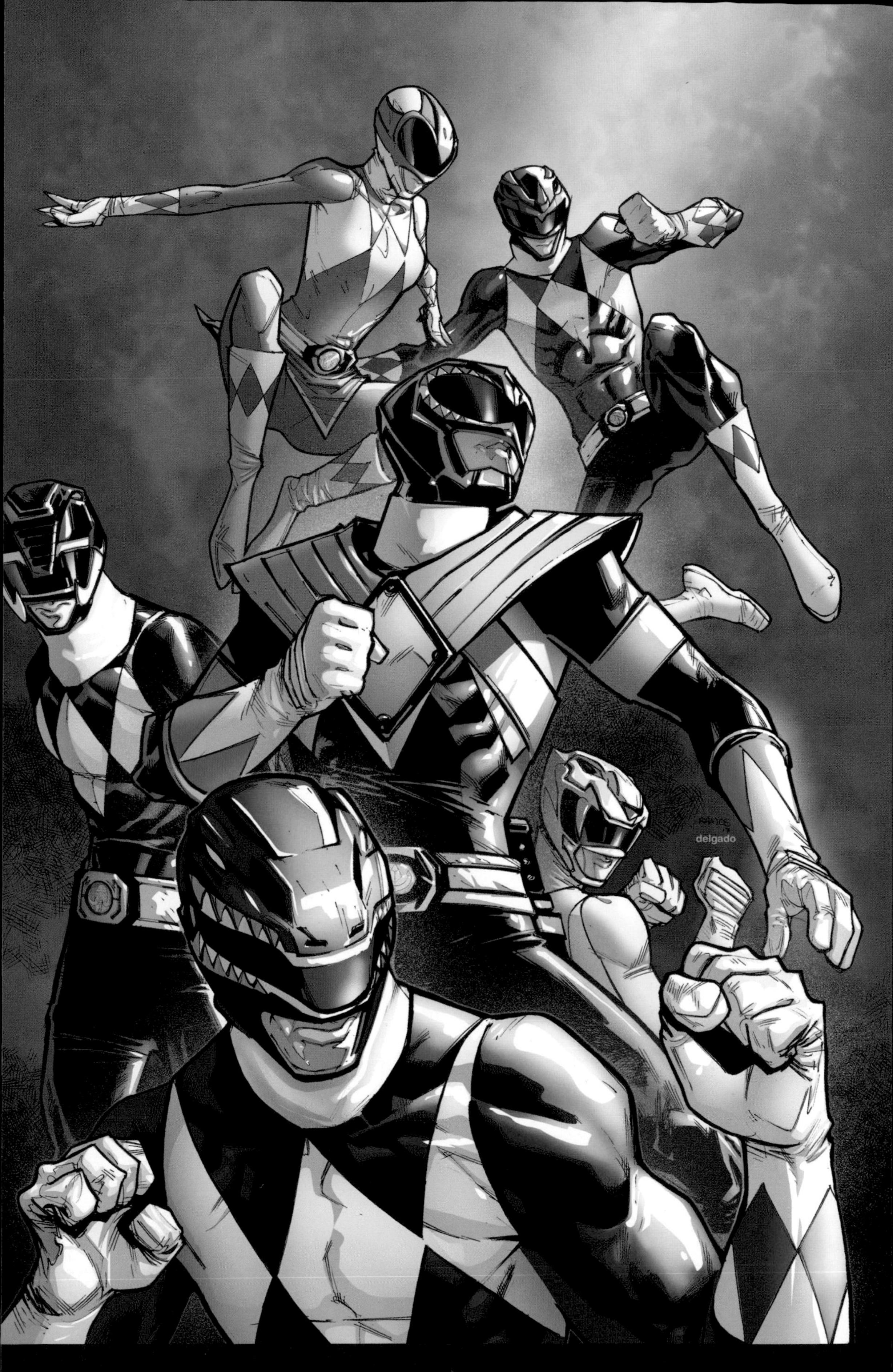
delgado

HUMBERTO RAMOS COLORS BY **EDGAR DELGADO** ISSUE TWENTY-FIVE ONE PER STORE VARIANT COVER

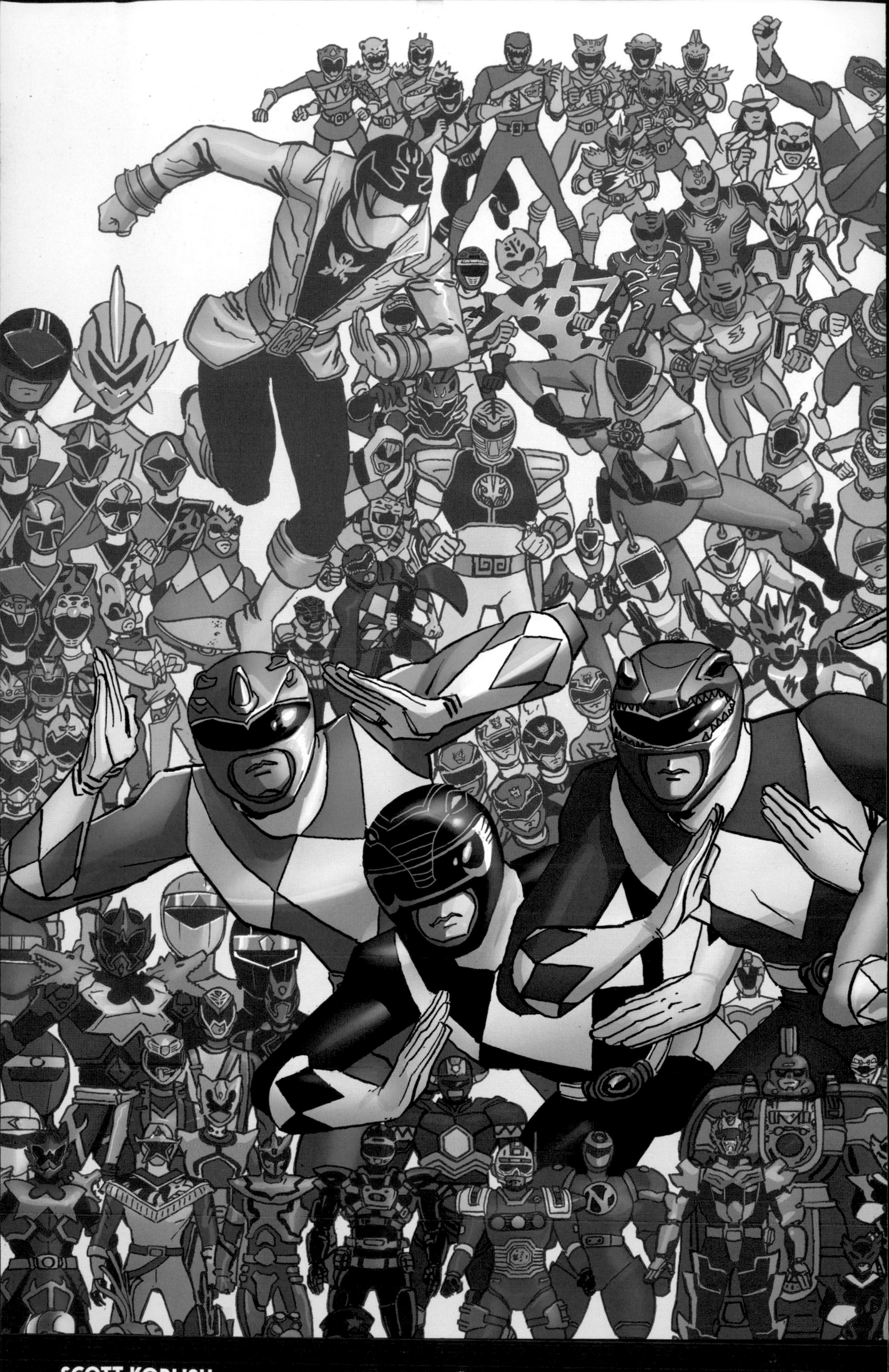

SCOTT KOBLISH WITH COLORS BY **ALEX GUIMARÃES** AND WITH SPECIAL THANKS TO **JAMES JAMESON**

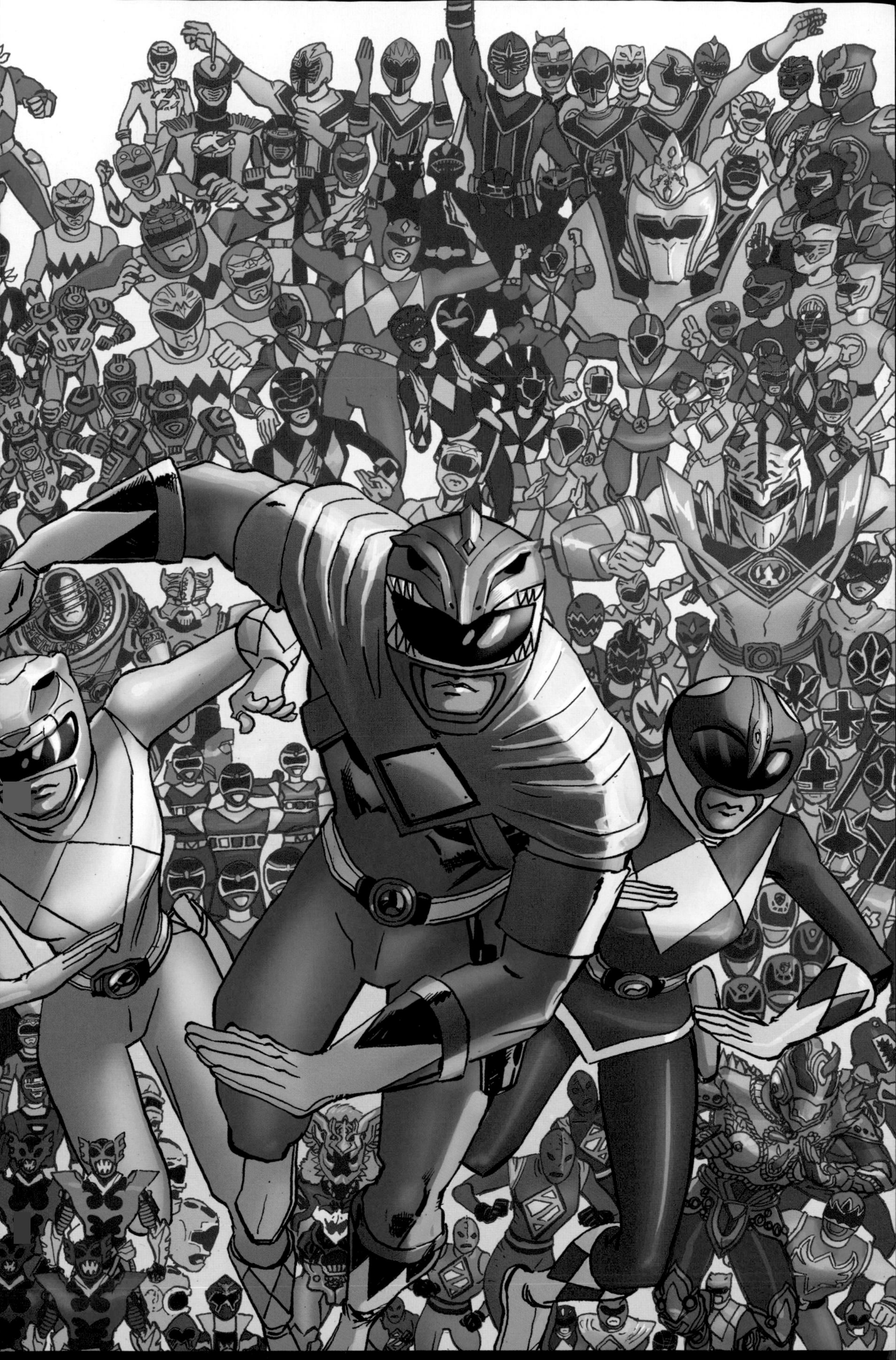

ISSUE TWENTY-FIVE WRAPAROUND VARIANT COVER

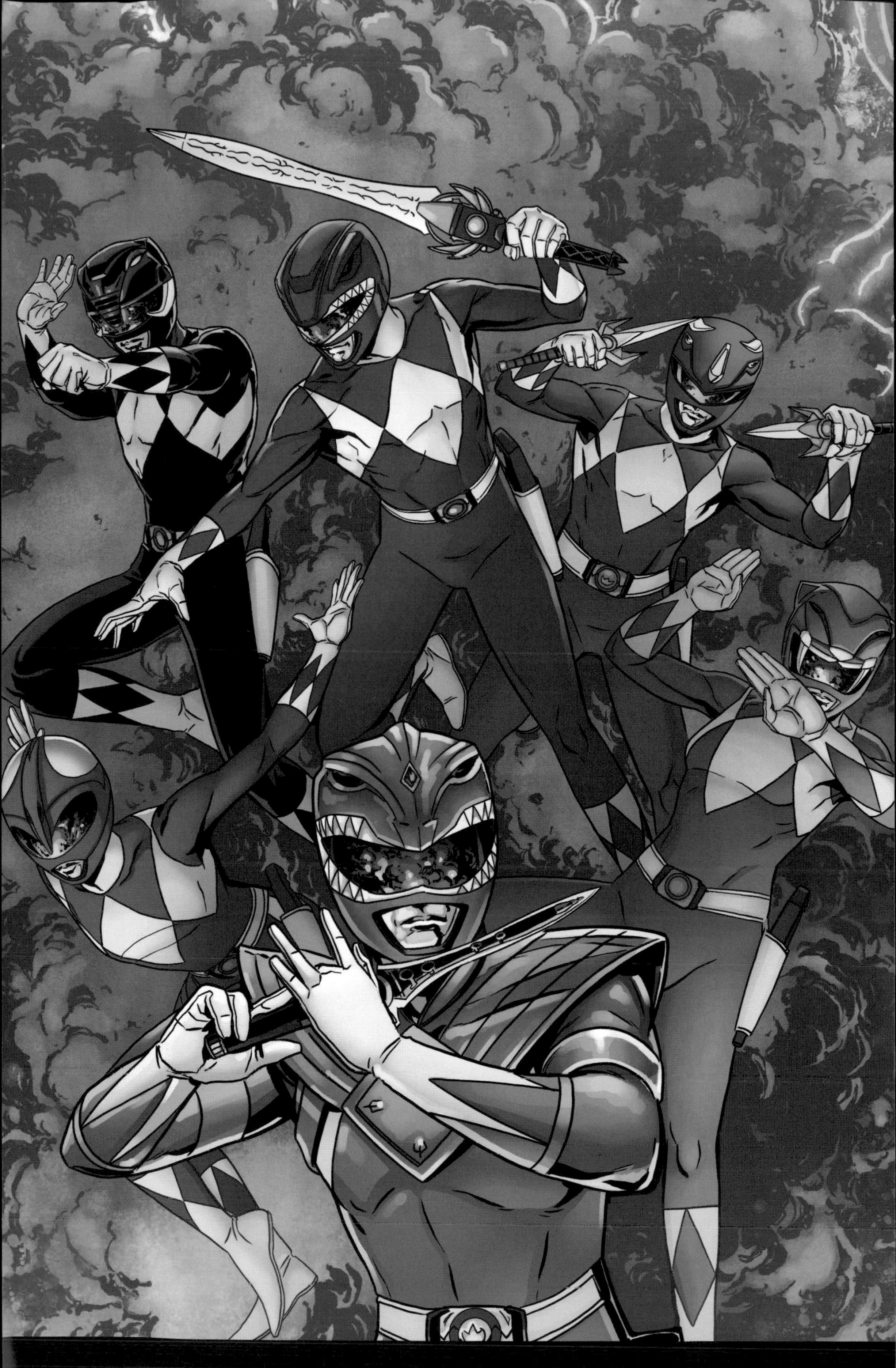

MARC LAMING COLORS BY **JORDAN BOYD** ISSUE TWENTY-FIVE C2E2 RETAILER SUMMIT VARIANT COVER

DERON BENNETT ISSUE TWENTY-FIVE WONDERCON BOOM! STUDIOS SHATTERED GRID PANEL VARIANT COVER

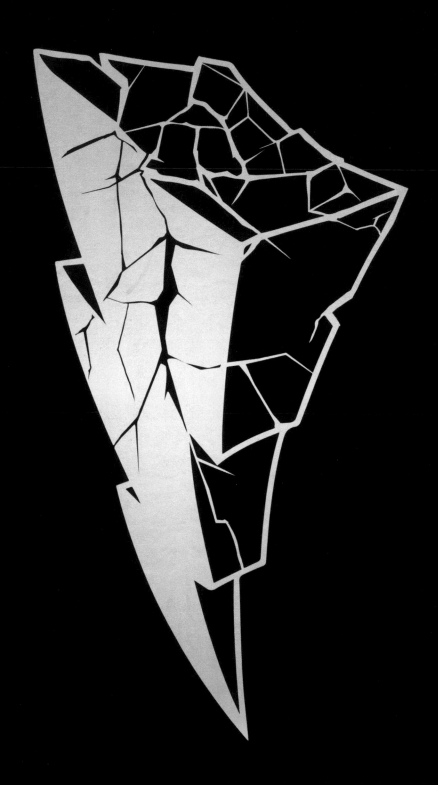

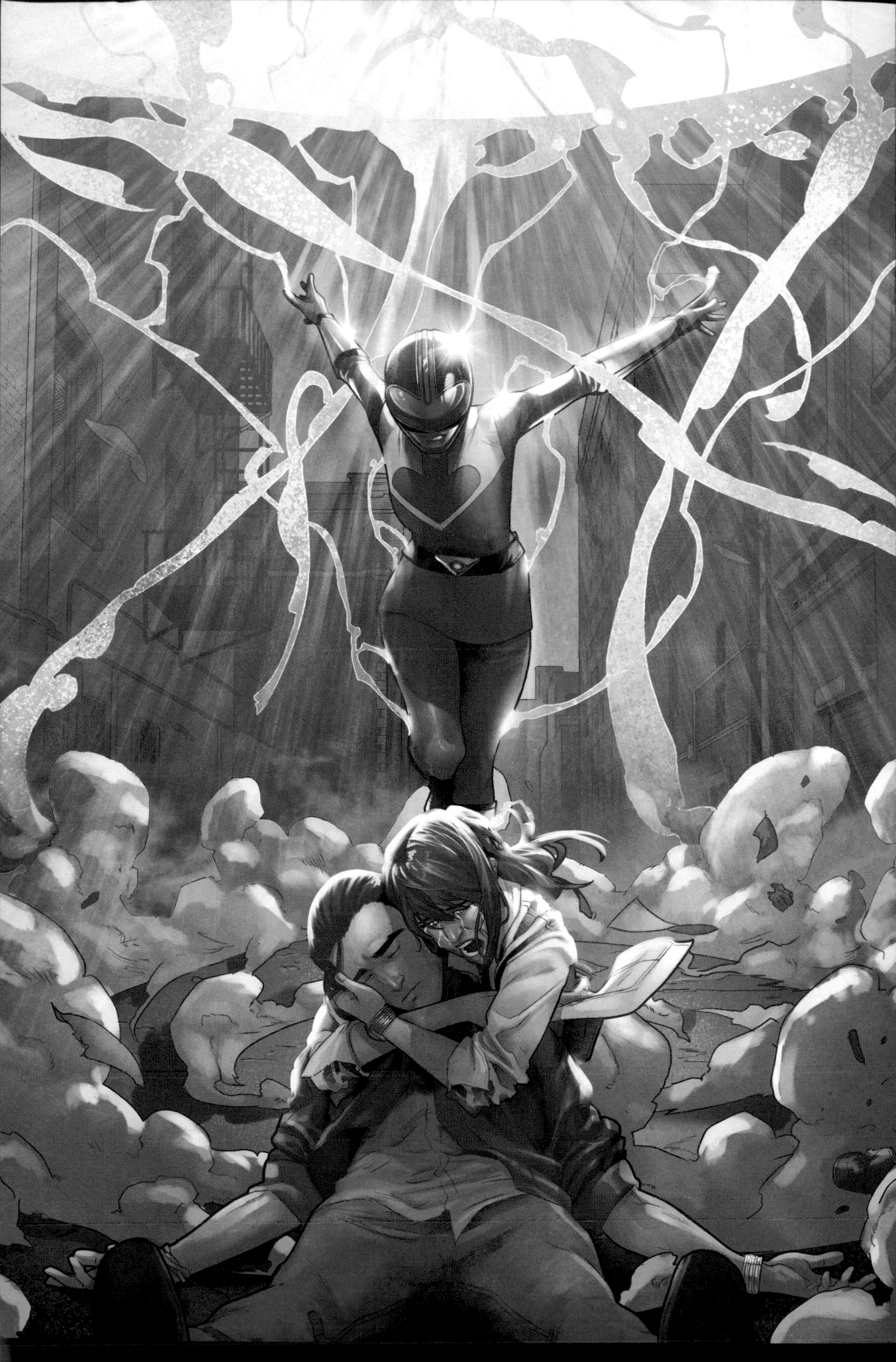

JAMAL CAMPBELL | ISSUE TWENTY-SIX MAIN COVER

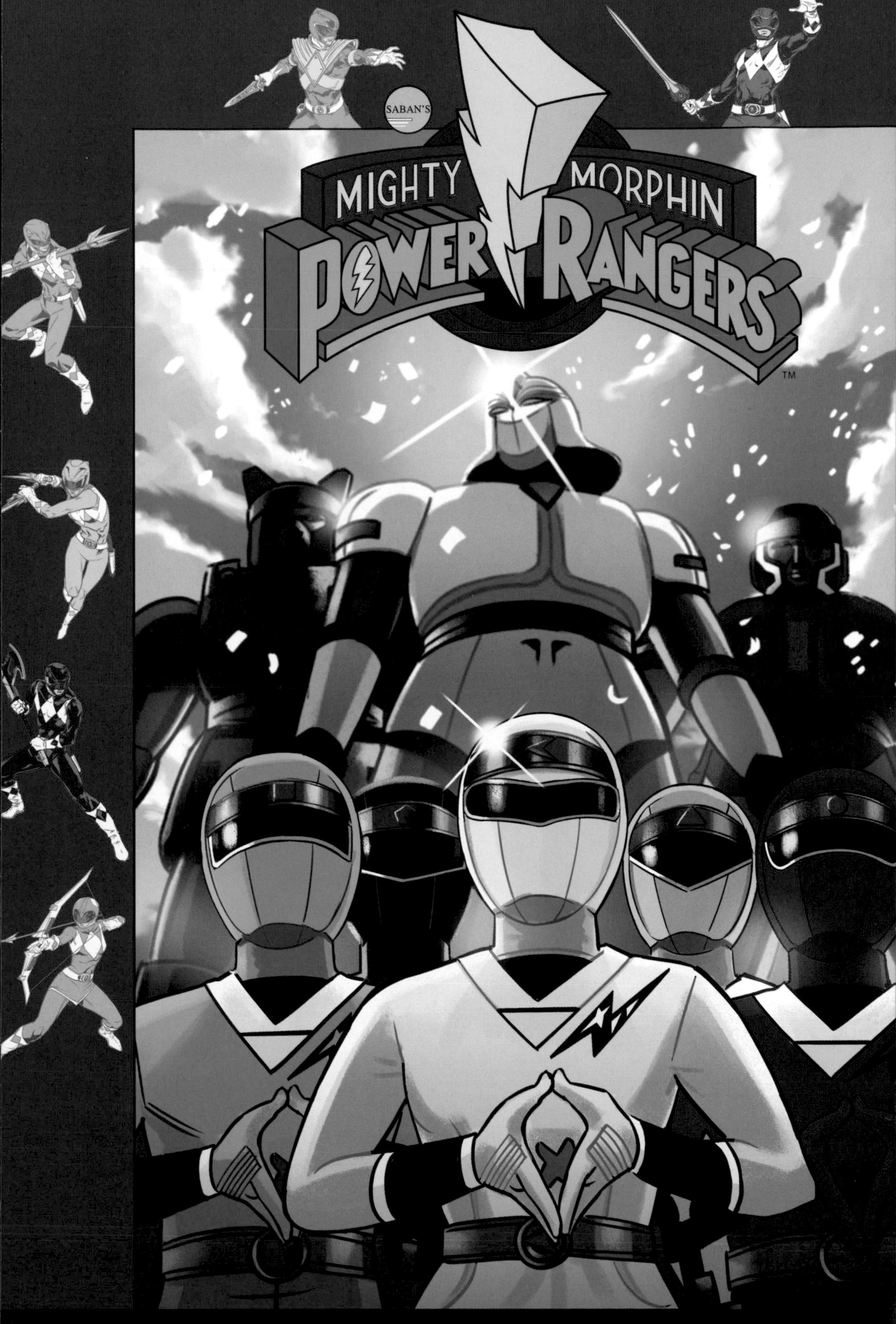
SABAN'S
MIGHTY MORPHIN
POWER RANGERS
TM

JORDAN GIBSON ISSUE TWENTY-SIX SUBSCRIPTION COVER

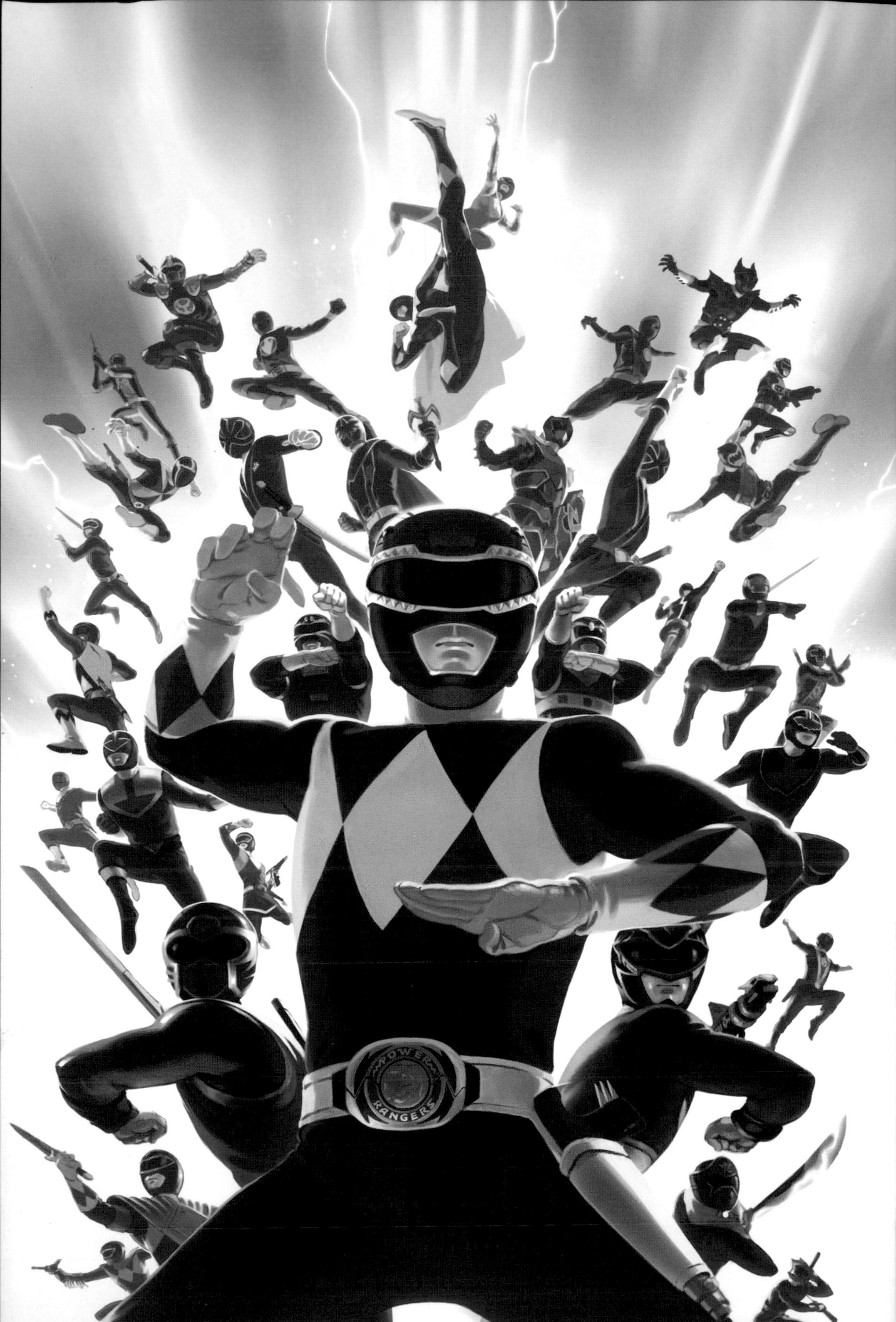
POWER
RANGERS

CARLOS VILLA | ISSUE TWENTY-SIX COLOR SPOTLIGHT VARIANT COVER

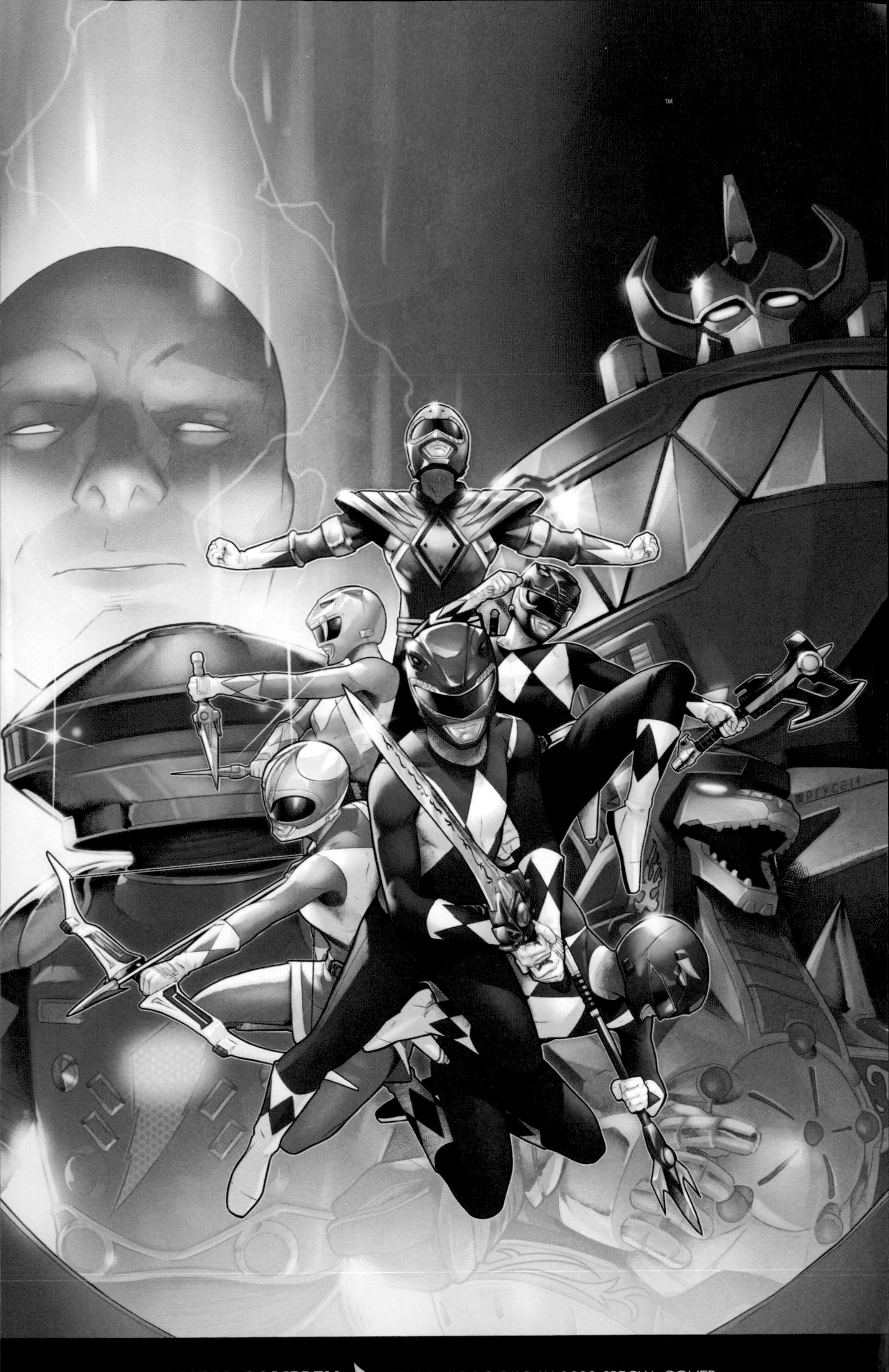

JAMAL CAMPBELL FREE COMIC BOOK DAY 2018 SPECIAL COVER

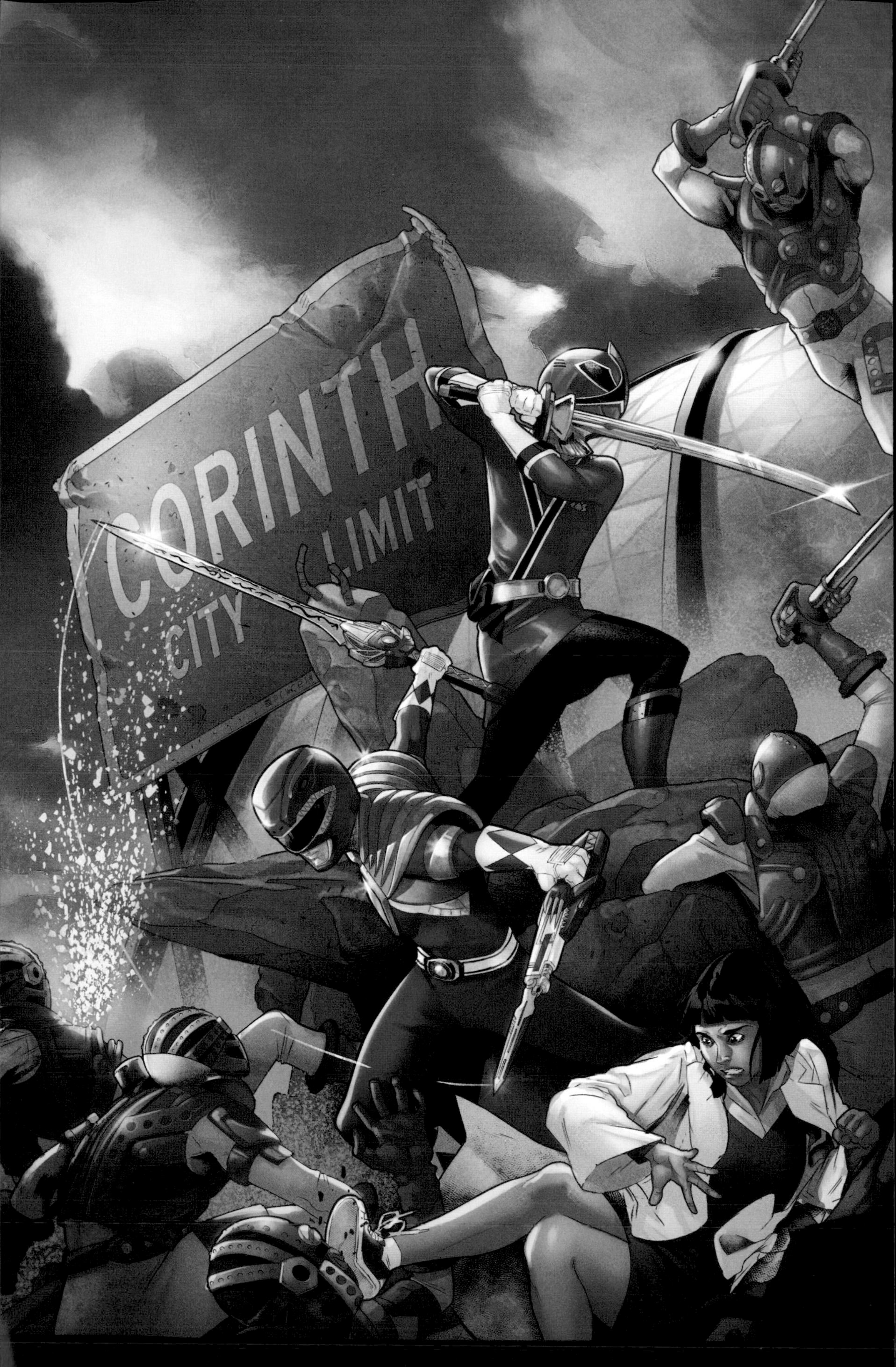
CORINTH
CITY LIMIT

JAMAL CAMPBELL ISSUE TWENTY-SEVEN MAIN COVER

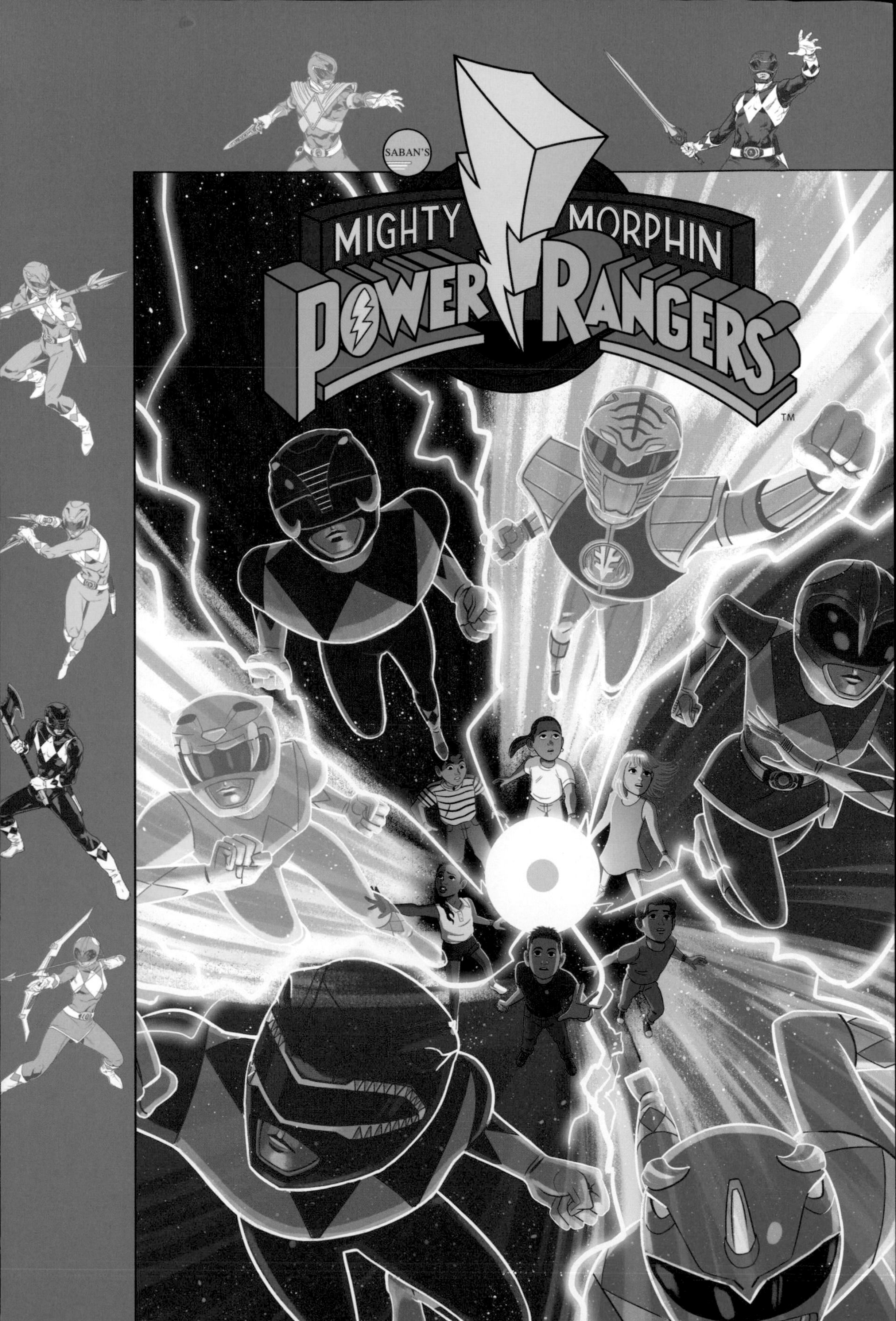
SABAN'S
MIGHTY MORPHIN
POWER RANGERS
TM

JORDAN GIBSON ISSUE TWENTY-SEVEN SUBSCRIPTION COVER

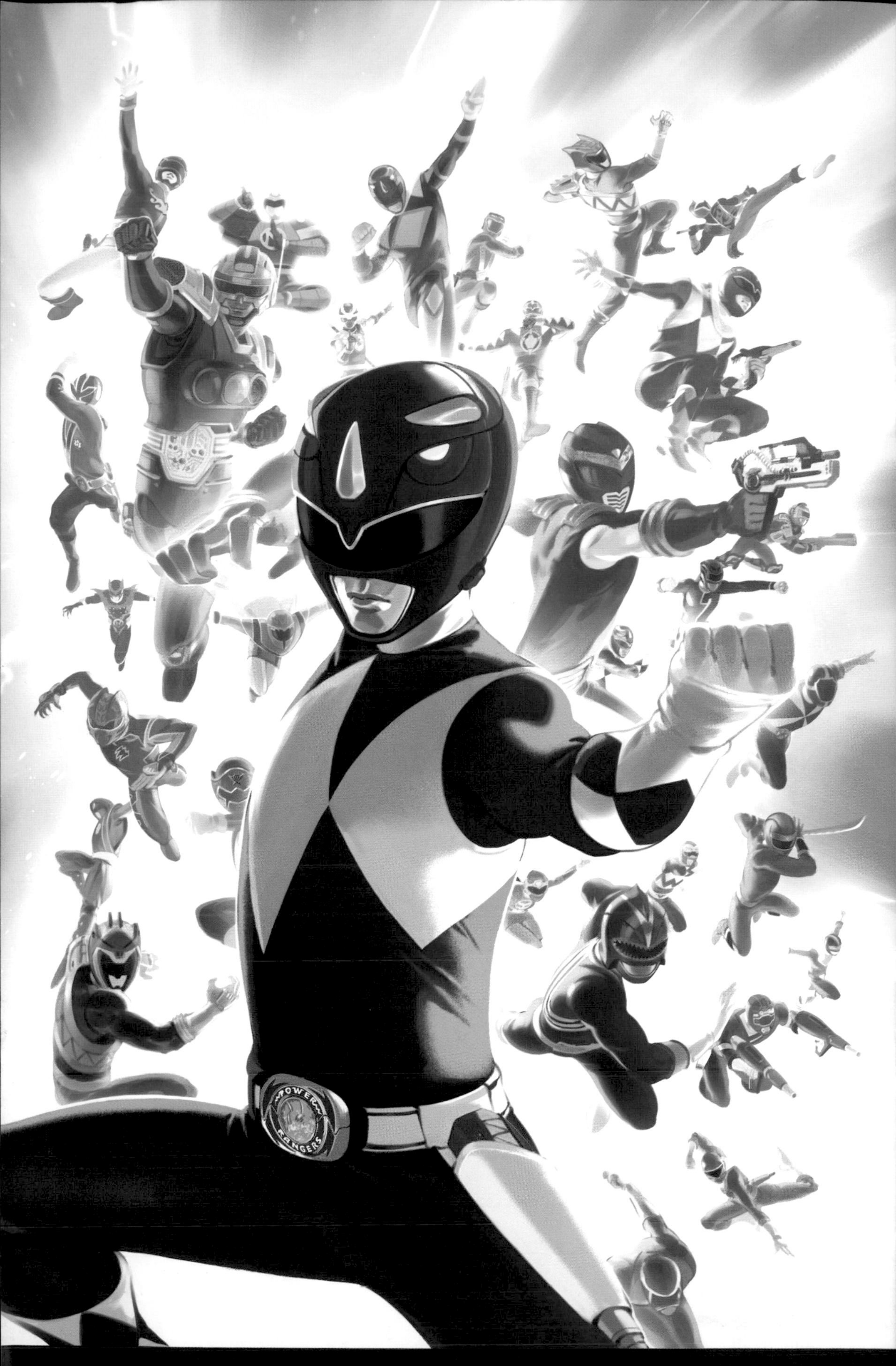
POWER RANGERS

CARLOS VILLA | ISSUE TWENTY-SEVEN COLOR SPOTLIGHT VARIANT COVER

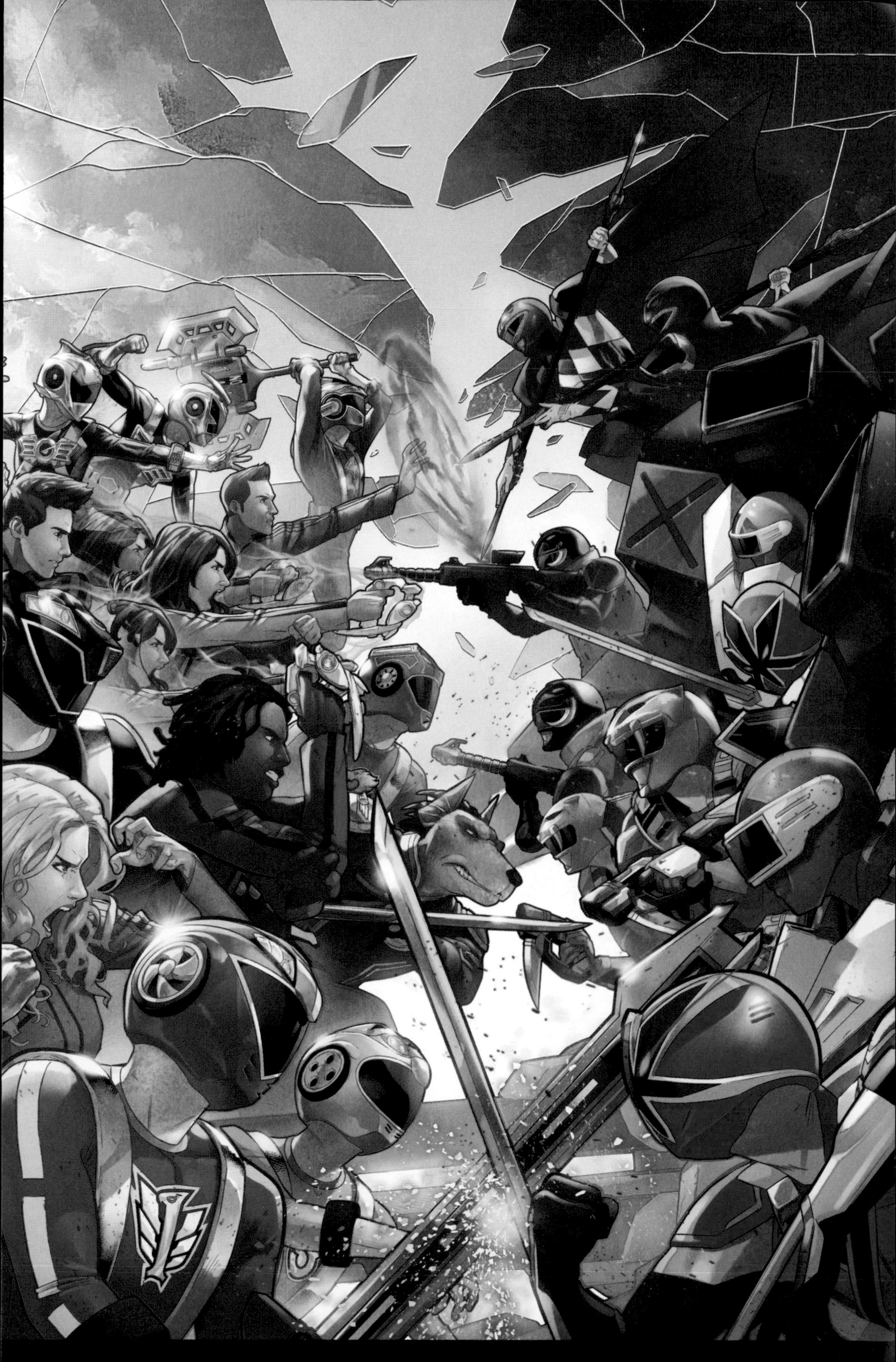

JAMAL CAMPBELL | ISSUE TWENTY-EIGHT MAIN COVER

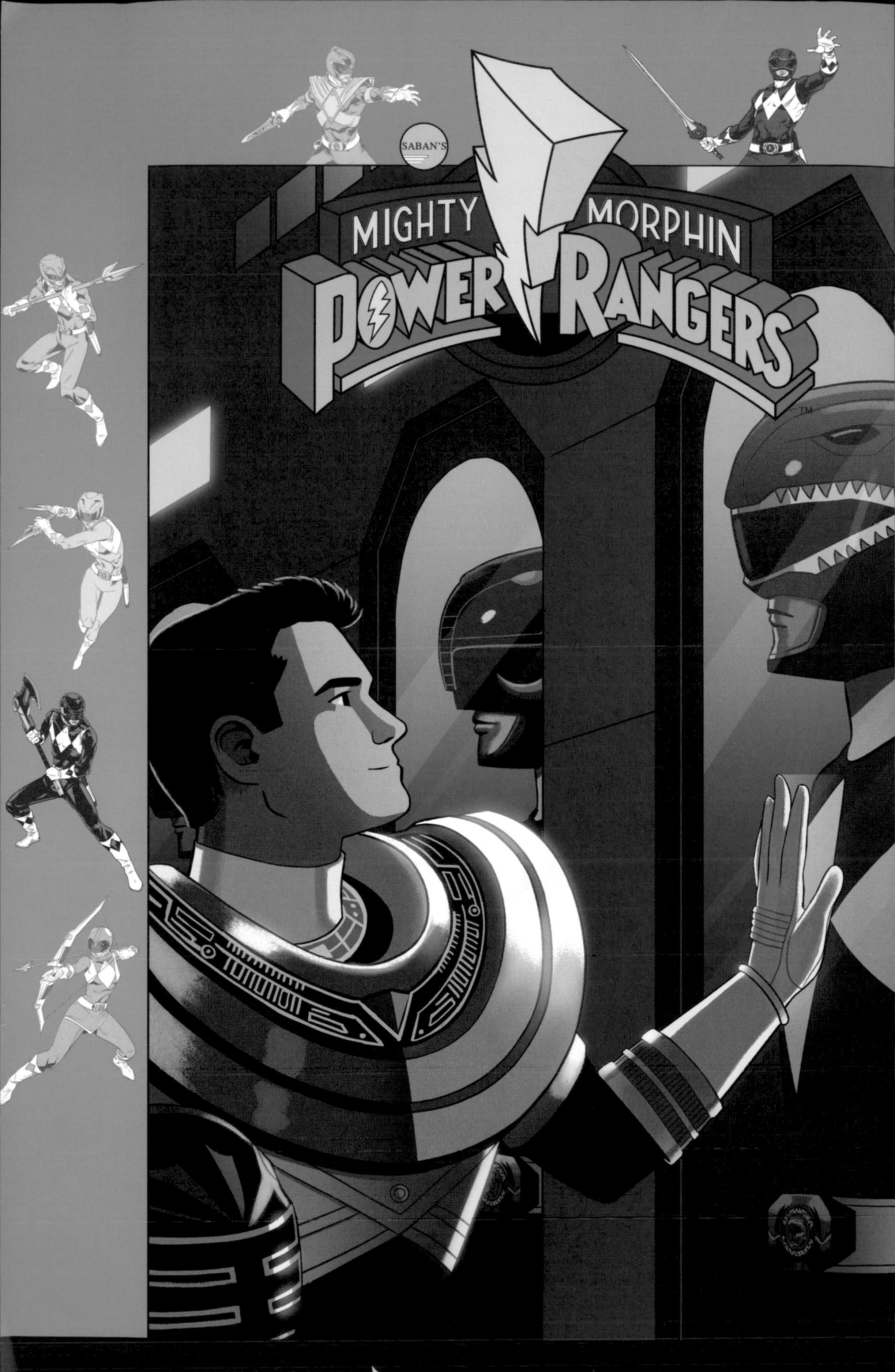
SABAN'S
MIGHTY MORPHIN
POWER RANGERS
TM

JORDAN GIBSON ISSUE TWENTY-EIGHT SUBSCRIPTION COVER

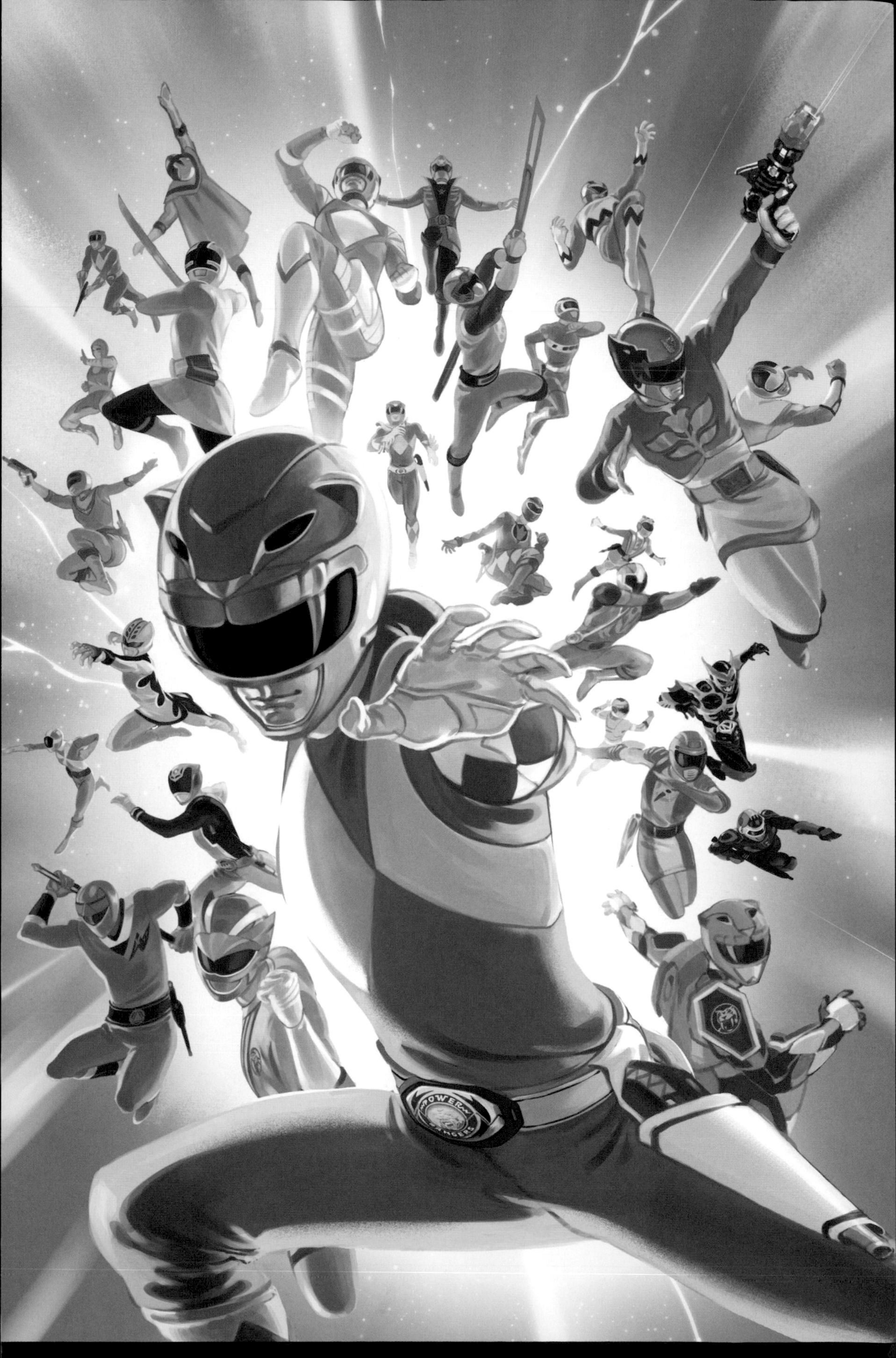
POWER RANGERS

CARLOS VILLA | ISSUE TWENTY-EIGHT COLOR SPOTLIGHT VARIANT COVER

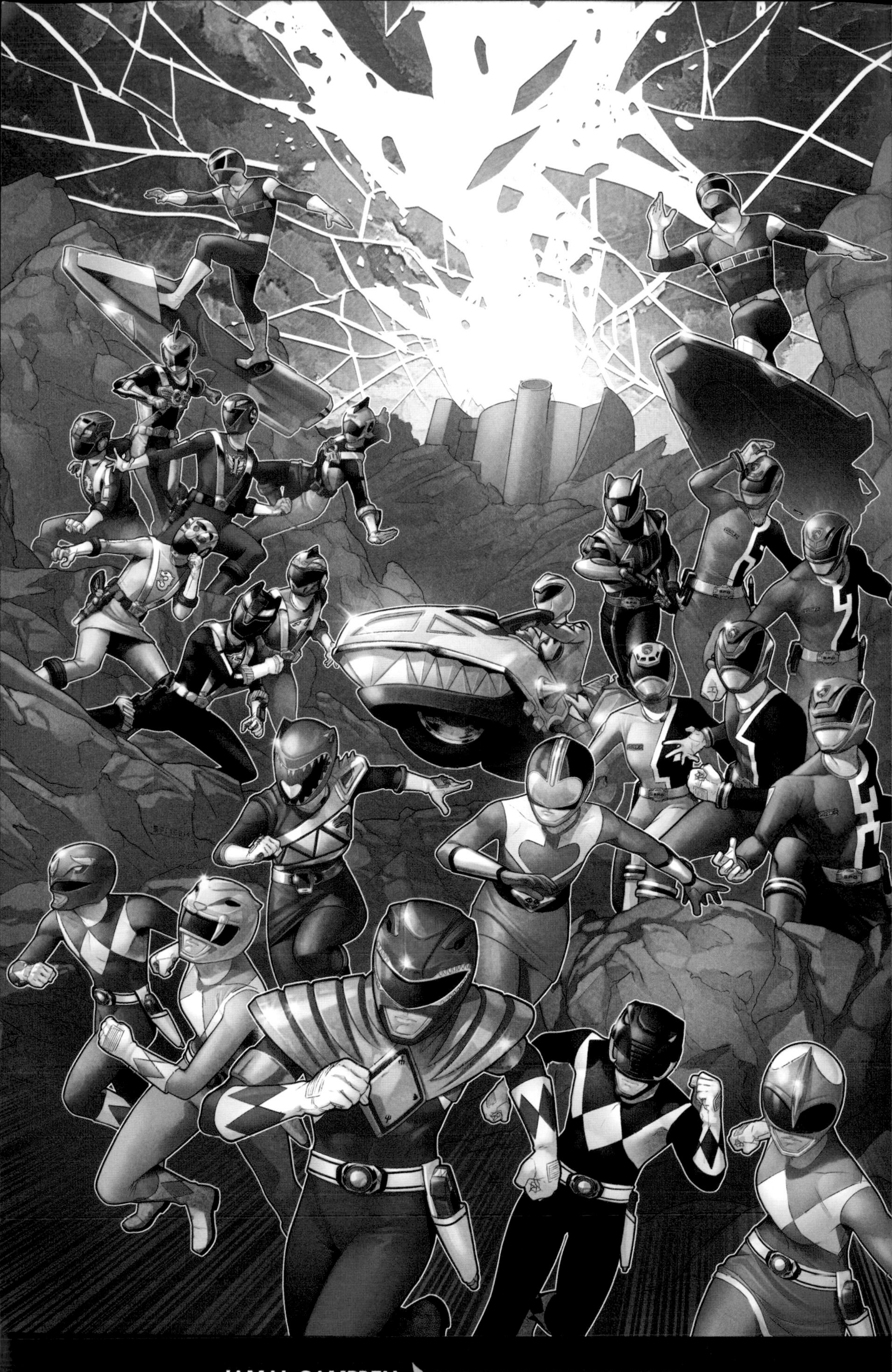

JAMAL CAMPBELL | ISSUE TWENTY-NINE MAIN COVER

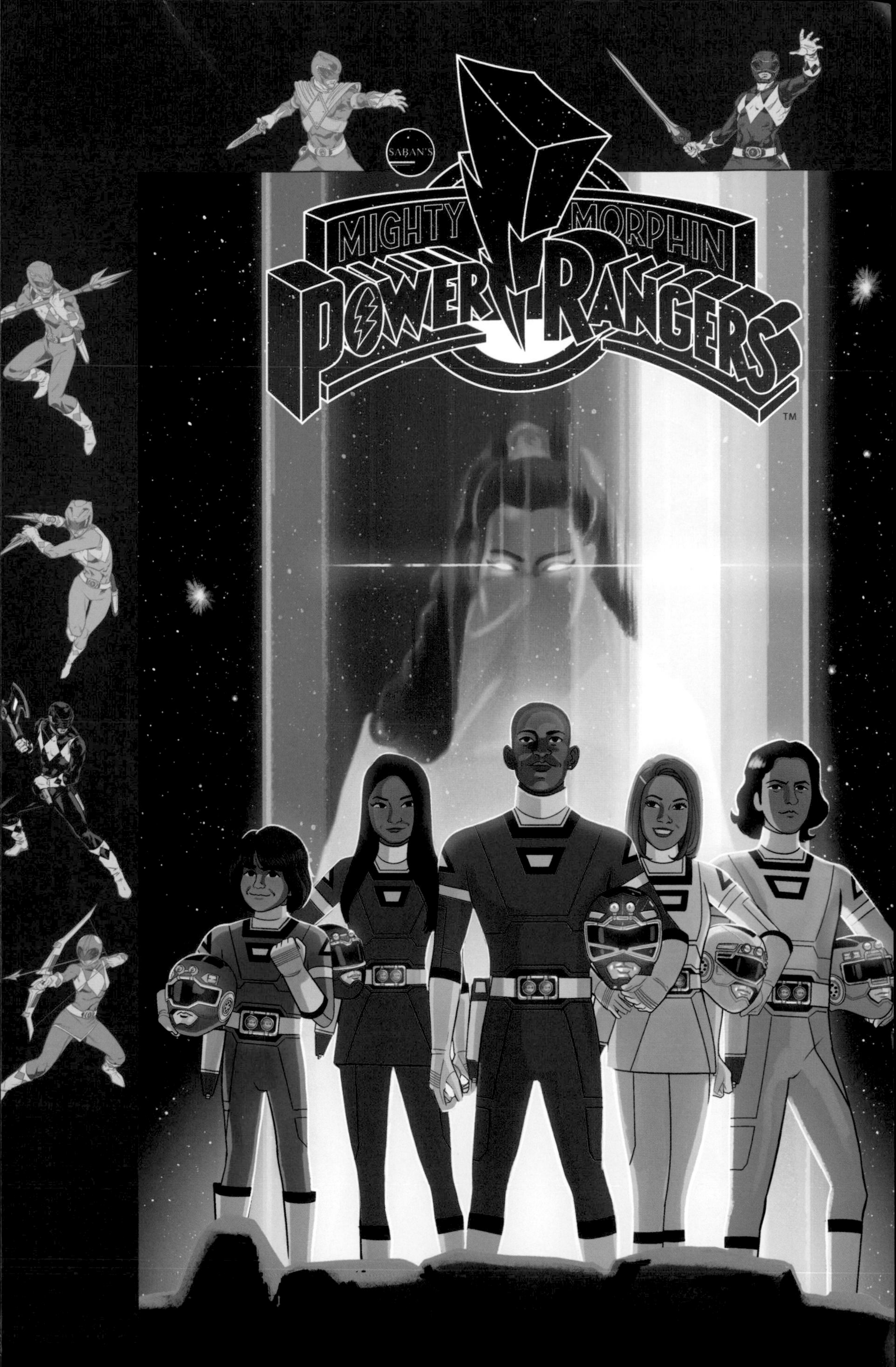
SABAN'S
MIGHTY MORPHIN
POWER RANGERS
TM

JORDAN GIBSON ISSUE TWENTY-NINE SUBSCRIPTION COVER

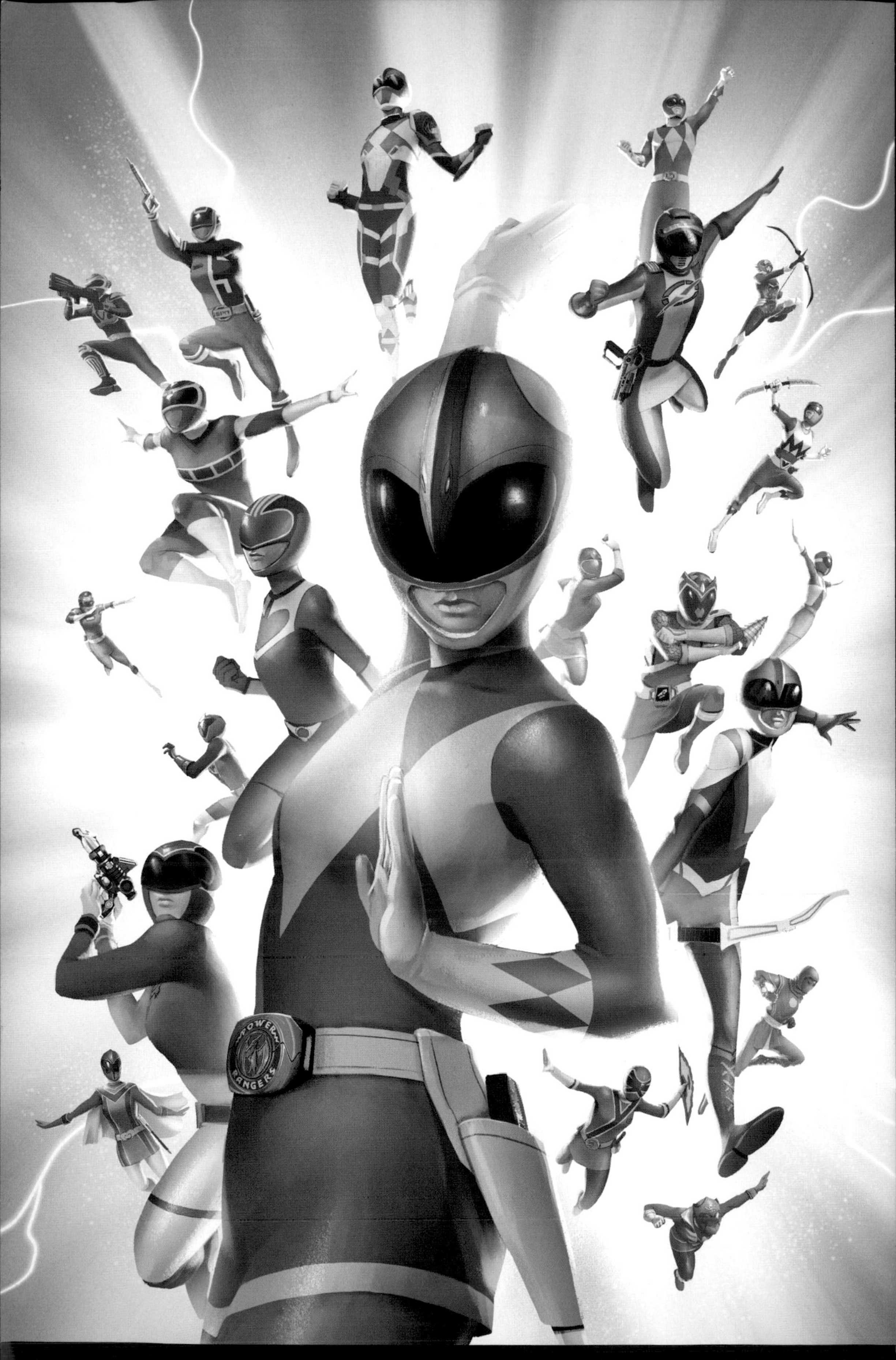
POWER
RANGERS

JOANA LAFUENTE WITH **CARLOS VILLA** | ISSUE TWENTY-NINE COLOR SPOTLIGHT VARIANT COVER

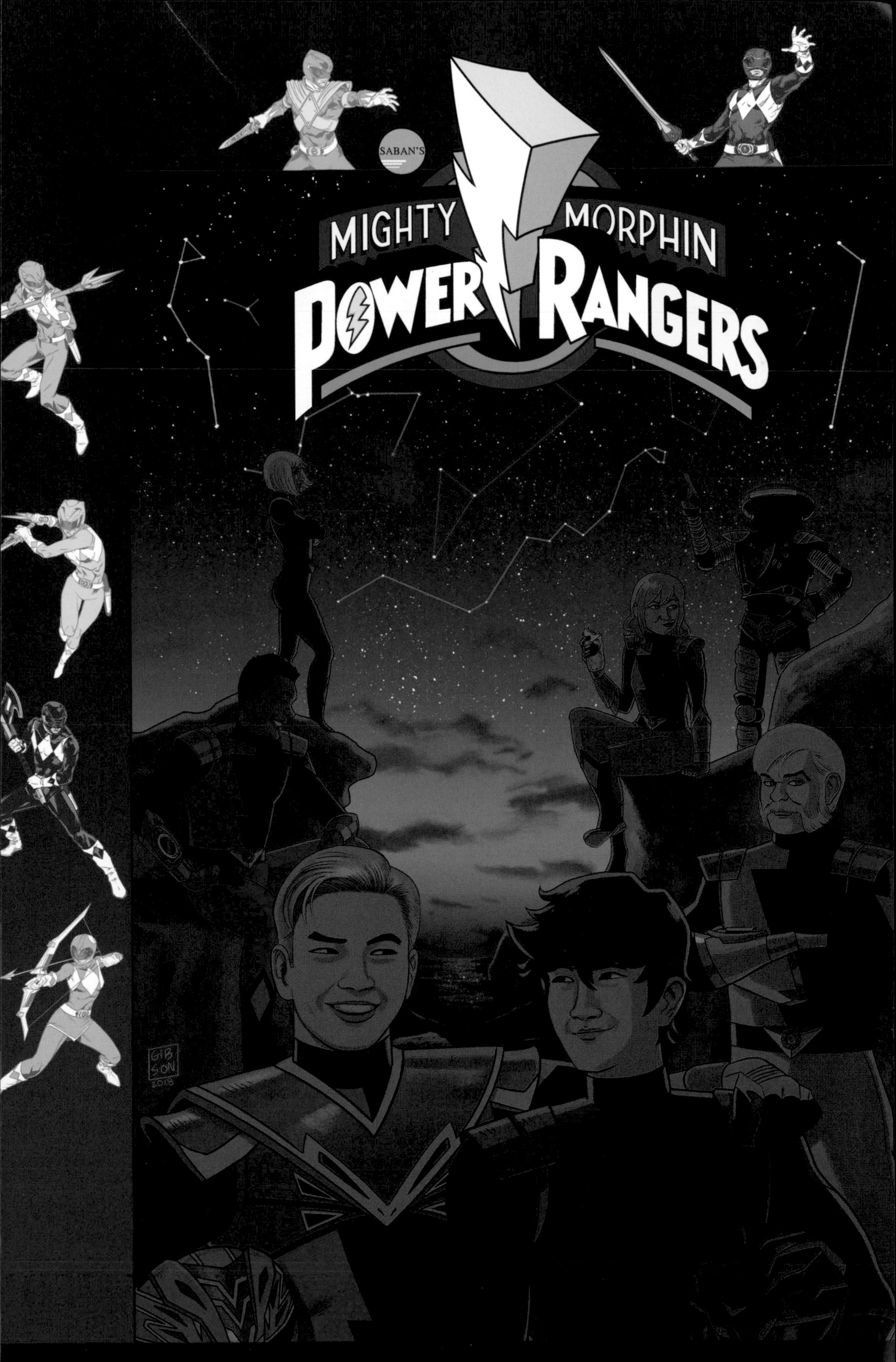
SABAN'S
MIGHTY MORPHIN
POWER RANGERS
GIB SON 2018

JORDAN GIBSON | ISSUE TWENTY-NINE HYPERFORCE VARIANT COVER

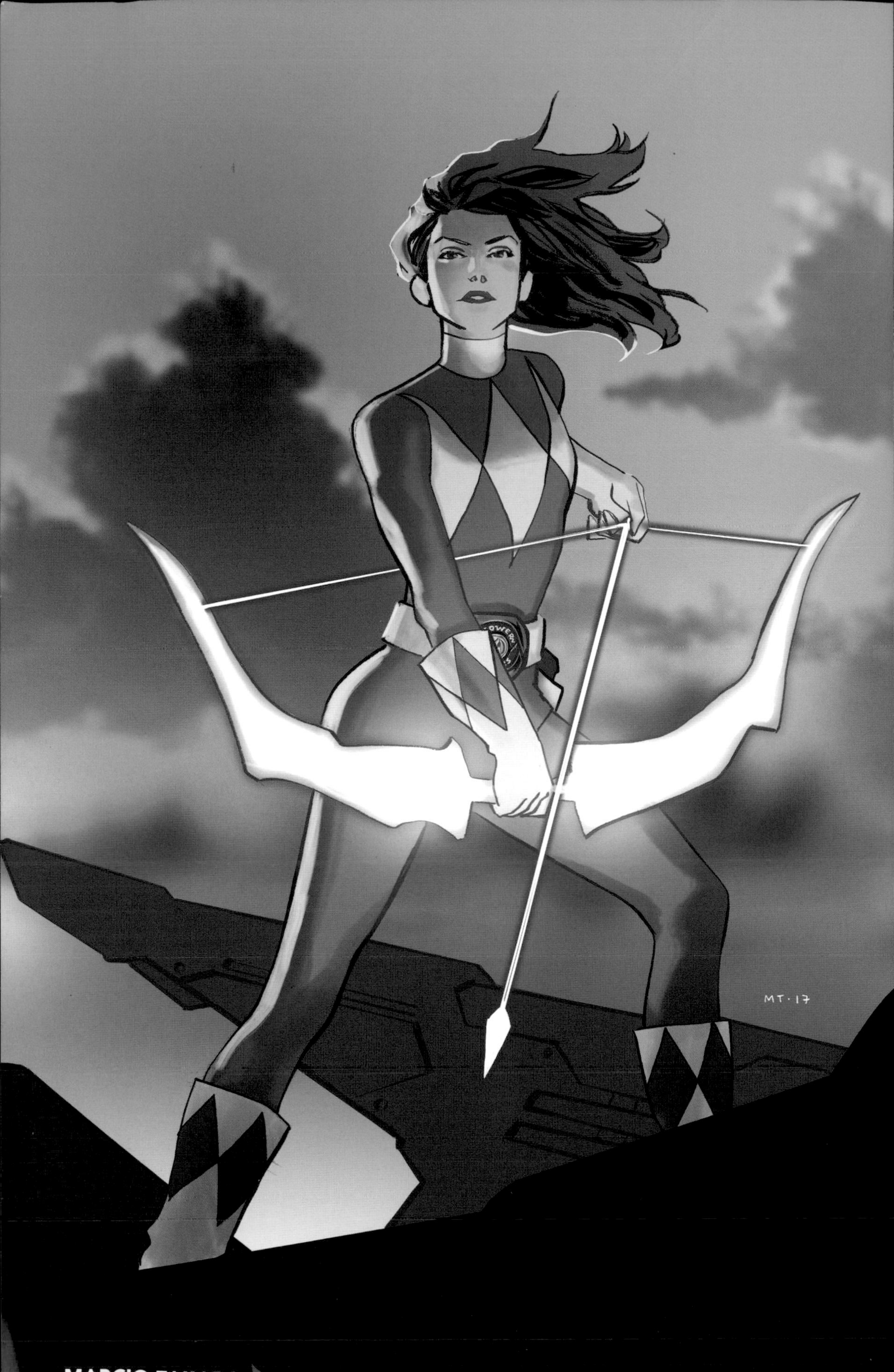
POWER
MT·17

MARCIO TAKARA ISSUE TWENTY-NINE SAN DIEGO COMIC-CON 2018 RETAILER EVENT EXCLUSIVE COVER

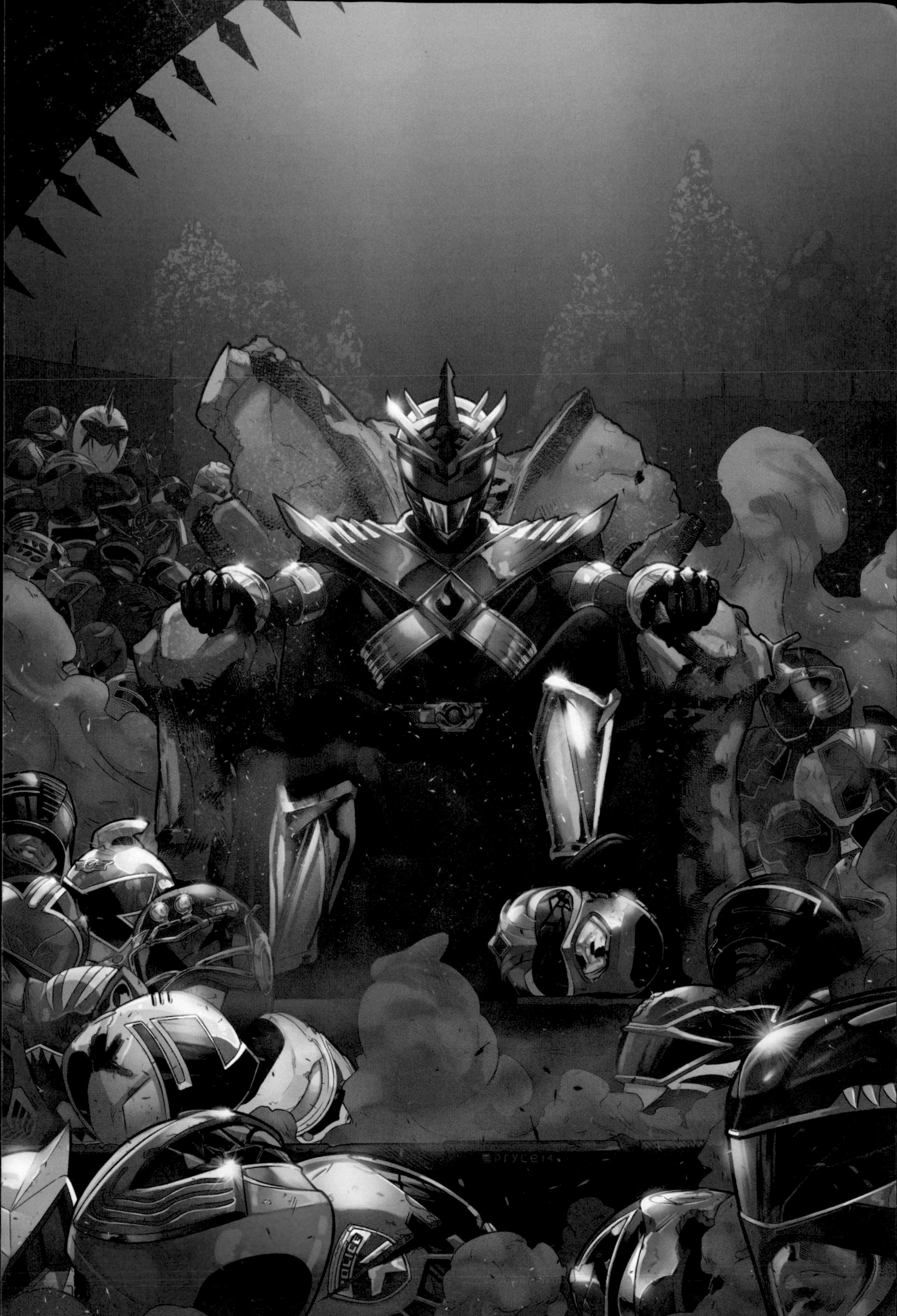

JAMAL CAMPBELL ISSUE THIRTY MAIN COVER

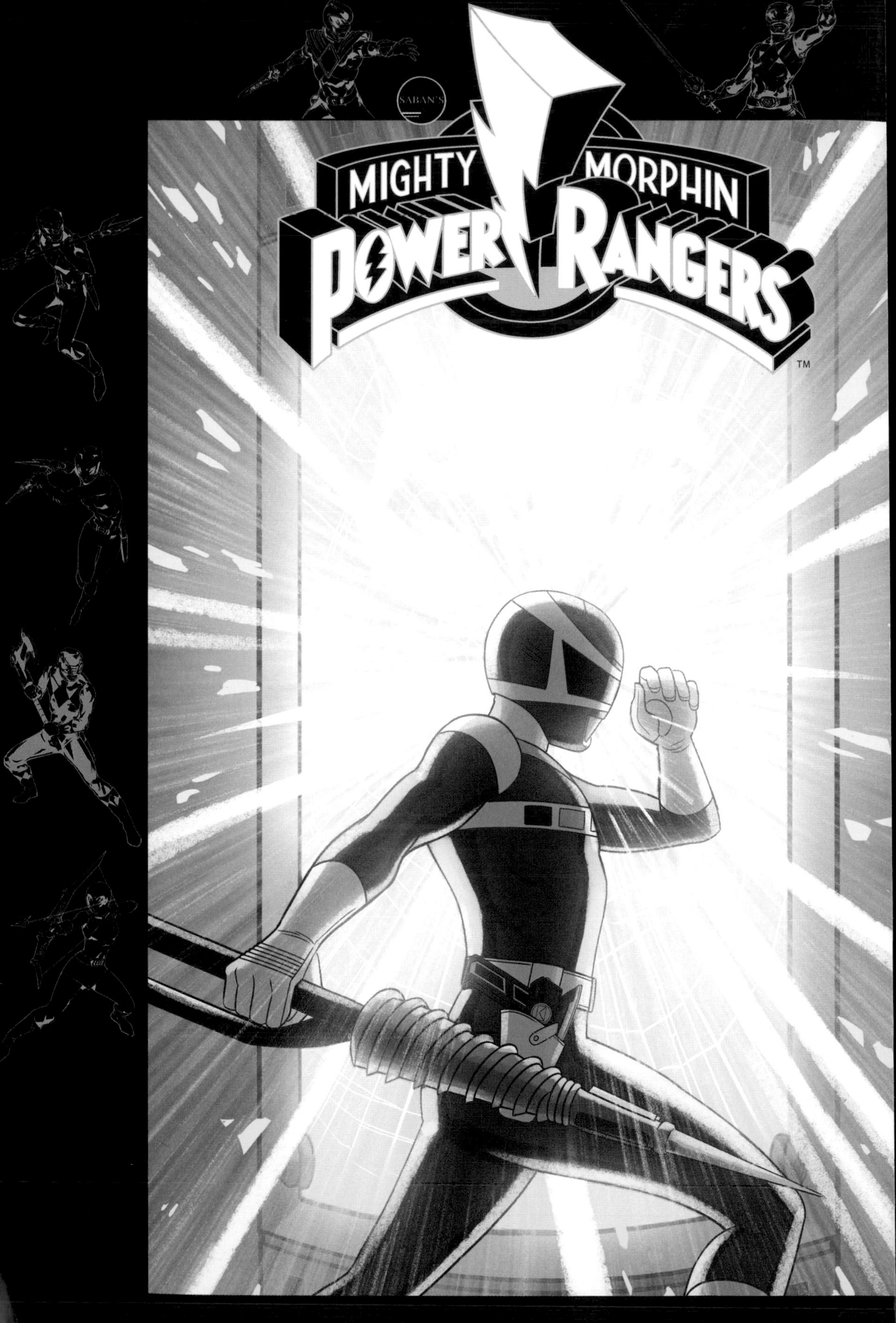
SABAN'S
MIGHTY MORPHIN
POWER RANGERS
TM

JORDAN GIBSON ISSUE THIRTY SUBSCRIPTION COVER

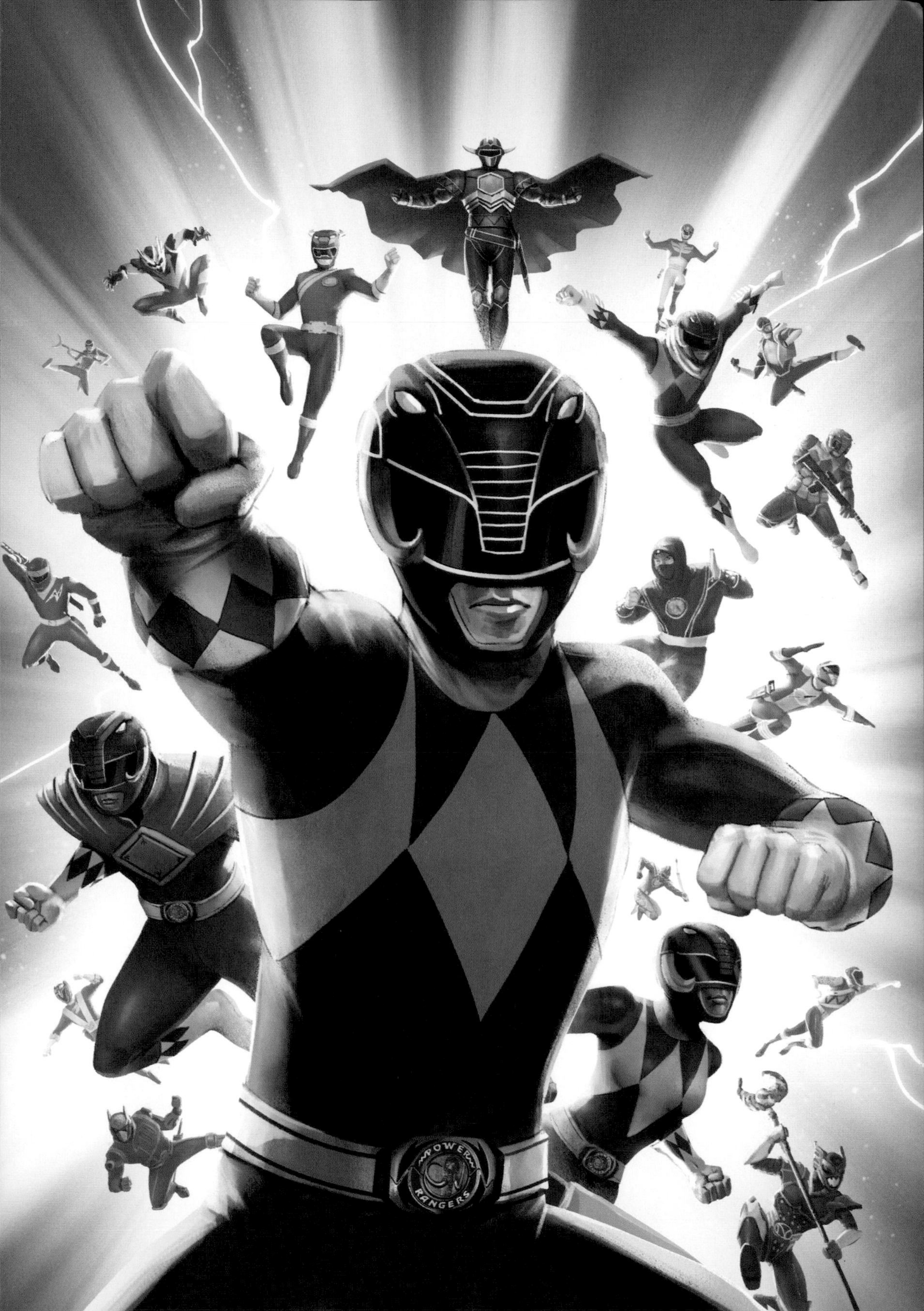
POWER
RANGERS

JOANA LAFUENTE ISSUE THIRTY COLOR SPOTLIGHT VARIANT COVER

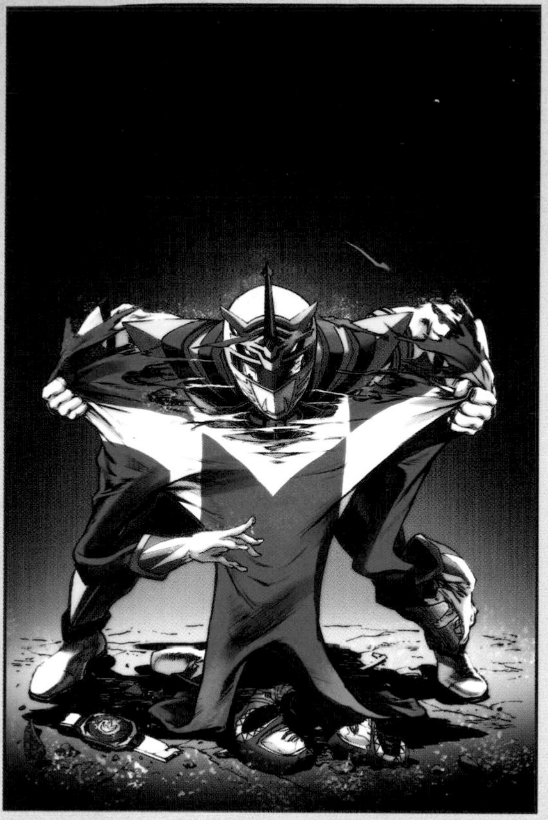

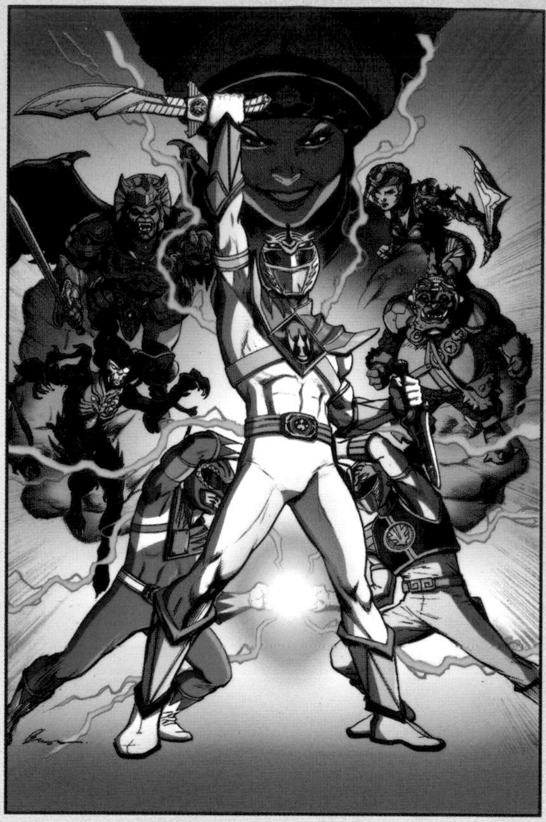

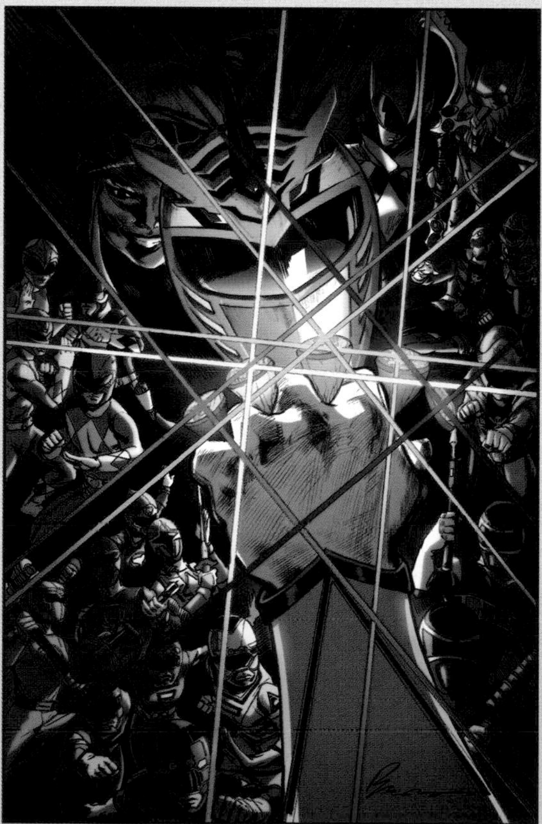

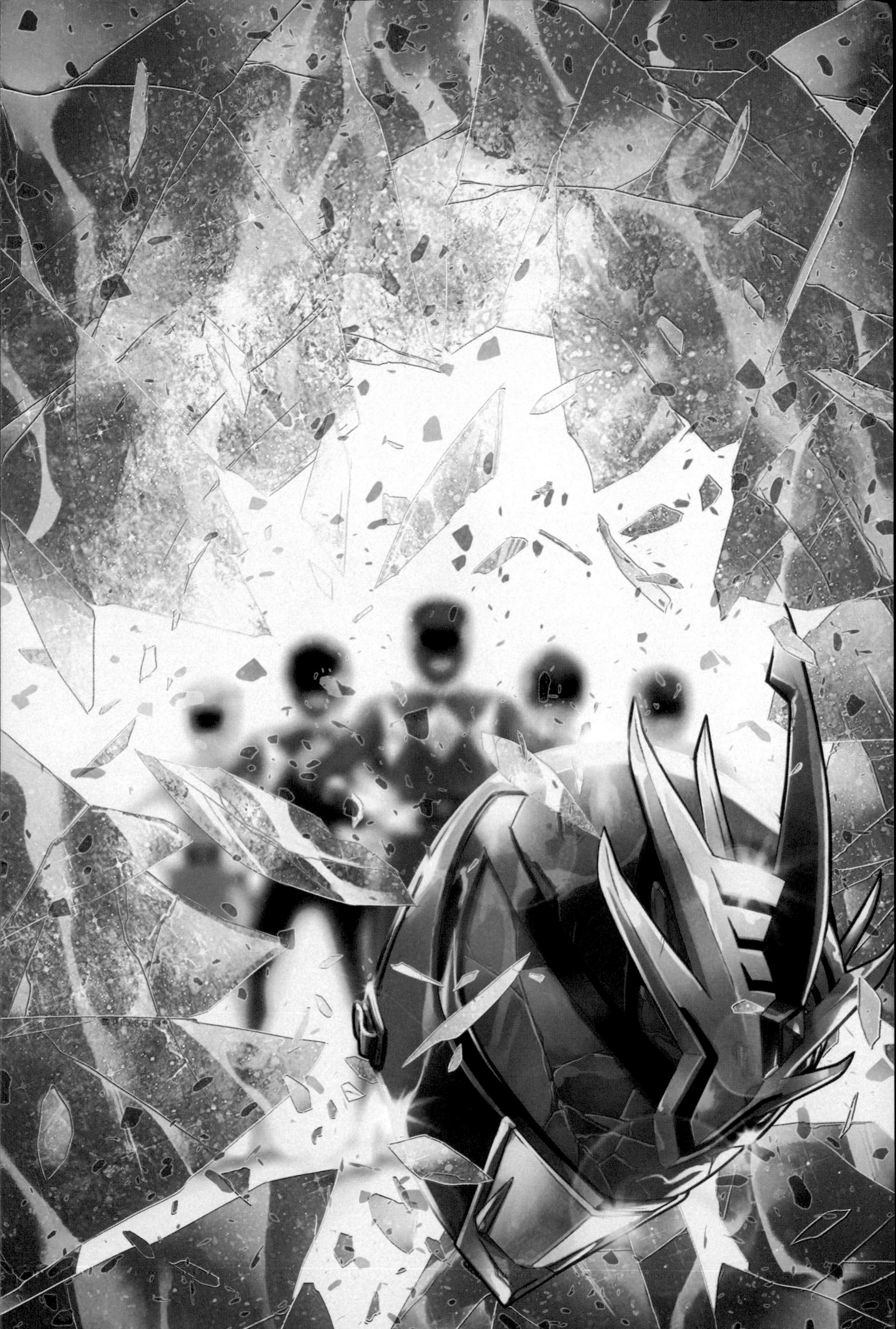

JAMAL CAMPBELL SHATTERED GRID ISSUE ONE MAIN COVER

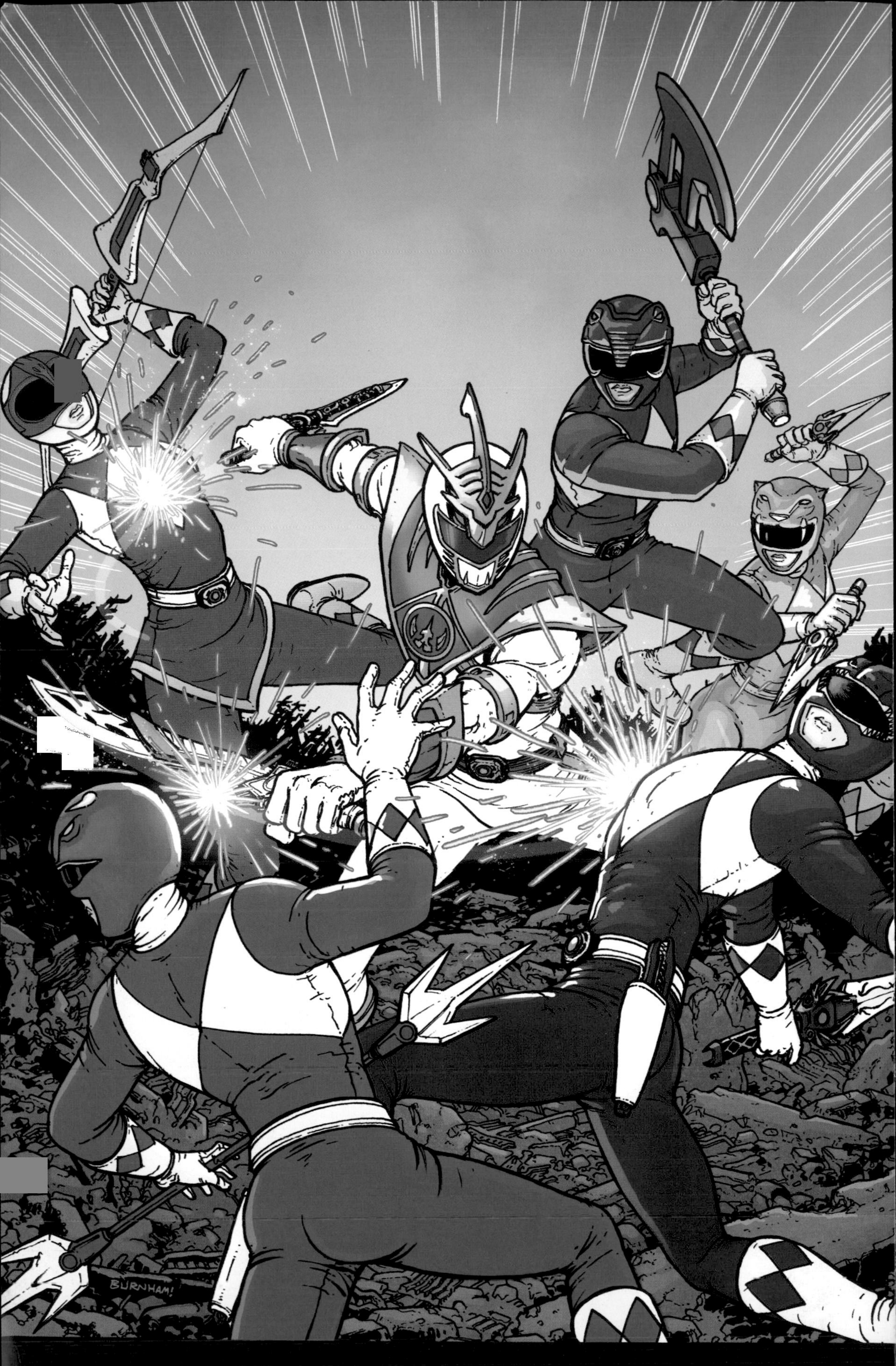
BURNHAM!

CHRIS BURNHAM WITH COLORS BY **JORDAN BOYD** SHATTERED GRID ISSUE ONE VARIANT COVER

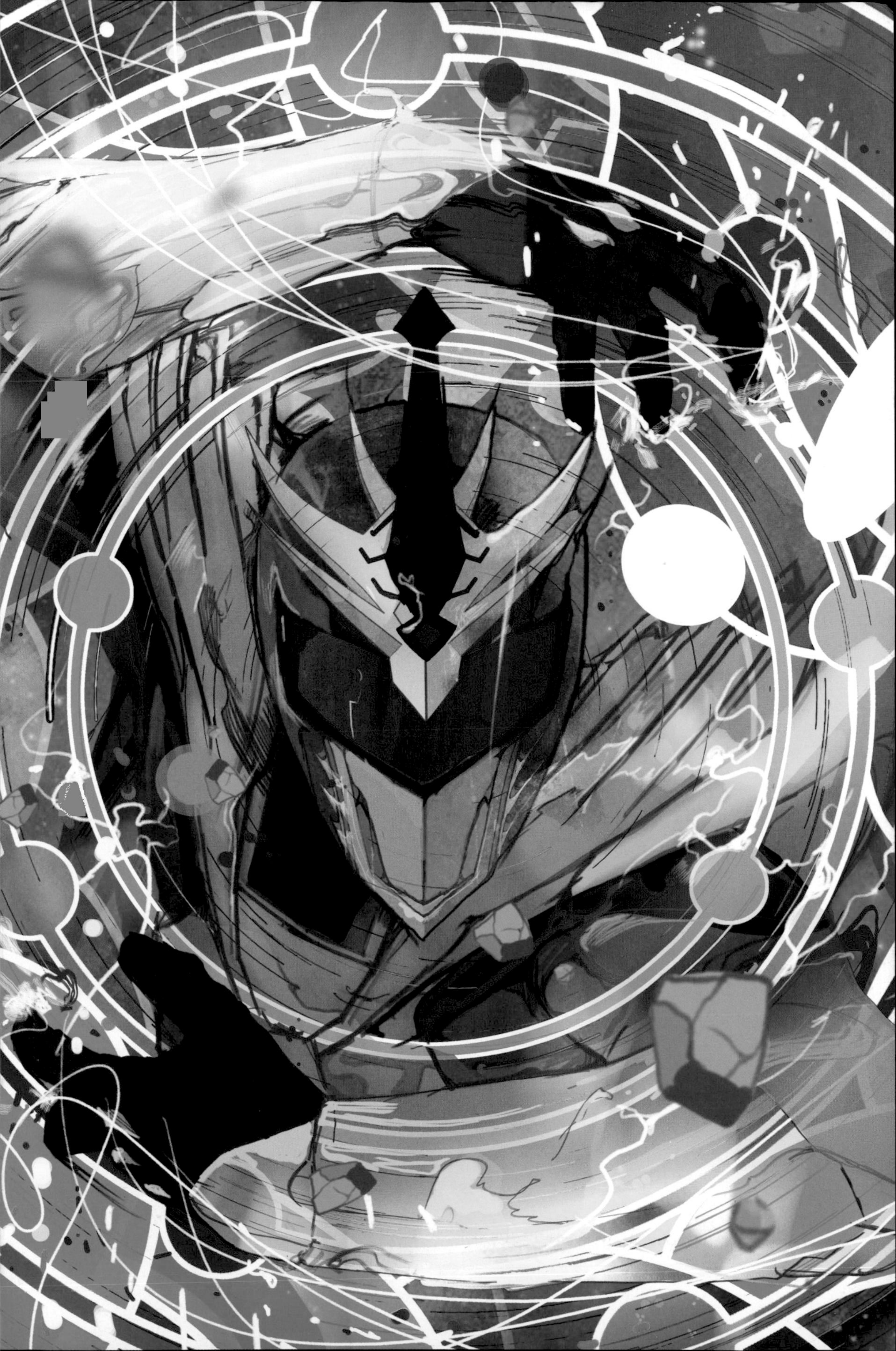

CHRISTIAN WARD SHATTERED GRID ISSUE ONE VARIANT COVER

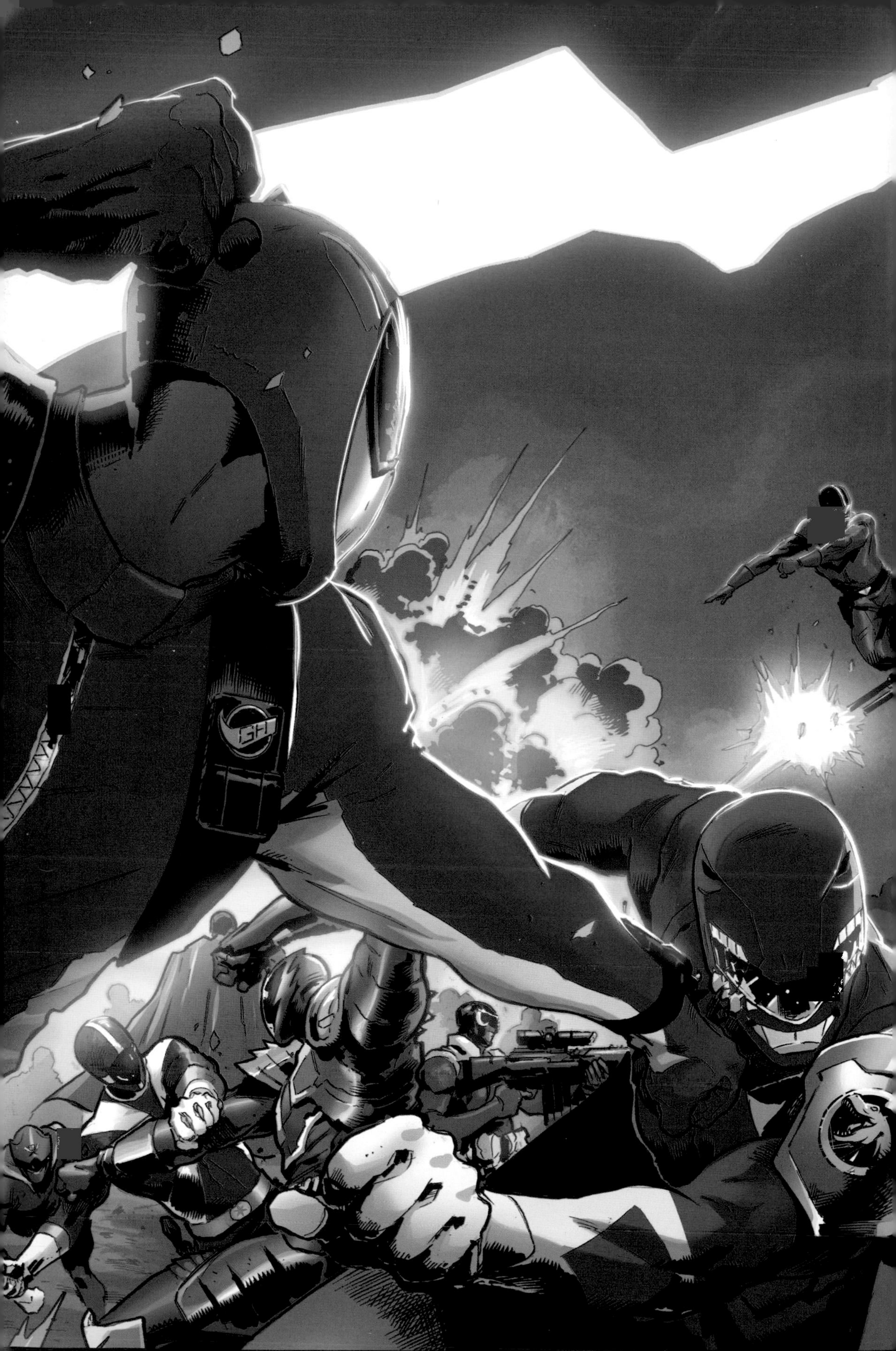

TREVOR HAIRSINE WITH COLORS BY **ALEX GUIMARÃES**

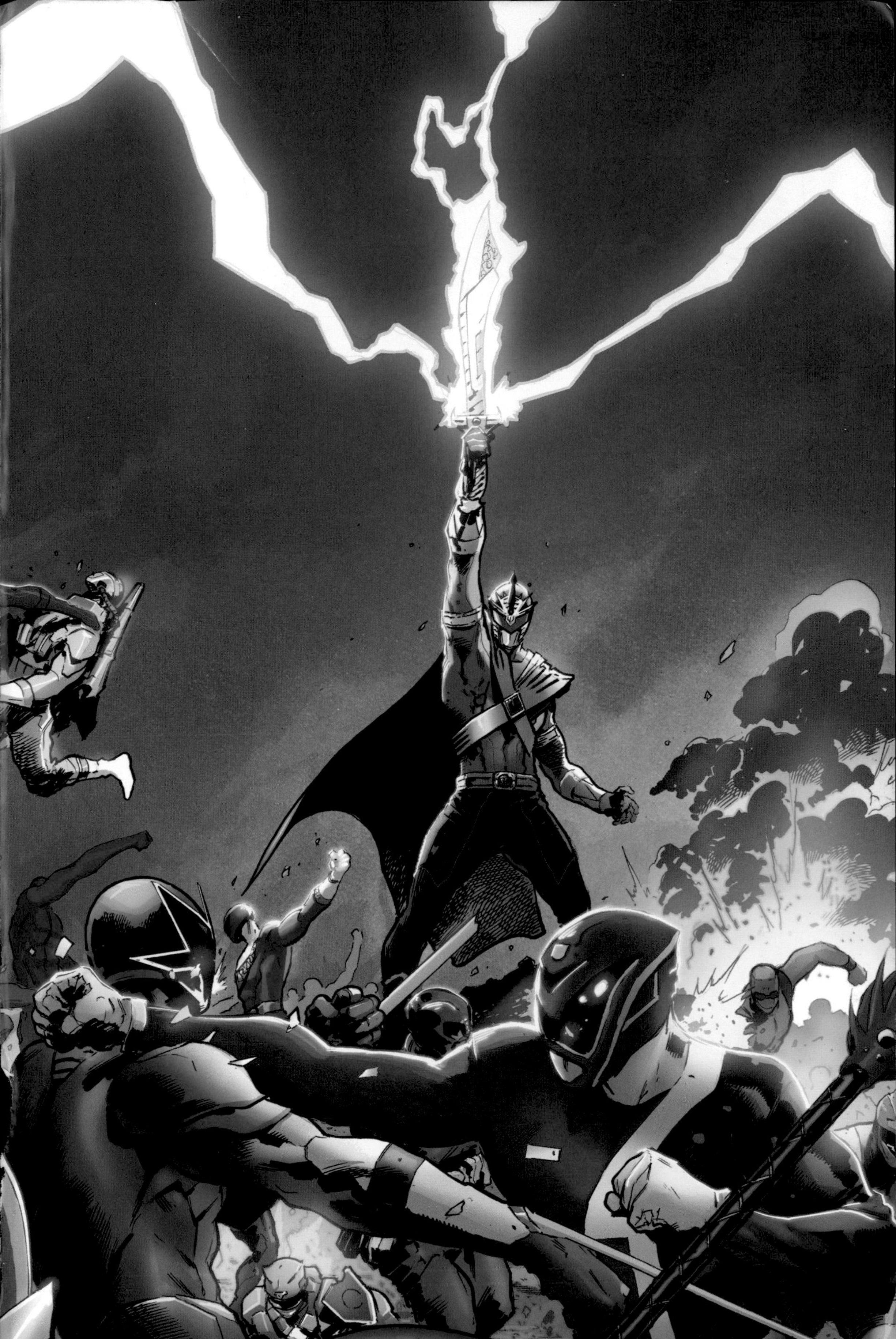

SHATTERED GRID ISSUE ONE SHATTERED HOLOFOIL VARIANT

DISCOVER
MORE POWER RANGERS!

Licensed by:

BOOM! Studios and the BOOM! Studios logo are trademarks of Boom Entertainment, Inc. All Rights Reserved. ™ and © 2020 SCG Power Rangers LLC and Hasbro. All Rights Reserved.